THE HARPER ATLAS
OF WORLD HISTORY

THE
HARPER ATLAS OF

WORLD
HISTORY

HarperCollins*Publishers*

THE HARPER ATLAS OF WORLD HISTORY *(Revised Edition)*. Copyright © 1992 by HarperCollins Publishers Inc. English translation copyright © 1987 by William Collins Son & Co. Ltd. All rights reserved. Printed and bound in France. No part of this book may be used or reproduced in any manner whatsoever without written permission except in the case of brief quotations embodied in critical articles and reviews. For information address HarperCollins Publishers, Inc., 10 East 53rd Street, New York, NY 10022.

HarperCollins books may be purchased for educational, business, or sales promotional use. For information, please write: Special Markets Department, HarperCollins Publishers, Inc., 10 East 53rd Street, New York, NY 10022.

Library of Congress Cataloging-in-Publication Data
Grand Livre de l'histoire du monde. English.
    Harper atlas of world history.—Rev. ed.
       p. cm.

    Translation of: Histoire de l'Humanité. Paris: Hachette, 1992.
    "Editor: Pierre Vidal-Naquet; cartographer: Jacques Bertin"—Acknowledgements.
    "Translation copyright 1987 by William Collins & Sons Ltd; copyright 1992 by HarperCollins Publishers Inc."—Copyright p.
    Includes index.
    ISBN 0-06-270067-7
    1. Historical geography—Maps. 2. Civilization—History.
I. HarperCollins (Firm). II. Title. III. Title: Atlas of world history.
G1030.G68513   1992 <G&M>
911—dc20   92-52538

92 93 94 95 96 10 9 8 7 6 5 4 3 2 1

ACKNOWLEDGEMENTS

Editor: Pierre Vidal-Naquet
Cartographer: Jacques Bertin

Text by:

Guillemette Andreu, Françoise Aubin, Michel Barbaza, Elie Barnavi, Irène Beldiceanu, Louis Bergeron, Jean-Noël Biraben, Robert Bonnaud, Jean Bottéro, Habid Boussouf, Olivier Buchsenschutz, François Caron, Roger Chartier, Jean-Pierre Darmon, Christian Décobert, Marie-Danielle Demélas, Elisabeth Deniaux, Jacques Dupâquier, Christian Duverger, Marc Ferro, André Fontaine, Raoul Girardet, Pierre Gouthier, Chantal Grell, Jean Guilaine, Ran Halévi, Mohammed Harbi, Daniel Hémery, Clarisse Herrenschmidt, Claudio Ingerflom, Christian Jacob, Pierre Jeannin, Gerard Jorland, Alain Joxe, Tamara Kondratieva, Ahmed Koulakssis, Alain Labrousse, Jean Lacoste, Jacques Le Rider, Jean Levi, Claude Lévy, Claude Liauzu, Claude Lutaud, Charles Malamoud, Elise Marienstras, Emilia Masson, Gilbert Meynier, Pierre Milza, Henri Moniot, Christos Mortzos, Jacques Népote, Claude Orrieux, Alain Piessis, Madeleine Rebérioux, Fabienne Reboul, Pierre Riché, Jean-Pierre Rioux, Agnes Rouveret, Yves Saint-Geours, Jean-Claude Schmitt, Pauline Schmitt, Irene Sorlin, Pierre Souyri, Jovier Teixidor, Wladimir Vodoff, François Weil, Claudie Weill

Translated from the French by Chris Turner (Material World Ltd), Leslie Hill, Jean McNeil, Stuart Hammond, Ruth Harvey, Barbara Lewis, Celia O'Donovan, Stuart McKinnon-Evans and Ivanka Roberts. Translation co-ordinated and edited by Chris Turner.

Introduction

1. A detail from Lopo Homen's Nautical Atlas, *(Portugal, c. 1519), showing the coasts of India and the 'islands of the East'.*

A History of Cartography

The history of the science of map-making is a story of continual development in succeeding cultures through the ages. To summarize the history of maps is also to enquire into their very identity: it is to examine how they are produced and to enquire into the nature of the traces that go to make them up, traces in which writing, painting and geometry are combined. It is also to examine their effectiveness – whether practical and political or imaginary and intellectual – for maps embody a society's knowledge. An historical atlas is, by its very nature, representative of this last function.

There are maps and maps. How maps are drawn depends to a large extent on their physical substratum. Some maps are portable while others are not; some stand alone while others form part of a book; some are hand-drawn while others are printed. These are all factors which make for different kinds of map, for projection on to a flat surface is only one solution among many. The Eskimos sculpt bone and wood to represent the outline of a coast; the inhabitants of the Marshall Islands assemble wooden sticks to produce a picture of the movements of wind and tide. The Touaregs make 'concrete maps' on the ground out of sand and gravel. A Babylonian clay tablet (from the end of the sixth century BC) has upon it a map drawn with compasses: the land is surrounded by the 'cruel' ocean and the stars. The first Greek maps were drawn on tablets of wood or metal. These bulky materials were doubtless very quickly supplanted by papyrus. It was on this fragile medium that the ancient Egyptians drew their maps (e.g. the chart of gold mines on the Turin papyrus, c. 1320 BC). In the first centuries of our era, parchment became the principal material. The use of this more solid and manageable medium made it easier for maps to be preserved. This was undoubtedly the case from Ptolemy's *Guide to Geography* (second century AD) onwards. The Portolan charts of thirteenth to fifteenth century Europe were drawn on sheepskin or calfhide. Not until the second century did the Chinese begin making paper. This new material, which did not reach the West until later, was to revolutionize writing and drawing.

There have also been maps of many different sizes. The *mappemondes* or planispheres of the Middle Ages had diameters ranging between 3 centimetres and 3 metres. The Ebstorf monastery map, which covers thirty sheets of parchment, has a surface area of 3.58 metres by 3.56 metres (c. 1284). Its monumental size reflects its decorative, religious function – which was to bear witness to God's majesty – as well as providing space for a great number of names and abundant ornamentation. A hand-drawn map like this is unique; any copy of it is a distortion.

Printing, which was first applied in the map-making field by the Chinese in 1155, was introduced into Europe around 1450. The first schematic printed world map is to be found in a book published by Isidore (Augsburg 1472). However, the main effect of the new technique was to make it possible for a great number of editions of Ptolemy (with maps from 1477 onwards) to be produced. This was how many Germans and Italians discovered map-making. Printing meant that a map could be republished, revised and corrected and, consequently, Ptolemy's map could now be modernized with the engraver replacing the scribe and the illuminator. In the days of wood engraving, only limited print runs and rough lines were possible; however, copperplate engraving, which was introduced in 1477, made more delicate work possible. In the nineteenth century, lithography, which was even more economical, enabled printers to introduce colour. With this step we reach the beginning of modern cartography. Maps were now produced either to stand alone or to be part of a larger work, as illustrations to a text or as a colour plate in an atlas. Alone, they were autonomous objects, serving either a utilitarian or a decorative purpose; in a book, they interacted with the text. In Greece, maps figured in scientific treatises as early as Anaximander (sixth century BC); they were particularly prominent in the work of Eratosthenes (third century BC), who explained how his map had been drawn, what sources he had used and provided a commentary on it; and lastly, they figured in the work of Ptolemy (second century AD) who accompanied his maps with lists of place-names and positions. The rediscovery of Ptolemy in the fifteenth century played a major role in the upsurge in the production of *Cosmographiae* in the sixteenth century (Münster, Thévet, Belleforest).

An atlas was initially a collection of maps assembled to order for a client. Each volume was unique, both in the selection and lay-out of its documents. But an atlas could also have a precise plan. Thus the hand-drawn *Atlas of Islam* (tenth century) included a map of the world, three charts of the principal seas and seventeen maps of individual countries. Printed atlases spread throughout Europe in the sixteenth and seventeenth centuries (the term itself being introduced in 1585 by Mercator), though the first modern atlas, Abraham Ortelius's *Theatrum Orbis Terrarum* had been published in 1570. An atlas gave its reader a symbolic mastery of the world (cf. Coronelli's *Atlante Veneto*, 300 maps, 1690–96).

Who were the map-makers? What was their place in society? When did maps begin to be drawn by professionals? The first Greek cartographers (Miletus, sixth century BC), who were geometers and astronomers, speculated on

2. A Babylonian clay tablet, Mesopotamia, sixth century BC.

abstract forms. Eratosthenes was a mathematician and geometer, as well as being a philologist and a grammarian. The profile of the medieval cartographer cannot be so clearly drawn. The men who made the hand-produced world maps were scholars: in their maps the earth was divided into three continents (the so-called T and O maps: 'the T in the O') or the globe was divided into climatic zones. These clerics and monastery scribes remained faithful to theological dogma and their maps were more symbolic than geographical. The development of Mediterranean trade in the sixteenth century gave rise to a new utilitarian cartography, providing up-to-date information. The 'Portolan charts' were drawn by specialists, the most celebrated of whom worked in Italy, Catalonia, Majorca or the Balearics. Map-making became a subject to be taught, as it was for example in Majorca (fourteenth century) and Dieppe (sixteenth century). German cartography developed in the universities in the sixteenth century, where it benefited from advances in mathematics and geometry (trigonometry). The methods of the cartographers, long kept secret, became public knowledge. They were now craftsmen working not in isolation, but as members of institutions – often religious institutions, for monks and missionaries played a major role in early map-making. The work of the Jesuits in China for example is well known. At the very beginning of the seventeenth century, Father Matteo Ricci imported a copy of Ortelius. This prototype was distributed and reproduced under the aegis of the Emperor. Subsequently, throughout the seventeenth century and in the eighteenth, the Jesuits re-worked 231 maps of Chinese origin and gathered them into an Atlas (1717–18). But theological dogma also played an inhibiting role. In Medieval times, the T & O map was more often reproduced than the map of terrestrial zones, all of which left unresolved the question of whether the antipodes were populated. Meanwhile, in the Islamic world, cartographers were faithful to another sacred text, the Quran.

It was not only religious power that influenced cartographers. They were also subject to political pressure, since it was sovereigns who provided most of the commissions for maps. Al-Idrisi, geographer to Roger II of Sicily (after

1140) dedicated his first map of the world to his king; the second was made for Roger's son and successor, William the Bad. From the sixth century BC onwards, the Chinese cartographer was a civil servant, charged with drawing up maps and keeping them up to date (Pei Hsiu, minister and map-maker, third century BC). In 1644, the first Manchu emperor instituted a reform of map-making, as if to demonstrate that political renewal required a re-affirmation of the symbolic mastery of space. Between the fourteenth and sixteenth centuries, the kings of Portugal and Castile employed official cartographers. These were men who moved easily from one court to another and some sovereigns paid fortunes to obtain recent maps of overseas discoveries. The great cartographic undertakings were financed by state power. The King of England gave Greenland Collins the task of mapping the country's coasts (1681): the result was a set of 120 charts. In 1666, Louis XIV founded the body of *Ingénieurs du Roi*, whose labours resulted in the *Neptune Français* of 1693 and the *Neptune Oriental* of 1745. Political centralization tended to stimulate greater production of maps. In 1747, the government financed a project to produce a topographical map of France, that had been proposed to them by F. Cassini de Thury. The undertaking continued until the revolution, though by then it was privately financed. The state intervened to complete the project in 1818. Similarly George Washington gathered senior military men together to draw up a map of the United States (1809: first general map of the USA). And we may add that in France, the *Atlas Universel de Géographie* of Vivien de Saint-Martin and Franz Schrader appeared in 1919–22 thanks to assistance from the War Ministry.

The cartographer has also been an actor in, and on occasion a hostage to, commercial strategies. Discoveries reveal untold sources of wealth. Can the map-maker be permitted to reveal this information to the world? Must he not rather conceal it from potential competitors? On Fra Mauro's map of 1459, there is no trace of the recent Portuguese discoveries along the coast of Africa. May we not perhaps attribute the rarity of sixteenth century Portuguese maps to a deliberate policy of concealing information? In the seventeenth century, the Dutch East India Company did not publish documents which could give its competitors information. W. Blaeu, the company's hydrographer had access to the most up-to-date charts, but he did not use these sources for his own publications. It was only in 1675 that the West India Company published its maps of North America. Similarly, the Napoleonic Wars were responsible for a curb on the circulation of sea charts, though in the nineteenth century, these ceased to be regarded as military secrets and the survey departments of the various navies exchanged charts with one another.

However, trading companies did also play a positive role: the Casa da India in Lisbon and its counterpart in Seville were centres of map production in the sixteenth century, as was the Hydrographic Bureau of Seville which, from 1508 onwards, supervised the drawing of charts, checked that they conformed to a fixed prototype and officially authenticated them. The cartographers had at their disposal pilots' logs and the notes made by navigators on old maps. The British companies played a similar role (Hudson Bay Company etc.). Three functions – those of draughtsman, engraver and writer – are involved in map production: historically these have either been assumed by a single individual or by persons joined together in a contractual relationship. From Mercator (1570) onwards, Holland was the main European centre of cartography; this was due particularly to the publishing houses (Blaeu, Hondius) that produced maps there and saw them through from conception to sale.

It was in the trading nations that maps were drawn. When, at the end of the sixteenth century, maritime supremacy passed from the Mediterranean nations to the Low Countries, map-makers followed, obeying the fluctuations of economic history. In the eighteenth and nineteenth centuries, Britain occupied the dominant position. Maps were also produced in the centralized, monarchic states, where a large territory had to be administered (e.g. France in the seventeenth century). We may be sure that where there were important printing centres map-makers were to be found nearby: from the fifteenth century onwards, these centres were in Germany and Italy. Later, supremacy

3. *The coasts of Europe. Map taken from the* Neptune Français *engraved by H. van Loon in*

passed to the Netherlands, which became famous for its atlases. In the eighteenth century, France dominated the market: it was there that the first scientific maps were produced.

Map-making developed over time into an institution. It was the aim of the French Academy of Sciences (seventeenth century), the *Ingénieurs du Roi* and the Royal Society of London (1660) to offer the scholar both a place of residence and a centre of learning, as the Museum of Alexandria (third century BC) and the Bayt al-Hikmah (House of Wisdom) in Baghdad (ninth century) had done before them. In the nineteenth century, geographical societies in France and Great Britain made an important contribution to the mapping of the colonial empires. The *Ordnance Survey* was founded in 1791 to draw up a map of England on the basis of a set of triangulations. The French Army Geographical Service, whose role its was to produce maps for the General Staff, was replaced in 1940 by the Institut Géographique National. Inevitably, the day had to come when international bodies would be set up to plan, co-ordinate and standardize maps. As early as 1891, a project was launched to produce an international map of the world, but it was hampered by a lack of co-ordination between the participants and by nationalist rivalries. The project was taken up again in its entirety after the Second World War by the Cartographic Department of the United Nations. Between 1919 and 1921, an attempt was made to standardize the symbols used on maps and they were re-drawn according to simpler, less expensive conventions. One of the routes through the history of map-making runs, then, right from the Portolan workshops to the UN.

Map-making techniques. How a map is made determines not only its appearance, but also its function. Purely geometrical maps were not intended to represent geographical reality, which knows no such straight lines and order. Anaximander's map (sixth century BC), which plays on the graphic possibilities of the circle, is of this type. The medieval map also stylized geographical reality to arrive at an essential structure, with the T & O map, which was divided into three by the Nile, the Don and the Mediterranean, and the map with climatic zones laid out in tiers on either side of the Equator. Perpendicular lines on maps brought them new depth. It now became possible to make calculations, as well as to check and correct a map. Eratosthenes (third century BC) could thus project positions and distances from one region of a map to another by employing the analogical operations that were available to him from Euclidian geometry. On Chinese maps of the Han dynasty (third century BC to third century AD), we also find a rectangular canvas with lines marking out regular squares. Ptolemy's grid (second century) allows us to find locations on the basis of their latitude and longitude: the network of parallels and meridians thus introduces a new rigour into position-finding. Between Anaximander and Ptolemy, maps change their meaning: we pass from the map as model to the map as inventory.

In the eighteenth century, the Portolan charts also had a linear framework. Their 'rhumb lines' were straight lines radiating out from the centres of adjacent circles in the direction of the compass-points and were usually thirty-two in number. If these circles were drawn, the points of intersection with the rhumb lines could be joined up to form a quadrangular figure. Rhumb lines were guides for the navigator, who followed a course parallel to them. They did not serve to locate positions on the map. The Portolan charts had, moreover, no 'projection': they neither took into account the spherical shape of the earth nor the convergence of meridians.

The rediscovery of Ptolemy in the fifteenth century made it possible to formulate the rules of map-making in a new way. He in fact advocated two systems of projection. In the first – conical projection – the meridians were straight lines running outwards from the North Pole (which was the centre to the arcs formed by the parallels); in the second, the meridians were curves which became increasingly accentuated as one moved outwards from a straight meridian in the centre. The parallels were drawn in conformity with the proportions of latitude.

In the fifteenth century, Ptolemy's maps were re-drawn. Nicholas Germanus (1466) became an authority in this sphere, both for his trapezoidal projection and the quality of his representation of relief. The editions of 1477 to 1482 were drawn using a rectangular projection. From 1482 onwards (the Ulm edition), the conical projection was used once again. Ptolemy thus introduced a new rigour into European cartography and on H. Martellus Germanus's map of the world (1488–90) we find meridians drawn and graduated. Ptolemy's grid was adopted in the Portolan charts, where it was added in over the rhumb lines. In this way, the representation of the east–west axis of the Mediterranean was rectified (1529, Ribero). Between 1500 and 1520, degrees of longitude and latitude began to appear on maps and from this point on, Portolan charts took account of the earth's spherical shape.

In 1569, Mercator invented a new projection: the meridians were drawn as parallel lines, and as latitude increased, so did the distance between the parallels, which distorted the shapes of the countries. In using this map, a sailor knew that a line drawn with compasses which intersected all the meridians at the same angle represented a straight line and he was therefore able to determine his course from one port to the next. The map was also embellished with topographical information, the quality of which depended on the instruments used. From the Han period onwards in China (third century BC to third century AD), surveying and geodesic instruments such as the chain measure and the plumb line were employed which the West did not discover until much later. It thus became possible to calculate distances and altitudes; in short, by using trigonometry, one could orientate oneself. The mariner's compass (which appeared in Europe in the tenth and eleventh centuries) gave a stimulus to the production of Portolan charts. In the fifteenth century, use of the astrolabe enabled sailors to determine their latitude. In the seventeenth century, the Germans worked out the principles of spherical trigonometry, published astronomical tables and systematized the calculation of latitude and longitude. In the eighteenth century, the telescope, the pendulum clock and logarithmic tables were all developed.

At the end of the nineteenth century, the use of radio signals introduced the greatest possible precision into the calculation of positions. Technical advances enabled countries to undertake cartographic projects on a national scale. A prime example of this is Cassini's map of France. In 1669–70, the Abbé Picard measured an arc of the Paris meridian using a chain of triangles. By 1718, the chain stretched from Dunkirk to the Pyrenees, enabling cartographers to make a great number of calculations of latitude and longitude. Using this triangulation of the national territory, the Cassini family was able to produce its 182-sheet *Carte Géométrique de la France* (1789). Even in the nineteenth century, national surveys were still carried out in much the same way. In the case of far-off lands, the explorer collected data, charted road networks, and measured noteworthy distances and relief features. From 1858 onwards, the technique of aerial observation was developed, using dirigible balloons. The two world wars gave a fresh stimulus to the development of aerial photography. This method, which made it possible to map coasts and inaccessible regions with great precision, created a need for the rigorous interpretation of photographs (nature of the soil, rock formations and vegetation).

The Map and the Text. In a geographical treatise, the text provides a gloss on the contents of the map. It renders it intelligible and the map, for its part, allows us to form a visual image of the over-abstract features of the description. This is the case in the treatises produced by Eratosthenes and Ptolemy or in Al-Khuwarizmi's *Curat al-Ard* (c. 820). Tenth century Islamic geography followed two paths. The Balkhi School, with its *Atlas of Islam* gave more prominence to the text than to the maps; the other school subordinated the geographical commentary to the construction of globe and maps. For them, the text had an informative function, whilst the map played a 'theoretical' role, visually condensing geographical science. Maps must provide the information that we need to understand them: the ascription of place names is the point at which the map as simple drawing meets the encyclopaedia. A proliferation of place-names does not necessarily represent topographical richness in a map, but it is evidence of a different project from that of the T & O schema. Naming places is a way of exorcizing the troubling power of blank spaces, as we can see from those Portuguese Portolan charts which are festooned with anachronistic or imagined place names (sixteenth century). The age of discovery was also an age of inventing place names. Everyone wished to impose their particular set of names, which on many occasions only lasted for the lifetime of a map. The New World had Catholic symbolism and hagiography, the names of sovereigns or even the names of European countries foisted upon it. Sometimes it was an intrinsic quality of the land being named that was emphasized, as in 'Tierra del Fuego', or in some cases a native name was borrowed, as with 'Canada'. We owe the name 'America' more to a decision of the map-makers (Waldseemüller's *World Map* of 1507, Mercator's *Map of the World* of 1538, which distinguished North from South America) than to any desire on the part of the man it was named after (Amerigo Vespucci). Meanwhile, Ptolemaic, Christian and Portuguese names co-existed merrily in the maps of the Old World. Place names were an integral part of maps, but names often proliferated at the expense of the map's readability or its decorative elements. A map's aesthetic value derived from the choice of typography or calligraphy (sixteenth century Italy and Holland). On the Portolan charts (thirteenth to fourteenth centuries), the names, which were written in black with the initial letter in red, served to pick out the coast lines more boldly. Written perpendicularly and to the left of the littoral, they formed a verbal fringe which marked the map's edge. The user of the Portolan chart could not simply view it at a single glance; he had to turn it round to read the legend.

Maps contain a great many other texts: the author's signature, the name and address of the printer and the engraver, the dedication and royal licence, the title written in its ornamental cartouche, the scale and sometimes even an explanation of the system of projection, along with fragments of description and references to sources. On his map of the world, Fra Mauro (fifteenth century) apologizes for not having enough space to report all the information brought back by explorers and declares his scepticism with regard to Ptolemy's maps. In some sixteenth century maps, authors provided

4. *Map of the Chinese Empire by Wang P'an, 1594.*

explanations and self-justifications. Certain of these notices are often as important as the map itself (Waldseemüller, Mercator).

In some cases, such commentaries were situated on the map itself. On N. Di Caveri's *Mappemonde* (sixteenth century) we read around *Chingirina* (Japan?): 'This island is very rich and there are Christians upon it; this is where Malacca porcelain comes from; benzoin, aloe and musk are also to be found there.' Thus the map-makers assessed potential wealth, determined levels of civilization and, on occasion, noted the names of contemporary rulers or sovereigns from the past of myth and legend; all these practices tended to transform maps into encyclopaedias.

Geometry and painting. As visual objects, maps lend themselves to aesthetic appreciation. A 'readable' map is, above all, one you can look at easily, one in which sea and land are distributed in harmonious proportion and where space is filled with clear graphic signs. The geometrical abstraction of Anaximander's maps or of the T & O renderings is not really compatible with a work of descriptive geography. A map must accommodate itself to the accidental contours of real forms even if it subsequently sublimates them in an image which is itself figurative. For example, there is a Chinese map of the world which uses the human profile, the head representing the central continent (China), the front part of the hair Korea and the back part the Western countries, while the chin and neck form India and Indo-china. Sometimes some small act of graphic violence is done to geographic forms to impose a familiar image on the eye. Maps doubtless suggested such parallels, which became proverbial in Greek texts: thus the Pelopponese were seen as the leaf of a plane tree, the Iberian peninsula a stretched-out ox-skin etc. The *Atlas of Islam* (tenth century) adopts this same procedure. To be legible, a map must include a figurative dimension which introduces an empirical motivation into its arbitrary lines.

Advances were also made in the recording of topographical data. The representation of towns, mountains and rivers developed from the figurative mode towards the symbolic. Until the end of the seventeenth century, a mountain was indicated by a picture which sought to represent it 'realistically'; it was an isolated shape, which, in late fifteenth century editions of Ptolemy, looked like the tooth of a saw or a mole-hill. It was not therefore possible to differentiate between a hill and a mountain, nor *a fortiori* to discover the structure of a mountain range or determine a particular altitude. But there was an increasing move towards abstraction. Efforts were made to project altitude onto the horizontal plane and to suggest valleys, peaks and mountain ridges by a graphic code. The nineteenth century saw two major innovations in this regard. In 1802, a decision was taken to take sea-level as the basis of all such calculations, enabling the surveyors who produced the so-called 'General Staff' maps in France (published, 1881) to put altitudes on them. In 1830 or thereabouts, the introduction of lithography made it possible to use colour to represent relief: this marked the passage from the 'landscape' to the 'abstract' map; later, the user would be able to determine altitudes with the aid of contour lines. The representation of towns underwent a similar development. The Portolan charts indicated them with flags or little castles: this generic symbol was often accompanied by veritable descriptive vignettes in the case of the most important towns. Cassini's map in fact contains plans of the main cities.

Another important element in the external appearance of maps is colour. Colour certainly plays a decorative role (sixteenth century maps painted *al fresco*); it also has a symbolic function. In the tenth-century *Atlas of Islam*, it is used to distinguish rivers from mountains. The medieval Portolan charts also used a precise and consistent colour coding.

For many years, printed maps were coloured by hand. In the seventeenth century, when an ordinary buyer acquired a Jaillot atlas, he bought one in which only the contours of the maps were highlighted with colour. More well-to-do clients, however, could purchase lavishly decorated atlases. On modern maps colour has an exact meaning and a contemporary map of the world requires the use of a wide range of colours sufficient to indicate the different bands of altitude, from the depths of the oceans to the peaks of the Himalayas.

The first maps were abstract and geometric in appearance. Figurative representation only appeared at a later stage. Medieval maps contain a plethora of miniatures (animals, plants and monsters) and with these the global overview provided by the world map becomes fragmented into a number of partial scenes. On one contract for a Portolan chart (c. 1400), both the quantity and the type of illustrations are specified: 165 persons and animals, 25 ships, 100 fish, 140 trees, 340 banners. Maps served as a microcosm and an inventory. The seas were studded with ships, which were both a means of discovery and functioned as guarantees that the New World could indeed be reached. This pictorial pedagogy acquainted the reader with exotic animals, Indians and cannibals, though the monsters of the sea could neither be conquered nor assimilated into the fund of human knowledge. The human monsters that inhabited the bowels of the earth were drawn from ancient encyclopaedias and represented a dream-horizon where the fantasy images of the Christian West could be exorcised. The Ebstorf *Mappemonde* (c. 1284) had as its background a picture of Christ crucified with his head at the top (the east) and his arms outstretched to north and south, holding up the world. It was an inventory of Creation in all its profusion and diversity. The Hereford map (c. 1300) is an encyclopaedia: its surface is a classification table for images that are organized into veritable taxonomies of history, ethnography and the natural sciences. These documents bear little resemblance to such 'scientific' works as the Ptolemaic maps.

As the Middle Ages drew to a close, map-makers were faced with a choice. They could either follow the tradition of decorative world maps and increase the figurative component at the expense of the map's geographical content and readability, or they could separate the figurative dimension from the cartographic project altogether. The printed Ptolemy maps mark a break with medieval map-making. The Catalan cartographers had already begun to limit the space given over to miniatures and, from the sixteenth century onwards, under the influence of Mercator and Ortelius, the pictures of natives, fruits, flora and fauna had been moved from the centre of maps to the edges. With his *Atlas de la Chine*, D'Anville introduced a new type of decoration; the titles of the maps were surrounded by large illustrations depicting the customs or resources of a particular area: from this point on, pictures left the map's interior to become part of its periphery.

Maps as images of the world. Maps provide the eye and the memory with a single complete picture. It is an essential feature that they should close off space. It matters little that until the fifteenth century, an entire continent remained unknown, and that in some maps there were many blank areas representing uncharted territories. Maps are organized around a centre and move outwards from the known and familiar towards the unknown and exotic. This was the case with the first Greek maps, which were circular and centred on Delphi. It was also true of medieval maps centred on Jerusalem, or of oriental planispheres centred on India or the Pamir plateau. A map's horizon corresponds to the needs and knowledge of a society. The first maps produced by the Japanese contained only those countries known to them by trading links (China and Korea). The map of the Islamic empire (tenth century) runs from Spain in the West to the Indus and Central Asia. The Italian Portolan charts cover only Western Europe and the Mediterranean, while the Catalan charts range as far as Scandinavia and even China. These maps are evidence of two different types of curiosity and two different commercial strategies.

The history of maps merges at points with the history of discovery. The fifteenth and sixteenth centuries represent a turning-point in this regard. While the knowledge of the Old World increased (1427: Nicolas Clavus's map of northern Europe), the Portuguese, by their explorations along the Atlantic coast, modified European perceptions of Africa. In 1448, Andrea Bianco mapped the coastline of Senegal and Cape Verde and in 1459 Fra Mauro completed this work, drawing perhaps on Arabic sources. The coasts of the Congo and the Cape of Good Hope, which were discovered by the Portuguese, are shown on Martellus's map of 1490. On a map printed in 1508, all of Africa south of the equator appears for the first time as a vast peninsula. Advances in the discovery of Asia occurred less rapidly. Martellus drew the islands of the Orient and Cipangu (Japan). Texeira's map of Japan was regarded as authoritative throughout the seventeenth century. Thanks to the British, the map of India became clearer during the eighteenth century.

In the midst of all these advances came a crucial event – the discovery of America. J. De la Cosa's world map of 1500 included information from Columbus's first three voyages and from John Cabot's discoveries in North America. In 1502, Cantino produced a map which drew together all the material from the new discoveries in America and Africa. There were, however, many problems to resolve. To begin with, was the newly discovered land an archipelago or a continent? Was it in Asia and, if so, was it far from

Cipangu and Cathay? Contarini was the author of the first map to show the New World. In the north, he recorded the findings of Cabot and Corte-Real, attaching these lands to the province of Tangut (Asia). He placed the West Indies in the centre and the south was occupied by a vast land mass. The cartographic birth of America in fact occurred in 1507, when Waldseemüller drew the intuitive conclusion that all these individual discoveries were connected. He separated America from Asia and, in the process, invented the Pacific Ocean eight years before it was actually discovered! Ribero produced a more precise map of the eastern coastline of America, including the Magellan Strait and Labrador. Cabot traced the outline of the Gulf of the St Lawrence, California and the complete course of the Amazon. From this point on, America was shown with a continuous coastline extending as far as Tierra del Fuego. Cook's voyages between 1773 and 1784 (which led to the production of seven volumes and an atlas) brought enormous progress in the mapping of the Pacific and Australia and New Zealand.

We can see, then, three key stages in the history of the representation of the earth. These were the discovery of America, the re-discovery of Ptolemy (and his model of projection) and the development, in the eighteenth century of surveying techniques that made it possible to fill in what had previously been blank areas on the map.

Maps, their uses and users. The primary function of a map is, of course, to allow users to determine their position and find their way. The Marshall Islanders' stick constructions, Portolan charts and road maps all have this same function. From the Islamic world to China and from ancient cadastral surveys to the modern land register, maps have provided a way of resolving problems of boundary lines.

But maps cannot be reduced to one single function. They may at one and the same time serve utilitarian, decorative, political and scientific purposes. They provide information in a condensed form and yet they may also at times be akin to works of art, especially when hand-drawn and illuminated, or printed from a fine engraving and hand-painted. In cathedrals, monasteries and palaces or in the houses of the well-to-do, maps have had a decorative role alongside their educative function. They have also been political gifts exchanged between kings; as such, they may be regarded as signs of 'social distinction'. In the seventeenth century, they were purchased by teachers, lawyers, clergymen, the older nobility and the bourgeoisie.

To read an atlas is to experience the joys of a journey in one's mind's eye. But maps can also be sources of religious edification. In both Christianity and in Islam, the map's order is seen as reflecting God's order. It allows the reader to decipher Creation. The 'T and O' maps were theological symbols: the tripartite division of the continents echoed the Trinity and the three sons of Noah. But maps are also bound up with temporal power. They are instruments of government; they have a preparatory role in military action and in decision-making 'in the field', whether it be the field of battle or that of broader geopolitical strategy. They offer the state symbolic control of its territory. Surveying the extent of that territory means stabilizing its frontier, making it available for organization into administrative units. The imperial geography of Islam was oriented towards the assessment of taxes, defence and the provision of messenger services. Chinese tax-collectors used atlases of the various provinces with statistical charts and maps of grain stocks.

Maps can provide a means for affirming national unity, or even nationalist sentiment. They are also a source of knowledge, and one that is indispensable to the decision-maker. Early in their development, it was seen as part of their encyclopaedic vocation that they should provide an inventory of a country's resources, modes of life and cultural heritage. However, as the decorative illustrations were squeezed out towards the edges, maps increasingly lent themselves to new uses. They became vehicles for transmitting any data that lent itself to treatment in terms of spatial distribution. They became heuristic objects, revealing to the eye what could only be imperfectly conveyed by a written text. The first geological maps appeared at the beginning of the nineteenth century. The thematic map was born in 1875 with Crome's comparative map of European populations, but it owes its development largely to German geographers. A. von Humboldt and K. Ritter used maps to reveal the spatial distribution and interaction of the natural phenomena studied by meteorology, climatology, hydrology and hydrography, geology, zoology, agronomy and ethnography, together with such variables as vegetation and terrestrial magnetism. These thematic maps later benefited from progress made in the field of statistics. The new tool was also used by history: in 1894, in his *Atlas Général*, Vidal de la Blache gave a visual representation of the relations between historical development and the environment.

Today, we are able to convey information through a map which is of equal status with that conveyed by a written text or a picture. A new discipline – 'graphic semiology' – has evolved to examine just what it is that determines the didactic or heuristic effectiveness of maps. Its theoretical principles have only recently been formulated by this volume's principal cartographer Jacques Bertin and *The Collins Atlas of World History* is just one of its most recent practical applications.

AUSTRALOPITHECUS AFARENSIS
Hadar, Ethiopia
– 3.4 million years ago

450 cm³

AUSTRALOPITHECUS AFRICANUS
Sterkfontein, South Africa
– 3 million years ago

450 cm³

HOMO HABILIS
Koobi Fora, Kenya
– 2.5 million years ago

500 cm³

HOMO ERECTUS
Koobi Fora, Kenya
– 1.8 million
years ago

825 cm³

HOMO ERECTUS "PRE-SAPI
Petralona, Greece
– 200,000 years ago

1200 cm³

ECCE HOMO

Hut
Acheule
Nice (Fra
Pre-Neanderthal fossils of *Swanscombe*
Patralona (Greece), Steinheim (German
Sw *P* *St*
Sinanthropus *(Peking)*
Hunting *Torralba (Spain)*
Mastery of fire *Nice (France)*
Tautavel (France) *Vertésszöllös (Hu*
Germany **Java Man**
France First Acheulean bifacial tools in Europe
First Acheulean bifacial tools in Africa
Homo erectus in Europe

E HOMO ERECTUS cranial capacity 825 cm³ *Koobi Fora (Kenya)*

Oldowan industry: bifacial tools *Oldoway (Tanzania)*
Structured habitat: *Melka Kunture (Ethiopia)*

H HOMO HABILIS cranial capacity 500 cm³, *Koobi Fora (Kenya)*
First tools single edged pebble tools *Shungura, Omo Valley (Ethiopia)*

Robustus
Africanus
Afarensis "Lucy" *Hadar*
Afarensis *Hadar (Ethiopia)*
Lukeino, Lothogam (Kenya)

Last australopithecines

**A AUSTRALOPITHECINES
ERECT POSTURE** *(Kenya)*

ABBEVILLIAN   A C H E U L E A N

◁ **L O W E R   P A L E O L I T H I C**

10 M 6 M
1 M
500,000   **200,000**

Years		5M	4M	3M	2M	1,5 M	900	800	700	600		400	300		150,000

Climate
warm
⬓ Glacial phases
⬒ Interglacial phases
DONAU ?   **GÜNZ**   **MINDEL**   **RISS**
cold

←—— Lower Pleistocene ——→ ←—— Middle Pleistocene ——→

Geological periods   **TERTIARY**   **Q U A T E R N A R Y**

HOMO SAPIENS
(NEANDERTHAL) 1500 cm³
La Ferrassie, France — 40,000 years ago

HOMO SAPIENS SAPIENS
(CRO MAGNON) 1500 cm³
Cro Magnon, France — 35,000 years ago

(PRESENT DAY) 1500 cm³

Iron
Anatolia Greece Italy France

■ **Writing** (Mesopotamia)

Bronze
Near East Egypt Greece Switzerland China

○ **Cast copper** (Southeast Europe, Iran, Sumer)
Anatolia Balkans
Ⓒ — Ⓒ **Hammered copper**

▮ **Towns** Sumer 4000 BC China 2000 BC

⊗ **Domestic ox** (Europe)   ⊗ **Domestic horse** (Central Asia)

Agriculture First farmers in Europe

Pottery
Asia   Near East

Wheat cultivated at Jericho

Rice cultivated at Ho-mu-tu (China)

? First cultivated cereals (Nile Valley)

● Microlithic tools, bone tools

● **Lascaux** ● Altamira (Spain) Font de Gaume (France)

● Homo sapiens sapiens in America?

● **Figurative art** Périgord, Lespugue, Brassempouy (France)

● **Cro-Magnon Man** (France)

Galilee skull
Mugharet-el-Zuttiyeh

Ss HOMO SAPIENS SAPIENS

● Neanderthal skulls of St Césaire and La Ferrassie (France)

● First settlement in hostile habitat (Moldova - Lat 53° N)

● **Neanderthal Man** (Germany)

S HOMO SAPIENS First burials

Gerona (Spain)

The time scale in the main table has been compressed in order to fit in all the events, particularly of the last 100,000 years.

EVOLUTION ON A NORMAL TIME-SCALE

HOMO SAPIENS SAPIENS
HOMO SAPIENS
HOMO ERECTUS
HOMO HABILIS
AUSTRALOPITHECINES

6 million years 5 M 4 M 3 M 2 M 1 M 0

PERIGORDIAN
GRAVETTIAN
AURIGNACIAN   SOLUTREAN   MAGDALENIAN

MOUSTERIAN   CHATELPERRONIAN

MIDDLE ▷◁ **UPPER** ▷ **MESOLITHIC**   **NEOLITHIC**   **METAL AGES**

00,000 50,000   20,000   **10,000** 5000   2000   **1000**   500 BC

80,000 60,000   40,000 30,000   15,000   9000 8000 7000 6000   4000   3000   1500   900 800 700 600

W Ü R M

Upper Pleistocene   Holocene

Q U A T E R N A R Y

The First Tools, Fire, Ritual

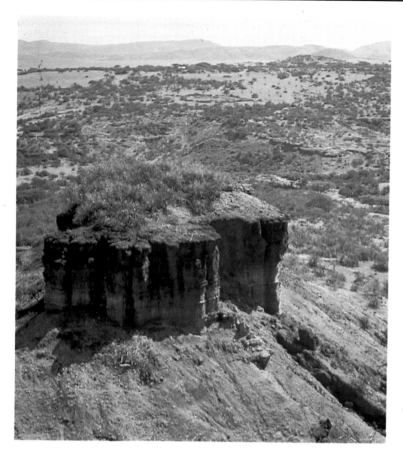

1. Olduvai gorges in Tanzania, site of Zinjanthropus skeleton, type of Australopithecus robustus contemporary of Homo habilis (1.7 million years ago).

THE RIFT VALLEY, a vast tear in the surface of the planet, where the secrets of the earth's history can be glimpsed, is where human life is thought to have begun. Geologists, paleontologists and prehistorians have focused their research here, on the horizon of the *Australopithecines*, a multiform, adaptable genus that gave birth, as far as we know today, to representatives of the genus *Homo*. The species *Homo habilis* began to differentiate themselves about 2.5 million years ago from *Australopithecus africanus*, a gracile, though not particularly specialized form with great evolutionary potential. Thanks to the

genetic vigour of some of its members, the evolutionary process was able to continue and give rise, about 1.8 million years ago, to *Homo erectus*.

Homo habilis lived in small groups in the varied habitat of the savanna, frequenting in particular, in an amphibian manner, the banks of lakes and rivers. For millions of years their lifestyle evolved little; they were eclectic in their eating habits, feeding as a rule on small animals that were easy to catch, gathering plants and even scavenging the odd carcass or carrion. What was new about these humans was that the dialogue between hand and brain had given birth to tools that developed their capacity for action and made it more effective, and these tools could be used in turn to make other instruments. The methodical chipping away at stones to produce a cutting edge is valuable evidence of coherent thinking and planning. Another particularly human feature of *Homo habilis* is their variety of habitats, from small temporary shelters to large encampments with specialized living areas. At Melka Kunture, an Ethiopian site 1.7 million years old, rest areas marked out with blocks of stone and pebbles but devoid of remains alternate with zones where carcasses were cut up, which are full of tools and fragments of bone.

The human group *Homo erectus* grew rapidly. They occupied the whole territory of Africa and their representatives spread over the totality of the warm and temperate zones of the Old World. Several branches have been found in numerous sites: *Atlanthropus* in Ternifine in Algeria, *Pithecanthropus erectus* in Java, *Sinanthropus pekinensis* at Chou-k'ou-tien in China, pre-Neanderthal humans in Europe etc. The tradition of chipped stone instruments persisted for a long time, then evolved around 1.5 million years BC in Africa (not until 700,000 BC in Europe) into an industry of bifacial tools which clearly show a sense of symmetry and a feeling for the beauty of an instrument. Patterns of life did not evolve at the same pace, haphazard gathering continuing for a long time to form the basis of the economic system. Gradually, perhaps under pressure from less favourable environments, this way of life changed and humans evolved genuine strategies for the hunting of larger mammals around 400,000 BC. At about the same time the use of fire began to be widespread and dwellings no longer consisted of natural shelters roughly adapted for use, but of caves or more elaborate enclosed structures in the open air. With archaic man a totally new dimension was introduced: cultural evolution, an intensification of the natural tendency towards creating ever greater complexity.

70 million years ago: End of Secondary Era, beginning of Tertiary. Appearance of first primates.

15 million years ago: Possible emergence of first Hominids. Erect posture.

6–3.7 million years ago: Earliest remains of *Australopithecus* genus in Kenya: Lukeino tooth, Lothogam jawbone, Kanapoi humerus.

3.7 million years ago: Various remains and footprints of *Australopithecus* at Laetoli, Tanzania, provide evidence of perfect erect posture. Oldest fossils of *Australopithecus afarensis* found in Hadar (Ethiopia).

3.4 million years ago: Probable date of fossilized skeleton of *Australopithecus afarensis* AL 288 of Hadar, known as 'Lucy'.

3 million years ago: Appearance of *Australopithecus africanus* and *Australopithecus robustus*.

2.5 million years ago: Probable appearance of *Homo habilis* and first tools.

2.3 million years ago: Chopper and adapted stone slab from Shungara in the Omo Valley (Ethiopia).

1.8 million years ago: Skull KNM-ER 3733 (cranial capacity 835 c.c.) from Koobi Fora,

east of Lake Turkana (Kenya). Attributed to *Homo erectus*.

1.7 million years ago: Structured habitat with specialized zones at Gombore, Melka Kunture (Ethiopia) built by *Homo habilis*. Industry found at Oldoway in Tanzania.

1.5 million years ago: Spread of *Homo erectus*, evidence of presence in Europe. Site of Chilhac in Auvergne occupied – the oldest tools in Europe.

1.2 million years ago: Upper portion of skull of Venta Micena (Granada, Spain).

1.1 million years ago: First *Acheulean* bifacial tools manufactured in Africa.

1 million years ago: Last *Australopithecines*.

900,000 BC: Cave of Vallonnet (Roquebrune-Cap-Martin, France) occupied.

700,000 BC: First early *Acheulean* bifacial tools made in Europe.

630,000 BC: Probable date of jawbone found at Mauer, Baden-Württemberg, Germany.

450,000 BC: Remains of pre-Neanderthal Man of Tautavel, Caune de l'Arago, France. *Homo erectus*.

400,000 BC: Hearths of Terra Amata, Nice

and Vértésszöllös in Hungary. *Homo erectus* masters fire.

300,000 BC: Sites of Torralba del Moral and Ambona (Spain). *Homo erectus* develops strategies for hunting very large mammals.

250,000 BC: Appearance of the Levalloisian method of cutting stone, enabling flakes of predetermined form to be produced.

130,000 BC: Building of *Acheulean* hut, Lazaret cave, Nice.

90,000 BC: Probable age of jawbone found at Bañolas (near Gerona, Spain), attributed to *Homo erectus*.

4. Bifacial tool found in the region of Liège, Belgium (Acheulean).

2. Skull of Australopithecus robustus *found in Kenya.*

3. Skull of Homo erectus: *Tautavel Man.*

5. Skull of Homo habilis *found in Kenya.*

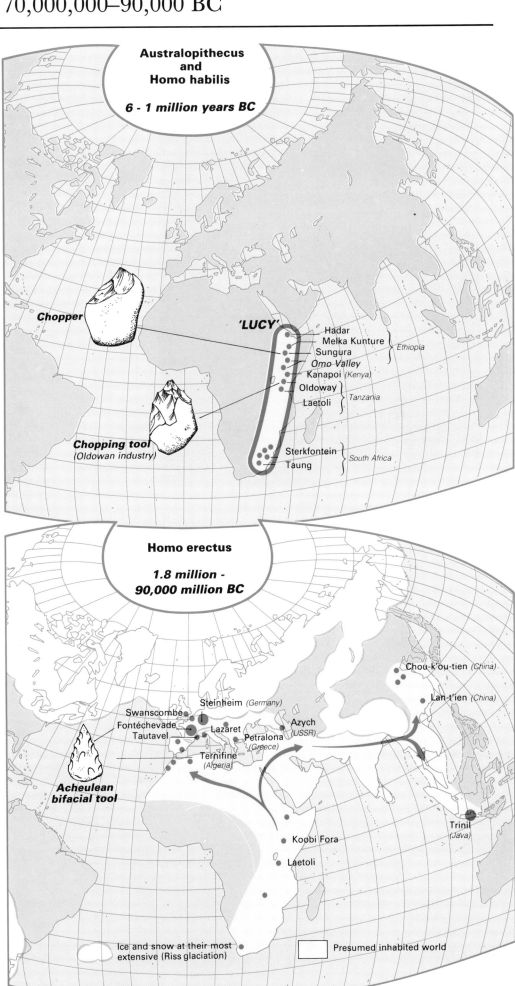

Australopithecus and Homo habilis

6 - 1 million years BC

Chopper

'LUCY'

Hadar
Melka Kunture
Sungura — *Ethiopia*
Omo Valley
Kanapoi *(Kenya)*
Oldoway
Laetoli — *Tanzania*

Sterkfontein — *South Africa*
Taung

Chopping tool
(Oldowan industry)

Homo erectus

1.8 million - 90,000 million BC

Chou-k'ou-tien *(China)*

Lan-t'ien *(China)*

Steinheim *(Germany)*
Swanscombe
Fontéchevade
Tautavel
Lazaret
Petralona *(Greece)*
Azych *(USSR)*
Ternifine *(Algeria)*

Acheulean bifacial tool

Trinil *(Java)*

Koobi Fora

Laetoli

Ice and snow at their most extensive (Riss glaciation)

Presumed inhabited world

Hunting and the Development of Man   200,000–20,000 BC

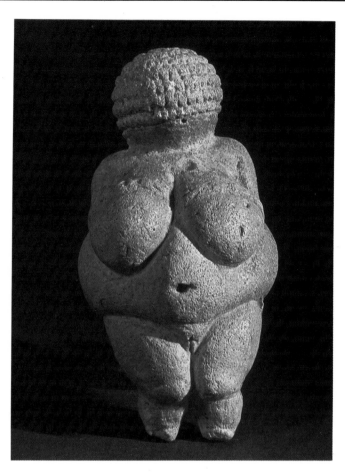

1. Venus of Willendorf, Austria. Limestone Gravettian statuette.

AFTER A MATURATION PERIOD lasting thousands of millennia during which major leaps in development occurred, in the last 100,000 years the daring experiment of intelligence at last began to pay off. Progress was irregular and took many false trails, but eventually *Homo erectus* gave way to a new form of humanity, *Homo sapiens*. The first group of these humans was located in Europe and western Asia and was possibly retreating before advancing glaciation: *Homo sapiens neanderthalensis* or Neanderthal Man. They date from between 80,000 and 35,000 BC and their anatomical features were still archaic. From the end of the Lower Paleolithic era, as shown by the fossilized remains of

Mugharet el-Zuttiyeh in Israel, a second human grouping began to form alongside the Neanderthalers and the last representatives of *Homo erectus*. The characteristics of modern humans were crystallized in *Homo sapiens sapiens*, who was to go from strength to strength.

Cultural evolution is not apparently sensitive to a profusion of minor variations; it tends to respond only to major ones. Implements that had already been tried out during the Lower Paleolithic evolution, standardized tools made from flakes of brittle stone, were produced in great quantities by all human groups of the Middle Paleolithic. These industries, known as Mousterian after the cave of Le Moustier in the Dordogne, usually comprise a great number of scrapers, points and serrated tools. Surprisingly, bifacial tools from the Acheulean tradition (early Paleolithic) have been found to exist side by side with lighter, smaller tools cut from slivers of stone (scrapers, burins, backed knives). In Europe and southwest Asia, after fifty millennia of Mousterian stability, material culture evolved rapidly in the Upper Paleolithic era, and the latter type of tool, more functional and varied, became increasingly important.

The Neanderthalers were not only concerned with the practicalities of life; as clearly shown by their burial customs, they had a very definite attitude to death, and must therefore have had a particular conception of life.

Homo sapiens now looked on the world with a new consciousness of their place in it. From then on, all cosmogonies and spiritual practices, in particular those shown in Paleolithic art after 30,000 BC, arise from the special place humans felt themselves to occupy among living things.

From the end of the Lower to the beginning of the Upper Paleolithic period, lifestyles changed little. This was the era of the great hunters; they did not specialise in a particular species, they knew how to exploit the resources of different environments to the full and were capable of tackling any game. They developed sophisticated, well-adapted dwellings: seasonal encampments of light tents along with much more solid constructions enabling them to withstand the rigours of the Würm Glaciation. Around 40,000 BC *Homo sapiens sapiens* reached Australia, and in 23,000 BC, if not earlier, penetrated America through the Siberian route.

The multiplicity of cultural responses made to daily problems by human societies was rapidly rendering synonymous the habitable and the inhabited regions of the world.

200,000 BC: Minimum age of pre-Neanderthal fossilized remains of Steinheim an der Murr (Germany).
130,000 BC: Beginning of Riss-Würm interglacial period.
100,000 BC: Probable date of remains found at Mugharet el-Zuttiyeh: possible ancestor of proto-Cro-Magnons of Near East. Rise of stone flake industries.
80,000 BC: Beginning of Würm glaciation. Appearance of stable characteristics of classical Neanderthalers (*Homo sapiens*) in Europe and Western Asia. Birth of Middle Paleolithic culture; Mousterian industries, first burials, beginnings of religious thought.
70,000 BC: Ritual cannibalism detected from remains of about twenty Neanderthalers found at Krapina (Yugoslavia).
50,000 BC: Site at Moldova on the Dniester (53°N), first permanent settlement in hostile habitat.
40,000 BC: Probable average date of Neanderthalers of La Chapelle-aux-Saints, La Ferrassie, La Quina (France) and of Cro-Magnon-type humans at Skhül and Kafzeh (Israel). Probable arrival of humans in

Australia.
35,000 BC: End of Mousterian stage,

2. Arrowhead found in Mauritania, Mousterian period.

beginning of Upper Paleolithic. Rise of stone implements cut from flakes and slivers of stone and of bone and horn industries. Probable average date of Cro-Magnon-type humans found at Combe-Capelle and Brno (*Homo sapiens sapiens*) and Neanderthaler found at Saint-Césaire (France).
30,000 BC: Average date of first obvious appearance of figurative art (Cellier shelter at Tursac, Blanchard shelter at Sergeac and Reindeer shelter at Belcayre, all in the Dordogne region of France).
27,000–19,000 BC: Gravettian culture (Paleolithic site of La Gravette, Dordogne). Period of female statuettes, in particular those of Lespugue and Brassempouy (France), Savignano (Italy) and Avdeeno (USSR) etc.
23,000 BC: Probable arrival of humans in America.

3. Grave at the 'Grotte des Enfants', Grimaldi, Monaco. Aurignacian period, Grimaldi race.

Homo sapiens
−100 000/−35 000 BC

Old Crow

Musashino

Fukui

Calico Hills

Neanderthal

Moldova

Techik-Tach

Lewisville

La Ferrassie

Mugharet
el-Zuttiyeh

Nyak

*Levalloisian
point*

Bir-el-Ater
El Guettar

**Mousterian
industry**

Scraper

- ● Neanderthalers
- ● Neanderthaloids
- ● Homo sapiens sapiens
- ○ Hypothetical sites

Broken Hill

Fauresmith

Homo
sapiens sapiens
−40 000/−10 000 BC

Yukon

Shishkino
Malta

Musashino

Sites of Périgord
and S-W France:
Cro Magnon
Aurignac, La Gravette,
La Madeleine, Lascaux
etc.

Afontova-
Gora

Fukui

*Cave paintings
of Lascaux*

Clovis

Hoa Binh

Shanidar

Parpallo

Taforalt
La Mouillah

Yabrud
Ksar 'Akil
Kafzeh

Renigunta

*Aurignacian
blade*

Ngangdong

Darwin

Guitarrero

*Gravettian
point*

Toca do
Boqueirao
da Pedra Furada

Kalambo Falls

Stillbay

	Snow and ice		Savannah
	Desert		Forest and zones of dense vegetation
	Steppe		

○ Hypothetical Saharan lakes

The Upper Paleolithic Explosion

THE RIGOROUS CLIMATE of the Würm Glaciation produced a mosaic of contrasting landscapes which were often surprisingly conducive to life. Between northern or mountainous areas covered with forbidding masses of ice and arid zones enlarged by a marked increase in rainfall lay an area where conditions were much more hospitable, offering sheltered valleys and sites exposed to favourable, temperate influences. Alternating with hilly, windswept regions and sparse plateaus of steppe and tundra lay zones of open parkland that became refuges for many vegetable and animal species and, of course, for humans.

By setting up permanent, sizeable shelters at the meeting point of several natural zones Paleolithic hunters benefited from complementary eco-systems. During the fine season in particular the clan could

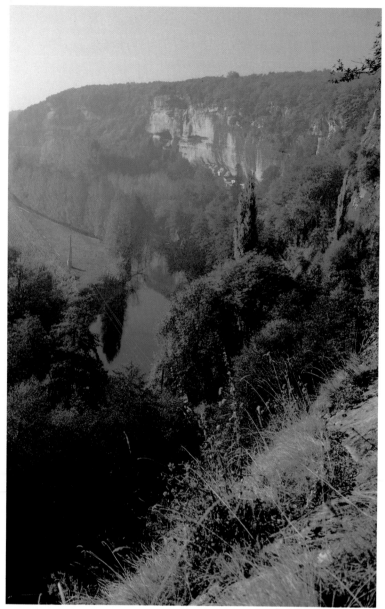

1. Valley of the Vézère, Dordogne, France. An important centre of hunting and settlement from Paleolithic times.

2. Magdalenian burial reconstructed by Abbé Henri Breuil (1887–1961), world authority on prehistory.

20,000–18,000 BC: Coldest point of Würm Glaciation.
20,000 BC: Last phases of various cultural horizons of European Upper Perigordian.
18,500 BC: Beginning of Solutrean civilization (European Upper Paleolithic) in France.
18,000 BC: Beginning of Ibero-Marusian civilization (cultural horizon of Late Paleolithic of North African Maghreb), development of arrowhead industry (lighter stone implements evolved), probably influenced by cultures further to the east. Mediterranean Epigravettian civilizations (named after materials found at Gravette site).
16,000 BC: Coldest point of glaciation. Mean date of monumental stone bas-relief sculptures. Solutrean sites of Roc de Sers (Charente) and Fourneau du Diable (Dordogne) in France. Probable signs of short-lived cereal cultivation in Nile Valley.
15,500–10,000 BC: Development of Magdalenian (evolution of bone industry, improvement in quality of portable and mural art) and Gravettian: climax of Paleolithic art.

4. Magdalenian bone sculpture of bison with turned head found in the cave of La Magdeleine, Dordogne.

15,000 BC: Probable date of paintings and engravings on cave walls at Lascaux (Dordogne), France.
14,000–11,000 BC: Development of El-Kebareh civilization in southwest Asia (Israel). First free-standing round cabins.
12,500–9500 BC: Flowering of Magdalenian civilization. Rise of bone and antler industries (assegais, harpoons, fishing spears) of Upper Magdalenian.
11,000 BC: Probable median date of Altamira paintings (Santander, Spain) and Niaux drawings (Ariège, France). Optimum climate of Natufian in Near East. Increase in rainfall changes arid land into grasslands with deciduous trees. Birth of Natufian civilization (from Wadi-al-Nattuf site near Jerusalem), formation of first permanent settlements. Hunting and systematic gathering, storing of wild cereals.
9800 BC: Beginning of climatic improvement of Allerod (Denmark). Last manifestations of Magdalenian culture in Europe. Rise of late Gravettian and Alizian cultures in

split up and station itself either next to a ford, on a migratory route or by a beaten track to exploit abundant if ephemeral resources. The obvious risks of an economy based on predation hardly affected its success, as shown by the diversity of material cultures, the strength of religious traditions underlying a cycle of artistic creation that lasted over twenty millennia and above all the multiplicity of sites. The systematic extension of hunting to smaller species such as birds and fish, aided by marked technological improvements such as the bow may have been due to the pressure of population growth.

We do not know what this tension might have produced had the environment remained unchanged; however, the improvement in climate around 12,000 years ago might well be seen in the context of Western Europe as a negative factor. It produced a profound renewal of eco-systems in an increasingly wooded, overgrown environment and for a while put an end to large groupings of people in favour of the most adaptive segment of society, the nuclear family. Hunting became less productive and was supplemented by intensive gathering of smaller animals such as rabbits and snails and new vegetable species such as pulses.

These groups of hunters now benefited from more diverse resources brought about by an increase in the biomass (total mass of living organisms) in a now temperate environment; they adapted their social structures and were able to respond to the post-glacial challenge, making a smooth transition to the Mesolithic period. According to data relating to southwest Asia, particularly the mountainous zones of Palestine, Commagene and Zagros in Asia Minor, the marked rise in rainfall around 13,000 years ago was a particularly dynamic factor.

The optimum climate of the Natufian (Mesolithic cultural horizon of Palestine) produced a sort of savanna with trees eminently favourable to human settlement. The natural presence of animal and vegetable resources, particularly wild cereals which were easy to store, favoured a sedentary existence and the formation of the first real villages about 12,000 years ago.

These successful adaptations began a process in which demographic forces played an essential role and which led – depending on the advantages and constraints of each zone – to an ever greater mastery of the natural environment.

3. Bisons of the Salon Noir, Niaux, Ariège, France. Magdalenian cave paintings.

5. The game found in the Vézère Valley. Magdalenian carved bone.

Mediterranean Europe. Alizian pebbles painted and engraved with abstract designs (from Mas-d'Azil, Ariège, France).
8200 BC: End of third and last glaciation.
8000 BC: Systematic harvesting of pulses at La Balma de l'Abeurador (Hérault, France). First one-off attempt at pottery at Mureybet (Syria).
7600 BC: First agriculture in southwest Asia.
7500–5000BC: Western European Mesolithic. Sauveterrian and Tardenoisian designs of triangles and trapeziums.
5500 BC: Appearance of early forms of cattle farming in Mediterranean regions of Western Europe.

6. Pebble decorated with geometric design found at Mas-d'Azil, Ariège. Azilian period.

The Domestication of Plants and Animals

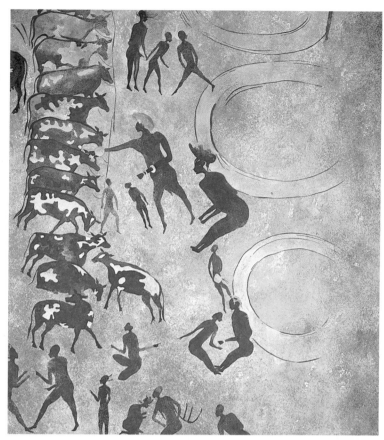

1. African herdsmen gathering their cattle. Cave painting of Tassili-n-Ajjer, Algerian Sahara, 4th millennium BC.

A MUTATION of tremendous importance in human history began to occur about 10,000 years ago with the appearance of animal breeding, agriculture and pottery and the first farming communities. These practices spread more or less rapidly to the main populated areas of the world apart from a few resistant pockets of isolated people still living from hunting and gathering. This new epoch – the Neolithic – when settlement in villages became widespread, was the beginning of a crucial stage in human evolution; it laid the foundations for past and present rural societies. This was no instant, decisive revolution; today's prehistorians see it rather as the outcome of a long condition-

ing of the natural habitat by humans, the establishment of new relations with the environment as societies became more developed.

Several regions of the world shared this development, each in its own way and quite independently. Southwest Asia or the Near East offer examples of advanced settlements with underground homes built of wood, clay and partly of stone, although the economy was still based on hunting (Mallaha-Eynan in Palestine, tenth millennium BC). This budding architecture was to make further progress as the climate became drier towards the end of the ninth millennium (Jericho). A millennium and a half later, around 6500 BC, Catalhuyuk in Turkey presents a typical example of a prosperous Neolithic settlement. Towards the middle of the eighth millennium, from Anatolia to Palestine, barley and certain types of wheat were grown for the first time. In the same geographical area sheep, goats, pigs and oxen were more or less rapidly brought into domestication; stone was still the preferred material for receptacles, with terra cotta coming into general use around 6500 BC.

The Near-Eastern Neolithic cultures were a powerful influence that encouraged the setting up of the first farming communities in Egypt and Europe; these also spread to the Caucasus and Iran and to Afghan, Indian, Yemeni and Cushitic lands. In Africa pottery was introduced very early, appearing in the Sahara before animal farming and agriculture, in the eighth and seventh millennia. On the African continent numerous indigenous plants were progressively brought into cultivation: sorghum, millet, African rice, yam. In China the first permanent villages took root along the Huang Ho River on land rich with deposits of silt (loesslands) (Yang-shao civilization of the fifth and fourth millennia). Rice-growing, either indigenous or imported from more southerly regions, appeared early on in the lower Yanze Valley at Ho-mu-tu.

Horticulture was established very early in Southeast Asia and Oceania. On the American continent permanent settlements predated the advent of agriculture (Anáhuac, Mexico); here marrows, beans and perhaps already maize were grown progressively from the sixth millennium. Around the same period the Andes (Guitarrero caves) then the Pacific coast of Ecuador and Chile were prime centres of agricultural development.

At different points of the globe production economies appeared and gradually took over until the process became irreversible.

11,000 BC: Japanese pottery with relief and intaglio decoration (Fukui cave, Kyushu) followed by Jomon cord-marked pottery (Jomon means cord-print). Early centre for pottery-making develops in East Asia.
From 10,000 BC: Near-Eastern Natufian 'villages' with round houses (Syria, Palestine), first permanent settlements. Stone polishing techniques applied to objects of adornment. Southeast Asia: horticulture in New Guinea (find of polished axes or adzes dating from c. 9000 BC at Kafiavana). Near East, northwest Europe and North America (Jaguar cave): dogs are domesticated.
c. 8500–8000 BC: First cereals – wheat and barley – grown at Jericho in Jordan, at Tell Aswad and Mureybet in Syria. Fleeting appearance of terracotta at Mureybet. Tower and wall of Jericho, pre-ceramic Neolithic.
c. 8000 BC: Pottery appears in the Sahara. Domestication of pigs in progress in Crimea.
c. 7500–7000 BC: Definitive domestication of goats and sheep in the Near East (Iran, Jordan). Oxen are domesticated a little later, in the Eastern Mediterranean (7th

millennium). First work of hammered copper at Cayonutepes, Turkey.
c. 6500–5700 BC: Catalhuyuk, important Neolithic village of Anatolia: houses and sanctuary made of unfired bricks and frescoes of goddesses and bulls.
c. 6000 BC: First farming communities of southeast Europe.
c. 5500 BC: Progressive cultivation of capsicums and beans in the Andes. Agriculture develops a little later on the Peruvian coast.
c. 5000 BC: First settlements in Anáhuac, Mexico (Zohapilco). First Western European farmer.
From c. 5000 BC: Beginning of domestication of camelids (lama, alpaca) in Andes (Lauricocha, Junin). Spread of marrow, bean and maize cultivation in Mexico (Tehuacán).
c. 4500 BC: First flowering of Megalithic phenomenon: dolmens, menhirs in Western Atlantic regions (Brittany, Portugal).
c. 4000 BC: Evidence of rice cultivation in Ho-mu-tu in China (Ch'ing-lien-kang

2. Mother-Goddess of Catalhuyuk, Turkey, 7th millennium BC.

3. Ceramic pot, Longshan culture, China, end of 3rd millennium BC.

11,000–2000 BC

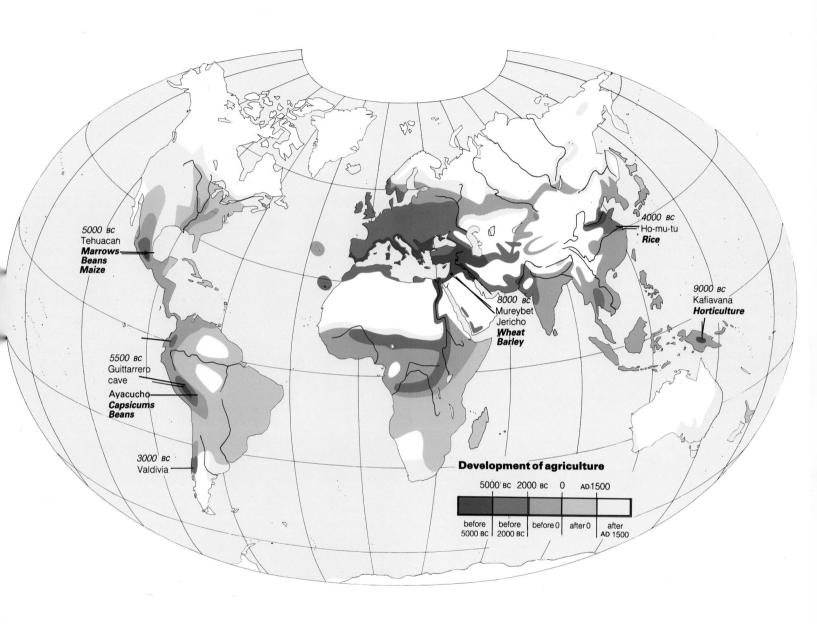

5000 BC
Tehuacan
**Marrows
Beans
Maize**

5500 BC
Guittarrero
cave

Ayacucho
**Capsicums
Beans**

3000 BC
Valdivia

4000 BC
Ho-mu-tu
Rice

8000 BC
Mureybet
Jericho
**Wheat
Barley**

9000 BC
Kafiavana
Horticulture

Development of agriculture

5000 BC	2000 BC	0	AD 1500	
before 5000 BC	before 2000 BC	before 0	after 0	after AD 1500

4. *Bone comb from the Island of Gotland, Sweden, 1st millennium BC.*

civilization). Large Chinese Neolithic villages (Yang-shao culture) with pottery, hoes, polished axes, weights for digging sticks and millet cultivation. Development of metalwork in Central Europe.
c. 3000–2500 BC: Progressive transition to Bronze Age in Central-western Asia, Europe, Egypt, China.

Climatic variations from the Neolithic age to the present day

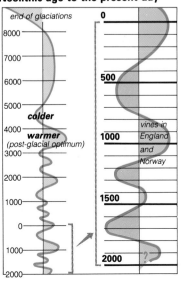

end of glaciations

8000

7000

6000

5000

4000

colder

warmer
(post-glacial optimum)

3000

2000

1000

0

1000

2000

0

500

1000

1500

2000

vines in England and Norway

The Birth of Art

ABSTRACT AND FIGURATIVE ART already exist side by side in the prehistoric world. There is no general chronological law governing the unfurling of prehistoric art: its canons and its evolution vary according to time and place. In Europe the Upper Paleolithic (between 30,000 and 9000 BC) produced exceptionally fine works, including engravings, sculptures and mural paintings in caves, rock shelters and in the open, and also objects of bone, ivory or stone. Portable artefacts are the most widely distributed, from the Atlantic to Siberia, from Belgium to the south of Italy, but mural art is only found in particular areas such as Périgord, the Pyrenees and Asturias, with a few exceptions such as the cave of Kapora in the Urals. Its main theme was the large fauna of the Quaternary period, which is depicted realistically; human forms are much rarer and are represented in a schematic or distorted manner; abstract or more or less unintelligible signs complete the motifs. The same differentiation is found in portable artefacts: in Périgordian art (25,000–20,000 BC) figures of women predominate (statuettes with rounded forms). The meaning of European Paleolithic art has been hotly debated: at first it was considered purely aesthetic, then the images were thought to be magical, serving to cast hunting spells. Today's researchers think it could be the expression of a complex cosmogony, a mythology based on sexual symbolism or perhaps the representation of systems of alliance between social groups.

In post-Glacial times (8000–5000 BC) Mediterranean Spain evolved an original art form known as Iberian Levant. It is characterized by fast-moving narratives full of vitality, such as boar and deer hunts and battle scenes.

The Sahara and regions bordering on it had their own particular cave art, the oldest of which dates from just before the sixth millennium BC. The earliest works are essentially naturalistic, with human figures and an abundant fauna; the paintings of Tassili-n-Ajjer are original in their portrayal of round-headed people. Oxen then became the favourite theme of the cattle herders of the Middle Neolithic period, and these in turn gave way, in the second millennium, to stiffer representations of equine animals and carts. The cave art of Southern Africa, most of which is attributed to the Bushmen or their predecessors, shows mainly predatory scenes. In northeast Brazil traces of paintings dating back at least 15,000 years BC are evidence of a very varied figurative cave art.

In general terms we can say that cave art in the last stages of prehistory and the first historical times was more or less universal, from the stone engravings of the Neolithic forest period in the USSR to the schematic Metal Age schools of the Val des Merveilles, the Iberian peninsula or Scandinavia.

Neolithic art in southern Asia, the Mediterranean and Europe often takes the form of a multiplicity of idols of stone or bone. The first statues in Europe – menhir statues – draw their motifs from deities or heroes of the period; the finest examples of these are in Anatolia and Malta.

Because it is found in so many different locations and spans such a long period, prehistoric art is a very complex phenomenon; the themes, styles and meanings of the recognized schools defy reduction to a single explanation.

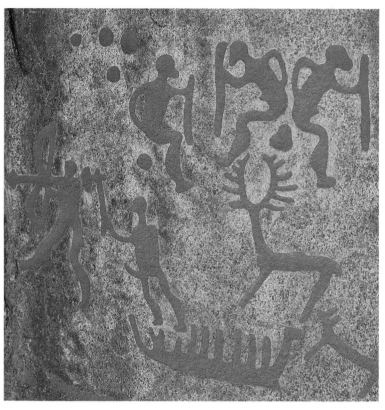

1. Hunters and animals. Cave engraving from Tanum, Sweden, 2nd millennium BC.

3. Cave of Lascaux, Dordogne, wild oxen of the rotunda. Early Magdalenian cave paintings.

c. 35,000 BC: Beginnings of European Paleolithic art. Pre-figurative period: Mousterian or Chatelperronian incisions in bone or stone slabs.
30,000–23,000 BC: Aurignacian art. Scribblings, vulvar forms, heads or forequarters of animals (stone slabs of La Ferrassie, rock shelters at Castenet and Cellier).
23,000–19,000 BC: Early Gravettian and Solutrean art. Depiction of animals with sinuous spines and ill-defined extremities. Bas-reliefs of Laussel (Dordogne). Carvings of Pair-non-Pair (Gironde). Sculpted 'Venus' figurines of Brassempouy, Lespugue, Willendorf (Austria).
19,000–13,000 BC: Early Solutrean and Magdalenian art. Sculpted blocks of stone of Roc de Sers, Cap Blanc and Bourdeilles. Cave drawings of Lascaux and Pech-Merle.
From 15,000 BC: Beginnings of cave art in South America (Brazil). Shelter of Toca do Boqueirao de Pedra Furada.
13,000–9000 BC: Middle and Upper Magdalenian art. Paintings of Font-de-Gaume, Niaux, Rouffignac, Altamira, engravings of Teyjat and Limeuil in the Dordogne. Bisons and modelled figures of bears (Tuc d'Andoubert, Bedeilhac, Montespan).
8000–7000 BC: Art of the Arctic zone, including Scandinavia, northern Russia and Siberia. Dotted figures of large mammals, birds, fishes, reptiles and also boats and people wearing skis. (The Neolithic art of Carelia (around 3000 BC) belongs to the same cultural area.) Beginnings of Iberian Levant art.
From 6000 BC: Art of Sahara and Maghreb, early phase (giant buffaloes). Around 4000 BC, art of cattle herders of Hoggar, Tibesti, Fezzan, Libya, Nubia, Harran. First South African art (engravings of Orange and Vaal Valleys, paintings of Drakensberg); beginning

4. Hares of Tassili-n-Ajjer, Algerian Sahara. Neolithic cave painting, c. 4500 BC.

35,000–1500 BC

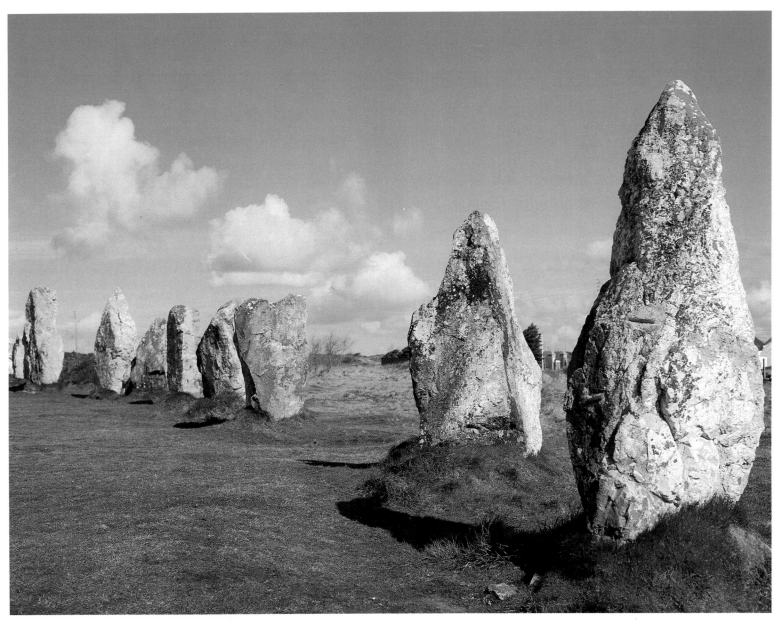

2. Alignment of stones at Lagat-Jar, Brittany, Neolithic period.

of a long line of development.

c. 6000 BC: Wall paintings of Catalhuyuk in Turkey.

From 5500 BC: Neolithic statuettes of South-Eastern Europe.

c. 5000 BC: Fish idols of Lepenski-Vir (Yugoslavia).

From 4000 BC: Megalithic art of Western Europe.

c. 2500 BC: Cycladic figurines. Menhir statues of Sardinia and southern France.

c. 2500–500 BC: Art of Val Camonica in Northern Italy.

c. 2000–1500 BC: Cave engravings of Mont Bego (Alpes Maritimes, France).

c. 1500 BC: Scandinavian bronze engravings. Horses and carts of Sahara.

c. AD 1800–1900: 'X-ray' art of Australian Aboriginals

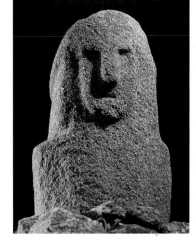

5. Carnac cave in the Lot, a reindeer. Early Magdalenian cave painting.

6. Marble Cycladic idol from Amorgos, Greece, c. 2500 BC.

7. Menhir statue from Filitosa, Corsica, c. 1500 BC.

Sumer and Akkad: Cities and Writing

1. A powerful and remarkably well-organized army.

2. A hierarchical society, a diversified economy and a rich, unifying culture.

MESOPOTAMIAN CIVILIZATION was born in the fourth millennium in Lower Mesopotamia. In this gradually emerging alluvial territory, there came together diverse populations who had come down from the mountain country to the north and east, as the ground drained. Vestiges of their cultures remain, but we have no means of identifying them. Only two groups, who came later on the scene and were more significant, have emerged into the light of history. These are the Sumerians, who came from the south-east, having severed all ties with the rest of their people (if indeed they left any of them behind) and who are totally isolated linguistically, and a Semitic population, who are connected to a known cultural and linguistic branch of humanity, which still flourishes today. The first people to arrive, as early as the fourth millennium, had originally belonged to the group of semi-nomadic sheep and goat rearers in the north of the Syrio-Arabian desert. From there, throughout the whole of history, they repeatedly came, singly or in waves, to settle among the Mesopotamians. First these Semitic peoples, who were more numerous in the north of the country, and the Sumerians in the south had to assimilate the old 'underlying' populations, and they grew progressively closer together in their cultural life, giving birth by this pooling of their cultural capital to the local civilization. The land was particularly well suited to livestock-rearing and to large-scale cereal cultivation, so long as the meagre levels of precipitation were supplemented by artificial irrigation. It was the undertaking of vast canal-building works which furthered both the prosperity of the region and the uniting of these populations under a single leader, who was capable of planning, commanding and governing, and ensuring the circulation of goods, even over long distances, as means of obtaining, by commerce or war, the materials lacking in this land of clay, reeds and asphalt, namely wood, stone and metal. These groupings of people gave rise to the formation of city-states, types of principalities which divided the territory into areas of land around the administrative and religious centre constituted by a city. At that point, along with a complex political organization of a monarchic type, monumental arts, metalworking, both in copper and later in bronze, underwent considerable development, together with a number of other techniques against the background of an ever-expanding economy. Around 3000 BC, to smooth the running of that economy, Sumerians developed the first forms of writing. At first picto- or ideographic, the phonetic value of signs was soon discovered and from being a mere aid to memory, this writing became a prodigious instrument for acquiring and propagating knowledge. The division into city-states was solely political: these all shared the same culture, as is very clearly shown by the establishment of a single pantheon and a single religious metropolis for the whole country. Quite early on, the Sumerians merged into the Semite population, the ranks of which were continually being swelled by new arrivals. It is, however, a sign of their acknowledged cultural supremacy that the Sumerian language continued to be used for cultural and liturgical purposes. Around 2300 BC the first unification of the country and the surrounding lands into an empire stretching from the Mediterranean to southwest Iran with Agade as its centre was achieved by Semites, who came subsequently to be known as 'Akkadians', under the leadership of the king known as 'Sargon the Great'. This enormous edifice lasted little more than a hundred years before it collapsed, but its political model was to mark the country for ever, as well as enshrining Semite hegemony. The kingdom of Ur (Ur III), which closes the millennium, would not weaken that hegemony, even though the official language was still Sumerian and the century turned out to be the golden age of Sumerian literature.

First Uruk archives.

Gilgamesh king of Uruk.

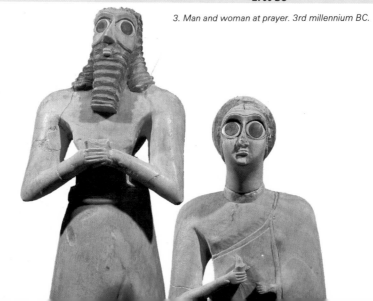

3. Man and woman at prayer. 3rd millennium BC.

3000 BC

2700 BC

4th millennium: Sumero-Semitic symbiosis: first towns (city-states) and emergence of local civilization.

c. 3000 BC: First Uruk archives. Writing invented: initially the tablets are used only for administrative operations and systematic lists of characters; they are pictographic and ideographic.

c. 2900 BC: First traces of the discovery of the phonetic value of written signs (in the Uruk archives).

2750–2650 BC: First Kish dynasty with the oldest known 'historic' king, Enmebaragesi (c. 2700 BC). First Uruk dynasty with its legendary kings: Gilgamesh. Fortifications are built around the towns. First dynasty of Ur: ancient archives and the 'royal cemetery' (the king's household is killed at his death to accompany him into the afterlife).

c. 2600 BC: At Fa'rah (Shuruppak) and Tell Abu-Salabikh, the first properly literary texts are produced (hymns, 'incantations' and myths).

2500–2350 BC: First Lagash dynasty (c. 2490 BC: Ur-Nanshe; c. 2400 BC: Eannatum:

c. 2350 BC: Uru'inimgina (Urukagina)) and royal archives. Ebla archives. First Mari kings.

2334–2279 BC: Sargon, a former officer of Ur-Zababa, King of Kish, kills Lugalzaggesi, takes over his kingdom, which he unifies around his capital Agade and expands it in the course of a series of military campaigns to the east and the west. He becomes master of a vast area of Near-Eastern territory, from the Mediterranean to the south-west marches of Iran. He thus founds and organizes the first Mesopotamian empire and inaugurates an important cultural fermentation of which few vestiges remain today. His descendants and successors – right down to Naram-Sin (2254–2218 BC) – will endeavour to maintain this edifice against both the internal revolts and external attacks which will ultimately destroy it in the reign of the Shar-kali-sharri, last king of the dynasty (2217–2193 BC). A period of anarchy ensues.

c. 2200 BC: The Gutians, mountain dwellers from the Zagros Mountains, invade and probably destroy a large part of the country, especially in the north.

3500–2000 BC

Modern names
of the Principal Sites:

Adab / *Bismaya*
Cuthah / *Tall Sifir*
Der / *Tall 'Agra*
Eshnunna / *Tall al Asmar*
Eridu / *Abu Shahrayn*
Girsu / *Tello*
Isin / *Bahriyat*
Kish / *Uhaimir*
Lagash / *Tall al-Hiba*
Larsa / *Senkera*
Nippur / *Niffer*
Shuruppak / *Tall Fa'rah*
Sippar / *Abu Habba*
Umma / *Tall Jokha*

• Main historic sites — - - - Ancient canals ○ Modern towns
● Sumerian and Akkadian sites ⇒ Extent of Sargon's penetration

Zone of Akkad influence
in the time of Sargon I
500 km
100 km

Sargon king of Akkad.   Gutian invasion. Gudea king of Lagash. Ur-Nammu king of Ur.

2334 BC   2200 BC 2141 BC   2112 BC

Between 2155 and 2111 BC: An
independent dynasty exists in Lagash which
seems to have brought prosperity to this
city-state. Its most famous sovereign is
Gudea (2141–2122 BC).

4. King Gudea.

2123 and 2113 BC: Ut-khegal of Uruk expels
the Gutians and recaptures a large part of the
country.
2112–2095 BC: Ur-Nammu, one of his
officers, supplants him and founds the third
Ur dynasty (Ur III), thus opening up a brilliant
and productive century in which Sumerian art
flourishes. This is also, however, a period of
many battles, both offensive and defensive
(largely against the Elamites of southwest
Iran, fought both by Ur-Nammu and his
successors, Shulgi (2094–2047), Amar-Sin
(2046–2038), Shu-Sin (2037–2029) and Ibbi
Su'en (2028–2004 BC). The last-mentioned
succumbs to the Elamites in 2004 BC and the
dominance of Ur dies with him. It is during the
Ur III period that the first Amorite Semites
began to infiltrate into the kingdom after
several threats against and attacks upon its
northwestern flank.

5. Land of clay, reeds and asphalt.

The Nile and the First Pharaohs

THE NILE VALLEY is bathed daily in the sun's rays and inundated each year by a flood that fertilizes the land around it at the height of summer. From 3000 BC onwards it was the cradle of an original civilization ruled over by a human god, the pharaoh. Menes, who, according to Herodotus, was the first Egyptian pharaoh, united Upper and Lower Egypt and imposed his authority upon a hard-working, disciplined peasant population. They were to show little inclination to challenge the foundations of a system that lasted for almost three thousand years. Exercising a power inherited from his divine forefathers, the pharaoh was master of the water and the land. A god among men, he was considered the guarantor of cosmic equilibrium and of the sound running of the country. As early as the first dynasty, the system of hieroglyphic writing was becoming highly developed; it would prove to be a vehicle for the expression of all the subtleties of human thought.

Menes, who had been born in the southern town of This, took up residence on the site of what was to become Memphis, on the borders of the Delta and Upper Egypt. The Old Kingdom (third to sixth dynasties) was the age of the great pyramid-builders. It was Imhotep, the architect of King Djoser (or Zoser) of the third dynasty, who had the revolutionary idea of abandoning sun-dried brick and using stone to build the step pyramid of Saqqarah. Djoser's successors would be buried beneath the famous Giza pyramids, then beneath those at Abu Sir (fifth dynasty) and along the whole of the Memphis plateau. The pyramids, which represented petrified sun rays, made it possible for the king to be united in the afterlife with the Sun God Ré, as did the magic formulas which covered their walls. These 'pyramid writings' are evidence of the dominant influence upon official theology of the priesthood of Heliopolis, who were sun-worshippers. By contrast, the popular pantheon was still very much influenced by archaic forms of worship, and major deities were beginning to be created by the amalgamation of the multitude of local animal gods. From Memphis, the administration organized the country's economy: at the head of this leading élite we find a class of privileged functionaries who had themselves buried in great 'mastabas' (low oblong tombs) built around the royal pyramids.

Being under no external threat, the pharaohs of the Old Kingdom launched no colonial wars; the major external activities of which there is evidence were commercial and mining expeditions (the former in Phoenicia and Nubia, the latter in Sinai). Following the long reign of Pepi II (2330–2240 BC), a grave social crisis shook the country: the provinces threw off the authority of the central monarchy and set

1. Djoser's pyramid at Saqqarah.

2. Scene from a wall of a princess's 'mastaba'.

themselves up as little kingdoms; Bedouins invaded the Delta and there was widespread famine and violence (seventh to eleventh dynasties).

The family of the pharaohs of the twelfth dynasty, which originated in Thebes in Upper Egypt, extended its rule over the whole of the country and transferred the capital to Lisht in Middle Egypt. Schools of scribes produced propagandist literature with the aim of restoring monarchist ideology. The great economic achievement of the Middle Empire was the development of the Faiyum region. Abroad, Nubia was colonised, Palestine fell under Egyptian tutelage and expeditions into Libya became more frequent. At the end of the Middle Kingdom the invasion of the Hyksos, who were Canaanite in origin, led to the break-up of the kingdom. A new capital, Avaris, became the residence of these foreigners who ruled over most of Lower Egypt.

First Pharaoh.   **First pyramid (Djoser).**   **Giza.**   **Jubilee shrine at Karna**

3000BC	2660 BC	2600 BC	1972 BC

3000–2660 BC: THINITE PERIOD (1st and 2nd dynasties). Menes and his successors organized the kingdom by developing irrigation. The establishment of the Sothiac (Sirius-based) calendar with a 365-day year. Building was carried out in sun-dried brick (Abydos, Saqqarah), and the making of statues developed.

2660–2180 BC: OLD KINGDOM (3rd–6th dynasties).
2660–2600 BC: 3rd Dynasty. Djoser, Sekhemkhet and Huni are the major figures of this dynasty, together with Imhotep, Djoser's vizier and architect. First stone pyramids; beginning of 'mastabas' for individuals.

2600–2480 BC: 4th dynasty. Snefru, Khufu (Cheops), Retdjedef (Djedfre), Khafre (Chephren) and Menkaure (Mycerinus), builders of the great pyramids (Maydum, Giza, Abou Roash). The statue of the Great Sphinx stands in front of Khafre's at Giza. Statuary, both royal and private, reached a

5. The seated scribe, 4th dynasty, Saqqarah.

peak of perfection which was to constitute a benchmark for artists of later periods.

2480–2330 BC: 5th dynasty. Userkaf, Sahure, Neferirkare, Shepseskare, Neuserre, Menkauhor, Izezi and Onas succeeded one another on the throne. Their pyramids were smaller and are today less well preserved than those of their predecessors (Saqqarah, Abu Sir). It is in Unas's pyramid that 'pyramid writings' first make their appearance. The great court figures had scenes from daily life depicted on the walls of their 'mastabas' (Giza, Saqqarah).

2330–2180 BC: 6th dynasty. Teti, Userkare, Pepi I and Merenre precede the long reign of Pepi II. Marked increase in the power of provincial governors, who began to gain some independence from central government. The provincial necropolises become more ornate. at Meir, Dayr el Gabrawi, Aswan, Edfu and Dendera the tombs are decorated with great refinement.

2180–1990 BC: FIRST INTERMEDIATE PERIOD (7th–11th dynasties). Anarchy and the dismantling of pharaonic organization. War between various kinglets, particularly between the Heracleapolitans (Middle Egypt) and the Thebans (Upper Egypt). With a few rare exceptions, art was very undeveloped, but under the 11th dynasty there was an appreciable renewal in this field with the accession of Intef and Montuhotep, who re-established unity.

1990–1780 BC: MIDDLE EMPIRE (12th dynasty). Amenhemhat I, Sesostris I, Amenhemhat II, Sesostris II, Sesostris III, Amenhemhat III, Amenhemhat IV and Queen Sebeknefru made up this glorious dynasty. The royal pyramids built in the Faiyum were of modest dimensions. From this point on, the funereal inscriptions were 'democratized' and the 'sarcophagus writings' helped each individual to accede to the realm of Osiris. Numerous sanctuaries were built in various parts of the valley. The royal sculpture workshops were reopened.

3000–1560 BC

Old Empire −2660 to −2180	−2180/−1990	Middle Empire −1990 to −1780	−1780 to −1560
Trade with the Phoenicians. MEMPHIS, SINAI (copper mines), LOWER EGYPT, THIS, UPPER EGYPT, Buhen, Nubia (gold mines), Trade with Africa	Heraclepolis Magna, Bedouins, Thebes, Nubians. 1st intermediate period disturbances, incessant struggles between Heraclepolis and Thebes	immigration, Control over Palestine, LIBYA, EL-LISHT, Development of the Faiyum, NUBIA	CANAAN, AVARIS, Hyksos

3. Nefertiti, wife of the high priest of Heliopolis, 4th dynasty, Maydum.

4. The royal symbol of the falcon, 6th dynasty, Hierakonopolis.

Classical Egyptian language established.

1878 BC

1780–1560 BC: SECOND INTERMEDIATE PERIOD (13th–17th dynasties). Hyksos invasion of the Delta. Social and political disturbances.

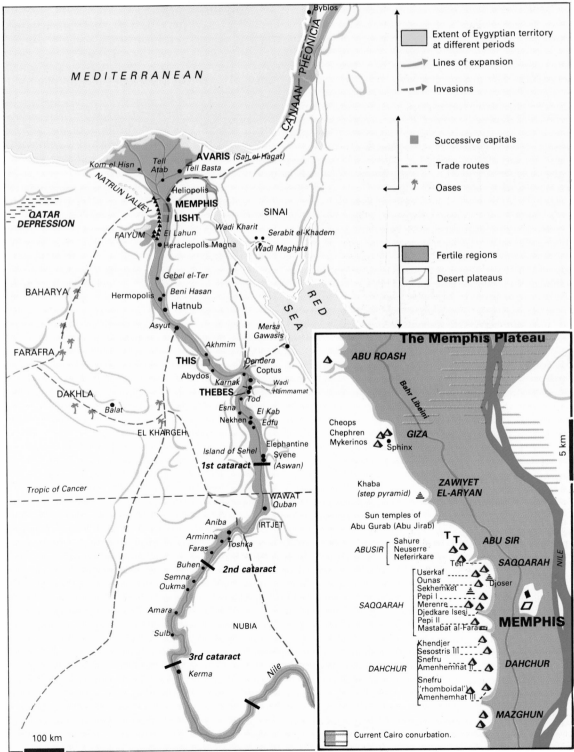

Legend

- Extent of Eygyptian territory at different periods
- Lines of expansion
- Invasions
- Successive capitals
- Trade routes
- Oases
- Fertile regions
- Desert plateaus

MEDITERRANEAN

Byblos

CANAAN – PHEONICIA

Kom el Hisn · Tell Atab · AVARIS (Sah el Hagat) · Tell Basta
Heliopolis
NATRUN VALLEY
MEMPHIS
QATAR DEPRESSION
LISHT
SINAI
FAIYUM · El Lahun · Wadi Kharit · Serabit el-Khadem
Heraclepolis Magna · Wadi Maghara
BAHARYA
Gebel el-Ter
Hermopolis · Beni Hasan
Hatnub
RED SEA
FARAFRA
Asyut
Mersa Gawasis
Akhmim
THIS
Dendera · Coptus
DAKHLA
Abydos · Karnak · Wadi Hammamat
Balat
THEBES · Tod
EL KHARGEH
Esna · El Kab
Nekhen · Edfu
Island of Sehel · Elephantine Syene (Aswan)
1st cataract

Tropic of Cancer

WAWAT · Quban
Aniba · IRTJET
Arminna · Toshka
Faras
Buhen · **2nd cataract**
Semna
Oukma
Amara
Sulb
NUBIA
3rd cataract · Kerma · Nile

100 km

The Memphis Plateau

ABU ROASH
Bahr Libeini
Cheops / Chephren / Mykerinos · GIZA · Sphinx
Khaba (step pyramid) · ZAWIYET EL-ARYAN
Sun temples of Abu Gurab (Abu Jirab)
ABUSIR { Sahure / Neuserre / Neferirkare } · ABU SIR
Tetr · SAQQARAH
SAQQARAH { Userkaf / Ounas / Sekhemket / Pepi I / Merenre / Djedkare Isesi / Pepi II / Mastabat al-Fara } · Djoser
MEMPHIS
DAHCHUR { Khendjer / Sesostris III / Snefru / Amenhemhat II } · DAHCHUR
Snefru 'rhomboidal' / Amenhemhat II
MAZGHUN

5 km

NILE

Current Cairo conurbation.

The Destiny of Babylon

AT THE BEGINNING of the second millennium BC, Mesopotamia was in the hands of the Semites, who had been joined nearly a century before by a new wave of invaders, the Amorites. Around 1750 BC the Amorites, headed by Hammurabi, put an end to the regime of city states which had been more or less revived after the third dynasty of Ur, and gave the country its definitive structure as a kingdom with Babylon as its capital. This political triumph marked the climax of the powerful cultural movement started by Sargon of Akkad. Institutions developed, techniques were perfected, thinkers ventured further into old and new realms, such as legal theory, lexicography and grammar, mathematics, divination, medicine, mythology (the 'philosophy' of the time). A great original literature was born.

1. Clay walls of the town of Nimrud, capital of Assyrian Empire, 9th century BC.

The invasion of the Kassites around 1600 BC plunged Babylonia into three centuries of political stagnation, but this was a climate propitious to the development of culture and literature in particular. Meanwhile, the Near East had changed its face: Egypt was increasingly involved in the international arena, and new and powerful kingdoms began to make their influence felt, the Hittites in Anatolia, the Mitanni in Syria and in northern Mesopotamia, and the Assyrians, who had regained independence around their original capital of Ashur. In addition, a new Semitic wave was unfurling, the Aramaeans, who were to prove resistant to assimilation. When Babylon, now reduced to its sole southern territory, finally awoke around 1100 BC it was not at first an impressive force. Between 1000 and 700 BC it was obscured by the military might of Assyria, which went from conquest to conquest, particularly on the western front, reaching its peak of glory after 700 BC with the Sargonid dynasty. But culturally it remained dependent on Babylon, the unrivalled intellectual and spiritual capital, which was alone capable of original thought and literature. When Nabopolassar, allied to the increasingly powerful Medes, destroyed Nineveh and forever wiped Assyria off the map, the glorious and awe-inspiring New Babylonian Empire had only a century to live. In 539 BC the founder of the Achaemenid Empire, Cyrus the Great, took Babylon without a struggle and reduced it to the provincial capital of one of his satrapies.

Babylon remained an intellectual centre, but the Aramaean language with its alphabet gradually replaced Akkadian in everyday usage. As Sumerian had done before, Akkadian became a high-brow language protected by its cuneiform script; it was confined, along with the culture it transmitted, to erudite circles whose task was not to create but to defend and promote the intellectual heritage. It was even transcribed in Greek for the Hellenistic world after Alexander's conquest of Mesopotamia in 331 BC, at the beginning of the Seleucid era. From now on, up to its final annihilation by the Parthians in 144 BC, Mesopotamia could only fade away. It had already dispensed the best of its creations over three millennia to lands as far distant as Israel and Greece, who, after adapting and assimilating this precious heritage, handed it down to us in turn.

Babylon sank into obscurity for two millennia. Then it took over fifty years, between 1800 and 1870, to unlock the secret of its extraordinary writing and its languages, to gradually unearth its clay archives spanning 3,000 years. Today we have managed to recover some 500,000 pieces, our oldest 'family archives'.

Hammurabi accedes to throne.

1792 BC

2000–1800 BC: The main political configurations – Isin (Ishbi-Erra, 2017–1985 BC), Larsa (thirteen sovereigns, 2035–1763 BC), Babylon from Sumuabum (1894–1881 BC) onwards, and outlying kingdoms of Assyria and Mari – all appear to be manipulated by the powerful Amorites.
1792–1750 BC: Hammurabi, sixth king of the first dynasty of Babylon, unites the whole country around Babylon in a centralized monarchic system never to be challenged. His illustrious reign marks the climax of the period known as Old Babylonian. All fields of thought and literature flourish; not only are old masterpieces in Sumerian copied out with zeal, but a new literature in Akkadian is born.
1750–1595 BC: Hammurabi's successors, from Samsuiluna (1749–1712 BC) to Ammisaduqa (1646–1626 BC) did their best to preserve his heritage until it was destroyed during the reign of Samsuditana, when the Hittites destroyed Babylon in 1595 BC.
c. 1570 BC: The Kassites from the northeastern mountains establish political domination over the country: this lasts three centuries.

Kassite domination.

c.1570 BC

1365–1330 BC: The reign of Ashur-uballith I marks the awakening of Assyria: it shines for a century or two under a few great sovereigns (Shalmanesar I, 1274–1245 BC, Tukulti-Ninurta I, 1244–1208 BC) and then falls into obscurity.
1124–1103 BC: Nebuchadnezzar I restores Babylon's greatness, freeing the city from the Kassites in 1157 BC. The *Creation Epic*, published at this time, confirms Marduk's promotion to head of the universe and makes Babylon into the spiritual capital of the country. But Babylon is repeatedly invaded by nomads; it never recovers its political ascendency.
911–891 BC: From the reign of Adad-Nirari, Assyria reappears on the scene and begins to build a formidable empire which reaches the height of its military, political, economic and intellectual glory under Sargon II (731–705 BC) and his successors, Sennacherib (704–681 BC); Esarhaddon (680–669 BC) and, above all, Ashurbanipal (669–627 BC). Under attack from Babylon and the Medes in 612 BC, Nineveh falls and Assyria disappears.

The *Creation Epic*.

c. 1120 BC

From 604–562 BC (Nebuchadnezzar II) **to 555–539 BC** (Nabu-Na'id), Babylon is left alone to bear the standard for Mesopotamia. It recovers its former supremacy for a while. Aramaean influence grows.

4. Cuneiform characters.

Library of Ashurbanipal.

c. 650 BC

539 BC: Cyrus conquers Babylon, relegating it to a mere local capital of a satrapy of the Achaemenid Empire. Mesopotamia survives, but its culture languishes under a total lack of political autonomy.
331 BC: Alexander conquers it along with the whole of the Orient. He dies in 323 BC and the Seleucid period begins in 311 BC.
144 BC: Arrival of Parthians in Babylon sounds the death-knell for Mesopotamia; it is taken over by new political and cultural systems, stripped of its original features, its fabulous innovations plundered by other cultures.

2000–144 BC

First Babylonian Empire
2000 – 1500 BC

Taurus Mountains
Hittites
ZAGROS MOUNTAINS
Tigris
Aleppo
Ashur
Ashur conquered
1745 BC
Euphrates
Katna
Mari
Eshnunna conquered
1755 BC
Eshnunna
Kassites
MEDITERRANEAN
SEA
Mari conquered
1758 BC
Kerkha
(Rud-e Karun)
Babylon
Susa
*Babylon conquered
by Hittites
1595 BC*
Isin
ELAM
Larsa
Ur
Persian
Gulf
Nile

□ Original zone of occupation
on advent of Hammurabi
● Principal sites first
and second millenia
⊙ Rival kingdoms of Babylon
fought by Hammurabi
□ Maximum extent of Empire (1750-1595 BC)
→ Invasions and destructions of Empire

2. Crowned woman. Ivory statuette, Nimrud, c. 800 BC.

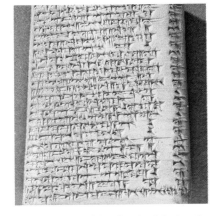

3. Fragment of Enuma elish or Creation Epic. Cuneiform
tablet, c. 600 BC.

Assyrian Empire
1800-1600 BC

Kanesh
Tigris
Medes
Carchemish
Haran
Nineveh
(Nimrud)
Dur Sharrukin
M E D I A
*Fall
of Niniveh
612 BC*
Ecbatana
Kalhu
Ashur
Ugarit
Tirqa
Divala
Rud-e
PHOENICIA
Euphrates
Kerkha
(Rud-e Karun)
MEDITERRANEAN
SEA
*Destruction
of Ashur
614 BC*
Babylon
Karun
ISRAEL
Chaldeans
Susa
PHILISTINES
ELAM
EGYPT
Nile
Persian
Gulf

□ Original zone of occupation
Successive extensions:
□ under Tukulti-Ninurta (1244-1208 BC)
□ under Sargon II (731-705 BC)
□ under Ashurbanipal (699-627 BC)
■ Successive capitals
→ Invasion and collapse
of Empire

Fall of Babylon. **Death of Alexander at Babylon**

539 BC 323 BC

5. Head count: two scribes record bows, quivers and heads of
the vanquished. Nineveh, 7th century BC.

New Babylonian Empire
600-500 BC

LYDIAN
KINGDOM
Tall Halaf
MEDIAN
Carchemish
Haran
Nineveh
KINGDOM
Haleb
Persians
Ashur
Tigris
Divala
MEDITERRANEAN
SEA
Euphrates
Kerkha
(Rud-e Karun)
Babylon
Susa
ISRAEL
*Conquest of Babylon
by Cyrus
539 BC*
ELAM
JUDAH
EGYPTIAN
KINGDOM
Persian
Gulf

□ Original zone of occupation
□ Conquests of Nebuchadnezzar II (604-562 BC)
□ Final conquests and maximum extent of Empire
→ Persian invasions

300 km

The Hittite Empire and its Legacy

HITTITE CIVILIZATION was born on the high Anatolian plain in the heart of Turkey. It is both a rather arid region, and inaccessible, being surrounded by mountains which offer excellent natural protection. The population which modern scholars have named the 'Hittites' after the term 'Hatti' (which designated the ethnic group that were the original natives of the region and who were, in the course of time, assimilated into the new population) began to penetrate into Anatolia around 2000 BC, settling initially in its southeastern corner. The Hittites spoke an idiom belonging to the vast group of languages known as Indo-European; indeed, their language is now its oldest known dialect. The creation of the Hittite State, which was to have Hattusa (the present village of Bogazkoy, 150 kilometres east of Ankara) as its capital, took place around 1650 BC. From that point onwards its power was continually extended and increased, until the little kingdom became a great power. It was to occupy a major place on the early political landscape of the Near East, alongside Egypt and Assyria.

The Hittites are one of the rare peoples to have used two parallel systems of writing. They used, first of all, a cuneiform script borrowed from Mesopotamia, in which their long texts were written on clay tablets. These documents were found in their thousands in the various archives of Hattusa. Along with Hittite, these archives reveal the use of a number of other languages on this site, including Palaite, Luwian (Indo-European dialects), Hatti, Sumerian, Akkadian and Hurrite. The same types of texts – political, religious and literary – were found there as had already been found in the neighbouring civilizations. The second system of writing, which was of the pictographic type (known, for that reason, as 'Hurrite hieroglyphics') was created in Anatolia itself around the year 1500 BC. It was used for ceremonial inscriptions which were most often carved on rocks. In the course of the centuries, the Hittites were to create a unique civilization in which Oriental influences and the underlying Hatti component would ultimately remain the essential ingredients.

The Hittite Empire collapsed around 1200 BC, radically modifying the ethnic and political geography of Anatolia and Syria. It was a violent end to a powerful state created by a warrior people, a state summed up in the following prayer: 'Strength and vigour to the King, the Queen, the Princes and their troops, and may their land be bounded on the left by the sea and by the sea on the right.'

2. The Lion Gate of Hattusa, 17th century BC.

After an obscure period lasting some two centuries and involving many transformations, a new situation emerged. Cohesiveness was followed by fragmentation. Though the high plateau was deserted, little kingdoms or Hittite city-states formed in the south-east of Anatolia and in northern Syria, where old traditions survived: chief among these were Tabal, made up of a federation of principalities located to the west of the Taurus Mountains, and Melitene, Gurgum, Commagene, Carchemish and Sam'al beyond that mountain chain. Whilst cuneiform writing disappeared, hieroglyphs remained in use and were indeed improved; they now came to be used in the writing of long texts. These so-called neo-Hittite states gave a three century reprieve (1000–700 BC) to the illustrious Anatolian civilization.

1. The armed gods of Yazilikaya. Rock carving, c. 1250 BC.

Assyrian merchants in Anatolia.

1900 BC

1900–1800 BC: Assyrian trading posts established in Anatolia between Kanesh (the present Kültepe) in the south and, following the Halys Valley (today, Kizil Irmak), the Black Sea in the north (Sinope). Assyrian tablets relating to commercial transactions represent the oldest vestiges of writing in Anatolia. The proper names of Indo-European origin which are found on these documents constitute the first evidence of the arrival in these regions of the Hittites, Luwians and Palaites.
c. 1650 BC: Accession of Hattusili I, who creates the Hittite state and sets up its capital at Hattusa.
1650–1600 BC: Period of the great military exploits of Hattusili I; they foreshadow the emergence of a powerful kingdom and mark the first territorial gains, notably Zalpa, Alalakh, Arzawa etc. The oldest texts in the Hittite language date from this same period. They are written in cuneiform characters and the most remarkable specimens are the historical annals, the laws and, above all, the political testament of Hattusili I, a unique document in ancient Near Eastern literature.

Hattusa capital.

1650 BC

The Hittites take Babylon.

1595 BC

1595 BC: Mursili I sacks Babylon.
c. 1500 BC: The first documents in hieroglyphic characters appear in the south-east of Anatolia. This script, which was a transcription of a Luwian dialect, spreads progressively over a large part of the territory.
c. 1300 BC: The Hittite Empire is at its height. Its frontiers are pushed forward in the east, south and west and it exerts substantial power and influence. Such a situation is not without its effects upon Hittite cultural and religious life, where syncretism becomes more and more evident. The majority of written documents date from this period.
1285 BC: Egyptians and Hittites fight at Kadesh for the domination of Syria. After the battle, its territory is divided up between them.
1250–1225 BC: Reign of Tudhaliya IV. The King completes the building of the Yazilikaya rock shrine (2 km from Hattusa), an extraordinary monument formed out of two

3. Early Bronze Age standard from the royal tombs of Alaca Hüyük. Beginning of 2nd millennium BC.

4. Cuneiform tablet in Babylonian syllabic script bearing the seal of King Mursili II (1344–1315 BC).

1900–700 BC

Hittite Sites

BLACK SEA

Zalpa

PAPHLAGONIA

Nerik?

BITHYNIA

Halys

Hatti

Tapigga

+ 3575   ‡ 3557

Etlik   **Hattusa**

Ankara   Bogazköy

Gordium

Halys

Kelkit

Euphrates

HIGH ANATOLIAN PLAIN

PHRYGIA

Sakarya

Samuha

Kanesh

Kültepe

CAPPADOCIA

Kayseri   + 3916

Lake Tuz

MELITENE

Malatya

Tyana

Kummanni

LYCIA   + 3734

GURGUM

Malash

COMMAGENE

TABAL

Ivriz

Karatepe

Sakçagöz

CARCHEMISH

Hupisna

Adana

TAURUS

Selçuk

Carchemish

Til Bersils

(Tell Ahmar)

CILICIA

SAM'AL

Arpad

Alakah

(Tell Acana)

Aleppo

Meskene

Euphrates

Tell Tayinat

UNQI-PATIN

MEDITERRANEAN SEA

Ugarit

(Ras Shamra)

Orontes

ALASHIYA (CYPRUS)

○ Kadesh

PHOENICIA

▨	Mountains and plateaus	■ Sites of the Imperial Period
▨	Low fertile regions	■ Neo-Hittite sites
□	Desert regions	⬭ City-states

100 km

1700 BC – 1200 BC
Imperial Period

Zalpa
1650BC

Troy

Hattusa

Halys

ASUWA
1430 – 1400BC

HASUWA

**MITANNI
(HURRITES)**

Tigris

Niniveh

ASSYRIA

MYCENEANS

Alalakh
1649BC

Aleppo

PHOENICIA

Kadesh
1285BC

Euphrates

KASSITES

Tyre

CANAAN

Babylon
1595BC

EGYPT

Nile

ARAMAEANS
1400BC

1000 BC – 700 BC
Neo-Hittite Period

Halys

PHRYGIA

URARTU

LYDIA

MELITENE

G.   C.

TABAL

S.   K.

Tigris

Niniveh

ASSYRIA

GREEK CITIES

U.P.

Euphrates

PHOENICIANS

Byblos

Sidon

Tyre

Babylon

EGYPT

Nile

Hittite
city-states

Sack of Thebes 680 BC

300 km

Battle of Kadesh.	Yazilikaya sanctuary is finished.	Fall of the Empire.
1285 BC	**c. 1230 BC**	**c. 1200 BC**

natural galleries, whose walls are covered with reliefs representing 71 divinities from the official pantheon. This king was also responsible for laying out the royal fortress of Büyükkale (in the centre of Hattusa).

c. 1200 BC: Fall of the Hittite Empire during the great disturbances which shook the Near East at this time and which are known as the Invasion of the Sea Peoples. Hattusa is destroyed.

c. 1000 BC: Formation of neo-Hittite principalities where multiple cross-fertilizations give rise to an art known as 'Syro-Hittite' as well as to the writing of bilingual or trilingual texts (Luwian, Phoenician, Aramaic) until 700 BC.

5. The town of Alaca Hüyük, c. 1300 BC.

6. Inscription in Hittite hieroglyphics from the neo-Hittite period, c. 800 BC, Carchemish.

The Aegean World

1. The first circle of royal tombs at Mycenae. 16th century BC.

DURING THE FIRST CENTURIES of the Bronze Age, civilizations of farmers, herdsmen and trading seamen, all virtually undifferentiated from a technological, economical or social point of view, succeeded each other in the Aegean, continental Greece and the Peloponnese. These civilizations, which might be termed regional, are nonetheless distinguished by certain individual traits: marble working in the Cyclades (statuettes, vases), funerary architecture of a monumental type in Crete (communal tombs in the Mesara Plain), production of gold artefacts at Troy and Poliochni (Lemnos).

In this same period, there are striking affinities in material culture between Troy and Lemnos, the Cyclades, Crete and mainland Greece, and the presence of imported objects reveals that there was a continuous movement of people and objects and doubtless also of ideas. Everywhere, except in Crete, sites were fortified, which testifies to the importance of war in these cultures. In Crete specifically, between 2000 and 1600 BC, we can see a civilization developing that was centred on the palace and the town. This was an isolated development in the Aegean world, but one linked to a process that

went back thousands of years in the Near East. The archaeological findings tell a story of the progressive formation of a stratified society and the increasing concentration of power in a few great cities, characterized by the presence of a central group of buildings – the palace – which was the focal point of economic, political and religious life. The development of writing using clay tablets (Linear A) helped to facilitate administration. In all the palace/urban centres, evidence of destruction is found, which is most often attributed to earthquakes. It is one such catastrophe which marks the end of the period of the 'first palaces'. The gradual reconstruction of Cretan towns and palaces around 1600 BC leads to the apogee of Minoan civilization and its period of greatest influence in the Aegean world.

In mainland Greece and in the Peloponnese, the transformations leading to a complex and stratified society appear some four centuries later than in Crete. Between 2000 and 1600 BC (Middle Helladic), there developed an homogeneous civilization at the same technological, economic and social level as the societies of the ancient Bronze Age period. It is generally thought that the bearers of this civilization, who came from the north, spoke an Indo-European dialect that was a forerunner of Greek. It is around 1600 BC that the Mycenaean civilization developed on this substratum (period of the deep shaft graves at Mycenae). The Mycenaean kingdoms of mainland Greece and the Peloponnese consolidated their position and prospered thanks to the systematic exploitation of agricultural resources (for example, by the draining of Lake Copais) and a highly centralized, bureaucratic administrative system: the centres of power were impressively fortified and detailed inventories of goods were kept on clay tablets (in Linear B and Greek). The progressive expansion of the Mycenaeans challenged the maritime supremacy of Crete and the Cyclades. The general destruction of Minoan sites around 1450 BC, which is attested by excavations, marks the end of Cretan domination and the beginning of Mycenaean power in the Aegean world. Between 1400 and 1200 BC, Mycenaean trade developed in the central and eastern Mediterranean, clearly promoting the establishment of permanent settlements in some part of the region. Mycenaean material culture, heavily influenced in its beginnings by Minoan artistic tradition and by that of the civilizations of the Near East, is remarkably homogeneous. The brusque and violent destruction of the towns and palaces and the progressive disintegration of the elements characteristic of Mycenaean culture were for many years attributed to the invasion of new Greek populations, the Dorians. But other factors may have played a part, such as climatic changes affecting agricultural production and, most importantly, social upheavals which might have weakened or even overturned the power of the ruling castes.

Arrival of the Greeks.

Destruction of the 'first palaces' on Crete.

2000 BC

1700 BC

3200–2000 BC: Early Bronze Age
Pre-hellenic regional civilizations:
Helladic (mainland Greece, Peloponnese and neighbouring islands. Main sites: Eutresis, Orchomenos, Hagios Kosmas, Lerna, Aegina).
Cycladic (Cyclades. Main sites: Myrtos, Vassiliki, Lebena, Mochlos, Knossos, Hagia Triada).
Civilizations of the north-east Aegean region (Main sites: Troy, Poliochni, Thermi, Emporion).

2000–1600 BC: Middle Bronze Age
Mainland Greece: Arrival of the first Greek-speaking Indo-European populations.
Crete: First rise of a complex urban civilization; 'first palace' period (main sites: Phaistos, Knossos, Mallia).
c. 1700 BC: Destruction layers in all the Minoan centres. End of the 'first palace' period.

1600–1100 BC: Late Bronze Age
1600–1500 BC: *Crete and Cyclades:* 'Second palace' period. Apogee of the palace/urban civilization (main sites: Kato Zacro, Palaikastro, Gournia, Mallia, Phaistos, Hagia Triada, Knossos, Khania-Kastelli). Expansion of Minoan culture in the Aegean (main sites: Phylakopi, Hagia Irini, Akrotiri).
Mainland Greece and Peloponnese: First rise of Mycenaean civilization; shaft graves of Mycenae.
c. 1500 BC: Volcanic destruction of Thera (Santorini). The town of Akrotiri buried under volcanic ash.
c. 1450 BC: Vast destruction in Cretan sites. Knossos occupied – possibly by Mycenaeans.
c. 1400 BC: Final destruction of Knossos.
1400–1200 BC: Great rise of Mycenaean civilization. Mycenaean kingdoms in mainland Greece and in the Peloponnese (main sites: Iolkos, Thebes, Orchomenos, Gla, Athens, Mycenae, Tiryns, Pylos, Peristeria). Mycenaean influence in the Aegean islands and Crete. Progressive expansion of the Mycenaean states in the

2. Pitcher in the Kamares style. Minoan art, beginning of 2nd millennium.

3. 'The lyre-player', Paros marble, found on the island of Amorgos. Cycladic art, c. 2300 BC.

3200–1100 BC

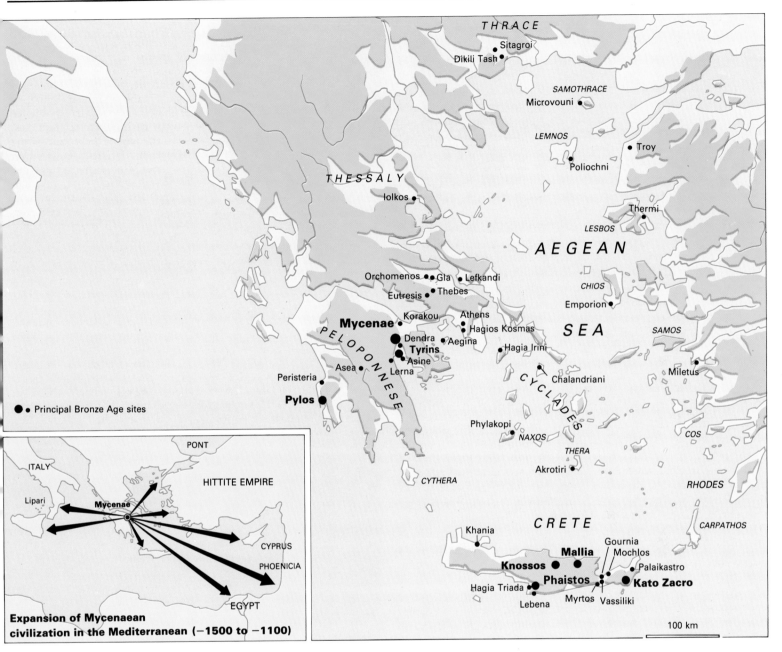

THRACE

Sitagroi
Dikili Tash

SAMOTHRACE

Microvouni

LEMNOS

Troy

Poliochni

THESSALY

Iolkos

Thermi

LESBOS

AEGEAN

Orchomenos • Gla • Lefkandi

CHIOS

Eutresis • Thebes

Emporion

Korakou

Athens

Mycenae •

Hagios Kosmas

SEA

SAMOS

Dendra

Aegina

Tyrins

Hagia Irini

Asine

CYCLADES

Miletus

Asea • Lerna

Peristeria •

Chalandriani

Phylakopi

COS

NAXOS

Pylos •

THERA

Akrotiri •

● **Principal Bronze Age sites**

RHODES

CYTHERA

CRETE

CARPATHOS

Khania

Gournia

Mallia

Mochlos

Knossos

Palaikastro

Phaistos

Kato Zacro

Hagia Triada

Myrtos

Vassiliki

Lebena

100 km

PONT

ITALY

HITTITE EMPIRE

Lipari

Mycenae

CYPRUS

PHOENICIA

EGYPT

**Expansion of Mycenaean
civilization in the Mediterranean (−1500 to −1100)**

Volcanic eruption at Thera (Santorini).	Destruction of the 'second palaces' on Crete.	Destruction of Knossos.	Invasion of the Sea Peoples.
1500 BC	**1450 BC**	**1400 BC**	**1200 BC**

central and eastern Mediterranean (southern Italy, Sicily, Sardinia, Malta, Asia Minor, Cyprus, Syria, Palestine, Egypt).
1200–1100 BC: Population movements. Disturbances in all the regions of the eastern Mediterranean. Invasions of the Sea Peoples in Egypt. Successive invasions of Dorian tribes in Greece. Destruction of Mycenaean centres of power. Disintegration of Mycenaean culture.

4. The two antelopes of Santorini, Minoan art, c. 1500 BC.

5. Woman bearing offerings, Santorini, c. 1500 BC.

6. Painted limestone head, Mycenae, 13th century BC.

The Indus Civilization

In 1921 AND 1922 archaeologists unearthed the remains of two cities in the Indus valley: Mohenjo-daro, 320 kilometres north of Karachi, and Harappa, 650 kilometres further north. The visible ruins of Harappa had already been described in 1834 by an English traveller who recorded local legends about its destruction. Excavations of the deepest strata of the cities established the existence of an Indian civilization contemporary with that of Egypt and Mesopotamia and covering a much wider area. Remains of the same type were found on the coast 500 kilometres east of Karachi, near Simla, near Delhi, and in the Gulf of Cambay. In all, there were about a hundred widely dispersed sites of this type. Older farming and cattle-breeding villages had paved the way for these two major towns; they were not, as had been thought, Mesopotamian colonies.

What is not known is whether they were capitals of two distinct states or alternate capitals of the same empire. Both have a perimeter of six kilometres and are built on a grid system, with rectangular blocks of dwellings; eight-metre-wide major streets are criss-crossed by smaller lanes. On the western flank stands a mound surrounded by fortifications of mud bricks: the 'citadel'. On the Mohenjo-daro citadel there is an enormous granary on a brick base, equipped with an air-drying system, and at Harappa twelve small silos with the same total capacity as the single one at Mohenjo-daro. The Mohenjo-daro citadel also includes a 'Great Bath', possibly for ritual bathing, with a flight of steps for access and a drainage system; it is surrounded by cells. The lower town was protected from flooding by a brick wall and houses and streets were equipped with a sophisticated system of drains also built of brick. At Harappa workers' barracks stood between the ramparts and the river.

The people of the Indus valley used not only stone tools but also copper and bronze implements. They domesticated horned animals, poultry and probably elephants. They grew wheat and barley, and the oldest traces of cotton have been found in the two cities. Their script is remarkable: they have left us thousands of square, round or cylindrical seals engraved with figures of animals or humans which also bear short inscriptions; these are based on 270 different signs undeciphered to this day. The seals are thought to have been used by traders to seal bundles of merchandise, as examples were found in Mesopotamia dating from 2300 BC; this is confirmed by Mesopotamian records of active trading with ports near the Indus. It is strange that this script should not have been used in longer texts or on material other than the steatite of the seals. Equally mysterious, it would seem, is the absence of temples or palaces in such a highly developed urban environment. We are left wondering also about the terracotta figurines and stone and bronze sculptures of human or divine beings: what religion do they point to? Are they forerunners of post- or para-Vedic Indian deities, proto-Śivas, Great Mothers? We know nothing of their language except that it may be related to the Dravidian group. The social structure and political history are equally mysterious, although these would appear to be centralized bureaucracies, judging by the standardized system of weights and measures (stone weights, for example), the regularly levied taxes on surrounding rich farmland and the fact that the two cities subsisted for six centuries without the slightest sign of change.

The final mystery is: how did this civilization disappear? All we can be sure of is that the skeletons found in the most recent stratum at Mohenjo-daro show signs of violent death. Could there have been a massacre by invaders and could these invaders be forerunners of the Aryans?

1. Site of Mohenjo-daro citadel with Great Bath in centre.

Neolithic settlements in Baluchistan. Beginnings of cattle breeding and agriculture.

Settlements in the Indus Valley.

c. 6000 BC

c. 3000 BC

3. Bust of a man known as the 'High Priest', found at Mohenjo-daro.

4. Detail of Great Bath surrounded by cells at Mohenjo-daro.

5. Bronze dancer, Mohenjo-daro.

6000–1700 BC

2. Steatite seals with animal designs and inscriptions.

2500-1500 BC: Indus Civilization

Principal urban sites: ○ Pre-Harappan ● Harappan

Zone of influence of Harappan civilization: secondary urban sites and trading relations

Zone of influence of Sumerian civilization

● Upper centres of Chalcolithic culture in Central India

500 km

January INDIAN OCEAN

July

The climatic conditions

Isotherms

Rainfall (July)
more than 200 mm
more than 400 mm

+ + + High pressure

Low pressure

⇨ Dry monsoon

➡ Wet monsoon

Pre-Harappan villages.

2800–2600 BC

Harappan civilization in the Indus Valley, Punjab and Gujarat.

2300–1700 BC

6. Mohenjo-daro: remains of brick houses and streets.

7. Ritual bronze statuette of buffalo, Mohenjo-daro.

8. The docks of Lothal in the Gujarat, dating from c. 2500 BC.

The Phoenician Middle East

IN CLASSICAL ANTIQUITY, the term 'Phoenicians' designated the Semitic peoples who inhabited the Syrian coast between Mount Casius in the north and Mount Carmel in the south, whose best-known towns were Aradus, Simirra, Byblos, Berytos, Sidon, Tyre and Akko (Acre). The origin of the word *Phoenicia* is unknown, since the words derived from the root *ponike* that are to be found in the Linear B texts of Knossos and Pylos (*c.* fourteenth century BC) and which signify not only 'purple' but also a type of spice and the fruit of the palm tree, do not seem to have had any precise ethnic connotation. The *Iliad* considers Phoenicians and Sidonians to be the same people, describing them first as artisans and then as navigators. On the other hand, the traditional accounts collected by Herodotus and Androsthenes, Alexander's explorer, present the Phoenicians as originating in the Gulf region, but these do not take account of the cultural elements which establish long-standing connections between the Phoenicians and the old so-called Canaanite culture of the Syro-Palestinian coast for which the texts of Ugarit are the best source. Some of the Phoenician ports must have been in contact with Egypt since very early times, as fragments of alabaster vases found in Byblos bear the names of pharaohs of the first dynasty who reigned at the beginning of the third millennium. Throughout the second millennium, the commercial relations of the coastal towns with Cyprus, Crete and Egypt became regular. The Akkadian texts from the age of Akhnaton (1364–1347 BC) found at Tell el Amarna reveal the existence along the coast of principalities like those of Byblos and Tyre whose fate was bound up with Egyptian policy in relation to other powers, such as the Hittite Empire. After the social upheaval that was produced in the whole of the Near East around 1200 BC by the invasion of the sea peoples, the Phoenicians acquired the historical identity which the classical authors attribute to them and they began to use alphabetic writing. The shape of the letters was inspired by hieroglyphic script and differs from the texts of Ugarit, which are in a cuneiform alphabet. In Mesopotamia, the Syro-Palestinian hinterland and the western Mediterranean at the beginning of the first millennium, the Phoenicians appear as architects, artisans and merchants. At that point, Tyre and Sidon became the most important cities, a fact recognized by the Assyrian kings, who only maintained diplomatic relations with those cities. Certain elements in Greek mythology and Phoenician religion suggest that the Phoenicians' genuine contacts with the outside world – and, in particular, with the Greeks – date from the beginning of the first millennium. The most recent researches within the domain of West-Semitic paleography show, moreover, that the Phoenician alphabet was taken over by the Greeks in this period and it is in the context of such exchanges that the similarities between the Greek and Phoenician gods must have developed.

Phoenician overseas expansion was the joint achievement of Tyre and Sidon, which were united in a single kingdom around the middle of the ninth century BC, but it was Tyre that played the leading role in that development. In general, the Phoenician cities did not form confederations as the Greek city states did, and their kings generally pursued individualistic policies towards neighbouring powers. But for a brief period after the conquest of Tyre by Nebuchadnezzar in

1. The ornamental pool of the Ugarit Palace, 14th–13th centuries BC.

573 BC, the cities were governed by a king. Under Persian domination (539–333 BC), Phoenicia formed part of a satrapate which also included Syria and Cyprus, and the navy of Sidon was placed at the service of the military interests of the Achaemenean kings. After the capture of Tyre by Alexander (332 BC), the Phoenician monarchies were abolished; in the Hellenistic period the cities were governed by Archons and by an assembly whose importance for the Phoenicians resident in overseas trading posts is attested in their inscriptions right up to the Roman epoch.

Akhnaton corresponds with the Phoenician kings.

c. 1350 BC

c. 2620 BC: Snefru, 4th dynasty Egyptian pharaoh, has cedar wood brought from Mount Lebanon.
c. 2320 BC: Pepi I (6th dynasty) directs military expeditions against the Syro-Palestinian coast.
c. 1468–1436 BC: Tuthmosis III (18th dynasty) maintains garrisons at Tyre, Aradus and Simirra.
c. 1200 BC: Invasion of the Sea Peoples. Destruction of Ugarit, Tyre and Sidon.
1177 BC: Rameses III's last military campaign (20th dynasty) in Syria and in Palestine. After his victory over the Sea Peoples, the Pharaoh, much occupied with internal strife, withdrew into Egypt.
1114–1076 BC: Tiglath-Pileser I, the King of Assyria, reaches Mount Lebanon, takes cedar wood and receives tribute from Byblos, Sidon and Aradus, 'the island in the deep sea'; with the ships of this latter, he reaches the coast again at Simirra.
c. 1095 BC: Zakarbaal, King of Byblos, asserts his independence vis-à-vis Wen-Amun, the envoy of Hrihor, high priest of Amun at Thebes. The Egyptian account of this voyage

The victorious Rameses III withdraws into Egypt.

c. 1177 BC

4. The Phoenician goddess, Anath.

shows that his father and grandfather had sent cedar wood to the temple of Amun.
c. 1000 BC: Ithobaal, King of Byblos, has a sarcophagus made for his father Ahiram bearing an inscription which, for the first time, uses the whole Phoenician alphabet but for two letters.
c. 995 BC: Hiram, King of Tyre, a contemporary of Solomon, develops a policy of trade with neighbouring kingdoms.
c. 887–856 BC: Ithobaal, high priest of Astarte and King of Tyre and Sidon, gives his daughter in marriage to Ahab, King of Israel.
883–859 BC: Ashurnasirpal II, King of Assyria, conducts a campaign against Phoenicia and exacts tribute from the Kings of Byblos, Tyre and Aradus.
c. 814 BC: Traditional date of foundation of Carthage by the Tyrians.
End of 8th century BC: Luli, King of Tyre and Sidon, crosses the sea and subjugates Kition (Cyprus) which has risen in revolt. Shortly afterwards he is deposed by Sennacherib, King of Assyria, and Luli seeks refuge in Cyprus.

Solomon and H

c. 960 BC

5. Helleno-Phoenician sarcophagus from Tyre, beginning of Hellenistic period.

2620–332 BC

2. Phoenician sphinx, an ivory from Nimrud (Assyria), 9th–8th centuries BC.

3. Byblos, landscape with Phoenician mortars.

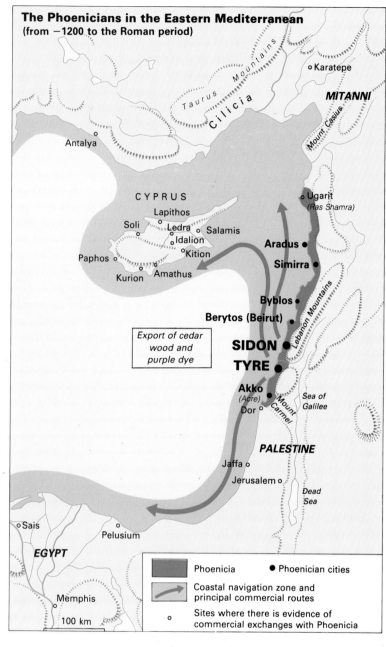

The Phoenicians in the Eastern Mediterranean
(from −1200 to the Roman period)

Export of cedar wood and purple dye

| | Phoenicia | ● | Phoenician cities |
| Coastal navigation zone and principal commercial routes |
| ○ | Sites where there is evidence of commercial exchanges with Phoenicia |

100 km

Capture of Tyre by Nebuchadnezzar II.

c. 573 BC

667 BC: Esarhaddon, King of Assyria and Babylon, imposes a humiliating treaty on Baalu, King of Tyre. The Akkadian inscriptions also mention a certain Abdimilkuti, King of Sidon, who was captured and decapitated by Esarhaddon.

573 BC: Nebuchadnezzar II, King of Babylon, captures Tyre after a thirteen-year siege.

539 BC: Cyrus captures Babylon. Beginning of Persian domination in the East.

First part of 4th century: The kings of the Eshmunazar dynasty at Sidon distinguish themselves by the military aid they bring to the Achaemenid kings. As a reward, they receive Dor, Jaffa and the Plain of Sharon in Palestine.

Middle of 4th century BC: Athens accords Strato I, King of Sidon, the title of *Proxenos*.

333 BC: Alexander arrives in Phoenicia after the battle of Issus. The Kings of Aradus and Byblos fall in with Alexander. Strato II of Sidon is deposed. After a long siege, Tyre is captured in 332 BC.

6. Phoenician ship on coin from Sidon, 375 BC.

Phoenicians and Greeks in the Mediterranean

| | Phoenician commercial zones and principal trading posts | | Greek commercial zone |

500 km

From the Hebrews to the Jews

THE ANCIENT HISTORY of Israel is mainly known to us through the documents and writings of various periods which, after undergoing revisions and adaptations, went to make up the Bible. The choice of these documents and the modifications made to them were determined by essentially religious criteria: not only must a great deal of critical work be done before they can be used as history, but we also have to expect to find in those documents that the past narrated there – the past of a people which has always claimed its radical religiosity – will be centred on its religion. The long wanderings of its ancestors in the 'Fertile Crescent' between Mesopotamia and Palestine very probably took place, but our information on them, which is provided largely by legends, does not allow us to say any more. After a more or less nomadic sojourn in the south of Palestine, part of this group settled in Lower Egypt, where life was ultimately made very difficult

1. The foothills of Mount Sinai, where Moses received the Tablets of the Law.

for them. Moses, the man who led them out of Egypt at the beginning of the thirteenth century BC, planned to reunite and consolidate his people by a covenant with the protecting deity, Yahweh, and perhaps also intended to launch them on the conquest of an area of Palestinian territory. This explains the detour via 'the Mountain' (probably beyond the Gulf of Aqaba) on which Yahweh manifested himself by means of seismic phenomena. The Covenant was formed there, marking out Israel as the special people of Yahweh, attached to him alone and ready to serve him by the observance of a sort of moral code of nomadic, tribal life. When they had returned to Palestine, the wanderers reunited with their brothers who had stayed at home and began their campaign of conquest. It took more than two centuries of peaceful penetration and wars to reshape the lives of these wandering shepherds, after they had settled down as peasants or town-dwellers. When finally they became the masters of the country, they gave themselves a king and made Jerusalem their capital. The prosperity and glory they enjoyed under their second monarch, David (*c.* 1010 BC) rapidly disappeared when a part of the population split off to found the northern kingdom of Israel, in opposition to the southern kingdom of Judah. Being richer and more closely involved in international politics, Israel found itself more exposed to the Assyrian conquerors who finally destroyed it in 722 BC. A group of more fervent religious teachers – the prophets – explained this tribulation and others as a punishment sent by Yahweh for their many failures to observe the Covenant after they had become settled, and warned that if things did not change radically the worst was to be feared. A reform organized on these lines, codified in *Deuteronomy* and sanctioned by King Josiah (*c.* 610 BC) failed to remedy matters. A new prophet, Jeremiah, then called for a more inward religious sense and prophesied that Judah would surely be ruined by Babylon. Events also proved him to be right. In 587 BC Jerusalem fell to the forces of Nebuchadnezzar and its elite was exiled to Mesopotamia. This collapse and the isolated exile which followed both confirmed the prophets' doctrines and turned minds towards fundamental reform. A great mind, of whom little is known but whom we call the Second Isaiah, called for Israel to devote its efforts henceforth to making known throughout the whole universe the teachings of its God, whose absolutely unique and universal character had now been discovered. Another doctrine, spread by Ezekiel in particular but probably responding more closely to the popular inclination, advocated that an Israel turned in upon itself should devote its energies exclusively to following the will of its God – now codified as the 'Law' – to the letter. When Cyrus the Great, the conqueror of Babylon (539 BC), opened the gates of their gaol to the exiles, it was this path they would choose and on this foundation that they would build Judaism.

The Exodus.	King David.	The separation of Israel and Judah.	The prophet Amos.	Death of prophet Is.
1260 BC	1010 BC	931 BC	c. 750 BC	687 B

Before the 13th century BC: The forerunners of the Israelites, a people of Aramean extraction, were nomads who wandered over an indeterminable period westwards along the 'Fertile Crescent' till they finally reached the central and southern regions of Palestine. A group of them – most likely a very small one – then travelled down the Nile delta and were detained there against their will.

c. 1280–1250 BC: Moses guided them from Egypt towards what was probably Midian, to make a covenant with Yahweh, whom he identified with their principal traditional god. In exchange for special ties ensuring them of divine protection, they undertook to serve only that god.

1250–1030 BC: The members of the various tribes of Israel mingled in with the local Canaanite population in some places, and in others made war on them. They gradually eliminated them, though they adopted both their sedentary way of life – becoming town-dwellers and peasants – and their customs, rendering all the more difficult the observance of those clauses of the Covenant based on a collective and frugal nomadic existence.

1030–1010 BC: After the election of a first king, namely Saul, his successor David (1010–970 BC) took Jerusalem as his first capital and brought the greatest success, prosperity and glory to his country.

931 BC: Under Jeroboam, the more numerous northern tribes broke away from the rest of the country, taking with them the name of Israel. They founded a kingdom based first on Tirzah and later on Samaria, which was ranged against that of Judah, which continued to have Jerusalem as its centre. The breaches of the Covenant increased and Israel, which had dealings with the neighbouring kingdoms, was attracted to their gods.

9th century BC: First religious literature and first zealots of Yahweh (prophets). The most vigorous of them, Elijah of the family of Tishbi, issued dire warnings against the choice of any other official god but Yahweh.

Middle of 8th century BC: The Assyrian conquest threatened all the western kingdoms. Second generation of prophets (Amos and Hosea, c. 760–750 BC, then Isaiah, 740–687 BC), who added written propaganda to preaching and threatened their compatriots who were unfaithful to the

4. Deportation of the Hebrews after the capture of Lachish by Sennacherib in 701 BC.

Covenant with the direst collective punishments.

722 BC: The capture of Samaria by Sargon II and the ruin of Israel confirm their prophecies, but the fall of Assyria (612 BC) and the unexpected death of the devout king Josiah, which seemed 'scandalous' to the pious, caused the failure of a first reform that had been prepared in accordance with the prevalent interpretation of the teachings of the prophets. A new prophet, Jeremiah (c. 630–580 BC), arose, calling for a personalized and more inward conception of the Covenant, but his efforts came to nothing.

587 BC: Nebuchadnezzar captured Jerusalem and sacked the city. All its leading personalities were exiled in Mesopotamia and, in its turn, Judah ceased to exist as a political entity. Both an important literary complement to what was to become our Bible and a permanent reorganization of religious life were born out of the remorse that was felt during that time of exile (which officially came to an end with the fall of Babylon in 539 BC).

16th–6th centuries BC

2. The captivity of the women of Israel at Nineveh. Relief at Sennacherib's palace, beginning of 7th century BC.

3. Pool of Siloam, engineered by Hezekiah in 700 BC.

Exile at Babylon.	Second Isaiah.
587 BC	c. 550 BC

5. The Assyrians torture the Hebrews after the capture of Lachish.

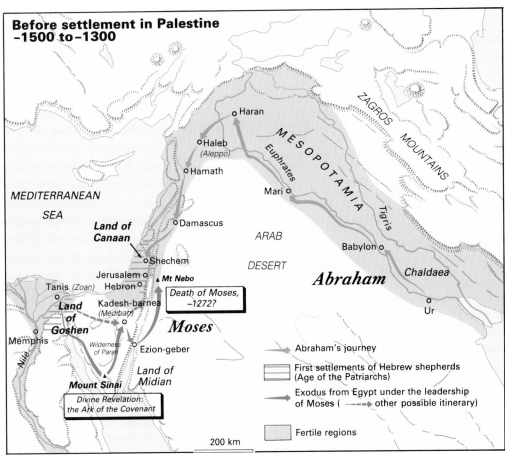

Before settlement in Palestine –1500 to –1300

Haran
Haleb (Aleppo)
Hamath
Mari
Babylon
Chaldaea
Ur
MESOPOTAMIA
ZAGROS MOUNTAINS
Euphrates
Tigris
MEDITERRANEAN SEA
Damascus
ARAB DESERT
Abraham
Land of Canaan
Shechem
Jerusalem
Hebron
▲ Mt Nebo
Death of Moses, –1272?
Tanis (Zoan)
Kadesh-barnea (Meribah)
Land of Goshen
Moses
Memphis
Nile
Wilderness of Paran
Ezion-geber
Land of Midian
Mount Sinai
Divine Revelation: the Ark of the Covenant

→ Abraham's journey
First settlements of Hebrew shepherds (Age of the Patriarchs)
→ Exodus from Egypt under the leadership of Moses (- - - ► other possible itinerary)
Fertile regions

200 km

The Twelve Tribes Circa –1200

— The Kingdom of David (–1010 to –970)
▪ Philistine cities

(Beirut)
Sidon
Tyre
PHOENICIANS
DAN
Dan
NAPHTALI
ASHER
Hazor
Lake of Genneserat
ZEBULUN
Yarmuk
ISSACHAR
MANASSEH
GAD
Samaria ○ Tidzah
Jabbok
EPHRAIM
DAN
Bethel
Rabboth-Ammon (Amman)
BENJAMIN
Jericho
Eglon
Gath
Ashdod
Jerusalem
Ascalon
JUDAH
RUBEN
Gaza
Lachish
Hebron
DEAD SEA
PHILISTINES
SIMEON
○ Beersheba
20 km
Tribe of *LEVI* had no territory of its own

The Kingdoms of Judah and Israel

(Beirut)
Sidon
→ Assyrian invasions
Tyre
Dan
Acre
Galilee
Lake of Genneserat
Yarmuk
Megiddo
KINGDOM OF ISRAEL
Jabesh
Samaria ⊙ ○ Tidzah
Shechem
Jabbok
Samaria
Siloah
Bethel ○
Ammon
Judaea
Heshbon
Jerusalem ⊙
Destroyed by Sargon II –722
Destroyed by Nebuchadnezzor –587
KINGDOM OF JUDAH
DEAD SEA
Moab
○ Beersheba
Kir
20 km

Imperial Egypt

FOLLOWING A PERIOD of invasions and disorder, the New Empire represents an era of renaissance, conquest and glory in the history of pharaonic Egypt, which can still be seen today in the enormous splendour of its architectural and artistic heritage. Freeing Egypt from domination by the Hyksos, Ahmose, the founder of the eighteenth dynasty, set the country on its feet again by restoring its unity and agricultural prosperity. His capital was at Thebes (Luxor), and it was to that city that wealth would flow, both to the pharaohs' courts and to the temples. In spite of a serious dynastic crisis, in which the personality of Queen Hatshepsut was the main factor (she reigned alone for twenty-two years, arrogating all power to herself and keeping from the throne the future Thutmose III), the Egyptian monarchy had its greatest years under the pharaohs of the eighteenth dynasty. The colonial empire was vast: Thutmose III imposed a protectorate upon Palestine, Phoenicia and Syria; Thutmose IV allied with the Mitannian kingdom of inner Asia by marrying a princess from that country. To the south, Theban domination extended as far as the fourth cataract of the Nile. Everywhere in these new provinces, royal agents levied labour and substantial tribute in raw materials and rare commodities. The privileged class of society was the army, and its power was enhanced by the appearance on the scene of horses and chariots. From the reign of Ahmose onwards the god Amun became the protector of the ruling dynasty. His sanctuaries provided it with wealth and its priests exercised a growing influence on the country's affairs. Gradually the temple of Amun at Karnak became a state within the state.

It was at that point that Amenhotep IV-Akhenaton had a revolutionary effect by radically opposing the policies of his forefathers and destroying the religious and social equilibrium which prevailed at the time of his accession to the throne. Akhenaton abolished Amun's privileges and confiscated his goods, founded a new capital at Tell el Amarna (Middle Egypt) and turned Aton from a celestial pharaoh into a universal god. Aton was the sun's disc that gave life and spread goodness: the new religion of Akhenaton and his wife Nefertiti was founded on a doctrine of love, goodness, justice and humanity. At the death of the heretical pharaoh, there was an almost immediate return to traditional orthodoxy and the former order was re-established. Under Tutenkhamun, whose original name was Tutankhaton, Thebes once again became capital and the Valley of the Kings on the western bank once again became the pharaohs' burial ground. It was there that Tutankhamun, who died in adolescence, was buried. The discovery of his intact tomb has enabled us to appreciate the refinement of eighteenth-dynasty art. At the end of that dynasty General Horemheb came to prominence. When he took power he completed the job of eliminating the last vestiges of the Atonian heresy.

2. Agricultural work. Fresco from Menna's tomb at Thebes.

The nineteenth and twentieth dynasties were the work of the pharaohs named Ramses, the most famous of whom was Ramses II. He covered the country with gigantic buildings (cities and temples) and fought unrelentingly in numerous battles in defence of the kingdom (the Battle of Kadesh, campaigns in Syria and Palestine). His reign was very long (sixty-six years). In spite of his efforts, the Egypt he bequeathed to his successors was very much weakened. Invasions, social upheavals, palace plots and scandals eroded the state's authority and the country's prosperity. At the end of the second millennium, poverty and decadence had overtaken the country, which once again forfeited its unity. In the first millennium Persian domination, followed by conquest by the Greeks and Romans, put an end to the local dynasties and reduced Egypt to being one of the larger provinces of these new empires.

1. The banks of the Nile, cradle of civilization....

First tomb in the Valley of Kings.　　　**Terraced temple of Dayr al-Bahri.**　　　**Temples of Karnak and Tell el Amarna.**

1506 BC	1490 BC		1364 BC

1552–1306 BC: 18TH DYNASTY
1552–1527 BC: Ahmose. End of Hyksos domination of Egypt.
1527–06 BC: Amenhotep I. Seeks political restoration of the country. Military campaign as far as the Euphrates.
1506–1494 BC: Thutmose I. Conquest of Nubia up to the third cataract and victory over the Mitannians. Beginning of the great works on Amon's temple at Karnak.
1493–1440 BC: Thutmose II, brother and first husband of Queen Hatshepsut. After his death, crisis over the succession.
1490–1468 BC: Hatshepsut rules as regent and arrogates to herself the powers and attributes of royalty. She has herself represented as a man and declares herself to be of the stock of the god Amon. The architect Senmut, the Queen's favourite, takes charge of the building of the funerary temple of Dayr al-Bahri.
1468–1436 BC: Thutmose III. One of the most brilliant reigns in ancient Egyptian history. 17 military campaigns in Asia (Megiddo, Kadesh). Numerous additions to the temple at Karnak.

4. Akhenaton, Karnak.

1438–1412 BC: Amenhotep II, the son of the previous king, maintained the expansionist policy and repressed two revolts in Asia.
1412–1402 BC: Thutmose IV. Pursued a policy of colonization towards the south and the east.
1402–1364 BC: Amenhotep III. Egypt is at the height of its glory and splendour. Building of the temple of Luxor.
1364–1347 BC: Amenhotep IV (changes his name to Akhenaton). The Asiatic kingdom is threatened by Hittite attacks. Diplomatic correspondence conducted in Akkadian (cuneiform tablets found at Tell el Amarna).
1347 BC: Smenkhkare. Brief reign of one of Akhenaton's sons-in-law.
1347-1338 BC: Tutenkhamun. End of the schism caused by Akhenaton: return to traditional ways.
1337–1333 BC: Ay, a commoner, legitimates his accession to the throne by marrying Tutenkhamun's widow.
1336–1306 BC: Horemheb, a soldier backed by the priesthood of the god Amun, marries a royal princess and reorganizes the country.

5. Nefertiti, wife of Akhenaton, Tell el Amarna.

1552–1070 BC

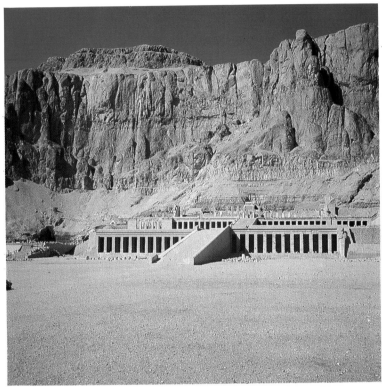

3. Hatshepsut's temple at Dayr al-Bahri, 18th dynasty, Thebes.

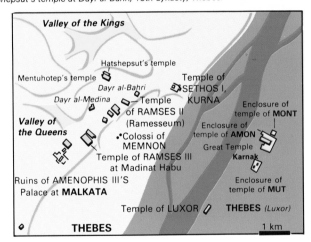

Valley of the Kings

Hatshepsut's temple
Mentuhotep's temple
Dayr al-Bahri
Dayr al-Medina
Valley of
the Queens
Colossi of
MEMNON
Temple of RAMSES III
at Madinat Habu
Ruins of AMENOPHIS III'S
Palace at MALKATA

Temple of
SETHOS I,
KURNA
Temple
of RAMSES II
(Ramesseum)
Enclosure of
temple of MONT
Enclosure of
temple of AMON
Great Temple
Karnak
Enclosure of
temple of MUT
Temple of LUXOR
THEBES (Luxor)
THEBES
1 km

ou Simbel.

Madinat Habu.

1290 BC

1184 BC

1306–1186 BC: 19TH DYNASTY
1306–1304 BC: Ramses I.
1304–1290 BC: Seti I. Consolidates the position of the new dynasty. Victory over the Hittites at Kadesh.
1290–1224 BC: Ramses II. Last great figure of the New Empire. Completion of the Great Hypostyle Hall of Karnak and the temple of Luxor. Building of the Ramesseum at Thebes.
1224–1186 BC: Merneptah (13th son of Ramses II), Seti II, Siptah and Tausert succeed one another on the throne. At the end of this period, under a Palestinian usurper, there is anarchy.
1186–1070 BC: 20TH DYNASTY
1186–1184 BC: The Egyptian Setnakht founds the 20th dynasty.
1184–1153 BC: Ramses III. Intense struggles against the Sea Peoples and the Libyans. Building of the temple of Madinat Habu at Thebes.
1153–1070 BC: Ramses IV to Ramses IX. Decline of the Egyptian Empire.

6. Dogs and a hyena; a sketch from the Ramses period.

Hittites — Carchemish — MITANNI — Aleppo — Euphrates — (SYRIA) — Kadesh: Victory of Ramses II over the Hittites −1285 — Byblos — Sidon — Tyre — (PHOENICIA) — MEDITERRANEAN — Meggido — (PALESTINE) — Gaza — Kom el-Hisn — TANIS — Tell el-Daba — Kom Abu Bellou — Tell Basta — Tell el Yahbudiyeh — Heliopolis — Giza — Saqquara — MEMPHIS — SINAI — Timna — El-Lahun — Serabit el-Khadem — El-Hibeh — Bir el-Naseb — Hermopolis — Tunah el-Gebel — AKHET-ATON (Tell el-Amarna) — Asyut — Akhmim (Panopolis) — RED SEA — Dendera — Abydos — Coptus — Mut — THEBES — DAKHLAH — Tod — El-Kab — Edfu — EL-KHARGEH — Elephantine — Syene (Aswan) — 1st cataract — Tropic of Cancer — Garf Hussein — Kuban — Aniba — Wadi es-Sebua — Armina — Abu Simbel — Toshka — Faras — Debeira — Buhen — 2nd cataract — Semna — Tangur — Amara — Sais — NUBIA — Sulb — 3rd cataract — Kerma — Tabo — 4th cataract — Napata

Frontiers of the Empire
in the XVth century BC
in the XIIIth century BC
Hittite Empire
Mitanni (or Hurrite) Empire
100 km

The Origins of the Chinese Empire

The Shang XVII - XI centuries BC

ALA SHAN DESERT
Huang Ho
Peking
KANSU
Lan-chou
T'ai-yüan
Dayi (An-yang)
W. Bo
KUNLUN MOUNTAINS
First CHOU centre in contact with barbarians of Kansu
SHENSI
Sian
Lo-Yang
E. Bo
HONAN
SHANTUNG
YELLOW SEA
Huai
Nanking
Shouyang
Present day dividing line between wheat
Yangtze
Lake Tung-t'ing
TIBET
Ch'ang-sha

The ancient kingdoms

**The Western Chou
End of XI century BC - 770 BC**

Barbarian people of steppes VIII century BC
Huang Ho
Peking
T'ai-yüan
KUNLUN MOUNTAINS
Wei
Hao (Sian)
Lo-Yang
Huang Ho
YELLOW SEA
TIBET
SZECHWAN
Yangtze
Hills of southern China

400 km

| | SHANG domain | | Relief contours | | Loess deposit: rich farmland | | Western CHOU |
| SHANG archeological site | | | | | | Their enforced expansion eastwards |

THE SHANG OR YIN DYNASTY made its appearance in the seventeenth century BC at the juncture of two Neolithic cultures, Yang-shao and Lung-shan, in the fertile, silt-enriched lands (loesslands) of the middle Yellow River basin. With it appeared features typical of ancient Chinese civilization, such as the harnessed cart, writing, bronze, divination by bones and tortoise shells and a political structure that revolved around the royal city. The society was governed by a unitary principle: ancestor worship provided a framework into which each individual was integrated. This enabled the Shang to expand over a vast territory (as far south as Lake Tung-t'ing) with a very elementary political organization mirroring patterns of kinship. Their relations with their neighbours were sometimes based on alliances or vasselage but more usually they were conflictual. They practised the immolation of prisoners to feed the souls of the ancestors, who were the true rulers of society. The expansion of Shang culture provoked tensions in a rigid society and brought about its eventual downfall.

The ancient monarchy was given a new lease of life by the Chou dynasty, founded by a people from the western borders. Family-based ancestor worship was transformed, leading to a more flexible, segmented society. Domains gave way to fiefdoms granted by the king to overlords who presided over the ancestor worship. Although progressively weakened by pressure from the 'barbarians', the monarchy was able to maintain religious and moral ascendancy over the powerful overlords up to the eighth century BC. Hierarchization of forms of worship reached its highest degree of sophistication. Confucius undertook to adapt and reinterpret behavioural roles in a humanist direction; this led to ritual becoming a universal norm of conduct and to the elaboration of classical Chinese codes of behaviour. The nobility was threatened by the formation of large, autonomous political units. While the central principalities remained fragmented into tiny feudal states jealously guarding their privileges, more peripheral states were wresting new territories from the barbarians; their conquered lands became provinces directly under central government. The Chin, the Ch'i, the Ch'u and the Ch'in began to play a dominant role (hegemon states) because of their military and economic power. The army was formed by conscripting independent farmers, which led to the downfall of the heroic code of the warlord; infantrymen were given precedence over charioteers. The previous balance was

Appearance of bronze.

17th century BC

2. Bronze wine vessel of Kuang type. Shang period, 17th–11th century BC.

First inscriptions on ritual vases.

12th century BC

771 BC: Raid by Rong barbarians in league with royal family forces King P'ing to move his capital further east, to Lo-Yang. Chou becomes dependent on rulers of Cheng, Wei, Chin and Song.
772 BC: Beginning of period known as 'Spring and Autumn' recorded in annals of Lu principality.
667 BC: Economic and fiscal reforms made by his prime minister, Kuan Chong, lead to Duke Huan Kung of Ch'i becoming head of Chinese confederation.
632 BC: Chin hegemony.
597 BC: Hegemony of Duke Chuang Ch'u following victory over Chin.
590 BC: Lu introduces first conscription system, which is soon copied by other states.
536 BC: First legal code inscribed on bronze braziers and put on public view.
c. 510 BC: Spread of iron smelting.
506–473 BC: Wars between Wu and Yüeh, two states of southeast China, started by a quarrel between two little girls gathering mulberry leaves and resulting in total destruction of Wu after a series of defeats suffered by Yüeh.

3. Chariot ornament, bronze encrusted with gold and silver. Ch'u dynasty.

481 BC: End of period recorded in Lu annals rewritten by Confucius.
479 BC: Death of Confucius.
453 BC: China is split among three high-ranking officers, thus creating three kingdoms of Chao, Han and Wei. This event marks the beginning of the 'Warring States' period.

17th century BC: Founding of Shang-Ying dynasty on site of present-day Erh-li-t'ou.
1384 BC: Capital moves to Ta-Yeh (now An-Yang).
1273 BC: Emperor Tsu Chia reforms religious practice by instituting regular sacrifices to ancestors linked to yearly cycle.

12th century BC: First ritual inscriptions on bronze vases.
11th century BC: Shang dynasty overthrown by Chou. King Wu Wang founds new dynasty, divides territory between members of his family and allies.

1600–250 BC

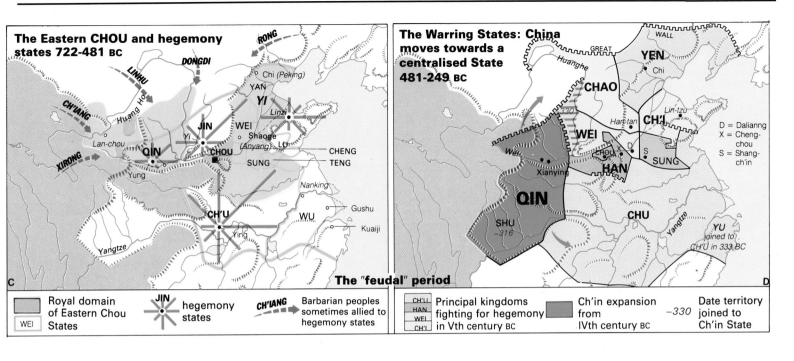

The Eastern CHOU and hegemony states 722-481 BC

The Warring States: China moves towards a centralised State 481-249 BC

The "feudal" period

Royal domain of Eastern Chou States / WEI	JIN hegemony states	CH'IANG Barbarian peoples sometimes allied to hegemony states

CH'U HAN WEI CH'I Principal kingdoms fighting for hegemony in Vth century BC	Ch'in expansion from IVth century BC	−330 Date territory joined to Ch'in State

1. Terracotta mould for casting bronze mask. Warring States period, 481–249 BC.

disturbed as ritual prestige gave way to naked power; the harsher side of society was reinforced. The sovereign – seen as an incarnation of social and cosmic laws – imposed a feudal system of duties on his subjects. At the same time the growth of iron smelting in the sixth century BC resulted in the peasants being subjected to central government or to large entrepreneurs linked to the state. Social upheaval led to intellectual ferment; a multitude of schools blossomed: Sophistry, Taoism, Legalism, Moism.

As the small principalities disappeared, power tended to be concentrated in the heads of the fiefs, who became veritable monarchs; they were now aided by competent administrators recruited according to ability, not birth. The state of Ch'in undertook a series of reforms that gave it ascendancy over its rivals. Neither reversals of alliances nor the banding together of the large states succeeded in containing the eastward march of the Ch'in. Their annexation of Chou territory merely sanctioned what had already been a fact for two centuries.

Iron smelting becomes widespread.	Writings of Lao-Tzu.	Suicide of poet Ch'ü Yüan for political reasons.
6th century BC	**4th century BC**	**277 BC**

386 BC: T'ien family usurp power in Ch'i.
c. 350 BC: Reforms made by lawyer-administrator Shang Yang give King Hsiao-Wen of Ch'in military superiority over other states.

311 BC: Ch'u is defeated in war against Ch'in.
c. 300 BC: Death of Taoist philosopher Chuang-tzu. Building of walls by states of Yen, Chao and Ch'in against incursions by barbarians of the steppes.

4. Bronze cooking receptacle, Ting type. Shang period, 17th–11th century BC.

284 BC: Yen, aided by Ch'in, Ch'u and the three kingdoms born of Chin secession, inflicts a bitter defeat on Ch'i. The capital is sacked and the sovereign forced to flee.
269 BC: Chao and Wei defeat Ch'in armies.
260 BC: During the battle of Changping the commanding general of Ch'in puts to death 200,000 Chao soldiers who had surrendered.
259–257 BC: Siege of Handan (capital of Chao) by Ch'in ends in defeat.
256 BC: King of western Chou surrenders his throne to Ch'in.
250 BC: Destruction of eastern Chou by Ch'in marks the end of the dynasty.

5. Knocker in shape of fabulous beast. Warring States period.

Celtic Europe

1. Frieze of Gundestrup cauldron representing the god Teutates receiving human sacrifices. Repoussé gilded silver, 1st century AD.

THE NAME 'CELTS' does not appear in texts until the fifth century BC, that of 'Germans' still later, but all the archaeological data seem to indicate that the population of temperate Europe was permanently settled, with a definable culture evolving steadily from the end of the Bronze Age up to the Roman conquest. Farmsteads occupied the richest plains as far north as Scotland, southern Scandinavia and west of the Vistula; hunter gatherers had virtually disappeared from these areas. The farmers divided the land into a complex system of plots ('Celtic fields'); they developed the swing plough, farmed heavy soils and corrected and fertilized poor soils. Intensive mixed farming enabled them to export their surplus: cereals and salt provisions were sent to southern Europe. Trade with the Greek colonies and Italy in other raw materials, such as tin, amber and copper reached a peak in the sixth century BC. Economic dependency of a colonial type

developed: the social group who benefited were those who controlled foreign trade and the distribution of imports, now seen as marks of social status. Their rise is linked to the end of the Bronze Age, when increased metal production led to hoarding and inequality of wealth, and also to the appearance of heavily armed professional soldiers in the style of the Greek hoplites.

Although horse-riding was introduced by oriental peoples, the cart was still typical of these cultures, for transport, war and funerary rites. Iron technology spread slowly at the beginning of this period, but in the fifth century BC it was put to good purpose for improving agricultural production, clearing new land and arming the surplus population that were making inroads into Italy and would soon be unfurling over the entire northern Mediterranean. Celtic mercenaries, in their contacts with local populations, introduced new

Peak of bronze production.	Chieftains, horsemen, tradesmen.	Spread of Celtic farmers.	Specialized craftsmen appear.
1250–800 BC	**750–450 BC**	**500–250 BC**	**250–100 BC**

1250 BC: Rise of Urnfield burial cultures in Lusatia, Central Europe, Switzerland-Rhine. Toughened bronze alloy produced in Atlantic regions. Explosion of bronze production; draught horses; climate becomes wetter. Development of rye, oats, millet and flax. First traces of stables.

1100–1000 BC: First burial chariots with furniture imported from the south.

750 BC: First Iron Age. Climate changes to very wet and cold sub-Atlantic, crops recede on impermeable soil and at higher altitudes. Iron produced locally. First horsemen. Burial mounds, ritual of burial.

600 BC: Massalia (Marseilles) founded by Phoceans.

600–450 BC: Chieftains' graves (Vix and Hochdorf), Hallstatt culture (Heuneburg). Imports and colonial-type contacts with Mediterranean. Poland: group of fortified dwellings at Biskupin.

500 BC: Development of Second Iron Age, known as La Tène culture, in agriculture-oriented environment. Cemeteries of burial mounds or flat tombs, linked to hamlets and organized in family groups. Appearance of 'Celtic Art' style.

400 BC: First Celtic raids in Italy. Celts settle in Italy, expeditions to Greece. Spread of La Tène culture to western France and colonization of heavy soils of Eastern Europe. Storage of agricultural produce developed in selected hill forts in Brittany.

4. 'Severed heads' from the hill fort of Entremont, France, 2nd century BC.

3. Mask and hands of hammered bronze from a tomb in Styria, Austria, 7th century BC.

techniques both in art and in production: compasses, the potter's wheel and the rotary millstone were the most spectacular innovations. In the second century BC artisans with specialized tools began to mass-produce objects which sometimes survived in the same form up to the eighteenth century AD. Iron was made in such quantities that it was employed for the first time in building.

The Roman conquest chased the Celts out of Italy, then southern Gaul. Massive commercial penetration by the Romans, as shown by the wine amphoras found on every site, preceded their occupation of Gaul and gave birth to a civilization based on *oppida*, or hill forts, stretching from Brittany to Hungary. Artisans, tradesmen and part of the landed aristocracy came together to found these important settlements, which were sometimes as big as 100 hectares. The use of bronze coinage and the very first Celtic texts mark the end of proto-historical times. The scene was now stolen by the Roman conquest and by invasions of northeastern European peoples. Today the Celts are still better known to us through what Caesar had to say about them than through the plentiful evidence they have left in the ground or in mediaeval manuscripts.

2. Entrance to hill fort of Finsterlohr, Baden-Württemberg, 1st century BC.

fort civilization.   **Celts retreat before Romans, Germans and Marcomanni.**

0 BC   **58 BC–AD 1**

225 BC: Defeat of Gauls at Talamone.

189 BC: Bononia (Bologna) founded. Italian Celts reduced to subjection. Development of craftsmen.

124 BC: Defeat of Celts and Salians at Entremont. Founding of Aquae Sextiae (Aix-en-Provence) in Roman Province of Narbonensis (created in 118 BC).

109–102 BC: Invasions of Cimbri and Teutoni. Rise of hill fort civilization. Circulation of first low-denomination coins.

58–52 BC: Caesar intervenes in Gaul, Brittany, western Germany. Conquest of Gaul.

c. 50 BC: Dacians defeat Boii in Pannonia.

25 BC: Romans pacify tribes of the Alps.

25–1 BC: Romans control south bank of Danube. Marcomanni invade Bohemia.

15–1 BC: Hill forts abandoned, founding of present-day provincial capitals.

AD 43: Romans occupy south of British Isles.

5. Breton helmet, 1st century BC.

The Grandeur of Carthage

PHOENICIAN EXPANSION in the western Mediterranean is amply illustrated by recent archaeological discoveries. Tyrians and Sidonians were guided towards Sicily, Malta, Sardinia, the North African coasts and southern Spain by a desire to extend their commercial activities, and perhaps also to alleviate the weight of Assyrian domination over the Near East which had reached its climax in the eighth century BC. However, the stages in this expansion are not well known, and attempts to establish a chronology are necessarily somewhat speculative. An inscription found at the archaeological site of Nora (Sardinia) does, however, provide evidence of a Phoenician presence at that location in the ninth century BC; pottery discovered in Malta and at Motya (Sicily) dates from the eighth century BC and the Phoenician settlements at Toscanos (Andalusia) are from the same period. This archaeological evidence cannot be taken to indicate the initial date of Phoenician presence in these areas; rather it suggests that there had been such a presence there for several generations. The same must also be true of Carthage. If the traditional date of its foundation by Tyre is 814 BC, it may be assumed that regular exchanges between the metropolis and the African coast must have taken place several decades before Kart Hadasht (the 'new city') was founded. With the founding of Ibiza by Carthage in 654–653 BC, the Phoenician presence in the Mediterranean took on a new dimension.

Carthage, governed by two sufets or annually elected chief magistrates, a council of elders and an assembly of the people, was itself capable of founding new colonies or developing existing ones. In this manner, an empire was created in the western Mediterranean basin in the centre of which Sardinia and Sicily were to become the principal stakes in the international political struggle. It was in Sicily indeed that the Greeks and the Carthaginians clashed on several occasions. In 264 BC the intervention of Rome in

1. Lid of Greco-Punic sarcophagus, Carthage, c. 300 BC.

the affairs of Messina caused the First Punic War, which ended in Rome's naval victory at the battle of the Aegates islands. After its seizure of Sicily, Rome forced Carthage in 237 BC to renounce its claim to Sardinia by a treaty which Carthage always considered an act of brigandage. The period preceding the Second Punic War (218–202 BC) saw the apogee of the Barca family, whose founder Hamilcar Barca undertook the conquest of Spain in the name of the government of Carthage. He was succeeded by his son-in-law, Hasdrubal, the founder of Carthago Nova (c. 227 BC), then by his son Hannibal: all three ruthlessly exploited Spain's mineral wealth.

The capture of Saguntum, an ally of Rome, by Hannibal in 219 BC was considered a *casus belli* by the Roman Senate and provoked a declaration of war. Hannibal then decided to cross Gaul and enter Italy by way of the Alps. His army remained there for fifteen years. After his victory at Cannae (216 BC) Hannibal gave a new turn to his Italian policy by signing a treaty with Philip V of Macedonia; however, isolated in Italy shortly afterwards and then recalled to Africa, he was defeated at Zama. From 150 BC onwards Rome decided to put an end to the Carthaginian threat and declared a preventive war against her. The city was disarmed by treason and besieged; after three years' resistance and a final battle fought out in the streets, Carthage was conquered and razed to the ground by Scipio Aemilianus in April 146 BC. At the moment of its fall, Carthage was said to be the richest city in the world (Polybius), and its political institutions had won the admiration of Aristotle, who considered the constitution of Carthage the equal of the best Greek regimes. The organization of its ports, the competence of its generals, its fleet and its cavalry, the possession of the Spanish mines and of a close-knit network of trading posts and colonies had made a clash between Carthage and Rome inevitable.

Himilco's expeditions to northwest Europe. Hanno's voyages on the coast of Africa.	First treaty between Rome and Carthage.	Himera and Salamis.	Beginning of the Punic Wars.	Hannibal's victory at Lake Trasimenus.
c. 520 BC	508 BC	480 BC	264 BC	217 BC

814 BC: Traditional date for the foundation of Carthage by the Tyrians.
8th century BC: Phoenician presence near Seville is attested by a statuette of the Phoenician goddess Astarte.
c. 600 BC: Naval victory of the Phocaeans, founders of Massalia, over the Carthaginians (according to Thucydides).
535 BC: Carthaginian and Etruscan victory over the Greeks at Alalia, Corsica (modern Aleria).
c. 508 BC: First treaty between Carthage and Rome (according to Polybius): mutual recognition of the right to trade.
c. 500 BC: Velianas, King of Caere (Cerveteri), dedicates a shrine in the port of Pyrgi (San Severa) to the goddess Astarte: the text is written in Etruscan and Phoenician.
480 BC: Hamilcar, son of Mago, is defeated by Gelon of Syracuse at Himera.
405 BC: Dionysius the Elder, 'tyrant' of Syracuse, signs a treaty with Carthage and recognizes the Punic possessions on the island.

2. Stelae of the Tophet of Tanit and Baal, 5th–4th centuries BC.

4th century BC: Power passes to the family of Hanno the Great, rival of the Barcidae during the Punic Wars.
348 BC: Second treaty of Carthage with Rome (according to Polybius).
264–241 BC: First Punic War. By the peace treaty of 241 BC, Rome forces Carthage to evacuate Sicily and to pay a war indemnity of 2,200 talents.
228 BC: Hamilcar Barca begins the conquest of Spain.
221 BC: Assassination of Hasdrubal. Hannibal, the son of Hamilcar Barca, is immediately chosen as leader by the army and is subsequently invested ruler by the Senate and people of Carthage.
218–202 BC: Second Punic War.
216 BC: Victory of Hannibal at Cannae. Treaties with Capua and other important Italian cities. Rome refuses to sign a treaty with Carthage.
207 BC: The army of Hasdrubal the Younger, Hannibal's brother, leaves Spain and manages to reach Italy to reinforce the

Carthaginian troops, but it is wiped out at the battle of the Metaurus, where Hasdrubal is killed.
203 BC: Hannibal is recalled to Carthage.
202 BC: Victory of Scipio Africanus at Zama followed by a peace treaty.

3. Molten glass mask, 4th–3rd century BC.

814–146 BC

Carthage's commercial hegemony in the Western Mediterranean

- Principal trading posts

Carthaginian domination

Conquests by the Barcas in Spain

Spanish mineral resources

✚ Silver   ▯ Lead

The struggle with Rome (Punic Wars)

⇨ First Roman intervention
(under Atilius Regulus, −256)

▨ Carthaginian losses after the First Punic War
(Sicily −214, Corsica and Sardinia, −237)

➤ Hannibal's campaign

★ Carthaginian victories

➤ Scipio Africanus's campaign

★ Roman victories

200 km

Hannibal poisons himself at Libyssa (Bithynia).

183 BC

196 BC: Hannibal is elected sufet and undertakes administrative reforms. He is denounced by his enemies at Rome.
195 BC: Hannibal seeks refuge with Antiochus III, King of Syria.
Beginning of 2nd century BC: Masinissa, chieftain of the Numidians, attacks and finally annexes a part of Carthaginian territory.
189–188 BC: By the Treaty of Apamea between Rome and Antiochus III, the latter is to deliver Hannibal to Rome. Hannibal is

Rome destroys Carthage and Corinth.

146 BC

forced to take refuge with Prusias, King of Bythinia.
c. 167 BC: Rome grants Masinissa authority to take over the emporia of Cirta (coasts of Cyrenaica and Tripolitania).
c. 153 BC: Cato the Elder visits Carthage; he is struck by its prosperity and the extent of its rearmament: *Delenda est Carthago.*
149 BC: The Carthaginians reject the order to abandon the city and prepare to resist. They inflict severe losses on the army of the consul Manilius.
146 BC: Destruction of Carthage.

4. Punic armour.

5. Barcide coinage in Spain in the Second Punic War period.

6. The mole of the war port of Carthage.

7. Punic razor in bronze with goose head.

Bronze and Iron, Commerce and Money

1. *Hauling up of the great winged bull of Nimrud at the entrance to the palace of Ashurnasirpal II, 9th century BC. Reconstruction by A. H. Layard.*

REVOLUTIONARY INNOVATIONS in technology happened in the Mesolithic and Neolithic periods, before the turning point of 3300 to 2800 BC, but the revolution that took place around 3000 BC was a socio-political one. The birth of the first nations marked the beginning of history seen in terms of growth. These nations could almost be compared to the 'mega-machine' of the modern state in their total regulation of the freedom and leisure of the individual: human labour was exploited, work systematically organized. What better evidence than the ancient myths and formidable constructions of the time: the pyramids of Egypt, the towers of Mesopotamia, the megaliths of Europe and the Mediterranean dating from the second and third millennia BC, monuments to the fabulous human effort that went into their making?

The use of metals, at least of copper which was hardened by hammering, dates from Neolithic times. But bronze, a copper and tin alloy, began in the third and particularly the second millennium to play a major role, linked to changes in society. The use of iron was introduced in Asia Minor from 1500 or 1400 BC and continued to develop well into the first millennium. The iron revolution – with the discovery of abundant ore that could easily be put to use – had tremendous consequences, transforming everyday implements and agricultural activity.

Beginning of 3rd millennium BC: Copper is common in Egypt, bronze is known in Mesopotamia. Grandiose constructions.

c. 2500–2400 BC: Businessmen in Mesopotamia.

c. 2200 BC: Horses are harnessed.

2100–1900 BC: Metalwork highly developed among Celts (the 'torque wearers', Anatolia, Europe).

From c. 2050 BC: Bronze becomes common in Mesopotamia.

c. 2000 BC: Bronze is made in Egypt.

c. 1600 BC: The Hittite cart. Cretan domination over the seas.

c.1500 BC: Egyptian trade developed with Black Africa. Trade between India and Near East. 'King Solomon's Mines' near the Red Sea, profusion of mines and metal works.

c. 1500–1400 BC: Marked development of iron working in the Hittite Empire.

4. *Gold dagger and sheath from Ur, second half of 3rd millennium BC.*

c. 1400 BC: Shang bronzes, the finest in the world, Shang-Yin and Chou in China. Period of commercial expansion. Cowrie shell money.

14th century BC: Rise of Achaean seafaring, progress of naval technology.

c. 1200 BC: Rise of Indian trade. Beginning of Iron Age in Greece. Breton metalwork (bronze axes). First known naval battle, the Egyptians against the Sea People. Specialized war ships developed. Appearance of Olmec civilization in Central America. Importance of trade.

End of 2nd millennium BC: Rise of camel-rearing in the Near East, herding and caravans.

c. 950 BC: Phoenician sea-going ships are perfected; use of bitumen and the ribbed hull. Kingdom of Solomon plays a role of intermediary in trading.

c. 900(?) BC: Chinese coins in form of knives.

c. 800 BC: Beginning of Hallstatt civilization (iron).

3000–200 BC

Around 200 BC the water wheel took hold in the countries of the Mediterranean and China; hydraulic power began to replace muscle power. This is probably the most important technical innovation of the period.

Meanwhile, in the field of transport important progress was being made. The horse was domesticated in two stages which affected both war and material life: from around 2000 BC carts and harnessed horses appeared, and from around 1300 BC mounted horses and cavalry. Ships, with both sails and oars, were perfected.

From the third millennium onwards Mesopotamia developed powerful corporations of businessmen. They stocked goods, speculated, used various types of goods as currency, and used ingots, especially of silver, carved into particular weights and sizes and sometimes bearing authentication marks. The period beginning around 1400 BC, although marked by catastrophic crises, was one of considerable commercial development in the Mediterranean, India and China. The usual means of exchange – heads of cattle (*pecus*, cattle, gave the Latin *pecunia*), iron brooches (the Greek *obolus*; a *drachma* is a 'handful' of brooches), ingots, shells, coins in the forms of spades and knives – no longer sufficed, being too imprecise and arbitrary. Coins as we know them appeared in the seventh century BC, as the small states of the Mediterranean and the Chinese principalities began to assert their independence and their prerogatives (the levying of taxes, recruitment of mercenaries or civil servants etc.). Coins were in abundant use from around 500 BC. In the Mediterranean the centuries that followed were so marked by the development of trade, money, banks, transport, that several historians have compared them to the capitalist era, an understandable if exaggerated opinion in view of the very real originality in this and other fields of the classical Greek and Hellenistic world.

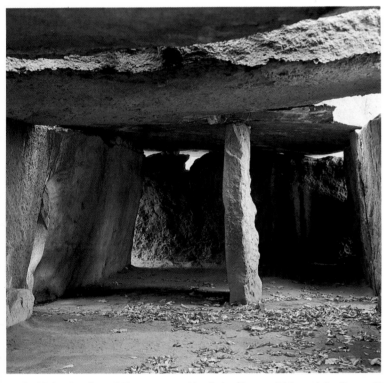

2. Burial chamber of megalithic monument with galleries, Bagneux, Maine-et-Loire, France, 4th century BC.

3. Detail of facing of Pyramid of Mykerinos, Egypt, built around 2600 BC.

7th century BC: Etruscans dominate the seas. Rise of the Phoenicians. Banks in Mesopotamia. Indian navigation. Building of Assyrian fleet. First naval battles in Greece (?). First triremes (ships with three rows of oars). First anchors (?). Greek and Chinese traditions date the appearance of proper coinage from these times; in China, the state of C'hi in Shantung may have played a role in their introduction.

c. 650–600 BC: Lydian and Ionian coinage (excavations of Ephesus).

Late 6th and early 5th centuries BC: Rise of the mercantile economies of Greece and the Mediterranean. Sea merchants play a role in primitive Buddhism. Proper coins appear in India.

From c. 500 BC: Abundant coinage in China, both copper and bronze. Rise of mercantile and urban economy in China. Celtic civilization of La Tène in continental Europe: iron, trade. Bronze Age civilizations in Southeast Asia. Iron working in Nigeria (?). Iron smelting in China.

4th century BC: Written texts on work. Major constructions. Progress of metalwork, particularly in China. Working of iron in Meroe in present-day Sudan (?).

From c. 200 BC: The water wheel.

5. Coin made of electrum minted in Asia Minor, early 6th century BC.

6. Greek trireme, 5th century BC, marble (Acropolis, Athens).

The Population of the Planet

LIKE ALL animal populations, prehistoric human populations were subject to the laws of biological equilibrium, with alternate periods of growth and regression according to the way the climate treated them.

However, by the adaptation of its techniques, humanity gradually liberated itself from environmental constraints. Certain technical advances were responsible for a substantial population growth. This was the case with fire and clothing, which allowed the human race at a very early – and very distant – stage to extend its habitat to almost all the climatic regions of the earth. A second demographic revolution occurred when there was a decisive improvement in hunting techniques in the Upper Paleolithic age. A third was produced by the Neolithic revolution. Although climatic variations were still an important factor, capable of producing prolonged declines in population, the cultural milieu began at that point slowly to take over from the natural one in importance and most of the advances made were lasting ones.

The graph shows these advances and declines from 40,000 BC

onwards for the whole population of the globe. The substantial leaps in population growth at the beginning of the Upper Paleolithic and Neolithic ages (similar to those which occurred during our own industrial revolution) can be clearly seen.

The elements making up the Neolithic period, which were developed over several millennia in a variety of different (relatively independent) centres and in quite diverse ways, formed, in certain places, particularly expansionist complexes. In a single millennium, the population of the globe was multiplied by a factor of 8 or 10.

More precocious, complete and dynamic than the others, the Near East centre was growing and spreading outwards as early as the seventh millennium. First of all, it expanded towards the Nile Valley in 6300 BC, then to the valleys of the Tigris and Euphrates from 5300 BC onwards. In 6000 BC population began to spread towards the north-west (Balkans, Ukraine, Central Europe) and the shores of the Mediterranean (Italy, southern France, eastern Spain, Andalusia, North Africa and as far as Portugal and Morocco). It expanded also towards the Caucasus in the north, towards Iran in the east, on to the southern shores of the Caspian Sea towards Turkestan in the north-east and Yemen in the south. Finally, far to the east, villages began to develop on the margins of the plateaus of Baluchistan which overlook the lower Indus Valley.

It is at this date that the map '4000 BC' gives a picture of the population of the world. At this period an important climatic change exacerbated the drought in the Sahara and the Near East, producing lower crop yields and casing occasional decreases in population. By contrast, in the Balkans, Ukraine and Central Europe, a peasant agriculture was developing in favourable conditions and was beginning to humanize the landscape. In northern China the same was true of peasant millet-growing, which spread into fertile valleys – particularly those in the east. In the south, however, rice-growing remained very basic and the yields remained at a derisory level, as did the yields of horticulture in Papua New Guinea. The same was true in Mexico and Peru, where the maize, bean and potato harvests were still at very low levels of productivity. Everywhere else, hunting, fishing and gathering were only able to support very sparse populations.

At the beginning of our era, the world population had again multiplied by a factor of 8 or 10 relative to 4000 BC. Every point on the lower map opposite is the equivalent of five points on the preceding map. Proportionally, the Near East, where the land was becoming exhausted or gorged with salt as a result of irrigation, lost some of its importance to India and, to a lesser degree, to China, where the population was expanding.

1. Transcription at Lyon of Claudius's speech calling for Gauls to be admitted to the Roman Senate, AD 48.

10,000 BC: Beginning of settlement in the Near East.
8000–6500 BC: Pre-ceramic Neolithic period in the Near East: the appearance of a first centre of high population density (from Iran to Greece, stretching through Anatolia, Syria and Palestine). This also extends, at a very early date, to Egypt.
6000–4000BC: First beginnings of population centres on the Mediterranean coasts, in the Balkans, Ukraine and Central Europe.
5000–4000 BC: First beginnings of centres of population in Mexico and, later, on the Peruvian coast. Colonization of the Tigris and Euphrates valleys in the Near East and the spread of population to Turkestan.
4500 BC: First Chinese population centre emerging in the Wei Ho basin. Beginning of population of Yemen.
4000 BC: First Indian population centre emerging in Indus valley. The populated Wei Ho area extends into the lower valley of the Huang Ho. In southwest China the beginnings of itinerant rice cultivation in areas of burnt forest produced no fixed population centres. In black Africa, the beginnings of

agriculture and settlement in the Sudan ran up against the hostility of the climate (desiccation of the Sahel, lateritization of the soil, tropical forest).
4000–3000 BC: Rapid extension of agriculture and population in Western Europe (France, north Germany, north Poland, southern Scandinavia, Netherlands, British Isles and Spain), in India (Indus valley), in China (Yellow Sea and China Sea coasts, first inhabitants of Yangtze or Chang Jiang valley). Population growth in the Near East was reduced by drought, as was that of North Africa. The discovery of writing in Sumeria furthered the accumulation of knowledge.
3000–2000 BC: Population growth in southern Japan and on the western coasts of Korea. In Ukraine, Western Europe and the Balkans, invasions by peoples from the steppes brought about a serious decline in both agriculture and population growth. In the Near East, too, wars produced devastation. In India, population extended into the Ganges valley, and in the south it spread along the western coast of the sub-continent.
2000–1500 BC: In the Near East and Europe

wars became more and more lethal and there was a substantial decline in population. In India, the Indus civilization collapsed suddenly and population levels with it. In China, population spread slowly towards the south, whereas in Japan it spread northwards. In America, the spread of population both in Mexico and in Peru was much slower.
1500–500 BC: After some large population movements in Europe and the Near East, societies became more stable and population began to increase again.
500 BC–AD 0: Founding of a number of great empires: Persian, Macedonian, Chinese, Indian (Maurya) and Roman – which took in almost all the world's organized states – promoted long-distance trade and stimulated the economy. Everywhere, population was in rapid progress.

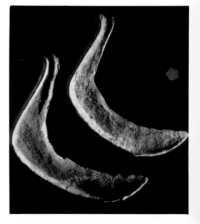

2. Bronze sickles, c. 1000 BC.

From the Neolithic Revolution to Jesus Christ

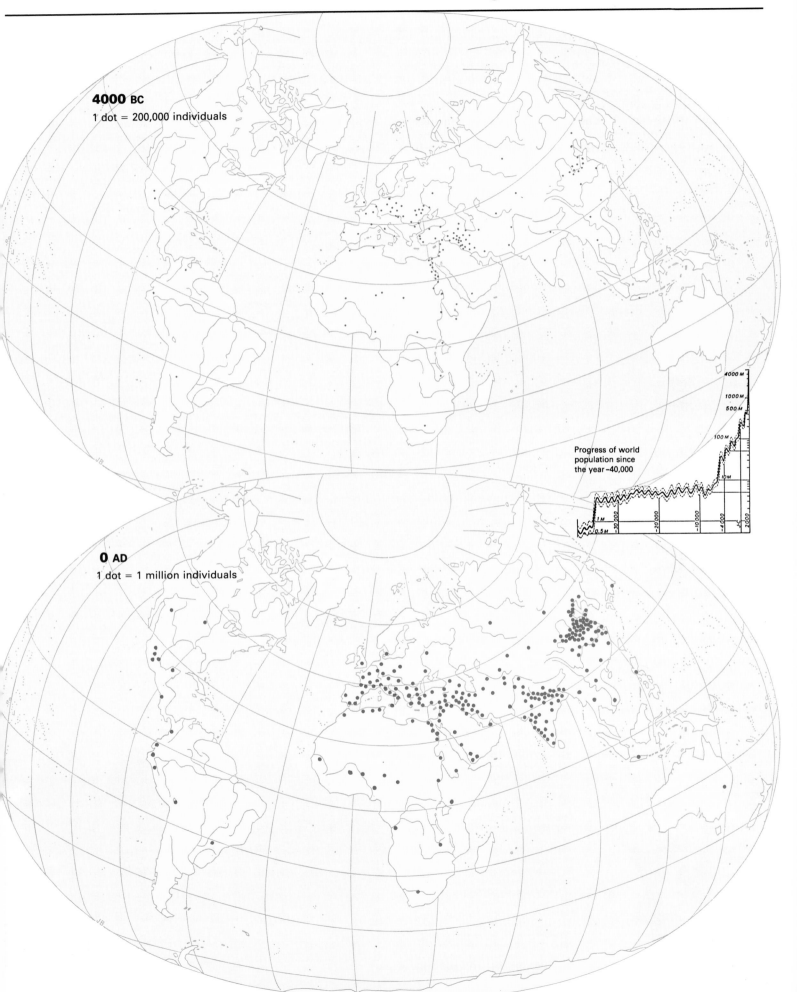

4000 BC
1 dot = 200,000 individuals

Progress of world
population since
the year –40,000

4000 M
1000 M
500 M
100 M
10 M
1 M
0.5 M

–30,000 –20,000 –10,000 –4,000 J.C. 2000

0 AD
1 dot = 1 million individuals

The Greek World between Myth and History

BETWEEN THE WORLD of the Mycenaean palaces and that of the Greek city-states, between, that is, the years 1200 and 800 BC, four centuries passed which are an enigma to historians. They are known as 'the dark centuries' or the 'Greek Middle Ages', formulae which reveal the irritation which this little-known period provokes among historians (though it has, for precisely the same reason, often stimulated the literary imagination). The absence of any written text (Mycenaean linear script had fallen out of use) confers a primordial importance upon the archaeological record, and it is the recent works of synthesis in this field that allow us to put together an, as yet fragmentary, picture of the Greek world.

1. The Lelantine Plain in Euboea. In the top left of the picture is the hill on which Lefkandi, the site of the first Eretria, stands.

The wave of destruction that occurred at the end of the thirteenth century BC was accompanied by the abandonment of the majority of the Mycenaean sites and by population movements towards safe areas where new habitats were created. The break-up of the Mycenaean world doubtless did not occur in an even manner; archaeologists have found that zones of continuity existed at such sites as Athens, Lefkandi in Euboea and in Cyprus. Certainly the collapse was not followed by any permanent settlement of populations that had arrived from elsewhere (the 'Dorian invasions' seem to have been a mirage). At most, what occurred was not a real conquest, but a rapid passing through of migrants. After more than a century of disturbances, from the eleventh century BC onwards, innovations were introduced in a number of fields. The ceramic art that is known as protogeometric made its appearance, iron replaced bronze in the

manufacture of tools and there were changes in burial practices. At the end of the century there began the long process of the migration and settlement of Greek communities from continental Greece along the coasts of Asia Minor and in the islands, whilst Cyprus played a major role as go-between with the Middle Eastern civilizations (there existed a Cypriot syllabic script). Little by little, the Aegean became a Greek sea.

Archaeology allows us to eliminate certain false theories which have attempted to project models derived from elsewhere on to these centuries. As a science, it lays stress on geographical diversity and encourages the historian to be prudent and develop a subtle view. Burial customs offer a good example of this. The map of necropolises reveals the variety of funeral rituals and casts doubt on the idea that there was a uniform transition from inhumation to incineration. It brings out the really new developments in this field: the spread of individual graves and the adoption of the cist tomb. The cemeteries also provide a glimpse of how the world of the living was organized. It is possible to perceive distinctive marks between ages, sexes and social groups in them, even if the step from tomb archaeology to social analysis is a difficult and necessarily speculative one. The documents which really bring this world to life are the *Iliad* and the *Odyssey*. These two epic poems attributed to Homer tell the story of the Trojan War and Ulysses's return to Ithaca. These were stories that had possibly been passed on in the oral tradition from as early as the Mycenaean period, but which were not written down until the eighth century BC. These stories essentially provide a picture of the world of the period between Mycenae and the Greek cities, the world of Greece's 'dark age'. They show Greece coming to life. It covered itself with a sprinkling of kingdoms, organized relations with the gods and between men, made the *oikos* (household, domain) the centre of economic and social power and the place in which kinship was expressed. It also peopled itself with 'heroes' – those who announced themselves 'the best' both as soldiers and as givers of banquets.

Our current knowledge of this period does not make it possible to draw up any detailed chronology. The major reference points are provided by the history of pottery. Other innovations cannot be dated in such a precise manner. They all relate to relatively long periods, whether we are considering population movements in Greece itself and in particular in the Peloponnese (1200–1000 BC), migrations in Asia Minor and in the Cyclades (c. 1100–800 BC), the spread of the use of iron (1100 BC onwards) or a particular burial site. The dark centuries are periods of long-term processes; within them, however, what one might call 'material culture' provides some markers to guide us.

Destruction of Mycenaean palace civilization.

Beginning of Iron Age. Protogeometric cerami

12th century BC

1100–900 BC

2. Cart drawn by three bulls, Crete, 11th century BC.

End of 13th century BC: Destruction of Pylos.
12th century BC: Destruction of Mycenae. Mycenaean palace civilization and Mycenaean script gradually disappear.
1150–1000 BC: Sub-Mycenaean ceramics. The motifs of Mycenaean ceramics are simplified.
1025–900 BC: Protogeometric ceramics. Vases are decorated with circles drawn with a compass and concentric semi-circles painted with a 'multiple brush'. The only other objects known are bronze buckles and clay statuettes. Nothing is known of domestic or temple architecture.
900–725 BC: Geometric ceramics. Decoration takes the form of continuous bands of triangles, wavy lines or zigzags separated by lines. The entire vase is decorated. Excavations have made it possible to reconstruct the structure of the living environment at the very beginning of the ninth century BC (modest cabins as at Smyrna) and of the structure of its defences. The sites whose chronology is best known

3. Small model granaries, Athens, c. 850 BC.

Necropolises 1500 BC to 1125 BC

Necropolises 1100 BC to 900 BC

100 km

Funerary rites: inhumation and cremation

Cist tombs

Other forms of inhumation

Cremation

From A. Snodgrass. *The Dark Age of Greece.*
Edinburgh, 1971

...ation of Greeks into Asia Minor.

c. 1100–800 BC

Geometric ceramics.

900–725 BC

The Mistress of Beasts (Artemis). Attic vase ...f the geometric period, 8th century BC.

are the necropolises. The first cities appeared in the course of the **9th century BC**.

It may be thought that there is one date missing from this brief chronology, that of the 'third Greek invasions: the Dorians'. This omission is deliberate. Did the 'Dorian invasion' really take place? The question has long been a controversial one, but the latest archaeological syntheses find no trace of such a phenomenon. The 'Dorian myth' and the central structuring opposition in Greek discourse between 'Dorians' and 'Ionians' are of the greatest historical interest. They are not, however, by any means proof of the arrival of vast numbers of invaders between the 13th and 12th centuries BC.

At the beginning of the **8th century BC**, figurative decoration appears. This same century sees the diversification of objects and techniques: the sanctuary sites and the rich tombs are filled with magnificent bronze tripod-cauldrons, weapons, bronze figurines, clasps, jewels and statuettes.

5. Stone tripod, Plataea, 7th century BC.

The 'Archaic' Greek World

DURING THESE THREE CENTURIES the geographical limits, mental universe and political structures of what the Greeks called *oukouméné* (the inhabited world) were set in place. The term 'archaic' is only accurate if one takes a view which assumes classical Athens as a model. It would seem more reasonable to view this period as a time in which an enormous number of innovations were tested out, ranging from the appearance of cities to the emergence of rational thought.

We have no means of knowing at what precise date the Greek cities originated; we see them only when they are already functioning, when they have emerged into history (from end of ninth/beginning of eighth centuries BC) and not all the regions of Greece developed at the same pace. A city (*polis*) was a group of people freely governing themselves: the Greeks always referred to the cities by the collective name of their citizens, e.g. the Athenians or the Megarans. Each city was independent, possessed its own institutions and often came into conflict with others. It was made up of a rural territory with a number of villages and a more or less urbanized centre which was the seat of common institutions. Greece was fragmented into several hundred cities, many of which are only names for us today. Lastly, there were a number of Greek regions where organization into cities was not known. The political unit in these regions was the 'people' (*ethnos*) (e.g. the Thessalians or the Locrians). Little was known of their history during these three centuries.

The various cities had very different histories. The close study of a specific community would reveal many features that diverge considerably from the broad outline we are able to present here. There are also gaps in the story owing to the lack of historical evidence. There are few written texts from the period and the archaeological record is often difficult to interpret.

A city was made up of different social groups. Some of these were free; others were slaves. Among the free men there was a fundamental distinction between citizens and non-citizens. As the cities developed, the boundaries between the various categories became more sharply drawn, and access to citizenship – which meant gaining the right to participate in assemblies, tribunals and the magistracy, to fight in wars and possess land – was either expanded or restricted depending upon the particular circumstances.

The lack of cultivable land and its inevitable consequences – debt, slavery and famine – were one of the causes of the great migratory movement which lasted for two centuries. This period of 'colonization' involved the creation of new cities all round the perimeter of the Mediterranean, land being claimed at the expense of the indigenous populations. It did not, however, resolve the internal problems of the cities of continental Greece, but it did ease them in certain cases and produced channels of cultural exchange which had a unifying effect

on a considerable area of the Mediterranean world, from Spain to the Crimea. The existence of these new cities and of what had now become metropolises gave legislators the task of framing new laws. These generally introduced more equity into social relations, though only in exceptional cases (as for example at Sparta) did they take account of the clamour for land reform. In some cases, a small number of great families shared power (aristocratic government); in others, one of these families held power illegally for several generations (tyrannic government). This was the only alternative that existed until Athens made equality before the law a principle of government.

1. The Temple of Apollo at Corinth, 6th century BC. In the background the Citadel of Acrocrinthus.

First cities.	First games at Olympia.		Beginning of Greek 'colonization'.	
800 BC	776 BC		770 BC	

End of 9th century BC: Appearance of first cities.

Beginning of 8th century BC: Adoption of a new alphabet with letters adapted from the Phoenician alphabet. The earliest extant inscriptions date from the end of the 8th/beginning of 7th century BC (scratched on pottery) and include the verse inscription on the Bowl of Nestor at Pithecusa (Ischia).

776 BC: Traditional date of the first Olympic Games. They were held during a festival in Zeus's honour at Olympia and comprised athletic, musical and poetry competitions. Of these, the athletic events were the most famous. They included running, throwing the discus and javelin, boxing, wrestling and chariot racing.

770–706 BC: Greek 'colonization' begins (in the west). Greek settlement at Pithecusai (island off the coast of Naples). Foundation of Naxos and Cumae by Chalcis, Syracuse by Corinth and Tarentum by Sparta.

Middle–end of 8th century BC: Iliad and Odyssey, epic poems attributed to Homer, written down. Writings of Hesiod.

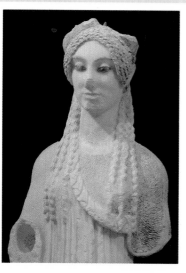

2. Dorian-style Attic Kore, late 6th century BC.

747–657 BC: The family of the Bacchiadae holds power in Corinth: an example of aristocratic government.

736–720 and 650–620 BC: Sparta stakes out its territory in the Messenian wars.

700–675 BC and after: Greek 'colonization' in the east. Megara founds Chalcedon (c. 687 BC); Paros founds Thasos (c. 682 BC); Megara founds Byzantium. Other cities were also founded along the coast of the Black Sea (Pontus Euxinus), such as Istros and Olbia (by Miletus) around 650 BC. New settlements were created in southern Italy and Sicily and in the far western Mediterranean. This expansion continued until the end of the century.

680–670 BC: First appearance of coinage in Lydia and in Ionia. The minting of coins did not develop in the Greek cities for another century. The pottery of this period is known as 'Orientalizing'. First stone temples built.

7th century BC: Saw the rise of 'tyrannies' (illegal government by one man) in the Greek cities. Examples are Kypselos and Periandres in Corinth (657–585 BC) or Orthagoras to Cleisthenes at Sikyon. Codes of law were also elaborated under the auspices of such 'legislators' as Zaleucus of Locri (660 BC?), Charondas of Catana and Draco (620 BC) and Solon at Athens.

600 BC: Massalia (Marseille) founded as a colony of Phocaea.

3. Gold buckle in the shape of a falcon. From the Temple of Artemis at Ephesus, c. 550 BC.

8th–6th centuries BC

Greek colonization 750 BC to 450 BC

● Principal metropolises
New cities founded by:
♦ Corinth
● Megara
■ the cities of Eubowa (Chalcis, Eretria, Andros)
● the cities of the Ionian cost (Miletus, Phocaea)
▬ by the cities of the Aegean islands (Thera, Rhodes, Paros)
○ diverse origins
⊙ Colonies of the new cities

500 km

● Principal metropolises
in this period

**First wave
of archaic colonization (750 BC to 675 BC)**

● Principal metropolises
in this period

**Second wave
of archaic colonization (675 BC to 540 BC)**

500 km

First coins.   Solon archon at Athens.   Cleisthenes's reforms at Athens.

c. 620 BC   594 BC   507 BC

7th and 6th centuries BC: Centuries of innovation in all fields: the 'origins of Greek thought' are indissociable from the history of the cities.
594BC: Solon, archon at Athens, abolishes enslavement by debt, removes the 'mortgages' that are oppressing the small landowners and introduces a new system of weights and measures. Certain of the constitutional reforms attributed to him (Areopagus council, etc.) were perhaps inventions of the 4th century BC (and Aristotle in particular).
561–528/7 BC: Peisistratos rules intermittently as tyrant at Athens.
528/7–510 BC: The tyrant Hipparchos (assassinated in 514 BC) is succeeded by the tyrant Hippias.
508–507 BC: Cleisthenes's reforms at Athens. The structures which will allow for the introduction of democratic rule are put in place.

. A hoplite. Detail from the 'Krater of Vix', Corinthian art (?), 6th century BC.

5. The cyclops intoxicated and blinded by Ulysses and his companions. Laconian bowl, 6th century BC.

A Universal Empire: Persia

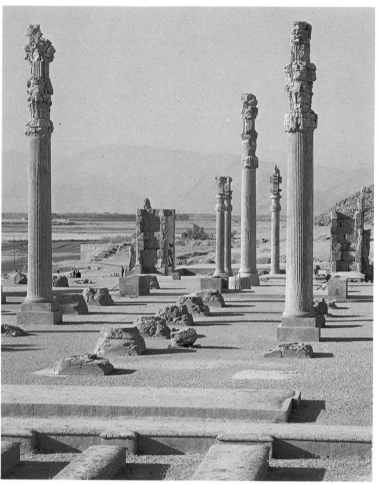

1. The Apadana (Hall of a Hundred Columns) of the palace of Persepolis, 6th–5th century BC.

THE PERSIANS AND THE MEDES were the foremost peoples among the 'barbarians' (the non-Greek-speakers). In forty years, they rose from being mere Oriental provincials to become masters of the world. The conquests of Cyrus, Cambyses and Darius I brought together the Indus region, the Scythians beyond Sogdiana, Egypt and Ionia into a vast single body whose heart beat in Persia. Though there were revolts within the Empire and though it suffered some defeats, particularly at the hands of the Greeks, a state of peace was established (albeit one defended by a vast deployment of arms).

Darius I played an organizing role in the Empire. Firstly, he placed garrisons in all the regions, especially those that were vital on account of their wealth (Egypt, Babylonia) or their location (Ionia, Bactria). The conquered populations were made to pay tribute by providing ships, soldiers or provisions. Secondly, he appointed satraps, governors and Persian officers who, being bound to the Great King by blood or honour, were entirely under his command. The king was the focus of the whole system: he was the theoretical owner of all land, commander-in-chief and supreme judge. He was also the representative of Ahura-Mazda among men, the junction between the divine and the human, the hub of the entire cosmic order. And within an immense network of land, river and sea communications (the royal road from Ephesus to Bactria; the Nile–Red Sea canal dredged in the reign of Darius I), each region continued to live under its own legal system. Greek money reached as far as Bactria, Iranian customs took root in Asia Minor and Egyptian, Greek and Ionian scholars and artists came together in Susa and Persepolis.

Evoking former nomadic times, the court had three residences. In winter it was based at Persepolis or Susa and in summer at Ecbatana(Hamadan). Persepolis was the domain of the Achaemenid clan and by that token, the capital. Built in the days of Darius I and enhanced by constant improvements, it was the centre of the royal economy, the theatre of the New Year festivals and the jewel of Achaemenid art. That art, which welcomed a variety of influences – it looked to Greece in matters of stone working, to Mesopotamia for iconography and to Iran for the representation of animals – was a royal art, in which the delegations lined up to offer their gifts to the king represented the vastness of the whole world showing allegiance to a single sovereign.

The Persians worshipped Ahura-Mazda; he was their great god, together with Mithra and the goddess Anahita; but the king acknowledged Amun-Ré in Egypt and Apollo at Delphi, whilst the Persian administration respected the cult of the Elamite gods at Persepolis.

A great number of centrifugal tendencies, constant dynastic difficulties, and the superior quality of the Greek hoplites, not to mention Alexander's good fortune, put an end to the Persian Empire. A whole chapter in the development of ancient oriental civilization was thus concluded, but Alexander's conquests brought the peoples of Central Asia and Iran on to the historical stage for the first time and opened up distant lands first to the Greco-Macedonians and later to the Romans. It is from these years of integration, in particular from the view that the contemporary Greeks had of the Persians, that we have derived the picture of the Orient that still haunts the Western imagination today, a picture made up of despotism and intrigue, lust and luxury. There is little difference between the writings of classical authors like Ctesias and Plutarch and those of seventeenth-century European travellers in Persia. Both share the same fascination made up of conflicting emotions of surprise, desire and repulsion.

Union of Medan princes at Ecbatana.

Cyrus builds Pasargades.

700 BC

c. 540 BC

2. King Darius says: 'This is the kingdom I possess. '... Here is what Ahura-Mazda has granted me.' Trilingual golden plaque, Darius I, c. 500 BC.

612 BC: A coalition of Median princes destroys Nineveh and the Neo-Assyrian Empire; the Persians become vassals of the Medes.
550 BC: Cyrus II the Great defeats the last Median king and conquers Asia Minor, including Croesus's Lydian kingdom and the whole of Iran.
539 BC: Cyrus conquers Babylon and allows the Jews, who were captive there, to return to Palestine and rebuild the Temple at Jerusalem.
525 BC: Cambyses II conquers Egypt.
521 BC: Dynastic problems enable Darius I to usurp the throne by eliminating Cambyses II's brother. With a section of the Persian nobility he represses uprisings throughout the Empire. The inscription at Bagistana in Media recounts his version of events in four languages (Old Persian, Akkadian, Elamite and Aramaic). He then conquers the Indus valley, Thrace and Macedonia.
510 BC: Building work at its height at Persepolis. The Elamite tablets – records of the wages paid to workers, peasants and artisans employed there – reveal a centralized, hierarchical economy.

3. Gold rhyton (animal-shaped vessel), Achaemenid art, c. 500 BC.

550–331 BC

557 BC

LYDIAN KINGDOM
M E D I A
Persia at the accession of Cyrus
NEO-BABYLONIAN KINGDOM
EGYPT

539 BC Cyrus's conquests

P E R S I A N   E M P I R E
Persepolis

500 BC Maximum extent of Empire under Darius

P E R S I A N   E M P I R E
Persepolis
Indus

Organization of the world's first great empire

Jaxartes (Syr Darya)
Lake Issyk-Kul
ARAL SEA
SOGDIANA
FERGANA
Maracanda (Samarkand)
Oxus (Amu Darya)
Danube
PONTUS EUXINUS
THRACE
MYSIA · Dascylium
Plataea –479
GREECE
Marathon –490
Salamis –480
Alliance of Greek cities against the Persians
LYDIA
Sardis · Ephesus
IONIA
PHRYGIA
CAPPADOCIA
Halys
CASPIAN SEA
ARMENIA
BACTRIA
· Bactria
MARGIANA
· Merv
Merv rud
GANDARITIS
Kabul
CILICIA
ASSYRIA
Niniveh
Tigris
Euphrates
PARTHIA
ARIA
Hari rud
Helmand
ARACHOSIA
INDUS
Rai (Tehran)
Salt deserts
Ecbatana (Hamadan)
MEDIA
MEDITERRANEAN SEA
Cyrene
Sidon
Tyre
· Damascus
BABYLONIA
Babylon
Nippur
Susa
ELAM
Dasht-e Lut
DRANGIANA
Thar Desert
Indus
LIBYA
Jerusalem
Pasargadae
Shiraz
· Persepolis
PERSIS
GEDROSIA
Memphis
EGYPT
RED SEA
PERSIAN GULF
SEA OF OMAN
SAHARA
Nile
· Elephantine

Mountainous regions, few inhabitants

Deserts and steppes

The three main centres of state power

Regions with close ties to these centres (Iranian populations)

Non-Iranian populations

Provinces ruled by a governor

Scythian population

Indian population

BACTRIA Grand satrapies (rich regions)

Royal road

300 km

Darius I.

521 BC

498 BC: The revolt of Ionia sparks off the Persian Wars. Darius is defeated at Marathon in 490 BC and dies in 486 BC. He is buried at Naqsh-i-Roustem.

482 BC: Revolt in Babylonia and Xerxes is defeated by the Greeks at Salamis (480 BC), Plataea and at the Mycale (479 BC).

c. 450–430 BC: Herodotus of Helicarnassus, a subject of Artaxerxes I, describes the Persian Empire in his *History*.

449 BC: Peace of Callias. This treaty, negotiated at Susa by Callias the Athenian, establishes a demilitarized zone along the coast of Asia Minor and puts an end to the Persian Wars.

404 BC: Artaxerxes II, son of Darius II, is challenged by his ambitious brother, Cyrus the Younger, who engages 10,000 Greek mercenaries in order to win the throne, but loses the battle of Cunaxa (401 BC) and dies. Xenophon describes the Retreat of the Ten Thousand in his *Anabasis*; on his return to Greece he writes the *Cyropaedia*, an idealized portrait of Cyrus the Great.

c. 403 BC: Revolt and secession of Egypt. Under Nectanebes I and his 30th dynasty, Egypt will enjoy independence and relative prosperity.

Elamite tablets of Persepolis.

519–465 BC

4. The tomb of Darius I at Naqsh-i-Roustem.

End of 5th/beginning of 4th centuries BC: The Greek doctor Ctesias, author of a *History of Persia*, lives at Susa and Persepolis.

386 BC: The Peace of Antalcidas dictated by Artaxerxes II, permits the Great King to act as a 'broker' among the Greeks. The Persian king makes good use of his gold both for war and for diplomacy.

362 BC: Revolt of the satraps of Asia Minor, amongst whom was a certain Mausolus whose tomb gave us the word mausoleum.

358 BC: Artaxerxes III endeavours to restore royal power within the Empire. He eliminates the opposition, reconquers Egypt (343–341 BC). He runs up against the ambitions of Philip II of Macedonia and dies at the hands of an assassin in 338 BC.

334 BC: Alexander III, the Great, lands in Asia Minor.

333 BC: The Persians lose the Battle of Issus in Cilicia; two years later they lose the Battle of Gaugamela.

331 BC: Persepolis is sacked and burnt. In Bactria and Sogdiana, Alexander becomes orientalized as Iran is hellenized.

Artaxerxes II.

404 BC

5. Lapis Lazuli head of an Achaemenid prince, Persepolis, end of 5th century BC.

Hellenism Triumphant

THERE HAS BEEN no shortage of positive expressions – the classical era, the Golden Age of city-states, the high point of Hellenism – deployed to describe this period, and yet it was also an era of incessant battles, plagues, famines, intolerance, civil war and confrontations between rich and poor. To see this, one has only to turn one's gaze away from the shining new statues of the Acropolis to the Ceramicus cemetery where the dead were buried, or from the processions of pilgrims who climbed the sacred path to the sanctuary of Apollo at Delphi to the inscriptions on the temple walls which, in their thousands, bear witness to the existence of slavery.

The fifth century BC was dominated by two conflicts. The one set the Greeks against the Persians, the other saw almost all the Greek cities, with Athens at their head, ranged against Sparta. What was at stake in the struggle against the Persian Great King was the freedom of the Greek world. The opposition between Athens and Sparta was, however, more complex and cannot be reduced to a confrontation between two models of government, one oligarchic, the other democratic. There was indeed a great divide – and one which constantly increased throughout the fifth century – between the rigidity of the Spartan social and political system, which had been frozen in its forms since the Archaic period, and the evolution towards greater power being given to the people (demos) which characterizes the internal history of Athens from Cleisthenes to Pericles. But war was in any event one of the primordial aspects of Greek life, an eternal competition which was carried on in every field by individuals and communities for whom rivalry was the only worthy mode of being.

The cult of war was bound inextricably together with the general life of the community through the medium of the gods. Not only fields of battle, from the farmland plains which offered opportunities for the skilful manoeuvring of infantry (hoplites) to the sheltered coves where the battleships (triremes) rammed each other, but also the more peaceful sites where only opinions clashed (assemblies, tribunals), and even the most humble domestic space, all were places where the gods were potentially present, invoked by a sacrifice, a libation, or a simple prayer. Greece certainly had its sanctuaries where marble statues were to be seen looming out of the smoke from roasting meat (who has not heard of Delphi, Olympia, Delos or the Acropolis at Athens?), but it should be stressed that every act of public and private life had a sacred dimension. This dimension was part and parcel of the daily round, which took the Greek from the gymnasium to the agora (public square), from the sanctuary to the banqueting hall, and from the field to the theatre where Aeschylus, Aristophanes, Sophocles and Euripides were performed.

A great deal of experimentation and innovation that had its beginnings in earlier periods was brought to completion in the fifth century. For the Greek city-states as a whole, there were more continuities than radical breaks. The most crucial new development was the immense breakthrough made by written documents, from stone-carved inscriptions to literary texts. Such documents both allow us to discover even the least significant little decree from some obscure city in the Pelopponese and at the same time they privilege a particular vision of the world of the city-states, namely that of Athens, whence most of the texts derive. The modern historian of the 'classical world' has a better understanding of the ethnocentrism of his 'sources', but it is very difficult for that historian to speak with anything but the voice of Athens, a city which saw itself as the model of the Greek world.

1. Athens: the Acropolis and the Parthenon. In the background, Mt Lycabettus (also known as the Hill of St George).

Marathon.	Salamis.	Delian League.	Birth of Socrates.
490 BC	480 BC	477 BC	470 BC

525–456 BC: Aeschylus.
508–507 BC: Cleisthenes' reforms at Athens.
499–493 BC: Ionian revolt. The Greek cities rise against the tyrants set in power by the Persians. In 498 BC the Persian town of Sardis is captured and burnt. In 494 BC Miletus is razed to the ground. Peace treaties between Darius and the cities.
497–406 BC: Sophocles.
492–479 BC: Persian Wars. The Persians under the direction of Darius and, later, Xerxes, invade Greece. They are defeated at Marathon (490 BC), Salamis (480 BC), Plataea and Mycale (479 BC) by a coalition of cities. Athens comes to the fore both by virtue of its place in the front line of the fighting (the Acropolis was burnt by the Persians) and of the part played by Themistocles, the strategic head of the Greek army. See Herodotus's History.
c. 485 BC: Birth of Herodotus.
485–406 BC: Euripides.
477 BC: Delian League founded. This was an alliance of Greek cities around Athens to prosecute war against the Persians; Athenian

hegemony became more and more marked and the allies were unable to leave the alliance (470 BC, the revolt of Naxos) even after a peace treaty, the Peace of Callias (449–448 BC) had been signed with the Great King.

2. Athenian decadrachma bearing motif of owl with outstretched wings. Persian Wars period.

3. Artemis and Acteon. Bell-shaped krater by the painter of Pan, c. 470 BC.

472 BC: Themistocles ostracized. Ostracism was a vote of the citizen body of Athens condemning to exile a political personality whose presence was thought to endanger the stability of the polis. Many Athenian politicians fell victim to it (Cimon in 461 BC; Thucydides in 443 BC).
472–387 BC: The tragedies of Aeschylus, Sophocles and Euripides and the comedies of Aristophanes made the theatre of Dionysos at Athens a significant site of civic discourse.
464 BC: Earthquake at Sparta. Revolt of the helots, a peasant population of serfs. These revolts, frequent in the 5th century BC, weakened Sparta, which was forced to struggle on several fronts at once. Athens, which employed vast numbers of bought slaves of non-Athenian origin, did not face such internal disturbances.
462 BC: Ephialtes' reforms at Athens. The aristocratic Areopagus Council lost part of its prerogatives to the People's Assembly, the Council of the Five Hundred (Boulé) and the Heliaea tribunal. An important step towards democracy.

5th century BC

The Greek cities in the Classical Age, Vth century BC

Magna Graecia and Sicily

100 km

100 km

Death of Pericles.	Death of Sophocles.	End of the Peloponnesian War.
429 BC	**406 BC**	**404 BC**

458 BC: Aeschyslus's *Orestes, Agamemnon, The Libation Bearers* and *Eumenides.*

447–438 BC: Rebuilding of the Parthenon temple on the Acropolis.

443–429 BC: Pericles repeatedly re-elected General at Athens.

431–404 BC: Peloponnesian War opposed Sparta and its allies to Athens and its allies (Delian League). Thucydides is its historian.

428 BC: Birth of Plato.

421 BC: Peace of Nicias.

415–413 BC: Athenian expedition to Sicily. Alcibiades takes on a political role.

411–404/3 BC: Attempts to install oligarchic governments at Athens with the support of Sparta. Double failure.

404 BC: Collapse of Athens. Sparta imposes its peace. The Athenian 'Empire' disappears.

4. Zeus or Poseidon? c. 460 BC. Bronze found in the sea off Cape Artemisium.

5. The tomb of the diver of Posidonia (Paestum). Greek painting, 5th century BC.

6. Poseidon, Apollo. Eastern frieze of the Parthenon, c. 440 BC.

Philosophers and Sages

1. Buddhas seated on lotus thrones. Dunhuang, 8th century.

THE IDEA that the years between 600 and 300 BC constitute an 'axial period' in human history is an old one given new life in the twentieth century in the works of Lewis Mumford and Karl Jaspers. On the one hand, we find radical innovation in the socio-political field, where some uniquely productive advances were made; on the other, significant advances in the dimension of intellectual creativity, of philosophical, scientific and artistic invention. From this second point of view, the period 600–200 BC is particularly exceptional and may be compared with the seventeenth and eighteenth centuries in the West or the years 1890–1920 in Europe. One is struck by the sudden burgeoning of genius in every corner of the inhabited world, by the emergence of philosophers, sages and scholars whose teachings and reputations will endure among later generations. What we know of the Olmec civilization, the mother of the Meso-American cultures, even allows us to add America to this panoramic picture. Another impressive feature is the sudden emergence of competing schools, which seem astonishingly modern to us even today (the 'hundred schools' of China, the 'sixty schools' of India). But are there, beyond this mere quantitative simultaneity, this planetary explosion of thought, qualitative similarities, analogies or homologies of content between these separate cultural achievements?

The sixth century BC was a century of intense moral disquiet, of religious agitation and reform; it was a century of mystics and ascetics. But something else was in gestation and even before the end of the century the precursors of world enlightenment were at work in the form of Ionian cosmologists, the Indian materialists, and the Chinese ancestors of legalist rationality and cynicism. Pythagoras, who was a priest and a thaumaturge, was also the forerunner of the mathematically-based science of the fourth century BC (and that of the eighteenth century AD). The monotheism of the Second Isaiah (the first true monotheism in history) is related to 'nationalist' fanaticism (the one God is the God of the Jews), but this purging of the sacred contributed to the 'disenchantment' of the world.

From the last decades of the sixth century BC onwards, this movement gained momentum. Gotama the Buddha with his godless wisdom undermined the hegemony of the priests. Confucius flaunted his agnosticism, desacralizing both writing and ritual. Theagenes rationalized Homer and Hecataeus mocked the Greek myths. The fifth century saw the flowering of a critical, utilitarian cast of mind, particularly after 450 BC (Sophists in Greece, Mozu (Mo-tsu) and his disciples in China, the Twelve Tables and their laicised law in Rome). The fourth century, with its immoralist tendencies, was the great

Jeremiah.	Zarathustra.		The Twelve Tables.
627–585 BC	627–585 BC		450 BC

1400 or 1300 BC to 300 or 200 BC: The formative millennium in Central America (the Olmecs), in Oceania (Fiji, Tonga, Samoa, the cradle of Polynesian civilization), in India (the *Vedas*) and in the Mediterranean and China.

600–200 BC: The 'axial' period.

c. 600 BC(?): Zoroaster and the dualism of Good and Evil.

6th century BC: Anaximander and Anaximenes: cosmologies.

2nd half of 6th century BC: Xenophanes criticizes Greek polytheism. Pythagoras. Second Isaiah.

c. 530 BC: Gotama the Buddha begins preaching. Rise of materialist schools in India. Confucius (Kong fu-tsu, or Kung-tzu) begins teaching. From about 495 BC onwards, he was a sort of itinerant political adviser: rites, history.

c. 525 BC: Theagenes.

522 BC (?): Massacre of the Magi (Zoroastrian priests) in Persia.

508–507 BC: Cleisthenes's reforms at Athens: rationalization.

c. 500 BC: Hecataeus, critical historian and geographer. Calendar and mathematics among the Olmecs.

4. Sun Stone, known as Aztec calendar.

5. Epicurus. Roman copy of a Greek original.

End of 6th/beginning of 5th centuries BC: The first great Greek philosophers. Heraclitus: universal flux and rhythm. Parmenides: the oneness of Being. Empedocles: the unity of opposites.

End of 6th to beginning of 3rd centuries BC: World Enlightenment.

Middle of 5th century BC: Sophist revolution in Greece (critical spirit, progressive anthropology).. Anaxagoras at Athens: rationalist humanism, friendship with Pericles. Herodotus: rationalist history.

c. 450 BC: The Twelve Tables at Rome, laicization of law.

444 BC: Calculation of the solar year in China (365¼ days).

c. 440 BC: Mozi reacts against Confucian traditionalism; strong utilitarian tendencies.

5th–6th centuries BC: Democritus: atoms and progress. Decline of prophetic activity among the Jews. The 'Chinese sophists': paradoxes and dialectics. Panini, Indian grammarian and linguist.

c. 400 BC: Thucydides: historical necessity.

600–200 BC

epoch of Greek, Chinese, Indian and Amerindian rationalism. Astronomy was the first of the sciences to be born. Naturalists produced classifications and general rules. History would never be the same again after Thucydides and the Bamboo Annals, nor politics the same after Aristotle and the Artha-sastra, Plato and Zou Yan (Tsou Yen). Logicians and theorists of all kinds flourished. Fourth-century rationalism leaned towards a mathematical, even mystical idealism (Plato, Mengzi, Zhuangzi). At its highest point, the invention of rationalism was internally contradictory and laid the ground for the movements that were to follow.

In the third century, observation reclaimed its due. Scholars designed machines, and moral and practical preoccupations won out

once again over ontology and theory. In the religious sphere, the great transformations which were to characterize the following period, either side of the birth of Jesus, were beginning to take shape. For the rationalism of the 500–300 BC period, this was the beginning of the end.

This rationalism, though quite different from ours, is nonetheless of the same lineage. This is particularly true of Greek rationalism, which has had inheritors in the West since the fifteenth century who have brought that inheritance to fruition, disciples who have followed and surpassed the masters. The Chinese or Indian rationalists of the 'axial' period have had only mediocre followers in modern times. Their own grandeur is not, however, thereby diminished.

2. Plato teaching geometry. Roman mosaic, 1st century BC.

3. Confucius. Chinese painting of 18th century.

Plato's Academy.

387 BC

Xun zi.

3rd century BC

6. Isaiah by Claus Sluter, Dijon, c. AD 1400.

399 BC: Trial of Socrates: conflict of free thinking with the state.

4th century BC: Rome provides itself with a history. In China, the *Bamboo Annals*; the *Zhouli*: highly systematic and utopian treatise of administration. Zou Yan: the cycles of the five elements, political cycles. Yang Zhu (Yang Chu) opposes all values. The Greek cynics oppose taboos.
387 BC?: Plato founds the Academy: idealism, mathematicism, political theories and utopias.
335 BC?: Aristotle founds the Lyceum. Deductive logic and encyclopaedism. High point of Greek rationalism.

End of 4th century BC: The Indian(?) *Artha-sastra*: politically rationalist, imbued with spirit of system, immoralistic. Mengzi (Mencius in Latin): idealist rationalism. Zhuangzi: mystical idealism. Shang Yang: Legalism. Euclid's(?) *Elements*.
306 BC?: Epicurus founds his school (atomism and happiness).
Since c. 300 BC: The Stoics.

3rd century BC: Greek scholars Aristarchus of Samos, Archimedes, Eratosthenes. Xun zi, Chinese empiricist philosopher.
Since 3rd century BC: Hellenistic technology. Signs of religious revival throughout the world.

8. Astronomical papyrus of 2nd century referring to the doctrines of Eudoxus of Cyzicus, 4th century BC.

7. Socrates. Roman copy of a Greek original.

The Division of the Hellenistic World

Alexander's Empire (323 BC)

- Macedonia at the accession of Alexander (−336)
- Alexander's Empire at its height
- −330 Alexander's route (−334 to −323)
- Craterus's return route (−325)
- Nearchus's return route (−325)
- −331 × Battles
- Alexandria • Towns founded by Alexander
- Cities and states that were Alexander's allies
- Independent states

IN THE MIDDLE of the fourth century BC, the idea of an inhabited world (*oikoumene*) with the Aegean Sea at its centre and the city as its model was to produce, among the Greeks, the fantastic ambition of establishing hegemony over the West and conquering the East. However, the high point reached in 325 BC and the decline which set in thereafter reveal the vulnerability of this goal to advances in military tactics: the Macedonian phalanx was all-conquering after Cheronaea, but the Roman legion became dominant after Cynoscephalae. Instead of remaining the centre of the world, as it had hoped, Greece reverted to being part of the periphery.

The years 403–338 BC appear to be a mere prolongation of the preceding century. The need to unite against the 'barbarian' (the argument Demosthenes applied against Philip of Macedon) still met resistance in the shape of the particularism of the individual city-states. We can also see here the renewed rise of the Persians – established in the position of power-brokers ('king's peace') – and of monarchy, in the person of Philip.

The sequence of events between 338 and 168 BC demonstrates the inability of the Greek states to administer a world empire. Setting out symbolically from Troy, within two years Alexander had conquered the Mediterranean façade of the Persian Empire. He needed only one more year to make the legacy of the assassinated Darius III his own. After difficult campaigns in the oriental satrapies, he crossed the Indus in 326 BC, but his troops forced him to stop on the Hyphases. After his death, the wars between the separatist kings (Diadochi) produced an unwieldy arrangement unsuited to the functioning of a great empire in which the principal seats of power were at capitals such as Pella, Alexandria and Antioch, none of which occupied a central position, either in relation to the hinterland or to the Mediterranean area as a whole.

Torn between Europe and Asia, the Antigonids inherited the divisions of the Hellenic world. From this point of view, 281 BC is a key date. The Battle of Corupedium put an end to the Asian ambitions of continental Greece and left the Ptolemies and the Seleucids face to

Restoration of democracy in Athens.	Persian 'King's Peace'.	Macedonian 'King's Peace'.	Foundation of Alexandria.
403 BC	386 BC	337 BC	331 BC

403 BC: After the bloody tyranny of the 'Thirty Tyrants', a moderate democracy restored the power of Athens.
401 BC: The revolt of Cyrus the Younger, supported by Sparta, against his brother Artaxerxes fails at Kunaxa.
386 BC: The Persians impose the 'King's Peace', which safeguards the autonomy of the cities.
377 BC: Athens reconstitutes its maritime league.
371 BC: Defeated at Leuctra, Sparta yields supremacy to Thebes.
355 BC: Philip, King of Macedon, extends his power over Thessaly and Thrace at the expense of Athens, which was defeated in the 'War for Amphipolis'.
338 BC: Philip wins the Battle of Cheronaea and gains hegemony over the new League of Corinth against the Persians.
336 BC: After Philip's murder, his son Alexander represses revolts in Greece (sack of Thebes) and conquers the Persian possessions as far as the Indus (334–324 BC).

331 BC: Alexandria founded.
323 BC: Death of Alexander at Babylon. War of the 'Diadochi' (successors) (→ 281 BC).
322 BC: Failure of revolt at Athens. Demosthenes commits suicide.

3. Portrait presumed to be that of Alexander the Great. Ivory from a royal tomb, Verghina, c. 330 BC.

2. Crown of gold oak leaves.

4th–1st centuries BC

The Hellenic and Hellenistic world on the eve of the Roman Conquest (185 BC)

■ Regions under Roman rule

→ Roman conquests after −188 (Peace of Apamea)

face. These two powers were to be exhausted by the 'Syrian Wars' of which there were six (culminating in the famous circle of Popilius Laenias). Tarentum's appeal to Pyrrhus, the king of Epirus, against Rome, then that of the Syracusans against Carthage, set in train a series of chain reactions in which the Greeks were soon to be reduced to playing only a marginal role. The Battle of Pydna concluded this process, finally eliminating Macedon from the political scene, at the very moment at which the two basins of the Mediterranean entered a common historical process, of which Rome was to be the arbiter.

The Ptolemies enjoyed the most homogeneous territorial base, in the form of Egypt. By methodically exploiting their dynastic possessions in the service of maritime supremacy, Ptolemy II (283–246 BC) and Ptolemy III (246–222 BC) were the only men to create a truly imperial economy.

The Seleucids possessed the most extensive continental land mass (4,000 km from the Aegean to Afghanistan). In spite of the energy of Antiochus I (281–261 BC), Antiochus III (223–187 BC) and Antiochus

IV (175–164 BC), their history is one of a progressive erosion. As early as 240 BC, a large strip of land had been lost in the north (Bithynia, Galatia, Cappadocia, Atropatenia), in the east (Parthia, Bactria) and in the west (Pergamum, Ptolemaic possessions). In the south, Coele-Syria, finally conquered in 200 BC, would in 143 BC, during the reign of the Hasmonean dynasty, have an independent Jewish state carved out of it.

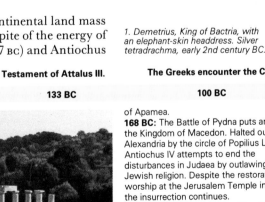

1. Demetrius, King of Bactria, with an elephant-skin headdress. Silver tetradrachm, early 2nd century BC.

The Greeks encounter the Chinese.

dom of Bactria founded.

Testament of Attalus III.

240 BC

133 BC

100 BC

306–304 BC: The Diadochi take the title of king. Macedonia remains in the hands of the Antigonid dynasty (→ 168 BC), Asia under the Seleucid control (63 BC) and Egypt under the Ptolemies (→ 30 BC).
303 BC: Alliance between Seleucus I Nicator and Chandragupta, founder of the Maurya Empire, opens India up to exchanges with the West.
300 BC: Antioch founded.
281 BC: Battle of Corupedium. Tarentum appeals successfully to Pyrrhos, King of Epirus, against Rome.
247 BC: East of the Caspian Sea, Arsaces founds the Parthian kingdom.
241 BC: Attalus proclaims himself king of Pergamum.
240 BC: Diodotus creates a kingdom of Bactria (→ 100 BC).
200 BC: Battle of Panium gives Coele-Syria to the Seleucids.
197 BC: Philip V of Macedon defeated at Cynoscephalae.
189 BC: After his defeat at Magnesia, Antiochus III abandons the Seleucid possessions beyond the Taurus by the Treaty

of Apamea.
168 BC: The Battle of Pydna puts an end to the Kingdom of Macedon. Halted outside Alexandria by the circle of Popilius Laenias, Antiochus IV attempts to end the disturbances in Judaea by outlawing the Jewish religion. Despite the restoration of worship at the Jerusalem Temple in 165 BC the insurrection continues.
155 BC: In the Indus Valley, Menander founds an Indo-Greek kingdom (→ 50 BC).
143 BC: Jerusalem becomes the capital of a Jewish state (→ 63 BC).
133 BC: Attalus III of Pergamum bequeaths his kingdom to the Romans.
100 BC: Conquest of Bactria by the Yueh'chih. China's first contacts with the West through Pamir.
95 BC: The Parthians sign a treaty of friendship with Sylla, fixing their frontier on the Euphrates.
66 BC: Pompey's Eastern Campaigns.
63 BC: End of the Seleucid monarchy and the Jewish state. Pompey organizes the eastern territories of the Roman Empire as far as the Euphrates.

4. View of the sanctuary of the great gods at Samothrace, Ptolemaic period.

5. The Delphi column of the dancers. Attic art, c. 330 BC.

Italy, the Etruscans and the Birth of Rome

THE IDEAS OF ANCIENT HISTORIANS on the appearance of cities and peoples were shaped by the model of colonial settlement. They attributed the birth of cities to founder-heroes like Romulus, combining local origins and migratory movements to explain the distribution of peoples or to justify their genealogical ties: the arrival of the Trojans and Aeneas in Latium; the departure of a group of Lydians for Italy under the leadership of Tyrsenos (the eponymous ancestor of the Tyrrhenians, which , as Herodotus tells us, was the Greek name for the Etruscans). Conditioned by these ancient sources, modern historians have until recently tended all too often to pose the problem of the formation of the cultures of Italy in terms of ethnic origins and population movements. Moreover, the heterogeneity of the Etruscan language in relation to the other Italic tongues, all of which are related to the Indo-European family of languages – a diversity emphasized in ancient ethnography, which regards language as a

primordial criterion in the differentiation of peoples – has contributed in no small measure to the invention of the 'Etruscan mystery'. This takes on all the more importance in the light of the fact that the Etruscans occupied an essential place in the very birth of Rome, the period of the Etruscan monarchy being a decisive one. Moreover, 'before the Roman Empire, the Etruscans had extended their power far abroad on land and sea' (Livy, Book V), acting as precursors of Rome's own foreign policy. Current analyses are based on the findings of archaeological research and propose a history of the populations of Italy which lays stress on two types of process. On the one hand, there is the internal structuring of economies and societies. We are thus looking here, between the end of the Bronze Age and the beginnings of the Iron Age, at sets of cultural features which can be more or less exactly related to the different peoples settled in Italy in this historical period. Secondly, there are external factors (Mycenaean sea voyages, contacts with the Phoenicians, Greek colonization) which produced real transformations in the parts of Italy where local cultures were sufficiently structured to react positively to outside influence. The single most important phenomenon in determining such transformations was the Greek colonization of southern Italy, which began with the settlement of the Euboeans at Pithecusa (Ischia). It was these settlers who purchased the ores which Etruria possessed in such quantities, and they also carried on trade between the eastern Mediterranean (Al Mina) and the West. This development gave rise to the formation of Etruscan, Latin and Campanian aristocracies, all characterized by the same luxurious, Hellenized style of life (consumption of wine and perfumed oil, the introduction of writing). Etruscan civilization is therefore a particular case of a more general evolution, not the result of a migration (the hypothesis of the transfer of a small nucleus of settlers from the East during the Bronze Age being of no relevance to the socio-economic transformation of the Villanovan milieu). The bipartite onomastic formula (forename plus family name), which distinguishes the peoples of Italy throughout the whole of antiquity and is the basis of our present system, also first appeared in this same period. At the end of this developmental phase, the coming of towns produced a decisive qualitative leap within these societies. The best-known case is that of Rome, where at the end of the seventh century BC a public and religious space appeared alongside the huts. Thus, at the end of the sixth century, a very sharp dividing line separated the regions which had an urban organization of one specific form or another (Roman and Etruscan cities being different in nature) and the rest of Italy, which had not yet reached this stage of development. The subsequent history of these populations is one of changes born out of their reactions to contact with the Greek city-states on the one hand and to interaction with the cities that had grown out of the Italian Iron Age cultures on the other.

1. An Etruscan couple represented on an urn in the Cerveteri necropolis, 6th century BC.

The Euboeans at Ischia.

775 BC

Rome founded.

753 BC

Syracuse founded.

734 BC

Middle of 2nd millennium: Middle Bronze Age (Apennine culture).
14th–13th centuries BC: Mycenaean interest in central Italy (they had been in southern Italy and Sicily since the 16th–15th centuries).
13th–12th centuries: Mention in Egyptian chronicles of the Sea Peoples: amongst them the Trs.w (supposed by some to be the Tyrsenoi).
11th–10th centuries BC: Late Bronze Age (Proto-Villanovan).
9th century BC: First Iron Age: development of Villanovan and Latin cultures (Latium), and the culture of deep-shaft graves.
814 BC: Traditional date for the founding of Carthage.
800 BC: Traditional date for the founding of Capua.
c. 775 BC: First Greek (Euboean) settlements at Pithecusa (Ischia).
21 April 753 BC: Traditional date for the founding of Rome by Romulus.
750 BC: Cumae, then Zancle and Rhegium (shortly after the middle of the century) founded by the Chalcidians.

734 BC: Founding of Syracuse, a colony of Corinth.
c. 730 BC: Beginning of the Orientalizing period: development of local aristocracies in Etruria, Latium and Campania; rise of Etruscan civilization.
728 BC: Date traditionally given for the founding of Megara Hyblaea, a colony of Megara.
720 BC: Achaean cities of Sybaris and Croton founded. They in turn produce further urban settlements, the former at Posidonia (Paestum) and Metapontum, the latter at Caulonia.
706 BC: Founding of Tarentum, a Spartan colony.
688 BC: Gela, a Rhodo-Cretan colony, founded.
640/630–580 BC: Transformation of the major population centres of southern Etruria and Rome into cities. Increased Etruscan presence in Campania. The texts mention the existence of a confederation of 12 cities, modelled on the organization of central Etruria.

2. Detail from a fresco in the Tomb of the Jugglers at Tarquinia, representing an Etruscan ritual dance, 6th century BC. .

628 BC: Selinuntum founded by settlers from Megara Hyblaea. The Ionians journey to the extreme west.
616–579 BC: Beginning of the Etruscan monarchy at Rome. The reign of Lucius Tarquinius, the son of the Corinthian Demaratus, exiled at Tarquinia.
580 BC: Agrigentum founded by settlers from Gela.
579–534 BC: Reign of Servus Tullius, known in the Etruscan texts (according to the Emperor Claudius) as Mastarna. Roman tradition attributes to him the census system and the division of the citizens into tribes.
c. 550 BC: Etruscan 'colonization' of the plain of the River Padus, where Villanovan culture had developed since the 9th century BC. Tradition relates that there was a confederation of 12 cities.
546–525 BC: Persians conquer Ionia and Egypt.
c. 535 BC: Victory of the Carthaginians and the Etruscans over the Phocaeans at Alalia (Aleria) which comes under Etruscan domination. The Phocaeans found Elea.

1500–470 BC

−530 to −520: The High Point of Etruscan Civilization

Regions structured around:

- Etruscan and Latin cities (◻ Etruscanized centres)
- Greek colonial centres
- Carthaginian colonies

Etruscan mineral resources

- ▲ Iron
- ● Copper
- ✦ Silver

→ Etruscan maritime trade

LIGURIANS
Genoa

Po
Adria
Spina
Felsina
(Bologna)
Ravenna
Marzabotto

Arno
Faesulae
(Fiesole)
PICENES

Volaterrae
(Volterra)
Siena
Arretium
Perusia

Populonia
ETRURIA
Clusium
Isle
of Elba
Vetulonia
Volsinii (Bolsena)
Vulci
Regisvilla
Tarquinii
SAMNIUM
Gravisca
Veii
Pyrgi
ROME
Caere
(Cerveteri)
LATIUM
Lavinio
Cales
Satrico
(Calvi Vecchia)
Telesia (Telese)
Capua
CAMPANIA
Neapolis (Naples)
Nola
Fratte
Cyme (Cumae)
Pithecusa
Posidonia
(Ischia)
(Paestum)
Pompeii
Pontecagnano
Elea
Pyxus

CORSICA
Alalia (Aleria)

Olbia

SARDINIA

Tharros

Sulci

Carales (Cagliari)
Nora

ADRIATIC SEA

IAPYDES

Tarentum
Metapontum
Heraclea
Sybaris
Croton
OENOTRII
Hipporium
Medma
Caulonia
Zancle
(Messina)
Locri Epizaphyrii
Rhegium

TYRRHENIAN SEA

Panormus
(Palermo)
SICANS
Motya
Etna
SICELS
Naxos
Selinuntum
SICILY
Catana
Agrigentum
Megara Hyblaea
Syracuse
Gela

Cathage

100 km

Circa −900 — Before the Etruscans

Golasecca culture
Este culture
Villanova
Cultures of the Adriatic coast
Iapydian culture
VILLANOVAN CULTURE
Culture of deep shaft graves

−530 to −520 — The Etruscans at the height of their power

Celts
Veneti
LIGURIANS
ETRUSCANS
Osco-Umbrian group
ETRUSCANS
Rome
Latins
ETRUSCANS
Messapians
CARTHAGINIANS
GREEKS
Sicels

Veneti, Celts . . . peoples whose languages are Indo-European

ETRUSCANS, LIGURIANS: Peoples whose languages are not Indo-European

−474 to −300 — Decline of the Etruscans. Rise of Rome

Celts
−390 Arrival of Celts in the Po Valley
ETRURIA
Veii −395
ROME
Cumae −474
Capua −423 Samnites

End of Vth century: Samnites occcupy the Greek and Etruscan cities of Campania

× Etruscan defeats
Progress of Rome c. −300

The Roman region of Etruria

TRANSPADANA
VENETIA
HISTRIA
LIGURIA
AEMILIA
ETRURIA
UMBRIA
PICENUM
SAMNIUM
Rome
LATIUM AND CAMPANIA
APULIA
CALABRIA
PROVINCE OF SARDINIA AND CORSICA
LUCANIA AND BRUTTUM
PROVINCE OF SICILY

The eleven regions established by Augustus
Roman provinces

---

e Cnidians at Lipari.

580 BC

Salamis and Himera.

480 BC

534–509 BC: Reign of Tarquinius Superbus. Temple of Jupiter on the Capitol completed (Vulca of Veii).
524 BC: Cumae defeats the Etruscans with the aid of the tyrant Aristodemus.
510 BC: Destruction of the luxurious city of Sybaris by Croton.
509 BC: End of Tarquinius's tyranny. Beginning of the Roman Republic.
508 BC: First trade treaty between Carthage and Rome.
480 BC: Victory of Syracuse over the Carthaginians at Himera.
474 BC: Syracusan victory over the Etruscans at Cumae. Hieron I offers sacrifices at Olympia.
473 BC: Victory of the Iapydians over Tarentum and Rhegium.

3. Votive offering glorifying maternity. Capua, 4th century BC.

4. Minerva the warrior. Votive statuette characteristic of the Oscan peoples, 2nd half of the 5th century BC.

China under the Ch'in and Han Dynasties

1. Dignitary and servant: Funeral statuettes made of bronze, from the era of the Eastern Han, 2nd century.

2. During the Han era, cavalry made a major contribution to reinforcing the power of the Empire.

AFTER THE COLLAPSE of the eastern Chou, the expansion of the kingdom of Ch'in proceeded more quickly. It led to the unification of the whole of China by 221 BC. This expansion was accompanied by the imposition of much greater uniformity across the country resulting from the application on quite a major scale of a system of administrative repression. The imposition of common standards on to society, the criss-crossing of the country by newly established administrative districts which took the place of the former fiefs and kingdoms, went hand in hand with a massive programme for the resettlement of the population. Over the same period, the first emperor undertook a policy of major public works, which resulted in the construction of a network of roads radiating out from the capital, Ch'ang-an, to the remotest towns in the country, in irrigation canals and defensive walls, as well as gigantic palaces and tombs. The reaction of the nobles and the peasants in the principalities of the east, and of the Ch'u under the second emperor, led to the fall of the dynasty and, after a period of confusion, to the arrival on the throne of the house of Han. They reapplied the administrative principles of their predecessors, but made more concessions to the nobles. Once the disturbances marking the change of dynasty had quietened down, the policy of imposing uniformity tried out earlier under the Ch'in emperor Shih Huang Ti was taken up again with greater determination. The threat from the Hsiung-nu, which already existed under the fighting kingdoms, became more substantial when the different tribes undertook to form a federation under the command of a single chief. A policy of reconciliation through marriage having failed, the Chinese government, under the Han emperor Wu, decided to extend its domination towards the west in order to take control of the trade and communication routes leading to and from Eurasia. As a result, Asia became almost totally Sinicized in progressive stages: the setting up of embassies and trading links and colonies was followed by total cultural integration. While the south remained resistant, the borderlands of the north-west were soon being defended by a number of half-Sinicized tribes who formed a buffer against the enemy and provided China with its troops. This cultural and military expansion soon began, however, to threaten the very state organization which had made it possible in the first place. The development of trade stimulated industry and business, and these were soon beyond the control of the central authorities. Social inequalities increased, bringing about the ruin of the peasant-soldier, who was the backbone of the Han system, provoking a number of serious difficulties in the state treasury. An agrarian crisis broke out at the end of the first century and after the aborted usurpation attempt of Wang Mang, which led to more unrest, the Han re-established order by moving their capital further east. This restoration of the eastern Han was the opportunity, in fact, for the arrival on the scene of a new social class of merchants and landowners with large estates. These estates in turn were the cause of the second agrarian and economic crisis, which dragged the dynasty into a series of messianic popular revolts. In parallel to the breaking down of the economic system, the political system itself became threatened by the ever-growing importance of the eunuchs, who had sole access to the emperor's private apartments, and who were a token of the isolation of the monarch.

The great book-burning incidents.

Discussions held on state monopolies.

213 BC

81 BC

247 BC: The Ch'in seize western Shansi. The coup attempt by Lao Ai, the lover of the mother of the Ch'in king and future first emperor, Shih Huang Ti, fails.
237 BC: Li Su, a legal expert, succeeds Lu Pu-Wei, who was a rich merchant become statesman, and had been implicated in the Lao Ai affair, as adviser to the Ch'in.
221 BC: Ch'in dynasty founded by King Shih Huang Ti, after the annexation of the principalities of Han, Chao, Wei, Ch'u, Yen and Ch'i. Chinese writing, weights and measures, and the axles on carts are all normalized as a result, and the Ch'in system is extended to the whole of China.
215 BC: Various expeditions to the south are undertaken.
213 BC: The burning of books, the banning of the classics, and the resettlement of many people nearer the Great Wall and further to the south are characteristic of the new regime.
211 BC: Intellectuals are persecuted (460 were buried alive), and there are massive deportations towards the Great Wall.
210 BC: First emperor dies.

3. Tomb of the Han emperors in Shansi province.

206 BC: Fall of the dynasty.
202 BC: Han dynasty proclaimed after the elimination of Hsiang Yu by Liu Pang. Fiefs are granted to his more humble comrades in arms.
200 to about 195 BC: First restrictions imposed on the nobility.
188/187 BC: Regency of Empress Lü, who introduces less harsh penal laws.
180 BC: After her death the clan of Empress Lü is exterminated.
158–144 BC: The pressure from the Hsiung-nu becomes more threatening.
141 BC: Emperor Wu Ti of the Han dynasty comes to the throne.
124–121 BC: Major Chinese offensives carried out against the Hsiung-nu.
119 BC: A monopoly on salt and iron production is imposed and a tax on boats and carts levied to replenish the coffers of the state.
110 BC: The kingdoms of Yüeh (Fukien) and of Nanyueh (Canton and northern Vietnam) are annexed.
108 BC: Annexation of Korea.
101 BC: The victory of Fergana follows the

Ch'in Empire from 249 BC to 206 BC

The Unification of China

▨	The Kingdom of Ch'in
	Its expansions in 221
−213	Its conquests after unification (with the date of annexation)
∿∿∿	Unification of the fortifying walls
══	Strategic routes
—	Canals

Han Empire from 202 BC to AD
Closer relations with the outside world

⊏⊐	Empire and Protectorate of the early HAN	═══	Silk route
→	Extent of the second HAN Dynasty (25-220)	—	Other trading routes
◀▮	Border settlements	●	Economic centres
◉	Military outposts	▦	Silk production
		▲	Iron
		°°°	Salt

First Buddhist community established.

Paper invented.

Revolt of the Yellow Turbans.

AD 65 — 105 — 184

conquest of the whole of Central Asia.
87 BC: Death of Emperor Wu Ti, whose place is taken by the regent Huo Kuang, an ally of the family of the Empress.
81 BC: Major discussions take place concerning how opportune it is to continue with the state monopolies.

76 BC: Liao-tung colonized by the barbarians.
AD 9: Throne usurped by Wang Mang, who introduces a number of reforms which lead to rebellion.
25: Han dynasty is restored by a descendant of the Liu house, Kuang Wu Ti.
42–3: General Ma Yuan puts down the rebellion of the Trung sisters.
91: The Han invade Mongolia.
c. 94: Campaign of repression in Central Asia under the leadership of General Pan Ch'ao.
125–150: Chinese control is re-established over Central Asia.
141: The power of the Ch'iang (who were proto-Tibetans) becomes threatening for the Han.
175: The eunuchs hold the real power.
184: The great popular uprising of the Yellow Turbans takes place. So called because of the colour of their turbans, which acted as a sign of allegiance, these were rebels who numbered 300,000 through Shansi, Shensi and Hupeh provinces.

192: The Revolt of the Yellow Turbans put down by Ts'ao Ts'ao, who became the new strong man of the regime after the assassination of Tung Cho, who had threatened to take over the throne for himself. The Celestial Masters, a Taoist sect, set up a community organization in Szechwan.
220: Fall of the Han dynasty and partition of the Empire into three parts.

6. Tiger and serpent attacking a wild boar: a bronze ornamental plaque from the era of the western Han.

4. Guardian of the tomb of Emperor Shih Huang Ti.

5. Model of a tower in varnished terracotta. From the era of the eastern Han, 2nd century.

The Indian Empire: From the Maurya to the Gupta

250 BC

Alexandria of Arachosia
GANDHARA
Indus
TIBET
Taxila
ARACHOSIA
Kalsi
Brahmapatra
Indraprastha
Sravasti
Kapilavastu
Lalita Patan (Katmandu)
Ganges
Mathura
MAGADHA
Campa
Seleucos I concedes the Sind to Candragupta (303)
Prayaga Kasi
Pataliputra
SIND
Sambodhi (Bodh-Gaya)
SUBASTRA
Narmada
Asoka crushes the Kalinga (−261)
Girnar
Tamralipti
PULINDA
KALINGA
PITINIKA
Godavari
ARABIAN SEA
ANDHRA
BAY OF BENGAL

Kingdom at the foundation of the Maurya dynasty (321 BC)

Probable extent of Asoka's empire around 250 BC

⊙ Capital

▼ Inscriptions (edicts)

around 150 AD

BACTRIA
KHOTAN
GANDHARA
KASHMIR
KAPISA
PUNJAB
Sui Vihar
Indraprastha
MARU
Mathura
SIND
Sarnath
AVANTI
Kasi
KACHHA
Ujjayini
Sanci
SURASTRA
Junagadh
Bharukacha
Ajanta caves
Surparaka
Kalinga Kingdom
Pratisthana (Paithan)
ANDRA
KERALA
COLA
PANDYA

500 km

Kushan empire (Scythians)

Western satraps

Andhra kingdom

INDIAN ANTIQUITY can be divided into two periods: before and after the expeditions of Alexander – the first really datable event in the history of India. For the period preceding that, the historian has to content himself with hypotheses and conjecture based on the interpretation of myths and legends. After this, there is much documentary evidence in the form of inscriptions, monuments, foreign reports (by Greeks and Chinese): India truly becomes part of history and fits into general chronology. Some uncertainty persists, however, in some cases over several centuries, as to the most notable figures in Indian civilization. There was Panini, the founder of grammar, Patanjali, creator of the theory of yoga, Kautilya, author of a treatise on the art of government, and even the emperor Kaniska (it is uncertain whether his reign began in 58 BC or in AD 78 or even AD 144), without mentioning texts like the two epics, Mahabharata and Ramayana or the Laws of Manu. The outlines of Indian historical development during these two millennia can, however, be described.

The Arya clans were dominant for about ten centuries over the country between the Persian Gulf and the Bay of Bengal, the Himalayas and the Vindhya mountains (the Aryavarta), and the Deccan north of the Godavari: the peoples of these regions adopting their language, religion and social system. Their language was Sanskrit, of Indo-European origin. The Indian-style languages developed from Sanskrit in the various regions of the Arya territory. The first inscriptions were written in these Indian-style idioms. Then Sanskrit, which had been kept as a religious language, became secularized and used as the vehicle for profane works of literature. The dividing line between the north and the south is in the language. In the north, only Sanskrit or languages drawn from it were used. The south, although it had adopted Sanskrit at the beginning of our period as a literary and religious language, kept alive the Dravidian languages, notably Tamil, which was used in the first centuries AD in some outstanding poetry.

In religion, beliefs and rites set out in the Veda (a form of polytheism which gave increasing precedence to sacrificial ceremonies) were the order of the day. But as it came into contact with native

Beginnings of the Iron Age. Irrigated rice farming in the Kaveri delta.

c. 1000 BC

Appearance of money in the Magadha.

c. 500 BC

1. Eastern portico of the Great Stupa, a Buddhist monument, at Sanci in Madhya Pradesh. 2nd century AD.

c. 1400 BC: The Arya moved into the Punjab. During the following centuries they would advance towards the east and the south; by 600 BC they would have conquered the entire Ganges Valley.

c. 650 BC: 'Second urbanization'; towns in the Magadha.

518 BC: Gandhara and Sind were satraps of the Persian Empire.

483 BC: Date normally given for the death of the Buddha.

467 BC: Presumed date of the death of the Jina.

327–325 BC: Alexander's expedition to India. Having seized Taxila, which was at that time a major centre of Brahman culture, Alexander vanquished the Indian armies of King Puru (Poros in Greek), but because his troops refused to go further he retreated towards the mouth of the Indus.

322 BC: In the Magadha, Candragupta the Maurya founded a state whose control extended in the end throughout northern India.

272–232 BC: Ashoka. Completely under the spell of Buddhism, this grandson of Candragupta built up an empire which covered the whole of the sub-continent apart from the south of the peninsula. Throughout the whole of the Empire, inscriptions/engravings on pillars and rocks proclaim (in various Indian idioms) the political and religious principles of Ashoka. After his death, the Empire broke up.

160–140 BC: The Indo-Greek king Milinda (Menander) ruled over the Punjab.

1st century BC: Scythians and Parthians destroyed the Indo-Greek kingdoms, and replaced them in the northwest of India with dynasties which quickly became Indianized.

1st century AD: The Kushans swept in. They came from Central Asia and seized Gandhara and the Punjab and conquered the Ganges Valley as far as Pataliputra. In the northern Deccan, around Pratisthana (Paithan), the Andhra (Satavahana dynasty) had supremacy. In the extreme south a powerful Cola kingdom was established. Indian kingdoms were created in Indochina and Malaysia.

around 400: Gupta

White Huns or Hepthalites
(held back until the end of Vth century)

TIBET

Purusapura
(Peshawar)
Sassanids

KASHMIR

MADRAKA

YAUDHEYA

Indraprastha

NEPAL

ARJUNAYANA   Kanyakubja

KAMARUPA

Vaisali

MARV   MAGADHA   1Patalipurra

Mandasor   Eran Prayaga   Campa

⊙2

SURASTRA   Ujjayini   Sanci

SAMATATA

Valabhi   Narmada

✳ Ajanta

VAKATAKA   KALINGA

SEA OF   ✦Katura

OMAN   BAY OF   BENGAL

PALLAVA

Kanci

COLA

CERA

PANDYMA

SINHALA

Unsuccessful
expeditions of
Samudragupta (335-375)

Extent of empire
at the death of
Candragupta II (414)
⊙1 ⊙2
Successive capitals

640: Harsa

KAPISA   KASHMIR

GURJARA   •Thanesar   NEPAL

SIND   Kanyakubja •Pataliputra   PUNDRA
              •(Patna)   VARDHANA
         Prayaga
VALABHI   Ujjayini   Kasi   KARNA
         Sanci   (Benares)   SUVARNA
                        SAMATATA
              Tamralipti

Ellora ✳Ajanta
      Calukya   KONGODA
      Kingdom   KALINGA

Badami •
  • Vatapi   PALLAVA

      • Kanci

CERA   COLA

PANDYA

SINHALA

500 km

Empire of Harsa
around 640

peoples, Vedism took up the cult of images, incorporated other gods, and balanced the ritual with a warm personal relationship between the devout and the divinity. This is Hinduism as we know it today. In the sixth century BC, two new religions came into being in the middle Ganges kingdoms, which advocated non-violence, detachment, and the formation of monastic communities: Jainism, founded by the Jina Mahavira, would remain exclusively Indian, and for the minority (but still alive today); Buddhism, however, would spread throughout the whole of Asia.

As regards society, because of what the Veda taught, the Arya were split into four 'classes' (varna): the Brahmans, religious specialists; the Ksatriya, warriors and political leaders; the Vaisya, wealth producers (farmers, craftsmen, merchants); and the Sudra, who served the first three varna. Outside the country, the tribal people were considered to be barbarians. These theoretical groups formed the framework within which were arranged hierarchically the real groups making up the whole of society: the castes (jati).

When they went into India, the Arya, who were shepherds and farmers, destroyed the towns. But in the sixth century BC a new urban civilization grew up in the Magadha. Later on, new towns appeared which were centres of an economic and intellectual lifestyle much admired by the Chinese pilgrims. They were linked by caravan trails: one linked Tamralipti to Taxila, another went from Prayaga to Ujjayini and Pratisthana (Paithan) and towards the ports of Surastra.

After the death of Candragupta the Maurya, the country was alternately divided into huge imperial blocks with changing frontiers, and small kingdoms. The most famous of the emperors, the most perfect ruler in the whole of India's history, was Ashoka, who, having taken over political power, declared his avowed hatred of war and his desire to bring about the Buddhist ideal of universal goodwill. Empires consisting of the whole continent were the work of the northern sovereigns, Indians or Central Asian invaders. The southern dynasties looked more towards foreign lands and trading links with Eastern Asia and the Roman world: from antiquity, the export of spices, precious stones and cloth brought gold from Europe to India.

Embassy of a Pandya king to the Emperor of Rome.   **Aryabhata's mathematical treatise: decimal numbering, zero, value of pi.**

AD 20   **c. 500**

c. 50: The Parthian king Gondophares of Taxila welcomed and then martyred Thomas the Apostle.

78?/144?: Presumed and contested dates given for the beginning of the reign of Kaniska, the most prestigious Kushan sovereign.

270–500: The Gupta Empire. From their initial territory, the Magadha, the Gupta princes extended their direct sovereignty or their protectorate over India to the north of Narmada and over part of the Deccan.

375–414: Reign of Candragupta II, who made Ujjayini his capital. Golden age of Indian civilization: the work of the poet Kalidasa symbolized this.

400–500: First Sanskrit inscriptions from Cambodia, Java, Borneo.

c. 450: The Hepthalite Huns (Hunas) moved into Bactria, then settled in the Indus basin. Skandagupta held them back. But the Gupta Empire fell apart.

c. 550: The Calukya of Badami became the major power in the northwest of the Deccan.

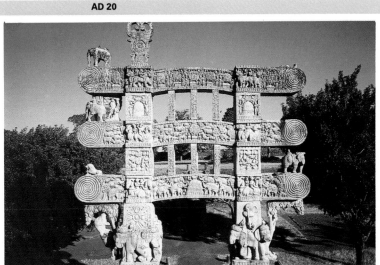

2. Ajanta Caves, Rupestrian (?) shrine in the Deccan. 3rd–6th centuries AD.

3. One of the 21 celestial, heavenly nymphs of the site of Sigirya. AD 485, Sri Lanka.

End of the 6th century: Supremacy of the Pallava of Kanci over the south-east of the peninsula, which would last until the 9th century. They attempted to conquer Ceylon and helped Indian kingdoms in Southeast Asia to develop.

606–47: Reign of Harsa. The capital of his empire was Kanyakubja (Kanauj): last truly outstanding period of the Hindu-Sanskrit culture in northern India.

630–44: Voyage of the Chinese pilgrim Hsuang-tang.

Rome: City of Conquest

ROME WAS INITIALLY similar in nature to the other Mediterranean cities. It formed itself into a state by assimilating Italy and conquered an empire by striving to extend its boundaries to the limits of the known world. The political centre of that empire grew into what, for the ancients, was the greatest city ever known. Greek observers like Polybius praised the excellence of its constitution and the cohesiveness of its social body: all its citizens served in the legions, paid taxes, elected the magistrates, and decided the laws, as well as questions of peace and war. Politics was everyone's affair; it was the *res publica*. In reality, it is possible to discern a political class of privileged individuals set apart from the mass of the citizenry, a citizenry from which women, foreigners and slaves were, in any case, excluded. The censors kept watch over the fortune and honour of each citizen and

1. The Appian Way linking Rome and Brundisium.

regulated his role in political life – along with his military and fiscal contribution. The richest citizens and those who were fortunate enough to be high born formed an oligarchy which shared out among itself the offices of magistrate, military commander and priest. The struggles between patricians and plebeians in the early years of the republic had led to an expansion of this 'nobility'. Later, however, it was only very rarely that this class opened itself up to 'new men' who had revealed outstanding political – or particularly military – talents.

The Roman city-state was first and foremost a community of warriors. The existence of military service, which meant that citizens could be mobilized between the ages of seventeen and sixty, distinguished it from Carthage and from the Hellenistic kingdoms which only possessed mercenaries. The defeated powers also had to provide soldiers for Rome's further conquests.

Control over the city-state's expansionist inclinations, which were bound up initially with its desire to ensure its own security, was in the hands of the Senate – a kind of permanent council consisting of former magistrates – which received ambassadors and ruled on the allocation of the budget.

Rome's early conquests were confined to Italy. Through the elaboration of a variety of diplomatic contacts with the peninsula's ethnically and culturally heterogeneous communities, and in organizing the Italian geographical area by building roads and founding colonies, Rome laid the basis of a unification which Hannibal's political strategy did little to damage. Presenting himself as the liberator of Italy, Hannibal was only able to win support among a section of the Campanians. The accession of more than a million Italians to Roman citizenship after the Social War was to revolutionize the structures of the city once and for all.

When Rome attacked Carthage, which controlled the western Mediterranean, it was entering upon a conflict with incalculable consequences. It was its first military intervention as a sea-power and its first outside Italy. The Second Punic War extended the field of hostilities to Spain, Italy, Sicily and Africa, as well as to the Greek world. The Third Punic War showed that Rome was henceforth capable of totally destroying those who resisted her. Rome conquered Carthage and also established her power over all the Hellenistic kingdoms. The profits from these conquests were so substantial that, after 167 BC, Romans no longer paid any direct taxes. But social tensions were growing. Rome had to modify its conditions for recruiting soldiers under Marius, and the way in which great commands were allocated in the first century BC. In spite of attempts at reform, such as those of the Gracchi, the economic and social system began to come under strain and the cohesiveness of the political system diminished. The clash of ambitions between the military leaders who had, in their turn, dominated parts of the East (Sulla, Pompey) or the West (Caesar) led to the Empire.

Brennus at Rome: *'Vae victis!'* (Woe to the vanquished!)	Rome mistress of southern Italy.	Birth of Hannibal.	Birth of Polybius.	Death of Cato the El●
390 BC	**272 BC**	**247 BC**	**c. 200 BC**	**149**

406 BC: Siege of Veii.
390 BC: Capture of Rome by the Gauls. A wall is built around Rome (the 'Wall of Servius Tullius').
367 BC: Consulship opened up to plebeians.
343–341 BC: First Samnite War.
338 BC: Rome dissolves the Latin League. Founding of the first Roman colony.
334–326 BC: Rome controls Campania.
326–304 BC: Second Samnite War.
312–308 BC: Appius Claudius becomes censor. Building of the Via Appia and the first aqueduct.
300 BC: The pontificate (civic priesthood) is opened to plebeians.
295 BC: Gauls, Etruscans and Samnites defeated at Sentinum.
287 BC: The votes of the plebeian assemblies given force of law.
279–275 BC: Expeditionary corps of Pyrrhus, King of Epirus, in Italy 'to defend the independence of the Greek cities'.
272 BC: Capture of Tarentum.
268 BC: Colonies of Ariminum (Rimini) and Beneventum.
265 BC: Fall of Volsinii and the subjugation of

the Etruscans.
264 BC: First Punic War. First funerary games in Rome with gladiator fights.
260 BC: Naval victory at Mylae.
256–255 BC: Failure of Roman campaign in Africa.
254 BC: Birth of the comic author Plautus.
242 BC: Creation of the Peregrine Praetor to judge legal disputes between Romans and foreigners.
241 BC: Rome is victorious over Carthage and occupies Sicily.
240–237 BC: The Romans in Corsica and Sardinia; revolt of mercenaries at Carthage.
239 BC: Birth of the poet Ennius.
222 BC: Occupation of Cisalpine Gaul.
220 BC: Flaminius is censor; the Via Flaminia and Circus Maximus are built at Rome.
219 BC: Capture of Saguntum. Beginning of the Second Punic War.
218 BC: Hannibal crosses the Alps.
216 BC: Hannibal victorious at Cannae. Defection of Capua.
215 BC: Creation of the companies of publicans to provide supplies for armies.
212 BC: Archimedes dies at Syracuse.

211 BC: Hannibal at the gates of Rome.
210 BC: Scipio in Spain.
204 BC: Scipio in Africa.
203 BC: Hannibal returns to Africa.
202 BC: End of the Second Punic War.
200–197 BC: Macedonian War against Philip V, who had supported Carthage.
197–181 BC: Cisalpine Gaul is annexed and colonized.
196 BC: The 'freedom of the Greeks' is proclaimed by Flaminius at Corinth.
192–188 BC: War against Antiochus III, King of Syria.
184 BC: Cato is censor. Construction of the first basilica at Rome.
168 BC: Polybius held hostage in Rome.
167 BC: Delos becomes a free port.
154–133 BC: Spanish Wars (Scipio Emilio at Numantia).
149 BC: First permanent tribunal to rule on the exactions of provincial governors.
149–146 BC: Third Punic War.
148 BC: Macedonia becomes a Roman province.
146 BC: Rome destroys Carthage and Corinth.

136–132 BC: First revolt of slaves in Sicily.
133 BC: Titus Gracchus becomes people's tribune.
129 BC: Creation of the province of Asia.
125 BC: Romans enter Transalpine Gaul.
118 BC: Colony of Narbo founded.
112–105 BC: War against Jugurtha.
107 BC: Marius's military reforms.
104–101 BC: Marius fights against the Cimbri and the Teutoni in Gaul.
91–88 BC: Social War: the defeated Italians receive Roman citizenship.
88 BC: Mithridates, King of Pont, invades the province of Asia and massacres the Italians at Delos. Sulla is given charge of the Roman troops.
87–83 BC: Marius and his associates in powe●
83–72 BC: Rising in Spain. Sertorius defeated.
82 BC: Sulla occupies Rome. 'Proscriptions'.
74 BC: Licinius Lucullus at war with Mithridates.
73–71 BC: Revolt of slaves in Italy (led by Spartacus).
70 BC: Prosecution of Verres, Governor of Sicily.

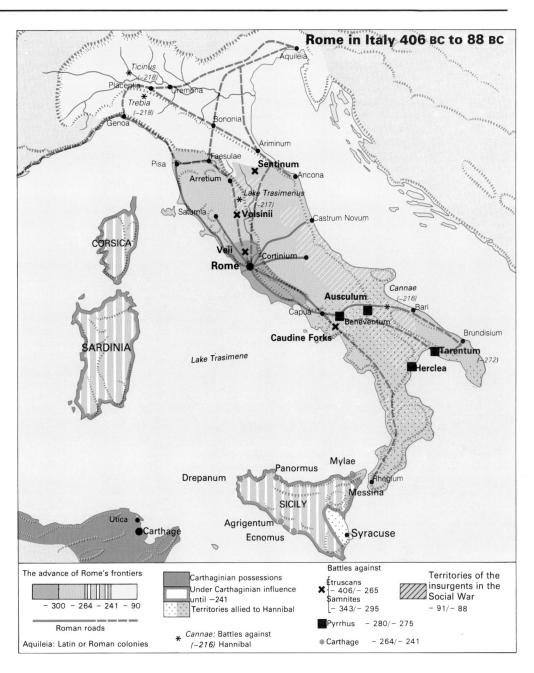

Rome in Italy 406 BC to 88 BC

Aquileia

Ticinus
(–218)
Placentia · Cremona
Trebia · Bononia
(–218)
Genoa
Ariminum
Pisa · Faesulae
Arretium **Sentinum** Ancona
Lake Trasimenus
Saturnia (–217)
✕**Volsinii**
Veji ✕ Castrum Novum
Rome Cortinium
Cannae
Ausculum (–216)
Capua · Bari
Beneventum
Caudine Forks Brundisium
Tarentum
Herclea (–272)

CORSICA

SARDINIA

Lake Trasimene

Panormus · Mylae
Drepanum · Rhegium
Messina
SICILY
Utica
Carthage Agrigentum Syracuse
Ecnomus

The advance of Rome's frontiers		Carthaginian possessions	Battles against	Territories of the insurgents in the Social War
– 300 – 264 – 241 – 90		Under Carthaginian influence until –241	✕ Etruscans – 406/– 265 Samnites – 343/– 295	– 91/– 88
Roman roads		Territories allied to Hannibal	■ Pyrrhus – 280/– 275	
Aquileia: Latin or Roman colonies		* *Cannae:* Battles against (–216) Hannibal	● Carthage – 264/– 241	

2. Samnite warrior, 3rd century BC.

Death of Spartacus.	Caesar crosses the Rubicon.
71 BC	**49 BC**

66 BC: Pompey's army fights Mithridates.
63 BC: Cicero consul. Catiline conspiracy.
59 BC: Caesar is consul.
58–52 BC: Caesar conquers Gaul.
53 BC: Licinius Crassus defeated by the Parthians.
52 BC: Pompey is made sole consul.
49 BC: Caesar marches on Rome.
48 BC: Pompey defeated at Pharsalus. Caesar in Egypt.
46–45 BC: The Pompeian forces defeated in Africa (Thapsus) and Spain (Munda).
46–44 BC: Caesar's dictatorship.
44 BC: Caesar assassinated on 15 March.
43 BC: The Triumvirate: Mark Antony, Lepidus, Octavian. Proscriptions.
42 BC: Victory over Brutus and Cassius at Philippi.
36 BC: Lepidus eliminated from Triumvirate.
31 BC: Antony defeated at Actium. Conquest of Egypt.

Rome in the world 241 BC to 27 BC

GALLIA
Alesia
COMATA
– 51
TRANSALPINE CISALPINE
GAUL GAUL ILLYRICUM
– 125 – 222
Narbo BITHYNIA – 74
NEARER MACEDONIA and PONT
Numantia ✕ SPAIN – 148 ✕Pydna – 65
– 197 Cynocephales Pergamum Carrhae
FURTHER Saguntum ✕ ASIA PHRYGIA ✕
SPAIN ROME Actium – 129 – 103 CILICIA
– 197 Carthago Nova – 241 Magnesia – 101 Antiochia
Carthage ACHAEA Corinth SYRIA
AFRICA – 146 Sparta – 64
– 146
AFRICA Jerusalem
NOVA – 63
– 46
Alexandria
CYRENE
– 74 EGYPT
– 31

Roman Possessions
– 241 – 197 – 133 – 101 – 27
✕ Battles

Towards an Integrated Roman World

AUGUSTUS, *Imperator Caesar Augustus*, was, first and foremost, 'the conqueror'. A commander-in-chief was hailed with the title *Imperator* after a victory. It was during Augustus's reign that the ideology of a victorious emperor unifying the world according to an order ordained by the gods was first elaborated. The military victories of Augustus and his successors – Trajan in particular – were always widely celebrated with triumphal arches and commemorative monuments and paved the way for certain military leaders to become emperors (Vespasian, Septimius Severus).

Augustus was also the founder of a political regime to which the name of empire was given. He transformed the republic into a monarchy. Caesar had attempted to achieve this by way of dictatorship. Paradoxically, his adopted son Octavian, presented as the providential saviour of republican institutions, was the man who established an hereditary monarchy in Rome. This was sustained by the Italian municipal oligarchies, who hoped to share the prerogatives of the traditional Roman nobility. He could not have acted without the existence of a very broad consensus. The Senate, which saw its role diminished, the population of Rome that was protected from crises by imperial benevolence and the provincial populations who organized to celebrate his cult, all wished for peace after the civil wars. Sure in the knowledge of this support, Octavian even assented to abandoning his exceptional powers; as a mark of gratitude the Senate accorded him the title of Augustus, which was subsequently borne by all his successors.

Augustus became the sole ruler of an immense empire in which the world of cities encountered that of tribes. That empire was run by an administrative service which would later assume specialized functions and be protected by a standing army. Within it, a regular fiscal system and a universally recognized legal system were established. It is this image of empire which is still ours today.

The peace Rome enjoyed under Augustus, which guaranteed it that prosperity celebrated by poets and artists, was an armed one. Maintaining peace required a solid military infrastructure of some 300,000 men, a road network that permitted them to intervene rapidly, and a frontier (*limes*) that was reinforced to a great depth by an agricultural colonization that had necessitated the organizing of large-scale population movements (into Germany and the Agri Decumates). The destabilization of this latter area only began in the reign of Marcus Aurelius. The *pax romana* was also largely guaranteed by a willingness to allow the former conquered peoples to share in the profits of empire. From as early as Augustus's time, a subtle diffusion of citizenship made certain privileged individuals the equals of Romans. Under Claudius, Gauls participated in the Roman Senate. Under the Antonine emperors, the senators of Rome were drawn from Spain, Gaul, Greece and the East, as well as from Italy. The knights (*equites*) who provided the Empire's civil service were most commonly recruited among notables from the various provinces. The most humble of them could also become Roman citizens by joining the army. Finally, in 212, Caracalla accorded citizenship to all the free inhabitants of the Empire. Caracalla himself provides a perfect illustration of this policy of integration, being the son of the first emperor of non-Roman origin, Septimius Severus.

This was the final stage in an earlier policy of assimilation: in the West, the progression of the Latin language, adaptation to the spatial and institutional framework of the city and to Roman models of behaviour, made for the development of a Romanization process, the traces of which can still be seen today.

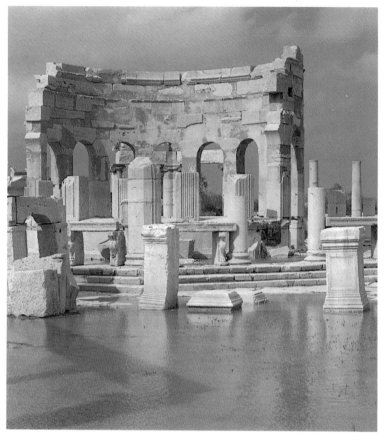

1. Forum of Leptis Magna, 3rd century.

Virgil begins the *Aeneid*.		**Death of Jesus.**	**Gauls in the Senate.**	**Destruction of Pompeii and Herculaneum.**
29 BC		**AD 30**	**48**	**79**

27 BC: Octavian receives the title of Augustus. Supervision of provinces shared between the Senate and the emperors. Dedication of the Odeon of Agrippa.
26–25 BC: Pacification in Spain and Gaul. Beginning of the imperial cult in Spain.
19 BC: Death of Virgil.
18 BC: Augustus receives the tribunician power.
13 BC: Altar of Augustan Peace built.
12 BC: Augustus becomes *pontifex maximus*. Beginning of the imperial cult in Gaul. Campaigns of Tiberius and Drusus (who goes as far as the Elbe) in Germania.
9 BC: The disaster which befalls the legions of Varius puts an end to the brief campaigns of conquest in Germania.
8 BC: Deaths of Horace and Maecenas.
AD 13: Testament of Augustus.
14: Death of Augustus. Germanicus's campaign on the Rhine.
14–24: African insurrections.
15–31: Sejanus becomes prefect of the Praetorian Guard.
17: Death of the historian Livy.
42: Construction of the port of Ostia.

43: Beginning of the conquest of Britain.
48: Claudius's speech in favour of the admission of Gauls into the Senate.
50: Adoption of Nero by Claudius.
55–65: Seneca, philosophical works.
58–63: Armenian campaigns.
64: Rome burns. Persecution of Christians. Nero's Golden House.
66–70: Revolt in Gaul (Vindex) and in Judaea. Nero's suicide. End of the Julio-Claudian dynasty. Civil wars: Galba, Otho, Vitellius.
69–96: Flavian dynasty.
70: Vespasian, proclaimed emperor in 69, becomes ruler of the Empire. Capture of Jerusalem by his son Titus.
71: Vespasian's Forum and Temple of Peace.
74: Spain receives Latin rights.
77–84: Agricola pacifies Britain.
79: Death of Pliny the Elder.
80: Dedication of the Coliseum. Arch of Titus built.
85–6: Wars against the Dacians.
96: Assassination of Domitian. Nerva adopts Trajan.
97–8: Forum of Nerva. Tacitus writes the *Life of Agricola* and the *Germania*.

2. Two legionnaires of the Roman army in Germany.

98: Trajan reinforces the *limes* of the Rhine.
101: First war against the Dacians.
105: Arabia becomes a Roman province.
108: Creation of the *alimentia*, an institution giving aid to young Italians.
111–13: Correspondence between Pliny, the governor of Bithynia, and Trajan.
111–14: Trajan's forum, the work of Apollodorus of Damascus.
114: War against the Parthians: annexation of Armenia.
116: Trajan conquers Assyria and Mesopotamia and reaches the Persian Gulf.
c. 116: Tacitus writes *The Annals*.
117: Hadrian withdraws from the eastern lands conquered by Trajan.
120: Suetonius writes the *Lives of the Caesars*. Death of Plutarch, author of the *Parallel Lives*.
122–7: Building of Hadrian's Wall in Britain.
125–35: The Villa Hadriana at Tivoli.
132–5: Second Jewish War.
135: Hadrian in Judaea. Capture of Jerusalem.
142: Antonine Wall in Scotland.

1st century BC–3rd century AD

The Roman Empire under Septimius Severus (193-211)

— Hadrian's Wall

• Eburacum
• Deva
BRITANNIA
• Isca Silurum

• Vetera
GERMANIA
Inf. Bonna
Moguntiacum
BELGICA Aregentoratum
Lutetia Castra Regina
(Paris) Vindobona
Carnuntum
LUGDUNENSIS Brigetio
RHAETIA Lauriacum Aquincum
AQUITANIA Germina **NORICUM** **PANNONIA** **Potaissa**
Sup. **Sup.** **Apulum**
Lugdunum Aquliea **DACIA**
Burdigala (Lyon) **NARBONENSIS** oMilan Sarmizegetusa
(Bordeaux) 2 Ravenna Singidunum • Durostoeum
• Gemina 3 Genoa **DALMATIA** Vininacium • Novae
Narbo **MOESIA** **MOESIA Inf.**
Rome **Sup.**
TARRACONENSIS **BITHYNIA**
LUSITANIA Tarraco Mosene **THRACIA** **AND** **ARMENIA**
Brundisium **PONTUS** **CAPPADOCIA**
Tarentum **MACEDONIA** • Satala
GALATIA
BAETICA **EPIRUS** • Samosata
Cathago Nova **ASIA** Pergamum Resaina
Corinth Athens Ephesus • Singara
ACHAEA **LYCIA** **CILICIA** Cyrrhus
MAURETANIA Syracuse **AND** Antioch
MAURETANIA **CAESARIENSIS** **PAMPHILIA** **COELE-SYRIA**
TINGITANA **NUMIDIA** Carthage **SYRIA–PHOENICIA** Phoenici
• Lambaesis • Ferrata
Caparcotna
Aelia Capitolina
ARABIA **MESOPOTAMIA**
Cyrene Alexandria
• Leptis Magna
AFRICA **CYRENE** **AEGYPTUS**

1 Alpes Graiae
2 Alpes Cottiae
3 Alpes Maritimae

▓ Rome	▨ Senatorial provinces which became imperial provinces
▒ Senatorial provinces	▨ Senatorial provinces which achieved autonomy under imperial rule

□ Imperial provinces

⬚ Protected kingdoms which became imperial provinces

⬚ Protected kingdoms

Military deployment under Septimius Severus
• Legionary camps (Latin name)
━ Fortified 'lines'
⛵ War fleet

Death of Tacitus.

All communities of the Empire enfranchised.

c. 120

212

143: Aelius Aristides writes his panegyric of Rome.
161–6: War against the Parthians.
167: Great plague in Rome.
169: Death of Lucius Verus, who had been made co-emperor by Marcus Aurelius.
172–5: Marcus Aurelius writes his *Meditations*.
172–80: Campaigns on the Rhine and the Danube.
184–5: Troubles in Britain. The Antonine Wall abandoned.
192: Assassination of Commodus. Political crisis. End of the Antonine dynasty.
193: Septimius Severus proclaimed emperor.
211: Death of Septimius Severus in Britain. He is succeeded by his sons, Caracalla and Geta.
212: Assassination of Geta. Edict of Caracalla granting citizenship to all the inhabitants of the Empire.
216: Baths of Caracalla built.
218–22: Development of sun worship (of Eastern origin) in Rome under Elagabalus.
226: The Sassanian dynasty in Persia.

3. Slaves serving at a banquet, Carthage, 3rd century.

234: The Alamanni invade Germania.
235: Assassination of Severus Alexander. End of the dynasty of the Severi.

4. The Emperor Caracalla.

Roman Gaul

THE GAULS burst on to the scene of Roman history in the fourth century BC: they swept through Italy and settled in the plain of the River Po, the future province of Gallia Cisalpina. Rome first took an interest in the Hellenized Gallia Transalpina in the third century BC, in response to an appeal from Marseille, which was concerned at the Carthaginian advance in Spain. Hannibal's campaign across the Alps had no lasting effects, and the *Provincia* of Transalpina was founded as early as the second century. The invasion of the Germanic tribes, the Cimbri and the Teutoni, and their repulsion by Gaius Marius, soon placed Rome in the role of protector of the Gauls, and the halt that Julius Caesar put to the migration of the Helvetii stabilized the frontiers of the cities. But Caesar needed a victory. His attempt to conquer the Gauls and Britons sparked off a general revolt. The leader of that revolt, Vercingetorix (who struck his own coinage

like a Hellenistic king), won great victories. However, Caesar, though he came near to disaster, emerged victorious at Alesia; the cities submitted to his rule and Marseille was taken after a long siege. On the death of Caesar in 44 BC, Rome controlled the whole territory of Gaul.

Augustus reorganized the conquered areas. Old *Provincia*, now known as *Provincia Narbonensis*, remained a senatorial province and received Latin rights: all the other Gallic cities were grouped into the three imperial provinces of Aquitania, Lugdunensis and Belgica. Colonies were founded, native population centres displaced and towns built on the Roman model, local aristocracies liberally receiving the benefit of Roman law. The death of Augustus reawakened desires for independence under his successor Tiberius, but Claudius, who knew Gaul well, opened the Roman Senate up to its élites and associated these provincials very closely with the destinies of the Empire. This decision set a precedent that was followed in the case of other provinces.

From this point on Gaul became an essential part of the Roman world. It provided soldiers, administrators and governors and each year, on the Altar of the Three Gauls at Lyon, it renewed its allegiance to the Empire. The wide reputation enjoyed by its centres of ceramic production (La Graufesenque and then Lezoux) attests to its prosperity, as do the thousands of inscriptions, mosaics, sculptures, bronzes, terracotta pieces and the rich hoards of coins and gold artifacts that have been discovered, not to mention its great architectural achievements, such as the Maison Carrée, the amphitheatre at Nîmes, the theatre at Orange, the Pont du Gard, the temples of Glanum, Vienne and Autun, and the Cluny thermal baths in Paris. Arles was a great port and received produce from the East. Jews were among those who landed there, and it became a centre of Christianity. These provinces retained their specific local features, as can be seen in such material symbols as the use of the *tonneau* and the wearing of breeches. Their gods and the forms of worship accorded to them retained local characteristics. During political crises, the Gauls willingly organized themselves as an autonomous empire, as can be seen in the troubled years of the third century AD when the Gallic emperors took charge of the Roman Empire's western defences.

Reorganized into two dioceses, they contributed to the fourth century Renaissance: Trèves (Trier) became the imperial capital and its Porta Nigra and Basilica are magnificent relics of that period. The villas of Aquitania and Mid-Gaul are proof of the continued prosperity of the country areas, in spite of the endemic agitation of the Bagaudae (bands of Gallic peasants in rebellion against Roman rule); the towns, which were fortified, in some cases retained their splendour. The aristocracy, converted to Christianity, provided the Empire with some personalities of the first rank. When the military defences fell, the Germanic peoples who had settled in Gaul were not long in becoming Romanized in their turn.

1. Roman Games in Gaul. Mosaic of chariot racing, Lyon.

Sack of Rome by the Gauls.	Caesar in Gaul.	Claudius's speech on the extension of the *jus honorum* to the Gauls.
390 BC	**59–49 BC**	**AD 48**

4th century BC: Gauls in northern Italy.
4th–3rd century BC: La Tène civilization in Gaul.
231 BC: Marseille seeks Roman diplomatic intervention in Spain.
218 BC: Hannibal passes through southern Gaul and crosses the Alps to attack the Romans in Italy.
122–121 BC: Domitius Ahenobarbus in Gallia Transalpina; foundation of Aix; defeat of the Allobroges, then of Bituitus, king of the Arverni; Rhône valley brought under Roman rule as Provincia.
118 BC: Foundation of the Roman colony of Narbo Martius (Narbonne).
109–103 BC: Invasion of the Cimbri and the Teutoni.
102–101 BC: Marius defeats the Teutoni at Aix, then the Cimbri at Vercelli.
1st century BC: La Tène III civilization.
87?–52? BC: Catullus, a Cisalpine poet of Verona.
70–19 BC: Virgil, a Cisalpine from Mantua.
?–26 BC: Cornelius Gallus, Gallic elegiac poet from Fréjus.

61 BC: The Aedui appeal to Rome against the Germanii.
59–17 BC: Livy, a Cisalpine from Padua.
59–58 BC: Migration of the Helvetii, halted by Caesar at Bibracte.
57–56 BC: Caesar in Belgium; Crassus in western Gaul; Caesar among the Veneti.
55–54: Caesar in Brittany.
53 BC: Vercingetorix leads revolt of the towns of Gallia Comata; Gallia Transalpina supports Caesar.
52 BC: Roman defeat at Gergovia; siege and capture of Alésia. Vercingetorix taken prisoner.
51–50 BC: Towns of Gaul surrender.
49 BC: Marseille, the last independent Greek city in the Mediterranean, is besieged and captured by Caesar.
46–44 BC: Colony of Arles created.
43 BC: Colonies of Lyon and Augst in Switzerland founded.
27 BC: Augustus at Narbo; Transalpine Gaul divided into four provinces.
6 BC: Definitive subjugation of the Alpine peoples; monumental trophy of La Turbie built.

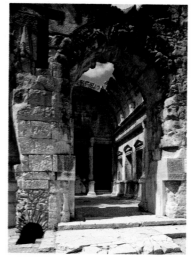

2. The Temple of Diana at Nîmes, 1st century.

1st century AD: Trogus Pompeius, Gallic historian.
2–4: Dedication of the Maison Carrée.
14: At the death of Augustus, Béziers, Fréjus, Orange, Valence, Vienne and Nyons also become *coloniae* under Roman law; Apt, Nîmes and Carcassonne become *coloniae* under Latin law.
21: Revolt of Florus and Sacrovir.
26–7: Dedication of the Arch of Orange.
41: Claudius, who spent his youth in Gaul, becomes emperor.
48: Aedui admitted to the Senate.
c. 50: Trèves becomes *colonia*; building of theatre at Orange.
68–70: Vindex, Civilis and the ephemeral first Gallic Empire.
69–79: Vespasian; Avenches becomes *colonia*; marble land survey map of Orange.
?–113: Pliny the Younger, a Cisalpine from Coma.
121–2: Hadrian visits the northwest provinces.
135–61: Reign of Antoninus Pius, who is partially of Gallic descent.
177: Christians persecuted at Lyon.

4th century BC–5th century AD

The Roman organisation of Gaul at the height of the Empire, between the Ist and IIIrd centuries

- Narbonensis: Province under *under jus senatus*
- Aquitania ⎫
  Lugdunensis ⎬ Imperial provinces
  Belgica ⎪
  Germania ⎭
- Alpes: Procuratorian provinces

BATAVI
MENAPII
Colonia Agrippinensis (*Cologne*)
Castellum Menapiorum (*Cassel*)
MORINI
TUNGRI
UBII
o Aquae (*Aix*)
GERMANIA INFERIOR (17)
Taruanna (*Thérouanne*)
Nemetacum (*Arras*)
ATREBATES
Aduatuca (*Tongres*)
NERVII
Bagacum (*Bavay*)
TREVERI
Augusta Treverorum (*Trèves*)
Samarobriva (*Amiens*)
AMBIANI
SUESSIONES
Augusta Suessionum (*Soissons*)
MEDIOMATRICI
GERMANIA SUPERIOR (17)
Juliobonna (*Lillebonne*)
Rotomagus (*Rouen*)
VELIOCASSES
BELLOVACI
Caesaromagus (*Beauvais*)
REMI
Durocortorum (*Reims*)
Divodurum (*Metz*)
Crociatonum (*Carentan*)
Augustodurum (*Bayeux*)
Noviomagus (*Lisieux*)
UNELLI
CALETI
BAIOCASSES
Mediolanum (*Evreux*)
EBUROVICES
Lutetia (*Paris*)
PARISII
Tullum (*Toul*)
LEUCI
Argentorate (*Strasbourg*)
Fanum Martis (*Corseul*)
Aregenvae (*Vieux*)
LEXOVII
VIDUCASSES
Autricum (*Chartres*)
CARNUTES
Agedincum (*Sens*)
SENONES
Augustobona (*Troyes*)
TRICASSES
Andematunum (*Langres*)
OSISMII
DIABLINTES
Sagii (*Sées*)
Condate (*Rennes*)
REDONES
Noviodunum (*Jublains*)
CENOMANI
Cenabum (*Orléans*)
Autessiodurum (*Auxerre*)
BELGICA
Vorgium (*Quimper*)
VENETI
Darioritum (*Vannes*)
NAMNETES
Juliomagus (*Angers*)
ANDECAVI
TURONES
Caesarodunum (*Tours*)
BITURIGES CUBI
Avaricum (*Bourges*)
AEDUI
Augustodunum (*Autun*)
Cabillonum (*Chalon s.S.*)
Vesontio (*Besançon*)
HELVETII
SEQUANI
o ALESIA
LUGDUNENSIS
Augusta Rauracorum (*Augst*)
RAURICI
Portus Namnetus (*Nantes*)
PICTONES
Limonum (*Poitiers*)
Argentoratum (*Argenton*)
Augustonemetum (*Cl. Ferrand*)
LEMOVICES
Augustoritum (*Limoges*)
SANTONES
Mediolanum Santonum (*Saintes*)
Forum Segusiavorum (*Feurs*)
SEGUSIAVI
Lugdunum (*Lyon*)
Aventicum (*Avenches*)
Noviodunum (*Nyon*)
Genava (*Geneva*)
Darantasia (*Moutiers*)
ALPES GRAIAE ET PENNINAE
Vesunna (*Périgueux*)
PETROCORII
ARVERNI
Ruessio (*St Paulien*)
VELLAVI
ALLOBROGES
Vienna
Valentia
Vasio (*Vaison*)
VOCONTII
Segusio (*Susa*)
ALPES COTTIAE
Brigantio (*Briançon*)
Ebruodunum (*Embrum*)
AQUITANIA
Burdigala (*Bordeaux*)
BITURIGES VIVISCI
VASATES
Divona (*Cahors*)
CADURCI
Anderitum (*Javols*)
GABALI
RUTENI
Arausio (*Orange*)
Carpentorate (*Carpentras*)
Vapincum (*Gap*)
ALPES MARITIMAE
NTIOBRIGES
Cassium (*Bazas*)
Aginnum (*Agen*)
Segodunum (*Rodez*)
Apta (*Apt*)
Cabellio (*Cavaillon*)
Reii (*Riez*)
Cemenelum (*Cimiez*)
Nicaea (*Nice*)
Antipolis (*Antibes*)
ELUSATES
Aquae Tarbellicae (*Dax*)
Elimberris (*Auch*)
Elusa (*Eauze*)
Nemausus (*Nîmes*)
G. Arelatae (*Arles*)
Aquae Sextiae (*Aix*)
Forum Julii (*Fréjus*)
TARBELLI
AUSCII
Tolosa (*Toulouse*)
VOLCAE TECTOSAGES
Baeterrae (*Béziers*)
Massalia (*Marseille*)
NARBONENSIS
Lugdunum Conveniarum (*St Bertrand de Comminges*)
CONVENAE
Carcaso (*Carcassone*)
Narbo Martius (*Narbonne*)
Ruscino
Castel-Roussillon

G = Glanum

Political Structures pertaining to the peoples of Gaul

□ The capital of a *civitas* (the basic administrative unit, based on the territory occupied by a Gallic tribe)

AEDUI Name of Gallic tribe organized in a *civitas*

The intensity of colonisation in the Augustan period
- ■ Colony under Roman law
- ◩ Chief (or other) towns enjoying certain privileges (*oppida latina*)

The development of the road network
- ═══ First route exploited by Rome, IInd century BC
- ━━━ Agrippa's network (-39 to -38)
- ─── Other Gallic and Roman roads
- ═══ Navigable rivers

100 km

[A] Before the conquest
MENAPII
BELGICA
TREVERI
AULERCI
REMI
VENETI
SEQUANI
BITURIGES
AEDUI
HELVETII
CELTICA
ARVERNI
BITURIGES VIVISCI
PROVINCIA (–120)
— Via Domitia military highway to Spain
The Romans 'aiding' the Gauls against the Teutoni (–102)
■ Roman Province
VOLCAE
AQUITANIA
TECTOSAGES
● Massalia *and its territory, allies of Rome since the IIIrd century BC*
HISPANIA

[B] Conquest of Gaul 58 BC to 52 BC
BATAVI
Coalition of the Belgae –57
EBURONES –55
Rhine crossings –55, –53
VENETI –56
CARNUTES
Agedincum
Cenabum
Alesia –52
(Ariovistus –58)
GERMANI
Avaricum –52
Bibracte –58
HELVETII
Gergovia –52
GALLIA CISALPINA
PROVINCIA
AQUITANI
● Massalia –49
— Gallic revolts before –52
▨ Rising of Gauls under Vercingetorix
o Gallic victories
➤ Caesar's campaigns and victories
▨ Subjugated Gaul

[D] The Late Empire, late IIIrd to beginning of Vth century
Colonia Agrippinensis
GERMANIA
Mogontiacum
BELGICA
Rotomagus
Treveri
LUGDUNENSIS
Parisii
Remii
Senones
Vesontio
PROVINCIA SEQUANORUM
Turones
Bituriges
ALPES GRAIAE ET PENNINAE
Lugdunum
Vienna
Mediolanum
Eburodunum
VIENNENSIS
↑ Diocese of the Gauls
AQUITANIA
Burdigala
Elusa
NOVEM POPULANA
NARBONENSIS
Narbo
ALPES MARITIMAE
Aquae Sextiae
↑ Diocese of Vienna
D = Darantasia

Second Gallic Empire.
–273

Trèves (Trier) capital of the empire in the West.
285

Eumenius's speech on the restoration of the schools of rhetoric at Augustodunum (Autun).
298

The Vandals in Gaul.
406–7

196: Albinus's rebellion in Gaul against Septimius Severus.
197: Battle of Lyon; death of Albinus.
212: Edict of Caracalla (*Constitutio Antoniana*) confers Roman citizenship on all the free men of the Empire.
258–68: Postumus, Emperor of the Gauls, defends against invasions by Germanic tribes.
268–73: Tetricus, Emperor of the Gauls, is ultimately forced to surrender to Aurelian.
269: First mention of the troubles caused by the Bagaudae.
275–7: Barbarian invasions.
276–82: Probus drives the invaders out of Gaul.
286: Maximian suppresses the Bagaudae.
303–4: Diocletian's persecution of Christians.
306–11: Constantine in Gaul.
309–90: Ausonius, Bordeaux poet and tutor of Gratian.
314: Council of Arles.
355: Invasions. Julian the Apostate Caesar.
356–7: Julian wins victories.

360?–425?: Sulpicius Severus Aquitanian historian.
361: Julian proclaimed Augustus at Paris.
363–4: Invasion. Jovian wins victories.
386: Council of Trèves.
430–80: Sidonius Apollinaris, letter-writer, Bishop of Clermont and poet.
435–7: Bagaudae.
455: Capture of Trèves by the Franks.

3. The tonneau, *a Gallic invention. 2nd-century relief, Rhineland.*

4. The Apollo of the Maison Carrée, Nîmes.

Christianity Persecuted and Triumphant

PLURALISM was at the heart of ancient religion: each group of humanity expressed its cohesion by honouring its own gods, who were adapted to the local setting and social needs. In Rome, as in Athens, the reception of new divinities obeyed the same rules as applied to the welcome of foreigners: that is to say their followers were required – upon pain of death – not to disturb the social order (Socrates' trial in 399 BC; Bacchanalian scandals of 186 BC). The Roman Empire even tolerated the exclusivism of the god of Israel, granting the Jews the right not to worship Rome and Augustus.

So long as the 'supporters of Christus' were identified with the Jews, they enjoyed the same privileges, which in part explains why Christianity was able to spread so rapidly (it was established in Damascus and Antioch before AD 38, in Asia Minor as early as AD 45, in Rome before AD 49, and at Corinth in AD 50). But the proselytism of the missionaries, which was often foolhardy, caused disruption almost immediately among the lower classes. The journeys of the apostle Paul are studded with civil disturbances which did not simply come from within the Jewish communities, who were indeed accustomed to showing discretion. The ease with which the unjust condemnation of the Christians as fire-raisers in AD 64 was accepted reveals a deep hostility towards them in public opinion. The persecutions unleashed by local magistrates when Christians were denounced were for a long time seen as simple public order measures. It was Trajan who brought these under control.

Everything changed at the beginning of the third century, when the barbarian threat became serious. Christianity, then quite widespread among the upper classes and even stretching beyond the frontiers of Rome as far indeed as Rome's enemies, the Sassanians, seemed to the soldier-emperors to smack of treason at a time when all energies had to be mobilized to save the Empire. This was a grave political error, for the Christians were generally loyalists where the state was concerned. Decreed from on high, the great persecutions were not reflections of popular pressure. Not only were they ineffective, they created new ferments of disintegration.

The 'conversion of Constantine' reflected the same concern as had inspired the Edicts of Diocletian: at all costs the unity of the Roman world had to be maintained. And one soon saw emperors – whether usurpers or not – imposing the same repressive measures on the traditional cults that had been decreed by their predecessors against Christianity. Thus the former sufferers became in their turn persecutors, even on occasion persecutors of their own co-religionists, accused of schism or heresy.

The church, though called upon by its founder to observe and promote unity, was in fact very soon prey to internal splits, in which local differences were revived, which neither the great schools of theology (Alexandria, Antioch, Caesarea) nor the development of monarchism would be able to contain. The mother community in Jerusalem, which inherited the divisions within the Jews, was split between 'Hellenists' and 'Hebrews' on the question of observance of the Mosaic customs. The Jewish–Christian schism (Ebionism) was the first of a long series, chief among which were Montanism in Phrygia and Donatism in Africa. The difficulty of reconciling the divinity of Jesus with monotheism was the cause of the first heresies (Gnosticism in Syria, Marcionism in Pontus, Sabellianism in Cyrenaica, Arianism in Egypt). To repress these disturbances of public order, the emperors in their turn became theologians and presided over synods. Thus was Roman continuity maintained.

1. The Good Shepherd. Catacombs of St Priscilla, c. 260.

Birth of Jesus Christ.

Peter and Paul killed at Rome.

First heresies.

4 BC	AD 64	c. 100

30: Jesus of Nazareth condemned to death by Pontius Pilate, Governor of Judaea, for having proclaimed himself King of the Jews.
37: Stoning of Stephen. The dispersion of the 'Hellenists', who proclaimed the Gospel to the Gentiles. Conversion of Paul.
45–9: Paul in Asia Minor. The Council of Jerusalem declares Gentiles free of obligations under the Mosaic law.
50: Claudius expels from Rome the 'Jews who are agitating at the instigation of Christus' (Suetonius).
50–2: Paul in Greece. Epistles to the Thessalonians.
53–8: Paul in Asia Minor. Epistles to the Corinthians and the Romans. Arrested in Jerusalem for disturbances in the Temple, he is judged at Rome before Caesar and discharged (63).
64: Burning of Rome and persecution of Christians accused of being fire-raisers.
66: Revolt of Judea. The Christians take refuge at Pella.
After 70: The synoptic Gospels. The Ebionites accept Jesus as Messiah but deny his divinity.

95: Under Domitian, new persecutions. Writings of St John.
c. 100: The Gnostics argue that Jesus's humanity is mere appearance.
111: Trajan's reply to Pliny the Younger fixes the procedure to be followed in the trials of those denounced for the crime of Christianity.

2. Judea vanquished. Coin struck by Vespasian in 71.

c. 150: The Marcionists reject the Old Testament.
c. 170: The Montanists form a charismatic church.
177: Martyrdom of the Christians of Lyon.
202: Edict of Septimius Severus forbidding proselytism.
217: Sabellius denies the personal distinction between Father and Son.
250: Edict of Decius ordering participation in a general sacrifice. Repression of those who refused. Many renunciations of Christianity ensue.
260: Gallienus's Edict of Toleration.
297: Diocletian's Edict against the Manichaeans.
303–5: Edicts of Diocletian forbidding Christian worship, ordering the torture of priests who refuse to renounce that religion and condemning to death or hard labour those refusing to take part in a general sacrifice to the tutelary gods of Rome.
311: Galerius's Edict of Toleration. Anthony the Hermit.
312: The Donatists reject the validity of the sacraments conferred by priests who had

3. Jesus giving the law to Peter. 4th century sarcophagus.

AD 30–392

The Spread of Christianity

-) Frontier of the Roman Empire at the death of Theodosius (395)
- ⇨ Barbarian incursions
- ➡ Sasanian incursions
- ▨ Regions with high proportion of Christians, IVth century
- ▨ Areas where Christianity had more limited influence
- ★ Main centres of diffusion of the doctrine
- ● Oecumenical councils
-)) Point of origin of major controversies
-)) Competing religions

MARCIONISM
Lyon ★ Milan ★
Armenia
Constantinople ★ (381)
Caesarea (Mazaca) ★
PRISCILLIANISM
Rome ★ Nicaea
★ Grenada
MONTANISM
★ Edessa
Babylonia
★ Carthage
DONATISM
Island of Patmos
GNOSTICISM
★ Antioch
MANICHEISM
★ Damascus
EBIONISM
SABELLIANISM
ARIANISM
Jerusalem ★
Alexandria

1000 km

The Journeys of Paul and the Churches of the *Apocalypse*

Paul's journeys

From Antioch
- ➡ First journey (45-49)
- ┅➤ Second journey (50-52)
- ➡ Third journey (53-58)

From Caesarea
- ➡ Journey in captivity to Rome (60-62)

The Seven Churches of John's *Apocalypse*

1 - Ephesus   5 - Sardis
2 - Laodicea   6 - Smyrna
3 - Pergamos   7 - Thyatira
4 - Philadelphia

• Rome
Thessalonica
• Troy
Pergamos
Ephesus
Athens
Corinth
Rhegium
Miletus
Perga
Myra
Syracuse
Kos
Crete
Rhodes
Cyprus
Sidon
Antioch
Seleucia
Damascus
Tyre
Caesarea
Jerusalem

200 km

Decian persecution.

Serdica Edict of Toleration.

Death of Julian the Apostate.

250

311

363

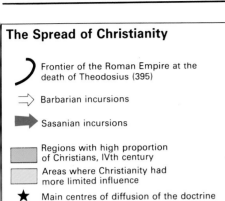

forsworn their religion during the period of persecution.
313: Constantine and Licinius accord freedom of worship to all the inhabitants of the Empire.
c. 320: In Egypt, Arius professes that the Father and the Son are not of the same nature. Pachomius founds the first

monastery.
325: The ecumenical council of Nicaea condemns Arianism.
c. 340: Wulfila spreads Arianism among the Goths.
347: Constant I orders the prosecution of the Donatists.
361: Julian gives aid to promote anti-Christian

4. Sarcophagus of Eutropos, a Christian sculptor, c. 350.

resistance.
381: The ecumenical council of Constantinople defines the consubstantiality of Father and Son.
385: Priscillian is executed at Trier as a heretic.
391–2: Theodosius outlaws all pagan cults.

5. Folio of the Gospel according to St John, Codex Sinaiticus, 4th century.

Expansionist Tendencies

THE HISTORICAL TURNING-POINT which marks the beginning of a clear trend towards homogenization, which the Greek historian Polybius situated around 220 BC – the point at which Rome began to exert its power over the other Mediterranean countries – can also be seen in Chinese history, where it is, if anything, even more marked. It was in 221 BC that China was first unified. These two parallel developmental processes make the third century AD one of the crucial moments in human history. Might it be said that the year 221 BC marked the end of an era for China and the beginning of a new one for Rome? In fact, the process of Roman conquest outside the peninsula began around 269 BC (according to Polybius himself). It quickened first around 260 BC, then in 229 BC and, once again, around 220 BC. It began again, after a pause, in 154 BC. The beginnings of the Chinese Empire obeyed a somewhat similar chronology.

Several factors do, however, to some degree temper the importance of the events of the late third century. The preceding period was an exceptionally fruitful one, since it saw the birth of such remarkable new phenomena as Greek democracy, Roman law, Jewish nationalism and the legalist Chinese state. It also saw the Persian Empire and Alexander's. Though these were not very long-lived and may even seem positively ephemeral alongside the Roman and Chinese Empires, they were more cosmopolitan, 'imperial' and adventurous. The fact was, however, that after the turn of the third century BC history passed into a phase of banalization and growing uniformity. And the socio-political units that emerged at that time were generally of a defensive, rather timid and prudent nature. The Chinese grouped together against the nomads from the Steppes. The Romans organized a common front of the Hellenized peoples against the Western Semites and the 'barbarians' of Germany. Central Asia, Iran and Mesopotamia rejected Hellenism. India, after Ashoka, reacted against Buddhist internationalism and reverted to Brahminism. Elsewhere, as ever, progress took an internally contradictory course: 'horizontal' integration occurred at the expense of 'vertical' segregation; the rich supported centralizing states, while the poor suffered.

There was, however, a great deal of progress, much of it occurring – most strikingly as it now seems – at around the same time. This can be seen in the many new peoples who 'entered history' (Vietnamese, Japanese, Ethiopians, the Slavs and the Numidians), in the numerous new contacts between peoples and in the evidence of the restless human spirit shown by the Jews in the West; the Teutons in Germany; the Polynesians in their travels to the Marquesas and Society Islands more than 3,000 kilometres from Samoa; the Bantus of the Cameroon and Congo forests advancing into the savannahs of the

1. Augustus imperator, marble, Rome, 1st century.

south and east of Africa, taking with them agricultural skills and iron; migrants from the Indian archipelago journeying to Madagascar and the east coast of Africa; the South American Arawaks sailing to the West Indies; Roman coins finding their way to Indochina etc. The face of progress could also be seen in those states which arose after the end of the third century BC in North Africa or in Celtic, Dacian and Hun territory, which opened the way to the development of empires. And it is also seen in the missionary religions, the sudden explosion of religious univeralism in Judaism, Mahayana Buddhism, the conversion of Southeast Asia to Brahminism (the Indian form of expansion – at once religious, political and commercial) and the conversion of the Mediterranean and Western Europe to Christianity. Then, finally, there was also the establishment of Teotihuacan on the Mexican plateaus which, by its immense political and religious influence, would leave its definitive stamp on the whole of Central American history.

272–232 BC: Ashoka – Indian unity and Buddhist missions. There followed a Brahman reaction and the Indianization of Southeast Asia.
c. 270–265 BC: The Ch'in state (which was to give its name to China, at least in European languages) adopted the markedly legalist orientation, which was to be the foundation-stone of its greatness. Rome became interested in Sicily, where she was subsequently to encounter Carthage.
c. 270–250 BC: Bible translated into Greek.
c. 260–241 BC: Roman victory over Carthage. The Ch'in state became the dominant power in China.
Second half of 3rd century BC: The Arsacid Parthians freed themselves from Greek domination. Central Asia detached itself from the Seleucid Empire. The Teutons left their peninsulas and marched towards the south. The Celts fell back and sought to unite. The Slavic people was taking form. A Japanese people and culture made its appearance. A Hun kingdom (Hsiung nu) and Numidian and Moorish kingdoms emerged. The King of Meroe conquered Ethiopia.

3. The soldiers of the dead ruler's army. Tomb of the first Chinese emperor, Shih Huang Ti, in Shensi province.

229–222 BC: The Romans crossed the Adriatic and occupied Cisalpine Gaul. The Ch'in state reduced its rivals to the status of provinces.
221 BC: The Ch'in Empire. Hannibal's Empire. The decisive conflict with Rome imminent.
219–202 BC: Second Punic War. In 202 BC the Han Empire replaced the rapidly dismembered Ch'in Empire: this had a 'federal' or 'feudal' structure, with great autonomy granted to the provinces.
2nd century BC: The Mongol Huns formed a bastion against the Indo-European Yueh-chih, who surged back into Central Asia, destroying Hellenism there. In their westward march the Jews reached Greece and Rome. Attempts at unification among the Dacians. First buildings at Teotihuacan. First Mayan layer.
154 BC: Rome, which had subjugated Spain, North Africa and Greece, was coming out of a relatively quiet period. New imperial impetus in China. End of provincial autonomy.
c. 130 BC: The Roman legions in Asia. Chinese offensives against the barbarian

3rd century BC–1st century AD

2. The Great Wall of China, built in the reign of Shih Huang Ti (221–206 BC).

north and south-west.
1st century BC: Aksum – the formation of historic Ethiopia. Hellenism again in retreat in the Near East. Expansion of Indian trade with the Mediterranean and the Far East.
Middle of 1st century BC: High point of Roman conquest. Stabilization and consolidation of the Empire. Rise of Italians and western provincials. Further successful Chinese expansion followed by a tendency for such expansion to decelerate. Promotion of provincial élites.
AD 50: Beginning of Christian expansion.
End of 1st millennium BC/beginning of 1st millennium AD: Bantu migration in Africa. Polynesian migration in Oceania. Indian migration into Southeast Asia and Indonesia. The Arawaks in the West Indies.

4. Capital of the pillar erected by Ashoka at Sarnath, India, 3rd century BC.

5. Mythic account of the migration of the Aztecs. Detail from the Boturini codex.

Fall of the Roman Empire in the West

AT THE END of the crisis of the third century, the 'Late' Empire – as it is known – underwent a profound transformation, becoming an absolute monarchy with capitals at Ravenna, Milan, Trier, Constantinople and Sirmium. Rome was now merely a cultural and religious centre. At the Empire's frontiers, the emperors had installed barbarian peoples as *foederati* and reinforced the *limes* – fortified lines between the Rhine and the Danube – to contain the Germanic tribes. Diocletian divided the Empire into fifteen large dioceses, each one being itself divided into provinces (of which there were seventeen in Gaul) and each province into cities. When, by the Edict of Milan,

Constantine decided to grant freedom to Christians, the ecclesiastical hierarchy was laid down: the 'metropolitan', later to be called an archbishop, was placed at the head of a province, whilst the role of a bishop was to direct the church in a city. Once converted to Christianity, Constantine considered himself head of the church. He called the first Ecumenical Council at Nicaea to fight against the Arian heresy. It was in the reign of Theodosios I that Catholicism became a true state religion. Contrary to common belief, the Late Empire was not a 'decadent' period; in the field of philosophy and the arts one might more accurately speak of a 'Constantino-Theodosian Renaissance'. On the death of Theodosios, the Empire was split into two. Ravenna became the capital in the west and Constantinople capital of the East. At the end of the fourth century, under pressure from the Huns – a Turco-Mongol people – the barbarians moved west in successive waves. Iranian nomads, Sarmatae and Alans were among the first, followed by the Goths. The Visigoth people requested asylum from the Emperor Valens in 376 and crossed the Danube. Two years later the Gothic cavalry defeated the Roman army at Adrianople and Valens was killed. The Visigoths dispersed about the Empire and captured Rome in 410. The fall of the Eternal City sent a shock wave through the Christian world, though Augustine did seek to reassure the faithful with his *City of God* (413–26). The Visigoths finally settled, with imperial authorization, in southern Gaul and Spain. Alans, Suebi and Vandals, who had crossed the Rhine in 406, passed through Gaul and Spain. Under the leadership of Genseric, the Vandals continued their advance into Africa. When he had conquered Carthage, the great grain exporting port, King Genseric persecuted the Catholics. Attila's Huns, who had settled in the Danube Basin, invaded the West in 451. They were unable to take either Paris, which was defended by Genevieve, or Orleans, and were finally defeated by Aetius and his barbarian soldiers at the Campus Mauriacus (near Troyes). Attila attempted to invade Italy in 452, but, yielding to the entreaties of Pope Leo the Great, he declined to advance south of Mantua.

In the second half of the century, the barbarian peoples formed themselves into political units. The Burgundi settled between Langres and Avignon in Sapaudia (origin of the modern 'Savoy'). The Angles, Jutes and Saxons invaded Britain and forced the Celts back to the west. The Visigoths extended the area of their domination from the Loire to southern Spain. Veritable playthings of the barbarian princes, the emperors succeeded one another rapidly at Ravenna until Odoacer decided to put an end to the fiction by taking the place of the last emperor, Romulus Augustulus, and by sending the imperial insignia back to Constantinople, a symbolic gesture which spectacularly sealed the refound unity of the Empire.

1. Diptych of the consul Boethius. Ivory carving, 5th century.

Diocletian's monetary reforms.	**Council of Nicaea.**	**St Martin becomes bishop of Tours.**	**Death of Augustine at Hippo.**
294	325	371	430

284–305: Reign of Diocletian. Maximian is nominated to serve alongside him in 287 (dyarchy). Constantius Chlorus and Galerius proclaimed Caesars in 193 (tetrarchy). He reorganized the tax system (297: first revision of the fiscal assessment or *indictio*) and controlled prices (*Maximum* edict, 301). In 303 he resolved to persecute the Christians and ultimately abdicated with Maximian in 305. Diocletian retired to his palace at Salonae (Split).
306–37: Reign of Constantine, son of Constantius Chlorus. He triumphed over his rivals and in 312 won the Battle of Pons Mulvius (Ponte Molle).
313: Edict of tolerance towards the Christians. 314: Council of Arles; 46 Western bishops meet – including two from London and York. In 325 Constantine calls the Council of Nicaea. In 330 he founds the new city of Constantinople. Pope Sylvester I, who has been given the Lateran Palace, dies in 335.
337–64: Constantine's successors come up against the Arian problem. Wulfila is made a bishop in 341 and converts the Goths to Arianism. 355: The Alamanni and the Franks

invade Gaul. 357–359; Three councils meet at Sirmium. In 360, St Martin founds Licugé, the first Western monastery. Julian the Apostate reigns between 361 and 363 and attempts to restore paganism.
364–78: Valentinian I and Valens divide up the Empire. In 370 the Huns arrive on the Don. The Visigoths cross the Danube in 376 and win a victory at Adrianople in 378. In 382 they will be considered as foederati in Lower Moesia.
379–95: Reign of Theodosios I in the East. Later, ruler of the whole Empire. The Second Ecumenical Council meets at Constantinople in 381. The pagan temples are closed down in 391.
395–450: Reign of Arcadius and his son Theodosios II in the East. Invasions of the Germanic tribes in the West. The barbarians cross the Rhine in 406 and the Visigoth, Alaric, takes Rome. Gallia Placidia, sister of Honorius, the second son of Theodosios, having been taken hostage, marries Ataulf in 413; the Visigoths are legally settled as foederati in the south-west of Gaul. Genseric's Vandals take Hippo, St

Augustine's city, in 431, then Carthage in 439. They sack Rome in 455. Aëtius governs the Western Roman Empire from 434 to 454 in the name of Valentian III. He allows the Burgundi to settle in Sapaudia, the Alans on the Loire. He fights back the Franks. Attila is beaten in 451 by Aëtius and his barbarian auxiliaries. 452: Attila fails in northern Italy. He dies in 453 and his 'empire' falls apart. Aëtius is assassinated in 454 and Valentinian III in 455.
455–76: The Visigoth Theodoric II as Avitus proclaimed emperor. Marjorian is the last great emperor (457–61). Ricimer, from the Suebi, has real power over the emperors until 472. The Frank Childeric governs the north of Gaul at the request of the Roman general Aegidius. Euric, the Visigoth, becomes chief at Narbonne (470), then in the Auvergne. The Christians are persecuted. 472: The Burgundian Gundobad in power at Lyons. He imposes Glycerius as emperor in 473. Orestes, Attila's former adviser, installs his son Romulus Augustulus as emperor. Odoacer re-establishes the unity of the Empire in 476.

3. Bronze colossus at Barletta in Apulia.

The Late Empire and first Barbarian kingdoms 285-451

Western Empire	Frontiers of the Empire under Diocletian · · · Diocesan boundaries · · · · · Provincial boundaries
Eastern Empire	Barbarian kingdoms · Invasions leading to formation of Barbarian kingdoms

Defeat of the Huns at Campus Maricacus (Moirey) · Towns attacked by the Huns

The Barbarian kingdoms 451-76

Eastern Empire in 476 · Barbarian kingdoms · New invaders · Merovingian heartland

2. *Chariot race in the Constantinople hippodrome. Ivory panel, c. 450.*

Sidonius Apollinaris becomes bishop of Clermont.

...odosian Code.

470

...ecorated bronze belt buckles from a prince's tomb, 5th ...ry.

Iran and Central Asia: Between Two Worlds

1. Royal hunt. Silver dish of the Sassanian period. c. 500.

AT THE END of the third century BC western Iran was under the control of the Arsacid Parthians, while the east was ruled by the Graeco-Bactrian sovereigns. Later the Kushan Empire appeared, from its centre in Kabul, linking Central Asia to India. If it is particularly remembered for its coinage, this is because its trade in precious goods flourished, especially with the Romans. Two centuries of peace under the Kushans enabled Afghanistan to become urbanized and also allowed the expansion of Buddhism and a flourishing of Graeco-Buddhist art, known as Gandhara, which combined local themes with Greek techniques and which became predominant in India and Asia as far as China.

It fell to the Sassanian Ardashir to re-found an Iranian empire based on Ctesiphon, which brought together Iran, Afghanistan and Mesopotamia. The latter was almost constantly at war with the Roman and Byzantine Empires; similarly the Iranians and the Romans (the Persian word for Roman – *roumi* – is the origin of the Arabic word for 'European') fought over northern Mesopotamia and Armenia. In the east, Iran was invaded first by the Hepthalite Huns and then the Oghuz Turks and lost the former Kushan region in the fifth century. In the end, neither the maintenance of the Arab vassal kingdom of Hira nor the Iranian presence on both shores of the Persian Gulf could prevent the Arabo-Muslim campaign of conquest in the seventh century.

Centralized state control, an objective of the first Sassanian kings, was only achieved under Khosrow I. By supporting the lesser gentry against the upper aristocracy, and by setting fixed rates of taxation and establishing a coherent legal system, he brought the Empire to the height of its power and laid the political and economic foundations for the Umayyad and Abbasid Empires. Art flourished in this period, with the accent on character and essential forms rather than on elements situated in a specific time or place; this was a period of Iranian artistic rebirth in which symbolic values and the search for new decorative forms combined in the celebration of an eternal glory.

Zoroastrianism became the state religion and its clergy, the magi, wielded enormous power. Whilst in Iran, the Avesta was being written down in a language which by that time was already dead, but certain parts of which had been preserved in the oral tradition for more than a thousand years, in Babylon the Jews, who formed an ancient and stable community, were writing the Talmud, which extolled the virtues of rabbinical discipline and study. However, the stringencies of the Zoroastrian ritual and a sense of social injustice led the Iranian Mazdak to found a new religion in which the victory of good over evil would be achieved by the redistribution of wealth. Though popular, the movement was brutally suppressed.

The Sogdians, who were still independent from the Iranian kingdom, continued to conduct trade between China and the West through the towns of Samarkand, Bukhara and Pendzhikent, providing a means of circumventing the taxes the Sassanians imposed in the sixth century on caravans passing through their territory. Though they founded no state, they were the ambassadors of the Turks to the Byzantine Empire, importers of wine into China, and they also supplied believers to all the religions of the age, especially to their own form of Zoroastrianism that was less strict and less priest-dominated than that of Iran. Their art bears the stamp of Iranian, Chinese and Indian influences.

The culture of Iran, Afghanistan and of the Russian Tadzhiks has its roots in these centuries. It is a many-faceted culture with its own distinctive place in the Islamic world.

Yüeh-chih invasions.	Kaniska.	Birth of Mani.	Ardashir I, founder of the Sassanian dynasty.	Kavadh I.
130 BC	AD 78?	14th April 216	224	488

2. Shapur I defeats the Emperor Valerian. Carving at Naqsh-i Roustem, c. 265.

130 BC: Saka (Scythians) and Yüeh-chih lay waste the Hellenized regions of Bactria and India and settle there.

AD 20–200?: Kushan Empire; reaches its peak in the reign of Kaniska (78?–120?). He initiates the *saka* system of dating still in use in India today and builds Purusapura (Peshawar).

224–40: Ardashir I defeats the last Parthian king: it is probably during his reign that eastern Iran (the former Kushan kingdom) is conquered.

240–72: Empire grows and is strengthened under Shapur I. Valerian, the Roman Emperor, is taken prisoner in 259 and works at Shushtar on the Karun dam, which is still known today as 'Caesar's dam'.

270: The Mani religion takes root in Iran.

273–6: Under Bahram I and Karter, the most influential magus, a Zoroastrian reaction sets in. The prophet is executed and his followers isolated.

309–79: Shapur II. During his reign the Roman Empire and Armenia are converted to Christianity. The borders with the Byzantines are bitterly disputed. The Iranian Christians

are seen as internal enemies until 484, when the Iranian Nestorian Church is founded (it is independent of Byzantium).

313: Tün Huang's letters show that the Sogdians were in western China.

5th century: Royal power weakened in Iran: nobility and clergy elect the kings. Situation stable in the west. In the east, the Hepthalite Huns appear and the Iranians are forced to pay tribute to them around the middle of the century.

488–531: Kavadh I ascends the throne, thanks to the Huns, uses the Mazdakites against the nobles and re-establishes the power of the monarchy.

531–79: Khosrow I Anushirvan ('of the immortal soul'). He defeats the Huns and welcomes the Neo-Platonists to Ctesiphon when Justinian closes the Academy in Athens in 529. The Persians claim (wrongly) that he invented the game of chess, though 'check mate' is indeed the English version of a Persian expression meaning 'the king is dead'. Regarded as both good and wise, he was the model pre-Islamic ruler.

565: Oghuz Turkish Empire founded in the

3. Horse's head in gilded silver, 4th-century Sassanian art.

130 BC–AD 751

Religions in Iran before Islam

MANICHEISM

EASTERN CHRISTIAN CHURCH

NESTORIAN CHURCH becomes autonomous in 484

MANICHEISM

EGYPT

ZOROASTRIANISM
State religion

Isfahan

Ctesiphon

BUDDHISM

✡ Judaism

The Sassanian Empire at its peak (531-579)

New silk route opened up by the Sogdians and Byzantines to avoid taxes

towards China

Lake Balkhash

EMPIRE OF

THE (OGHUZ) TURKS

HUNS

Turfan

Lake Nop Nor

Frunze

ARAL SEA

SOGDIAN

CIVILIZATION

Takla Makan Desert

Tashkent

Samarkand

Kashgar

Amu Darya

Sougdi

Bukhara

PAMIR

Old Kushan Empire (Ist - IInd centuries)

BLACK SEA

CAUCUSUS MTS

CASPIAN SEA

Gilgit

Constantinople

against Constantinople

Ankara

EASTERN ROMAN EMPIRE

ARMENIA

Lake Van

Amida

Nisibis

Ghandzhe

AZERABAJAN

Merv

Bactria (Balkh)

Peshawar

HIMALAYAS

Nishaper

Edessa

Dara

Rai (Tehran)

KHORASAN

Herat

Kabul

Antioch

Euphrates

Hamadan

Salt desert

Helmand

Kandahar

Palmyra

Tigris

SASSANIAN EMPIRE

INDIA

GHASSAN

□ Ctesiphon (Baghdad)

Isfahan

Indus

HIRA

Shushtar

FARS

Persepolis

KERMAN

towards the Yemen

Shiraz

MAKRAN

KINDAH

PERSIAN GULF

Daybul

RED SEA

Medina

Mecca

Nile

500 km

⬜ Frontier towns (under alternate Sassanian or Byzantine domination)

⬜ Permanent conflict and temporary conquests

⬜ Victories over the Hepthalite Huns (under Khosrow)

Lines of future Islamic expansion

Trade:

Silk routes

Other trade routes

✴ Sogdian commercial centres

Khosrow I.

531

Fall of Samarkand.

712

steppes of Asia and Sogdiana: the Sogdian merchant Maniakh is sent as Turkish ambassador to Byzantium. A new silk route is opened and a Sogdian trading post is opened on the Black Sea at Sougdi, which, in years to come, will be one of Marco Polo's ports of call.

591–628: Khosrow II Parviz ('the victorious') leads lightning campaigns in Asia Minor, Syria and Egypt. While he is away, the Byzantine Emperor Heraclius sacks Ctesiphon (627).

628–36: Five sovereigns, including Queen Boran, succeed one another. The last of them, Yazdegerd III, loses the Battle of al-Qadisiyah against the Arabs and is assassinated in 651 during his flight to the east.

650: Sogdiana under the nominal protectorate of Tang China and the mercantile oligarchies of Pendzhikent prosper. However, the country is ravaged by the Arabs in 712–22. The Sogdians appeal in vain for China to come to their aid. Victory of the Arabs over the Chinese in 751 at the Battle of the Talas. The Abbasid caliphate effectively takes control of Sogdiana.

4. Boddhisattva.

5. The preaching of the Buddha. Fresco at Qizil, Hsin-hsiang, influenced by Sogdian art, c. 600.

6. Episode in the life of the Buddha. Graeco-Buddhist art, Paitava.

The Barbarian Kingdoms of Europe

THE BARBARIAN KINGDOMS took shape during the sixth century, but were very different from north to south. In Britain, pagan Anglo-Saxon states were established. In Gaul, the Franks under Clovis, the son of Childeric, advanced from Tournai to Soissons, where Syagrius, 'the last of the Roman rulers', was defeated, then to Paris and the Rhine. Clovis, the first barbarian king to be baptized according to Catholic ritual, defeated the Arian Visigoths at Vouillé before being recognized as king by the Eastern Emperor. His sons completed the conquest of Gaul with the occupation of the Kingdom of Burgundy and of Provence. But the Germanic influence was still dominant, and resulted in the Kingdom of the Franks being partitioned into Neustria, Austrasia, Burgundy, and Aquitaine, the last of these being the most Romanized area. In the barbarian kingdoms on the Mediterranean, Roman influence was maintained. Theodoric the Ostrogoth won Italy from Odoacer and surrounded himself with Roman senators, like Cassiodorus and Boethius. But the barbarian kings were Arians, the result of which was that the Eastern Emperor, Justinian decided to reconquer the western kingdoms. He retook Carthage, and took control of Italy after twenty years of war and settled his representative in Ravenna. Italy, which was ruined, fell to the Lombards in 568. The Visigoths resisted and made Toledo their capital. Justinian was able to repossess only the south of Spain. The Arian Leovigild, king of the Visigoths, dreamed of bringing about religious and political unity in the Iberian peninsula. He subjugated the Basques and founded Vitoria. But when his son Recared abandoned Arianism and became a convert to Catholicism in 587, a new era in the history of Spain began. In Italy, the Middle Ages began with the Lombard invasion. These Arian barbarians settled in northern Italy, in Spoleto and Benevento, while the Roman Empire retained only the Tiber valley, Ravenna, the coast and islands. Pope Gregory the Great, the first monk to be pope, was caught between the Byzantines and the Lombards whom he hoped to convert to Catholicism. He decided to convert the pagan Anglo-Saxons, and the conditions of religious and cultural life in the West were to be profoundly altered as a consequence. During the same period, Celtic monks settled in Gaul. In Spain, the Catholic kings drove out the Byzantines and took control of a prosperous kingdom. St Isidore, the Bishop of Seville, gave his name to a kind of 'Renaissance'. In Gaul, Chlotar II and Dagobert I re-established the unity of the kingdom. The Irish monks restored religious life. But after 639 the kingdom was partitioned once again, and the aristocracy, controlled by the mayors of the palace, held power. Over this period the Byzantine Empire was being attacked on all sides: in Italy by the Lombards, in the Balkans by the Slavs, and in particular by the Arabs, who left them holding only Asia Minor. In addition, religious issues set the emperors at odds with the papacy. At the beginning of the eighth century Arabs and Berbers from North Africa invaded Spain, drove the Goths back as far as the Asturias and tried to enter Gaul. But the Austrasian mayors of the palace re-established their authority in the Kingdom of the Franks. Charles Martel triumphed over the aristocrats and the neighbouring barbarian peoples. His sons Pepin III and Carloman reigned in the name of the Merovingian kings and, with St Boniface, reformed the Frankish Church. The popes, who were increasingly threatened by the Lombards and were opposed to the religious policy of the emperors, turned to the West and to the Franks.

1. Visigoth manuscript illustrating an episode from the life of Moses. 7th century.

Baptism of Clovis.	Rule of St Benedict.	Luxeuil founded by Columban.	The Venerable Bede retires to the Monastery of St Paul in Jar
498	**534**	**590**	**685**

481–511: Reign of Clovis, the son of Childeric I. 486: Victory at Soissons. 494: Clovis comes to the assistance of the Rhenish Franks attacked by the Alamanni at Zülpich (Tolbiac). Under the influence of the Burgundian Princess Clotilda, Clovis becomes a convert to Catholicism, and is baptized in Reims by Bishop Remigius. He defeats the Arian Visigoths (under Alaric II) at Vouillé in 507 and calls a Church Council at Orleans in 511 to reorganize the Church of the Gauls.

4. Merovingian eagles in cloisonné enamel. End of the 5th century.

493–526: Reign of Theodoric, the Ostrogoth king, who restores Italy, builds churches and allies himself with the Vandal, Burgundian and Visigoth princes. In 508–9 he prevents Clovis from reaching the Mediterranean coast. In 523 he breaks with the Emperor. Boethius is condemned and executed in 524. **527–65:** Reign of Justinian I. 533: Vandal North Africa is reconquered in an effort to come to the aid of the persecuted Catholic community. 536: Belisarius recaptures Naples, then Rome. 538: The Ostrogoth Witiges lays a year-long siege to Rome. 540: Ravenna is captured. 543–6: The Ostrogoth King Totila retakes Naples, then Rome. 552: Totila is defeated and killed. Italy is rebuilt as a result of the promulgation by Justinian of the *Pragmatic Sanction* (13 August 554). 555: The Ostrogoths capitulate. The Byzantines take southern Spain. Toledo becomes the Visigoth capital. **568:** The Lombards, pressed by the Avars from Pannonia, invade Italy. Pavia is captured in 569–72. The Byzantines set up the Exarchate of Ravenna in 584. Benedictine monks from Monte Cassino arrive in Rome.

590–604: Gregory I, 'the servant of the servants of God', is pope. Rome is besieged by the Lombards. 600: The Slavs attack Salona. 601: Recared, the first Catholic Visigoth king, dies. 605: Augustine of Canterbury, who had been given the task of evangelizing the Anglo-Saxons by Gregory the Great, dies. **610–41:** Reign of the Eastern Emperor Heraclius. 613: King Chlotar II has sole power in the Frankish kingdom. 614: The Irish monk Columban founds the monastery at Bobbio with the help of Agilulf. 626: The Avars lay siege to Constantinople. 629: The Byzantines are driven out of Spain. 633: Bishop Isidore of Seville presides over the Fourth Council of Toledo, and dies in 636. **629–39:** Reign of Dagobert I. He embarks on campaigns against the Basques, the Bretons and the Slavs. 632: Death of the prophet Mahomet. 634: Start of the Arab conquests. 636: Heraclius is defeated at the Battle of the Yarmuk River. **641–68:** Constant II becomes Eastern Emperor. 643 sees the Edict of the Lombard king Rothari, which codifies Lombard

customs. 650: Founding of Saint-Wandrille and Nivelles. 653: The Lombards convert to Catholicism. Pope Martin I is deported to Constantinople. 654: Foundation of Jumièges. 663–79: Struggles break out between Léger, the aristocratic Bishop of Autun, and the mayor of the palace, Ebroin. **687–751:** The Merovingian mayors of the palace govern Gaul. 711: The Arabs defeat the Visigoths at the Rio Guadalete. 714: Pepin II of Herstal dies. 718: Pelayo defeats the Arabs at Covadonga. 732: Battle of Poitiers. **715–44:** Conflicts break out between the popes Gregory II, then Gregory III, the Lombard king Liudprand and the Byzantine Emperor, Leo III. The Lombards make further inroads. The Iconoclastic Controversy begins. **735–51:** Anglo-Saxon monks are sent as missionaries to Frisia and Germania. 735: The Venerable Bede dies. Councils of reform are held. 744: Founding of the monastery at Fulda. 751: Ravenna captured by Aistulf the Lombard. Pepin III, the Short, becomes king.

5th–8th centuries

2. Apsidal chapel in Venasque (Vaucluse). An example of Christian art in the 7th century.

3. Inlay of a Lombard shield in the form of a horseman. Gilt moulded bronze, 7th century.

Ravenna captured by the Lombards.

751

5. Ornamentation from the helmet belonging to Agilulf, the 7th-century Lombard king.

Empire in 476
Empire in 568
Territory controlled by the Franks
Vandal Kingdom
Ostrogoth Kingdom

ANGLO-SAXON KINGDOMS · London · Tournai · Le Mans · Vouillé · Bordeaux · Soissons · Tolbiac · THURINGIA · ALAMANNIA · BAVARIA · Lombards · Saxons · Avars · Gepids · BLACK SEA · Empire of Persia

KINGDOM OF THE FRANKS · BURGUNDY · Lyon · Toulouse · Narbonne · Marseille · PROVENCE · Ravenna · Constantinople

KINGDOM OF THE SUEVES · Braga · KINGDOM OF THE VISIGOTHS · Toledo · Barcelona · Valencia · Basques · Rome · Naples · Antioch

Merida · Seville · Cartagena · Carthage · Syracuse · EASTERN EMPIRE · Beirut · Jerusalem · Tripoli · Alexandria

The Barbarian Kingdoms and the Reconquest of Justinian 476-568

500 km

Empire in 636
Visigoth conquests

ANGLO-SAXON KINGDOMS · Canterbury · Slavs · Slavs · Avars · BLACK SEA

AUSTRASIA · NEUSTRIA · ALEMANNIA · BAVARIA · FRANKS · AQUITAINE · BURGUNDY · Lyon · Milan · Pavia · Lombards · Ravenna · LOMBARDS · Spoleto · Salona · Thessalonika · Constantinople

Toulouse · PROVENCE · Marseille · Braga · Barcelona · Toledo · VISIGOTHS · Valencia · Cartagena · Rome · Benevento · Antioch · BYZANTINE · Syracuse · Carthage · EMPIRE · Jerusalem · Alexandria

The Three Great Barbarian Kingdoms 568-636

500 km

Empire in 750
Arab invasions
Battles

ANGLO-SAXON KINGDOMS · Canterbury · Frisians · Slavs · Avars · Khazars · BLACK SEA

Bretons · Metz · Ratisbon · Slovenes · Slovenes · Croats · Serbs · Bulgars · FRANKS · Tours · Poitiers · Milan · Ravenna · Constantinople

Covadonga · KINGDOM OF ASTURIAS · Basques · Toulouse · Pavia · LOMBARDS · Spoleto · Rome · Benevento · Narbonne · BYZANTINE

Toledo · Cordoba · Jerez · Gibraltar · Carthage · Kairouan · Syracuse · EMPIRE · Antioch · Yarmuk River · Jerusalem · Alexandria

AURASIAN MOUNTAINS

Arab Conquests 636-751

500 km

Constantinople and the Byzantine Empire

1. A naval battle illustrates a Greek manuscript of the 11th century.

THE TRANSFER of the Roman capital to Constantinople in 330 was a sign of the Emperor Constantine's desire to reunite the western and eastern parts of the Empire, which had been effectively divided by Diocletian in 286. In spite of such attempts at unification, the distance between east and west continued to grow.

Constantinople was 'the new Rome'. As the phrase suggests, the Byzantine Empire was thus founded under a dual impetus, on the one hand towards continuity and on the other, change. Though Byzantium inherited a territory whose boundaries were continually changing as a result of invasion, the same theoretical frontiers were always claimed by the emperors. It thought of itself as the inheritor of the Roman Empire (its emperor would always bear the title 'Emperor of the Romans'), which indeed it was in terms of its institutions, even though these underwent some transformation over the centuries. The Byzantine state was based upon a strictly hierarchical central administration, which lasted in an effective form into the thirteenth century. Social exchanges were regulated by Roman law, which was recognized and taught throughout the Empire. A healthy level of monetary circulation made for an active economy. Byzantium derived profit both from its gold reserves and its role as intermediary in the East-West trade in luxury goods. From the reign of Constantinople onwards, it imposed upon its subjects the use of its gold currency, which remained stable right up to the eleventh century and became the standard currency of Mediterranean commerce.

Here the Roman legacy ends, for it was its Hellenistic culture, rather than its institutions, which gave Byzantium its unity. In the seventh century the Empire consisted of all the Greek-speaking territories under the emperor's rule. Greek, which was the language of culture for the Oriental elites, and which after Justinian became the language of administration, was also, most importantly, the language of the Eastern Christians. The Hellenistic tradition (Byzantium was never to reject the heritage of secular Greek culture) and the language of the Gospels and the liturgy gave the diverse peoples who made up the Empire an identity which at a very early stage was formed by setting itself against the Western and barbarian worlds. This opposition is emphasized in the organization of the church. The church was modelled on the administrative structures of the Empire, which led to ecclesiastical jurisdiction being split between east and west. Byzantium's loss of its western territories after the Teutonic invasions led the bishops of Rome, as early as the fourth century, to claim independence from the temporal power. In the east, by contrast, the imperial power over the church became more precise. Theodosios I made Christianity the state religion. From that point onwards, the internal history of Byzantium merges with that of Christianity. The Eastern Orthodox Church, which was more conservative that its Roman counterpart, would seek to preserve the tradition of the original Christian church, a tradition expressed in its forms of worship and liturgy. It therefore resisted the theological innovations introduced in Rome. Right up to the twelfth century there would be many political and theological disputes between the two churches, without the unity of the Christian faith being compromised. It was a political crisis – the diversion of the Crusades on to Constantinople and the conquest of that city by the Westerners – that was to make the division irreversible.

Definitive division of Eastern and Western Empires.	Collapse of the Persian Empire.	Arab attack on Constantinople.
395	**628**	**674—8**

330: Constantine inaugurates the new capital, giving it his own name. Constantinople develops on the site of the old Hellenistic town of Byzantium. The fortifications built by the emperors will make Constantinople impregnable for many years. Situated at the junction of many East-West trade routes, Constantinople enjoys enormous economic prosperity; it will be the greatest town in the medieval world (almost 500,000 inhabitants in the 6th century).

337–518: The Empire is threatened by the Huns and the Teutons, whom the emperors divert, by conceding territories and tribute, towards the West. Between 410 and 493, Italy, Gaul, Spain and North Africa are lost. But the oriental territories remain intact.

518–610: The Emperor Justinian (527–65) reconquers North Africa, Sicily, southern Spain and the great Italian cities. But he ruins the Empire and leaves its eastern front exposed. His successors, attacked in the east by the Persians and by the Slavs and the Avars (a Turko-Mongol people) on the Danube, abandon Italy. Byzantine civilization is at its height at this point. Roman law and

2. The central nave of Hagia Sophia, Constantinople, 6th century. Lamps and coat of arms from the Ottoman period.

3. Capital and mosaic from St Vitale, Ravenna, 6th century.

jurisprudence are enshrined in the Justinian Code.

537: Building of Hagia Sophia completed: this domed edifice is a fine example of Byzantine architecture. The mosaics at Ravenna mark the birth of a new figurative style.

610–717: Heraclius (610–41) and his successors have difficulty defending the Empire. The Persians are contained, but the Slavs cross the Danube. The Bulgars set up a powerful kingdom in Thrace. The Arabs conquer Syria, Egypt, Palestine and North Africa. Though halted before Constantinople in 677, they remain a threat.

717–867: The Empire is reduced to Greece and Asia Minor. It is shaken by a deep religious crisis. Outbreak of iconoclasm (or the destruction of images). This is in keeping with oriental sensibility which sees representations of the divinity as a form of idolatry. The emperors, who are natives of Asia Minor, support the movement from inner conviction and also to detach the eastern provinces from Arab influence. They are supported by the higher clergy (the

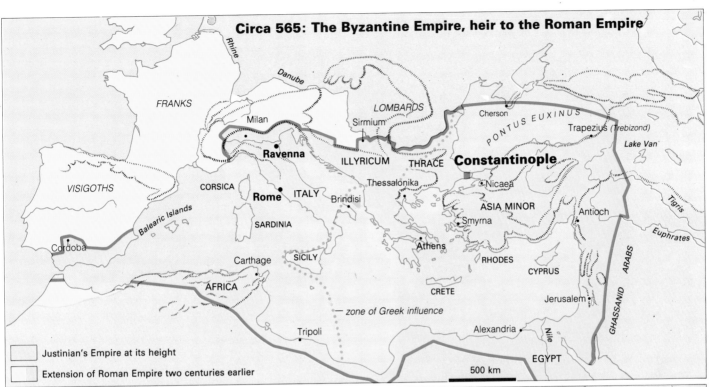

Circa 565: The Byzantine Empire, heir to the Roman Empire

FRANKS

Rhine

Danube

LOMBARDS

Milan

Sirmium

Cherson

PONTUS EUXINUS

Trapezius (Trebizond)

Lake Van

Ravenna

ILLYRICUM

THRACE

Constantinople

VISIGOTHS

CORSICA

Rome ITALY

Thessalonika

Nicaea

ASIA MINOR

Tigris

Brindisi

Antioch

Cordoba

Balearic Islands

SARDINIA

Smyrna

Euphrates

Carthage

SICILY

Athens

RHODES

CYPRUS

GHASSANID ARABS

AFRICA

CRETE

Jerusalem

Tripoli

— *zone of Greek influence*

Alexandria

Nile

EGYPT

500 km

☐ Justinian's Empire at its height

☐ Extension of Roman Empire two centuries earlier

Constantinople

☐ Ancient Byzantium
☐ Town of Constantine and his successors

1 Forum of Constantine
2 Hippodrome and Great Palace

Wall of Theodosios

GOLDEN HORN

Wall of Constantine

AQUEDUCT

Bosphorus

Cistern of Mocios

FORUM BOVI

FORUM TAURI

ACROPOLIS

ST EIRENE

HARBOUR OF ELEUTHERIUS

FORUM OF ARCADIUS

Ancient Wall

HAGIA SOPHIA

SEA OF MARMORA

1000 m

Circa 1050: Byzantine Empire, heir to the Greek world

Singidunum (Belgrade)

Cherson

PONTUS EUXINUS

Trapezius (Trebizond)

Sirmium

ARMENIA

Serdica (Sofia)

THRACE

Constantinople

Ragusa

Bari

BULGARIA

MACEDONIA

Tigris

LONGIBARDIA CALABRIA

Amorium

Edessa

Euphrates

Athens

Seleucia

Antioch

Taormina Syracuse

RHODES

CYPRUS

CRETE

Beginning of the Iconoclastic Controversy.

726

Eastern Church's first break with Rome.

867

Constantinople's second break with Rome.

1054

councils of 730 and 754 forbid the worship of images) but opposed by the monks whose possessions they seek to confiscate. The worship of images is restored in 843.

867–1057: With the descendants of Basil I (867–86) in power, the idea of the family as a source of political legitimacy develops. The 'Macedonian' emperors conquer Syria, Crete and Cyprus. Armenia is subjugated. In the West, Byzantium establishes a foothold in southern Italy. In 1014, Bulgaria has to bow to Byzantine rule. The new economic prosperity is paralleled by a remarkable burgeoning of cultural activity (legislative writings of the emperors, flowering of humanist culture, etc.).

4. *Imperial Quadriga, silk and gold, Constantinople, 8th century.*

5. *Scenes of pastoral and farm life. Illustration from an 11th-century manuscript, Constantinople.*

6. *The baptism of Christ. Mosaic at St Luke's Monastery, Phocis, c. 1050.*

From Arab Conquest to Islamic Empire

THE ARAB CONQUESTS were the direct product of the preaching of Muhammad (Mohammed). In his teachings, monotheistic revelation is accompanied by exaltation of a way of life based on warrior virtues. The Quran (Koran), God's word, says precisely this: the sincere believer is the warrior, the one who accepts exile, and the spoils of war shall be his viaticum. These conquests, which Islam needed if it was to survive beyond its early years, proceeded swiftly. When Muhammad died in 632, western Arabia was under his control. The caliphs who followed him as leaders of the true believers roved far and wide in their campaigns of conquest, sweeping aside the Sassanian kingdom and amputating the Syrian and Egyptian provinces from the Byzantine Empire. The Arab advance, which slowed under 'Ali, quickened again under the Umayyads: in 711 the Berber Tariq ibn Ziyad entered Spain and the following year Hajjaj's troops advanced up the Indus as far as Multan.

This sweep of conquest was blocked by some effective resistance put up by opposing armies and populations, especially by the Berbers and the Byzantines, who sealed off the north of Syria against them. It was also disrupted by internal conflicts: a model of a closed community of equal warriors was set against one based on a spiritual hierarchy. The origin of the various Muslim sects (Kharijites, Shi'ites etc.), these two models constituted, broadly, the two poles between which the Islam of the first centuries oscillated, without really settling on any one solution and without confronting the problems of caliphal power and the status of converts.

The pattern of Arabs stationed in garrisons levying tribute was fast disappearing. At the end of the seventh century some converts joined the army, others entered the administrative service of their conquerors. In the following century conversions were carried out on a much greater scale and increasingly in country areas. The regions under Islamic rule were not so much occupied as administered, and were so in a way that took account of the local cultures, whether Persian, Syrian or Coptic. A nascent system of law aimed at unifying all the conquered lands, whilst the science of geography developed to provide a conceptual grasp of the different regions.

Under the Umayyads (660–750) an empire was built, though it was one in which control of territory by the arts of war was replaced by submission to the divine order. Among its first acts were the choice of ancient Damascus as capital (far from the sanctuary of Mecca) and Arabic as the official language. They also began minting their own coinage and introduced a new division of the provinces along military lines. The garrisons were moved into the towns, where they grew rapidly (at Kufa, Basra, Fustat, Kairouan etc.). What is known as the Abbasid 'Golden Age' (middle of eighth to middle of ninth centuries) was characterized, in spite of the disturbances which occurred at the time, by a gigantic siphoning off of levied goods towards a few metropolises, where mosques, palaces and canals were constructed. In these centres the Greeks were translated. The authority of the caliph was both divine and human in its essence; this meant that he embodied the cohesiveness of the community and guaranteed the application of the law. However, the forces which provided the Islamic state's strength in the provinces were also its undoing: in the ninth century the governors became autonomous and founded local dynasties, first on the margins of the Empire, then later at its centre. The demands of the leaders of the Turkish warriors became more pressing, as did those of the jurists and doctors of the law ('ulama), who sought a share in the heritage of the prophetic mission. From the tenth century on, other caliphates, including the Fatimids in the Eastern Maghreb (909) and the Umayyad caliphate of Cordoba (929) competed with that of the Abbasids.

1. The Great Mosque of Cordoba with its nineteen naves, each with a double layer of vaults. 8th–10th centuries.

Hijra.	Capture of Syria.	'Ali becomes caliph.		Arabs land in Spain.	Defeat at Poitiers.
622	633	656		711	732

622: Flight (Hijra or Hegira) of the prophet Muhammad and his followers from Mecca to Yathrib (Medina): beginning of the Hegiran era.
624: Victory of Muhammad's troops over the Meccans at Badr.
632: Death of Muhammad: Abu Bakr becomes caliph (successor).
634: Beginning of the caliphate of 'Umar.
636: Victory in the Battle of the Yarmuk over the Byzantines; Arab settlement in Syria.
637: Capture of al-Qadasiyah on the Euphrates and sack of the Sassanian capital Ctesiphon.
640: 'Amr ibn al-'As enters Egypt. Fustat founded.
642: Capture and sack of Alexandria; victory at Nehavand which opens up the Iranian plateau.
644–56: Caliphate of 'Uthman: conquest of Khorasan, Kirman and, in the west, of Cyrenaica.
656: Controversial choice of 'Ali, son-in-law of the Prophet, as caliph: civil war.
660: Mu'awiyah, the Umayyad governor of Syria, proclaims himself caliph and takes up residence at Damascus.
661: Assassination of 'Ali.
670: Conquest of Ifriqiya (Eastern Maghreb). Kairouan founded.
680: Death of Mu'awiyah: his son Yazid succeeds him; al-Husayn, second son of 'Ali and Fatima is killed at Karbala.
685–705: Caliphate of Abd al-Malik: supported by the remarkable governor of Iraq, Hajjaj, he creates an Arabized administration and divides the provinces into military districts under Syrian control.
711–14: In the west, Tariq ibn Ziyad enters Spain: conquest of Cordoba and of the Visigothic kingdom of Toledo; in the east, the Indus is reached.
732: The Arabs are defeated by Charles Martel at Poitiers.
744–50: Revolt of Arab settlers and converts in the Khorasan: this will bring the Abbasids (another branch of the Prophet's family) to the office of caliph.
750: Caliph Marwan II is killed. Abu al-Abbas as-Saffah takes over power.
756: Umayyad amirate of Cordoba.
762: Abbasid capital of Baghdad founded.

2. From Byzantium to Islam: façade of the Umayyad mosque, Damascus, 8th century.

777: Beginning of the first regional Islamic dynasty, the Rustamids of central Maghreb.
786–809: Caliphate of the colourful Harun ar-Rashid.
821: Beginning of the Tahirid dynasty in the Khorasan.
833: The caliph al-Ma'mun dies shortly after ordering that those writers who claim the Quran to be 'not of God' be subjected to inquisition; the dispute masks a struggle for the legacy of the Prophet's teaching and for religious power.
836: Foundation of the short-lived capital at Samarra; al-Mu'tasim settles there and surrounds himself with an army of Turkish slaves.

3. 9th-century ceramic dish.

7th–10th centuries

Expansion (622- c.740)

FRANKISH KINGDOMS

Poitiers
732
725

Toledo
Cordoba
Jerez
711
Fez
808

Tahuda
683
Kairouan
670
667

IFRIQIYA

Constantinople
678

BYZANTINE EMPIRE

Rhodes
654
Damascus
Siffin
657
SYRIA
Yarmuk
636

Barca 643
CYRENAICA
Alexandria
Fustat
640
EGYPT
Copts
Nile

Badr
624
Medina
622
Mecca

ARABIA

YEMEN
San'a

Tiflis

Rai
Hamadan
Nehavand
IRAN
Isfahan
KERMAN
Samarra
Baghdad
Karbala
Ctesiphon
Kufa
Basra
al-Qadasiyah
PERSIAN GULF

Nishapur
Herat
KHORASAN
SEISTAN
Zaranj

Merv

Bukhara
712
Samarkand
Oxus
Ghazni
Kabul
Multan
712
Indus

Talas
751
Tashkent
Kashgar

Break-up (760 - c.865)

Bukhara
SAMANIDS
875
Nishapur
TAHIRIDS
821
SAFFARIDS
867
Zaranj
Baghdad
ABBASID KINGDOM IN 875

UMAYYADS
OF CORDOBA
756
Cordoba
Kairouan
AGHLABIDS
800
Fez
Tahart
IDRISIDS
788
RUSTAMIDS
777
TULUNIDS
869
Fustat
(Cairo)

1000 km

Expansion of Islam

⟳ Under the first four caliphs (632-650)

⟳ Under the Umeyyads (656-740)

Break-up of Islam

▨ Abbasid kingdom in 790

▨ Abbasid kingdom in 875

✕ Battles

1000 km

Foundation of Cairo.

969

867: The Saffarid amirs take over power in the province of Seistan.
868: The governor of Egypt, Ahmad ibn Tulun, secedes.
909: Conquest of Ifriqiya by the Fatimids (Ismailian Shi'ites).
928: The Qarmatians (a populist Ismailist movement) occupy Mecca.
929: The Umayyad amir of Cordoba, Abd ar-Rahman III proclaims himself caliph.
945: The Buyid amirs (Shi'ites from the Daylam region) occupy Baghdad; end of the imperial age of Islam.
969: The Fatimids conquer Egypt and found Cairo.
972: Inauguration of the al-Azhar Mosque at Cairo.
996: al-Hakim becomes caliph of Cairo at the age of 11; his (25-year) reign is marked by bizarre deeds and even more by rigorous anti-Coptic policies.

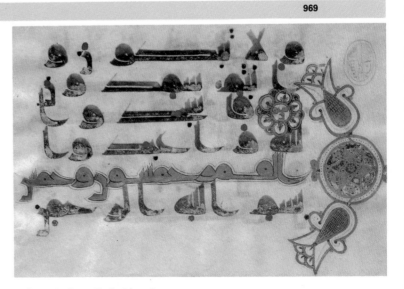

4. Minaret of the Great Mosque of Samarra, Iraq, 850.

5. Page of a Quran, Tunis, 9th century.

The New Western Empire: Charlemagne

BETWEEN THE MIDDLE of the eighth century and the middle of the ninth, the Carolingians proceeded to combine a large part of the West into a single unit once again. Having first struck an alliance with the papacy, Pepin the Short was elected and crowned king of France. He defeated the Lombards and created a separate political state for the Pope: from this point until 1870 the popes were to be both temporal and spiritual potentates. He also expelled the Arabs from Spain in preparation for the reign of his son. Charlemagne made Austrasia, which was richly endowed with abbeys and palaces, the centre of his kingdom. After thirty years of warfare, he brutally subjugated Saxony. He also annexed the kingdom of Lombardy and Bavaria and thwarted the powerful Avars on the Danube. When he had finished building his empire, Charlemagne set about protecting its frontiers by creating 'marches': those of the Slavs in the east beyond the Elbe, those of Slovenia and Friuli in the south-east, in the south that of Spain (after the defeat at Roncesvalles) and in the west that of Brittany. Ruler of a kingdom extending over a million square kilometres, he was crowned emperor by the Pope. The Byzantine Emperor, who found Charlemagne's elevation difficult to accept, held on to Venice, southern Italy and Sicily.

After the fashion of the Byzantine Emperor, Charlemagne considered himself master of the church. He intervened in theological questions and had an impressive palace built for himself at Aix-la-Chapelle (Aachen). In order to govern his empire more effectively, he divided off the kingdoms of Aquitaine and Italy, which he bestowed on his sons. Bavaria became a prefecture, responsibility for which he delegated to his brother-in-law. Lastly, the Austrasian aristocrats who allied with the imperial family were designated counts, bishops and *missi* (agents of the king who travelled about the Empire in his name and submitted their findings to him). In his way of life, Charlemagne remained a Frank. He loved hunting and swimming and had numerous concubines.

His son Louis the Pious was very different in character. During his reign the bishops played a genuine political role: as guarantors of the unity of the Empire, they stood out against the Emperor's sons, who favoured the division of the territory along the lines laid down by Germanic tradition. This tension was to give rise to the wars between Louis and his sons and, after his death (840), to the famous Treaty of Verdun, by which the Empire was divided into three parts in 843 and then into five in 855. Popes Nicholas I and John VIII took advantage of this situation to recapture the authority they had lost. They intervened in the churches of the various kingdoms – and even in the lives of the princes – and sought to recover some influence over the Eastern Church.

Charlemagne and his successors stimulated a religious, intellectual and artistic renaissance. Dozens of monasteries, cathedrals and palaces were built in this period, particularly north of the Loire in France, in Germany and in Italy. Schools and scriptoria were established in the monasteries. Some 8,000 manuscripts from this period are still extant: thanks to them, numerous classical authors have been saved from oblivion.

We should note that the Carolingians did not conquer the whole of Europe. The Celtic and Anglo-Saxon kingdoms remained independent, but maintained good relations with the emperors. The kingdom of Asturias was governed from its capital at Oviedo by the Visigothic kings, who dreamed of recapturing Spain from the Arabs. The Basques of Navarre also retained their independence.

In sum, the Carolingian Empire achieved a successful balancing of the perennially opposed tendencies towards unification and fragmentation.

1. The Eagle of St John. Carolingian ivory, northern Italy, 9th century.

Pope Stephen II at Ponthion.

Alcuin abbot of Saint-Martin-de-Tours.

754

796

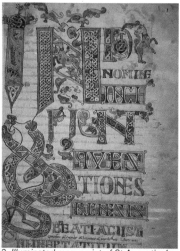

2. Illuminated manuscript of St Augustine's Quaestiones, copied in the 8th century, northern France.

751–68: Reign of Pepin the Short. 754: Stephen II comes to Ponthion to meet Pepin, whilst Emperor Constantine V assembles the iconoclastic Council of Hiereia. Boniface dies a martyr's death at Dokkum in Frisia. In 755, and again in 756, Pepin intervenes against the Lombards and gives the territories won in the battle to the Pope. But the new Lombard king Desiderius refuses to submit.
752–68: Septimania won back from the Arabs and first stages of the subjugation of Aquitaine. Tassilo III, Duke of Bavaria, asserts his independence. The Irish monk Virgil is appointed Bishop of Salzburg. 765: Exchange of ambassadors with Baghdad. 767: Synod of Gentilly with the Byzantine envoys.
768–72: Early years of Charlemagne's reign. 771: Death of his brother Carloman; break with Desiderius. 772: Accession of Pope Adrian I. Beginning of war with the Saxons.
772–8: Policy of expansion. 774: Kingdom of Lombardy annexed. First journey to Rome. 776: Saxons subjugated. 777: Paderborn Assembly, which lays the basis for ecclesiastical organization of the defeated countries. 778: Expedition to Spain.

3. The Ark of the Covenant. Mosaic in the Chapel of St Theodulf's Palace at Germigny-des-Prés (Loiret), early 9th century.

Roncesvalles disaster. Revolt of the Saxon Widukind and Arichis of Benevento.
778–92: The decisive years. 780: Second stay at Rome. 781: Pepin King of Italy. Louis King of Aquitaine. 783–5: War in Saxony. 785: Third stay in Rome. Benevento subjugated. 788: Bavaria annexed. 789: *Admonitio generalis* capitulary. Frisia subjugated. Conquest of Gerona.
792–3: Crises – revolts of Benevento and Saxony, Muslim attacks, famines.
793–814: End of period of conquest.
794: Council of Frankfurt in response to 2nd Council of Nicaea of 787. Conflict with Byzantium over icons. Charlemagne moves to palace at Aix-la-Chapelle. 796: The Avars defeated. 797: Rising in Saxony quelled. 797–801: Spanish march constituted. Capture of Barcelona. 799: Pope Leo III takes refuge at Paderborn. Empress Irene reigns alone in Byzantium. 800: Imperial coronation. The *De villis* capitulary lays down how the royal domains are to be organized. 811: Campaign in Bohemia. 812: Peace between Charles and the Byzantine Emperor. 813: Louis made co-emperor.

8th–9th centuries

The Carolingian Kingdom from Pepin the Short (751) to Charlemagne (814)

DANISH MARCHES
Hamburg
Bremen
Óbotrites
Wiltzes
London
SAXONY Verden
Dorestad Nijmegen Minden
Canterbury FRISIA Xanten Corvey
Boulogne Paderborn
Quentovic St Amand Ghent
St Bertin
St Wandrille AUSTRASIA (AACHEN)
Erfurt Sorbes
Mainz Fulda
Quierzy Attigny Frankfurt
St Denis Lorsch BOHEMIA
MARCH OF BRITTANY NEUSTRIA Reims Metz Wurzburg
Ponthiou ALAMANNIA
Ferriéres Murbach Ratisbon Moravians
Nantes Auxerre Flavigny BAVARIA (Regensburg) Slovaks
Tours Bourges Remiremont Reichenau
Poitiers Luxeuil St Gall Salzburg
AQUITAINE BURGUNDY CARINTHIA PANNONIA
St-Maurice Avars
Lyon MARCH OF FRIULI
Bordeaux LOMBARDY
KINGDOM OF ASTURIAS GASCONY Toulouse SEPTIMANIA Pavia Venice
Roncesvalles Arles Ravenna
Pamplona Ahiane PROVENCE Nice TUSCANY Croats
Saragossa NAVARRE Narbonne PAPAL STATE
EMIRATE SPANISH MARCH Rome DUCHY OF SPOLETO
Barcelona CORSICA Monte Cassino
OF Tarragona Naples
CORDOBA SARDINIA DUCHY OF BENEVENTO APULIA
Valencia CALABRIA
SICILY
Syracuse

200 km

The Treaty of Verdun (843)

CHARLES THE BALD
WEST FRANKISH KINGDOM
LOTHARINGIA (Lothar II)
LOUIS THE GERMAN
EAST FRANKISH KINGDOM
LOTHAR I
BURGUNDY
(Charles the Young)
ITALY (Louis II)

•••••• Division of the kingdom of Lothar I after his death (855)

- ⬭ Carolingian heartland
- ▨ Carolingian kingdom in 751
- ▨ Conquests of Pepin the Short
- ☐ Conquests of Charlemagne
- ☐ Territories paying tribute to Charlemagne
- ⬈ Charlemagne's zone of influence in 814.
- ⊏ Frontiers of the Carolingian Empire at the Treaty of Verdun
- ▨ Byzantine possessions
- ▨ Arab possessions
- ▮ Carolingian palaces
- ◼ Archbishoprics
- ☐ Bishoprics
- ● Monasteries
- ✚ Mints

Building of Saint-Riquier.

Discovery of relics of St James of Compostela.

Oath of Strasbourg.

Treaty of Verdun.

800	839	842	843

814: Death of Charles I.
814–29: Imperial unity maintained by Louis the Pious and his eldest son Lothar. 816–7: St. Benedict of Aniane presides over the Councils of Aachen (Aix-la-Chapelle).

4. The crystal of Lothar II. Gold and quartz, depicting the biblical episode of Susannah and the Elders, 9th century.

5. Copy of the Breviary of Alaric, made in the 9th century, representing the organization of power in the Carolingian Empire: the king, the bishop, the duke and the count.

Ordinato imperii: Lothar becomes co-emperor. 818: Louis the Pious marries Judith of Bavaria. 821: Birth of Charles the Bald. Louis's brother Drogo Bishop of Metz. 824: Embassy of Emperor Michael II to Louis's court. 826: Harald I of Denmark baptized at Ingelheim. Ansgar leaves with him.
829–40: Revolt of the sons against the father. 829: Plan for Empire to be divided in Charles's favour. Revolt of Lothar. 831: New plan for a division. Revolt of Pepin and Louis. 833: Louis the Pious deposed at Soissons. 835: Restoration of Louis. 838: Death of Pepin in Aquitaine. Lothar in Italy. Norman incursions.
840–3: Fighting between the three brothers. 843: The Treaty of Verdun.

6. Charlemagne depicted in a 10th-century manuscript.

The Nordic Peoples

1. Prow of the Oseberg ship, southern Norway, 9th century.

BY THE START OF THE FIFTH CENTURY the Roman legions had left Britain, giving the Celts the opportunity to organize themselves. The Britons now fought against the Picts and the Scots. The Welshman Patrick converted Ireland to Christianity around 430. The Briton chief, Vortigern, called on the Saxons to fight the Picts. The Jutes invaded Kent, the Angles the eastern coasts. Small kingdoms were set up named after those who invaded them. The Christian Celts gathered in Wales, Cornwall and Cumberland, taking no notice of their pagan neighbours. Britons moved into Armorica. At the end of the sixth century Gregory the Great sent the Roman monk, Augustine, to convert the pagans in Kent. Canterbury became the episcopal centre of the new church. The other kingdoms were converted gradually. The Irish founded monasteries in Northumbria

(Lindisfarne, Whitby) and ended up by taking over Roman liturgical customs. Between Christian Britain and the Continent there were important links. The Channel and the North Sea became a sort of 'Nordic Mediterranean'. The ports of Quentovic, Dorestad, London and Hedeby were used by the Frisians. It was through the tradings of these pirates and merchants that coins (sceattas) spread through Northern Europe. The Carolingian *denier* was based on them. The Frisians held out for a long time against conversion. The Anglo-Saxon Willibrord's follower, Boniface, died a martyr at Dokkum.

In the eighth century the Scandinavians began their attacks. The Vikings ('bay men') steered their fast-moving and steady boats, with rectangular sails and ornamental monsters on the prows, towards the river mouths. For a century Danes and Norwegians pillaged the West. Eastern Ireland was occupied, as was the north of England and the islands off Scotland. King Alfred the Great, one of the most remarkable princes of the time, succeeded in stopping the Danes after the Treaty of Wedmore. His successors gradually took over the Danelaw lands. In France, Charles the Simple set up the Normans of Rollon on the Lower Seine (Treaty of Saint-Clair-sur-Epte). The Norwegians colonized Iceland and Greenland, and arrived around the year 1000 in Canada in a land they called 'Vinland'. The Swedes, known by the name 'Varangians', traded with the Baltic countries, Courland and Novgorod, and contributed to the formation of the first state of Kiev. They formed the 'Varangian guard' in Byzantium.

Christianity spread into the Scandinavian countries through Hamburg, and three bishoprics were created in Jutland. Harald Bluetooth was converted around 960, and had the Jelling Stone erected to commemorate the event. The first Christian Norwegian king, Olaf Tryggvason, brought in priests and bishops from Britain. These first steps towards the conversion to Christianity did not prevent the Scandinavians from preserving many aspects of their pagan past.

At the end of the tenth century the Danes, the toughest soldiers in this region, went to conquer England. King Ethelred fled to Rouen and left his kingdom to Svend I (Swein) Forkbeard. Many generations would come and go before his ancestors' plan would finally work out, and all his descendants would play their part. When Svend disappeared, his son Cnut the Great extended his power over southern Sweden and Olaf's Norway. The empire was divided between his sons in the following generation. Edward the Confessor, son of Ethelred II, finally returned to England, and it was William of Normandy who eventually had the honour of conquering England.

Victory of Britons over Picts and Saxons at Verulamium.		Death of St Patrick.	Plague.	Dublin founded.	Sack of Dorestad.	Dunstan Archbishop of Canterb•
429		**460**	**668**	**839**	**863**	**959**

408–600: Period of invasions. 408: The Romans leave Britain. 432: Patrick begins the conversion of Ireland. Great Welsh monasteries set up. 444: Mission of Germain, the Bishop of Auxerre, against the Pelagian heretics. Vortigern in conflict with Ambrosius Aurelianus, the Briton equivalent of King Arthur. Middle of the 5th century: The Anglo-Saxon invasions. Briton victory at Mount Badon. 500: Resumption of invasions. 563: The Irish on the island of Iona. 590: Columban in Gaul. 597: Augustine of Canterbury converts Kent.
600–99: Beginnings of Christianity in England. Ethelbert of Kent dies in 616. Paulinus, the Archbishop of York, baptizes Edwin, King of Northumbria, in 627. c. 630: The tomb at Sutton Hoo. 633–55: Disputes between Mercia and Northumbria. 664: Synod of Whitby. 668: Arrival of Theodore and Hadrian in Canterbury to reorganize the Church after the plague epidemic. 681: Foundation of Jarrow. Coinage struck at Dorestad.
680–754: Conversion of Frisia. 680: Radbod's attacks against the Franks. 690:

3. Helmet from the royal tombs of Sutton Hoo, Great Britain, gold and silver, 7th century.

Willibrord in Frisia. Victory of Pepin II over Herstal. 717: Boniface in Frisia. 733: Charles Martel conquers Frisia. Wera Bishop of Utrecht. 754: Boniface martyred.
757–96: Reign of Offa of Mercia who constructed Offa's Dyke separating England from Wales. 766: Alcuin in control in York. 787: First Viking raids on England. Pillage of Lindisfarne. 795: The Norwegians in Ireland.
802–39: Reign of Egbert of Wessex. Beginning of this kingdom's supremacy. 820: Ansgar at Hedeby. 830: First church at Birka. 839: End of Frisian trade with Jutland.
850–910: Great Scandinavian invasions. 851: They set up winter quarters on the Thames and the Seine. 863: Destruction of Dorestad. 867: Capture of York. 870: *Annus terribilis.* King Edmund martyred by the Danes. 875: Foundation of Reykjavik in Iceland. Victories of Alfred the Great over the Scandinavians. 879: Peace of Wedmore. Military reforms, revival of scholarship. 900: Death of King Alfred.
910–91: Height of the Anglo-Saxon kingdom. 911: Treaty of Saint-Clair-sur-Epte. 921:

Edward the Elder joins with Constantine III, King of the Scots. 924–39: Aethelstan reconquers York. 957–9: Reign of Edgar the Peaceful, King of all England. 966: Baptism of Harald Bluetooth. 980: Colonization of Greenland.
991–1035: More Danish attacks on England. 991: Ethelred the Unready beaten at Maldon. Olaf I Tryggvason beaten by Svend (Swein). 1014: Svend (Swein) King of England. Death of Ethelred in Normandy. 1016–35: Reign of Cnut the Great. 1018: Alliance between England and Denmark. 1028–30: Conquest of Norway. Death of Saint Olaf. Cnut's pilgrimage to Rome. 1042–66: Reign of Edward the Confessor, the last Anglo-Saxon king.

5th–11th centuries

2. Irish Celtic cross, St Columcille's Monastery, Drumcliff (Sligo), 10th century.

William the Bastard Duke of Normandy.

1035

4. Ornament from the Oseberg ship, which served as a tomb for a Viking princess.

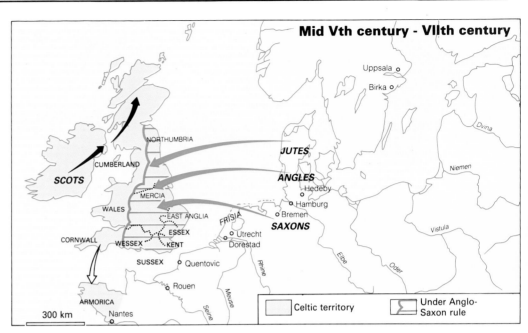

Mid Vth century - VIIth century

- Celtic territory
- Under Anglo-Saxon rule

300 km

VIIIth - IXth century

- Danish conquests
- Norwegian conquests
- Towns occupied by the Danes
- Wedmore dividing line
- Offa's Dyke
- Archbishoprics
- Bishoprics
- Monasteries

300 km

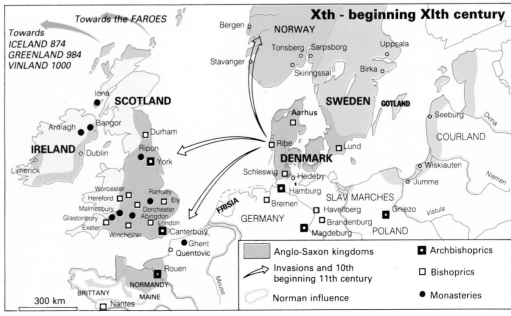

Xth - beginning XIth century

Towards the FAROES
Towards ICELAND 874 GREENLAND 984 VINLAND 1000

- Anglo-Saxon kingdoms
- Invasions and 10th beginning 11th century
- Norman influence
- Archbishoprics
- Bishoprics
- Monasteries

300 km

China from the Six Dynasties to the Sung

Four Centuries of Barbarian invasions
The same fate befalls China as Europe

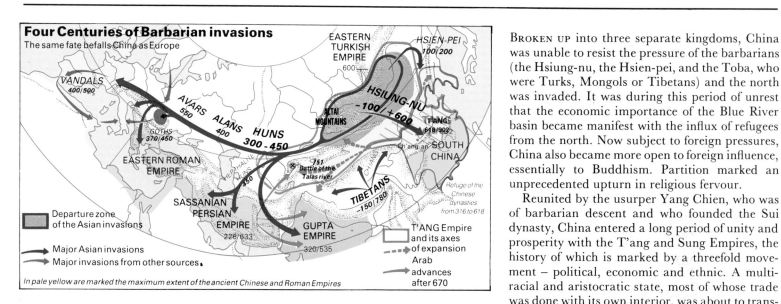

Departure zone of the Asian invasions

→ Major Asian invasions
→ Major invasions from other sources.

In pale yellow are marked the maximum extent of the ancient Chinese and Roman Empires

T'ANG Empire and its axes of expansion
Arab advances after 670

BROKEN UP into three separate kingdoms, China was unable to resist the pressure of the barbarians (the Hsiung-nu, the Hsien-pei, and the Toba, who were Turks, Mongols or Tibetans) and the north was invaded. It was during this period of unrest that the economic importance of the Blue River basin became manifest with the influx of refugees from the north. Now subject to foreign pressures, China also became more open to foreign influence, essentially to Buddhism. Partition marked an unprecedented upturn in religious fervour.

Reunited by the usurper Yang Chien, who was of barbarian descent and who founded the Sui dynasty, China entered a long period of unity and prosperity with the T'ang and Sung Empires, the history of which is marked by a threefold movement – political, economic and ethnic. A multi-racial and aristocratic state, most of whose trade was done with its own interior, was about to transform itself into a trading state, governed by a class of civil functionaries whose view of the world was entirely xenophobic. The dynasty of the T'ang, more in its administrative organization than in the make-up of its ruling class, was the direct heir to the barbarian states. Having at its disposal a strong military tradition as well as vast troops of horses (which were the main tool it used in service of its policy of conquest), the dynasty established control over Eastern and Central Asia from the seventh century. The practice of setting up military colonies had eased the process of conquest, but the victory of the Arabs in the battle of the Talas River put a final stop to expansion. Having gained control of the mainland communication routes, China became very open to foreign penetration. This was the golden age of Buddhist pilgrimages to India. Persian and Arab influence was evident in every field, particularly in religious matters. In addition to the might of their armies, the success of the T'ang rested on the remarkable organization of their system of government. It owed its integrity to the recruitment by special competition of state officials whose influence counterbalanced the

1. Ladies-in-waiting belonging to the Princess Yung T'ai, from the T'ang tombs at Ch'ien Hsion.

China partitioned.

Great Canal built.

220

605

220: Han Empire divided up into the kingdoms of Wei, Wu and Shu-Han.
280–316: Reunification of China (under the Chin dynasty).

3. A celadon jar, from the Chin era, at the end of the 3rd century.

316: Barbarian invasions force the Chin to retreat to the Yangtze.
386: Kingdom of the Toba, or northern Wei, founded.
557: Northern Chou founded.
577: North China unified by the Chou.
581: Sui dynasty founded.
589: China reunited by the Sui dynasty.
618: Generalized uprisings bring the T'ang dynasty to power.
666–8: After Central Asia, it is the turn of Korea and Manchuria to come under Chinese control.
690: Reign of Empress Wu Han, who founded the Chou dynasty.
700: Death of Judge Ti.
751: Imperial armies defeated by the Arabs at the battle of the Talas River.
756–63: Rebellion of An Lush-an. The Emperor flees to Szechwan.
762: The capital, Ch'ang-an, looted by the Uighurs.
763: The Tibetans, after breaking their alliance with the Chinese, sack Ch'ang-an.

4. Pagoda of the Great Wild Goose at Hsian, which was erected in 652.

780: A harvest tax is substituted for the family tax levied in copper coin. The salt tax is instituted.
790: The T'ang lose control of all the territories to the west of western Kansu.
845: Buddhism and foreign religions are proscribed.
860–70: The southern kingdom of Nanchao extends to Vietnam and Szechwan.
879–84: As a result of economic difficulties,

5. A vase from the T'ang era.

3rd–13th centuries

2. Apsaros, the Buddhist spirit, from a silk painting from Tun-Huang in the 9th century.

power of the nobles. The conflict, which was initially latent between the two classes, came to the surface in the great military rebellion of the non-Chinese generals led by An Lu-shan in the middle of the eighth century. The date marked a turning-point in Chinese history. Foreign traditions became highly suspect (Buddhists were persecuted and Muslims massacred), and attempts were made to find the authentic source of tradition in Confucianism. The loss of its stud farms made China very vulnerable to invasion from the nomads, from the Tibetans in the west and before long from the Khitans in the north-east, who took possession of Manchuria and north China and founded, on the Chinese model, the dynasty of the Liao, before falling victim in their turn to another nomadic people, the Jürcheds. These, after driving out the Khitans, their former masters, towards the west, pushed the Sung back to the Yangtze. This retreat accelerated the process of economic redeployment begun two centuries earlier. The building of the Grand Canal by the Sui had turned east-central China into the crossroads for all trade between the north and the south, by linking together the Yangtze basin with that of the Yellow River. The Yangtze, because of its high output, fed the northern region, which was no longer self-sufficient in food. The economic and then political centre of gravity shifted from the north to the south: a technical (printing, compasses, gunpowder), commercial and cultural blossoming ensued.

The development of South China during the Sung era

Crops:
- Rice
- Tea
- Silk worms

Mineral ore:
- Silver
- Lead
- Commercial centres
- Copper
- Bronze
- ● Southern
- ○ Northern

The monk Hsüan-tsang returns from pilgrimage to India.

Introduction of reforms by Wang An-shih.

Death of the neo-Confucian philosopher Chu Hsi.

645   1067   1200

rebellion breaks out under the leadership of Hung Ch'ao. Lo-yang is destroyed, Ch'ang-an is occupied and the head of the rebels is proclaimed emperor.

902–60: The Empire is broken up into ten kingdoms, founded by the commanders of the military regions.

947: Liao Empire founded by the Khitans.

960: The Sung dynasty is founded by Chao K'uang-yin, who adopts K'ai-feng as his capital.

977: Official recruitment competitions are reintroduced.

991–7: Khitan influence is extended.

1004: A peace treaty is signed between the Sung and the Liao according to the terms of which the Sung are to pay a tribute of silks and silver.

1038: The kingdom of Hsi Hsia is founded by the Tanguts.

1044: The Sung conclude a peace treaty with the Hsi Hsia in return for a tribute of silks, silver and tea.

1067–1100: Struggle for influence between conservative forces (led by Sima Kuang) and reformers (led by Wang An-shih).

1126: The Jurcheds, having taken the title of Chin, destroy the kingdom of the Liao and take possession of K'ai-feng, thus reigning over the whole of north China and the Yellow River.

1135: After retreating to the Yangtze, the Sung use Lin-an (the present-day Hangchow) as their capital.

1142: The Sung sign a peace treaty with the Chin after the death of Yo Fei, who advocated the reconquest of the lost territory.

1162: The Sung win a great victory over the Chin at Kai-shi after the Chin had invaded the north of the territory.

1225: The Mongols seize the northern Chin capital (Peking).

1234: The alliance between the Chinese and the Mongols leads to the destruction of the Chin Empire.

1279: The Mongols take over the whole of China. The last Sung emperor commits suicide.

6. Boddhisattva, found in Kuan-yin, from the 11th century.

7. Portrait of the poet Li T'ai-po, by Liang Kai, from around 1200.

Ancient Japan

JAPAN WAS MENTIONED for the first time by Chinese chronicles in the first century of our era. It was a country then divided into a large number of communities already familiar with techniques of metallurgy and paddyfield rice-growing brought in from the continent. In 239, Himiko, a queen of the Yamatai kingdom, sent an embassy to China. But the first real evidence of a political centre in the Kinai plain dates only from the fourth century. Japanese society was then controlled by an aristocracy known to historians by the ornamental tombs or *kofun* which they had built. During the fifth and sixth centuries, Yamato dominance continued, both over Japan and beyond its frontiers. They had acquired a base of operations in the territory of Mimana, and this was maintained until 562, when it was finally destroyed by the Korean kingdom of Silla. During the whole period, Korean cultural influences were of great importance and were instrumental in bringing about the rapid transformation of Japanese society.

Between the end of the sixth century and the beginning of the eighth, Japan passed from protohistory to a high degree of civilization. The Yamato became the centre of a state which followed the Chinese model. Buddhism was introduced around 538 and adopted by the court, although Shinto animism was not rejected. The regent Shotoku Taishi (593–622) decreed a constitution styled on the Confucianist ethic. After the great reform of Taika in 646, the principles of an imperial government were set out. Land reform was instituted which would transform the aristocracy into a bureaucracy paid by the state. Cultivated land was declared state property and there was a census of peasant families, who would now have to undergo periodic redistribution of their land. Finally, at the beginning of the eighth century, the imperial court promulgated administrative and penal codes and had great historical chronicles compiled.

The bureaucratic monarchy of the Codes operated only for a short time, because the families of the court tried to monopolize the remunerated posts. After the capital of Nara had been transferred to Heian (Kyoto) in 794, the Fujiwara clan took more than a century to take full control. By installing their grandsons as emperors, the Fujiwara ministers were able to acquire the role of regent. The system reached its peak around the year 1000 under Michinaga. For several centuries the Heian aristocracy had a cultivated life style, with a host of ceremonies and poetry competitions. The break in official relations with China in 894 is a sign of the extent to which Japanese culture and aesthetics had reached maturity.

From the eighth century onwards the law had made provision that land reclaimers were allowed to maintain possession of their fields. Local officials and monasteries gradually formed estates, the *shoen*, with various tax exemptions and immunities. These were outside the control of central government. To ensure that they kept possession their property, the land-clearing barons kept in favour with those power at court. They became the local managers of the *shoen* of t Heian aristocracy. At the end of the ninth century the empero succeeded in breaking away from the supervision of the Fujiwara a established *Inseid* (rule by the retired emperor). In the east of t country in particular, where the minor officials were taking up arm groups of vassal warriors of independent spirit were formed and the bands began to threaten order in the provinces.

1. *The monk Ganjin in meditation, Nara period.*

PROTOHISTORY.   **ANTIQUITY.**

| 100 | 200 | 300 | 400 | 500 | 600 | 7(|

STATE OF THE YAMATO.

STATE OF THE COD

645

57: A king of the country of Wa (Japan) sends an embassy to the Han.
107: Further embassy.
235–9: Himiko (a Shaman priestess?) reigns over the country of Yamatai (?).
391: The Yamato advance into Korea and take over there, at the expense of the Koguryo and Silla kingdoms. Japan seems to have been unified by the Yamato dynasty, ancestors of the imperial clan.
538: Introduction of Buddhism.
587: Fall of the Mononobe clan and rise of the Soga clan, who seek Chinese-style reform.
604: Proclamation by the regent Shotoku Taishi of the '17-article Constitution'.
607: First official Japanese embassy to the Sui emperors. Construction of the Horyuji near Nara.
630: First embassy to the Tangs.
645–6: Coup d'état against the Soga clan and beginning of the great Taika reform.
701: Promulgation of the Daiho code.
712: Compilation of the *Kojiki – Chronicle of*

Ancient Things.
718: Yoro code.
720: Compilation of the *Nikon Shoki – Chronicle of Japanese History*.

2. *Funerary ornament from the period of the Kofun tombs.*

3. *Pagoda at the Temple of Horyuji, Japan's oldest sanctuary, beginning of the 7th century.*

743: Land reclaimers granted possession rights. First step towards the appearance of private estates.
770: The fall of the monk Dokyo brings abou a decline in the influence of the monks of Nara on the court. Around this time the *Man'yoshu*, a great anthology of poetry, is written.
801: Tamuramaro is appointed shogun to fight against the barbarian peoples of the north, who are still undefeated.
805: The monk Saicho, on his return from China, founds the Tendai sect at Mount Hiei.
806: The monk Kukai founds the Shingon sect at Mount Koya.
858: Fujiwara no Yoshifusa is imperial regent.
901: Dismissal of Sugawara no Michizane the scholar, who opposes the policies of the Fujiwara.
Early 10th century: Publication of a large number of literary works – *The Tale of the Bamboo Cutter, The Tale of Ise, Anthology of Things of Yesterday and Today*.

1st–12th centuries

KINGDOM
OF
KOGURYO

KINGDOM
OF
PAEKCHE

KINGDOM
OF
SILLA

KOREA

MIMANA
(under Japanese
control until 562)

SEA

OF

JAPAN

HOKKAIDO

*Boundaries of regions
controlled by the state*

c. 850

Akita

• 2041

40°

c. 700

c. 600

△ 2105

HONSHU

1268

Chugoku Mountains

1510

1330

1358

YAMATAI ?

• Fukuoka

c. 600

c. 800

KYUSHU

△ 1759

3015

3780

Hida Mountains

2542

Mikuni Mts

2578

Kanto Mountains

2899

Fuji-Yama
3778

△

KANTO
Plain

PACIFIC

OCEAN

Heian (Kyoto)

Mt Hiei △

Lake Biwa

N▫ ▪

Nara

Na ▫ A

Na △ A

△ 1981

SHIKOKU

△ Mt Koya

YAMATO
(YAMATAI?)

*First Warrior
risings
935-941*

35°

130°

100 km

135°

140°

◯ Possible areas of Yamato domination, IIIrd century

▫ Successive Yamato capitals

N. = Nagaoka
Na. = Naniwa
A. = Asuka

MIDDLE AGES.

800	900	1000	1100	1200

PERIOD OF FUJIWARA DOMINANCE. | RULE BY THE RETIRED EMPERORS. | SHOGUNATE OF KAMAKURA.

...ra Period. | 784 | Heian Period. | 1185

4. *The Buddha of the future, sitting
prophesying. Wood from the* Asuka *period, 7th
century.*

935–41: Revolts of Taira no Masakado in the
Kanto and of Fujiwara no Sumitomo in the
Inland Sea.
995–1016: Fujiwara no Michinaga
all-powerful at the court.
c. 1000: *Pillow Book* by Sei Shonagon and
Tale of Genji by Murasaki Shikibu; women's
writing at its height.
1051–87: Violent wars in the northern
provinces for control of these regions by the
warrior clans. Beginning of the rise of the
Minamoto in eastern Japan.
1053: Fujiwara no Yorimichi has the Byodoin
built.
1086: The emperor Shirakawa abdicates and
continues to hold real power at court from his
'retirement' residence.
c. 1120: Stories of *What Is Now Past*.

5. *'The prince playing backgammon', scroll from the* Tale of Genji.

Southeast Asia

Circa 500

Circa 800

Agrarian states
Thalassocracies

Sea routes
Continental routes

Circa 1100

Circa 1400

Areas controlled by the Majapahit

1000 km

THE PROTOHISTORIC SOCIETIES of Southeast Asia, endowed as they were with precious goods, such as spices, gold or camphor, developed in their own indigenous manner, as was the case, for instance, in Burma in the second century BC, when there were already signs of the beginnings of urbanization. In the following centuries, these societies were progressively influenced by the Chinese and, later, Indian civilizations. Chinese influence, which was based on the country's importance as a commercial and technological centre, went hand in hand with a policy of annexation, the effects of which, however, did not extend beyond the Tonkin delta (the present-day North Vietnam). Beyond this line, China contented itself with the increasingly symbolic policy of placing the local leaders in the position of tributaries. On the other hand, Indian influence, outside of any political link, endowed these selfsame local communities with more sophisticated cultural offerings (from religion, writing and art to political expertise) which reinforced their identity. The combination of these two influences created fertile ground for the transformation of the indigenous principalities into kingdoms which, in the main, appeared 'Indianized'. Given this dual heritage, the geopolitical logic of the region was for it to maintain the movement of trade between India and China by the establishment of maritime kingdoms centred on the trading network. The first of these thalassocracies was Funan, which for almost three centuries dominated the shipping lanes from the Malay peninsula to the mouth of the Mekong. By the sixth century, its inability to control Champa, and the region around the Malay straits and the strait of the Sunda, brought about its collapse. In the course of the seventh century, the shift in the central focus of trade to the straits region provided the basis for a more ambitious thalassocracy in the shape of Srivijaya. On its periphery, some communities which were already established in the agricultural basins found that it was possible to follow a different continental and territorial course, as a result of a new idea of royalty and the perfecting of irrigation techniques. This gave rise to a fresh disposition of agrarian land, as is demonstrated by the great religious monuments of the region. The finest example is that of the 'hydraulic city' of Angkor. From the second half of the eighth century, the new policy was already burgeoning on Java, as is shown by the building of Borobudur, although the states centred there still clearly entertained maritime ambitions. At the end of the ninth century, the new approach was developed most of all in Angkor by the Khmers, then in the eleventh century in Pagan by the Burmese ethnic group. The Mongolian surge of the thirteenth century split this regional balance into two competing halves, each of which attempted to accomplish the synthesis between maritime state and agrarian state. On the Indonesian archipelago, the Majapahit Empire was partly successful in this and managed to recentre the maritime trade network on Java. In Indochina, on the other hand, the efforts of the Thais, who were newcomers to the area, were more or less in vain: although they dominated the region territorially, they remained nevertheless largely dependent on Chinese traders for the management of their trading networks. These two attempts at synthesis remained all the more partial because the new peninsular order rested on 'Small Vehicle' (Hinayana) Buddhism, which maintained the divisions between the different kingdoms and bore the seeds of future clashes between the Thais and the Burmese. As for Majapahit, it did not control the markets at the end of the Chinese sea networks and Islam was soon to take over.

First inscriptions in the Khmer language.	Campaigns by Śrivijaya.	Nan chao founded
611	683–6	728

3. Site of the former capital of the kingdom of Pagan, in present-day Burma (9th–13th centuries).

2nd century BC: Earliest archaeological evidence of urbanization can be dated to this century (on the site of Bekthano, in Burma).
1st century BC: Trade grows in the China Sea.
1st century AD: Appearance of the first 'kingdoms' for which there is historical proof.
2nd century: There are beginnings of some political harmonization along the trade routes between the Malay archipelago and the Mekong delta.
Mid-3rd century: The thalassocracy of Funan has links with India and China.
4th–5th centuries: There is significant archaeological and epigraphic evidence of Indianization.
Late 5th century: Funan makes unsuccessful attempts to take control of the kingdom of Champa with Chinese support.
Early 6th century: Funan is at its height.
Second half of 6th century: Funan is dismembered and its regional economic role is taken over by Champa.
Late 6th century: The earliest architectural monuments to be preserved date from this period. The major states are organized, and

2nd century BC–16th century AD

The hydraulic city of Angkor
14th century

ANGKOR THOM ANGKOR WAT

Preah Khan Phnom Bakheng Ta Keo

THE EASTERN BARAY

Bayon

30 m

25 m

4 km

THE WESTERN BARAY

JB

TONLE SAP

Great reservoirs (called baray), held in by high dams, are fed by rivers and rainwater. They provide water for irrigation during the dry season.

1. Frontal of Khmer dancing women in the Bayon of Angkor Thom (late 12th century).

2. The Khmer temple of Angkor Wat (12th century).

Building of Borobudur.	Angkor founded.	First inscriptions in the Burmese language.	Nan chao occupied by the Mongols.	Ayuthia founded.	Khmer court is transferred from Angkor to Phnom Penh.
c. 800	889	1058	1253	1350	1431

there is the development of a local style of art in sculpture and building.

7th century: The Khmers are unsuccessful in their attempt, from a continental base, to take over the pre-eminent role previously filled by Funan.

Late 7th century: The new thalassocracy of Srivijaya is formed.

Second half of 8th century: The Śailendra rulers establish in Java a dominant agrarian state, but one which still harbours maritime ambitions.

822: Nan chao invades the territory of the Pyu, followed by the ethnic Burmese, who take control of the country.

877: Unification of the two Chenla (Land Chenla and Water Chenla) by Indravarman I (the nephew of the first Angkor king), and the building of the first Khmer 'hydraulic city'.

Early 10th century: The Javanese centre of government shifts to the east of the island, which begins to spread its trade network towards eastern Indonesia.

Mid-10th century: Vietnam becomes independent and the Cham withdraw.

Mid-11th century: The Burmese conquer the territory belonging to the Mon and set the seal on the unity of Burma.

Late 12th century: The last 'hydraulic city' is built.

Mid-13th century: The Thais rise up against the authority of the Khmer.

Late 13th century: Independence is restored to the Mon and Pagan is overrun by the Mongol armies (in 1287).

Early 14th century: The rise of the kingdom of Majapahit (on Java) puts an end to Srivijaya.

Mid-14th century: Re-establishment of a Khmer state beyond the influence of the Thais in the lower Mekong valley.

1446: Islam triumphs in Malacca.

1471: Champa is reduced to three principalities.

Early 16th century: Majapahit is no longer a powerful state.

4. Terraces of rice fields on Bali.

5. The Buddhist stupa of Borobudur, in the centre of Java, built around 800.

The Last Barbarian Invasions

1. Panel of an altar frontal made of gold, belonging to Otto II, depicting Christ as judge.

AFTER THE PARTITIONS of 843 and then 855, the former Carolingian Empire was broken up into various separate kingdoms and principalities. Despite the resistance of the church, the Germanic practice of partition at each succession prevailed over the principle of unity. Nonetheless the imperial dignity was safeguarded, at least until the beginning of the tenth century. Pope John VIII crowned Charles the Bald emperor in 875, then, after his death, Charles the Fat, who was

forced by ill-health to abdicate in 887. The various royal titles fell to representatives of the great aristocratic families, such as Arnulf in Germania, Guy of Spoleto then Berenger in Italy, Rudolph I in Burgundy, Boso in Provence, and Eudes (the ancestor of the Capetians) in France. The last Carolingians competed for power with the Capetians until 987. Within these kingdoms themselves, dukes sought to set up independent principalities, as in Germania (Saxony, Swabia, Bavaria, Lorraine and Franconia) or Italy (Friuli, Ivrea and Tuscany) or in France (Aquitaine, Gascony, Burgundy, Normandy, Flanders etc.). Both dukes and counts endeavoured to appropriate for themselves the various regal privileges, like levying indirect taxes, minting coins, building castles, or administering justice.

Fortifications had become all the more essential, since, from the middle of the ninth century, the Vikings had been invading the Western countries, looting rich monasteries and laying siege to cities, notably Paris, first in 845, then again in 885. Princes had to pay a tribute (or *danegeld*), and monks fled, taking their holy relics with them, like those from Noirmoutier who ended up in Tournus. Charles the Simple installed the Normans along the lower Seine and made Rollo count of Rouen, though this did not stop the Normans pushing into Brittany and the Maine area. From Africa and from Spain came waves of Muslim pirates. They looted Rome in 846 and forced Leo IV to surround the Vatican with a defensive wall, which can still be seen today. They destroyed Monte Cassino, captured Bari and settled in Sicily, where they remained for 200 years. The Italian princes and the Pope stopped them in 911 along the Garigliano. In Provence, the Muslims used Fraxinetum (La Garde-Freinet) as a base for their raids. Last, arriving from Asia as the Huns and Avars had done, were the Magyars, who settled in the Danube basin and launched attacks into Lorraine, Burgundy and Italy. Indeed, more than thirty Magyar incursions took place within the first fifty years of the tenth century. Without being as aggressive, the Slavs sought to set up their own states like the Slavic kingdom of Moravia, which was Christianized by the Byzantine monks Cyril and Methodius and then was broken up by the Magyars.

It was not until the middle of the tenth century that the kings counter-attacked. Henry I of Germania, then his son Otto the Great, won convincing victories over the Magyars. In defence against the Slavs, Otto organized buffer territories between the Elbe and the Oder and along the Danube. He brought Christianity to these areas and created bishoprics dependent on the archbishopric of Magdeburg. Bohemia was converted, as well as Poland and Hungary. In the year 1000, Otto III and Pope Sylvester II bestowed a national hierarchy on the two states. The frontiers of Roman Christianity henceforth reached as far as the Vistula and the Danube.

Nicholas I becomes pope.

858

840–55: The Empire is partitioned and invaded. 841: Lothair is defeated at Fontenoy-en-Puisaye by Charles the Bald. 842: Meeting between Charles the Bald and Louis the German to swear the Oath of Strasbourg. 843: Treaty of Verdun sees the Empire partitioned between the three brothers. The Normans reach the Loire Valley. 845: First siege of Paris. 846: The Muslims attack Rome. 850: The Normans overrun Frisia. 855: Lothair I dies, and his kingdom is divided up between Lothair II, who claims the north (Lotharingia), Charles (Burgundy and Provence) and Louis II, who receives Italy and is given the title of Emperor.
855–88: The Carolingians resist invaders. 860: The Muslims reach Campania. The Magyars reach the Dnepr. 866: Robert the Strong, the ancestor of the Capetians, is killed at Brissarthe. In Bulgaria, Boris asks Pope Nicholas I to send him missionaries. 869: Death of Lothair II and of Cyril, who had introduced the Slavonic liturgy. 871: Emperor Louis II and the Byzantines recapture Bari. 875: Pope John VIII bestows the title of emperor on Charles the Bald and calls for his assistance against the Muslims. The monks

The Normans lay siege to Paris.

885

of Noirmoutier arrive in Tournus. 879: Boso becomes king of Provence. 881: Charles III, the Fat, becomes emperor, and restores the unity of the Empire in 884. The Normans are defeated at Saucourt-en-Vimeu. 885: Paris is under siege. 887: Emperor Charles III, the Fat, is deposed.
888–936: Invasions continue, and many principalities are created. 888: Eudes wins a victory over the Normans at Montfaucon. The Muslims establish their base in La Garde-Freinet. 898: Magyar invasions into Italy and Bavaria. The Slavic kingdom of Moravia is destroyed. 911: Treaty of Saint-Clair-sur-Epte. Lorraine is annexed by Charles the Simple. 918: Count William I of Aquitaine, founder of the Abbey at Cluny, dies. 919: Henry I the Fowler, Duke of Saxony, becomes king of Germania. 926: Hugh of Arles becomes king of Italy. 927–35: Herbert of Vermandois pursues his campaign against King Rudolph of Burgundy. Henry I the Fowler recaptures Lorraine and defeats the Magyars at Lechfeld. 932: Alberic II takes control of Rome and the papacy.
936–1000: The kingdoms reassert themselves. Otto I becomes king of Germania. In France the Carolingian

Synod of Ingelheim.

948

3. La Garde-Freinet (Fraxinetum), the site of a Moorish fortress.

Building of Langeais Castle.

992

Restoration takes place. The kingdom of Burgundy is annexed. 942–8: Struggles break out between Duke Hugh the Great and Louis IV d'Outremer ('from overseas'). Otto intervenes on Louis's side. The Synod of Ingelheim is held. 951: Otto I becomes king of Italy. 955: Otto defeats the Magyars and the Slavs at Lechfeld and Recknitz. Pope John XII, the son of Alberic II, crowns Otto emperor. Otto is deposed in 963. The Polish Duke Mieszko is Otto's first vassal, and is baptized in 966. The dioceses suffragan to the archbishopric of Magdeburg are established. 972: Otto II marries the Byzantine princess Theophano and succeeds his father in 973. The Bishopric of Prague is founded. 982: Gerbert of Aurillac is abbot at Bobbio. Otto II is defeated by the Arabs in southern Italy (in 982) and dies a year later. The Slavs revolt. 985: Stephen I of Hungary is baptized and is king from 1000 to 1038. 987: Death of Louis V, the last Carolingian monarch. Hugh Capet accedes to the throne. 996: Otto III, the Emperor, takes up residence in Rome. 999: His master Gerbert is appointed Pope and takes the name of Sylvester II. Otto II undertakes a pilgrimage to Gniezno and Aix-la-Chapelle (Aachen).

2. St. Paul. Ivory of the Ottonian era.

ace Assemblies take place.

94

4. The Judgement of Solomon. A Catalonian manuscript of the Bible from Saint-Pierre de Rodas, c. 1000.

Invasions in the IXth–Xth Century

NORWAY
Bergen
Stavanger
Uppsala
Novgorod
Birka
SCOTLAND
SWEDEN
IRELAND
Dublin
York
DENMARK
PRUSSIA
Hedeby
Gniezno
ANGLO-SAXON KINGDOMS
Magdeburg
Kiev
Canterbury
KINGDOM OF GERMANIA
Slavs
Aix-la-Chapelle (Aachen)
Cracow
Paris
Khazars
Nantes
KINGDOM OF FRANCE
Lechfeld
955
Magyars
968-971
Lyon
Pechenegs
BLACK SEA
KINGDOM OF ASTURIAS
Bordeaux
Valence
Luna
Croats
Serbs
860-968
La Garde-Freinet
890
Pisa
Rome
Bulgars
Constantinople
Barcelona
859
Bari
Lisbon
Valencia
846
Naples
Brindisi
BYZANTINE EMPIRE
Cordoba
Seville
844-859
Cartagena
Palermo
Syracuse
Carthage
827

500 km

	Islamic regions
Arab invasions	Norman invasions
Norman incursions	Advance of the Varangians

Principal Territories in the Xth Century

NORTHUMBRIA
MARCH OF THE BILLUNGS
NORTH MARCH
Weser
Rhine
DUCHY OF SAXONY
MERCIA
WALES
EAST-ANGLIA
MARCH OF MISNIA
Oder
ESSEX
THURINGIA
CORNWALL
WESSEX
KENT
COUNTY OF FLANDERS
DUCHY OF LOWER LORRAINE
DUCHY OF FRANCONIA
Elbe
Corbie
Meuse
Beauvais
Laon
Reims
Danube
BAVARIAN EAST MARCH
DUCHY OF NORMANDY
DUCHY OF BRITTANY
MAINE
Paris
DUCHY OF UPPER LORRAINE
COUNTY OF CHAMPANGE
Langres
DUCHY OF SWABIA
DUCHY OF BAVARIA
MARCH OF STYRIA
Le Mans
Loire
ANJOU
Tours
DUCHY OF BURGUNDY
Saône
COUNTY OF BURGUNDY
MARCH OF CARINTHIA
MARCH OF CARNIOLA
POITOU
MARCH OF VERONA
Lyon
Rhône
KINGDOM OF ITALY
Venice
DUCHY OF AQUITAINE
AUVERGNE
Pavia
Po
EMILIA ROMAGNA
Viviers
COUNTY OF PROVENCE
Agen
COUNTY OF ROUERGUE
Arles
TUSCANY
MARCH OF ANCONA
DUCHY OF GASCONY
MARCH OF GOTHIA
CORSICA
DUCHY OF SPOLETO
KINGDOM OF NAVARRE
ARAGON
COUNTY OF TOULOUSE
COUNTY OF BARCELONA
Rome, Patrimony of St Peter
ASTURIAS
Ebro
UMAYYAD CALIPHATE

200 km

Kingdom of France	Kingdom of Germania
Royal lands in 987	Kingdom of Burgundy-Provence under the protection of the Empire
Ecclesiastical lands	Byzantine Empire

The Innovations of the Dark Ages

1. *Chinese pilgrim monk, carrying scrolls of manuscripts. Painting of the Tun-huang school, 9th century.*

THE PERIOD FROM the fourth to the tenth centuries remains mysterious and uncertain, yet numerous technical innovations were introduced. In China, for instance, it was the age of the first major upsurge in irrigated rice cultivation, of the crucial introduction of the technique of planting out, and of the emergence of tea and sugar cane (as a result of these changes the economic centre of gravity moved south, towards the Yangtze River). Cambodia had considerable success in the use of hydraulics. India adopted the elevating wheel for irrigation, and Ethiopia started growing coffee. In the Islamic world, which shared with China the passion for horses, whole agricultural estates were established, as notably at Tahert (in North Africa). In the West, the forests were slowly being turned into grazing land: the use of ploughs with wheels, and ploughshares with mouldboards and coulters, became systematic. The recourse to scythes, to marling, to the three-field system of crop rotation (itself the most important agricultural innovation of the European Middle Ages), became generalized. The energy of animals was mastered with the domestication of the horse: the use of stirrups, shoeing, 'modern' harnesses with shoulder collars (representing a true technical revolution) spread throughout the ancient world. In addition to the utilization of animal energy, other new energy sources such as water and wind-power began to be harnessed to human activities. The water-mill, which first appeared in the second century BC, became quite common and its many technical applications grew in number. The windmill, which was used in Iran and Afghanistan in the sixth or seventh century, was used in China in the ninth century, during which period gunpowder was also discovered. From the seventh century onwards, Byzantium possessed 'Greek fire' (a mixture of saltpetre and bitumen). The Buyyids of Iraq-Iran, in the tenth century, used burning missiles, while China and Europe at the same period were armed with crossbows with metal springs. By the tenth century Western Europe had perfected the chimney and stained glass. The spread of new materials was spectacular: by the tenth century silk came to be used by the Byzantines and the Arabs, and no longer just by the Chinese and Indians. Paper had been used in China since the sixth century and had reached the Islamic and Byzantine world by the eighth centuries. China had been making proper porcelain since the seventh or eighth century. In the tenth century Western architects began using stone again, while the Pueblo Indians (from what is now the south-west of the United States) did the same. The progress made in the use of metals, iron and steel, was enormous.

The efforts to explore and master space, in these centuries of the nomad, were sometimes sufficient to overcome the long periods of stagnation in trade (conditions improved somewhat between 750 and 900). Particularly worthy of mention are the explorers and travellers of the sixth and seventh centuries (like St Brendan of Ireland, Cosmas from Byzantium, and the Buddhist pilgrims), the Vikings and

6th century: The breeding of silkworms begins in the Byzantine world. John Philiponus, in Alexandria, merges pagan science and Christianity, while Dionysius Exiguus invents the Christian calendar.
c. 540: Chinese book written on methods of cultivation.
After c. 550: Growth of steel-making in China.
From the 6th or 7th centuries: Introduction of the technique of planting out, of new tools, and cranking gear for the raising of water in China.
6th–7th centuries: Writing of *Geoponica*, a Byzantine treatise on working the land. 'Indian' and 'Frankish' swords are used. Chain-mail is introduced. Growth in the use of gold for fine metalwork. This, in turn, spreads across Turkey, Central Africa and America. Almost everywhere the trend is towards 'industrialization', with the standardization and mass production of tools, jewellery and weapons. In India, the decimal system (nine digits and zero) is devised, as is algebra. The golden age of the Mayas is reflected in their dizzying preoccupation with complex calculations. The *Codex Justinianus* is written and Western custom law is codified. The

influence of these was to be long-lasting.
Late 6th–7th centuries: Collapse of Mediterranean trade. Contacts between India and the Mediterranean become looser. The circulation of money in the majority of the developed areas slows down considerably.
After c. 600: In India, the number of trading groups declines, and the number of artisan castes increases. 'Greek fire', a mixture of sulphur and saltpetre, is invented.
Early 8th century: Japanese legal code written down. It was to remain in force till 1868. The T'ang code in China, similarly, remained in force till the 20th century. Sugar cane and tea are grown in China. Paper is made in the Muslim and Byzantine countries. China has its first escapement clock.
c. 710: Liu Chi-shi, the first Chinese theorist of history.
After c. mid-8th century: There are signs of economic recovery in Europe and the Mediterranean, in North Africa and the Sahara region, in India and China.
8th–9th centuries: Invention of the shoulder collar and of horseshoes.
After 800: Chinese xylography (the engraving in relief on wooden slabs) is used for calendars and books as well as pictures.

Szechwan seems to have played a central role in this.
c. 800: Harun ar-Rashid offers Charlemagne a water clock. New writing systems are introduced, including Carolingian minuscule, Greek minuscule and the Japanese syllabary. The Carolingian, Byzantine and Chinese 'Renaissances' take place, leading to the rediscovery of ancient writers.

4. *Horse and harness: a three-coloured pottery figure of the T'ang era, 7th–8th century.*

5. *Remains of the palace built by the Umayya sultan Hisham (724–43) at Rusafa, near Jericho*

6th–10th centuries

arangians (especially in the ninth century), the wonderful map-
makers (from the ninth century onwards), the sea compasses
invented by the Chinese (in the eighth or ninth century) and, in the
same spirit, the introduction of 'flying money' (or paper currency) by
the ninth-century T'ang dynasty, or the use of gold in the Sudan. ...

The struggle to conquer time was equally active during this period.
It gave rise to inventions such as Harun ar-Rashid's water clock and
the Chinese forebear of the mechanical escapement clock. It also
produced the transformation represented by Chinese xylography,
and other new, and quicker, modes of writing. It slowly became
possible to reach back into time, through memory, history and writing. The result was the various rediscoveries of ancient writers,
notably the renaissance of Greek science and philosophy in the
Islamic world, saved by translators to be enriched and passed on later
to the Western world.

The pragmatism of the sixth to tenth centuries, the technical
approach it promoted, was of a piece with its abstract rationalism,
and fostered the establishment of major legal monuments and the
development of the law as a practical discipline, though one dedicated
to generalization and uniformity. Abstract rationalism was also
behind the mathematical computations of the Mayas and the
Indians, whose major achievements were quickly taken up in China
and by the Islamic world. The same combination of pragmatism and
abstraction also lay behind philosophy, behind the desire to master
the world by philosophical concepts. ...

3. Water clock with automatic movement, from a painting in the Book of Knowledge of Mechanical Processes, by Al-Djazani, from the Seljuq copy of 1206.

Traditional architecture of the Pueblo Indians (New Mexico).

A Saxon ploughman directing a team of oxen. Pen drawing from England, 8th century.

800–50: The Indian Philosopher Sankara (780–820) elaborates his monistic idealist system. The Irishman Johannes Scotus Erigena combines rationalism and Platonism, while the Arab philosopher al-Kindi mingles Aristotelianism with Platonism.

832: al-Mamun founds the House of Wisdom in Baghdad. Translations are made from the Greeks. A world atlas is made. There is much traditionalist resistance to the rationalist offensive.

After c. 850: Muslim map-makers are active.

9th century: Invention of gunpowder in China.

10th century: Growth of cotton as a crop and of new farming methods in Mexico. The West goes back to stone building. Chimneys and stained-glass are perfected. The Pueblo Indians construct their buildings (in the south-west of the United States). The Japanese have sabres. The Toltecs show their prowess as workers in fine metal. The metal-spring crossbow is introduced.

c. 960: Chinese treatise on the history of technology is written.

7. 'Greek fire' used to set a tower alight. From a Byzantine manuscript, 10th century.

Europe in the Year 1000

ON THE EVE of the millennium, Europe was experiencing radical changes in all fields. Unprecedented demographic and agricultural growth meant that Europe had developed considerably more than neighbouring regions and, in the course of the resulting drive to expand, it acquired firm territorial outlines which, broadly speaking, remain the same today. The old Holy Roman Empire still constituted Europe's central axis. In theory this comprised Italy and Germany, to which in the eleventh century were added Provence and Burgundy.

1. The Four Horsemen of the Apocalypse. Illumination from an 11th-century manuscript from St Sever in southwest France.

In the year 1000 the emperor Otto III and Pope Sylvester II (Gerber of Aurillac, one of the most learned men of his day) dreamed restoring the Roman Empire', but new geopolitical powers we forming in the West: from 987 Capetian France and, from 1066, th Anglo-Norman kingdom would play an increasingly important pa in events. The changes taking place on the fringes of Europe were n less significant: the Carolingians had already subdued and converte the Saxons to the east. The archbishopric of Magdeburg on the Elb became a base for expeditions against the Slavs. The conversion these peoples, however, was achieved less by means of armed forc than by missionary activity and as a result of the matrimoni alliances of princes whose subjects followed their example in observ ing the new faith. Christianity had already been adopted throughou most of Bohemia in the tenth century. In 973 Duke Boleslas I, wh had recognized the imperial suzerainty, established the see of Prague whose second incumbent, St Adalbert, died a martyr's death i Prussia. Duke Mieszko I of Poland was baptized in 966, and the whol of his kingdom constituted the diocese of Gniezno, which was directl subject to Rome. The Hungarians had settled the land following thei decisive defeat by Otto I at Lechfeld in 955: they were converted t Christianity during the reign of Vaik (997–1038), who was baptize as Stephen and later canonized. The incorporation of all these king doms into Latin Christendom halted the further advance of th Eastern Church, which by this time had established itself in th Russian principality of Kiev, and then in Bulgaria and Serbia. Th schism between the two churches had in actual fact been brewing for long time, fostered as much by mutual linguistic and cultural incom prehension as by divergence of dogma: when it finally came in 105 the frontiers of the two observances were fixed once and for all. Th Christianization of Central Europe also prevented the 'Drang nac Osten' of the German peoples, a barrier breached only by the violen conquest of pagan Prussia by the Teutonic Knights in the thirteent century. Around the year 1000 the Scandinavians had also becom Christian: Denmark under Harald Bluetooth (950–986); Norwa under Olaf Tryggvason (995–1000) and lastly Sweden. Between 100 and 1035 Cnut, King of Denmark, created an empire comprising hi own country, southern Sweden and Norway and extending as far a England. Expansion was equally vigorous in the Mediterranean: th Norman Robert Guiscard conquered Campania, and his brothe Roger, Sicily. Roger II united the whole kingdom of 'greater' Sicily under his control. In Spain the *Reconquista* first opened up the pilgrim route to Santiago de Compostela and in 1085 Toledo was taken. The decisive battle was fought at Las Navas de Tolosa in 1212 and by the mid-thirteenth century only the kingdom of Granada was left in Arab hands: this finally fell to the Christians in 1492.

Vikings settle in Normandy.

Baptism of Mieszko I.

Accession of Holy Roman Emperor Ot

911: The Vikings settle in Normandy under the terms of the Treaty of St-Clair-sur-Epte between Rollo and Charles the Simple. This region forms their base for expeditions against England (1066) and southern Italy.
955: Hungarians defeated by Otto I at Lechfeld (Bavaria). This marks the end of their raids across Europe: they settle the land and adopt Christianity.
966: Baptism of Mieszko I of Poland, who founds a centralized state ruled by 'ducal law'. Creation of the archbishopric of Gniezno.
973: Creation of the see of Prague, but Duke Boleslas I accepts the suzerainty of Emperor Otto I.
985: Baptism of Vaik (St Stephen), founder of the Christian kingdom of Hungary, who is crowned in 1001 in the new metropolitan see of Esztergom. The pagan uprising which follows his death is put down by King Béla I.
996–1002: Reign of Otto III, son of Otto II, and the Byzantine princess Theophano. The Emperor installs his old tutor, Gerbert of Aurillac, in the Holy See as Pope Sylvester II. Both dream of restoring the Roman Empire,

the Senate and the Code of Justinian. The Emperor orders the tomb of Charlemagne at Aix-la-Chapelle to be opened and venerates his relics. He is deeply influenced by the apocalyptic ideas which become widespread as the millennium approaches.
1000: The terrors foretold for this time fail to materialize, but ecclesiastics find in the Book of Revelations the prediction that the Devil, bound in chains since the coming of Christ, would be set free and would reign on earth. Wonders, the appearance of comets or the birth of monsters are interpreted as signs of the impending end of the world.

2. Reliquary of St Foy de Conques, 9th–10th century.

3. Monogram of Hugh Capet, King of France 987–96.

4. Ivory box inscribed with the name Al Mughira, Cordoba, 10th century.

Tenth and eleventh centuries

European expansion after the year 1000

Lübeck

NORMANDY

Lechfeld

Venice

Aigues-Mortes

1000

Reconquista

1492

Tunis

MALTA
1090

Palermo

Messina
Syracuse

1030

Bari

Brindisi

Constantinople

Jerusalem

Damietta

Riga

**Crusade of the
Teutonic Knights
1198-1411**

Kulm
1226

Thorn

The Reconquista   **1000**

Santiago de
Compostela

LEON

N

A COUNTY OF
BARCELONA

CALIPHATE
OF
CORDOBA

Lisbon

Cordoba

C CASTILE
N NAVARRE
A ARAGON

1085

L

N

PORTUGAL

C

A COUNTY OF
(BARCELONA
(= CATALONIA)

Toledo

ALMORAVIDS

1157

L

N

P

C

A

ALMOHADS

1212

N

P

C

A

Valencia
1238

Cordova
1236

Las Navas
de Tolosa
1212

Balearic Islands
1229-1235

GRANADA

→ Crusades not directed
towards the Holy Land

1 ⇒ First Crusade

2 ⇒ Second Crusade

Lands occupied by the
Teutonic Knights

1309   1382   1411

• Cities established by the
Order of Teutonic Knights

Norman Conquests

Death of Cnut the Great.

5. *St Stephen, King of Hungary. Fragment of coronation robe, 1031.*

1018–35: Reign of Cnut the Great, King of
Denmark, which was converted to
Christianity in the 10th century. The bishopric
of Lund rapidly becomes independent of the
see of Hamburg.

1060–91: Norman conquest of Sicily. By 1131
Roger II controls the whole kingdom of Sicily,
including Calabria and Apulia. In 1194 the
kingdom passes to the Hohenstaufens of
Swabia as a result of a marriage alliance.

1066: Norman conquest of England. Duke
William the Bastard had been designated heir
by the last Anglo-Saxon king, Edward the
Confessor. Harold opposes William but is
defeated at Hastings. These events are
illustrated in the Bayeux Tapestry.

1075–1122: Construction of the cathedral of
Santiago de Compostela. The *Reconquista*
makes progress. Toledo is captured from the
Moors in 1085.

6. *Stave church of Hopperstad, Norway, c.
1150.*

The Crusades in the East

WESTERN EXPANSION was not slow to upset the balance of power in the Mediterranean world. In the west there was Latin Christendom; to the north-east the Byzantine Empire; and in the south Islam, stretching from Almohad Spain to the Middle East, which was gradually conquered by the Seljuk Turks, who cut off Christian pilgrims' access to the holy places. Already in the eleventh century the Spanish *Reconquista* had familiarized the French and Burgundian knights who took part in it with the notion of 'Holy War', while at the same time the impulse for religious reform had glorified Christian values: promotion of the 'Peace of God', which sought to limit the violent depredations of the warrior classes within Western society, made it possible for this energy to be turned against the infidel to liberate the Holy Sepulchre. For a society deeply imbued with millenarian ideas, 'taking the cross' meant identifying oneself with the Redeemer and, in the certainty of salvation, going to relive the sufferings of His Passion at their actual scene. The First Crusade was preached by Urban II at Clermont in 1095. Flemish and northern French knights such as Godfrey of Bouillon set out in response to this appeal, preceded by crowds of humbler folk, many of whom perished on the way, victims of the hardships of the journey and the attacks of the Turks. A third contingent under the leadership of Raymond, Count of Toulouse, set out from southern France; they, too, followed the overland route. Jerusalem fell to the crusaders on 15 July 1099, but the crusade also led to the creation of four Latin states in the East: the County of Edessa, the Kingdom of Jerusalem, the Principality of Antioch and the County of Tripoli. Thenceforth the defence of these lands became the prime consideration in the launching of crusades: St Bernard preached the Second Crusade (1147–9) at Vézelay following news of the fall of Edessa, and again in 1189–92 a third expedition set off in response to the loss of Jerusalem. Apart from their disappointing results, these new enterprises were notable for the participation of Western monarchs (Louis VII and Philip Augustus of France, Richard the Lionheart of England, and the German emperors Conrad III, Frederick Barbarossa and finally, in the thirteenth century, Frederick II). In all cases the faster sea-route was used, though this meant that political and commercial agreements had to be reached with the Italian cities, who alone possessed the necessary fleets, with the result that rivalry of interests among the crusaders themselves, considerable as these already were, became ever more pronounced. If the Muslims benefited from this trend, the Byzantines were its first victims: in 1191 Richard the Lionheart took from them Cyprus, which became a Frankish kingdom under the Lusignan family, and, after the capture of Zara in Dalmatia (which the Venetians demanded as compensation), the Fourth Crusade culminated in the crusaders' sack of Constantinople (1204) and the partition of the Byzantine Empire among the Frankish lords, who established the Principality of Morea (Achaea), the Lordship of Athens and the Kingdom of Thessalonika. The attention of the West was thus diverted from the Holy Land: Jerusalem was recovered only temporarily between 1229 and 1244, and it was in the face of public opinion that Louis IX went on crusade to Egypt and the Holy Land (1248–1254). He died on crusade outside Tunis in 1270, fulfilling an anachronistic dream.

1. Crusaders' assault on Antioch. Manuscript of Chronicles of William of Tyre, 12th century.

Urban II preaches the First Crusade.	Crusaders take Jerusalem.	St Bernard preaches the Second Crusade at Vézelay.
1095	1099	1146

2. Ramparts of Caesarea in Palestine, 13th century.

1062–4: Pope Alexander II grants a plenary indulgence – the forgiveness of all sins – to those who fight the Muslims. This encourages the participation of many northern French and Burgundian knights in the *Reconquista*. Toledo is taken in 1085.
1095: Pope Urban II preaches the First Crusade at Clermont.
1096–9: First Crusade – involving knights and separate contingents of simple people led by itinerant preachers such as Peter the Hermit. Many pogroms against the Jews take place in the course of this movement. Jerusalem is taken on 15 July 1099 and the Kingdom of Jerusalem, governed by Godfrey of Bouillon, is created, along with the Principality of Antioch and the Counties of Edessa and Tripoli.
1147–9: Second Crusade, prompted by the loss of Edessa to the Muslims and preached by St Bernard at Vézelay in 1146. Louis VII of France and the emperor Conrad III take part.

3. Cross of a knight who participated in the First Crusade, end of 11th century.

11th–13th centuries

The Latin States in the Middle East

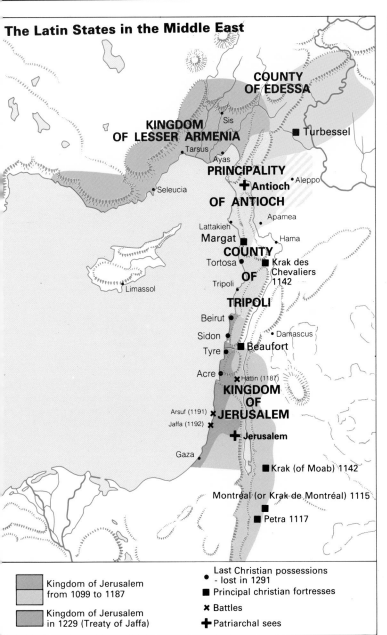

COUNTY OF EDESSA

KINGDOM OF LESSER ARMENIA

Sis

Turbessel

Tarsus

Ayas

PRINCIPALITY

Seleucia

Aleppo

+ Antioch

OF ANTIOCH

Apamea

Lattakieh

Margat

Hama

COUNTY

Tortosa

Krak des Chevaliers 1142

OF

Tripoli

TRIPOLI

Limassol

Beirut

Sidon

Damascus

Tyre

Beaufort

Acre

× Hattin (1187)

KINGDOM

Arsuf (1191) ×

OF

Jaffa (1192) ×

JERUSALEM

+ Jerusalem

Gaza

■ Krak (of Moab) 1142

Montréal (or Krak de Montréal) 1115

■ Petra 1117

Kingdom of Jerusalem from 1099 to 1187
Kingdom of Jerusalem in 1229 (Treaty of Jaffa)

● Last Christian possessions - lost in 1291
■ Principal christian fortresses
× Battles
+ Patriarchal sees

1096-1099
First Crusade

Bruges
Paris
Hugh of Vermandois
Godfrey of Bouillon
Ratisbon
Vézelay
Lyon
Raymond of Toulouse
Toulouse
Constantinople 1097
Nicaea
Bari
Dorylaeum
Edessa
Antioch 1098
Bohemond
Jerusalem 1099

☐ Roman Catholic Church
☐ Greek Orthodox Church
☐ Islam

1147-1149
Second Crusade

Worms
Ratisbon
Vézelay
Louis VII
Constantinople
Damascus
Conrad III
Acre

━━ Overland route
━━ Sea route

1189-1192
Third Crusade

Ratisbon
Frederick Barbarossa
Genoa
Marseille
Pisa
Nish
Constantinople
Amalfi
Adrianople
Lisbon
+
Richard the Lionheart
Philip Augustus
Acre 1191

1202-1204/1217-1221
Fourth and Fifth Crusades

Boniface of Montferrat (4th)
Venice
Zara
Spalato
Constantinople 1204
MOREA
Hungarian Crusade (5th)
Acre 1217
Damietta 1219

1228-1229/1248-1254/1270
Sixth, Seventh and Eighth Crusades

Louis IX
Aigues-Mortes
Frederick II (6th)
Constantinople
Bari
Acre (7th)
Tunis 1270 (8th)
Jerusalem 1229
Damietta

---

din recaptures Jerusalem.

Death of Louis IX outside Tunis.

87

1270

1189–92: Third Crusade, following the recapture of Jerusalem by Salah ed-Din Yusuf (Saladin) in 1187. Emperor Frederick Barbarossa takes the cross but is drowned in Anatolia. Richard the Lionheart and Philip Augustus, King of France, take part.
1202–4: Fourth Crusade, instigated by Pope Innocent III. The demands of the Venetians – who provide the crusaders with sea transport – lead to the capture of the Byzantine town of Zara, then of Constantinople itself (1204). A Latin empire replaces the Byzantine and its capital is established at Nicaea. Frankish nobles carve out fiefs for themselves in Greece.
1208–13: Albigensian Crusade against the Cathar heretics of southern France.
1217–21: Fifth Crusade, originated by Innocent III. The crusaders take Cyprus, Acre and Egypt. Damietta is taken but then lost. This expedition is preceded by the Children's Crusade – in reality composed of young people, the majority of whom die on the journey.
1228–9: Sixth Crusade, organized by Frederick II although he has been

excommunicated. The Emperor negotiates with the Sultan for the right to reoccupy Jerusalem, which is finally lost in 1244.
1248–54: Seventh Crusade, to Egypt. Led by Louis IX: he takes Damietta but is defeated and captured at Mansourah. After he is freed on payment of a ransom, he spends four years in the Holy Land.
1270: Eighth Crusade, to Tunisia, under the leadership of Louis IX, who dies outside Tunis.
1291: Fall of Acre, last bastion of resistance among the Latin kingdoms in the East.

Kiev and the Birth of the Russian State

1. *The Annunciation by Ustiug. Novgorod school, 12th century.*

AT THE END OF THE NINTH CENTURY Russia emerged as a geographical and political unit. But the word Russian, which is often used to refer to its population, is somewhat misleading and the reality is more complex. Slav peoples had occupied the vast area of land spreading from the Baltic to the Black Sea and from the Bug to the Oka. There is clear evidence of settlements along the coastal regions of the Black Sea going back to the fourth century. The Slavs mixed with older populations of Iranian origin (the Scythians and Sarmatians), who, living from agriculture and from animal husbandry, had taken up a sedentary existence and reached a high level of civilization. In the north, settlements followed later. Slav tribes settled in the region around Novgorod and along the upper reaches of the Dniepr River around the seventh century. These were nomadic peoples and made their living as hunters and gatherers. Their mode of life was similar to that of the Finno-Ugric peoples who were their near neighbours to the northeast of the Volga. But these small autonomous groups with their own local leaders remained separate from the Finns and the Balts essentially because of their language, which also laid the foundation for their own unity. Between the eighth and ninth centuries urban centres sprang up along the rivers (which were the only means of communication), the first of these being Novgorod. Very early on, the area around Novgorod was occupied by Scandinavian peoples, no doubt coming from Norway. In the ninth century the arrival of the Vikings added to these peaceful settlements. The rivers criss-crossing Russia gave the Scandinavians more direct access than was possible by sea both to the Arab countries, along the River Volga and the Don, and to Byzantium. Coming down the Lovat from the Dniepr, the Scandinavian warrior traders (Varangians) reached the Black Sea, then Constantinople, where their goods and services were paid for in gold: they brought with them slaves as well as furs, wax and honey levied from the Slavs on their route. The first Russian leaders were drawn from these bands of adventurers. By forming alliances or by force of arms, they subjugated the Slav tribes who lived along the commercial routes, founded cities, and carved out vast properties for themselves. In the tenth century Kiev, which was an ancient city occupying a key position on the 'road from the Varangians to the Greeks', fell into the hands of the Rurikid princes, the first royal line for whom there exists documentary evidence. These princes subjugated Novgorod and put their families in control of neighbouring towns. Very quickly they became integrated into the Slav population. To reach the markets in Constantinople, which they at first attempted to win over by force, the Russian princes concluded treaties of alliance and trade with Byzantium. In order to negotiate successfully with the emperors they had to demonstrate their own unity and organize themselves according to some definite hierarchical order. This is emphasized, after the conversion of the Russians to Christianity, by their ecclesiastical structure. Directly subordinate to the patriarch of

The Russians lay siege to Constantinople.	Oleg becomes prince of Kiev.	Baptism of Prince Vladimir and the Christianization of Russia.	Reign of Jaroslav the Wise.
860	**c. 900**		**988–9** **1019–54**

860: The first date in Russian history according to Byzantine sources. The Russians lay siege to Constantinople. The Patriarch Photius attempts to convert them to Christianity (864–7).

911–71: At the beginning of the 10th century a prince from the line of Rurik, Oleg, settles in Kiev and subjugates Novgorod. In 911 he signs a peace and trade treaty with Byzantium. The alliance is renewed in 955 by his successor, Igor, after a short campaign against Constantinople in 943. These two documents, preserved in the first Kievan Chronicle, almost certainly had Greek originals. Together with a document from the middle of the 10th century, from the hand of Emperor Constantine VII Porphyrogenetus, they are extremely informative about social and political conditions in Russia. After Igor (who died in 945), his son Svyatoslav seeks to consolidate his control over the commercial routes. In the east, he attacks the Khazar kingdom, and threatens the Byzantine lands in Cherson (965–6). In 968 he undertakes an expedition against Bulgaria and attempts to occupy the lower regions of the Danube.

Byzantium counter-attacks. Defeated at Dorostolon, Svyatoslav signs a new peace treaty in 971. In 972 he is killed by the Pechenegs (a nomadic Turkic people established since the beginning of the 10th century on the northern shores of the Black Sea), almost certainly at the instigation of the Byzantines.

972–1015: Vladimir, Svyatoslav's younger son, captures Novgorod in 978, and then Kiev, with the help of Scandinavian mercenaries. Emperor Basil II asks for his assistance to quell a military rebellion; in exchange he receives the hand in marriage of the Emperor's sister Anne. The alliance is preceded by the Prince's conversion to Christianity (989). Though Christianity had begun to penetrate into Russia before this official ceremony, the attempts at the forced conversion of the Russian people, particularly in rural areas, were to meet with strong resistance.

1019–54: Jaroslav takes power in 1019. Under his reign, Kievan Rus enjoys its most successful period. The Prince concludes alliances with several European courts. The

Patriarch of Constantinople bestows the status of metropolis on Kiev. Cathedrals are built, including the cathedrals of St Sophia in Kiev and Novgorod, which are amongst the finest examples of stone architecture. There is intense literary activity. The first Russian chronicles are written.

1054–1110: After Jaroslav, the influence of Kiev collapses. The Kievan princes are no longer able to restrain the internal feuding between the principalities or prevent their break-up. External threats become more serious, both in the west, in Poland, and in the east, where the Cumans had settled permanently in the plains of southern Russia, making trade with Byzantium more difficult. From this period of upheaval date many important literary landmarks: the first versions of Russian law (*Russkaja Pravda*), which ordered social relations according to princely law, and the *'Russian Primary Chronicle'* or *'Tales of Bygone Years'*, the first Russian historical work, which was written around 1110.

3. *The Vladimir Madonna, an icon of the early 12th century from Constantinople.*

9th–12th centuries

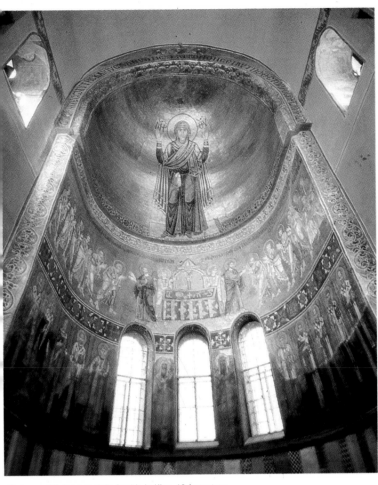

2. Apse of Cathedral of St Sophia in Kiev, 12th century.

Constantinople, Kiev became the metropolitan centre of 'all of Russia'. The political image of Russian unity was sustained by a religious ideal, which was much called upon in times of crisis. The culture of Kievan Rus, which was at its height in the eleventh and twelfth centuries, owed its first literary works and first monuments to the clerics and artists of Byzantium. After the destruction of Kiev by the Mongols in 1240, the Russian principalities of the north were to invoke this cultural and spiritual heritage as a way of consolidating their own hegemonic position.

nastery of the Caves founded in Kiev.	Reign of Vladimir II the Monomakh.
1	1113–25

4. The first occurrence of the name Moscow, in a page from the Ipatiev Chronicle, *1147.*

Popes and Emperors

1. Christ blessing the Emperor Otto II. Byzantine ivory, 10th century.

973. Holy Roman Empire at the death of Otto I

Frontiers of Holy Roman Empire in 973

Expansion of Kingdom of Germany between 912 and 973

Dependent territories of the Empire

Territory under imperial protection

BETWEEN THE RHINE AND THE ELBE, which is to say between the Latin world and the Slavic, the process of disintegration of the Carolingian Empire gave birth to four duchies: Saxony, Franconia, Swabia and Bavaria. This group of territories was soon augmented by the addition of Upper and Lower Lorraine, then in 1033 of Burgundy, giving a western border that ran along the Seine and the Rhône, as established by the Treaty of Verdun of 843. In the east, between the Elbe and the Oder, Bohemia, Austria, Carinthia, Styria, the Marches of Brandenburg, and Upper and Lower Lusatia were progressively conquered and converted to Christianity. Around 1190, the old Empire was then divided up into some seventeen duchies. In the south the Kingdom of Italy and the Mark of Verona also theoretically belonged among this number, though the emperors had repeatedly to return to assert their rights against the claims of local dynasties or towns or the Holy See. The reunification of the Empire, with the German regions as its new focus, was the work of the Saxon dynasty: Otto I, conqueror of the Hungarians at the Lech (955) received the imperial crown from the hands of the Pope at Rome, in exchange for the re-affirmation of papal

Gregory VII's *Dictatus Papae*.	Henry humiliated at Canossa.		Frederick Barbarossa crowned emperor.
1075	1077		1155

962: Otto I crowned emperor at Rome.
962–1002: Ottonian dynasty of Saxon origin.
996–1002: Otto III emperor. With Gerbart of Aurillac, who becomes Pope Sylvester II, he dreams of re-establishing the Roman Empire.
1024–1138: Salian dynasty of Franconian origin.
1075–1122: 'Quarrel over investiture of bishops' between the Pope and the Emperor. In 1075 *Dictatus Papae* (the Pope's instructions) is promulgated by Gregory VII (1073–85), the former Cardinal Hildebrand – central figure in the 'Gregorian Reforms' – whose object is to prevent church appointments being controlled by the laity and who declares the pope's right to depose the emperor. In 1077 the emperor Henry IV is forced to make submission to the Pope at Canossa. In 1122 the two parties come to an agreement in the Concordat of Worms: the Pope reserves the right to the spiritual induction of prelates, the Emperor receives rights of temporal investiture. This accord is ratified by the First Lateran Council in 1123.
1122–1250: 'Struggle between the priesthood and the Empire': revival of the

2. Emperor Otto the Great among the monks. 13th-century illuminated manuscript.

quarrel between the Emperor and the Pope on the more general question of universal sovereignty.
1138–1250: Hohenstaufen dynasty, of Swabian origin.
1155–90: As a descendant of the two rival families, the Guelphs and the Ghibellines, Frederick Barbarossa is chosen as emperor. He proves to be a bitter adversary of Pope Alexander III. Dies during the Third Crusade, drowned in a Cilician river, thus gathering around his name the legend of 'the Emperor of the Last Days', according to which he is waiting on the Kyffhäuser mountains to return to lead the German people.
1177: Peace of Venice between Frederick Barbarossa and the Pope. It allows the Emperor, though weakened, to recover his power very quickly in Italy.
1179: Third Lateran Council, which decides that the Pope will henceforth be elected by a two-thirds majority of the cardinals and takes various measures aimed at bringing about church reform.
1202: Innocent III's *Venerabilem* decretal affirms Pontifical Theocracy, the doctrine of

10th–13th centuries

987. Beginnings of the Capetian monarchy

Royal lands in France

Territory lost by the Holy Roman Empire

Expansion of Poland

995-1035. Empire of Cnut the Great

Danish conquests

Territories temporarily occupied by Poland

---

rights over the Patrimony and over southern Italy, which was held by the Byzantines. The emperor did, however, obtain a right of supervision over the election of the pope and gained control of the German church; for their part, the German prelates took a considerable share in the exercise of and benefits accruing from imperial power. However, the emperor, unlike the French king, for example, possessed no lands of his own; and, most importantly, the elective principle put in question the extent of his power at each succession. The princes, who were mainly ecclesiastics, chose the new emperor from one of the ducal families. The emperors certainly attempted to designate successors during their own lifetimes, thus ensuring a certain dynastic continuity to the Ottonians of Saxony, the Salians of Franconia (1027–1152) and the Swabian Hohenstaufens (1138–1250). But, by contrast with the kingdom of France, for example, the Empire was not in the hands of a single dynasty that might have strengthened it vis-à-vis the papacy. The Pope, undertaking a general reform of the church and Christianity, denied the Emperor his right of intervention in the papal election (*Dictatus papae* of 1075) and his right of ecclesias-

tical investiture. With the emperor Henry IV and Pope Gregory VII the conflict came to a head. In 1122, the Concordat of Worms recognized that the pope alone had control over the spiritual consecration of bishops ('by the ring and staff'), the emperor merely retaining the power of temporal investiture ('by the sceptre'), but the political and ideological question as to which of these powers took precedence over the other was not resolved. In the Peace of Venice (1177), Frederick Barbarossa had to acknowledge that the cardinals were free to elect the pope. Worse still from the emperors' point of view, Innocent III was able, at the beginning of the thirteenth century, to affirm his right to arbitrate between two candidates for the imperial crown (in the decretal *Venerabilem* of 1202) and he also elaborated the theory of the universal power of the pope in juridical terms (pontifical theocracy). Frederick II did not succeed in restoring dignity, or its former power, to the imperial throne, which, shortly after his death in 1250, was to remain vacant for many years (interregnum of 1256–73). The Empire would never recover from this two-century-long confrontation with the papal monarchy.

Innocent III's decretal, *Venerabilem*.

Death of Frederick II.

1202

1250

the universal sovereignty of the Holy See.

1220–50: Frederick II becomes emperor. He is son of Emperor Henry IV and Constance, daughter of Roger II of Sicily, which enables him to become king of Sicily in 1198. He resumes the struggle against the papacy, now represented by Innocent III and Honorius III. In 1229, though excommunicated, he leads the Crusade and negotiates the return of Jerusalem. At Palermo, with his harem and menagerie, he leads the life of an oriental prince. He is a fascinating character who, like Barbarossa before him, is thought of as incarnating the legendary idea of the 'Emperor of the Last Days'.

1250–73: Interregnum. The imperial throne remains vacant, the princes being unable to agree on a candidate. The Empire comes out of the struggles with the papacy very weakened. This is also the end of the Hohenstaufen dynasty.

3. The imperial globe. 12th-century Germanic.

4. Castel del Monte, the castle of Frederick II of Hohenstaufen in Apulia.

Feudal France

As EARLY AS 888–898 the crown of the kingdom of 'Western Francia' passed out of the hands of the Carolingian dynasty to King Eudes. Hugh Capet, one of his descendants, was elected king by the magnates of the realm in 987, and thereafter the crown remained with the Capetians. Thanks in part to their practice of having their eldest sons crowned during the king's own lifetime – a practice observed even by Louis VII – the Capetian succession was remarkably untroubled. Moreover, they excelled in exploiting the concept of sacral kingship, which was glorified by symbolism, ritual and myth such as the legends of the holy oil of consecration borne by the Holy Spirit to Clovis's baptism and the king's purported ability to cure scrofula. The king also made the most of his demesne, which was extremely well placed in the heart of the rich wheat-fields of the Ile-de-France. Powerful barons such as the Dukes of Normandy and Aquitaine, held lands much more extensive than the king's but his symbolic authority offset his comparative lack of effective political power. The Capetians also benefited from their alliance with the church and, in contrast to the German emperors, generally supported the reform movement. Even in the south of France 'royal bishoprics' served as the advance guard of Capetian influence in the kingdom. In the twelfth and

1180-1223: Europe during the reign of Philip Augustus of France

Royal demesne of France

Possessions of the King of England as vassal of the King of France

Expansion of the Holy Roman Empire

Lands occupied by Denmark

Venetian possessions

1. *Philip the Fair receiving a sealed document from a monk. Illumination from the* Livre de Dina et Kalila *(collection of fables), 1313.*

thirteenth centuries the increase in royal authority was evident everywhere. In the east Louis VI forced the Emperor to withdraw from Champagne in 1124. In the west the accession to the English throne of the seigneurial family of the Counts of Anjou, the Plantagenets, had catastrophic consequences for the French king when Henry II married the Duchess Eleanor of Aquitaine and thereby acquired sole control over England, Normandy and all western France with the exception of Brittany. The first hundred years of conflict between these two powers, which were marked by Philip Augustus's noteworthy victory at Bouvines (1214), culminated in the Treaty of Paris in 1259, according to which Louis IX accepted Henry III as his vassal for Guyenne and the county of Ponthieu. In the south the crusade against the Albigensian heretics (1208–1213) enabled the French crown to drive back the Aragonese in Catalonia and to annex the seneschalcies of Nîmes-Beaucaire and Béziers-Carcassonne (Treaty of Paris, 1229), while the county of Toulouse, which had formed the apanage of Alphonse of Poitiers, reverted to the crown at Alphonse's death in 1271. By the mid-thirteenth century the king

Accession of Hugh Capet.

Louis VII repudiates Eleanor of Aquitaine.

987

1152

987–96: Reign of Hugh Capet. Hugh, a descendant of King Eudes, is elected king over Charles of Lorraine, the Carolingian candidate. Archbishop Adalbero of Reims, and Gerbert, master of the schools and future Pope Sylvester II, play a decisive part in this change of dynasty.
996–1031: Reign of Robert the Pious, consecrated during his father's lifetime. His sanctity is praised by Archbishop Adalbero in his *Life of Robert the Pious*, although he is excommunicated by the Pope for marrying his cousin, Bertha of Burgundy, and has to repudiate her.
1031–60: Reign of Henry I, during which the first conflicts arise with the increasingly powerful Duke of Normandy.
1060–1108: Reign of Philip I, who adds the Gâtinais, the French Vexin and Berry to the royal demesne. Once Philip's conflict with the papacy is resolved, the Capetians, in contrast to the German emperors, maintain good relations with the Holy See.
1108–37: Reign of Louis VI, who pacifies the Ile-de-France, subduing in particular the Sire de Coucy. In 1124 he repels an invasion of

3. *Nave of the Abbey of St Denis, 13th century.*

Champagne by the emperor Henry V, ally of the King of England.
1137: The union of the kingdom of Aragon and the county of Barcelona creates a threat to the south of France which is removed only in 1213.
1137–80: Reign of Louis VII. He marries Eleanor, daughter of the Duke of Aquitaine, only to repudiate her in 1152 after the Second Crusade. She marries Henry Plantagenet, who becomes king of England.
1151: Death of Suger, Abbot of St Denis and Louis VI's chief advisor.
1180–1223: Reign of Philip Augustus, who crushes the King of England and his allies at Roche-au-Moine and Bouvines (1214).
1208–13: Albigensian Crusade, led by Simon de Montfort. He defeats and kills Peter II of Aragon at the Battle of Muret in 1213. After Louis VIII's intervention the Treaty of Paris in 1229 leads to the royal annexation of the seneschalcies of Nîmes and Beaucaire. The war against the Cathar heretics continues until the fall of Montségur in 1244.
1223–6: Reign of Louis VIII, who annexes the Poitou region.

4. *Knight on a prancing horse. 13th-century French manuscript.*

1223-1270: Europe during the reigns of Louis VIII and Louis IX of France

- → Conquests of the Teutonic Knights
- Land returned to the King of England by Louis IX in 1259

1270-1328: Europe at the accession of the Valois dynasty

2. Hand of Justice of the kings of France, 12th century.

controlled almost all of a kingdom of some 14 million inhabitants, by far the most populous in the West. Paris was already generally thought of as the political capital and centre of learning. Under Philip Augustus and Louis IX there emerged stable organs of monarchical government and administration which were already highly centralized: the *Parlement* developed from having been an offshoot of the feudal *curia* into the supreme judicial body; bailiffs and seneschals were the king's representatives throughout the country and they submitted annual accounts to the *Chambre des Comptes* (Accounting Chamber). The Grand Ordinance of 1254 set out in detail the administrative organization of the kingdom. Under Philip the Fair the French monarchy emerged strengthened from its conflict with the papacy: the humiliation which Gregory VII had inflicted on the Emperor in 1077 was reversed when in 1303 the King's envoys seized the Pope; the King's lawyers pointed to Roman law to justify royal sovereignty, but the destruction of the Templars (1307–1314) also demonstrated the awesome degree of efficiency which state policing had by then attained.

Battle of Bouvines.	Treaty of Paris between France and England.	Canonization of St Louis.
1214	**1259**	**1297**

1226–70: Reign of Louis IX (his mother, Blanche of Castile, is regent until 1242). The King of England is defeated at Taillebourg and Saintes, but in 1259 (Treaty of Paris) Louis IX restores to him Quercy, Perigord and the Limousin. After Louis's unhappy experiences on the Seventh Crusade, he dies outside Tunis during the Eighth Crusade. His piety, concern for justice and death on crusade lead to his canonization in 1297.

1270–85: Reign of Philip III. At the death of his uncle, Alphonse of Poitiers, in 1271 he incorporates Languedoc into the kingdom of France.

1285–1314: Reign of Philip the Fair. He endows France with an efficient and modern government but clashes with Pope Boniface VIII (1294–1303), who is humiliated by the King's officers in 1303, and destroys the Templars (1307–1314).

5. Statue of St Louis, painted wood, c. 1300.

6. Illumination from The Coronation Ordines of the kings of France, *c. 1250.*

Feudal England

THE ENGLISH MONARCHY in the eleventh and twelfth centuries was essentially the product of conquest. King of England by his victory at Hastings in 1066, William the Conqueror, Duke of Normandy, replaced the Anglo-Saxon monarchy with a political system modelled for the most part on the centralized administration of Normandy. The continental influence dominated every aspect of English society, institutionally as well as linguistically, and French remained the language of the aristocracy until at least the beginning of the thirteenth century. With the lands confiscated from the Anglo-Saxon nobility the King created a substantial personal demesne (amounting to one-seventh of the country) and endowed his companions-in-arms, who became his tenants-in-chief owing him personal allegiance. In 1085 he ordered the compilation of the Domesday Book, an inventory drawn up under oath of his kingdom's estates and wealth. The crown

1066-1087: The Anglo-Norman Kingdom of William the Conqueror

was, however, also obliged to accommodate existing Anglo-Saxon traditions, in particular the right of all free men to sit in session at the local courts of shires and hundreds. The local office of sheriff was preserved, with its judicial and fiscal responsibilities, but these people became the king's personal representatives in the counties and were inspected regularly by itinerant justices. At the level of central government the king legislated for all the realm through the holding of general assizes: at the Assize of Clarendon in 1166 steps were taken to deal with lawlessness in the country, the Grand Assize of 1179 reorganized the administration of justice, and both the Assize of Arms (1181) and the Assize of the Forest (1184) introduced important new measures. From an early date a highly organized system of taxation provided the crown with large revenues, which account for England's military strength relative to the more populous France. In the same period England also acquired permanent and centralized institutions of government: King's Bench became a court of appeal from local tribunals, and the Exchequer audited the sheriffs' accounts. In the thirteenth century the King's Council replaced the feudal *curia*. Eng-

1. Chapter house of Wells Cathedral, 13th century.

Battle of Hastings.

1066

Marriage of Henry II to Eleanor of Aquitaine.

1152

1066: Conquest of England by William, Duke of Normandy and designated heir of the last Anglo-Saxon king, Edward the Confessor. William crushes his rival, Harold, at Hastings.

The Bayeux Tapestry, which depicts these events, is completed shortly afterwards. William reigns from 1066 to 1087.
1085: Commissioning of the *Domesday*

Book, an exhaustive inventory of land-ownership in England after the Conquest.
1087–1100: Reign of William Rufus

3. Harold meeting William. Bayeux Tapestry, 11th century.

4. West front of Salisbury Cathedral, 13th century.

11th–14th centuries

1087-1127: Plantagenet Expansion (House of Anjou)

Lands held of the King of France

Plantagent possessions (Geoffrey of Anjou)

1127-1180: The Angevine Empire

Angevine possessions

Kingdom of England after the conquests of Henry II

Possessions of King of England as vassal of King of France

Lands acquired through marriage

land distinguished herself from France by the early introduction of central governmental institutions. Paradoxically, however, while France later came to be governed by a powerful centralized authority, England's institutional history was one of development towards a limited monarchy. During Henry II's reign the English crown

2. Richard the Lionheart fighting Saladin during the Third Crusade. Luttrell Psalter.

seemed to reach the height of its power: following Henry's marriage to Eleanor of Aquitaine in 1152 the king ruled over all western France with the exception of Brittany. But conflicts with baronial factions (who rebelled in 1173–4), with the Church (culminating in the murder of Thomas Becket, Archbishop of Canterbury, in 1170 – a grave political miscalculation from which the monarchy never quite recovered), the war against Capetian France and the defeats of 1214 finally forced the crown to accept the conditions of Magna Carta in 1215 and the Provisions of Oxford in 1258. Thereafter power would be shared with Parliament, which represented the various communities of the kingdom and whose consent was needed for the raising of any taxation. On this basis the English monarchy recovered a measure of stability during the reign of Edward I (1272–1307), while the conquest of Ireland, the subordination of Wales to the crown and the pressure exerted on Scotland set the seal on its increasingly insular destiny. The outbreak of the Hundred Years' War in 1337 was to upset this balance again.

Magna Carta.

1215

Organization of Parliament.

1294

5. The Sower. Window of Canterbury Cathedral, 13th century.

(William II), son of the Conqueror.
1100–35: Reign of Henry I, brother of William Rufus. 1106: Defeat of Robert Curthose at Tinchebrai. Henry I becomes Duke of Normandy as well as King of England.
1135–54: Reign of Stephen of Blois.
1138: Outbreak of civil war between the supporters of Matilda – whom her father, Henry I, designated as his successor – and Stephen of Blois, grandson of William the Conqueror through his mother.
1154–89: Reign of Henry II, grandson of Henry I through his mother Matilda, and Count of Anjou through his father Geoffrey Plantagenet. By marrying Eleanor, the recently repudiated wife of the King of France, he also rules over all Aquitaine. Conflict between Henry and the French king is henceforth inevitable. But the murder of Thomas Becket, Archbishop of Canterbury, in 1170 turns the church against Henry II. In 1173–4 the barons rebel. Between 1166 and 1184 the King reforms the administration of the kingdom through several important assizes.

1189–99: Reign of Richard the Lionheart, son of Henry II. Between 1189 and 1192 he participates in the Third Crusade, but on the return journey he is captured by Duke

6. 14th-century enamelled casket depicting the murder of Thomas Becket in 1170.

Leopold of Austria and handed over to the German Emperor Henry VI, ally of the King of France. During this period his brother, John Lackland, usurps power in England. Once he is freed, Richard reassembles his troops and makes war on Philip Augustus of France.
1199–1216: Reign of John Lackland. In 1214 he is defeated by the Capetian Philip Augustus at Roche-au-Moine, and his allies (Otto IV of Brunswick and the Counts of Flanders and Boulogne) are crushed at the Battle of Bouvines. His barons take advantage of this to force him to accept the conditions of Magna Carta.
1216–72: Reign of Henry III. He is forced to agree to the Provisions of Oxford (1258) and also to conclude the Treaty of Paris (1259), by whose terms Henry retains Quercy, Perigord and the Limousin as a vassal of Louis IX.
1272–1307: Reign of Edward I. In 1265 he puts down Simon de Montfort, leader of the rebellious barons, and as king conquers Wales (Treaty of Aberconway, 1277), but Scotland holds out against him. The basis of Parliament's organization is settled in 1294.

Monasticism in the West

1. *Episodes from the life of St Dominic by Fra Angelico.*

MONASTICISM, a way of life quite distinct from that of laymen and clerics living in the community, is a characteristic feature of Christianity from the first centuries onwards. Between the eleventh and thirteenth centuries it underwent many changes as it adapted to new conditions in the surrounding economy and society. New religious orders appeared which claimed to reform the Benedictinism that had been prevalent since the sixth century. The diversity of orders is particularly characteristic of the central period of the Middle Ages, reflecting a society marked by an increased division of roles and occupations. By setting up networks of congregations independent of political and linguistic frontiers, the new orders gave the Christian world a systematic structure. The Benedictine order underwent two very important reforms – those of Cluny and Citeaux in 910 and 1098 respectively. Directly dependent on the Holy See, Cluny flourished under its first six abbots, who had total control over more than 1,100 affiliated priories and abbeys, mainly situated in France, Spain and Italy. Other less important congregations appeared at the same time: Hirsau in southern Germany, Gorze in Lorraine. The 'White Monks' of Citeaux, who were also from Burgundy, rapidly spread outwards from that abbey and its four 'daughter-houses' (La Ferté-sur-Grosne, Pontigny, Clairvaux – founded by St Bernard – and Morimond). In 1153 the order had some 350 houses; by 1200 it had 530. The emphasis was on asceticism and humility rather than (as at Cluny) on the liturgy. Alongside traditional monasticism there was a new interest in the reclusive life, and a number of new orders were created: the

Camaldolesi (1002), Vallombrosa (1039) in central Italy and the Carthusians founded by St Bruno in 1084. Combining hermit-like solitude with community life, this latter order had 39 monasteries by 1200 and almost 200 by the end of the Middle Ages. The 'Rule of St Augustine', which married communal life to secular action, inspired the foundation of new congregations of regular canons: in 1120 Norbert of Xanten founded the Premonstratensians, an order which after his death in 1134 had 614 monasteries, particularly in Flanders, northern France and Germany. The same rule was followed by the nursing and military orders such as the Templars (1118–1314), the order of St John's Hospital of Jerusalem (1113) (the origin of the Order of Malta), the Teutonic Knights and the Order of the Brothers of the Sword (these last were the principal agents of German penetration into Prussia). However, the need to work among the laity, particularly in the towns, the urgent need for a more effective fight against the rebirth of heresy, and the promotion of the spiritual value of poverty as a reaction to the growth in the wealth of the monasteries and of the church, led to the creation of mendicant orders at the beginning of the thirteenth century. The Order of Preachers – founded by St Dominic to combat the Cathar heresy – followed the rule of the canons of St Augustine; the Friars Minor, founded by St Francis, set even more store by poverty, which was to be the source of internal rifts within the order throughout the thirteenth century. The less important orders, the Carmelites and the Hermits of St Augustine, completed the 'family' of mendicant orders during this century.

Cluny founded.

Foundation of Citea

910

10

2. *'St Matthew'. Masterpiece of Irish illumination, taken from the* Great Gospel of St Colomba, *Kells, early 9th century.*

910: Foundation of Cluny on land given by the Count of Aquitaine, William the Pious: the Abbot Odon restores the Rule of St Benedict. The order is directly dependent on the Holy See. The abbots Maieul, Odilon and Hugh ensure its prosperity, which lasts until the abbacy of Peter the Venerable (middle of 12th century). But the economy of Cluny – too closely linked to the manorial system – adapts badly to the growth of trade links from which the Cistercians profited.

1002–39: Foundation of two congregations of ascetic monks in Tuscany: the Camaldolese Benedictines set up by Romuald and the congregation of Vallombrosa by John Gualberto.

1059: Foundation of the reformed Benedictine congregation of Hirsau, which rapidly spreads throughout Germany.

1084: Foundation of the Grande-Chartreuse near Grenoble. Each monk has a small cottage and hermit's garden in which to do both mental and manual work; communal services.

3. *Consecration of the high altar of the Abbey of Cluny by Pope Urban II in 1095. Painting taken from the manuscript of the* Chronicle of Cluny.

1098: Foundation of Citeaux by Robert de Molesmes in a deserted region south of Dijon. The legate Hugues de Die approves the austere and contemplative life of the Cistercian monks. The lay brothers, who perform the material tasks, are not subject to that rule. In 1112 Bernard de Fontaines joins the community with a group of young knights. The first 'daughters' of Citeaux are founded in the following three years: La Ferté, Pontigny, Clairvaux run by St Bernard and Morimond. With the general economic boom, the order grows to 530 monasteries at the end of the 12th century.

1110: Foundation of St Victor de Paris (Regular Canons of St Augustine) by William of Champeaux.

1113, 1118: Foundation of the military orders of the Knights Templar and St John of Jerusalem, who were to defend the Latin states in the East.

1117: Death of Robert d'Arbrissel, founder of the double monastery of Fontevrault, where the abbess also has authority over the monks.

Monasticism Xth–XIIIth Centuries

- ● Cluny (910)
- ⋮ Abbeys affiliated to Cluny
- ● Citeaux and its four 'daughters' (1098)
- ⋮ Cistercian Monasteries
- ○ Other orders

Prémontré

Gorze   Hirsau

Clairvaux

Pontigny   Morimond

Fontevrault   **CITEAUX**

La Ferté

CLUNY

La Grande-Chartreuse

Camaldoli

Vallombrosa

500 km

Death of St Bernard.

1153

Foundation of Dominican and Franciscan Orders.

1207–9

1120: Foundation of the Abbey of Prémontré by Norbert of Xanten: these regular Canons who follow the rule of St Augustine, of whom there are a large number in Germany, turn to preaching.

1153: Death of St Bernard.

4. Seal of the Templars.

5. St Benedict receives the Commentary on the Rule of the Order from the hands of the Abbot John. 11th-century manuscript, Monte Cassino.

1198, 1202: Foundation of the German military orders – the Teutonic Knights and the Brothers of the Sword – who subdue Prussia.

1207–12: Foundation of the Order of the Friars Preachers by St Dominic, in Languedoc (1221), to convert the heretics and preach to the laity. He adopts the Rule of St Augustine. In the 13th century he plays an important intellectual role, alongside Albert the Great and Thomas Aquinas.

1209: Foundation of the Minor Friars by St Francis of Assisi. He receives the stigmata of the wounds of Christ in 1224 and dies in 1226. He imposes strict poverty on his friars. But only the Spiritual Franciscans follow this rule to the letter. The Conventuals take over in the order, with St Bonaventura among them, after a very violent struggle.

1243–7: Foundation of the Hermits of St Augustine and resettlement of the Holy Land by the Carmelites: these two orders are linked to the mendicant orders.

6. Teaching monk. Illumination from a Latin vocabulary, Austria, c. 1350.

Religious Dissidence: Jews and Heretics

THE UNITY OF FAITH and of practices of worship is a fundamental principle of medieval Christianity and one that was forcefully reaffirmed from the eleventh century onwards when the rapidly expanding West came up against Islam (first in Spain, then in the Holy Land), Slav and Magyar paganism, and the Greek schism (from 1054 onwards). Within the Christian world attitudes also changed towards the Jews and the church had to confront a new upsurge of heresy. The period – especially from the thirteenth century onwards – is characterized by a hardening of attitudes and the establishment of a system of social exclusion which was also directed against the poor, lepers, prostitutes and homosexuals. The First Crusade was accompanied by numerous pogroms which are attributable to Christian anti-Judaism; there was as yet, however, no anti-Semitism as we know it. The Fourth Lateran Council gave a juridical basis to the exclusion of Jews and imposed on them the wearing of a distinctive mark (a piece of yellow or crimson cloth). At the dawn of the fourteenth century Jews were banished from the kingdom of France.

The birth of popular heresies at the beginning of the eleventh century was in part a product of the church's success, the result of the spread of its teachings and a manifestation of the moral exigencies consequent upon the reform of manners and society which it had itself proposed. The resonances of such movements among the laity were all the greater for the fact that social tensions, caused by the rise in Europe's material prosperity, had produced aspirations towards greater social justice, and the church was by far the richest and most powerful institution in Christendom.

Medieval heresies were various in nature, but they all had in common a desire to return to the letter of the Gospels, to the precept of poverty and the apostolic spirit; they criticized the church's worldly dealings, the clerical monopolization of holiness and particularly of preaching; they wished to strip the Christian religion of the rites and beliefs that had been added to it in the course of history, such as the cults of the Virgin and saints, belief in Purgatory etc. The first seedbeds of heresy appeared in France and northern Italy around the year 1000. At the end of the century the movement first accompanied, then violently overspilled from, the campaign for ecclesiastical reform (Milanese *Paterines*). In the twelfth century heresiarchs sprang up everywhere (Peter of Bruys, Tanchelm). The most important group, the Waldensians, was formed in Lyon in the 1170s; in spite of persecution, it spread rapidly in Italy and even as far as Central Europe. Catharism was not so much a genuine heresy as a wholly different religion, inspired by the Balkan Bogomils and founded on a doctrinal dualism between good and evil, discounting the Fall. It was an awareness of the danger represented by the Cathars that was at the origin of the creation of the Dominican order, the crusade against the Albigensians and the formation of the Inquisition (which was entrusted to the mendicant orders in 1232). Heresies, however,

merely grew in number and intensity at the end of the Middle Ages, even undermining the Franciscan order itself (the *fraticelli*, inspired by the eschatology of Joachim of Flora) and becoming more and more bound up with social demands – or even revolts. Thus the preaching of John Wyclif in England inspired the English Lollards and, more importantly, Jan Hus's teachings lay behind the Hussite rising against the church and the Empire in Bohemia.

1. *Episode from the* Legend of the Profanation of the Host *by Paolo Uccello, 1469.*

Leutard, the heretic, in Champagne.		Organization of the Cathar Church in Languedoc.	Waldo at Lyon.	Albigensian Crusade.
1000		1167	1170	1208

1000: Leutard, the heretic at Vertus (Champagne): first manifestation of popular heresy. In the same period, other seedbeds of heresy at Orleans, Chalons, in Aquitane, Arras and around Milan.

2. *Sarcophagus of a follower of the Bogomil heresy, prevalent in Serbia in the 11th century.*

The Paterines are poor people vigorously critical of the unreformed clergy. A long period of mutual incomprehension and doctrinal divergences ends in schism from the Byzantine Church.

1096–7: Departure of the First Crusade. Anti-Jewish pogroms.
c. 1140: Death of the heretic Peter of Bruys. His disciple, Henry of Lausanne, is denounced by St Bernard.
1146–55: The heretic Arnold of Brescia, a disciple of Abelard, in power at Rome.
1167: Cathar Council of Saint-Felix-de-Camaran; this organizes the Cathar Church of the Languedoc with its bishops and clergy made up of the 'perfected', who are distinct from simple 'believers'. The third Lateran Council pronounces the first condemnation of the Cathars.
1170: Waldo preaches at Lyon: he advocates voluntary poverty and presses the right of lay people to preach. Waldensians condemned in 1184.
1184: Creation of Episcopal Inquisition. In 1232 it is entrusted to friars of the Dominican order. The Inquisition uses the procedure of

3. *Edict of Louis VII banishing relapsed Jews from the kingdom of France, 1145.*

interrogation and also torture to obtain confessions from suspects charged with heresy. The guilty, once reconciled with the church, are condemned to the 'broad' or 'narrow' 'wall' (*murus largus* or *murus strictus*), i.e. life imprisonment. Relapsed heretics are handed over to the secular arm – the temporal powers – and burned at the stake.
1202: Death of the Calabrian Cistercian, Joachim of Flora. His conception of universal history being divided into three ages – those of the Father (Old Testament), the Son (incarnation in the present age) and the Holy Spirit (yet to come) – led him to predict the imminent disappearance of the church and the coming of a reign of saints and monks; this millenarianism inspired the Spiritual Franciscans (fraticelli) who will later be accused of heresy.
1207: Preaching of St Dominic in Languedoc. At Fanjeaux he founds a community of converted female heretics.
1208–13: Crusade against the Albigensians, led by Simon de Montfort. This prepares the ground for the King of France to intervene in

11th–15th centuries

Religious differences and dissidence

- ◉ Movements of heretics
- XIth century and first half of XIIth
- Second half of XIIth century
- XIIIth, XIVth and XVth centuries

THE CHRISTIAN WORLD IN THE THIRTEENTH CENTURY

Oxford
Lollard movement inspired by John Wyclif

Arras

Vertus

Orléans

Dijon

LIMOUSIN birthplace of the first Cathar movement

BOHEMIA
Prague ◉
Hussite rising

Lyon
Waldensian movement. Poor of Lyon

Area of high concentration of Waldensians

Monteforte
Cathars

Bogomils

Constantinople ○

BYZANTINE

Cathar Council of St Felix-de-C.

Cathars
Toulouse
Foix
Montégur
Albi
Narbonne
Carcassonne
Béziers

Arnold of Brescia

EMPIRE

Madrid ○

Rome ◉
Lateran Council

Athens ○

Boundaries of Islam

500 km

Jan Hus executed at Constance.

1415

4. Chateau de Peyrepertuse in the Aude (France), a Cathar bastion besieged during the Albigensian Crusade.

5. Inquisition scene: the exhibition of condemned heretics. Detail from a painting by Pedro Berruguete.

the south. The last outpost of Cathar resistance, the Château of Montségur, falls in 1244.
1215: Fourth Lateran Council. Canon 21, *Omnis utrusque sexus*, obliges all Christians to make confession once a year – a measure which some see as directed at identifying heretics – and forces Jews to wear a piece of yellow or crimson cloth as a distinguishing mark.
1240: Dispute over the Talmud between clergy and rabbis at the court of the King of France. The copies of the Talmud are burnt.
1306: Jews expelled from the kingdom of France.
1377–82: Lollard movement in England.
1415: Council of Constance posthumously condemns John Wyclif for heresy. Execution of Jan Hus, a Bohemian reformer who was in fact less radical than Wyclif. In Bohemia, after the moderate Hussites or Calixtines – who demanded the communion in both kinds – returned to the fold, the radical Hussites or 'Taborites' are crushed at the Battle of Lipary (1434).

6. Death of Jan Hus at the stake in 1415. From Diebold Schilling's Spiezer bilder-chronik, 1485.

Decline and Fall of Byzantium

1. *Mistra (Peloponnese), showing the Church of the Hodegetria, 14th century.*

THE BYZANTINE EMPIRE reached its zenith between the ninth and eleventh centuries. By that point it had consolidated its territorial possessions and enjoyed great economic prosperity. The renewed circulation of gold in the Mediterranean in the period following the Arab conquest made the Empire for a while the great beneficiary of East-West trade. However, this wealth, which took on mythic proportions in Western accounts, provoked on the one hand the greed of the Normans and on the other the rivalry of the Italian republics, who as a result sought direct trading access to the Levant. The Western drive to go in search of the wealth of the Orient is at the origin of the crusades; it was the principal cause of the ruin of the Empire and its incapacity to defend itself against the Turks. Internal factors also contributed to this decline. The end of the Macedonian dynasty (1057) opened up a power vacuum which was only filled by the

coming to power of provincial military families, whose fortune was based on the ownership of great estates. In the course of the eleventh and twelfth centuries the emperors distributed territories, privileges and tax exemptions to their own families and to those military families to which they were allied. The division of the land into small estates on which the fiscal assessment was based began to disappear and large sectors of land fell outside of the control of the central administration. Independent governments were formed even before the Empire was divided up by the Latins. The state's monopoly on the sale and production of luxury goods and the aristocratic tendencies of Byzantine society did not help to promote the development of a class of merchants capable of competing with the Italian republics. Byzantine trade was a passive trade. The customs concessions granted to Venice, then later to Pisa and Genoa, in exchange for aid against the

2. *'The Sufferings of Job'. Byzantine manuscript, 1362.*

Normans and Turks, and the monopoly granted to Venice in the eastern Mediterranean after the Fourth Crusade, deprived the Empire of all its revenue. The sack of Constantinople by the crusaders in 1204 took from it its last remaining wealth and precipitated its dislocation. A Latin emperor was crowned at Constantinople, whilst the Frankish lords divided up the western regions of the Empire between them, founding principalities of a feudal type. In the second half of the thirteenth century the Greek emperors succeeded in reconquering the capital, but the emperors of the Paleologus dynasty

The Normans take Bari; Seljuq Turks win a victory at Manzikert.   **Capture of Constantinople by the crusaders.**   **Michael VIII Paleologus signs the Treaty of Nymphaeum with Geno**

1071	1204	13 March 1261

1057–81: The Empire is attacked on all sides. In the west the Normans settle in Byzantine Italy. In the Balkans the Petchenegs (Turkish tribes) take control of Macedonia and Thrace. In the east the Seljuq Turks (so named after their first chief, Seljuq) penetrate into Asia Minor, inflicting defeat on Byzantium at the Battle of Manzikert (1071). They establish the Sultanate of Iconium.
1081–1185: The Comneni dynasty provides a period of internal stability, but external attacks continue. In the Balkans the Petchenegs are repulsed in 1091, but the Hungarians and Serbs pose a new threat. In Asia Minor the Seljuq Turks consolidate their position and win the decisive victory of Myriokephalon in 1176. In the west the Normans occupy Dyrrachium (Durazzo) and threaten Constantinople (1081). To combat them, Alexis Comnenus calls on aid from Venice and accords that republic a monopoly on trade throughout the Empire (1082). The mistrust between Greeks and Latins (Westerners of Roman Catholic obedience) leads to the massacre of the Latin population of Constantinople (1182).

4. *Carpenter at work. Mosaic of St Mary of Otranto, 12th century, southern Italy.*

1185–1204: The failure of the first crusades has in the West been unjustly attributed to the treachery of the Greeks. The Fourth Crusade is openly directed against Byzantium by Venice. In 1204 Constantinople, overrun by the crusaders, is looted and pillaged. Baldwin, Count of Flanders, is crowned at Hagia Sophia. He appoints a Venetian patriarch. Venice takes over Byzantium's ports and most of its islands.
1204–1261: The Greek emperor Theodore Laskaris founds the Empire of Nicaea in the west of Asia Minor. His successors recapture territory in Thrace, Macedonia and Epirus. In 1261 the Latin Empire of Constantinople collapses.
1261–82: The Empire is reduced to the territory of the Empire of Nicaea, Thrace and a part of Macedonia. Serbs, Bulgars and Turks threaten its frontiers. Michael VII Paleologus turns to the West and achieves some diplomatic successes. To thwart Charles of Anjou, who has designs on the Empire, he accepts papal supremacy over the Eastern Church at the Second Council of Lyon in 1274. This decision is met with strong

5. *The wedding at Canaa. Mosaic in the Monastery Church of Chora, 13th century.*

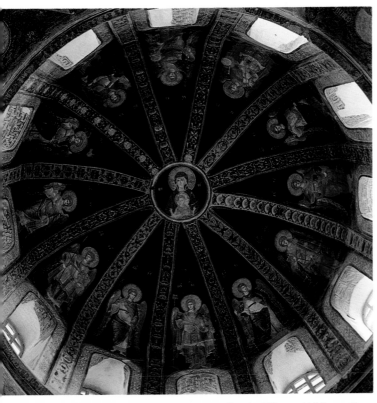

3. *The Virgin and the Apostles. Dome of the Monastery Church of Chora, which is now the Kariye Mosque, Constantinople, early 14th century.*

(1261–1453) were unable to prevent the disintegration of the Empire, nor to restore the economic situation. Under threat from their Slav neighbours and, more importantly, from the advancing Turks, they appealed in vain to the West. Their attempts at *rapprochement* with Rome, which were viewed very unfavourably by a population hostile to the Latins, only exacerbated tensions within the Empire, and the aid they requested did not materialize. The political decline of Byzantium was accompanied, paradoxically, by a remarkable flowering of culture. Great artistic centres emerged in the provinces at Mistra (in the Peloponnese) and at Mount Athos. Byzantine painting exercised a profound influence upon the Greek Orthodox Slav countries. There was also a brilliant renaissance of philosophical and theological speculation, and we are indebted to the Byzantine humanists who took refuge in the West after the Turkish conquest for our knowledge of many of the great authors of classical antiquity.

ncil of Lyons.   **Reunion of Eastern and Western Churches at Council of Florence.**

74   1438–9

religious opposition in Byzantium, which leads eventually to schism.
1282–1453: The greatest danger now comes from a new Turkish tribe, the Osmanlis or Ottomans (so called after their chief, Uthman), who carved out for themselves a state in Asia Minor (at the expense of the Seljuqs), then continue their advance into Byzantine territories. By 1341 they have become masters of Asia Minor and enter Europe. Between 1363 and 1389 they conquer Thrace, Macedonia, Serbia and Bulgaria. In 1444 they defeat the Hungarians at Varna and become masters of the Balkans. Constantinople, defended only by its own troops, is taken on 29 May 1453. Sultan Mehmed II goes on to take Morea and Trebizond (1460, 1461), after which nothing remains of the old Empire.

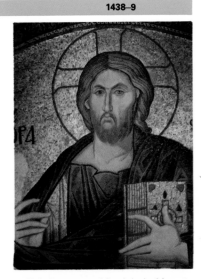

6. *Christ Pantocrator. Mosaic in the Monastery Church of Chora, early 14th century.*

1080-1204

Venice
Genoa
PETCHENGS
Danube
PONTUS EUXINUS
Adrianople
Dyrrachium
Thessalonika
Constantinople
Trebizond
NORMANS
Myriokephalon
Manzikert
SELJUQ TURKS
Athens
Antioch
MEDITERRANEAN SEA
Euphrates

☐ Last great Byzantine Empire, c.1180
✕ Byzantine defeats in Asia Minor
Trade routes
→ Venetian
→ Genoese
.... Itinerary of first Crusades
●●●●►► 4th Crusade (1202-04)

1204-1261

Venice
Danube
Zara
Ragusa
KINGDOM OF BULGARIA
LATIN EMPIRE
Constantinople
EMPIRE OF TREBIZOND
KINGDOM OF SICILY
Durazzo
DESPOTATE OF EPIRUS
NEGROPONTE
EMPIRE OF NICAEA
Nicaea
Smyrna
SULTANATE OF ICONIUM
KINGDOM OF LESSER ARMENIA
Antioch
CRETE
RHODES
KINGDOM OF CYPRUS
Euphrates

☐ Greek States (Byzantine)
☐ Latin Empire of Constantinople   ☐ Venetian possessions
☐ Other Latin States in the East

400 km

1261-1460

Venice
Genoa
Danube
MONGOL EMPIRE
KINGDOM OF BULGARIA
Constantinople
1453
EMPIRE OF TREBIZOND
KINGDOM OF NAPLES
KINGDOM OF SICILY
OTTOMAN EMPIRE
Smyrna
OTTOMANS
Euphrates
RHODES (Order of St John of Jerusalem)

☐ Byzantine Empire around 1340   ☐ The Ottomans around 1360
☐ What remained of it in 1450   ☐ Their expansion around 1450
☐ Latin States   ● Genoese trading posts
                                     → Genoese trade routes

Islam's New Edifice Breached

AT THE END of the tenth century the Islamic world had lost its imperialist designs. They had been laid to rest by forces to which it had itself given rise. Local administrations became more powerful, wealth was distributed on a more regional basis and institutional life and legal matters were structured by the diffuse group of *'ulama* (doctors of the law). The Empire, which had been founded on war, could not survive Islamization and the adherence of the majority to Islamic law. In the period of change which followed, religious values (based in theory either on a community of equal believers or a spiritual hierarchy) became mere rationalizations of other interests: the Almoravids (Sanhaja Berbers, 1056) from the outer Maghreb saw themselves as a community of warriors for the faith and stood out against the Fatimids – with their 'inspired' caliph – who were installed in Cairo. Whilst the latter imposed their foreign rule over a non-Shi'ite population, the Almoravids were striving to extirpate Kharijitism from the Maghreb. In the east, the Seljuq Turks moved over a few years from Transoxiana to Iraq, passing through Aleppo (Haleb) as they went and forcing the Byzantines back to a narrow coastal strip of land. With the support of an Islamic Iranian aristocracy, they established solid administration everywhere and defended strict observance of tradition (*sunna*), though they in fact used their power to subordinate the caliph to their own authority. Also in the eleventh century, the Islamic world discovered the Christian West. Trading links began cautiously, with southern Italy and the Normans in Sicily. But the arrival of the crusaders (First Crusade, 1095) came as a shock. The Latin states created by the knights were isolated entities with few settlers. They paid little heed to the Eastern Christians who spoke Arabic and who saw themselves as belonging to the Muslim world come what may. They were also unable to turn to

advantage the commercial routes which were developing between the Italian towns on the one hand (Pisa, Venice and later Genoa) and Egypt and Syria on the other. In response to the interest shown in Islamic philosophy and science in cultured Western circles, Muslim scholars travelled to Sicily and Spain.

One man, Salah ad-Din Yusuf ibn-Ayyub (Saladin), destroyed the Fatimid caliphate (1171) and through a holy war against the infidel brought about unity in the Near East and dealt a lethal blow to hopes of a Latin Orient (Battle of Hittin, 1187). His real achievement was to turn Islam into a system in which the power exercised by the strong man – the amir or sultan (usually not an Arab) – was recognized and ratified by a caliph whose only power was that accorded him by the political authority. The sack of Baghdad by the pagan Mongols of Hülegü (1258) and the seizure of power by the Cairo Mamluks

2. Aristotle and his followers. 13th-century Seljuq manuscript by the Arab author Al-Mubassir.

(emancipated slaves) in Egypt (1250) came as a confirmation of that development.

Eastern Islam now became centred on Egypt, where the Mamluks (1250–1517), though welcoming a powerless caliph to Cairo, imposed a strictly military regime, which in the time of the Circassians was not dynastic. It was an efficient system which provided protection against the Mongols: however, a long series of epidemics (from 1348 onwards) and the decline of certain internal commercial routes weakened a country whose economic exchanges with the northern coast of the Mediterranean were becoming increasingly unequal.

1. The citadel of Haleb (Aleppo).

Conquest of the Punjab.	The Seljuq Turks at Baghdad.	El Cid captures Valencia.	Saladin takes power in Egypt.	Capture of Jerusalem.
1001	1055	1094	1171	1187

1001: Muslim troops penetrate into the Punjab.
1009: Destruction of the Holy Sepulchre by order of al-Hakim; this will later be taken as a pretext for the Crusades.
1031: Quarrels over succession lead to the demise of the Spanish caliphate.
1036: The Almoravids leave the western Sudan and march on the Maghreb.
1038: The Seljuq amirs take Nishapur (in Khorasan).
1052: The Banu Hilal tribe are sent by the Fatimids to ravage Ifriqiya.
1055: The Seljuqs at Baghdad; the caliph al-Qa'im confers the title of sultan on Toghril Beg. Despite their dislike of the settled life and the fact that there are younger independent dynasties, the Seljuqs are to dominate the Middle East for more than two centuries (1038–1194), during which they will impose an occasionally hectoring religious guardianship on the caliph.
1085: Alfonso VI of Castile recaptures Toledo.
1091: Normans take Sicily.
1094: El Cid (El Campeador) takes Valencia.

1095–9: First Crusade and capture of Jerusalem. Four states created: Kingdom of Jerusalem, County of Edessa, Principality of Antioch, County of Tripoli.
1130: The Almohads take the eastern Maghreb, then Spain and the rest of the Maghreb: Abd al-Mu'min, a disciple of the founder Ibn Tumart, becomes caliph.
1147–9: Second Crusade.
1169: Shirkuh, a Kurd, the new vizier of the Fatimid caliphate, dies and is succeeded by his nephew Saladin.
1171: Saladin overthrows the Shi'ite caliph and returns Egypt to Sunni orthodoxy and the rule of the caliph.
1187: Saladin defeats the Crusaders at Hattin and retakes Jerusalem.
1191: Capture of Acre by the Third Crusade: Richard I ('the Lionheart') occupies the Byzantine island of Cyprus.
1228: Hafsids in Ifriqiya (until 1574); this puts a definitive end to the unity of the Maghreb.
1235: Abd al-Wadid dynasty in Tlemcen (until 1557).
1236: The Castilians recapture Cordoba.
1248: Recapture of Seville.

1250: The Cairo Mamluks take over Egypt: Louis IX taken prisoner at El-Mansura (Egyptian delta), then freed after the surrender of Damietta and payment of a ransom.

1256–60: Mongols in Iran, Iraq and Syria.
1269: End of the reign of the Almohads in the Maghreb.
1269–1465: Marinid dynasty in the western Maghreb (Morocco).
1279–1290: Sultanate of the great Qala'un in a prosperous Egypt.
1291: Mamluks destroy the last Latin bastion at Acre.
1382: The Circassian Mamluks take power.
1387: Taking of Isfahan by Tamerlane: at least 70,000 beheaded.
1492: The Catholic kings complete the 'Reconquista' by taking the small Nasrid amirate of Granada.
1517: Selim I's Ottoman Turks invade Egypt.

4. Arab astrolabe.

circa 950

- Bukhara
- SAMANIDS 875
- Ghazni
- GURJARAS
- Constantinople
- EMPIRE BYZANTINE
- Aleppo
- BUYIDS 945
- Baghdad
- QARMATIANS
- UMEYYADS OF CORDOBA 756-1156
- Cordoba
- HAMDANIDS 929
- Tahart
- Kirouan
- Fustat (Cairo)
- Fez
- IDRISIDS 788-974
- FATIMIDS 909
- IKSHIDIDS 935-969
- Mecca
- ZAYDIS 893
- Sana

circa 1150

- Genghis Khan 1167-1227
- HOLY ROMAN EMPIRE
- GHAZENEVIDS 962-1187
- Constantinople
- SELJUQS 1037-1194
- Baghdad
- LATIN STATES 1099-1291
- ALMORAVIDS 1056-1147
- ALMOHADS 1147-1269
- Cairo
- FATIMIDS 969-1171
- AYYUBIDS 1171-1250
- (Saladin 1138-1193)

circa 1400

- Samarkand
- BYZANTINE EMPIRE
- Timur Lenk (Tamerlane 1336-1405)
- Delhi
- DELHI SULTANATE
- FRANCE
- Constantinople
- OTTOMANS
- GRANADA → 1492
- Tunis
- HAFSIDS 1228-1574
- Fez
- Tlemcen
- Cairo
- MARINIDS 1269-1465
- ZAYYANIDS 1235-1557
- MAMLUKS 1250-1517

circa 1550

- UZBEKS
- Luther
- Constantinople
- SAVAFIDS
- Francis I
- Charles V
- OTTOMANS

3. Manteq ot-teyr (The Conference of the Birds). *15th-century manuscript.*

Tamerlane.	Fall of Granada.
1336–1405	1492

5. *Detail from a manuscript copy of the* Suwer al-Kawakib al-thebitah (Book of the Fixed Stars) *by Abd ar-Rahman ibn 'Umar as-Sufi.*

The Nomadic Empire of the Mongols

1. Letter written by Arghun, Mongol ruler of Persia, to Philippe le Bel (Philip the Good), announcing the Mongol victory over the Arabs in Egypt.

GENGHIS KHAN, the thirteenth-century 'Conqueror of the World', did not appear from nowhere. For fifteen centuries before his day the 'Empires of the Steppes' – unstable confederacies controlled by the ancestors of the Turks, the Mongols or the Manchus – succeeded one another in Central Eurasia and even, from time to time, took power in the north of China. These were original civilizations of great richness, as the archaeological record reveals, and their whole economy was based on nomadic pastoralism.

The Mongols burst on to the world scene with a cleverly organized campaign of terror. Their history is composed entirely of conquests, sieges and massacres. When Genghis Khan died in 1227 the Mongol Empire stretched from the Pacific to the Black Sea, from northern China to the Siberian taiga, the Volga Plain and Persia. Fourteen years later the horsemen of the Steppes went even further, reaching right to the gates of Vienna. The Western world trembled, convinced that the Anti-Christ had come to sweep away Christianity, when suddenly the terrible invaders turned back, recalled by domestic intrigues of imperial succession. They were never to return. China was less fortunate. For the first time in its long history, it fell totally under the domination of a dynasty of barbarian origin. The Mongols' conquests stretched as far as Cambodia, Burma and Annam.

European travellers – missionaries and traders – started to journey through Eurasia. Luxury goods from the Far East now became an essential feature of life in the upper echelons of Italian and French society. The rulers of Christendom nurtured dreams of allying with the Mongols to destroy the forces of Islam. But the decline of the Mongol Empire was as sudden as its growth had been quick. From the 1250s onwards the khanates, founded by sons or grandsons of Genghis Khan, began to assert their independence. Those in the west became Turkish and Islamic in character. The Great Khan now only ruled over China. The epic period of Genghis Khan's rule was, however, more than just a series of wars of conquest and domestic strife; it was also more than might be gleaned from the tales of Marco Polo. It marks the period in which the Mongol peoples finally settled in the territories that were to become their own. The unity of the population assisted in the creation of a cultural identity – both material and spiritual – which can be seen to have been remarkably continuous from the thirteenth century up until our own times. We possess written records of this process in both Eastern and Western languages – Chinese, Persian, Syriac, Armenian, Russian, Greek, Latin, Italian etc. The abundance of such material contrasts markedly with the poverty of sources from earlier periods of civilization in the Steppes.

To understand thirteenth-century Mongol civilization from the inside, the key document is the *Secret History of the Mongols*, a splendid chronicle in narrative form, written to glorify Genghis Khan and the line descended from his youngest son (that of Möngke and Kubilai, who were in conflict with the descendants of Ogedei). Its pages reveal the operation of a morality based on loyalty and respect for age which is still very much alive in the Steppes. In the name of the 'Eternal Blue Sky', Genghis Khan and his successors also imposed a code of law whose influence is visible in the Mongol legal codes of later centuries. So much so, indeed, that up until recent times Genghis Khan was seen as the great protector of his people; in all Mongol regions his name was venerated and his glorious return awaited. In 1980 the People's Republic of China reconstructed his pseudo-mausoleum in the Ordos Desert (Inner Mongolia), in order themselves to share in some of the glory still attaching to his memory.

Genghis Khan.

c. 1155–1227

2nd century BC: Confederation of the Hsiung-nu: rich Bronze Age civilization, powerful cavalry.
6th–8th centuries AD: Confederation of the T'u-chueh (Chinese transcription of 'Turk'); first Turkish Empire.
8th–10th centuries: Confederation of the Uighur Turks, a great civilization which was to influence the Mongols.
907–1118: Khitans control northern China (Liao dynasty).
1115–1234: The Jurchen tribes control northern China (Chin dynasty).
1206: Temujin takes name Genghis Khan and founds the Mongol state.
1215: Capture of Peking, capital of the Chin, and northern China is gradually conquered.
1219–23: First invasion of the Muslim world and the Russian Steppes.
1227: Death of Genghis Khan.
1229–41: Reign of Ogedei, third son of Genghis Khan; capital at Karakorum.
1231–44: Conquest of Asia Minor resumed.
1234: Whole of northern China occupied (end of the Chin).
1236–40: Conquest of Russia.

Ogedei.

1229–41

1241: Invasion of Europe is halted after reaching its most westerly point.
1245–7: John Plano Carpini is sent by Pope Innocent IV to the court of the Great Khan.
1245–48: Reign of Guyuk, son of Ogedei.
1251–9: Reign of Möngke, son of Genghis Khan's fourth son.
1253–5: William Rubrouck, a Flemish Franciscan, journeys to the court of the Great Khan on behalf of Louis IX.
1260–94: Reign of Kubilai Khan, younger brother of Möngke and founder of the Chinese dynasty of the Yuan.
1271–95: Journey of the young Venetian Marco Polo through Europe and Central Asia to China.
1276–7: Conquest of China completed.
1294–1328: John of Montecorvino is sent to Khanbaliq (Peking) as apostolic legate by Pope Clement V. He becomes bishop there and later Oriental Patriarch.
Late 13th century: Mongol Empire breaks up into rival states. In the Russian steppes, the Golden Horde, led by the descendants of Jochi, eldest son of Genghis Khan, is won over to Islam. The khanates of Crimea,

Guyuk.

1246–8

3. The Mongol ruler of Persia, Mahmud Ghazan, and his wife surrounded by their court. Mongol manuscript, late 13th century.

Möngke.

1251–9

Astrakhan, Bukhara, Kasimov, Khiva and Khokand were to result from this process. Until 1335: Iran is governed by the Likhans, descendants of Möngke and Kubilai Khan converted to Islam. Chagatei khanate in Turkestan, founded by the second son of Genghis Khan, was Turkish and Islamic. Dominated by Timur Lenk (Tamerlane) in 1370; khanates of Transoxiana, Mogholistan and Kashgar result. In the east, the Yuan dynasty, Sinified and Buddhist.
1345–6: Journey of the Arab writer Tanger Ibn Battuta to southern China and Khanbaliq (Peking).
1368: Yuan overthrown by the Ming. Mongols return to the steppes.

12th–14th centuries

Hunting scenes. Details of a painting on silk by Zho Mongfu, a Chinese painter in the service of the Mongols.

...ubilai Khan.

...260–94

13th-century tortoise at the entrance to the ...ite of Karakorum, former capital of the ...enghiskhanids in Mongolia.

Genghis Khan's first Mongol Empire

Genghis Khan's original territorial base
The Mongol Empire in 1206
The Mongol Empire at Genghis Khan's death (1227)

Itineraries of armies led by:
→ Genghis Khan
→ His sons and generals
● Towns destroyed or pillaged

The Mongol Empire in the XIIIth century

Frontier of Genghiskanid Empire at beginning of XIVth century
Borders of the Khanates, c. 1310
→ Great campaigns

Dates of annexation or subjugation of a territory
✝ Catholic bishoprics in the XIVth century
Vassal territories of the Mongols

500 km

Medieval Japan

IN THE KANTO at the end of the twelfth century the warriors were becoming increasingly active. In 1156, and again in 1159, the aristocracy called upon the great warrior clans to settle their internal disputes. For some twenty years the Taira clan eclipsed the Fujiwara at court, but they were themselves displaced by the head of the Minamoto clan, who set up his government at Kamakura and took the title of *shogun* in 1192. The old imperial regime, which had been based on an aristocracy dedicated to state service, lost power to the warriors, who took over the administration of the landed estates to carve out fiefs for themselves. As in the West, the Japanese chivalric system was based on vassalage. The suzerain of the warriors (the shogun), or his regent from the Hojo clan, took over political power, while the former Kyoto aristocracy which remained the titular owner of the *shoen* existed alongside. The liegemen of the shogunate were given key positions in the provinces and in the estates. It could be said that the power held by the warriors in a way complemented that of the civil and religious aristocracy.

The thirteenth century was a relatively stable period, which saw slow but even commercial expansion. The attempted invasions by the Mongols forced the warriors to bear the costs of war, with Kamakura in no position to pay its vassals. Outbreaks of fighting, banditry and private wars started up again. In 1333 the Emperor succeeded in restoring the old regime, but was unable to control the warriors' lust for land. Ashikaga Takauji founded a new shogunate at Kyoto, but the civil war continued with only occasional interruption by truces.

The thirteenth and fourteenth centuries were periods of great religious activity. New sects advocating salvation through a simple faith in the Buddha Amida (Amidaist sects) took root among the lower levels of society. The Zen sects, with their rigid moral standards, meditation techniques and mastery over the body, exerted a strong influence on the thinking and way of life of the warriors. The shogunate encouraged the Zen monasteries, which were arranged in a hierarchical system known as that of the Five Mountains. 'Intimist' and poetic literature gave way to great war epics. In the fifteenth century increased homogeneity between local economies, technological advances in farming and the exploits of pirate-traders at sea brought Japanese civilization to one of its highest points. The former aristocracy, the shogunal court and the growing bourgeoisie invented new artistic forms: Zen gardens and the tea ceremony, architectural masterpieces and the Noh theatre. But this growth brought social upheavals in its train. Some warrior clans collapsed; others extended the area of their control. Revolts in the countryside, sometimes organized by the Ikkoshu (Single-Minded sect), made the control of central

Japan impossible for the shogun, who was now a mere puppet of his vassals. Merchant oligarchies at the head of 'free towns' liberated themselves from seigniorial tutelage. It was a prosperous but divided land that the Portuguese found when they landed in 1543, bringing with them Christianity and firearms.

1. *Portrait of Yorimoto, ruler of Japan from 1192.*

ANTIQUITY   **MIDDLE AGES**

1100	1150	1200	1250	1300	
RÉGIME OF RETIRED EMPERORS		TAIRA RÉGIME	SHOGUNATE OF KAMAKURA		
Heian period.	1159	1185	Kamakura period.	1333	1338

1156: The aristocracy in the capital calls upon the Taira and Minamoto warriors to control its internal conflicts.
1159: New coup d'état. The Taira take over from their rivals, the Minamoto.
1167: The head of the Taira family, Kiyomori, is 'prime minister' at court.
1175: Honen founds the Pure Land sect (or Jodo).
1180: Revolt of Minamoto-no-Yoritomo in the Kanto.
1185: The Minamoto are victors over the Taira in the west. Yoritomo makes his followers military governors (*shugo*) and land stewards in the estates (*jito*).
1191: Eisai founds the Rinzai sect.
1192: Yoritomo appointed *sei-i-tai shogun*.
1203: Hojo Tokimasa becomes regent of the shogunate. Beginning of the dominance of the Hojo family.
1221: The retired emperor Go-Toba tries to suppress the shogunate. Unsuccessful, he is exiled. The Hojo confiscate many estates and

2. *13th century silk scroll depicting an episode in the war against the Mongols.*

consolidate their power. Shinran founds the True Sect of the Pure Land.
1227: Dogen teaches the Zen doctrines of the Soto sect.
1232: The regent Hojo Yasutoki establishes a legal code, the *Joei Shikimoku*.
c. 1240: Composition of the greatest warrior epic, the story of the Taira family, *The Tale of the Heike (Heike Monogatari)*.
1253: Nichiren founds an original sect committed to the teachings of the Lotus sutra; they wished to make Japan the birthplace of a doctrine that would be spread throughout the world.
1274: Failure of the first Mongol invasion on the coasts of Kyushu.
1281: Further failure for the Mongols.
c. 1320: *Tsurezure gusa (Idle Jottings)*.
1333: General revolt against the Hojo of Kamakura. Kemmu restoration.
1338: Ashikaga Takauji founds his shogunate. The imperial dynasty is divided into the northern court, supported by the

12th–16th centuries

Legend:

- ▓ Paddy-field rice growing predominant (western plain)
- ░ Dry farming predominant (eastern plain)
- ⌒ Limits of Japan before 1600
- ☐ Shogunate capitals
- ☆ Great people's revolt area (about 1430-1570)
- (ODA) Fiefs of principal warlords around 1560
- ⋯⋯ Raids of Japanese pirates
- — — — Trade routes of Japanese merchants

*Map labels:*

KOREA

SEA OF JAPAN

HOKKAIDO

NORTH-EAST PROVINCES

40°

H O N S H Ū

Unsuccessful Mongol raids (1274/1281)

towards China

MORI

WESTERN

JAPAN

Hakata

OTOMO

KYUSHU

SHIKOKU

Kyoto

Mt Hiei

Hyogo

Sakai   Nara

ODA

IMAGAWA

TAKEDA

Mt Fuji-Yama

UESUGI

EASTERN JAPAN

HOJO

KANTO

Kamakura

Odawara

PACIFIC OCEAN

35°

Cultural dividing line

towards China

Island of Tanegashima

1543 Portuguese landing

130°   135°   140°

100 km

MODERN TIMES

350	1400	1450	1500	1550	1600

ASHIKAGA SHOGUNATE

between the southern and northern courts. 1392   Muromachi period. 1477   Warlord/Shokuho period. 1573

Ashikaga, and the southern, which refuses to recognize the shogun.
1378: The third shogun, Ashikaga Yoshimitsu, has the 'Villa of Flowers' built at Muromachi.
1392: Reunification of the two imperial courts.
1395: Yoshimitsu has the 'Golden Pavilion' built.
c. 1400–20: Zeami fixes the rules of the Noh Theatre.
1401: Yoshimitsu re-establishes official links with Ming China. He takes the title in Chinese of 'King of Japan'.
1428: First great peasant revolt.
1441: The shogun Yoshinori is assassinated. The peasants around Kyoto rise up and demand the abolition of debts.
1467–77: Civil wars in Onin.
1485: Start of the great revolt of the province of Yamashiro. The shogun Yoshimasa has the 'Silver Pavilion' built.
c. 1530: The peasant and religious leagues, the *ikki*, at their peak. The warlords consolidate their fiefs.
1543: The Portuguese land in the south of Japan.
1546: The first firearms are made by the Japanese.
1573: Oda Nobunaga drives the last Ashikaga shogun out of Kyoto.

3. *The moss garden at Kyoto, created in the 15th century.*

4 *Old Age, 15th century.*

Muslim India

THE CONQUEST of the Sind by the troops of Muhammad ibn al-Qasim was one aspect of the spectacular Arab expansion in the first decades of Islam, yet it happened at a time when everywhere else the momentum was declining: the new Arab province could not act as a base for the conquest of the rest of India. The Arabs showed tolerance and subtlety in the way they treated their Hindu subjects: they gave them the status of *dhimmi* or 'protected ones' (which is normally only applied to the 'People of the Book'), leaving them free to practise their religion and to live by their own customs as long as they paid the special tax known as the *jaziyah*. They also took an interest in the culture and in particular in the accumulated knowledge of the Indians. In the next three centuries, then, Islam was to remain on the margins of India.

The situation became quite different when the Turk, Mahmud of Ghazna, began a series of raids and massacres in the Indian towns and Hindu temples. Some two centuries later the process was repeated, this time under Muhammad of Ghur, who carried out campaigns of extermination and created the sultanate. The rise of Islam resumed, this time in the hands of warriors from Central Asia whose power base was located in a number of Afghan principalities. The end result was the creation of a Muslim state which was to dominate India, though which was only to become Indian slowly and partially, bringing about profound transformations in Indian society in the process. Three stages can be distinguished. First there was the Slave (or Mamluk) dynasty. Iltutmish introduced a bureaucratic administration that consolidated the sultanate's power over the whole of northern India. Then came the Khaljis. The sultanate – under Ala ud-Din – was now at the height of its political, territorial and cultural power. Last of all came the Tugluqs, under whose rule regional Muslim states were founded: Indian Islam would now no longer be a mere emanation of the sultanate, the break-up of which was soon to be hastened by Tamerlane's incursions.

At the end of the thirteenth century Muslims apparently made up a quarter of the population. There were several different groups, including people who were of Muslim origin, Turkish and Afghan courtiers who were paid hereditary tenures (*jagir*) by the sultan, and warriors from Central Asia, who along with their families and sometimes their entire clans came to replenish and reinforce the ranks of the conqueror's armies. Their common language was Persian and this became the language of government and prestige (even for Hindus). Persian culture was their ideal. The largest part of the Muslim population was, however, made up of converts, of whom there were a great number throughout the north and particularly in the Punjab and Sind regions and also in Bengal, where Islam had supplanted the previously dominant Buddhist faith. Hinduism proved more durable because it was solidly built into the social structure. A large number of converts were, however, made from Hinduism. It is not the case, as has been argued in the past, that most of them came from the lower castes, seeking to escape the oppression of the system, for in Muslim society, though technically egalitarian, the caste system was to some degree re-established: this was how Islam became integrated into Indian culture. The Hindu Indians – especially upper-class ones – adopted Muslim customs, such as *purdah*. There also developed an Indo-Muslim style in the arts and the Urdu language, a mixture of Persian and Hindi, appeared at this point. In spite of the savagery of its wars, India prospered. The account of the Hindu town of Vijayanagar given by the Muslim Abd al-Razzaq is an eloquent testimony to the splendours of India in the later part of this period.

1. *The great monolithic Buddha of Pollonnoruva, Sri Lanka (Ceylon), 11th century.*

Kashmir: independent Hindu kingdom and centre of Sanskrit culture.

Sultanate of Delhi: dynasty of the 'Slaves'.

Khilji dynasty

| 725–1339 | 1206–90 | 1290–1320 |

712: The Arab Muhammad ibn al-Qasim conquers Sind for the Umayyad caliphate.
c. 760: The Great Temple of the Kailasa is hewn out of rock at Ellora.
780–820: The Hindu philosopher Sankara lives in Kerala. He professes 'Nondualism'.
783: Gurjara-Pratihara dynasty founded. It dominates northern India until 885, constituting an obstacle to Arab expansion.
c. 850: The Cola become the ruling power in southern India. Cola 'thalassocracy' lasts for two centuries.
950–1050: The Chandelas of Prayag build the temples of Khajuraho.
933: Founding of Delhi.
1000–27: Mahmud of Ghazna launches looting raids against towns and temples in India, including Mathura, Thanesar and Kanauj. During his reign, al-Biruni, the historian, geographer and astronomer, compiles an important anthology of observations and reflections on India.
1173: The Afghan princes of Ghur seize Ghazni.
1192: Battle of Thanesar. Muhammad of Ghur conquers and kills the Rajput king,

Prthviraja. His troops enter the Ganges valley, destroy Benares and the Buddhist and Hindu centres of Bihar and Bengal.
1206: Qutb-ub-Din Aybak founds the Sultanate of Delhi.
1211–36: Iltutmish becomes Sultan of Delhi. He fights off Genghis Khan's Mongols and builds the Qutb Minar.
c. 1250: Construction of the Temple of the Sun at Konarak in Orissa.
1288 and 1293: Marco Polo visits southern India.
1303: Ala ud-Din Khalji seizes Chitor in Rajasthan. Queen Padmavati burns herself alive along with thousands of women to avoid being captured by the conquerors (*jauhar* rite).
1310: Malik Kafur, Ala ud-Din Khalji's general, brings almost all of the Deccan under Delhi's rule: the extreme south and pockets of resistance in Rajasthan and on the Malabar coast are the only parts to escape his control.
1325–51: Muhammad Tugluq, Sultan of Delhi. He has part of the population of Delhi transported to his new capital at Daulatabad. Bold but unsuccessful attempts at monetary

3. *Illustration from a Kalpasutra, a Jain text portraying the life of the Jina Mahavira.*

8th–16th centuries

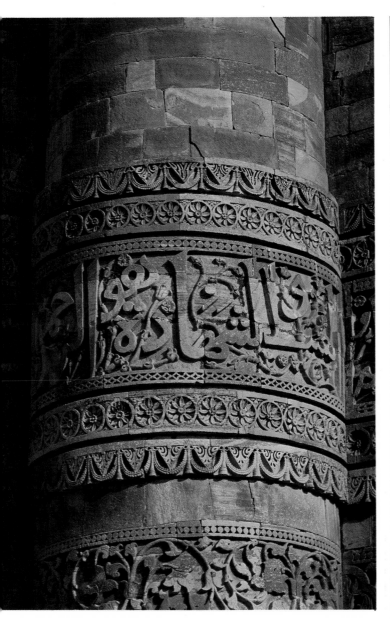

2. Verses from the Quran on a column of the Mosque of Quwat ul-Islam, near the Qutb Minar tower (Delhi), 13th century.

XIth century: Muslim conquests

Empire of Mahmud of Ghazna

Muslim expeditions of conquest, early XIth century.

XIIIth–XIVth centuries: Delhi Sultanate

1236 Sultanate of Delhi under Iltutmish (1211-36)

1335 Empire of Muhammad Tugluq

Uchch names of provinces

⊙ Capitals

1398 Invasion by Timur Lenk (Tamerlane)

Sultanate of Delhi in revolt

500 km

Tugluq dynasty.	Lodi dynasty.
1320–88	1450–1526

reform and fiscal centralization.

1336: Foundation in Mysore of the Hindu kingdom of Vijayanagar, which was to control southern India until 1565. A centre of Sanskrit culture.

1347: Bahman Shah establishes an independent sultanate based on Bijapur, Bidar and Gulbarga, which will develop fruitful relations with the whole of the Muslim world. Constantly in conflict with Vijayanagar over two centuries.

1387: Death of Sayana, author of a commentary on the Veda.

1398: Tamerlane raids Delhi.

1420: The Italian voyager, Niccolo dei Conti, visits Vijayanagar.

1470: The Russian merchant Nikitin visits Bidar.

1440–1518: Life of Kabir, a mystic poet, who dreams of uniting the Hindu and Islamic cultures.

1469–1539: Life of Nanak, founder of the Sikh community.

1498: Vasco da Gama lands at Calicut: first time a European journeys to India entirely by sea.

1510: Portuguese admiral Albuquerque seizes Goa and massacres the Muslim population.

1534: Bishopric of Goa founded.

The Rise of the Towns in the West

BETWEEN THE TENTH and the thirteenth centuries Western Europe underwent a series of profound material and social changes on a scale not seen again until the Industrial Revolution. Since medieval society was organized around cultivation of the land, it is in the great expansion of agricultural production that we must seek the origins of these transformations. New social bonds were created which reflected the organization of manorial demesnes and an increase in the feudal dues which the aristocracy exacted in kind, in labour (the *corvée*) and, more and more frequently, in money. Greater productivity was therefore required of the only class able to furnish it – the peasantry. A number of other factors contributed to this agricultural boom. Europe was entering a period of drier, colder climatic conditions which favoured the growth of cereals, the Hungarian and Scandinavian invasions came to an end and workers were now better protected, thanks to the 'Peace of God'. More efficient tools and machinery (such as the wheeled plough with mouldboard, the collar-harness, the harrow, the water-mill and later the wind-mill) came into widespread use,

1. Town walls and towers of Carcassonne. 13th century.

together with improved agricultural techniques. Three-year crop rotation became the practice in the most fertile areas in the thirteenth century. In these conditions cereal harvests increased to give a yield of 5 or 6 to 1. The dramatic rise in production was, however, due less to intensified cultivation than to the increase in the area of arable land through scrub clearance, marsh drainage and reclamation of land in coastal regions (*polder*), and the expansion was sustained by that universal driving force of land acquisition – demographic growth. Over three centuries the population of Europe more or less doubled, to reach a figure of around 60 million inhabitants. They settled either in the villages which sprang up in this period or in the towns, whose growth picked up again for the first time since late antiquity. In

addition to the long-established episcopal cities, there grew up *portus* (urban centres of trade and craft industries), and 'new towns' (or the French *sauvetés*) were built from scratch. Town life gave rise to new forms of organization of trades (guilds), new political structures (the communes) and new religious associations (the confraternities). All these were concessions which the townspeople extracted from the lay and ecclesiastical overlords. The urban economy increasingly dictated that of the surrounding countryside (the Italian *contado*), but it was above all tied up with long-distance trade. Commerce benefited greatly from increased monetary circulation, which boosted the minting of silver *deniers* (necessary for large transactions) and later, in the thirteenth century, the issue of gold coins. The entire European economy was stimulated by trade between the two great economic zones – on the one hand the Italian ports of Pisa, Genoa and Venice with their maritime trading links with the Levant, and on the other the northern European cloth towns of Ghent, Ypres and Bruges. The merchants of these two complementary regions met annually at the fairs in Champagne, which reached their peak during the twelfth century at Troyes, Provins, Bar-sur-Aube and Lagny. Merchants there employed new financial and commercial practices such as using bills of exchange which enabled them to circumvent the church's prohibition of usury. Towards the end of the fourteenth century, however, there were increasing signs that Western Europe's economic and demographic boom was running out of steam.

2. The Lendit Fair at St Denis. Manuscript of the Grandes Chroniques, 14th century.

First 'Peace of God'.	Creation of the Commune of Laon.
989	1112

941–2: Famine in western France.

c. 950: Earliest evidence of land clearance and of use of water-mills for grinding grain and also in dyeing, forging and pressing: this is a crucial factor in the economic expansion of Europe.

989: Synod of Charroux – beginning of the 'Peace of God' imposed by the church on the knightly classes. Most of the time, however, the church has to settle for imposing the 'Truce of God' on certain days of the week or dates of the year. This nevertheless affords some degree of protection to church property as well as to the defenceless peasantry and to the material basis of the economy. In this respect the 'Peace of God' movement contributes significantly to the economic revival.

992: First commercial treaty between Venice and Byzantium. This marks the beginning of Venetian maritime power in the Mediterranean.

1005–6: Famine in Western Europe.

1032–3: Chroniclers, alert to signs announcing the coming of the Antichrist, record a famine in France.

3. The windmill. Illumination from a 14th-century French manuscript of the Roman d'Alexandre.

c. 1097: Completion of the Bayeux Tapestry, which carries in its lower border the earliest picture of a harrow.

c. 1100: Increasing importance of the fairs in Champagne – halfway between the towns of Flanders and those of northern Italy. The counts of Champagne have an interest in protecting and promoting these fairs. The scratch plough tends to be replaced by the wheeled plough, whose mouldboard and heavier ploughshare enable farmers to increase their yields.

1112: Creation of the Commune of Laon. The townspeople assassinate the bishop who is also their secular lord. King Louis VI intervenes to put down the uprising.

1120–50: First statutes of the trade guilds, which are drawn up under the aegis of the princes or town governments. They are intended to preserve equality between master craftsmen or merchants and to protect them from competition, either internal or external. In 1121 Louis VI grants privileges to the Parisian corporation of water-carriers, whose provost becomes in effect mayor of the capital city.

10th–13th centuries

European Trade in the XIIIth century

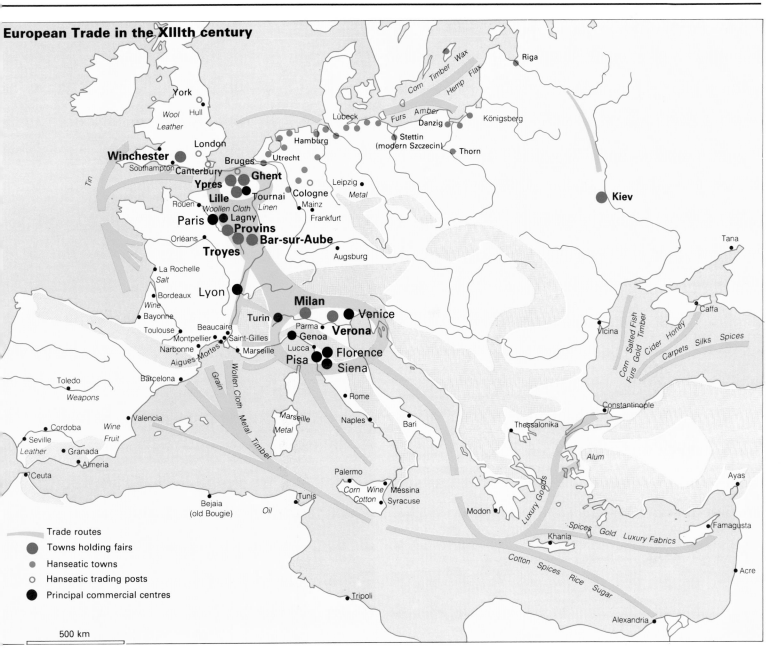

York
Wool
Leather
Hull
London
Winchester
Southampton
Canterbury
Bruges
Ghent
Ypres
Lille
Tournai
Cologne
Rouen
Woollen Cloth
Linen
Lagny
Paris
Provins
Bar-sur-Aube
Troyes
Orléans
La Rochelle
Salt
Lyon
Bordeaux
Wine
Bayonne
Milan
Turin
Venice
Toulouse
Beaucaire
Parma
Verona
Montpellier
Narbonne
Saint-Gilles
Genoa
Aigues-Mortes
Marseille
Lucca
Florence
Pisa
Siena
Barcelona
Grain
Woollen Cloth
Metal Timber
Toledo
Weapons
Rome
Marseille
Metal
Naples
Bari
Cordoba
Wine
Valencia
Fruit
Seville
Leather
Granada
Almería
Ceuta
Bejaia (old Bougie)
Oil
Tunis
Palermo
Corn Wine Cotton
Messina
Syracuse
Tripoli

Hamburg
Utrecht
Leipzig
Metal
Mainz
Frankfurt
Augsburg
Lübeck
Furs Amber
Danzig
Stettin (modern Szczecin)
Thorn
Königsberg
Riga
Corn Timber Wax
Hemp Flax
Kiev
Tana
Caffa
Vicina
Corn Salted Fish
Furs Gold Timber
Cider Honey
Carpets Silks Spices
Constantinople
Thessalonika
Alum
Ayas
Luxury Goods
Modon
Khania
Spices Gold Luxury Fabrics
Famagusta
Cotton Spices Rice Sugar
Acre
Alexandria
Tin

Legend:
- Trade routes
- Towns holding fairs
- Hanseatic towns
- Hanseatic trading posts
- Principal commercial centres

500 km

Sack of Constantinople by the crusaders. | Minting of gold coins resumed.

1204 | 1252

4. *The punishment of adulterers: the guilty couple are paraded through the town. 13th-century Cistercian manuscript.*

1124–6: Severe famine in the countryside of Flanders.

c. 1180: Appearance of windmills in the West. A mill represents a considerable capital investment: ownership is consequently restricted to lords, who reserve the exclusive right to operate them as a public right or 'ban': the fees charged for use of the mill make up an increasingly important part of the lord's income.

1204: Capture and sack of Constantinople during the Fourth Crusade, enabling the Genoese to set up trading posts on the shores of the Black Sea.

c. 1237: The St Gothard Pass is opened up: this assists the economic growth of southern Germany.

1250: Great increase in the numbers of charters of liberties granted to rural communities. Large numbers of serfs are freed. The peasants' tithes and labour services are commuted to monetary dues.

1252–82: Resumption of minting of gold coins and of the bimetallic currency system (gold and silver) which had disappeared in late Antiquity. In 1231 Emperor Frederick II issues the *augustale*, Genoa mints the *genovino*, Florence the florin and, from 1284, Venice issues ducats. The King of France issues the *ecu* (1263).

5. *Seal of town of Saint-Omer depicting the échevins (aldermen). 13th century.*

Romanesque Art

AROUND THE YEAR 1000, in the monk Rodulfus Glaber's words, Christendom became covered with a 'white mantle of churches'. The flowering of art and architecture during this period is best understood in the context of a whole range of mutations, economic, demographic, technical and religious. It is directly linked with the dynamism of religious orders such as Cluny and later Cîteaux, the rapid growth in the number of monasteries, the birth of villages and towns which needed places of worship and the abundance of gifts received by the church, enabling them to finance expensive buildings. Important, too, was the development of hoisting, stone-cutting and vaulting techniques and, finally, the increasing popularity of relics and pilgrimages: Santiago de Compostela, Vézelay and Conques have magnificent churches.

Romanesque is characterized above all by its new architecture. Between 1000 and the twelfth century techniques of construction which were already known but had not found the right context for their development were brought together in an original synthesis. The basilical plan with nave and two aisles and the column with a capital came from Antiquity. The use of the dome and the taste for polychromy may have had oriental and Arab origins. The Romanesque style derived directly from the Carolingian (Germigny-des-Prés, Aachen) but the synthesis was new, whether the plans adopted the transept with dome over the crossing or the circular or octagonal form. The forms of worship were important in structuring space: chapels radiating from the apse were built to accommodate separate altars (Oliba Monastery at Ripoll in the Spanish Pyrenees has seven), ambulatories for processions, crypts for the relics of the saints. However, it was the revolution in building techniques which allowed the realization of daring projects: exclusive use was made of hewn stone, which called for vaulting on a grand scale. Within this framework various formulae were used: the barrel vault (Saint-Savin-sur-Gartempe) or the vault formed by intersecting arches. Where two barrel vaults met, groin vaults had to be erected.

Around 1125–1130 in the Ile de France (Morienval and ambulatory of Saint-Denis) rib vaulting was used for the first time; it soon became characteristic of Gothic architecture. But a major technical problem was caused by the considerable pressure on the outer walls; the answer was increasingly thick, windowless walls and powerful buttresses. In some regions such as Aquitaine (Saintes, Périgueux, Angoulême, Cahors) the solution was a series of domes rather than barrel vaults. The variety of styles – according to 'school', region (Catalonia, Burgundy, Auvergne, Germany, Lombardy etc.) or monastic order financing the church (Cluniac, Cistercian styles) – is as important as the unifying influence of Romanesque.

Other forms of art were closely linked to architecture: the sculptures of tympana and capitals (great Romanesque tympana of the first half of the twelfth century, Moissac, Vézelay, Conques, Autun etc.) were the church's way of explaining Christian eschatology. Mural paintings (San Clemente de Tahull in Catalonia) had an edifying function, but the harmony of their colours was also designed to accompany the liturgical chants. Gold and silverwork and illuminations represent the most precious expression of the spirituality of the times.

1. Apse of Cistercian Abbey of Le Thoronet, Provence, c. 1160–80.

Book of Miracles of Saint Foy of Conques.

1030

2. Elephants and flowers. Capital of Perrecy-les-Forges, Saône-et-Loire, 12th century.

997–1004: Building of Saint-Martin at Tours, one of the first important Romanesque churches, now almost entirely destroyed. The choir was surrounded by an ambulatory with five radiating chapels.

1000–30: Statue of Saint Foy at saint's shrine, Conques: wooden figure covered in gold leaf and precious stones; the head probably dates from 5th century. It was worshipped as an idol and was the object of an important 11th-century pilgrimage.

1006–13: Building of the abbey church of Saint-Philibert at Tournus, remarkable for the Saint-Michel Chapel above the entrance porch and for transverse barrel-vaulted aisles.

1007: Rotunda of Saint-Bénigne at Dijon based on basilical plan.

c. 1015–24: Basle altar-front in repoussé gold, one of the masterpieces of Romanesque work in precious metals, now in the Musée de Cluny, Paris.

Fleury Abbey completed.

1068

3. Head of Christ at Lavandieu, Loire, 12th century.

Work begins on Santiago de Compostela.

1075

c. 1025: Frescoes of Saint-Savin-sur-Gartempe painted on the barrel vaulting of one aisle. Old Testament scenes: the Flood and Noah's Ark, the Tower of Babel, etc.

1045: Building of octagonal church of Ottmarsheim (Upper Rhine), inspired by the Palatine Carolingian chapel of Aachen.

1067–8: Construction of Fleury Abbey (Saint-Benoît-sur-Loire) with vast narthex (vaulted porch beneath belfry).

1075–1122: Cathedral of Santiago de Compostela built to accommodate crowds of pilgrims coming to St James the Great's tomb. A Moslem raid in 997 had destroyed the primitive church. The porch (Pórtico de la Gloria) is related to those of Moissac and Saint-Sernin at Toulouse.

1088–1130: Building of Cluny III to replace two other abbey churches: Cluny I which dates from the early 10th century and Cluny II dating from 955–91. The new church is

10th–12th centuries

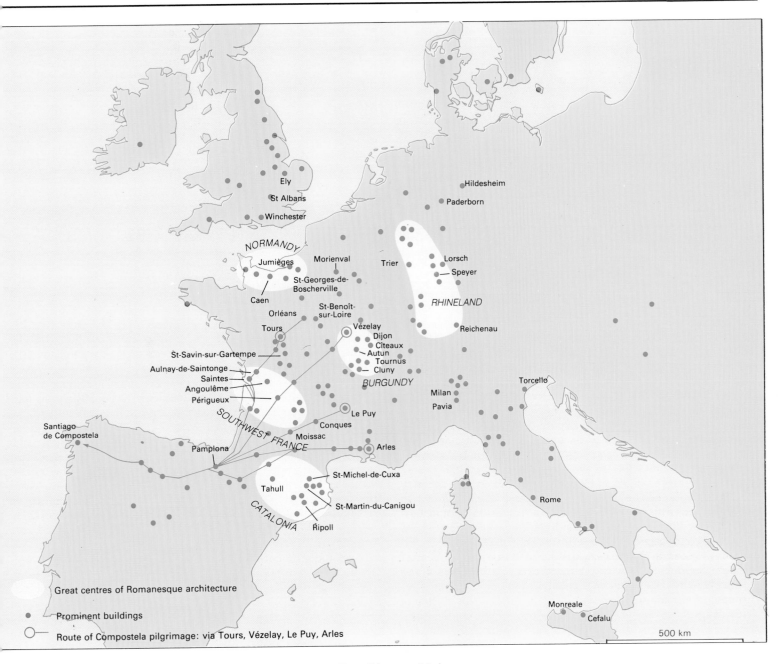

Great centres of Romanesque architecture

● Prominent buildings

◯ Route of Compostela pilgrimage: via Tours, Vézelay, Le Puy, Arles

500 km

Moissac tympanum.

1115

Cluny Abbey completed.

1130

4. The Animals of Creation. Catalan tapestry, 12th century.

181 metres long, has four aisles and a double transept; its scale reflects the power of the Cluny order. It was unfortunately almost entirely destroyed during the French Revolution.

1096–1132: Construction of Vézelay Abbey, famous for the sculptures of the main tympanum and those of the capitals in the nave.

1115: Moissac tympanum heralds the series of great Romanesque tympana of the first half of the 12th century: Saintes, Aulnay in Saintonge, Conques in Rouergue, Vézelay, Autun in Burgundy. All show themes of the Apocalypse and are organized around the figure of Christ presiding over the Last Judgement and the Resurrection of the Dead.

1130–47: Construction of the Cistercian Abbey of Fontenay, still remarkable for the close relation between its religious and its utilitarian buildings, such as the forge.

1132: Ambulatory of Morienval: its groin vaults emphasized by thick cylindrical mouldings mark the transition from Romanesque to Gothic.

5. The porch at Aulnay-de-Saintonge, 12th century.

Gothic Art and the Twelfth-Century Renaissance

1. Porch of Cologne Cathedral, 13th century.

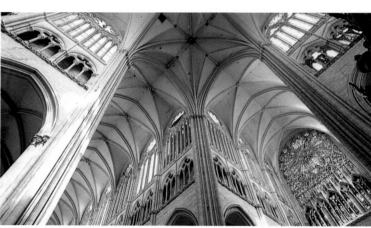

2. Nave and north transept of Amiens Cathedral, 13th century.

IN THE MID-TWELFTH CENTURY towns became the main centres of material and intellectual life, the source of all innovation. The founding of universities and the building of cathedrals are vivid evidence of this urban renaissance. The transfer of learning from the monasteries to the city schools went along with a complete transformation of the content, form and object of intellectual activity. To begin with, schools remained dependent on the bishop and chapter, as in Laon, Chartres and Orleans. They were also identified with new religious communities, such as the Abbey of Saint-Victor in Paris. The rediscovery of ancient philosophy and science (Plato, Aristotle, Hippocrates) through Arab authors (Avicenna, Averroës) stimulated the most advanced thinking. The seven liberal arts – 'literary' trivium, 'scientific' quadrivium – formed the basis of study. In the thirteenth century universities emerged, at Paris, Bologna and Oxford, at first in the form of corporations of masters and students. Paris included an Arts faculty and three specialized faculties: Medicine, Canon Law and Theology. The masters were either clerics paid by the students or, increasingly, members of mendicant orders. Teaching and examinations were based on the *disputatio*, the confrontation and synthesis of opposite arguments. The effort to reconcile Christian culture and pagan philosophy caused serious tension, with the church authorities stepping in to maintain orthodoxy. In 1270 and 1277 the Bishop of Paris, Etienne Tempier, proscribed the doctrine of the 'double truth' taught by the followers of Averroës. In 1337 William of Ockham's Nominalism was denounced as a source of scepticism in matters of faith. The great theological *summa* of the scholastic age have been compared to the cathedrals of the same period, in that they present the same logic of articulation and subdivision, the same breadth. They also both originated in the prosperous heart of the Ile-de-France, where Abbot Suger of Saint-Denis erected around 1140 the first example of the new art. New architectural techniques took Romanesque a step further: the crossing of pointed arches meeting in a crown enabled the force of gravity to be spread equally among four pillars. Walls were freed of their load-bearing function; large windows could now be cut in them, and stained glass could express Gothic aesthetics and spirituality in glowing colours. The edifice could reach undreamt-of heights; storeys of arcades, tribunes, triforia and clerestory windows graced the interior, while the structure was visible outside in the design of the façade framed by towers and spires. There was, however, great variety among Gothic churches, depending on the finance available, the size of the population and the period, from the first buildings of the twelfth century (Noyon, Senlis, Laon, Notre-Dame, Paris) to the 'classical' period of Reims, Amiens, Bourges and the Sainte-Chapelle at Paris and finally the 'flamboyant' Gothic of the late Middle Ages. Regional variations play a part, too (the brick cathedral of Albi, the Mudejar style of Spain, the rectangular forms of English cathedrals with flat chevet, as in York, Lincoln, Durham), as do various specific requirements, as can be seen in the spacious churches of the mendicant orders which were adapted to preaching and are similar all over Europe.

Suger abbot of Saint-Denis.

The *Sentences* of Peter Lombard.

1122	1152

1132–44: Suger builds abbey church of Saint-Denis. The ambulatory is the first example of Gothic art.
1140: Council of Sens. Abelard condemned at the instigation of St Bernard. Two conceptions of theology are revealed, rational for the master of dialectics, mystical for the monk.
c. 1140: *Decretum Gratiani*, critical synthesis of church legal texts or canon law.
1145–55: Royal portal of Chartres. On the tympanum, Christ in His Majesty and symbols of the evangelists above figures of the apostles. On either side of the porch the *pieds-droits* (column-statues) represent the prophets and kings of Israel.
1152: The Parisian master Peter Lombard writes the *Four Books of Sentences* or *Sentences*, which becomes the basic text of biblical interpretation at the university.
1152–1211: Construction begins on principal Gothic cathedrals of northern France: Le Mans, Laon, Notre-Dame, Paris, Chartres, Bourges, Reims.
1168–83: French romances in verse by Chrétien de Troyes: *Lancelot* or *le Chevalier à*

3. Stained-glass window of Saint-Denis basilica, 12th century.

la Charette, Yvain or *Le Chevalier au Lion, Perceval* or *Le Conte du Graal*.
1215: Statutes of the University of Paris deriving from the schools of the 12th century. The 'University of Masters and Students', governed by the Pope, soon becomes independent of royal and episcopal power. Fourth Lateran Council takes a stand on all major questions of the period.
1220–70: Stained-glass windows of Chartres.
c. 1234: First part of *The Romance of the Rose* by Guillaume de Lorris, French didactical and allegorical poem in octosyllables. Completed by Jean de Meung (1275–80), who gave it an encyclopaedic form.
1240: Translation of Aristotle's *Ethics* by William of Moerbeke. Now better known, Aristotle's works revolutionize orthodox theological, political and scientific ideas.
1243–8: Louis IX has the Sainte-Chapelle built to accommodate Christ's Crown of Thorns.
1245–59: Dominicans Albertus Magnus and Thomas Aquinas teach at Paris University.

4. Psalter of Queen Ingeborg of Denmark, wife of Philip II Augustus, 1210.

12th–14th centuries

Gothic architecture and universities, XIIth - XVth centuries

Uppsala

Roskilde

Danzig

York

Cambridge

Oxford
London
Canterbury

Magdeburg

Cologne

Chichester
Arras
Amiens
Rouen
Noyon
Laon
Soissons
Reims
Senlis

Mont St Michel

Prague

Nuremberg

St Denis
Paris
Chartres
Châlons
Sens
Strasbourg

Angers
Candes
Le Mans
Orléans
Dijon

Poitiers
Bourges
Beaune

Vicenza
Vercelli
Treviso
Milan
Padua
Grenoble
Reggio
Bologna

Cahors
Montpellier
Florence
Avignon
Arezzo
Albi
Pisa
Perugia
Bayonne

Leon
Toulouse
Carcassonne
Perpignan
Aigues-Mortes
Rome

Burgos
Palencia
Valladolid
Salamanca
Lérida
Gerona
Naples
Salerno

Batalha
Coimbra
Lisbon
Tomer

Seville

Toledo

500 km

○ Cradle of new architecture (Ile-de-France)
● First examples of new architecture. XIIth century Gothic
○ Gothic architecture: XIIIth and XIVth centuries
Area of development of XVth century flamboyant Gothic; main buildings
| Universities founded before 1270
| Universities founded after 1270

Fourth Lateran Council.

1215

Averroism condemned.

1277

From 1266 to 1273 the latter publishes his *Summa Theologiae*.
1265–1321: Dante Alighieri, author of *The Divine Comedy*.
1270–7: Averroism condemned by Bishop of Paris, Etienne Tempier. The Arab philosopher Averroës (died 1198) originated a doctrine unacceptable to the church, of a 'double truth', that of reason and of faith.
1310–15: William of Ockham teaches Nominalism at Oxford. This doctrine, originated by Abelard in the 12th century, stipulates that general ideas (or universals) do not have any reality in themselves but are only names, thus demolishing the traditional realism of medieval theology.

5. Virgin and Child, painted stone statue from the Ile-de-France, early 14th century.

6. The Virgin of Calvary, 14th-century English embroidery work.

7. Statute book of Hubant College, French manuscript of 1387.

Italy: The Era of Merchants and Artists

1. *Commercial activity at Bologna. Manuscript illumination, Bologna, 1345.*

As THEY SHOOK THEMSELVES free of the imperial yoke (the Holy Roman Empire was weakened by the death of Frederick II and the subsequent interregnum) and as their role in international trade grew more powerful, the towns of central and northern Italy became the centres of a flourishing culture that heralded the Quattrocento Renaissance. This was where capitalism was born, both private (Genoa, Florence) and state (Venice), linking the profits of industry, maritime trade and banking. In Florence banking was tied up with major political affairs: debts incurred by the King of England and the Pope caused the Bardi and Peruzzi to go bankrupt (1343–6), while the Strozzi and Medici, who came later, were able to consolidate their economic power by gaining political power. Economic rivalries resulted in the political fragmentation of Italy: Genoa and Florence were at war, as were the Guelfs and the Ghibellines (partisans of Pope and Emperor, respectively). An important phenomenon was the formation of territorial states which increased the hold of cities over the surrounding regions: Milan under the Visconti, Venice, who, breaking with her exclusively seafaring tradition, annexed the lower Po Valley at the beginning of the fifteenth century (including Verona and Padua, where the University of Venice became based). Tuscany, more and more dominated by Florence, was from the end of the thirteenth century the cradle of Italian literature. This was where Dante Alighieri wrote his masterpiece, *The Divine Comedy*, inspired by Virgil's *Aeneid*, between 1307 and his death in 1321. In the *Canzoniere* – more than 300 sonnets and songs – Petrarch sang of his impossible love. In the *Decameron* Boccaccio defined the rules of a new narrative genre, the novella. Classical literature also returned to favour from 1320 or 1330 onwards: corrupt church Latin was compared unfavourably with the purity of Cicero, whose works were being rediscovered. The Chancellor of the Florentine Republic, Coluccio, was the patron of Italian humanism. Greek authors were no longer ignored; they began to be taught at Bologna in 1424.

Milan cathedral was the most monumental adaptation of French Gothic to Italy, but Tuscan churches generally took a different direction: simple façades adorned with alternate bands of white and black (Santa Maria Novella), classical pediments (Santa Croce) and vaulted ceilings. For civic buildings Gothic usually dominated (Signoria and loggia of the Palazzo del Commune of Florence). Another remarkable phenomenon was the birth of monumental painting, with Giotto's frescoes at Assisi and the Scrovegni chapel at Padua, Simone Martini's at the Palais des Papes, Avignon, and Ambrogio Lorenzetti's *Allegory of Good and Bad Government* at the Palazzo Pubblico of Siena (1338). Religious painting on wood, influenced by Byzantine

Maestà of Siena Cathedral by Duccio.	Death of Dante Alighieri.	Death of Giotto.
1311	**1321**	**1337**

1228: Construction begins on basilica at Assisi, two years after death of St Francis.

1240–1302: Cimabue, Tuscan painter influenced by Byzantine art. Painter of crucifixes of Arezzo and Santa Croce at Florence (the latter damaged in 1966 flood).

1245–1302: Arnolfo di Cambio. Begins work on Duomo at Florence in 1300. Santa Croce and Palazzo Vecchio attributed to him.

1250: Death of Emperor Frederick II. As King of Sicily he was mainly concerned with Italian affairs. At his court at Palermo he was host to Greek, Arab, Jewish and Italian scholars. A man of wide culture, he wrote a treatise on hunting, had Aristotle and Averroës translated, founded Naples University in 1224.

1255–1319: Duccio di Buoninsegna. Painter of the *Maestà* of the Virgin in Siena Cathedral, 1311.

1265–1321: Dante Alighieri. From a

3. *The Virgin with Angels by the Sienese painter Cimabue, Pisa, 13th century.*

Florentine Guelf family, he played a diplomatic role before being exiled. In *De monarchia* he advocates the independence of temporal power from spiritual power. *Il convivio* (The Banquet) is a philosophical treatise in the classical tradition. *De vulgari eloquentia* is written in Latin but advocates the use of Italian as a literary tongue. His lyrical works include the *Canzoniere*, in which he celebrates his love for Beatrice, *Vita nuova* and, above all, *The Divine Comedy* (1307–21), inspired by Virgil, a vast portrait of the human condition.

1266–1337: Giotto di Bondone. Painter of frescoes in upper church at Assisi (1296–9) and Scrovegni chapel at Padua (1303–5).

1284–1344: Simone Martini. Painter of the *Maestà* at the Palazzo Pubblico of Siena and frescoes at Notre-Dame-des-Doms and the Palais des Papes, both at Avignon.

1303–74: Petrarch. Lived mainly in Avignon; his *Canzoniere*, which include *I trionfi* and *Le rime*, inspired by Ovid, Seneca, Cicero and

4. *Portrait of Dante illustrating a manuscript of* The Divine Comedy, *Sienese studio, 1403.*

13th–15th centuries

art and Franciscan spirituality, is represented by Cimabue (1240–1302) in Florence and Duccio di Buoninsegna, who painted the *Maestà* of the Virgin in 1311 for Siena cathedral. Nicola Pisano was the first in a brilliant line of sculptors, notably, Giovanni Pisano, Arnolfo do Cambio (who began the Duomo at Florence around 1300) and Andrea Pisano, who sculpted one of the bronze doors of the Baptistery at Florence, completed by Ghiberti in the next century.

The Fragmentation of Italy XIIIth to XIVth centuries

100 km

Italy at the Peace of Lodi 1454

100 km

2. The prosperity of the city, a result of 'Good Government'. Fresco by Ambrogio Lorenzetti, Siena, 1338.

Death of Boccaccio.

1375

Virgil, tell of his lost love for Laura.

1313–75: Giovanni Boccaccio. Born of a Tuscan father and a French mother, lived in Florence and at the court of Charles I at Naples. Between 1348 and 1353 he wrote the *Decameron*, founding the literary genre of the Italian novella. In 1360 he wrote *De claris mulieribus*, a collection of biographies of illustrious women.

1337–9: Ambrogio Lorenzetti paints *Allegories of Good and Bad Government* at the Palazzo Pubblico of Siena.

1424: Teaching of Greek introduced at Bologna.

1429: Venice conquers Po valley up to the Adda. Padua becomes university of Venice and a flourishing centre of humanism.

1434: Cosimo de' Medici takes de facto power in Florence.

5. The Palazzo d'Este, Ferrara, 14th century.

6. Lady with the arms of the Visconti. Miniature illustrating Cicero's *De natura deorum*, early 15th century.

The Hundred Years' War and the Great Schism

THE MODERN STATE was born in the later Middle Ages. The economic crisis which occurred at that point both adversely affected the resources of the various states and contributed indirectly to their formation. The survival of governments, confronted with the expenses incurred by permanent warfare, depended on their capacity to raise taxes, if necessary by submitting to the prior consent of assemblies such as the Parliament in England or the Estates – both national and provincial – in France, which met at the moments when the monarchy was at its weakest (in 1356–8, during Étienne Marcel's revolutionary uprising and the 'Jacquerie' which followed, in 1380–2 on the accession of Charles VI and in 1415–20 when Paris was occupied by the Anglo-Burgundians). The growing role of representative assemblies and the attempts to have the élites participate in decision-making were characteristic features of the political and institutional evolution of the period. This tendency could also be seen in the church with the Conciliary movement, which, given further impulsion by the Great Schism, considerably weakened the papal monarchy (Councils of Constance, Ferrara, Basle). Another striking feature was an increasing national particularism, which crystallized in wars but which also expressed itself in a rise in nationalist sentiment. The clearest examples of this are to be seen in anti-English feeling in Scotland, Bohemian disaffection with the Empire and Rome, and Polish opposition to the Teutonic Knights. For its part, the church, in its divided condition, was unable to avoid espousing these nascent nationalisms: national forms of Christianity found expression in Gallicanism, Anglicanism and Bohemian Utraquism. At the time of the Great Schism, the two (and subsequently three) rival allegiances flowed quite naturally into the pre-existing mould of the political alliances between the various states. The 'Clementine' party – partisans of the Avignon Pope – consisted of France, Scotland, the Iberian Peninsula and the Kingdom of Naples. Ranged behind the 'supporters of Urban', who favoured the Pope of Rome, were England, and with her Burgundy, the Empire, Flanders and Northern Italy. The internationalization of conflicts was therefore a further dominant characteristic of fourteenth and fifteenth-century Europe. It explains their generality and their inevitable repercussions, both on the level of rivalry between nations (France, England, Burgundy etc.) and that of the schism within the church and the struggle between rival ecclesiastical allegiances. For the first time, the whole of Europe seemed to suffer and fear at the same rhythm. Thus around 1380 the social upheavals which struck England, Italy and France coincided with the beginning of the Great Schism. In 1417 the Schism was healed, but France was torn by the bloody struggle between the Armagnacs and the Burgundians; the Lollards rose in England, the Taborites in Bohemia and the Conciliary movement seemed to be winning out within the church. After 1453 England and France were no longer in conflict, but the former was entering upon the Wars of the Roses, which set the houses of York and Lancaster against each other, and over the latter there hung the increasingly dangerous threat of encirclement by the states of the Duke of Burgundy, Charles the Bold. Only the defeat and death of Charles in 1477 would see an end to that threat.

1. Charles the Bold presiding over a chapter of the Order of the Golden Fleece. From the book of the same name by Guillaume Filastre, late 15th century.

Great Schism begins.

Battle of Agincourt.　　**Council of Constance: end of Schism.**

| 1378 | 1415 | 1417 |

1309–77: Papacy installed at Avignon, where seven popes succeed one another.
1311–12: Council of Vienna, which orders the suppression of the Templars.
1337–1453: Hundred Years War. The King of France, Philip IV, is initially defeated by Edward III of England, who takes Calais. In 1356 John the Good is defeated and taken prisoner at Poitiers. By the Treaty of Brétigny (1360), France loses Calais, le Ponthieu and Aquitaine.
1348–51: Black Death.
1364–80: Charles V king of France. With his constable, Du Guesclin, he reconquers the territories occupied by the English.
1378–1417: The Great Schism divides the church into two allegiances – 'Clementine' in Avignon, 'Urbanist' in Rome. In 1409 the Council of Pisa causes the birth of a third allegiance. The election of Martin V puts an end to the Schism in 1417.
1380–1422: Charles VI king of France. His madness promotes rivalry between the Armagnac party (that of Duke Louis of Orleans, assassinated in 1407) and the Burgundian party. The latter allies with the

2. Court life. Scene from a falcon hunt. Fresco by Matteo di Giovanetti da Viterbo, 14th century, Palais des Papes, Avignon.

English king Henry V, who has triumphed at Agincourt (1415). After the assassination of the Duke of Burgundy, John the Fearless, at Montereau in 1419, his party choose Henry V, the king of England, as king of France (Treaty of Troyes, 1420).
1386: The Swiss Confederation defeats Leopold III of Austria at Sempach.
1411–33: King Sigismond II calls the Council of Constance.
1414–18: Council of Constance. Execution of Jan Hus (1415).
1422–61: Charles VII denounces the Treaty of Troyes and reconquers his kingdom (in 1429 Joan of Arc liberates Orleans). The King is crowned at Reims, but Joan is executed in 1431. The alliance with Philip III the Good, Duke of Burgundy, allows the King to recapture Paris in 1436, then to reconquer Normandy (1449–50) and Guyenne (1450–53).
1431–9: Council of Basle, where the conciliary theory limiting the Pope's authority triumphs and where an agreement is struck with the Hussites (*Compactata* of 1436).
1438: Pragmatic Sanction at Bourges

3. The future emperor, Sigismond, receives homage from his Hungarian subjects at the Council of Constance in 1414. Engraving, 1483.

14th–15th centuries

The Hundred Year's War 1340-1360

★ Sluis (Sluys) 1340
Calais 1347 ★
Crécy 1346 ★
KINGDOM OF FRANCE
Brétigny ■
★ Poitiers 1356
Bordeaux ●

■ English possessions
■ Lands acquired by the Treaty of Brétigny, 1360
★ English victories

1360-1429

KINGDOM OF ENGLAND
Calais
Agincourt 1415 ★
Reims ●
Orleans
Chinon ●

◿ Territory owing allegiance to the King of England
⦁ Territory loyal to the King of France
■ Possessions of the Duke of Burgundy
■ Territory under the Duke of Burgundy's control
↪ Path followed by Joan of Arc

1429-1453

KINGDOM OF ENGLAND
Calais
Arras ■
Formigny 1450 ✪ Paris ● Reims ▼

◿ Burgundy allied to the King of France by the Peace of Arras (1435)
✪ French victories
▼ Coronation of the King of France in 1429
← Lands recaptured by Charles VII

The State of Burgundy

FRIESLAND
HOLLAND
GELDERLAND
ZEALAND BRABANT
FLANDERS Cologne
Calais
HAINAULT ARTOIS
Ricquigny LUXEMBURG
Amiens • Luxemburg
Reims
Nancy Strasbourg
LORRAINE
DUCHY OF BURGUNDY
Nevers Dijon Besançon
COUNTY OF BURGUNDY
• Macon

■ The Burgundian State at the accession of Philip the Bold, (1363)
■ 1364-1404 Lands acquired by Philip the Bold
■ 1419-1467 Lands acquired by Philip the Good
■ 1467-1477 Lands acquired by Charles the Bold
⦁ Ecclesiastical principalities under the influence of the Dukes of Burgundy

The Great Schism 1378-1417

WALES
CLEVES MARK
BRABANT NAMUR
BRITTANY HAINAULT
Constance
Basle STYRIA
GUYENNE Vienne CARINTHIA
TYROL
Avignon Ferrara
Pisa Florence
Rome

■ Regions of obedience to Avignon
□ Regions of obedience to Rome
⦁ Regions of variable obedience
◿ Avignon regions after 1409
■ Neutral regions

Execution of Joan of Arc.
1431

Defeat and death of Charles the Bold.
1477

between the Pope and Charles VII. The election of French prelates henceforth requires the king's consent.
1438–9: Councils of Ferrara and of Florence, which oppose the Pope. The union of the Greek and Latin churches is proclaimed, but the capture of Constantinople by the Turks (1453) will render it obsolete.
1450–85: Wars of the Roses in England between the houses of York (White Rose) and Lancaster (Red Rose). A scion of the latter house will found a new dynasty in 1485.
1461–83: Louis XI king of France. He opposes François II of Brittany and Charles the Bold, Duke of Burgundy. In 1468 at Péronne, where Charles is holding Louis prisoner, Charles forces him to cede Champagne. But the King makes an agreement with Edward IV of England against Charles (Treaty of Picquigny, 1475). Charles is finally defeated and killed at Nancy in 1477. His states fall to the Emperor Maximilian, husband of Mary of Burgundy. By the Treaty of Arras (1482), Burgundy and Picardy are ceded to Louis XI.

4. Ferdinand I re-entering Naples after his victory over the Angevins at Ischia in 1462. Anonymous Neapolitan artist.

Crisis and Change in the West

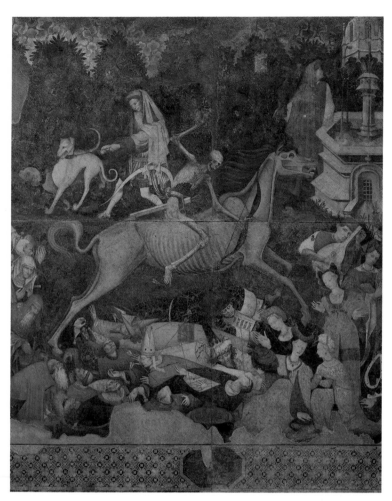

1. The Triumph of Death. 15th-century Sicilian fresco.

FROM THE END OF THE THIRTEENTH CENTURY Western economic and demographic expansion began to show definite signs of stagnation. The general depression which then set in was to last until the mid-fifteenth century, making deep inroads into medieval life, yet also creating the conditions for a new social and economic order.

The crisis first appeared in the rural economy. The consistent fall in agricultural prices, the tendency of a reduced pool of labour to increase wages, and an even more marked rise in the cost of manufactured products combined to cause growing instability. Grain crop failures, as in 1315 and 1316, brought famine and unrest for short periods to town and country. The years of dearth rendered the population particularly vulnerable, and in 1348–50 it suffered the full impact of the Plague. Not since the sixth century had the West experienced a scourge of such magnitude: in the space of three years the Black Death claimed a quarter to a third of Europe's population. Demographic and economic factors thus combined to alter the face of society drastically. Whole villages were deserted; agricultural activity converted away from staple food products to more profitable specialized crops and stock-rearing; rural populations moved into the towns, causing mass impoverishment.

It is against this background – further aggravated by constant war and political tension – that the numerous uprisings characteristic of the period must be set. On occasion, as in Flanders after 1323 or in the Ile-de-France in 1357, peasant insurgents sought to join forces with groups in the towns, where the issues of pay and working hours, the exclusion of journeymen from the mastery, and the effect of monetary changes on purchasing power were the source of extremely violent conflicts.

The depression, however, gradually brought about a modification of social and economic structures, the most obvious being the growing influence of state intervention, which henceforth determined fiscal and monetary policy and even attempted by decree to limit salaries and control the labour market. The economic attitude of the state was principally one of protectionism, defending home markets and granting monopolies to privileged merchants, e.g. Jacques Coeur in France under Charles VII, and the Medicis in the Papal States with their monopoly on Tolfa alum. New forms of capital organization emerged: the Medicis introduced affiliated companies, while large international monopolies were built up by the Hanseatic League in the Baltic. Equally evident is the shift in centres and axes of the European economy, the opening of the Saint Gotthard Pass in 1237 providing new impetus to central and northern Switzerland and southern Germany. The decline of trade fairs in the Champagne region was accompanied, on the one hand, by the rise in importance of the Rhône-Saône axis, the development of Marseille as a port, and fairs in Lyon and Chalon; and, on the other hand, by increasing activity on the Atlantic seaboard (La Rochelle, Brouage) and the growing importance of maritime countries such as Spain and Portugal – soon to discover the New World – England with its nascent woollen industry, and Holland, developing at the expense of Flanders, especially Bruges.

Bardi and Peruzzi bankruptcies in Florence	Black Death.	'Ciompi' revolt in Florence.
1343–6	**1348**	**1378**

1315–16: Grain crisis.
1323–7: Revolt in coastal Flanders.
1337–45: Strike by weavers in Ghent. Notable among their demands: a cut in working hours.
1343–6: Failures of the Florentine bankers Bardi and Peruzzi, following non-repayment of debts on the part of the Pope and the King of England.
1348–50: Black Death. Introduced via the Mediterranean, the Plague spread within three years to almost every country, killing up to a third of the European population.
1356–8: Political and fiscal disruption in Paris. Taking advantage of the imprisonment of French king, John II, the Good, merchants' provost Étienne Marcel imposed on Dauphin Charles the 'Grande Ordonnance' of 1357 which rendered the levying of taxes subject to the approval of the Etats Généraux. The Dauphin's escape and the subsequent murder of E. Marcel enabled the rebellion to be quelled.
1358: Peasant uprisings ('Jacquerie') in the Ile-de-France, Champagne and Picardy, suppressed by Charles II of Navarre at the

cost of 20,000 dead.
1377–83: Revolts throughout Europe. In Florence textile workers (the *'Ciompi'*) forced the inclusion of commoners (*'il populo minuto'*) in the Republic's political bodies.

4. Leper-house in France, 14th century. Miniature from Vincent de Beauvais's Miroir Historial.

Peasant revolts in England, also affecting London. Their leader, a priest named John Ball, preached equality for all. Rebellion in Rouen against new tax levies. 'Maillotin' uprising in Paris (so called after the insurgents' leaden hammers) in protest against a new tax. 'Tuchin' revolts in rural areas. Revolt, turning to insurrection, of the Lollards, a popular heretical movement in England inspired by the doctrines of John Wyclif.
1397–1456: Jacques Coeur, French merchant, native of Bourges, where he erected a magnificent palace. Established trading posts in all commercial centres in Europe and the Middle East. Banker to Charles VII, who entrusted important public functions to him. Financed the reconquest of Normandy before being arrested for embezzlement.
1411, 1434, 1438, 1441: Popular revolts in Scandinavia.
1413–14: Revolution in Paris led by butcher Simon Caboche in alliance with the Burgundians against Dauphin Charles VI. Imposition of the 'Ordonnance

Cabochienne'. The revolution was later quelled by the Armagnacs.
1414–20: Hussite uprising in Bohemia, rapidly weakened by its division into the moderates of Prague, who negotiated with the Council of Basle, and the 'Taborites', a popular radical movement based at Tábor. The latter, who preached social revolution, were finally defeated at Lipany in 1434.
1420: Royal charters granted by French king to Lyon fairs.
1450–70: Beginning of European economic revival.
1476: Niklashausen revolt in Thuringia, prelude to the Peasants' War of 1525.
1494–8: Florence: the waning power of the Medicis succeeded by the theocratic régime of Savonarola. Savonarola excommunicated by the Pope and later assassinated.

14th–15th centuries

7: Massacre at Meaux after revolt of the 'Jacques'. From
uscript of the Grandes Chroniques de France, 15th
ry.

nish fortress, c. 1450. Artist unknown.

Execution of Savonarola.

1498

uit and grain merchants, 15th century. Italian manuscript.

Europe at the time of the Black Death

▥ Peasant Revolts	★ Urban revolts

Propagation zone of the Black Death

1346 1347 1348 1349 1350 1351 1353

European Trade in the XVth century

Commercial routes
● Hanseatic towns
● Towns with fairs
● Principal trading centres

500 km

Medieval Africa

MUSLIM AND, LATER, European sources reveal to us that external forces exerted some influence within Africa during the 'medieval' period. The taming of the camel and Islamic dynamism opened up the Sahara, through which there had previously only been a trickle of travellers, and linked the Sudan, both intellectually and economically, to the outside world. The traditional openness of the eastern coast to the countries of the Indian Ocean took on a new dimension in this period, particularly on account of Islam. The Atlantic, however, was still one of the ends of the earth: this would not really change until the fifteenth century, when it first became a historic frontier.

These external forces have, however, often blurred the issue. Progress in archaeology and the development of more cogently argued historical theories have combined to cast some doubt on the aptness of applying the term 'medieval' to Africa. Settlements, developments in agriculture and animal husbandry and advances in metal-working are thought to have predated, in some instances, the medieval period, and indeed to have done so quite considerably. The political entities referred to in 'medieval' written (or sometimes oral) sources clearly stood on ground prepared by long processes of technological development of indigenous origin, however much these societies may subsequently have benefited from external contributions.

The foundations of the fifteenth-century Luban political society, for example, were laid by the earlier Kisalian culture. Another case is that of the peoples found on either side of the mid-Limpopo and from there to the Zambezi. The industrious society of that plateau – which was rapidly strewn with enclosures (Zimbabwe) – derived an important source of wealth from cattle-rearing. Evidence of the blossoming of that civilization can be seen at Mapungubwe, Mapela and, most importantly, at Great Zimbabwe, a major political and monumental centre. The flame of that culture is taken up in the fifteenth century by the Matapa and Butua states. On the eastern coast, from the ninth century onwards, an influx of Arabian, Persian and even more distant immigrants and cultural influences contributed to the formation of trading centres. To the south of Kismayu these factors also combined, over a number of years, to produce the Swahili language and civilization, which are African in origin but which contain some imported elements.

Though the kingdom of Aksum withered away in the tenth century, Christian Ethiopia continued to survive. After 1270 it enjoyed a two-century-long revitalisation which saw it assert its power over its – Muslim and non-Muslim – neighbours and consolidate the unity of Church and State. By contrast, though Christian Nubia flourished for several centuries, the influence of Islam eroded its power in the twelfth and thirteenth centuries and the Christian kingdoms finally disappeared between 1365 and 1500.

In the west, Jenne, Niani, Igbo-Ukwu and the Sao sites of the lower Chari are evidence of settled societies and the development of ancient techniques. From the eleventh century onwards Ife became the political and religious centre of the Yoruba country, and Benin was later to take certain technical and ideological elements from that source. The new trans-Saharan links stimulated the growth of empires. A western centre of power was provided successively by Ghana, Mali and the Songhai empire, whilst in the east Kanem-Bornu held sway. Alongside these empires, the Hausa and Senegambian states, amongst others, contributed to the rich political and human tapestry of that region.

1. Rock church in Lalibela, Ethiopia, 13th century.

Cathedral of Faras, Nubia.

Empire of Ghana.

7th century	8th–13th centuries
400–900: Development of the Jenne settlement. **7th–8th centuries:** Faras (or Pachoras) Cathedral (architecture, painting). Empire of Ghana, traces of which date back to the 8th century. **8th–9th centuries and after:** Kukiya kingdom, then that of Gao, another partner in trans-Saharan relations. **9th century:** Igbo-Ukwu remains (Bronzes, burial chamber of a high-ranking figure, long-distance trade links). **9th–10th centuries:** Emergence of Kanem. New dynasty in second half of 12th century and sovereign converted to Islam. **10th century:** Major disturbances in Christian Ethiopia. **10th–11th centuries:** High point for the trading city of Awdaghost. **10th–14th centuries:** Kisalian culture in the Upemba valley and around Lake Kisale (fishing, agriculture, long-range trade links, crafts). **11th century:** Islam in Takrur (mid-Senegal). **Second half of 11th century:** Almoravid militancy, originating among the Sanhajah	Berbers of Mauritania. In the Sudan its effect is to reinforce the presence of Islam and increase relations with the Maghreb. **11th–15th century:** The Ife assert political, technical, artistic and religious dominance in Yorubaland. **Beginning of 12th century:** King of Ghana converted to Islam. **12th–13th century:** Boom years for Mogadishu on the east coast. **c. 1200–c. 1450:** Intensive occupation of the (long inhabited) Great Zimbabwe site; clear signs of its political dominance and its distant economic relations. **13th century:** Kanem becomes very powerful and subjugates the Fezzan for a time at the end of the century. **First quarter of the 13th century:** Reign of Lalibela in Ethiopia; rupestrian churches in his capital (which takes his name). **Mid-13th century:** Mali becomes prominent under Sundiata (d. 1255); the Empire remains at its peak until the mid-14th century (reign of Mansa Musa, 1312–37). **1270:** New dynasty in Ethiopia which proclaims legitimate descent from Solomon.

3. Part of the ruins of Great Zimbabwe, discovered by Europeans in 1868.

Medieval Africa 700-1500

EMPIRE OF GHANA
Taghaza
Tichitt
Awdaghost
Awlil
Walata
TAKRUR
Kumbi Saleh
JOLOF
Jenne
Kangaba
Niani
MALI EMPIRE
Begho
Tadmekka
Timbuktu
Kukiya
SONGHAI
Daora
Katsina
Kano
AIR
NOK
Ife
Benin
Igbo-Ukwu
Takedda
Bilma
KANEM
Lake Chad
BORNU
Njimi
Zaria
KANEM BORNU EMPIRE
Niger
Faras
NOBATIA
MAKURRA
Dongola
'ALWA
Saba
Masawa
Aksum
Lalibela
Zeila
Berbera
CHRISTIAN ETHIOPIA
ADAL
Nile
BACHWEZI
Bigo
Lake Victoria
Brava
Merca
Mogadishu
Manda Island
Engaruka
Malindi
Mombasa
Pemba Island
Ungula Island (Zanzibar)
Mafia Island
Kilwa Kisiwanii
Anjouan Island
Iharana
Nosy Manja
Congo
KONGO
MBUNDU
LUBA
Sanga
KISALIAN
Lake Tanganyika
Lake Malawi
MARAVI
Ingombe Ilede
MATAPA
GREAT ZIMBABWE
LEOPARD'S KOPJE
MANYIKA
UTEVE
Sofala
Manekweni
Great Zimbabwe

Empires or kingdoms
Sanga — Sites
KISALIAN — Cultural areas
Equatorial forest
Savannah with more or less degraded forest
Plain or bush land
Sub-desert vegetation
Desert
Mediterranean vegetation

1000 km

The king and the camel-driver, a detail from the Great Catalan Atlas, 1373.

Great Zimbabwe.

c. 1200

Reign of Mansa Musa in Mali.

1312–37

Mwene Matapa kingdom.

c. 1450–1500

14th century?: Rise of Benin. Empire of Jolof.
1314–44: Reign of Amda Tseyon; militant religious policies based on a combination of Ethiopian nationalism, Christian tradition and

the conversion of conquered peoples.
End of 14th century: Decline of Mali. Around 1400, its capital is pillaged by the Songhai Empire, which is in the ascendant during the first half of the 15th century. The Empire of Kanem is reduced to the Bornu territory.
c. 1400?: Kongo kingdom.
14th–15th centuries: In the interlake zone, the Bachwezi political culture (nothing is known of the people involved). Kilwa on the east coast is powerful and prosperous.
1434–68: Reign of Zara Yacob in Ethiopia; warrior leader and spirited reformer, who combated heresy both practically and intellectually.
Mid-15th century: Rapid decline of Great Zimbabwe; Matapa in the north and Butua in the south-west rise in its place.

4. Bronze bust, made by lost wax technique, representing a king of Ife, Nigeria, c. 12th to 15th centuries.

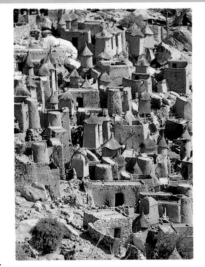

5. Traditional Dogon urban habitat, Mali.

6. Ivory breastplate. 15th century Benin art.

The Aztec Empire and its Antecedents

1. Teotihuacan, metropolis of the central plateau: the Pyramid of the Sun.

WHEN THE SPANIARDS invaded Mexico at the beginning of the sixteenth century, the Aztecs ruled over a powerful empire which opened on to two oceans, controlling the trade routes through Central America. That rapidly expanding empire was, however, quite a new creation. The ruling dynasty had only been in power for 150 years, whilst the history of the indigenous civilizations of Meso-America went back several millennia.

Around the year 1500 BC there existed in various parts of Mexico villages of sedentary farmers who had learnt how to cultivate maize and make pottery and who modelled feminine figurines which, it is assumed, represent the first images of the native gods. The population was already large, heterogeneous and differentiated. It is from this context that the Olmecs emerged. Originating in the low tropical lands along the coast of the Gulf of Mexico, they were to extend their influence over the central high plateau and the Pacific coast as far as Costa Rica. They were the bearers, in particular, of a religion based on the worship of the jaguar. It is the Olmecs who are responsible for

the first ceremonial centres in Central America, the first monumenta[l] sculpture, the first carved jade objects and the first traces of writing Around the year 300 BC the Olmecs disappeared as suddenly as the[y] had appeared. Regional cultures then developed, amongst which w[e] can distinguish those of the west (Colima, Jalisco, Nayarit) and thos[e] of the Basin of Mexico (site of Cuicuilco).

It was to be some six centuries before two new cradles of civilizatio[n] – Teotihuacan and the Mayas – emerged. If there was no 'Teoti[-]huacan Empire' in the strict sense of the term, the great metropolis o[f] the central plateau nonetheless exerted an influence across a wid[e] zone, stretching from Nayarit to Guatemala, by way of Monte Alba[n]. Teotihuacan thus disseminated certain cultural features – like th[e] step pyramid or the cult of the rain god – all of which contributed t[o] establishing a homogeneous culture in Central America.

In the same period the other contending centre of power wa[s] located in the lands of the Maya, a constellation of city-states which[,] contrary to a widespread fallacy, fought a great deal among them[-]selves. This highly cultivated society, which produced an exuberan[t] art, declined during the course of the ninth century. It seems that[,] having turned in upon itself, it collapsed from within.

It is at this point that northern Mexico saw great migrations[.] Tribes of nomadic hunters who came from the north and spok[e] Nahuatl invaded the central plateau and rapidly won control of tha[t] region. Among the first to rise to prominence were the Toltecs. B[y] contrast, the first Aztecs would be the last Nahuas to arrive in th[e] valley of Mexico, at the end of a long migration. The Aztecs settled i[n] Mexico-Tenochtitlan on an island in the middle of a vast lake. Afte[r] modest beginnings, the town soon took on the appearance of a capital[.] Sustained by an élite army, the Aztec regime asserted its crushing superiority. It organized the state not only in its administrative functioning but also, and most importantly, in its ideological under[-]pinnings. Emperor Motecuhzoma I and his brother Tlacaele[l] invented a new religion, a synthesis of northern tribal traditions and the preceding indigenous cultures. Holy war and its correlate, huma[n] sacrifice, which skilfully united the priesthood and the army, serve[d] as the cornerstones of a systematic expansion policy pursued fro[m] 1428 onwards. This policy would find only one obstacle in its path[:] the Tarascan empire of Michoacan which was definitively to bloc[k] the Aztecs' westward thrust. In 1519 Motecuhzoma II reigned over 20 million subjects and the valley of Mexico, which probably alone had five million inhabitants, was at that time the greatest urba[n] concentration in the world.

It was this empire which Cortes would conquer with the aid of 60[0] soldiers, sixteen horses, ten cannons and thirteen arquebuses.

850: Beginning of the great Nahua invasions from the north of Mexico. Founding of Tula by the Toltecs.
900: Collapse of the Maya civilization (Yucatan and Guatemala).
970–985: Reign of Topiltzin Quetzlcoatl at Tula. The death of the sovereign marks the beginning of the dispersion of the Toltecs throughout the whole of Mexico.
1100: The Nahuas dominate the central plateau. Mexican dynasties also rule over most Mayan cities. The Aztecs are still merely a nomadic tribe wandering through northern Mexico.
1325: Aztecs settle at Mexico-Tenochtitlan.
1376: Accession of Acamapichtli, founder of the Mexica (Aztec) dynasty.
1428: Victory of Tenochtitlan over the rival city of Azcapotzalco; the Aztecs rule over the Basin of Mexico. Enthronement of Itzcoatl.
1429: Triple Alliance constituted (Mexico, Tetzcoco, Tlacopan).
1440: Motecuhzoma I crowned. The Aztecs reign over Cuernavaca and the hot lands of Morelos.

1450–4: Natural calamities produce a long and deadly famine.
1468: Axayacatl succeeds Motecuhzoma I and pursues expansionist policies.
1469: Occupation of the Totonac region on the coast of the Gulf of Mexico.
1478: Failure of Michoacan's campaign. The Tarascans will remain outside the Empire.
1486: Emperor Ahuitzotl, seventh Aztec sovereign. Newly elected, he extends the Templo Mayor in Mexico City and inaugurates it by sacrificing 20,000 prisoners of war.
1487–8: Beginning of the campaigns of conquest over the Huaxteca, Guerrero and Oaxaca.
1492: Christopher Columbus discovers the Bahamas.
1496: Conquest of Tehuantepec by the Aztecs.
1500: Conquest of Soconusco at the frontier of Mayan territory.
1502: Motecuhzoma II succeeds Ahuitzotl: the expansion of the Aztec Empire marks time; Mexico's rivalry with Tlaxcallan becomes exacerbated.

4. Codex tro-cortesianus or Madrid Codex. Mayan divinatory manuscript.

1517: First reconnaissance of the coasts of Mexico by Hernandez de Cordoba.
1518: Juan de Grijalva's expedition reaches the Veracruz region. The Spaniards are forced back.
1519: Having set out from Cuba, Hernan Cortes lands near the site of modern Veracruz (22 April), marches on Mexico (August), enters Tlaxacallan (23 Sept.), destroys Cholula (18 Oct.), and enters Mexico (8. Nov.), where he takes power.
30 June 1520: The *Noche triste*; rout of the Spaniards and their flight from Mexico.
1521: Cortes besieges Mexico, which falls on 13 August. The Aztec Empire becomes New Spain under the authority of Cortes, who is named Captain General.

850–1521

*a: columns of the front hall of the Toltec Temple of the
ing Star.*

*ull decorated with mosaic of turquoises and ivory, Oaxaca
y.*

	Inaugural sacrifices at the Templo Mayor	Fall of the Aztec Empire
	1486	1521

tatue from Las Limas (Vera Cruz), Olmec civilization.

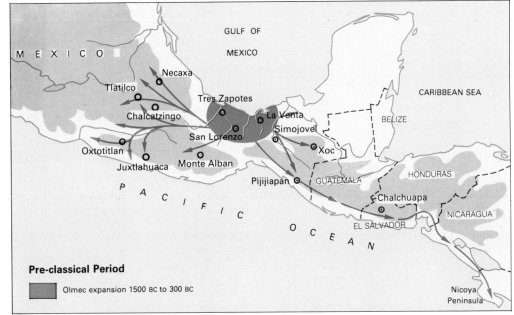

Pre-classical Period

Olmec expansion 1500 BC to 300 BC

Map labels: GULF OF MEXICO, MEXICO, CARIBBEAN SEA, Necaxa, Tlatilco, Tres Zapotes, La Venta, BELIZE, Chalcatzingo, Simojovel, San Lorenzo, Xoc, Oxtotitlan, HONDURAS, Juxtlahuaca, Monte Alban, PACIFIC OCEAN, Pijijiapan, GUATEMALA, Chalchuapa, EL SALVADOR, NICARAGUA, Nicoya Peninsula

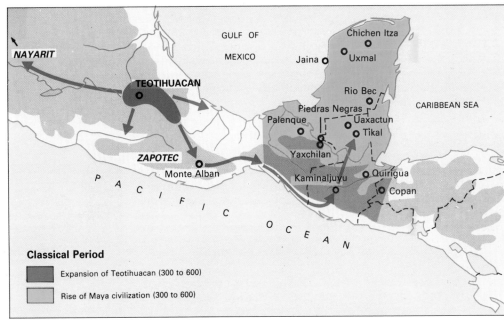

Classical Period

Expansion of Teotihuacan (300 to 600)

Rise of Maya civilization (300 to 600)

Map labels: NAYARIT, GULF OF MEXICO, Chichen Itza, Jaina, Uxmal, TEOTIHUACAN, Rio Bec, CARIBBEAN SEA, Piedras Negras, Palenque, Uaxactun, ZAPOTEC, Tikal, Monte Alban, Yaxchilan, Kaminaljuyu, Quirigua, Copan, PACIFIC OCEAN

Post-classical Period

Aztec Empire on the eve of conquest by the Spaniards (1519)

The Maya-Toltec region (1100 to 1400)

The Quiché-Cakchiquel (1200 to 1500)

Map labels: NAYARIT, Ixtlan, Tula, Cempoala, Mayapan, Chichen Itza, Tulum, MACHOACAN, Cortes 1519, Champoton, Tzintzuntzan, Mexico-Tenochtitlan, Tlaxcala, Tayasal, Oaxaca, Acapulco, Mitla, Tehuantepec, Utatlan, Iximche

500 km

The Inca Empire and its Antecedents

As though there existed some kind of historical symmetry between North and South America, the chronology of pre-hispanic Peru is not appreciably different from that of pre-Columbian Mexico. It is around the year 1500 BC that the first farming settlements appear, together with the first monumental constructions, which had a religious function. Then the dawn of the first millennium BC sees the emergence of the parent civilization of the Andean world: Chavin culture, characterized by the worship of a feline god, was to see its influence spread not only in the north of Peru but also on the southern coast. The theme of the semi-human, semi-divine jaguar, for example, recurs on the pottery and multi-coloured cotton funeral garments of the inhabitants of Paracas. This Chavin influence, which in certain respects is reminiscent of that of the Olmecs in Mexico, seems to have produced the beginnings of a uniform culture in Peru.

Towards 300 BC, however, the influence of Chavin declined and regional variations began to assert themselves. Peru became fragmented. Each coastal valley, each Andean basin developed its own original culture. On the coast, metalwork, weaving and ceramics attained an artistic quality which remained unsurpassed. In the north, the most dynamic civilization was that of the Mochica; in the south, the Nazca, the brilliant inheritors of Paracas traditions, were dominant. By comparison, the highlands of the interior did not experience the same magnificent development. It was not until the ninth century that Peru's cultural centre of gravity shifted. The motive force for this shift came from Tiahuanaco, which was situated 4,000 metres above sea level near Lake Titicaca. A much more militarist culture soon emerged and the government of Tiahuanaco, after having built a second capital at Huari (Ayacucho), succeeded in unifying the previously very fragmented Andean world. This supremacy of the high plateaus over the coast lasted for approximately two centuries.

Around 1200 AD the country again became split. In the south the Inca state was founded, whilst in the north the Chimu established themselves in the ancient territory of the Mochica. They founded a capital at Chanchan and ruled for more than two centuries over a sort of coastal empire, controlling some 1,200 kilometres of littoral. Their advance was not to be halted until the rise of the Incas in the middle of the fifteenth century.

The Inca state was born at Cuzco, in the heart of the Andes. Its origins are obscure. In the thirteenth and fourteenth centuries the Incas were not really distinguishable from the other tribes who lived a half-peasant, half-warrior life on the Andean plateau. But after the enthronement of Pachacuti, which followed victory over the Chanca (1440), the Inca triumph was stunning. Pachacuti behaved like a

1. The Inca city of Machu Picchu, looking towards Huyana Picchu.

Cuzco capital of the Incas.

The Incas reach Qu

1250

14

1250: Incas settle at Cuzco.
1400: Reign of Viracocha, eighth sovereign of the Inca dynasty: his authority only extended over a 40 km radius around Cuzco.

3. Mochica pottery.

1440: Battle of Cuzco: the Incas defeat the Chanca. In triumph, Viracocha's son deposes his father and reigns under the name Pachacuti.
1441–4: Campaigns of conquest – Vilcas in the west, Lake Titicaca in the east, Arequipa in the south.
1463–70: Expeditions of Capac Yupanqui, brother of Pachacuti Inca – conquest of the north, subjugation of the Chimu; the Incas reach Quito (Ecuador).
1471–4: Inca domination extends as far as the southern coast of Peru.
1473: Death of Pachacuti; accession of Topa Yupanqui, his son.
1473–5: The Amazonian dream. Topa, at the head of the Inca army, descends the Amarumayu (Rio Madre de Dios) and reaches the tropics. Expedition ends in disappointment. A rebellion on the Shores of Lake Titicaca brings him back to Cuzco.
1480: The 'pacification' of Bolivia.
1484: Conquest of northern and central Chile. Garrison set up at Coquimbo, at the southernmost tip of the Inca Empire.
1485–9: Topa's Great Progress. The Inca

took four years to travel around and inspect the whole of his empire.
1492: Christopher Columbus lands on the coast of the West Indies.
1493: Death of Topa at Chinchero, near Cuzco. Palace intrigues. Accession of Huayna Capac, aged five, who governs with his elder brothers.
1500: Portuguese explorer Cabral discovers the Brazilian coast.
1511: Huayna Capac leads a military campaign into the far north against the Carangui of Ecuador.
1511–26: The Inca king dedicates himself to the 'pacification' of the north. A regent is installed in Cuzco.
1513: Having crossed the Panama isthmus, the Spanish conquistador Balboa discovers the Pacific.
1514: Smallpox, brought by the Spaniards, begins to decimate the Indian populations.
1523: Induced to do so by the Portuguese, who have gone into Brazil, the Chiriguano launch a raid on the Inca Empire's Bolivian frontier.
1524: First expedition of Francisco Pizarro,

from Panama to the Columbian coast.
1526: Huayna Capac dies of smallpox at Quito. Pizarro's second voyage, which touches land on the coast of Ecuador.
1527: Pizarro reaches Peru, then returns to Panama. Huascar proclaims himself king of Cuzco, whilst his brother Atahuallpa has himself acclaimed sovereign of Quito. Partitioning of the Empire.
1530: War between the feuding brothers; defeat of Huascar.
1531: Pizarro's third voyage. The conquistador lands with less than 200 soldiers.
16 November 1532: Battle of Cajamarca. The Spaniards impose their superiority. Atahuallpa is taken prisoner.
29 August 1533: Atahuallpa is hanged by Pizarro at Cajamarca.
15 November 1533: The Spaniards enter Cuzco.

1250–1533

conqueror, but also like a wise organizer. In order to integrate the conquered populations, he imposed *Quechua* as the common language of the entire empire, set in train a policy of forced resettlement and made sun worship obligatory. Tribute and corvées made possible the opening up of roads, the building of terraces to grow maize and the construction of forts built in cyclopean blocks. When Topa Inca progressed around his empire at the end of the fifteenth century it extended over more than 900,000 square kilometres, and covered 4,000 kilometres of coastline. The very size of the Inca Empire was the cause of its fragility. Before the Spanish conquistadors landed the state had split in two and various hotbeds of agitation were appearing. It was easy for Pizarro to exploit these internal rivalries and conquer the country.

2. Pre-Inca ceremonial knife (Chimu culture).

pa Inca journeys
t around his empire.   **Fall of the Inca Empire.**

85–9   1533

4. The Inca fortress of Sacsahuaman, near Cuzco.

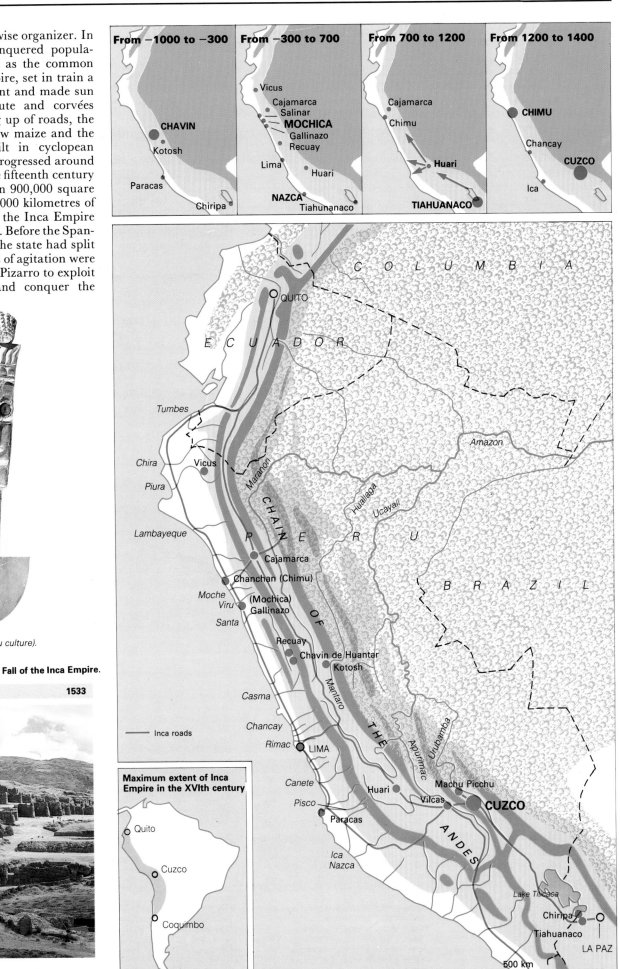

From −1000 to −300

CHAVIN
Kotosh
Paracas
Chiripa

From −300 to 700

Vicus
Cajamarca
Salinar
MOCHICA
Gallinazo
Recuay
Lima
Huari
NAZCA
Tiahunanaco

From 700 to 1200

Cajamarca
Chimu
Huari
TIAHUANACO

From 1200 to 1400

CHIMU
Chancay
CUZCO
Ica

COLUMBIA
QUITO
ECUADOR
Tumbes
Chira
Vicus
Piura
Maranon
Amazon
Lambayeque
Cajamarca
Huallaga
Ucayali
Chanchan (Chimu)
Moche
Viru
(Mochica)
Santa
Gallinazo
Recuay
Chavin de Huantar
Kotosh
Casma
Mantaro
Chancay
Rimac
LIMA
Canete
Huari
Pisco
Vilcas
Paracas
Machu Picchu
CUZCO
Apurimac
Urubamba
BRAZIL
Ica
Nazca
ANDES
Lake Titicaca
Chiripa
Tiahuanaco
LA PAZ

Inca roads

Maximum extent of Inca Empire in the XVIth century

Quito
Cuzco
Coquimbo

500 km

China, Europe and World Exploration

THE FIFTEENTH CENTURY is one of those turning-points in history, like the centuries around 3000 BC and the first three decades of the twentieth: it laid the foundations of capitalism and the world market. But it also had its own distinct sub-periods and turning-points, the most important of which was the period 1465–70. This was when the Equator was crossed, the terrors of the unknown overcome; the circumnavigation of Africa was within sight and Africa's gold fell into European hands. In fact, the West had begun to take off. The last third of the fifteenth century is the period that recurs whenever historians try to locate the beginnings of 'modern' economic development in the regions of Western Europe.

The medieval world (like that of Antiquity) was less unbalanced than our own; development was more even, countries did not progress at such widely different rates. In spite of this, Europe before the fifteenth century lagged behind the Orient – particularly China – in almost every field. Admiral Cheng Ho, who headed Chinese maritime exploration from 1405 to 1433, had enormous resources at his disposal. The cockleshells and paltry fleet of Dias and Columbus were no match for the enormous junks and tens of thousands of men under Cheng Ho's command. The Chinese made seven expeditions to the South Seas; they visited Southeast Asia, Indonesia, India, Persia, Arabia, Somalia and Kenya. They exchanged sumptuous and exotic presents, received promises of friendship and vows of submission. Then, strange as it may seem, they ceased their wanderings. They were not there when the Portuguese reached the Cape; they did not overtake them at La Miña, nor did they encounter them at Cape St Vincent or Lisbon. Why was it the Westerners who, almost without realizing it, ended the isolation of separate civilizations? Why were they the ones who, to their own glory and great profit, put the peoples of the world in touch with each other? Answers suggest themselves when we compare the two blocs. The West was poor, it coveted gold and spices. China, on the other hand, had banknotes, the silver of Japan, the tropics on its doorstep; it had no need to seek the solution of forging new geographical links. The West was under threat: the Turks occupied the Near East and were moving westwards; trade with Eastern countries meant parting with precious metals and was not advantageous to the middle man. Alternative solutions were imperative. The 'middle part' of China was peaceful and stable; if it were to push southwards too forcibly it would leave the northern frontier vulnerable and risk unleashing the only real peril – the perennial peril of the Steppes. The West was divided into many weak states, even if the rivalries between them could be positive (Venetians and Genoese, Portuguese and Spaniards). Whereas imperial China was strong and it was not easy to evade its grasp or disobey its commands. The West needed to come out of itself, but how? Its physical space was beset on all sides by the sea, so it was naturally drawn to navigation. Portugal, because of the Trade Winds, was drawn to the southern seas. The West had for centuries been fed on Greek cosmography, Latin cartography, Italian and Norman naval daring, not to mention the Crusades. For a long time technology in the West had been far ahead of political and social organization, which had remained rudimentary, feudal. And for some time now, Western high culture, particularly painting, had been obsessed by space, by the rendering of perspective, the pushing back of horizons....

The West was not alone in this adventure. Discovery was not simply the monopoly of the Portuguese and Spanish, aided by numerous Italians, a few French at the beginning of the century and a few English at the end. On the contrary, many and diverse lands were caught up in the fascination for distant parts, but the West preceded and outdistanced them all. For four centuries the world was to become Western.

1. Western Africa according to a Portuguese atlas of 1563.

From c. 1400: Major improvements made in Western sailing ships.
1402: Korean map shows tip of Africa.
1402–6: French explore the Canary Islands.
1405: First major Chinese sea expeditions.
1406: Ptolemy rediscovered in the West.
From 1407: Chinese missions to Central Asia.
1409–11 and 1411–15: Second and third Chinese sea expeditions to Indonesia, India etc.
1413: Pierre d'Ailly's work *Imago mundi* inspires Christopher Columbus.
1415: Ceuta in Morocco captured. Portuguese maritime expansion begins. Kenyan giraffes shown at court of Nanking.
1417–19: Chinese ships reach east coast of Africa.
c. 1418: Gypsies reach Western Europe. In 1418 Henry the Navigator, Prince of Portugal, organizes Cape St Vincent as a base for Portuguese expeditions.
From 1419: Portuguese on Madeira. Voyages of Venetian Niccolo Dei Conti to Vijayanagar in India (1420) and Southeast Asia.
1419–22: Persian traveller in China.
c. 1420: First caravels (?). Indian or Arab ship rounds Cape of Good Hope and sails into the Atlantic.
1425: Celebrated Korean geographical work.
1431–3: Seventh and last Chinese expedition in Indian Ocean. Chinese ships again reach Africa (Somalia, Kenya and possibly Tanzania and Mozambique).
c. 1436: Cape Bojador is rounded (coast of western Sahara); Portuguese reach Rio de Oro.
1437: Tangier expedition proves disastrous for Portuguese.
c. 1442: Development of caravel. Pope recognizes African 'Crusade'. First African base on Arguin Island. First black slaves to Portugal. Discoveries multiply. Cape Blanc reached in 1441, Cape Verde in 1444.
1455: First African spices reach Portugal.
1461: Major geographical directory printed in China.
From 1462: Nautical treatise of Ahmad ibn Madjid, possible future pilot of Vasco da Gama on Indian Ocean expedition.
From 1465: Russian expeditions to Siberia. Abortive Chinese plans for sea expeditions.
From 1465–70: Marked progress of stellar navigation in West. Portuguese explore Gulf of Guinea and cross Equator. Gold from La Miña (now Ghana) reaches Europe. Slave trade develops. Idea of sailing round Africa spreads. Portuguese crown now allied to private capital.
1466–72: Russian Nikitin travels to India.
c. 1470: An Italian visits Timbuktu. English reach Newfoundland (?).
From 1470: First pivoted front axles developed on four-wheeled vehicles.
1476: Christopher Columbus in Portugal.
Last decades of 15th century: Migrations of Nilotic peoples to East Africa. Arrival of Somalian-Ethiopian peoples in Madagascar. Migration of Brazilian Indians. Inca expansion. Aztec expansion.
c. 1484–5: New developments in navigational techniques.
1485–6: Columbus leaves Portugal for Spain, where he is welcomed by Queen Isabella.
1485–8: Diego Cão and Bartholomeu Dias reach the tip of Africa.
1487: Chinese memorandum advocating maritime trade.
1492: The 'Columbus of mountaineering' climbs the Mont Aiguille in the French Alps. Martin Behaim produces a globe in Germany. Columbus discovers the Caribbean Islands.
1493: Pope dictates limits of Spanish and Portuguese expansion ('Inter caetera' Bull).
1496–7: John Cabot, an Italian in the service of the King of England, explores North Atlantic and discovers Labrador.
1497–8: Vasco da Gama reaches India via the Cape.
1498: On his third journey Columbus discovers American continent.

1400–1500

Giraffe brought back from Africa by Chinese
miral Zheng He in 1414, by the artist Shen Tu.

Portuguese warrior portrayed by Benin artist.
th-century brass plaque.

1400-1460

Nanking

MING Empire

HONAN

Poulo Condor

Azores

Cape St Vincent

PERSIA
Conti

Madeira

Canary Islands

Ceuta

INDIA

Melaka

EQUATOR

Jiddah
Mecca
Aden

Calicut

CEYLON

SUMATRA

Surabaya

Cape
Verde Islands

Maldives

JAVA

SOMALIA

St Vincent

Cape

KENYA

MOZAMBIQUE

Cape of Good Hope

Area of Chinese and African
exploration

Expeditions of Chinese admiral
Cheng Ho

African migrations

European expeditions and area
of exploration

1460-1520

1547

SIBERIA

LABRADOR

John Cabot

Nikitin's journey 1466-1472

Macao

FORMOSA

Caribbean

Death of
Magellan

Sea

Christopher Columbus

Hormuz

Diu

Calicut

M O L U C C A S

EQUATOR

1498

Cape Blanc

Cape Verde

Aden

São Jorge de Mina

Natal

São Tome

Natal

Magellan

Treaty of Saragossa 1529

S P A I N   P O R T U G A L

Treaty of Tordesillas 1494

The First Division of the World

AFTER THE ERA of the discoverers came the age of the 'conquistadors'. Strengthened by the blessing of the Pope ('Inter caetera' Bull, 1493) and the agreement of the Chancelleries (Treaty of Tordesillas, 1494), urged on by the taste for riches and adventure, and by missionary zeal as well, intrepid men left to conquer new worlds. In 1519, with 600 men and sixteen horses, Hernán Cortez seized Mexico, the great Aztec Empire. Ten years later, with fewer than 200 men and twenty-seven horses, Francisco Pizarro decided the fate of the Inca Empire of Peru. In one generation, Central and South America became 'Latin', that is to say Spanish or, in the case of Brazil, Portuguese. Between 1540 and 1550 the discovery of the silver mines in Mexico and Peru – especially Potosí in upper Peru – was to help the Spanish maintain a fifty-year political and military hegemony over Europe.

The Portuguese pushed down towards the south, along the west coast of Africa and then up the east coast, moving out into the Indian Ocean. They settled on the west coast of the sub-continent, took Ormuz, then Malacca, seized the principal spice market, the Moluccas (or Spice Islands) in 1512, and finally gained a foothold in Japan (1543) and China (1557). At the same time they colonized Brazil, which had quickly become the world's main sugar producer. But Spanish and Portuguese hegemony could not last. The future of imperialism belonged to the northern nations, who were richer in human and material resources and more modern in terms of state and social structures. Late entrants in the race and confined to 'lands of no worth' in North America and seeking the famous 'passage' to India, the French and Dutch settled where they could, the former in the St Lawrence valley and around the Great Lakes and the latter in the Hudson valley. Although they arrived last, the British moved in in more tightly closed groups and enjoyed the support of the mother country. They were eventually to acquire control of the continent.

The latecomers did not resign themselves, however, to a Spanish and Portuguese monopoly over the 'prime' sites, from which flowed gold, silver, spices, sugar and slaves. Practising first piracy (French and Dutch Calvinists, and English corsairs such as Drake and Hawkins), then open war, they eventually seized entire colonies, the British through the East India Company, founded in 1600.

In 1602 the Dutch created their own company, which was by far the most powerful, and systematically chased the Portuguese from their bases along the length of the spice route to the Moluccas, then – from their stronghold at Batavia (Djakarta) – from Malacca and Ceylon. All the while, the coasts of India, the Caribbean and Africa became the private property of the British and the French. In the seventeenth

century the Spanish and Portuguese imperial monopoly was finally broken in favour of the northern powers – a situation which was repeated in Europe itself (see below).

Within three generations the face of the whole globe had changed

1. Beginnings of Spanish America: Francisco Pizarro, conqueror of Peru.

The sword of the conquistadors, the 'microbic unification of the world' and the brutality of the colonists had depopulated the American continent. The slave trade had bled Africa and given a tremendous lift to the European economy, now effectively a 'world economy', and the white man had imposed his total rule and his civilization everywhere. From this time on, even those adversaries who attacked him were to do so with his weapons and his concepts.

Voyage of Christopher Columbus.	Cabral discovers Brazil.	Cortez among the Aztecs.	Pizarro among the Incas.
1492	**1500**	**1519**	**1531**

1479: Treaty of Alcacovas between Spain and Portugal concerning the Atlantic islands.
1493: 'Inter caetera' Bull recognizing Castillian sovereignty over lands already discovered and as yet undiscovered beyond an imaginary line passing 100 leagues west and south of the Azores and Cape Verde.
1494: Tordesillas Treaty: Portugal and Spain divide the New World between them.
1501: Beginning of the African slave traffic to the Americas.
1505–15: The viceroys Almeida and Albuquerque build the Portuguese trade empire – Ormuz, Goa, Ceylon, Malacca, East Indies.
1508–11: Conquest of Puerto Rico. Colonization of Jamaica.
1511–15: Conquest of Cuba by Diego Velasquez.
1519–21: Hernán Cortez conquers the Aztec Empire and refounds Mexico.
1521–30: Portuguese colonization of Brazil.
1523–35: Conquest of Guatemala, El Salvador, Honduras, Yucatan.
1524: Seville receives the monopoly of Spanish colonial trade.

1529: Treaty of Saragossa between Spain and Portugal fixes the demarcation line in the Far East.
1531–4: Francisco Pizarro conquers the Inca Empire.
1535–8: Conquest of Columbia by Gonzalo Jimenez de Quesada.
1546: Foundation of Potosí, silver mining centre of Peru.
1557: The Portuguese gain foothold in Macao.
1562: John Hawkins is the first Englishman to trade in slaves between West Africa and the New World.
1565–71: Legazpi subjugates the Philippines and founds Manila (1571).
1565: The Portuguese found Rio de Janeiro.
1574: Beginnings of Portuguese colonization in Angola.
1577–80: Voyages of Francis Drake along the Pacific coasts.
1584: Sir Walter Raleigh founds Virginia.
1600: Founding of the British East India Company.
1602: Dutch East India Company.
1608: Samuel de Champlain founds Quebec.

2. Francisco de Almeida.

3. Alfonso de Albuquerque.

15th–17th centuries

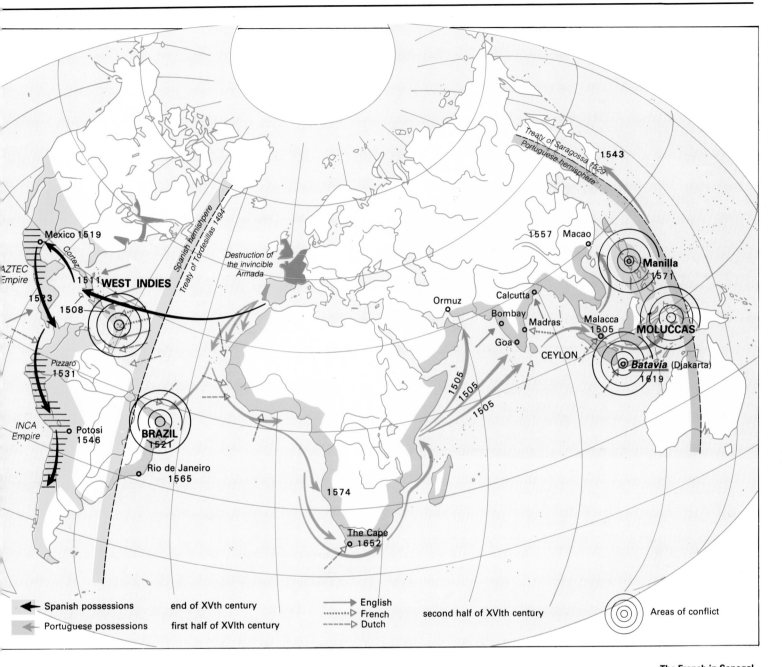

Mexico 1519

Cortez

1511 **WEST INDIES**

AZTEC Empire

1523

1508

Pizzaro 1531

Potosi 1546

INCA Empire

BRAZIL 1521

Rio de Janeiro 1565

Spanish hemishpere Treaty of Tordesillas 1494

Destruction of the invincible Armada

Treaty of Saragossa 1529 Portuguese hemisphere

1543

1557 Macao

Manilla 1571

Ormuz

Calcutta

Bombay

Madras

Goa

Malacca 1505

MOLUCCAS

CEYLON

Batavia (Djakarta) 1619

1505

1505

1505

1574

The Cape 1652

Symbol	Meaning		Symbol	Meaning
←	Spanish possessions	end of XVth century	→	English
←	Portuguese possessions	first half of XVIth century	▷	French
			▷	Dutch

second half of XVIth century

Areas of conflict

1609: The Portuguese lose Ceylon to Holland.
1619: The Dutch found Batavia.
1620: Voyage of the Mayflower, the vessel of the Pilgrim Fathers.
1621: Dutch West India Company.
1624: The Dutch gain a foothold in Taiwan.
1624–54: Dutch-Portuguese wars over Brazil.
1625–64: The French settle in the West Indies.

1637: French settlements throughout the length of Senegal.
1641: The Dutch take Malacca from the Portuguese.
1642: Founding of Montreal (Ville-Marie).
1652: The Dutch found the Cape.
1664: Colbert founds the French East India Company; New Amsterdam, founded in 1626, becomes New York.
1682: Cavelier de la Salle takes possession of Louisiana.
1686: Louis XIV annexes Madagascar.
1697: Treaty of Ryswick; France receives Haiti.
1699–1702: Start of French colonization in Louisiana.

4. A caravelle.

5. The massacre of Aztec chiefs at Tenochtitlan in 1521, codex of Diego Duran, 1579.

The Expansion of Financial and Commercial Capitalism

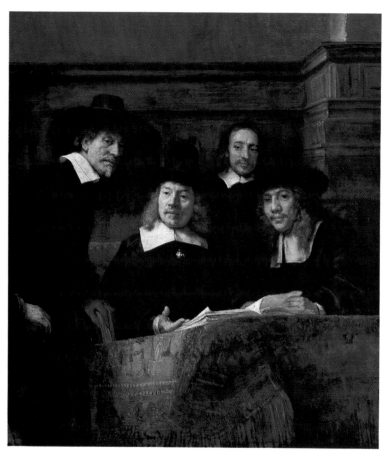

1. Urban oligarchic forces: the cloth-making syndics of Amsterdam, as seen by Rembrandt.

FROM THE SECOND HALF of the fifteenth century the crisis during the latter part of the Middle Ages was brought to a halt, the population curve stabilized and the Western world entered a long period of economic progress. Although the structures remained essentially medieval, beyond any doubt the advent of colonialism, the emergence of 'new monarchies', the enormous concentration of capital in the hands of great 'merchants' (whose role was that of banker, manufacturer and trader) and the appearance of state and private monopolies of international size and scale all created the conditions for the first capitalist age. The powerful bourgeois – individualistic, hardworking, something of an adventurer, concerning himself with the business of princes (in order to improve his own) and dealing even more effectively with them – became a perfectly defined social type, the complete opposite of the medieval *miles christianus*. In Europe itself, the main axes of trade did not undergo significant changes. In the fifteenth century Venice had a virtual monopoly in spices from the East, which were distributed by Venetian and German merchants along a southwest–northeast trade route (from France and Spain to Germany, the Baltic and Scandinavian states) with an extension towards the north-west (Netherlands and England). From the Scandinavian countries came wheat, wood and skins to be exchanged for salt, wine and manufactured goods from the more developed European countries. Arab merchants brought to Mediterranean ports exotic products from those parts of the world with which Europe had not yet forged direct links: slaves and African gold, Chinese silks, Indian spices. ...

The great fortunes of the late Middle Ages and the beginnings of the modern era had their origins in the south and were centred on the Mediterranean. There were first of all the Florentines, then the Genoese and the south Germans. The organization of trade may well have been archaic still, but commercial techniques had made notable progress and the first commodity markets allowed speculative business to be carried out on a large scale. Later, the appearance of public banks was to bring new facilities to international trade. In the wake of further discoveries, direct contacts were established and the Venetian monopoly declined. Europe, Africa and America formed an enormous three-way trading bloc: ships loaded with alcohol, arms and glass beads traded their cargoes all along the African coast against slaves destined for the sugar plantations of America; there, in the holds of the same boats, sugar cane, and later tobacco and cotton were loaded destined for the European ports, replacing human flesh. The American money that passed through Seville paid for the products needed by the colonists and flooded the money markets in Genoa, Piacenza, Lyons, London and Antwerp. At the same time, the Portuguese maintained trade with India and the fabulous Spice Islands of eastern Asia. Spices were used to pay for German copper, iron and silver among other things. But the Portuguese and the Spanish were soon to be shouldered aside by the French, the British and the Dutch.

In the sixteenth century Antwerp was the centre of European and Atlantic trade. The bankruptcies suffered by nations in the fifties and sixties, war and the religious troubles all hastened its decline, and in the seventeenth century Amsterdam took over the torch before itself being supplanted by London a century later. The significance of this enormous shift to the west and north is clear: the Spanish and Portuguese had revolutionized the world economy and the Protestant powers and France were to benefit from it.

Casa de Contratación.	Le Havre.	Muscovy Company.
1503	1517	1554

2. A builder of empire: Jakob II Fugger 'The Rich' and his accountant.

1462: Protectionist edict of Louis XI ensuring the prosperity of the Lyon fairs.
1487: The Fuggers secure control over the silver mines in the Tirol, then Thuringen and Hungary, and become the sponsors of the imperial crown.
1488: Bruges loses its commercial advantages to Antwerp.
1503: Founding of the Casa de Contratación in Seville.
1506: The King of Portugal reserves the monopoly in spices for himself.
1513: The Fuggers become agents for the distribution of indulgences in Germany.
1517: François I founds Le Havre de Grâce.
1519: The Fuggers ensure the election of Charles V to the Empire.
1522: François I inaugurates the system of irredeemable securities on the Hôtel de Ville in Paris.
1525: Death of Jakob Fugger, whose capital, destined to double in twenty years, is valued at two million florins.
1526: Rise of the Genoese Bank.
1531: Opening of the new Antwerp Stock Exchange.

3. The centre of the Western economy: the Antwerp Stock Exchange at the height of its power.

15th–17th centuries

Circa 1450

Visby
Riga
Danzig
Lübeck
ENGLAND
London — *wool*
Dortmund
Breslau
Antwerp
Ghent — *arms*
Bruges
HOLY
ROMAN
EMPIRE
Cracow
Paris
FRANCE
Geneva
Lyon — *silk*
Milan
cloth
Venice
Avignon — *silk*
Genoa
Bologna
PORTUGAL
Madrid
Saragossa
Florence
The Medicis
Rome
alum
Lisbon
Naples
SPAIN
Seville

• *St George's Bank*

A

Circa 1530

London
Antwerp
Cologne
Leipzig
Danzig
Frankfurt
Breslau
Nuremberg
gold
Cracow
Paris
copper
Ausburg
The Fuggers
Innsbruck
Milan
Venice
Genoa
Bologna
Florence
Madrid
Rome
Lisbon
silver
Naples
Seville
American silver
(Peru)

B

1600-1700

Liverpool
HOLLAND
Hamburg
London
Amsterdam
To the Americas
Bristol
Antwerp
Bruges
Ghent
**Growth of large
Trading Companies**
Vienna
Paris
Augsburg
FRANCE
Lyon
Milan
Venice
To Africa and the East Indies
Bordeaux
Genoa
Bologna
Florence
Marseille
Rome
Lisbon
Madrid
Naples

C

Trading Areas:

Hanseatic	
Genoese	*Map A*
Venetian	

⟹ Main maritime trade routes

Empire of Charles V (1519-1556) *(Map B)*

Trading networks of the first bankers:

◼ Parent Company	
◾ Branches	*Maps A and B*
X Mines	

◯ Centre of European capitalism in XVII century — *Map C*

▨ Main centres of metal industry

Towns

○ 50,000 to 100,000 inhabitants
○ 100,000 to 200,000 inhabitants
◯ more than 250,000 inhabitants

500 km

British East India Company.

French East India Company.

1600

1664

1540: Decree of Charles V in connection with the Netherlands, legalising bank interest.
1540: Start of massive influx of American money.
1545: Calvin refutes scholastic arguments against loans with interest.
1554: Creation of Muscovy Company.
1556: The 'Grand Parti' of Lyon.
1557: Bankruptcy of the King of Spain.
1559: Bankruptcy of the King of France.
1560: Death of Anton Fugger: beginning of the decline of the house.
1566: M de Malestroit. *Remonstrances . . . on wealth . . .*
1568: In his *Reply to the paradoxes of M de Malestroit . . .* Jean Bodin examines the mechanism of inflation and shows the main cause to be the influx of precious metals from America.
1581: Creation of the British Company of the Levant.
1600: British East India Company.
1602: Dutch East India Company.
1609: Creation of the Bank of Amsterdam.
1614: Dutch North Company: Levant Company.

1615: Antoine de Montchrestien, *Treaty on Economic Policy*.
1619: Creation of the Bank of Hamburg.
1621: Dutch West Indies Company.
1627: Richelieu creates the Company of One Hundred Associates.
1660–80: General fall in prices due to the economic crisis.

1664–7: Colbert's protective tariffs.
1664: Colbert creates the French East India Company and the French West India Company.
1669: French North Company. Jacques Savary *The Perfect Merchant*.
1670: Colbert creates the Levant Company.
1685: Creation of the Guinea Slave Trade Company and the Privileged Royal Company of Senegal.
1694: Creation of the Bank of England.
1698: Creation of the China Company by Jourdan: creation of the Saint-Dominique Slave Trade Company.

4. Trade in Venice in 1616.

5. Louis XIV visiting the Gobelins factory.

The First Industrial Age

CAN WE CALL THIS a period of industrial capitalism in the same sense as we have spoken (above) of commercial and financial capitalism? Only to a certain extent, for traditional craft production remained the most widespread form of manufacture. This was organized in small workshops where the independent producer worked with one or two assistants, produced for a local market and was a member of a guild with its strict regulations, quality control and fixed prices. In short, this was an economy much closer to that of the twelfth than the nineteenth century. However, in certain branches of industrial production a class of entrepreneurs possessing capital and the means of production could be seen clearly emerging, whilst opposite them there arose a class of workers selling their labour power. The classic example of a purely capitalist – in fact state-capitalist – enterprise was

1. Work in the Kutna Hora mine.

the Venice arsenal, where thousands of workers built, repaired and armed the republic's fleet. The mining and iron industries, which required large quantities of investment, were organized along similar lines, as increasingly was the textile industry. If there was nothing spectacular about the technological innovations that took place between the Middle Ages and the Industrial Revolution (rather than producing new developments, the spread of printing in fact enabled the sixteenth century to make available to a wider audience what had been invented in the Middle Ages), the organization of work developed rapidly: 'rural' industry allowed the 'merchant' to escape the tentacular grasp of municipal regulations. In the large production units, more rational methods of exploiting labour power, growing demand from both courts and armies and a great number of technological innovations, especially in mining, metallurgy (notably with the introduction of the high furnace, forerunner of the present blast furnace) and the textile industry all indubitably created the conditions of a modest but genuine 'industrial age'. At the beginning of our period, this was particularly true for the area stretching from Flanders to Tuscany, including southwest Germany and northern Italy. This was an area on which the rest of Europe was largely dependent. In the course of the sixteenth and seventeenth centuries, other centres of production emerged – especially France, Holland, Sweden and England (we may again observe here a displacement of the centre of gravity of the European economy towards the north-west, cf. p. 140). Textiles remained the dominant industry with Florentine, Flemish (Hondschoote, Lille) and, increasingly, Dutch (Leyden, Haarlem) and English woollen cloth. Linen came from Saxony and Picardy, and silk, initially the Italian product par excellence (Lucca), was later produced by the Spanish (from Seville and Toledo) and, finally, by the French with the development of the Lyon silk industry. The mining industry – without doubt the most 'modern' – was undergoing rapid expansion: silver came from the Tyrol, Carinthia and Upper Silesia, areas that were soon to lose their dominant position with the arrival of American imports; iron and copper from Sweden, coal from the Liège region and the north of England, which towards the end of the sixteenth century had become the principal source of energy for iron-smelting. As the sixteenth and seventeenth centuries were indisputably an age of war, they saw a real boom in the armaments industry. We must also mention printing, an industry in the forefront of technology (see below), naval shipbuilding (England, France – especially in the second half of the seventeenth century – and the Netherlands) and the glass industry (Venice, France and England).

Spain lost ground considerably in these years; the old centres of production – Italy, Flanders and south Germany – also showed a relative decline; meanwhile England, France, the Netherlands and Sweden emerged as economic powers. Industrial Europe was some way off, but it was already possible to discern its future contours.

Arms manufacture at St Étienne.   *De re metallica.*

1516   **1556**

1460: Discovery of the Tolfa alum mines.
1460: Introduction of the blast furnace.
1464: Edward IV prohibits the importation of foreign cloth.
1470: Manufacture of precision astronomical instruments at Nuremberg (Regiomontanus).
1500: Rise of the Venetian, English and Dutch woollen industries and decline of the Flemish and Florentine. Appearance of the musket (Germany).
1516: First firearms manufactured at St Étienne (France).
1529: Strike of the Lyon printing workers (Grande Rébeyne).

1531: Beginnings of Lyon silk industry.
1540: V. Biringuccio, *De la pirotechnia.*
1540: Use of railways in mines; casting of iron cannons in England.
1543: 400 ironworks in France.
1552: Prohibition of the export of Spanish cloth to the Americas.
1556: Georg Agricola, *De re metallica.* The *patio* amalgam process for the extraction of silver is introduced into the mines of Peru and Mexico.
1563: Elizabeth I's *Statute of Artificers.*
1569: The textile industry is prohibited in the Spanish colonies.
1570: Increased iron and copper production in Sweden. Mining begins at the Huancavelica mercury mine.
1572: First use of gunpowder in mining (Sicily).
1578: Jacques Besson, *Théâtre des instruments.*
1580: The windmill-driven saw; the Dutch freighter (fluyt); Delftware; coal is increasingly used in England.
1588: Agostina Ramelli, *Le Diverse Artificiose Machine.*

3. One of the first known pistols.

4. Rapidly expanding industries: a cannon foundry in the 16th century.

15th–17th centuries

2. Stages in the search for and processing of ore in a German silver mine, drawn by Heinrich Gross (16th century).

Alchemia.   **The royal Gobelins manufactory.**   **The steam engine.**

1597   **1667**   **1687**

1589: William Lee's knitting machine.
1590: Introduction of railways into English coal mines.
1597: Andreas Leibau, *Alchemia*, the first manual of chemistry.
1600: Claude Dangon's loom (Lyon). 800 ironworks in England.
1611: Royal foundries at Seville for the Indies fleet.
1615: Use of coal in the manufacture of glass in England.
1650: Leyden becomes the major centre of the woollen industry.
1667: The Gobelins company becomes a royal manufactory.
1670: Cannon-making works set up in the Angoumois, Périgord, Nivernais, Lyonnais, Dauphiné and Burgundy by Colbert; creation of the great royal factories of France: cloth at Abbeville (Van Robais), tapestries at Beauvais (Hinard), glass (Du Noyer).
1687: Denis Papin's steam engine.
1692: Creation of the Saint-Gobain company.
1695: H. Gautier, *Traité de la construction des chemins*.

5. Few inventions, many innovations: a crane, as seen by Agostino Ramelli.

6. First products of applied science: Pascal's calculator.

The Development of Printing

THE MODERN WESTERN BOOK is a product of two revolutions. The first of these in the first centuries AD introduced a new form of book, the stitched book (or codex), which gradually supplanted the scroll (volumen). The second in the mid-fifteenth century revolutionized the conditions of reproduction of texts: we refer, of course, to the invention of printing.

It was from 1452–3 onwards that Gutenberg, in Mainz, produced the first European printed texts using movable metal type: the type was pressed onto paper with the aid of a hand press. The technique, which greatly reduced the cost of book manufacture and allowed the reproduction of several hundred copies of an identical text (an average print run in the fifteenth century was of the order of 500 copies), had evolved in response to unprecedentedly high levels of demand that had been poorly met by the manual copying of books, where manufacture was on an individual basis and remained slow and expensive. Increased demand arose in part because the lay community was becoming more literate and educated; there was, in this period, an unprecedented thirsting after a new spirituality to be achieved through the reading of works of piety. In part also it was due to the new demands of emerging state structures. Two sets of technological developments had made Gutenberg's invention possible in the fifteenth century. On the one hand, there was the newly-acquired expertise in metalworking, in particular by German goldsmiths (Gutenberg was the son of a goldsmith and was himself a member of the goldsmiths' guild of Strasbourg before his return to Mainz); on the other, there was a great increase in the number of paper mills, which had spread across the whole of Europe from Italy, where they had first appeared at the end of the thirteenth century.

The printing of texts by means of movable type was not peculiar to Europe. During the Sung dynasty (between the eleventh and thirteenth centuries) printing had reached a peak in China, whilst in Korea movable metal characters had been used for the first time during the thirteenth century. However, in neither of these two countries was printing to find the place it was to have in the West, a fact doubtless to be explained by the large number of characters required (several tens of thousands), which meant that its use was confined to state publications alone. Interestingly, it does not seem that Gutenberg, or, indeed, any of his European contemporaries, knew of these earlier Oriental examples.

In the fifteenth century the new invention quickly spread throughout the whole of Europe, carried initially by the early German printers on their travels. Between 1452 and 1470 the new art conquered nine German towns, four Italian centres, Paris, which had its own printing shop at the Sorbonne in 1470, and Seville. Six years later, William Caxton began printing at Westminster, and by 1480 printing had won a temporary or permanent place in 108 towns, and by the year 1500 it was established in 226. In the age of incunabula (i.e.

1. Printing shop in the 15th century. Manuscrit des chants royaux.

before 1500) we may suppose that the European printing shops printed between 35,000 and 40,000 publications, of which more than three-quarters were in Latin. At that stage Venice was the printing capital, followed by Rome, Paris and Cologne, and the three great bastions of book production were Italy (42% of incunabula), Germany (30%) and France (15%).

In the sixteenth century the spread of printing continued, but production became concentrated in the university towns and the great trading centres. Venice continued to dominate the book market and Paris maintained its position (production there was doubled between 1500 and 1540), but some new centres appeared – Lyon, Basle, Antwerp and Frankfurt – and a first shift in European printing became evident, the balance moving from Italy towards Northern Europe, where Gutenberg's invention lent its support to the spread of humanism and the Reformation.

Movable type in use in China.

First paper in the W

1000

1276

2. 'Thousand Buddha' scroll. Chinese xylograph, 7th–9th centuries.

Beginning of the 11th century: Appearance in China of printing with movable type.
11th century: First use of paper in Western manuscripts, in Spain. The technique of paper-making had been introduced to the West from China by the Arabs.
13th century: Oldest known Korean publication, printed with metal movable characters.
c. 1276: Beginning of paper-making at Fabriano in Italy.
c. 1340: Paper mills set up at Troyes.
c. 1452–3: First pieces printed at Mainz with movable type.
c. 1455: Gutenberg's forty-two line Bible (perhaps 150 copies).
1457: Mainz Psalter – first book with a title page and publisher's name: Fust and Schöffer of Mainz.
1461: Albrecht Pfister prints the first known illustrated printed books at Bamberg.
1465: First book printed outside Germany in the printing shop of the Monastery of Subiaco in Italy.
1470: Foundation of the printing shop at the Sorbonne and the first book printed in France.

3. Illuminated folio from Gutenberg's thirty-six-line Bible.

4. Portrait of Gutenberg engraved by Larmessin, 1682.

11th–16th centuries

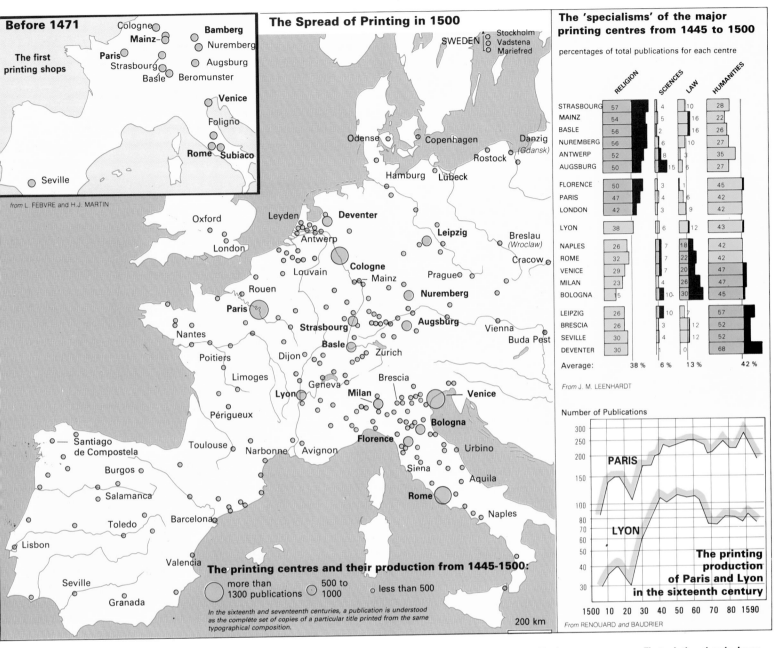

Before 1471

The first printing shops

Cologne · Bamberg · Mainz · Nuremberg · Paris · Strasbourg · Augsburg · Basle · Beromunster · Venice · Foligno · Rome · Subiaco · Seville

from L. FEBVRE and H.J. MARTIN

The Spread of Printing in 1500

The 'specialisms' of the major printing centres from 1445 to 1500

percentages of total publications for each centre

	RELIGION	SCIENCES	LAW	HUMANITIES
STRASBOURG	57	4	10	28
MAINZ	54	5	16	22
BASLE	56	2	16	26
NUREMBERG	56	6	10	27
ANTWERP	52	8	3	35
AUGSBURG	50	15	6	27
FLORENCE	50	3	1	45
PARIS	47	4	6	42
LONDON	42	3	9	42
LYON	38	6	12	43
NAPLES	26	7	18	42
ROME	32	7	22	42
VENICE	29	7	20	47
MILAN	23	4	26	47
BOLOGNA	15	10	30	45
LEIPZIG	26	10	7	57
BRESCIA	26	3	12	52
SEVILLE	30	4	12	52
DEVENTER	30		0	68
Average:	38 %	6 %	13 %	42 %

From J. M. LEENHARDT

Number of Publications

PARIS

LYON

The printing production of Paris and Lyon in the sixteenth century

1500 10 20 30 40 50 60 70 80 1590

From RENOUARD and BAUDRIER

The printing centres and their production from 1445-1500:

- more than 1300 publications
- 500 to 1000
- less than 500

In the sixteenth and seventeenth centuries, a publication is understood as the complete set of copies of a particular title printed from the same typographical composition.

200 km

Death of Gutenberg.	William Caxton at Westminster.	Aldus Manutius in Venice.	First printing shop in Japan.
1468	1476	1494	1590

1476: William Caxton begins printing from Westminster.
1494: First publications of Aldus Manutius in Venice.
1501: First book printed in italic by Aldus Manutius.
1514–17: Alcala de Henares's polyglot Bible.
1522: Publication at Wittenberg by Melchior Lotter of the first vernacular translation of the New Testament by Luther (with an exceptional print-run of 3,000 copies).
1531: Publication at Augsburg of Andrea Alciati's *Liber emblematum*, which fixes the iconographic repertoire employed by book illustrators.
1539: First printing shop set up in Mexico.
1545: First catalogue of condemned books, published at the instigation of the Sorbonne.
1544–5: First papal *Index* of books banned by the church. First printing shop in India.
1559: Christopher Plantin printer at Antwerp.
1564: Publication of the Council of Trent's *Index* by Paul Manuce at Rome.
1564: First general catalogue of books sold at the Frankfurt fair.
1569–73: Plantin's Polyglot or Royal Bible.

1584: First printing shop in Peru.
1588: Introduction of printing to Macao.
1590: First printing shop in Japan.
1592: Publication of the papal Vulgate at Rome.

5. Buddhist treatise printed using movable type, 1377, Jik ji sim kyong.

6. Death and the bookseller. A Danse macabre, Lyons, 1499.

Renaissance Europe

THE RENAISSANCE was born in fourteenth-century Tuscany, came to maturity in the fifteenth century and, in the sixteenth, swept through the whole of Western Europe. Seen by contemporaries as a genuine revolution that would put an end to a thousand years of medieval barbarism and revive the splendours of classical antiquity, it was, first and foremost, a cultural and intellectual phenomenon. The key concept here is humanism. Strictly speaking, this referred only to the *studia humanitatis* (philology, languages, ancient literature), by opposition to medieval scholasticism. In this sense, the humanist was the person who studied the ancients in a new spirit free of dogmatic prejudices; the key features of that spirit were intellectual curiosity, sympathy, the free exercise of critical reason and the appreciation of human values (truth, beauty, glory) for their own sake. In the broad sense, humanism was a system of thought which put the human being in the centre of a universe designed for the greater glory of humanity. The view of the human being as a miserable creature, forever shackled by original sin, gave way to a vision of the free, autonomous, creative being, whose nature was innately good and whose faculties were unlimited. Thus, rather than being a specific philosophy, humanism was a method of working, a doctrine of life and a system of education. In the Graeco-Latin works, the humanist pursued a (moral, aesthetic and social) model of human perfection.

The search for ancient documents put forgotten texts within the reach of scholars. But it was not so much the quantity of ancient treasures that changed as the way they were regarded, the desire to become impregnated with them and identify with them. That divine spark which Pico della Mirandola discerned in every human being had to be brought out. This was the work of the educators of the Renaissance, who developed methods which are even today considered revolutionary, aimed at bringing about the blossoming of the intellectual, moral and physical capacities of the child. Men like Erasmus, Rabelais and Montaigne wrote scornfully of medieval education and sang the praises of the liberal arts of their day, and the humanist schools formed an élite that was small in number, but significant on account of its social position.

We find humanism again in the field which, more than any other, epitomizes the contribution of the Renaissance, the plastic arts. Every theme – even the religious – is treated in a human perspective. The artist imitates nature – for it is beautiful and good – and produces endless representations of the nude male and female forms, seen as the fruit of divine love rather than the miserable product of an original transgression. And in order to paint the human form as it is, or rather as the canon of human beauty requires it, all its aspects – anatomy, perspective, proportions and colour – are studied; where, in Leonardo, for example, does science end and art begin? Delivered from their association with architecture, the plastic arts claimed their autonomy and dignity: accordingly, the painter, who was now fully an artist, would sign his works and deal with princes as an equal.

This handful of heroes invented a social ideal: the *uomo universale*, the most developed representative of which was Leonardo. To those who had not been granted genius, the *Zeitgeist* of the century left a choice between financing the genius (without patrons there would have been no Renaissance) and apeing him, like that 'Courtier' of whom Castiglione demands all the virtues, except that of being a good Christian. But *virtù* is not virtue, and Machiavelli's 'Prince' has nothing of the contemplative about him. We must not forget that the Renaissance was also the crucible in which the modern state was forged (see below) and much blood was shed in the process.

1. Antonello da Messina, Annunciation.

Birth of Petrarch.

1304

1304–74: Petrarch, the father of Italian humanism.
1348–53: Boccaccio writes the *Decameron*.
1396–7: Manuel Chrysoloras, a Byzantine scholar, settles in Florence.
1425: Vittorino da Feltre founds his *Casa giocosa*, the celebrated humanist school.
1440: Cosimo de Medici founds the Platonic Academy.
1449: Lorenzo Valla, *Annotationes in Novum Testamentum*.
1462–92: Rule of Lorenzo the Magnificent. Peak of the Florentine Renaissance.
1469: Marsilio Ficino begins the translation of the Platonic *Dialogues*.
1486: Pico de la Mirandola, *De hominis dignitate*.
1493: Dürer, *Self-portrait*.
1495: Leonardo da Vinci, *The Last Supper*.
1500: The *Adagia* of Erasmus; Botticelli, *Mystic nativity*.
1501: Michelangelo, The *Pietà* in St Peter's.
1504: Michelangelo, *David*.
1506: Jimenez de Cisneros founds the University of Alcala de Henares.
1507: Dürer, *Adam and Eve*.

1508: Michelangelo begins the ceiling of the Sistine chapel.
1510: John Colet founds St Paul's School.
1511: Erasmus, *In Praise of Folly*.

2. Façade of Santa Maria Novella.

1512: Michelangelo, *Moses*. Lefèvre d'Étaples publishes his *Commentaries on the Epistles of St Paul*.
1514–17: Publication of the Complutensian Polyglot Bible.
1515–17: Ulrich von Hutten, *Letters of Obscure Men*.
1516: Machiavelli, *The Prince*; Thomas More, *Utopia*; Ariosto, *Orlando furioso*; Erasmus publishes the New Testament.
1518: Titian, *The Assumption*.
1520: Lefèvre d'Étaples joins the 'Meaux Circle'.
1528: Baldassarre Castiglione, *The Courtier*. Jean Clouet appointed painter to the king.
1530: Francis I founds the *Collège des lecteurs royaux*.
1532–4: Rabelais, *Pantagruel* and *Gargantua*.
1541: Michelangelo, *The Last Judgement*; Marot's *Psalms*.
1543: Copernicus, *De revolutionibus orbium coelestium*; Vesalius, *De corporis humani fabrica*.
1549: du Bellay, *Defense et illustration de la langue francaise*.

1550: Vasari's *Lives*, the first systematic history of art.
1553–7: du Bellay, *Antiquités de Rome*.
1555: Veronese, *The Coronation of the Virgin*.
1559: Amyot translates Plutarch's *Lives*.
1561: F. Guicciardini, *History of Italy*.
1564: Lescot finishes the façade of the Louvre. Delorme begins his Tuileries façade. Birth of Shakespeare.
1566: Bodin, *Methodus ad facilem historiarum cognitionem*.

3. The solar system according to Copernicus, by Andrea Cellarius.

14th–16th centuries

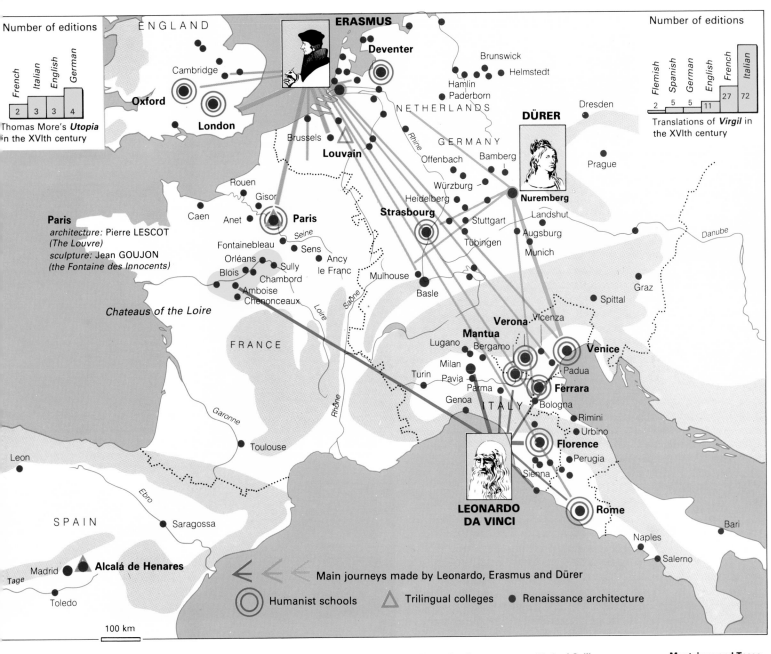

Number of editions

French	Italian	English	German
2	3	3	4

Thomas More's *Utopia* in the XVIth century

ENGLAND

ERASMUS

Deventer

Cambridge

Oxford

London

Brussels

Louvain

Rouen

Gisor

Caen · Anet

Paris

Seine

Fontainebleau

Orléans · Sens · Ancy

Blois · Sully · le Franc

Chambord

Amboise

Chenonceaux

Chateaus of the Loire

Paris
architecture: Pierre LESCOT
(The Louvre)
sculpture: Jean GOUJON
(the Fontaine des Innocents)

FRANCE

Garonne

Toulouse

Leon

SPAIN

Ebro

Saragossa

Madrid **Alcalá de Henares**

Tage

Toledo

Brunswick

Helmstedt

Hamlin

Paderborn

NETHERLANDS

GERMANY

Rhine

Offenbach · Bamberg

Würzburg

Heidelberg

Strasbourg

Stuttgart

Tübingen

Mulhouse

Basle

DÜRER

Nuremberg

Landshut

Augsburg

Munich

Dresden

Prague

Danube

Graz

Spittal

Verona · Vicenza

Mantua

Lugano · Bergamo

Milan

Turin · Pavia

Parma

Genoa

ITALY

Venice

Padua

Ferrara

Bologna

Rimini

Urbino

Florence

Perugia

Sienna

**LEONARDO
DA VINCI**

Rome

Bari

Naples

Salerno

Rhône · Saône · Loire

Number of editions

Flemish	Spanish	German	English	French	Italian
2	5	5	11	27	72

Translations of *Virgil* in the XVIth century

100 km

⟨ ⟨ ⟨   Main journeys made by Leonardo, Erasmus and Dürer

◎ Humanist schools   △ Trilingual colleges   ● Renaissance architecture

rth of Leonardo da Vinci.	Birth of Michelangelo.	Machiavelli, *The Prince*; Thomas More, *Utopia*.	Birth of Galileo.	Montaigne and Tasso.
1452	1475	1516	1564	1580

5. A manuscript by Francis I and Henry II's Greek copyist, Ange Vergèce, who inspired the French expression 'to write like an angel'.

1567: Bruegel the Elder, *The Land of Cockaigne*.
1572: Ronsard, *La Franciade*.
1576: Bodin, *Six livres de la République*.
1580: Montaigne's *Essays*; Tasso, *Jerusalem Delivered*.

4. Domenico Ghirlandaio, Four Italian humanists: *Ficino, Landino, Politian and Gentile de'Becchi.*

6. The anatomist Vesalius *by Pierre Poncet*.

The Empires: Machiavelli and the Modern State

IT WAS IN THE LATER MIDDLE AGES that the modern state was born, out of the ruins of the imperial concept of a universal, double-headed *Respublica christiana* and of feudalism. First France and England – nations which had emerged fully armed from the Hundred Years' War – then Spain – unified morally by the Reconquista and politically by the will of the Catholic monarchs – emerged at the end of the fifteenth century as 'new monarchies'. That is to say, they were solid political entities based upon a broad national consensus with a suitably centralized political system, in which the king's authority over his subjects knew no bounds other than those dictated by custom, morality and religion, and where the only limits to external action were set by the extent of a state's power. Royal absolutism – de jure in Valois France and Hapsburg Spain and de facto in Tudor England – made the prince an 'emperor within his own kingdom' and a 'power' outside it.

Two great political entities did not reach this stage of development. These were the Holy Roman Empire and Italy. The former was a mosaic of principalities, bishoprics and free cities, kept in balance by a constitution which reduced the (elected) emperor to the role of a president-mediator without royal power. For the latter, even this theoretical unifying factor was absent. *Italianità* was powerless to unify a peninsula torn apart by the intense rivalry that existed among the five 'powers' – Venice, Milan, Florence, the Papal States and the Kingdom of Naples – and their satellites. All these states, not to mention the smaller ones, spied on and fought each other, negotiated, made and unmade military coalitions and volatile political alliances. It is easy to understand why Italy was the diplomatic school of the modern age and the laboratory in which *raison d'état*, that cynical ideology, born essentially of impotence, was forged. One can also easily understand why Italy became the major bone of contention between the great national monarchies – and also the battlefield on which they fought out their rivalries. The Angevin heritage of Charles VIII and the Milanese claims of Louis XII dragged France down into the Italian quagmire. Francis I's crushing defeat of the Swiss at Marignano left the French and the Spaniards alone in the field. Four years later Charles V united the Aragon heritage (Naples) with the imperial heritage (Milan). From that point on, the houses of Hapsburg and Valois were engaged in a fight to the death, which finally laid to rest the fiction of Christian unity. Between Charles V's imperial dream and France's desire to break out of Hapsburg encirclement, nothing – not even the Turkish threat – could produce grounds for compromise. Charles V's victories ultimately led nowhere. In the end the Protestant counter-offensive, his inability to bring France to its

1. Niccolo Machiavelli, *by Rosso Fiorentino.*

3. Elizabeth I of England, *by Zuccaro.*

knees and serious financial problems exhausted the knight-emperor. The rickety Augsburg compromise (see below) set the seal upon his failure. His abdication and the partition of the Empire ensured that Spanish interests would predominate. In 1557 bankruptcy and the acute nature of the religious problem led the weakened belligerents to the negotiating table. At Cateau-Cambrésis, France gave up its

2. Catholic monarchs, Ferdinand of Aragon and Isabella of Castile.

unrealistic Italian ambitions but kept Burgundy. The treaty reflected the drifting of the political centre of gravity towards the West; it opened up a half-century of 'Spanish preponderance', enshrined the lasting decline of Germany and Italy and marked the rise of the great centralized states.

The Protestant Reformation

AT THE TIME when Luther stood out against Rome, the 'seamless robe' of the Christian West had already been damaged by the long crisis that affected both the church and the faith of the declining Middle Ages, by the 'new monarchs' and by the critique of the humanists, but it was still entire. A generation later it was in shreds. The revolt of this Augustinian monk against the church's abuses (indulgences etc.) and the solution he found to the agonizing problem of his own personal salvation (the omnipotence of Grace, justification by faith alone, the revelation of the Word by Scripture in a church constituted by the community of the faithful, who are all equal in the sight of God) found favourable conditions in a Germany that was disunited, eager for reforms, riven by rivalries between princes and by social tensions and increasingly impatient with Rome's tutelage. A fraction of the lower and middle clergy, humanists, a good proportion of the nobility and the urban bourgeoisie rallied to the movement. Luther offered the towns the means to rid themselves of a rich, idle and detested clergy; to the princes he offered a power that they would at last no longer have to share; to everyone, his was a simple, national, intelligible faith, drawn from Gospel sources. Those whom the revolutionary implications of the Lutheran message might have troubled were reassured by the reformer's reaction to the Peasants' War and subsequently to revolutionary Anabaptism as it manifested itself in Munster in 1534. From the popular movement that it initially seemed to be, the German Reformation became socially and politically conservative, an instrument of state and royal control. On the reformer's death, three-quarters of Germany, fifty-one cities of the Empire out of sixty-five, the Scandinavian countries, Prussia, the Baltic states and Finland were of the Lutheran confession. In a different socio-policial context and under the rule of men of a different sensibility, who in some respects were closer to Erasmus than to Luther – Zwingli in Zurich, Bucer in Strasbourg and, most importantly, Calvin in Geneva – the Reformation established itself in the towns of Upper Germany and Switzerland. From there, it spread to France, the Netherlands, Scotland, England, Bohemia, Poland and Hungary. After some difficult beginnings, the Reformation had become solidly established in Geneva and, from 1541 onwards, Calvin set about turning that city into a theocratic republic. At the same time he directed the French Reformation from afar, imposing doctrinal cohesion and a set method of pastoral training upon it.

It was England which engaged upon the most original Reformation. This was made possible, as on the Continent, by a long hostility to Rome and by the work the lay intellectuals in the great universities had done to undermine the church and its teachings. But it had its immediate origin in a problem that was legal rather than theological, namely the matrimonial difficulties of Henry VIII. The English Reformation stemmed from the King's decision to be divorced, whatever the obstacles. Once he had become 'supreme head of the Church of England', Henry VIII silenced the Catholic opposition and suppressed the monasteries, but the English church was, nonetheless, only 'Anglican' in the way that the French church was 'Gallican'. All that was missing was the pope. After the reign of the Catholic Mary, the pendulum swung back wildly, producing the Elizabethan compromise of an Anglican Church that was Catholic in appearance but Calvinist in inspiration.

The unique character of the English case should not obscure the general truth: the Reformation became established in those places where the secular power wanted it. Luther understood that perfectly, as did the Pope and the Catholic princes, who did all they could to block the Protestant advance. There would indeed be a Catholic Reformation, but there would also be a half-century of religious wars.

1. Martin Luther.

2. Melanchthon, painted by Cranach.

3. Calvin.

4. Zwingli, painted by Hans Asper.

Luther posts his theses at Wittenberg.

Luther translates the Bible.

Peasants' War.

| 1517 | 1522 | 1525 |

5. Martin Luther's rendering of the Bible, 1534 edition.

1517: Luther's 95 theses at Wittenberg.
1519: The Leipzig disputation with the theologian Johann Eck.
1520: Papal bull, *Exsurge domine.* Luther, who is condemned and ordered to retract, burns the bull in public; his three famous treatises: *An den christlichen Adel deutscher Nation* (To the Christian nobility of the German nation), *Von der babylonischen Gefangenschaft der Kirche* (On the Babylonian captivity of the Church) and *Von der Freiheit eines Christenmenschen* (On the liberty of the Christian).
1521: Diet of Worms. Luther is placed under the imperial ban and is given refuge at Wartburg Castle. Melanchthon, *Loci communes*, the first work of Lutheran theology; an anti-Lutheran pamphlet earned Henry VIII the title 'Defender of the faith'.
1522: Luther's German Bible. Rising of the imperial knights led by Hutten and Sickingen: agitation of the (Carlstadt) radicals at Wittenberg, defeated by Luther.
1523: Zwingli establishes the Reformation in Zurich: the movement spreads to Basle (Oecolampadius), Berne and then Strasbourg (Bucer).
1524: Erasmus, *De libero arbitro.*

6. Leo X flanked by two cardinals, painted by Raphael.

1525: Luther, *De servo arbitro*; the Peasants' War; Luther's violent pamphlet, *Wider die mördischen und räubischen Rotten der Bauern* (Against the murderous and thieving peasant bands); defeat of the peasants at Frankenhausen and death of Münzer; bloody repression encouraged by Luther. Grand Master Albert of Prussia secularizes the state of the Teutonic Knights and transforms it into a secular duchy: birth of Prussia.
1526: Luther lays down the form of the German communion service; the ecclesiastical organization of the electoral Duchy of Saxony becomes the model for the Lutheran churches.
1527: Founding of the first Protestant university at Marburg, followed by Königsberg (1544) and Jena (1588); Riksdag of Vesteras: Gustavus Vasa introduces the Reformation into Sweden.
1529: The Marburg Colloquy between Luther and Zwingli runs into difficulties over the problem of the communion: fall of the cardinal-legate Wolsey in England.
1531: Death of Zwingli in the Battle of Kappel. Bucer presses for union with the Lutherans. Bullinger opposes this move.

1517–1566

Protestant universities and academies

Anabaptists

Charles V's Empire

E. Erfurt
F. Frankenhausen
K. Kappel

NORWAY 1536 · Vesteras · Uppsala

SWEDEN 1527

DENMARK 1536

John Knox SCOTLAND 1567

Königsberg 1544

Greifswald 1539 · PRUSSIA

Rostock · POLAND

Henry VIII London 1534

Cambridge · Oxford · Leyden · Franeker · Utrecht · Munster

Luther Wittenberg 1517 · Frankfurt · F. · Leipzig

Antwerp · Ghent · Cateau-Cambrésis · Marburg 1527 · Wartburg · SAXONY · E. Jena 1588 · Schmalkalden

Sedan · Worms · Heidelberg · Tübingen · Vienna

Paris · FRANCE · Strasbourg

Saumur · Basle · Buda · Pest

Zwingli · Zurich · K. · Bern · SWITZERLAND · HUNGARY

Calvin Geneva 1536 · Trent

Orthez · Montauban · Nimes · Die · Orange · Genoa · Venice · OTTOMAN EMPIRE

Montpellier · Florence

SPAIN · Madrid · Rome

400 km

VIII founds the Anglican Church.   **Calvin at Geneva.**   **Michael Servetus is burnt at Geneva.**

1534   1541   1553

1533: Divorce of Henry VIII, who marries Anne Boleyn.
1534: Henry VIII supreme head of Church of England; the millenarianist kingdom of Johann Matthiesen and John of Leyden at Munster.
1535: Execution of Thomas More.

1536: Christian III introduces Lutheranism into Denmark and Norway; Calvin publishes *Institutio religionis christianae.*
1541: Calvin, French translation of *Institutio.*
1547: Death of Henry VIII; in the name of the minor, Edward VI, Cranmer gives the Anglican Church a resolutely Protestant direction.
1549: *The Book of Common Prayer.*
1553: Execution for heresy of Michael Servetus at Geneva.
1556: Execution of Cranmer during the Catholic reaction of Mary Tudor.
1559: Academy of Geneva; Elizabeth I's restoration of Anglicanism; first national synod of the reformed churches of France in Paris.
1560: Establishment of the Scottish Presbyterian Church, which in 1567 became the established state church.
1563: The '39 Articles' of the Church of England.
1566: The Synod of Antwerp founds the Calvinist Church of the Netherlands.

7. The Peasants' War, by David Vinckboons.

8. Henry VIII, by Hans Holbein the Younger.

152

The Counter-Reformation and the Wars of Religion

1. The Holy League in Procession.

THE TERM COUNTER-REFORMATION is an ambiguous one. The nineteenth-century liberal historians who coined it saw the actions of the papacy and Catholic princes as nothing more than an obscurantist reaction to that deeply portentous event, the Protestant Reformation. Incomplete as the view of those historians may have been, it would be wrong to seek to deny this aspect of the phenomenon. There were indeed desperate attempts to arrest the advance of Protestantism and, as far as possible, to win back lost ground. At the local level, this was a matter for the princes, who were the natural defenders of the faith. The first round was fought in Germany, where twenty years of war between Charles V and the Lutheran princes of the Protestant League ended in the compromise of Augsburg: *cuius regio, eius religio* –

the ruler alone was to determine the religion of his subjects. This spelled the end of the concept of the universal empire, and it set the seal on the definitive division of the Christian West. The maelstrom then shifted westwards, to France and the Low Countries. The accidental death of that great persecutor of heretics, Henry II, initiated a long power struggle which resurrected the fortunes of the noble families and fostered the development of politico-religious 'parties'. The militarization of the Huguenots after the peace of Cateau-Cambrésis, the crown's devious policies, the rivalry between Catholic Guises and Protestant Bourbons, popular fanaticism and the ambition of faction leaders were all features of the backdrop to the 'Wars of Religion'. In the Low Countries, religious strife also took on a nationalist dimension, since the Calvinist cause became indistinguishable from the struggle for independence. Everywhere extremism and violence were generated by the weakness of central authority and by ancient enmities (dynastic, feudal and social), exacerbated ideologically by religious passions. Increasingly from the end of the 1560s, the battle was fought out on an international stage. Coalitions were formed with French and Dutch Calvinists supported by England on the one side and Catholic French Leaguers and Spain on the other. Philip II's grand design had been to put Mary, Queen of Scots, on the English throne and a Spanish puppet on the throne of France, to reconquer the Low Countries and thus put an end once and for all to heresy. His ambitions foundered with the Spanish Armada. Henry IV finally triumphed over the League and France was to remain Catholic. By the Edict of Nantes, however, for the first time in the Christian West, a religious minority was accorded a place within the national community. This marked a first victory for religious toleration – though admittedly one that was dictated by overwhelming practical considerations. Moreover, even Alexander Farnese, with all his military and diplomatic skills, was unable to restore to the bosom of Spain the seven northern provinces of the Low Countries which had acquired independence under the leadership of Holland.

In the meantime, the church pursued its own reforms. These began in Spain and Italy, scenes of a remarkable Catholic renaissance, and continued under the aegis of the papacy, which armed itself with the instruments of reconquest – the Inquisition, reconstituted on the Spanish model, and, most particularly, those formidable soldiers of the faith, the Jesuits. At the same time, the church was, at the Council of Trent, undertaking the immense task of doctrinal clarification and ecclesiastical reform which left an indelible mark on modern Catholicism. Rome can by no means be said to have succeeded in 'rooting out heresy', but the combined effects of armed action, propaganda, religious art, education and a less corrupt church with a more responsible clergy, made it possible to avoid the worst deviations, and prepared the way for the great Catholic revival of the 'Century of Saints'.

Birth of Ignatius Loyola. 1491

Foundation of the Society of Jesus. 1534

Beginning of the French Wars of Religi 1562

1524–5: Foundation of the Theatine, Capucin and Ursuline religious orders.
1526: *The Spiritual Exercises* of Ignatius Loyola.
1531: The Protestants of the Empire form the Schmalkaldic League.
1534: Loyola founds the Society of Jesus.
1540: Paul III confirms the new order.
1542: Roman Inquisition introduced on the Spanish model.
1545: First session of the Council of Trent.
1548: Charles V imposes the Interim of Augsburg on the Protestants.
1555: The Peace of Augsburg.
1559: The Peace of Cateau-Cambrésis: death of Henry II; accession of Francis II to the French throne; government by the Guise family.
1560: Conspiracy of Amboise; accession of Charles IX to French throne; regency of Catherine de Medici.
1561: Colloquy of Poissy; failure of Michel de l'Hospital's policy of conciliation.
1562: Massacre of Wassy; beginning of the Wars of Religion.
1563: Assassination of François, Duc de Guise; Edict of Amboise; dissolution of the Council of Trent.

2. Ignatius of Loyola, by H. P. Seghers.

3. Saint Bartholomew's Day, Nuremberg print.

1524–1635

Map legend

- States claiming to be Protestant
- • Safe havens for Protestants
- ● Safe havens still in existence after the Edict of Nantes
- States claiming to be Catholic
- Areas won back from the Reformation
- ● Jesuit establishments
- Charles V's Empire
- × Battles

L. Longjumeau
Pe. Péronne
P. Poissy
S. St Germain
A. Arras

Map labels

NORWAY 1536
SCOTLAND 1567
SWEDEN 1527
1561
DENMARK 1536
• Edinburgh
PRUSSIA
ENGLAND 1534
• Berlin
POLAND
Brielle
• Utrecht
• Magdeburg
London
FLANDERS
Antwerp
• Breslau
A
BRABANT
Arques
• Schmalkalden
Cateau-Cambrésis
Pe
Vervins
• Augsburg
P S
Paris L
Vassy
Ivry
HUNGARY
Nantes   Blois
• Amboise
La Rochelle   FRANCE
• Trent
• Venice
OTTOMAN EMPIRE
• Pau
• Parma
Montpellier
SPAIN
• Florence
• Madrid
Rome

400 km

Timeline

Massacre of St Bartholomew's Day.
1572

Union of Utrecht.
1579

Edict of Nantes.
1598

Trial of Galileo.
1633

1564: Publication of *Index* of works forbidden by the Holy Office.
1565: Protestation of the Dutch nobles dismissed as 'beggars' by Berlaymont).
1567: Military dictatorship ('Council of Blood') by Duke of Alva in the Netherlands.
1568: Execution of the Counts of Egmont and Hoorn; treaty of Longjumeau; departure of Michel de l'Hospital.
1570: Peace of St Germain, favourable to Huguenots.
1572: St Bartholomew's Day Massacre; the Sea Beggars' take Brill in Zeeland.
1573: Publication in Geneva of Francois Hotman's *Franco-Gallia*.
1574: Death of Charles IX; accession of Henry III to French throne.
1576: The 'Peace of Monsieur'; formation of the first Catholic League at Péronne; the 'pacification' of Ghent; Union of the seventeen provinces against Spain; Philip Neri founds the Congregation of the Oratory in Italy.
1578: The Union of Arras returns the southern provinces of the Low Countries to Spain.
1579: Union of Utrecht concluded among the northern provinces.

1581: Declaration of independence by the Union of Utrecht.
1582: Reform of the calendar by Gregory XIII.
1584: Assassination of William of Orange; constitution of the United Provinces; Alexander Farnese, Prince of Parma, becomes governor of the Low Countries in the name of Philip II and occupies Flanders and Brabant.
1585: Fall of Antwerp to the Spanish; formation of the second Catholic League in Paris.
1588: 'Day of Barricades' in Paris; the Estates General meet in Blois; assassination of Duc

4. A hanging in Brabant, 1570.

de Guise and Cardinal de Guise; defeat of the Spanish Armada.
1589: Death of Catherine de Medici; assassination of Henry III.
1590: Battle of Ivry; Henry IV besieges Paris; new edition of the Vulgate produced in Rome.
1593: Meeting of Estates General in Paris dominated by the Catholic Holy League; conversion of Henry IV to Catholicism.
1594: Henry IV enters Paris; *Menippean Satire*; execution of the regicide Jean Chatel and expulsion of the Jesuits.
1598: Edict of Nantes; Peace of Vervins; death of Philip II.
1603: *Introduction to the Devout Life* by St Francis of Sales.
1609: Twelve-year truce between Spain and the United Provinces.
1627: Company of the Holy Sacrament founded.
1632: Galileo's *Dialogue Concerning the Two Chief World Systems, Ptolemaic and Copernican.*

5. The golds and blacks of the Gesu church (Giacomo della Porta).

Philip II's Spain: The Golden Age

In 1556 THE SON of Charles V inherited the western half of his father's immense empire. This reserved, hard-working and conscientious man, a home-loving bureaucrat and a fervent Catholic, the master of Spain during the half-century in which Castilian power was at its height, had great ambitions and, it seemed, the means to realize them. Thanks to a tentacular bureaucracy, his empire was as centralized as possible; Spain had been spared religious troubles and, since the failed revolt of the *Comuneros* of Castile, the kingdom had been peaceful. His troops, the redoubtable *tercios*, were reputed to be the best in the world, and the flow of American money was apparently inexhaustible.

During the first half of his reign Philip fought in the Mediterranean against the forces of Islam. Then, when he had removed the Turkish threat at Lepanto, he turned his attentions to the Atlantic, where he opposed the Protestants. The annexing of Portugal and its empire in 1580 marked the high point of his power. This was the period of Philip's 'Grand Design' (see above, p. 152). He dreamt of establishing his domination over a Catholic West from which heresy would be forever banished. So great was the power of Spain and so magnificent its civilization – one thinks of the Christian humanism of a Francisco de Vitoria, the neo-Thomism of Suarez and Molina, the mystical spirituality of Theresa of Avila and of St John of the Cross, but also of *Don Quixote* and *Amadis de Gaul* – that there were very few at the time, apart perhaps from the Venetian ambassador (who portrayed the misery of the Spanish people) or Jean Bodin (1530–1596, French philosopher and economist, who described the dependence of the kingdom on French manufactured goods), who recognized it as a colossus with feet of clay. The fact was that Philip II's Spain was a poor, badly unified country, which produced very little, had to import almost everything, including corn, and whose trade was in the hands of foreign merchants. Its political and military power was artificially preserved by the flow of American ingots. The Reconquista had left the Spaniards with a *hidalgo* mentality (whereby they scorned trade and manual labour), archaic and rigid social structures, and an ardent and exclusive religious faith. The final collapse of Philip's 'Grand Design' was a logical consequence of the country's economy and demography and the outcome of his European war was disastrous: not only did he not succeed in taking France and England, but he also lost the rich 'Low Countries'.

After the peace of Vervins and the death of the King, the decline accelerated. The expulsion of the Moriscoes (Muslims theoretically converted to Catholicism), the great plagues of the beginning and middle of the century and emigration decimated the population and completed the ruin of the economy. The international position of Spain felt the consequences of this. Under mediocre sovereigns and ambitious ministers – Lerma and then Olivares – Spain engaged in ill-fated wars against Holland and France, had to recognize the de jure independence of the former and cede areas of its territory (Roussillon, Artois, Franche-Comté) to the latter. Incapable of internal reform, Spain remained on the margins of Europe's expansion and its imperial power did not usher in capitalism. It would not, for example, occur to the twentieth-century French historian Fernand Braudel, when writing a history of the Mediterranean in the seventeenth century, to include the names of Philip III, Philip IV or, even less, Charles II. All the same, literature and art suffered hardly at all from this decadence; the Spanish 'Golden Age' was still a glowing reality even when the glory of Spanish military deeds had become but a pale memory. The plays of Lope de Vega and Calderon, and the paintings of El Greco, Murillo and Velazquez bear witness to this.

1. Don John of Austria, champion of Christendom: the Battle of Lepanto definitively ended the Turkish threat to the West.

Theresa of Avila, *The Castle of the Soul.*	El Greco, *The Burial of the Count Orgaz.*	Cervantes, *Don Quixote.*
1577	**1586**	**1605**

1556: Philip II becomes king of Spain.
1556–9: War against France (see p. 148).
1557: Beginning of building of Escorial: bankruptcy.
1559: Treaty of Cateau-Cambrésis (see p. 148).
1568: St John of the Cross founds the order of the Descalzos or Barefoot Carmelites; mysterious death of Philip's son Don Carlos.
1568–71: Revolt of the Moriscoes of Granada.
1571: Victory at Lepanto over the Ottoman fleet.
1575: Bankruptcy.
1577: St Theresa of Avila, *The Castle of the Soul.*
1579: El Greco, *Trinity.*
1580: Annexation of Portugal. El Greco, *Adoration.*
1581: Act of Abjuration: Dutch states reject Philip's claim to sovereignty.
1584: Alliance with the Guises and the Leaguers. Alexander Farnese takes Ghent. Completion of the Escorial. Cervantes, *Numancia.*

3. American treasures flood into Spain but do not remain there: the port of Seville in the 16th century.

1586: El Greco, *The Burial of the Count Orgaz.*
1587: Francis Drake raids Cadiz.
1588: Wreck of the Invincible Armada. Molina, *Liberi arbitrii cum gratiae donis, divina praescentia, providentia, praedestinatione et reprobatione, concordia.*
1593: Molina, *De justitia et jure.*
1595: War against France.
1596: An English fleet destroys Cadiz. Bankruptcy.
1597: Francisco Suarez, *Disputationes metaphysicae.*
1598: Peace of Vervins. Death of Philip II. Philip III abandons the management of national affairs to the Count of Lerma. Lope de Vega, *Arcadia, La Dragontea.*
1605–16: Cervantes, *Don Quixote.*
1608: High point of trade between Seville and America.
1609–14: Expulsion of the Moriscoes.
1612: Francisco Suarez, *De legibus.*
1613: Cervantes, *Novelas exemplares.*
1618: Velazquez, *Old Woman (frying eggs).*
1621: Philip IV King of Spain. Olivares initiates an ambitious foreign policy.

16th–17th centuries

?. The king of all Spain at the height of his power. Portrait of Philip II by Antonio Moro.

...eron, La Vida es Sueño.　　　　　　　　　　**Velazquez, Las Meninas.**

1631　　　　　　　　　　　　　　　　　　**1656**

*EL INGENIOSO
HIDALGO DON QVI-
XOTE DE LA MANCHA,
Compuesto por Miguel de Ceruantes
Saauedra.*

DIRIGIDO AL DVQVE DE BEIAR,
Marques de Gibraleon, Conde de Benalcaçar, y Baña-
res, Vizconde de la Puebla de Alcozer, Señor de
las villas de Capilla, Curiel, y
Burguillos.

Año, 1605.

CON PRIVILEGIO,
EN MADRID, Por Iuan de la Cuesta.

Vendese en cafa de Francisco de Robles, librero del Rey nro señor.

4. First edition of Don Quixote.

1628: War against the United Provinces recommences. Zurbaran, *Saint Serapian.*
1631: Calderon, *La Vida es Sueño.*
1632: Lope de Vega, *La Dorotea.*
1635: Calderon, *El Médico de sa honra.* Zurbaran, *The Painter before Christ Crucified.* Richelieu declares war on Spain.
1636: Taking of Corbie (near Amiens) by Spain.
1640: Spain loses Portugal.
1643: Lope de Vega, *El castigo sin venganza.*
1647–52: Plague kills half a million. Revolt of Naples.
1647: Velazquez, *The Surrender of Breda.*
1648: End of the Thirty Years War. De jure recognition of the independence of the Netherlands.
1656: Murillo, *Vision of St Anthony.* Velazquez, *Las Meninas* (The Maids of Honour).
1657: Velazquez, *Las Hilanderas* (The Spinners).
1659: Peace of the Pyrenees.

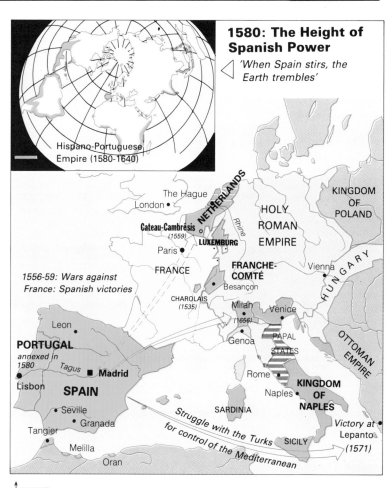

1580: The Height of Spanish Power

◁ *'When Spain stirs, the Earth trembles'*

Hispano-Portuguese Empire (1580-1640)

The Hague
London
NETHERLANDS
Cateau-Cambrésis *(1559)*
LUXEMBURG
Paris
FRANCE
HOLY ROMAN EMPIRE
KINGDOM OF POLAND
Rhine
FRANCHE-COMTÉ
Besançon
Vienna
HUNGARY
1556-59: Wars against France: Spanish victories
CHAROLAIS *(1535)*
Milan *(1656)*
Venice
Leon
Genoa
PAPAL STATES
OTTOMAN EMPIRE
PORTUGAL
annexed in 1580
Tagus
■ **Madrid**
Rome
Lisbon
SPAIN
Naples
KINGDOM OF NAPLES
• Seville
• Granada
SARDINIA
Victory at Lepanto (1571)
Tangier
Struggle with the Turks for control of the Mediterranean
SICILY
Melilla
Oran

Spanish possessions	⇨ Victorious campaigns
Holy Roman Empire and Austrian Hapsburg possessions	⦸▬✗ Reverses and defeats
Territories lost by Spain after 1580	★ Revolts

1580-1659: The Beginnings of Spanish Decline

UNITED PROVINCES *gain independence (1648)*

1588: Wreck of the invincible Armada

London
The Hague
★ Ghent
HOLY ROMAN EMPIRE
KINGDOM OF POLAND
ARTOIS (1659)
Vervins
SPANISH NETHERLANDS
Paris
FRANCHE-COMTÉ
Vienna
HUNGARY
SWITZERLAND
1635: Richelieu declares war on Spain
DUCHY OF SAVOY
Milan
Venice
Avignon
TUSCANY
PAPAL STATES
OTTOMAN EMPIRE
30,000 men
10,000 men
1595-1598
Corunna
Santander
PORTUGAL
lost in 1640
★ ROUSSILLON (1659)
Rome
■ Madrid
★ CATALONIA (1640-1652)
SPAIN
KINGDOM OF NAPLES (1648) ★
SARDINIA
Cadiz
destroyed by the British fleet in 1596
SICILY (1648) ★

250 km

England: Towards a Bourgeois Monarchy

THE FIRST TUDOR, Henry VII, had put an end to the civil wars. His son Henry VIII succeeded, at the height of the humanist Renaissance and the Lutheran Reformation, in asserting the national, independent character of the English throne. Drawn, whether by concern for a son and heir or by kingly ambition, into a crisis over Rome's refusal of his divorce, he in his turn rejected Rome and proclaimed himself head of the Church of England. There followed a long period of instability. Edward VI, who favoured the Reformation priests, was succeeded by a 'Spanish-style' Catholic reaction under Mary Tudor.

After 1558, Elizabeth I ended the uncertainty. Consolidating the Acts of Supremacy and Uniformity, in the face of the (foreign) 'Pap-

ists' and the (rebel) Puritans, she imposed a national religion, later to be called 'Anglican'. This was a compromise between Protestant dogmatism and episcopal discipline and hierarchy, which was based on two documents, the 'Thirty-nine Articles' and the Book of Common Prayer. By manipulating her parliament, the Queen 'allowed' her Franco-Scottish rival Mary Stuart to be executed. She also profited greatly from the catastrophic failure of the Spanish Armada (1588). The forty-five-year-long 'Elizabethan Era' consolidated the English national identity by opening it up to influences from the four corners of the earth. It was also a period of great cultural Renaissance in which Shakespeare stands out as the leading figure.

The year 1603 does not simply mark a change of dynasty. The explicit absolutism of the Stuart, James I, and the financial disorder he created, exasperated both the gentry and the city bourgeois, who were the masters of the Commons, 'God's elect', and therefore men with a vocation to govern. In the great city of London, the word on everyone's lips was 'reform'. Under Charles I, this pressure mounted, and Parliament demanded the power to share in decision-making. Its Petition of Right was punished by eleven years of tyranny in which both crown and bishop joined forces. The failure of the attempt to extend Anglicanism to Calvinist Scotland unleashed revolution in 1640. The key word was now 'revolt'. Under great financial pressure, the King accepted the Remonstrances of the Parliament, which voted to 'extirpate' the bishops and the prerogative courts. Censorship ceased, in practice, to exist. The revolt of the Catholics in Ulster and the violation of the immunity of the Commons provoked civil war. When the 'New Model Army' of the independent parliamentarian Cromwell had crushed the Royalists in 1645, freedom seemed won. Equality, however, was not. 'Leveller' fever ran rife in the towns and among the soldiery. Once Cromwell had purged his ranks of this radicalism, the rest of Parliament judged the King and condemned him to death for having violated the political contract. After the proclamation of the republic, the City found itself in favour (Navigation Act) with the result that from 1653 on it affirmed the personal power of the Lord Protector of the Commonwealth. After his death, there were two years of great upheaval, following which Charles II, the executed king's son, returned from exile.

In a framework of economic vitality, with both dissidents and Papists removed from the scene, the Restoration saw sharply opposed Whig and Tory administrations exchanging power. It also, paradoxically, saw the introduction of the law of *Habeas Corpus*. But the Catholic James II had learnt nothing. He was to be put to flight by a revolution made by the Whigs and spoken of as 'Glorious' (1688). His son-in-law, Stathouder of Holland, and his daughter were crowned monarchs on the basis of a contract by which the king was to be controlled 'in Parliament'.

1. William and Mary crushing tyranny, painted by J. Thornhill.

Thomas More, *Utopia*.

1516

1485: End of the Wars of the Roses. Tudor Age begins.
1517: Luther's 95 theses produce resonances in Britain.
1527: Beginning of the controversy surrounding Henry VIII's divorce from Catherine of Aragon.
1533: Excommunication of Henry VIII.
1534: Act of Supremacy: King becomes head of the Church of England.
1535: Execution of the Catholic humanist Thomas More.
1536–9: Dissolution of the monasteries: creation of a nobility based on wealth who were loyal to the state.
1559: Act of Uniformity: Elizabeth I head of the episcopal hierarchy of the new Church of England.
1563: The Thirty-Nine Articles: faith and order.
1577: Francis Drake sets off to circumnavigate the earth.
1587: Mary Stuart executed.
1588: The 'miraculous failure' of the 'invincible' Spanish Armada.

c. 1590: Beginning of Shakespeare's magnificent *oeuvre*.
1600: East India Company granted its charter.
1603: Beginning of reign of Stuart dynasty (which will end in 1714): uniting of English and Scottish crowns.
1605: Failure of the (Catholic) Gunpowder Plot.
1611: Authorized version of the Bible.
1620: Pilgrim Fathers sail for America.
1628: Parliament's Petition of Right.
1638: Revolt of Scotland to defend its religious freedom.
1640: Long Parliament meets.
1641: Execution of the minister Strafford and the Grand Remonstrance.
1642: Civil War. Charles I leaves London.
1644: Milton's *Areopagitica*: for the freedom of the press.
1645: Cromwell's victory over the Royalists at Naseby.
1647: Organization of the egalitarian movement, the Levellers.
1649: Trial and execution of the King. Republic. Diggers phenomenon (rural socialism). Cromwell crushes Ireland.

The Thirty-Nine Articles

1563

2. Charles I is beheaded.

1485–1713

The Civil War 1642-49

England divided at the end of 1643
(after two years of civil war)

SCOTLAND
revolt 1638

1643 alliance with Parliament

Scotland-England Border

IRELAND

Rebellion 1641

WALES

Marston Moor 2-7-1644
First defeat for the king against Parliamentarians and Scots

London

Zone under 'Roundhead' (pro-Parliament) control

Zone under Charles I's control

Cromwell's victory 1645-50

1648 Scottish intervention on the king's side

Scotland-England Border

1650 Cromwell to occupy Scotland

Preston 1648

Drogheda 1649

Naseby 14.6.1645

London

Royalist bastions the end of 1645

British outposts
XVIth-XVIIth century

NORTH OF THE AMERICAN CONTINENT

NORTH-EAST EUROPE

NEW ENGLAND

WEST INDIES

CENTRAL AMERICA

Gibraltar

AFRICA

INDIA

Spanish territory

Portuguese territory

British outposts

Colonised areas

Zones of exploration

West Indies. Central America
1595 Trinidad
1596 Guyana
1624-50 Lesser Antilles
1655 Jamaica
1670 Bahamas

Africa (in tandem with Slave trade)
1580 Guinea coast
1588-92 Coast of Gambia, Sierra Leone, Gold Coast

New England
1584 Landing in Virginia (colonised - with Florida - after 1606)
1620 Massachussets ('Pilgrim Fathers')
1637 Maryland
1667 New York and New Jersey and Delaware regions recaptured
1670 Carolina (visited in 1585 by Raleigh)

1683 Pennsylvania

North of the American Continent
1497 J. Cabot discovers Newfoundland, but it is not annexed until 1713
1567-1610 Reconnaissance of Baffin Island, east and south coasts of Greenland, coast of Labrador and Hudson's Bay which is annexed in 1713 (search for North West Passage)

North-East Europe and 'North-East Passage'
1607-08 Spitzbergen and Novaya Zemla

Gibraltar
1704 and officially in 1713

India
1639 Madras
1661 Bombay
1690 Calcutta

'Anti-Spanish voyages of exploration'

Drake 1577-80

Cavendish 1586-88

Raleigh sails up the Orinoco, the Caroni and visits the Guyanas

---

ng James Bible.

1611

Death of Shakespeare.

1616

Charles I executed.

1649

Death of Locke.

1704

1651: Navigation Act: Cromwell the 'City's man'. Hobbes: *Leviathan*.
1653–8: Cromwell Lord Protector. Personal rule.
1660: General Monk restores the monarchy (Charles II).
1661–5: Anti-Puritan Restoration (Clarendon Code).
1665–7: War with Holland. Acquisition of New York.

1666: Great Fire of London. Reconstruction under the guidance of Christopher Wren.
1673: Test Act: confirmed exclusion of Catholics.
1679: *Habeas Corpus*.
1687: Newton formulates his theory of universal attraction.
1688: Birth of a Catholic heir to the throne. Appeal to William of Orange. James II flees to France.
1689: Bill of Rights accepted by William and Mary. Act of Religious Toleration (did not include Catholics).
1690: Locke, *Treatise on Civil Government*, a justification of 1688.
1694: Bank of England. End of censorship.
1701: Act of Settlement: Catholics excluded from the throne.
1707: Act of Union between England and Scotland.
1713: Treaties of Utrecht: Britain henceforth the major maritime and colonial power.

3. Cromwell Lord Protector. Portrait attributed to G. de Crayer. 4. The Royal Exchange, London.

Contemporary Revolutions

1. *The orator Genuino haranguing the mob during the revolt in Naples, led by Masaniello, 1657.*

WHAT HAD THE various disturbances of the middle years of the seventeenth century in common, if not 'the mood of giddiness which prevailed at the time'? (Voltaire). To this we should add Vauban's equally famous observation, 'There is nothing which stirs and angers the people more than food shortages and the cost of bread.' In Europe, these 'stirrings', both urban and rural, like those in Andalusia in 1652, caused by hunger or, to be more exact, by the fear of hunger, tended to remain circumscribed. But in China, the catastrophic droughts which began in 1627 shook and eventually overturned the power of the Ming dynasty (1644) and paved the way for the Manchurian invasions.

Most uprisings against central government were anti-fiscal in character. Thus, for example, in Russia the common townspeople (*posadskie*), particularly in Moscow, rose in revolt (1648), and this led to the drafting of a new code of law (*Sobornoe Ulozhenie*); the representative assembly, the *Zemski Sobor*, was not summoned after 1653. In England, Charles I's attempts at absolutism encountered the fierce opposition of the Independents, who took full advantage of the general hostility to ship-money (a levy intended to finance the building of warships). The conflict between France and the nebulous Hapsburgs meant an increase in fiscal pressure and imprisonment for debts, and this added to the state of tension in the country. Mazarin was reputed to have put in irons 25,000 prisoners for non-payment of the taille (the major direct tax) and of this large number 6,000 died of starvation in the prisons. In many cases the rebels' justification was the defence of traditional liberties (long-established privileges, representative assemblies). The *Va-nu-pieds* (literally 'those who go barefooted') of Normandy wanted to preserve their right of *quart-bouillon* (a salt tax paid at a lower rate than the standard *gabelle*). The leaders of the 'secret diet of peasants' in Lucerne (Christmas 1652) dressed themselves symbolically in the old costume of the Swiss confederates. Prudently, the revolutionaries claimed to respect legitimate authority; the *croquants* (a group of French peasants) intended to take their taxes directly to the king in the Louvre palace (1637). Cries of 'Long live the King!' punctuated the most unruly outbreaks; Stenka Razin called on the Cossacks to march against the 'enemies of the Tsar'. The antipathy to centralization was fuelled by regionalist and nationalist feeling. The agents of authority were regarded as outsiders. During the Fronde revolt, the fact that the chief minister (Mazarin) was a foreigner was exploited to the full. The rebellion in Naples (1647) was helped by the anti-Spanish sentiments of the nobility, epitomized by Generalissimo Marco Antonio Brancaccio (1570–1650). In 1668 the Sardinian nobility, taking advantage of the War of Devolution, tried to set their island on an anti-fiscal and autonomous adventure. The only successful revolt was that of Portugal, where the long tradition of nationalist feeling kept resistance going until Spain was forced to concede defeat (1 December 1640–January 1668). The Cortes (national assembly) of Catalonia was persuaded to offer sovereignty over the country to Louis XIII (23 January 1641). The Cossack insurrection led by Bogdan Chmielnicki (1648), which began as a defence of ancient privileges, changed into a nationalist movement against the Poles and ended with the Zaporozhians putting themselves under the protection of the Tsar of Moscow.

In the early days of colonialism, anti-colonial uprisings were rare: the people of Ulster, driven from their lands by the Plantations of 1607–11, revolted in October 1641. Cromwell, who in 1637 had been refused permission to emigrate to New England, led the repression. This was a prelude to the confiscation and colonization of land by the British, effectively keeping the Irish confined in Connaught.

Masaniello's revolt in Naples.	Barricades in Paris.
1647	1648

1637: Revolt against Shogun by 40,000 Christian peasants in Nagasaki region.
1 June: *les croquants* (peasant revolutionaries) crushed at La Sauvetat.
July–November 1639: Revolt of the *Va-nu-pieds* (lit. 'those who go barefooted') in Normandy.
7 June 1640: Viceroy of Catalonia murdered in Barcelona by insurgents disguised as harvesters (*segadores*).
22 October 1641: Irish rebellion in Ulster. Institution by Puritans in January 1642 of public national fast on last Wednesday of each month for duration of revolt.
1642: Refusal by parishes of Val d'Aran, led by their priests, to pay taxes to King of France.
22 August: Charles I's standard raised at Nottingham.
1644: Taking of Peking by Li Zicheng: suicide of last Ming emperor.
2 July: Battle of Marston Moor.
1647: Disturbances in Seville.
19 May: Uprising in Palermo to cries of *'Fuera gabelle. Viva il re e muora il mal governo.'* (Down with the salt tax. Long live the King and death to bad government.)

7 July: Insurrection in Naples. Masaniello killed 16 July but struggle continued by partisans until February 1648 against Spanish troops of viceroy Arcos and fleet of Don John of Austria. Republic proclaimed 23 October 1647.
1648: Riots in Moscow. Insurrections in Ukraine (1648–54).
26 August: Barricades in Paris following arrest of Broussel (a leader of the Parlement).
9 February 1649: Execution of Charles I.
11 September: Population of Drogheda massacred by Cromwell's army.
1650: Riots in Pskov and Novgorod.
12 January 1651: Following death (on 6 November 1650) of William II of Nassau, sovereignty of individual Dutch provinces declared at The Hague by general assembly of the seven provinces.
21 May 1653: Bern besieged by peasant army of 16,000 men: army defeated on 8 June at Herzogenburg.

3. *A fight between peasants and soldiers, as seen by Gallais.*

2. Soldiers pillaging a farm. France, 17th century.

Death of Cromwell.	Spinoza's *Tractus Theologico-politicus*.	Execution of Stenka Razin in Moscow.
1658	1670	1671

1658: Cossack revolt.
April–August: Revolt of the *sabotiers* (clog-makers) of the Sologne.
May–July: Revolt of the Lustucrus in the Boulogne region put down on 11 July at Hucqueliers.
28 May 1668: Assassination of Marquis of Camarassa, viceroy of Sardinia.
24 June 1670: Capture of Astrakhan by Stenka Razin.
15 June 1671: Execution in Cagliari of Marquis of Cea, leader of Sardinian conspiracy.
20 August 1672: John and Cornelius de Witt assassinated at The Hague.

4. 'We are right to rebel' – engraving from the period of the Fronde.

Thirty Years of European Wars

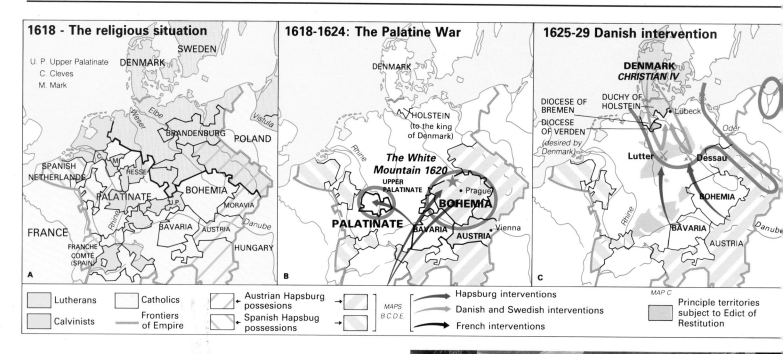

1618 - The religious situation

U. P. Upper Palatinate
C. Cleves
M. Mark

SWEDEN
DENMARK
Weser
Elbe
Vistula
BRANDENBURG
POLAND
SPANISH NETHERLANDS
HESSE
PALATINATE
BOHEMIA
Rhine
U.P.
MORAVIA
FRANCE
BAVARIA
AUSTRIA
Danube
FRANCHE COMTÉ (SPAIN)
HUNGARY

A

1618-1624: The Palatine War

DENMARK
HOLSTEIN (to the king of Denmark)
Rhine
The White Mountain 1620
UPPER PALATINATE
• Prague
BOHEMIA
PALATINATE
BAVARIA
AUSTRIA
• Vienna

B

1625-29 Danish intervention

DENMARK CHRISTIAN IV
DIOCESE OF BREMEN
DUCHY OF HOLSTEIN
• Lübeck
Oder
DIOCESE OF VERDEN (desired by Denmark)
Lutter
Dessau
Rhine
BOHEMIA
BAVARIA
AUSTRIA
Danube

MAP C

C

Lutherans	Catholics	← Austrian Hapsburg possesions	→	MAPS B.C.D.E.	→ Hapsburg interventions	Principle territories subject to Edict of Restitution
Calvinists	Frontiers of Empire	← Spanish Hapsbug possessions	→		→ Danish and Swedish interventions → French interventions	

BOHEMIA, AN ELECTIVE MONARCHY, was not subject to the principle, *cuius regio, eius religio*. Protected by the Letter of Majesty (1609), which guaranteed freedom of worship, the Utraquists, exploiting an aristocratic reaction against the Hapsburgs on the death of the Emperor Matthias (1619), prompted the inauguration of a *Confederation Bohemica*, and appealed to the leader of the Evangelical Union, Frederick V the Elector Palatine. After the Battle of the White Mountain, the states of Bohemia and Moravia capitulated. The Letter of Majesty was torn to shreds by the public executioner. The Elector Palatine was placed under the imperial ban, his possessions were confiscated and his electoral dignity was transferred to his Bavarian cousin. On the death of the Archduke Albert (1621), the Netherlands became once again a group of Spanish provinces. When the twelve-year truce ended, hostilities recommenced between Spain and the United Provinces: the latter gradually conquered the 'Generality Lands' and won independence.

After the Peace of Augsburg (1555) the Lutherans retained possession of the secularized church property. But the Ecclesiastical Reservation prevented bishops who abandoned Catholicism from conserving their temporal power. In the north of the Empire this clause was often violated, a provisional administrator of the temporal power occupying the vacant episcopal seat until such time as it could be

1. The Plague at Ashdod, by Nicolas Poussin, 1630.

Battle of the White Mountain.

Wallenstein leader of Empire's armies.

Nicolas Poussin, *The Plague at Ash*

1620

1625

1630

3. Battle at Prague, 16 September 1620. German engraving.

23 May 1618: Defenestration of Prague.
4 November 1619: Frederick V crowned King of Bohemia.
3 July 1620: At Ulm, the Protestants undertake not to intervene in the Bohemian war; the Catholics agree to respect the Elector Palatine's states.
8 November: Protestants defeated at the Battle of the White Mountain.
14 May 1621: Evangelical Union disbands at Heilbronn.
August: War between Spain and United Provinces recommences.
5 March 1626: Treaty of Monzon: Spanish troops evacuate the Valtelline, whose inhabitants are forced to pay tribute to their old rulers, the Grisons.
17 January 1628: Charles I of Gonzaga, Duke of Nevers, takes possession of Mantua, his cousin Vincent II having died on 26 December 1627.
6 March 1629: Edict of Restitution.
22 May: By the Treaty of Lübeck, Christian IV of Denmark renounces his claims to bishoprics within the Empire.

4. Count Wallenstein, leader of the imperial mercenaries. A. van Dyck, c. 1630.

1618–48

630-35: Swedish intervention

SWEDEN
GUSTAVUS ADOLPHUS

POMERANIA

BRANDENBURG

Lützen
1632

SAXONY

Death of Gustavus Adolphus

Peace of
Prague
1635

BERNARD OF SAXE-WEIMAR'S offensive at the head of the Swedish armies

Nordlingen
1634
partial setback by the Swedes

• Munich

1635-48: French intervention

Spanish offensives from Netherlands bases

TREATIES OF
WESTPHALIA
• Osnabruck
Munster

BRANDENBURG

SAXONY

Corbie

Rocroy
1643

ALSACE

BOHEMIA

Breisach   BAVARIA

FRANCE
allied to Bernard of SAXE-WEIMAR

E

Human cost of 30 years of warfare

POMERANIA

UNITED
PROVINCES

BRANDENBURG

SAXONY

SILESIA

H O L Y
R O M A N   E M P I R E

BOHEMIA

PALATINATE

WURTEMBERG   AUSTRIA

FRANCE   BAVARIA

SWITZERLAND

F

▢ Territories occupied by Sweden and its allies in 1633	·········· Swedish positions in 1635

MAPS B.C.D.E ✕ Successive theatres of operations and decisive battles

Human losses, as a % of the population

—   15 %   30 %   **65 %**   +

200 km

secularized. This explains the clashes over Aachen, Cologne and Strasbourg (1592–1604). Christian IV of Denmark, who had had his youngest son elected administrator of the Bishopric of Verden and arranged matters so that the same son would acquire control of the Archbishopric of Bremen, had a great deal to fear from the success of the Counter-Reformation, and threw himself into war in June 1625. The military genius of Wallenstein forced him to desist (Lübeck, 1629). The Edict of Restitution (6 March 1629) annulled all the secularizations effected since 1555.

Since the Treaty of Vervins (1598), France had sought to weaken Spain's positions. In 1601 she acquired Bresse and Bugey. And in response to the occupation of Jülich-Cleves by imperial forces, she allied with the Evangelical Union and Savoy, though this was interrupted by Henry IV's assassination in 1610. She cut the lines of communication between Spanish and Austrian Hapsburgs in the Valtelline. She intervened against the Spaniards who were laying siege to Casale (Montferrat) in 1629–30. Spain's American money having been cut off (Admiral Piet Heyn had captured it at Matanzas Bay), France remained at Pinerolo, while the Duke of Nevers retained Mantua (1631). With the help of French subsidies he received under the Barwalde Treaty, Gustavus II Adolphus conducted a dazzling campaign throughout the Empire until his death at Lützen. When the

Swedes were crushed at Nördlingen, France had itself to enter the war. After some difficult beginnings (Corbie, 1636), her efforts were eventually sufficient to cause the Iberian bastion to totter: Louis XIII was proclaimed Count of Barcelona and concluded an alliance (1641) with the new king of Portugal. If, however, the Emperor was resigned to losing his patrimonial lands in Alsace and what real sovereignty he retained within the Empire, Spain – in spite of Rocroy (1643), Dunkirk (1646) and Lens (1648) – was not so ready to give up the fight. ...

2. The Miseries of War. *Jacques Callot, 1634.*

Jacques Callot, *The Miseries of War*

1634

June 1630: Gustavus II Adolphus lands in Pomerania.
July: Diet of Ratisbon.
23 January 1631: By the terms of the Treaty of Barwalde, France promises an annual subsidy of a million pounds to Gustavus Adolphus, who undertakes to respect the neutrality of Bavaria and the Catholic League.
20 March: Sack of Magdeburg by Tilly's army rallies the undecided Protestant princes to Gustavus Adolphus's cause.
16 November 1632: Victory – and death – of Gustavus Adolphus at Lutzen.
6 September 1634: Victory of imperial troops over the Swedes at Nördlingen.
19 May 1635: France declares war on Spain.
30 May: Treaty of Prague between Emperor Ferdinand II and the Princes of Saxony and Brandenburg.
11 July: By the Treaty of Rivoli, Victor Amadeus I of Savoy takes command of the Italian League against Milan.
7 August 1636: Spaniards take Corbie.

5. The end of a long war: the French copy of the Treaty of Münster.

Peace of Westphalia.

1648

9 August 1640: French take Arras.
25 December 1641: Preliminary peace treaties between France and the Empire signed: date for negotiations is fixed as 25 March 1642.
19 May 1643: Duke of Enghien victorious at Rocroy.
May 1644: Münster and Osnabruck conferences open.
30 January 1648: At The Hague, Spain recognizes the independence of the United Provinces and cedes the 'Generality Lands' to them (Treaty ratified at Münster, 15 May 1648).
20 August: Condé victorious at Lens. Treaties of Westphalia.
7 November 1659: Treaty of the Pyrenees between France and Spain.

The Ottoman Empire: Grandeur and Decline

THE CAPTURE OF CONSTANTINOPLE began the second phase of the Turkish expansion which had come to a halt after the victory of Tamerlane over Bayezid I in 1402. Indeed, less than a century later, the Ottoman state stretched from the Red Sea and the southern coasts of the Mediterranean to the gates of Vienna. There are many reasons for this success. The sultans had at their disposal a powerful army made up of timariots (salaried cavalrymen) and janissaries (infantrymen receiving a fee, recruited from among Christian children instructed in the Muslim faith). This enlistment also allowed capable men of humble origin to rise to high positions, even to the rank of grand vizier. The talent for exploiting internal struggles in neighbouring countries was another strong point. The sultans would be called in to help and would end up taking over power for themselves (cf. the fate of Hungary after the death of Louis II (1526)). The state thus very soon included a large number of ethnic groups, among whom the only common denominator was the duty to serve the ruling dynasty. When a country had been conquered and its military and judicial administration taken over, its ancient customs and laws were left intact. This disparity between the various systems was the source of some of the Empire's earliest problems. Mehmed II, seeking new resources after his costly campaigns, realized that he could not make decrees without knowing what laws governed his empire. It is to him, then, that we owe the first 'book of laws' or legal code. He tried to unify legislation relating to land ownership by reforming the property laws, but created widespread discontent, particularly among the dervishes and the timariots in Anatolia who had hereditary revenues.

In the sixteenth century the conquest of Egypt by Selim I and the surrender of the sherifs of Mecca made possible the appearance of a further unifying factor. Rather than create a single secular constitution, the Holy Law (Shari'a) was glorified as the arbiter supreme. This last conferred on those who applied it even greater recognition, since it brought religious prestige to add to military glory. The reign of Süleyman the Magnificent was the high spot of this development, with illustrious jurisconsults such as Kemalpashazade and Abu Su'ud. Constantinople and its court were seen by all as the model to copy. Following the example of the capital, the provincial centres had mosques, schools, libraries, hospitals, soup kitchens, public baths and fountains. Religious foundations also saw it as part of their role to provide for the welfare of the community. In the literary field, writers cultivated a refined style by introducing Persian and Arabic elements into the Turkish texts (the poets Bâkî and Fuzuli).

However, the state had serious economic problems. In the euphoria of conquest, little thought was given to the careful management of the riches so gained. Large sums of money were given to the dignitaries, and the queues of timariots waiting for promotion lengthened. The constant debasement of the coinage diminished purchasing power and had an effect on the equipping of the army. What is

more, the young princes, isolated in the harem, no longer learned the art of government in the provincial capitals. The sultans shut themselves away in the seraglio and fell under the influence of the sultan's mother and the favourites. Corruption became rife and even able viziers like the Köprülü in the seventeenth century could only temporarily stall the decline. The overwhelming successes of the Ottomans forced the West to co-ordinate its defence more carefully, with the resulting victory over the Ottoman fleet at Lepanto in 1571, and, on land, with the victory at the Battle of Saint-Gotthard in 1644: this process climaxed with the relief of Vienna in 1683. The wars against Russia, which became frequent from the end of the seventeenth century, would hasten the downward trend.

1. The siege of Vienna, 27 September 1529, as seen by a Turkish artist (1588).

Mehmed II.	Fall of Constantinople.	Bayezid II.	Selim I.	Süleyman the Lawgiver.		Selim II.
1451	1453	1481	1512	1520		1566

1453: Capture of Constantinople by Mehmed II; death of last Byzantine Emperor.
1458–9: Conquest of Serbia.
1460: Conquest of Morea.
1461: Conquest of Trebizond; end of the great Comneni state.
1463–4: Conquest of Bosnia.
1463–79: War against Venice.
1464: Occupation of Konya, capital of the Karaman emirate; the conquest of the emirate was completed in 1474.
1468: Death of Skanderbeg, leader of the Albanian rebels.
1473: Mehmed II defeats Uzun Hasan, head of the Ak Koyunlu or White Sheep dynasty, at Otluk-Beli.
1475: Capture of Kafa from the Genoese and defeat of the Crimean Khanate.
1484: Conquest of ports of Kilia and Akkerman in Moldavia.
1514: Defeat of Shah Esma'il I of the Safavid dynasty in Chaldiran.
1516–17: Conquest of Syria and Egypt.
1521: Capture of Belgrade.
1522: Süleyman the Magnificent (also called the Lawgiver) overthrows the dynasty of Zu'l

Kadr. Conquest of Rhodes: the Knights now settle on the island of Malta.
1526: Victory over Louis II, King of Hungary, at Mohács and capture of Buda.
1529: First siege of Vienna.
1533: Süleyman appoints Barbarossa (Khayr ad-Din) *kapudan* of Algiers.

2. Portrait of Süleyman the Magnificent by a Venetian artist, 17th century.

3. The fortress of Roumeli Hisari facing Constantinople, 15th century.

4. Pottery from Iznik (Nicaea), c. 1580.

1534: Capture of Baghdad.
1535: Treaty between Süleyman and Francis I.
1566: Conquest of Szigetvár; Süleyman dies during the siege.
1571: Capture of Cyprus from the Venetians, but defeat of the Ottoman fleet at Lepanto.
1577–89: War against Persia; peace treaty signed in 1590.

15th–17th centuries

Ottoman victories
Ottoman defeats

Kamieniec · Chigirin
Vienna
Buda
Kilia 1484 · Kaffa 1475
Belgrade · Akkerman
Venice
BOSNIA · SERBIA
Constantinople 1453
Sinop
Trebizond 1461
Otluk-Beli 1473
Chaldiran 1514
CRIMEAN KHANATE
Caucasus
Elburz
Carpathians
Alpes
Lepanto 1571
MORÉAL
Konya 1464
KARAMAN
Baghdad 1534
I R A Q
Algiers · Bizerte 1574
Oran · KABYLIA
Malta
Rhodes 1522
Cyprus 1571
SYRIA 1516
Crete 1645-69
Ouargla (Wargla)
EGYPT 1517
Nile
Jeddah · Mecca
Sawakin
Mitsawa
Aden

Kamieniec 1672
Vienna
Zsitvatörök
Eger 1596
Esztergom
Tisza
MOLDAVIA
Carpathians
Alpes
Stuhlweissenburg (Székesféhervár)
Buda
Debreczin
Grosswardein
St Gotthard 1664
Mochács 1526
Szegedin
Szigetvar 1566
Zenta 1697
Venice
Karlowitz 1699
Slankamen
WALLACHIA
Belgrade 1521
BOSNIA · SERBIA
Danube
200 km

1000 km

1451	1503	1520	1566	1683	
Mehmed II Bayezid II	Selim I	Suleyman I		Maximum extent of Empire	Vassal states

Timeline (rulers):
ad III. | Mehmed III. | Ahmed I. | Mustafa I. | Murad IV. | Ibrahim. | Mehmed IV. | Mustafa II.
4 | 1603 | 1617 | 1623 | | 1640 | 1648 | 1695

5. *The Mosque of Sultan Selim II, designed by Sinan (1569–74).*

1594: Capture of Esztergom by the Hapsburgs, who will lose the fortress ten years later.
1596: Conquest of Eger by the Ottomans.
1602: The Ottomans recapture Szekésfehervar (in present-day Hungary), lost one year previously.
1606: Ahmed I signs the Peace of Zsitvatörök, favourable to the Hapsburgs.
1645–69: Conquest of Crete.
1656–61: Ahmed Köprülü is Grand Vizier.
1664: The imperial troops, with French assistance, defeat the Ottomans at St Gotthard.
1672: Capture of Kamieniec from the Poles.
1678: Capture of Chigirin from the Russians.
1683: Defeat of the Grand Vizier Kara Mustafa Pasha at Kahlenberg, near Vienna, due to the arrival of Polish troops under their king, Jan III Sobieski.
1691: Defeat of the Ottomans at Slankamen.
1697: Victory of Eugene of Savoy over the Ottomans at Zenta.
1699: Peace of Carlowitz signed by the Ottoman Empire, the Holy Roman Empire, Poland and Venice (with Russia in 1700).

6. *The Great Hall of the Seraglio, Constantinople.*

China under the Ming and the Early Manchu

In the course of four centuries Chinese society underwent a dual process of change. After an initial agrarian phase there began to appear, towards the end of the sixteenth century, small pockets of an embryonic capitalist economy, which the bureaucratic apparatus sought to restrict. The founder of the Ming dynasty, who was of peasant stock, proceeded to reconquer territory from the Mongols and gave a firm foundation to future prosperity by introducing a policy of major public works (irrigation, reforestation, the building of dams). At the same time, a strict system for control of the population was introduced, accompanied by a massive programme of resettlement. This policy of national reconstruction was a major success. China, rediscovering its former prosperity, saw its influence spread over Mongolia, Manchuria, and over Vietnam, which was momentarily under Chinese rule. Major sea expeditions, the purpose of which was diplomatic as much as commercial, spread the grandeur of Ming culture. Chinese junks sailed the oceans. Nonetheless the maritime expansion was short-lived. Within a short space of time the emperors' lack of interest in the fleet left the way open for the exactions of Japanese pirates, whose incursions into Chinese territory became more and more daring, while the Europeans entered on to the scene, at first discreetly, with the Portuguese, then more assertively with the Dutch. The remarkable prosperity the Empire enjoyed paradoxically undermined its autocratic and agrarian foundations. Industrial development threatened the privileges of the state and its bureaucracy.

While the sixteenth century did mark the development of an urban trading economy, it also confirmed the pre-eminence of the region around the Yangtze within that economy. While cash crops (like cotton or tea) were developed in the area, food crops moved more to the south (to Fukien and Kweichow), which thus became the granary of China. The impoverishment of the peasants as a result of the re-establishment of the great estates and the discontent amongst the city dwellers who felt hemmed in by state regulations led eventually to disturbances which, in conjunction with the external threat from Manchuria, brought the dynasty to an end.

Nevertheless it did prove necessary for the Manchu princes to declare their allegiance to Confucian values and for the mandarin system to be restored before the élite were willing to serve their new masters. The Manchus brought to China immense lands and a remarkable war machine. The Ch'ing ruled the Steppes without challenge. Endowed with vast buffer zones and with well-defended borders, China experienced a period of great prosperity, some measure of which was due to the remarkably efficient use of the land and the introduction of new crops (such as groundnuts, sweet potatoes and maize). A side-effect of this prosperity was a demographic upsurge across the country. Though this was in some respects a positive thing, it turned out to be a major handicap once traditional society had reached the threshold of growth imposed on it by its own pre-industrial mode of production. From the end of the eighteenth century the threat to China became more and more clearly visible, in the shape of Russian and Japanese expansionism in the north and east, and the increasing influence of the Western countries at sea, while internally the regime had to confront a number of social crises of its own.

1. The entrance to the imperial palace under the Ch'ing dynasty (18th century).

Dissertations in eight parts for official examinations.

1387

1368: The Ming dynasty is proclaimed by Chu Yuan-chang, a former peasant who had become leader of the anti-Mongolian rebellion.
1370–87: The whole of China is liberated.
1380: Purges culminate in the execution of Chu Yuan-chang's comrade-in-arms, Hu Wei-yang.
1395: A policy of major public works is introduced.
1403: Chu Di, the younger son of the founder of the dynasty, usurps the throne.
1405–33: Great sea expeditions set out for the China Sea, Southeast Asia and to Africa, under the command of the Muslim eunuch, Admiral Cheng Ho.
1421: The capital is transferred from Nan-ching to Peking.
1424: Successful expeditions are launched against the Oyrats (Kalmycks).
1449: The Emperor is imprisoned by the Mongols after a raid.
1470–80: A wall is built in northern China to restrict the incursions of the peoples of the steppes.

Death of Wang Yang-ming, the author of a philosophy of the spirit.

1528

From 1500: The conflict hardens between eunuchs and Intellectuals.
1550: Mongol offensives are launched against the Chinese.
1555: Hangchow is sacked by pirates.
1563: Japanese pirates run amuck in Fukien.
1570–80: The use of money, based on the silver ingot, becomes more widespread.
1592–4: First attempted Japanese invasion of Korea is repelled.
1596–8: Second invasion attempt of Korea fails.

2. The Temple of Heaven, built under the Ming dynasty in Peking in 1420.

3. Porcelain ewers from the Ming dynasty with an armillary sphere as a motif (16th century).

1368–1800

China opens up to the outside world

China's main exports: tea, porcelain, lacquer-ware and silk

PORTUGUESE
SPANIARDS
DUTCH

EUROPE

Jesuit Priests from Europe

The Growth of China

Under Ming Dynasty (1368-1644)

Under the first Ch'ing dynasty (1644-1800)

1731: Date of conquest

Means of communication and contacts with the outside world

----- Canals

Major Roads

Main Ports

→ Sea Expeditions (Cheng Ho 1405-1433) and Chinese Commercial Routes

→ Journeys to China of the Jesuit Missionaries (XVIth-XVIIth Century)

RUSSIA

HEILUNG KIANG 1689

MONGOLIA 1697

1757

TIAN-SHAN 1758

CH'ING-HAI 1724

TIBET 1731

Peking

Nanching

Hsi-an

Su-chow

Yang Chou

JAPAN

Japanese pirate raids

Jedda

Ormuz

ARABIA

Aden

Mogadishu

AFRICA

INDIA

Yunnan

Macao 1557

Canton

TAIWAN (FORMOSA)

SPANIARDS (Silver from the New World)

Manila

PHILIPPINES

PORTUGUESE

DUTCH

PORTUGUESE

INDONESIA

Rebellion of Li Tzu-ch'eng.

1644

The Dream of the Red Chamber, by Ts'ao Chan.

c. 1750

Death of Ch'ien-lung.

1799

1596–1602: Disturbances in the cities and mines become widespread.
1601: The Jesuit priest Matteo Ricci reaches Peking.
1610: The Tung-lin Academy, a semi-secret society of anti-government intellectuals, is banned.
1615–27: Eunuchs and Tung-lin intellectuals compete for influence.
1627–30: Peasant rebellions break out.
1644: The rebellion of Li Tzu-ch'eng puts an end to the Ming dynasty. The Ch'ing take control of the north of China and order the wearing of pigtails.
1657: After the conquest of the whole of China, official competitions for recruitment begin again in Peking.
1661: Koxinga drives the Dutch out of Taiwan, where they had been settled for 30 years. The end comes of the southern Ming and of resistance to the Manchurians.
1665: The Ch'ing progress to north of the Amur River.
1689: Treaty of Nerchinsk fixes the border between Russia and China in Manchuria.
1697: Outer Mongolia is occupied.

4. The Jesuits in China: on the left, Father Matteo Ricci in mandarin dress, as seen by Father Athanasius Kircher in 1607.

1722: Emperor K'ang-hsi dies.
1727: Treaty of Kiakhta, which settles the new border between China and Russia and the number of private trade missions which will be allowed.
1731: Occupation of Tibet.
1736: Ch'ien-lung accedes to the throne.
1739: Treaty signed between the Ch'ing and the Dzungars, which settles the issue of the border in the Altai Mountains region.
1756–7: The Dzungars are exterminated and the area around Lli conquered.
1758–9: Conquest of the Tarim basin.
1775: The population of China reaches 264 million inhabitants.
1788: China extends its sovereignty over the upper basin of the Irrawaddy River in Burma.
1795–1803: White Lotus Rebellion.
1799: Death of Ch'ien-lung.

5. The process of drying in paper-making. From an album on the paper industry (17th century).

Japan under the Tokugawa

AROUND 1550, civil war was a constant feature. Whilst the warlords wanted merely to settle in the capital, the Amidaist sects recruited the peasants (farmers) of central Japan, and the city dwellers took over control of the municipal administration. The introduction of firearms and the construction of citadels revolutionized the nature of the war. Oda Nobunaga, and then Toyotomi Hideyoshi, succeeded in breaking up regional resistance and reunified the country under their hegemony. The lords or *daimyo* were overcome or made into vassals (military), the lesser samurai were made to leave the land and to live in towns below castles, and the farmers were disarmed (sword hunt). Thorough land-survey registers were kept enabling taxes relating to real productivity to be levied. When he had wiped out his enemies, Tokugawa Ieyasu took over: in 1603 he took the title of shogun and settled in his new capital, Edo (Tokyo). Christianity was prohibited, and the ports were closed to overseas trade with the exception of Nagasaki, where the Dutch trading post of the East India Company was set up in 1641. Japan closed in on itself.

The seventeenth century was also a century of great economic growth. The population tripled, reaching more than 30 million by about 1700. The daimyo in their fiefs, and the shogun in his estates, increased the range of uses of hydraulic power, allowing land to be reclaimed and the rice fields to be extended. The land-survey registers and the reduction in the number of those having the right to land simplified production procedures. It was in the interests of the farmers to increase and commercialize their production. The samurai, who were forced to live in the towns near to their lord, were cut off from the land and became fief administrators, managing the revenue of the shogun or the daimyo. They had to learn to be efficient and so attended special schools set up for them. The official philosophy of Neo-Confucianism provided an appropriate framework for these warriors-cum-bureaucrats. The shogunal state and the great lords attracted a hard-working population of artisans and merchants to the towns. A bourgeois society grew up in the main towns: by about 1700 Edo had a million inhabitants, Osaka nearly 400,000, and Kyoto almost as many.

A new aesthetic awareness flourished in this urban society. The puppet theatre which came into being at Osaka, and the Kabuki, had rich repertoires, with Chikamatsu Monzaemon the greatest of the playwrights. Basho was one of the great masters of haiku poetry, and in his novels Ihara Saikaku described the 'floating world' of the *ukiya* (pleasure quarters).

In the eighteenth century expansion gave way to stagnation. Social inequalities became more pronounced. Peasant famines and uprisings started up again, and got worse and worse until the final collapse of the regime. Reforms were seen to be inadequate. Literature became more ironic and critical, and new currents of thought, based on the national heritage, untainted by foreign ideas, attacked the official Confucianism, which was now stagnant. Other thinkers were interested in 'Dutch studies' which filtered in through Nagasaki. From the beginning of the nineteenth century uprisings in the country and the towns became more and more common: the southwestern fiefs, which were more prosperous, shook off shogunal control, and pressure from the West to re-open Japan became stronger and stronger. In 1853 the Shogun had to give in to the demands of the American, Perry. The days of the Tokugawa *ancien régime* were numbered.

1. Castle of the White Heron, erected at Himeji, late 16th century.

MIDDLE AGES   **MODERN (OR PRE-MODERN) A**

1500	1550	1600	1650	17
	ASHIKAGA SHOGUNATE			
Warlords Period.		1573 Azuchi-Momoyama Period. 1603		

1549: Francis Xavier lands in Japan and preaches Christianity. Half a century later there are 600,000 Christians.
1568–82: Oda Nobunaga eliminates his rivals, drives out the Ashikaga shogun and destroys the military power of the Buddhist sects.
1582–98: Toyotomi Hideyoshi continues the task of unification started by Nobunaga. He conducts a land survey and carries out the 'sword hunt'.
1600: Tokugawa Ieyasu wins the Battle of Sekigahara and reaps the political legacy of Hideyoshi.
1603: Tokugawa Ieyasu is appointed shogun.
1615: With the capture of the citadel at Osaka, the last opposition is defeated.
1636: Inauguration of the great temple of Mikko dedicated to the memory of Ieyasu.
1637: The great Christian revolt of Shimabara ends in a bloodbath with the aid of the Dutch.
1641: Only the Dutch are tolerated in their trading post of Deshima at Nagasaki.

2. Detail from a door at the Toshugu Sanctuary at Nikko, revealing the Chinese influence on Japanese architecture, 17th century.

c. 1685: Poetry by Basho and novels by Ihara Saikaku.
1688–1703: Genfoku period. The régime of the Tokugawa shoguns at its peak.
c. 1715: Chikamatsu Monzaemon writes the major plays in his theatrical repertoire.
1716–51: Reign of the shogun Tokugawa Yoshimune. His reformist policies stabilize the shogunal economy, but the social situation deteriorates.
1772–86: The minister Tanuma Okitsugu in power. Failure of his reformist and 'liberal' political ideology.
1782: Great famine of the Temmei era.
1787: More and more revolts, even in the towns. Matsudaira Sadanobu, the Shogun's chief minister, embarks on a new series of reforms aiming to reinforce control of the country by the shoguns, and reverses Tanuma's liberalization programme.
1792: Russians in Hokkaido. Sadanobu refuses any opening up of the country.
1808: The Japanese explore Sakhalin.

3. Portrait of an actor, by Toshusai Sharaku. Late 18th-century print.

1550–1853

The formation of the modern Japanese State
unification, centralisation, isolation

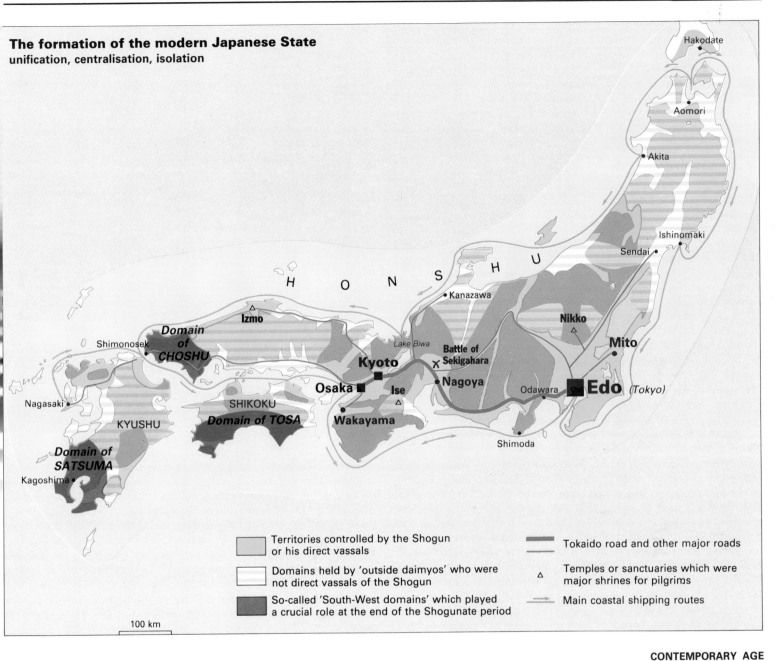

Hakodate

Aomori

• Akita

Ishinomaki

Sendai •

H O N S H U

• Kanazawa

Nikko
△

Mito

△ Izmo

Domain of CHOSHU

Shimonosek

Lake Biwa

Battle of Sekigahara

Kyoto

Osaka ■

× Nagoya

Odawara •

■**Edo** *(Tokyo)*

Ise △

Nagasaki •

SHIKOKU

KYUSHU

Domain of TOSA

Wakayama

Shimoda

Domain of SATSUMA

Kagoshima •

	Territories controlled by the Shogun or his direct vassals		Tokaido road and other major roads
	Domains held by 'outside daimyos' who were not direct vassals of the Shogun	△	Temples or sanctuaries which were major shrines for pilgrims
	So-called 'South-West domains' which played a crucial role at the end of the Shogunate period		Main coastal shipping routes

100 km

CONTEMPORARY AGE

| 1750 | 1800 | | 1900 |

OKUGAWA SHOGUNATE | | | **MEIJI ERA**

EDO PERIOD | 1853 'End of the Shogunate' Period. 1868

1809: First engravings in the style known as Ukiyoe.
1833: Hiroshige paints his famous '53 views of the Tokaido'.
1836: Serious famine of the Tempo era.
1837: Great revolt of the people at Osaka.
1840–5: The minister Mizuno Tadakuni passes a new series of measures, known as the Tempo era reforms, along the same lines as the previous reforms. These also fail.
1844: William II, King of the Netherlands, demands that the Japanese ports should be opened. The shogunate refuses.
1853: The American commodore, Perry, moves into the Bay of Edo with his fleet. In the following year, the shogunate agrees to sign a treaty with the United States. End of the political isolation of Japan.

4. Fishing for shellfish. *Hokusai painting on silk.*

5. The Portuguese arrive in Japan. Detail from a decorated screen, early 17th century.

The India of Akbar and the Great Mughals

1525-1561

Surviving area
of Sultanate
of Delhi in 1525:
Kingdom of the Lodi

Rajput confederacy

Babur's key campaigns

Annexation of
urban centres

Akbar's kingdom in 1561

Portuguese trading posts

1561-1605

1594
Dates of conquests

Urban centres annexed
between 1561 and 1605

Mughal empire on the
death of Akbar in 1605

Agra
Names of provinces

Portuguese trading posts

500 km

ON THE DEATH OF AKBAR, the empire which Babur had founded on the ruins of the old Sultanate of Delhi was at the height of its greatness. It had unified the whole of the country north of the Narbada (and Afghanistan too) and it was on the point of absorbing the sultanates of the Deccan. At that stage a very great number of India's 100 million inhabitants were among its subjects. Sher Shah's land reform had proved effective: the peasants had received rights to land and paid taxes directly to the state (a third of their harvests), assessed on the basis of their plots as they appeared on the land register. The civil servants, now closely supervised, received money wages and were no longer rewarded by large estates, which had a tendency to become hereditary. Artisanal labour remained a great source of wealth (at least for the merchants and the state): European innovations were turned to good account (e.g. book printing inspired colour printing on cotton). There were changes in the relations between Hindus and Muslims: by suppressing the *jiziya* (a poll tax on non-Muslim subjects) and by striving to create a synthesis of Hinduism and Islam, Akbar intended to show that India had ceased to be a conquered country.

But if the splendours of the Mughal courts became even more magnificent under Akbar's successors, many of the reforms he had instigated were reversed. Aurangzeb re-established the jiziya in 1679, which caused a rift with the Rajput warriors with whom Akbar had managed to make an alliance. And the state allowed the tax collectors to develop into a landed aristocracy once again. Moreover, in 1681 Aurangzeb embarked upon a war of conquest in the Deccan which impoverished and weakened the Empire. The decline which set in at the end of the seventeenth century was exploited by the Marathas, who now became the prominent power in the region. Under Sivaji's leadership, the *svarajya* (autonomous kingdom) of the Marathas harassed the armies of Delhi, and extended its power rapidly into the Deccan. It even built a fleet that was capable of defeating the English off Bombay in 1680. Sivaji was regarded as the Hindu national hero and his successors, or rather the chief ministers of their house, the Peshwas of Poona, forced the Mughal emperor to recognize the legitimacy of the power of the Maratha state (now the *samrajya* or imperial confederacy) in the areas where it had supplanted Delhi.

However, India had made its entry on to the stage of world politics,

Tulsidas: *Ramcaritmanas.*

Under Akbar, the *Ain-e Akbari.*

1533–1623		1542–1605	
1504: Babur (Zahir ud-din Muhammad), a descendant of Tamerlane and Genghis Khan, conquers Afghanistan.	**1582:** Akbar creates a new religion, the Din-Illahi or 'Divine Faith', which finds followers only among his immediate entourage.	**1605–27:** Reign of Jehangir. Political and cultural pinnacle of Mughal civilization in India.	

1526: Battle of Panipat. Babur, the Great Mughal, takes control of the capital.
1530: Death of Babur. He leaves memoirs written in Turki.
1533–1623: Tulsidas, author of a vast epic poem in Hindi, the *Ramcaritmanas.*
1540–5: Reign of Sher Shah, who had defeated Humayun, Babur's son. A lasting, efficient administration is set in place.
1542: Arrival in India of the Spanish Jesuit, Francis Xavier.
1542–1605: In Akbar's reign, the *Ain-e Akbari* is composed in Persian by Abu'l-Fazl; it is a systematic description of the resources and the administration of the Empire. A work that is unique of its kind in pre-colonial India.
1556: Battle of Panipat. Akbar, son of Humayun, restores the sovereignty of the Great Mughals.
1569: Akbar defeats the Rajput Rana Pratap and overcomes the resistance of the Gondwana, who are led by Queen Durgavati.
1572: Abolition of taxes on non-Muslims.

1600: British East India Company founded.
1602: Dutch East India Company founded.
1605: Death of Akbar. The Spanish Jesuit Roberto de Nobili arrives in India. He settles in Madura.

2. The Emperor Akbar crosses the Ganges. Detail of a Mughal miniature, late 16th century.

1615: Delhi grants Thomas Roe the right to open a trading station at Surat.
1627–58: Reign of Shahjahan.
1630–32: Terrible famine in Gujerat.
1631: Death of the Empress Mumtaz. Shahjahan has the Taj Mahal built as a mausoleum for her at Agra.
1640: British East India Company establishes a trading post at Madras.
c. 1640: Dara Shikoh, son of Shahjahan, has the *Upanishads* translated into Persian.
1650: British trading post established at Hooghly, near what will become Calcutta.
c. 1650: The great temple to Shiva at Madura (now Madurai) is built.
1658–1707: Reign of Aurangzeb. A strict Muslim, he reacts against the tolerant universalism that had been prevalent under Akbar.
1664: French East India Company founded.
1666: Sivaji, Hindu prince of the rebellious Maratha states, signs a (very temporary) settlement with Aurangzeb.

3. The temple to Vishnu of Srirangam at Tiruchchirappalli in the state of Tamil-Nadu.

16th–18th centuries

1605-1700

Extent of the Mughal empire circa 1700

Maratha territories on the death of Sivaji in 1680

States in rebellion against the Mughal Empire circa 1700

European settlements
- ▲ Portuguese
- ● French
- ■ British
- ◆ Dutch
- ▬ Danish

1700-1761

Maratha Confederacy founded in 1732-38

Hindu States

Kingdom of Delhi greatly weakened in 1761

European presence:
- ▲ Portuguese (P) and Dutch (D)

British

French

500 km

1. Krishna tells how he fell in love. . . . Miniature taken from an 18th-century erotic treatise.

which is to say the stage of European rivalries. What was now beginning was the last phase of a process that had begun at the very moment when the foundations of the Mughal Empire were being laid. As early as 1535, in fact, the Portuguese had obtained the fortress of Diu from the sovereign of Gujerat and established a series of trading posts along the coasts. Their objective was to ensure a monopoly of the seaborne trade between India and Europe and also to obtain a foothold in India from which to spread the Catholic religion. However, they were only able to hold on to the enclave of Goa. Everywhere else they had gradually to give way, first to the Dutch and the Danes, then later to the English and the French. For the Indian sovereigns themselves, these 'trading stations' became an essential element in the export system. A decisive change took place in 1741, when Dupleix, the governor of the French East India Company, received a *jagir* (gift of land) from the Great Mughal. France became a territorial power in India. Britain, which was at war with France, could not allow her a free hand on the sub-continent. Once her army had defeated the French on Indian soil, Britain stood on the verge of what was to be the long adventure of her conquest of India.

Sivaji, the founder of Maratha power.

Gobind Singh, founder of Sikh power.

1627–80

1675–1708

1669: Rising of the Jats, Hindu peasants of the Mathura region.
1674: On the initiative of François Martin, the French trading post at Pondicherry is opened.
1700: The Punjab becomes a Sikh state.
1714–40: Maratha territory extended to the gates of Delhi and as far as the southern Deccan.
1757: Battle of Plassey. Robert Clive defeats the troops of the Nawab of Bengal.
1760: Battle of Wandiwash (near Madras). The British inflict a decisive defeat on the French.
1761: Battle of Panipat. The Great Mughal is defeated by an Afghan warlord, in spite of Maratha support. There is no longer an Indian army to stand out against British penetration.

5. Jaipur, Rajastan. Jantar Mantar astronomical observatory. In the foreground, a solar clock (18th century).

4. Fort of Golconda, built to resist the Mughal invasion in Andhra Pradesh, 16th–17th century.

Africa at the Time of the Slave Trade

BETWEEN 1450 AND 1600, Europeans voyaged to the African coasts, but their presence remained limited and their influence marginal until the nineteenth century; the appearance of this new Atlantic front did not reduce the importance of the Saharan one. The old kingdom of Gao became the great Songhai Empire. It was, however, destroyed in a battle at the end of the sixteenth century. Meanwhile Bornu, which had reconquered Kanem, became a major power. The century is characterized by the rise of a variety of states, including, for example, the kingdoms of the Volta (Mossi, Dagomba) and Sennar. This was also the period in which the Christian and Muslim kingdoms of Ethiopia clashed violently, leaving both sides weak and drained. On the east coast, the Portuguese dismantled the existing trading net-

1. The king of the Kongo receiving Dutch ambassadors. From an engraving of 1700.

Black Africa from the XVth to the XIXth centuries 1450-1600

SONGHAI EMPIRE

- Direct domination at its peak
- Partial domination
- Portuguese colonisation
- Desert
- Dense forest

1000 km

work between the cities and replaced it with their own. Matapa and Butua prospered and the kingdoms of Luba and Lunda became prominent. The Kongo kingdom took the risk of opening itself up to Christianity and Portuguese technology, though in the long run it lost its vigour.

Between 1600 and 1800, the Sudan was more fragmented than before, though its territory was still the site of intensive interactions between some old protagonists (Hausa states, Bornu) and some new ones (Segu and Wadai kingdoms). Its coastal traffic mainly centred on the slave trade, which had negative effects in the long term. However, the West African states, particularly the Ashanti and Abomey — two of the new powers — used that trade and adapted it to their own ends, without becoming solely dependent upon it. Oyo was dominant among the Yoruba states. In the southern savannahs, the Luba and the now reduced Lunda kingdoms extended the field of

Sonni 'Ali Ber Emperor of Songhai.

1464–92

1464–92: Reign of Emperor Sonni 'Ali Ber, a great conqueror and administrator, in the Songhai.
1483: The Portuguese come into contact with the Kongo kingdom.
1493–1528: Reign of Muhammad I Askia, who continues the work of Sonni 'Ali Ber, though in an Islamic framework.

End of 15th–beginning of 16th centuries: Restoration of Bornu.
1504: Destruction of Soba; emergence of the Funj kingdom.
1505: The Portuguese at Sofala.
1506–43: Afonso I Christian king of the Kongo.
1521–42: Invasion of Ethiopia by Ahmad Gran: intense wars; Ethiopia imperilled but eventually survives.

Mid-16th century: Growth of Fouta-Toro.
c. 1570: Portuguese settlements around Luanda and in the Zambezi valley.
1571–1603: Glorious reign of Idris Alawma in Bornu.
1591: Defeat and collapse of the Songhai at

Afonso I, Christian king of the Kongo.

1506–43

Tondibi at the hands of Moroccan soldiers (conflict over the Teghaza salt mines).
1593: Portuguese fort built at Mombasa.
1606–32: Reign of Suseynos in Ethiopia: forced to abdicate upon conversion to Catholicism.
1632–67: Reign of his successor, Fasilides, who drives out the Jesuits and makes his capital at Gonder in 1636.
1668: Battle of Ambuila; Portuguese kill the king of the Kongo, which now declines.

End of 17th–beginning of 18th centuries: Portuguese driven out of Mombasa. Osei Tutu founds the Ashanti political state (c. 1695).

Beginning of 18th century: Creation of the Dyula kingdom of Kong (now Ivory Coast). Reign of Mamari Kulibali (known as the 'Commander'), the Bambara king of Segu (1712–55); successful conqueror and unifier of his people.
1725: Muslim state of Fouta Jallon.
1726: Muslin state of Fouta Toro.
1785–1810: Reign of Andrianampoinimerina in Madagascar.

Reign of Fasilides in Ethiopia.

1632–67

2. The Ashanti receive the British ambassadors, c. 1815. Anonymous engraving.

15th–19th centuries

1600-1800

CAYOR · Timbuktu · Agadès · DARFUR · Nile · FUNJ
FOUTA TORO · SEGU · MOSSI · BORNU · Warra · ETHIOPIA
FOUTA JALLON · Segu · HAUSALAND · WADAI · Sennar · Gonder · Zeila
Kong · MAMPURSI DAGOMBA · Oyo · BENIN · BAGIRMI · ADAL · Harar
ASHANTI · Benin · Mogadishu
Abomey · KITARA · BUGANDA · Kismayu
Congo · NKORE · RWANDA · Malindi
TEKE · KUBA · Mombasa
LUANGO · LUBA · Kilwa
Luanda · KONGO · LUNDA · Mozambique
Benguela · LUNDA · KAZEMBE
LOZI · Tete · Sera
MWENE MATAPA · Sofala
BUTUA

‖‖ Dutch settlements
⬭ Portuguese settlements
▨ Desert
▨ Dense forest
⊢⊣ 1000 km

1800-1870

TUKULOR EMPIRE · Timbuktu · Agadès · DARFUR · EGYPTIAN SUDAN · Suakin
FOUTA TORO · Segu · MASINA · BORNU · Abeche · El-Fasher · Masawa
FOUTA JALLON · Sokoto · Kano · Kouka · WADAI · Gonder · ETHIOPIA
MAMPURSI DAGOMBA · SOKOTO · Ibadan · Yola · BAGIRMI · Harar
ASHANTI · Benin · Mogadishu
Abomey · Congo · BUGANDA · Lake Victoria
TEKE · RWANDA · Mombasa
KUBA · BURUNDI · SULTANATE OF ZANZIBAR
LUBA · BEMBA · Kilwa
LUNDA · Lake Nyasa · YAO
LOZI · Zambezi · NDEBELE · MERINA
SWAZI · ZULU · LESOTHO

← Great Trek
←- Ngoni raids (continuation of the Zulu campaign)
▨ Desert
▨ Dense forest
⊢⊣ 1000 km

their tributary economy and forged links with coastal traffic through intermediaries (Kasanje etc.). In the east, the coastal cities underwent something of a revival, thanks partly to the presence of Omanis. Ethiopia, which was initially reunited around Gonder, again became fragmented.

Between 1800 and 1875 the slave trade – though now repudiated by Europe – continued, remaining particularly lively in Islamic areas. A dizzy rise in trade links with Europe put the various coastal societies to the test: where states were able to respond to this new situation their power was consolidated; otherwise they were plunged into crisis. There was a generalized penetration of the continent, spurred on by European and Arabo-Swahili trade. However, these developments cannot all be ascribed to a single logic. In the Sudan, as early as the eighteenth century, a series of social and political revolutions gave birth to a number of dynamic, resolutely Muslim states. The process

repeated itself throughout the nineteenth century. In Natal, after 1816, Shaka brought the Zulu state to prominence. Dissidents from and imitators of this military society spread its example far and wide in dramatic raids. In Madagascar, around the year 1800, Andrianampoinimerina brought unity, organization and power to the Merina people in the centre of the island. In the middle of the century, Tewodros reconstructed Ethiopia, though not without much bloodshed. Buganda also, which had, by its own efforts, formed itself into a centralized state, opened its frontiers to external trade and foreign ideas.

Should we then regard this as a period in which indigenous African forces dominated? Or did the slave trade economy simply prefigure later relations of dependence? Both perspectives can provide some understanding of nineteenth-century Africa, but only up to 1860. When we reach the 1870s the 'scramble' for the continent begins.

Reign of Andrianampoinimerina in Madagascar.	**Muhammad Bello King of Sokoto.**	**Reign of Tukulor al-Hajj 'Umar.**	**Tewodros II King of kings in Ethiopia.**
1785–1810	1817–37	1852–64	1855–1868

1804: Fulani *jihad* (holy war) of the marabout Shehu Usman dan Fodio in the Hausa country, leading to the birth of the Sokoto caliphate.

c. 1805–1815: Sabun becomes *kolak* (king) of the Wadai.

1812: Muhammad al-Kanami saves the Bornu kingdom from the Sokoto threat and gives it a new lease of life.

1816–28: King Shaka creates the Zulu society and state.

1817–37: Reign of Muhammad Bello, sovereign and brilliant intellectual, in the Sokoto.

1818: Muslim state of Masina.

1823: Ndebele kingdom.

1830: Disintegration of the Oyo kingdom.

1833: Mshweshe unites the Sotho people in a single state.

1835: Beginning of the Great Trek of the Boers.

1852–64: Tukulor al-Hajj 'Umar conquers Kaarta (1855–6), Segu (9 March 1861) and Masina (16 May 1862).

1855: Tewodros II crowned Emperor of Egypt (c. 1868).

1862–86: Lat Dior, leader of the Cayor (Senegal), resists the French.

3. Ethiopian popular art: Menelik II depicted as King Solomon, 19th-century manuscript.

4. Three elephants, an Ashanti golden ornament.

Art in Europe: A New Vitality

1. Tromp-l'oeil ceiling by Ignazio Birajo di Borgaio in Aglie Castle, Piedmont.

As STAGES ON THE road to modernity, the Renaissance, Mannerism, and the Baroque were each different facets of a multidisciplinary inquiry into the world which drew no distinction between science, art and technology. At the same time as Michelangelo was designing the dome of St Peter's, Cardan, in his *Ars Magna* (1545), was setting out the concepts of positive, negative and imaginary numbers. The catenary curve was used to calculate the arches of Saint-Eustache, even before its function had been defined by Pascal. Stereotomy, the art,

according to Charles Perrault, 'of using the weight of stone against itself and supporting it in the air with the same weight as that which makes it fall', through the efforts of Desargue, La Hire, Frézier and Monge, led directly to descriptive geometry.

Challenging Aristotle, a whole sector of European thinking abandoned functionality and privileged appearance. The structure of edifices could no longer be grasped simply and clearly by the eye but was masked by the rigid application of the laws of symmetry. Artists undertook to conquer space, movement, light. The vertical perspective imagined by Mantegna for his *Camera degli Sposi* (wedding chamber) frescoes in Mantua was taken up and extended by Andrea Pozzo, who, in effect, doubled the height of the nave of St Ignazio's in Rome. Michelangelo's *Moses* was ready to leap to his feet, but Giulio Romano's giants in the Sala dei Giganti in the Palazzo del Te on the outskirts of Mantua strained to break down the very walls which contained them. The flame from St Joseph's candle in the *Nativity* attributed to the Master of Flémalle (in the Musée de Dijon) was replaced by the glow of the sun setting over the Roman ruins of a Claude Lorrain. Baroque virility was disciplined into classical virtue, but degenerated into rococo virtuosity.

Classicism was a struggle for order amidst this teeming surge of energy. Order reigned in the rules of perspective, and the gruff accuracy of the engravings of Abraham Bosse was the very reverse of the generous creativity apparent in the etchings of Rembrandt. Order reigned, too, in the use of the palette, and Poussin, emulated by Lebrun, laid the emphasis on clarity of meaning and propriety. The warmth of Rubens was not rediscovered until the time of Watteau. Classicism could soften the impact of the Baroque to the point of freezing it entirely. The façade of the Louvre palace, filled with movement by the skill of a Bernini, lost all its vitality in the hands of a Perrault. In Gabriel's drawings the Place Louis XV was scrupulously arranged and laid out.

The Rococo made its appearance when the dynamic energy of the Baroque had become mere dispersion and movement little more than agitation. Even as Monteverdi's music was being acclaimed in Mantua, the spectacle of the opera in the Tuileries offered only the creaking of machines and monstrous apparitions lit by fireworks. Caravaggio expressed the conversion of Saint Paul with stunning economy, whereas the minor masters found their delight in the illusions of the trompe-l'oeil and the ambiguities created by anamorphosis. The old demons of excess and overstatement re-emerged once order was no longer respected. As a result the achievement of the Escorial remains isolated in the whole of Castile, while elsewhere on the Iberian Peninsula and in Latin America medieval retables were being overlaid with colour. Whilst Saenredam gives an indication of the sobriety of Dutch churches, the gilt decorations of the German churches were periodically brightened up.

3. The statuette of the Immaculate Conception by Alonso Cano (1601–67) in the sacristy of Granada Cathedral.

Death of Palladio.	Birth of Boromini and Velázquez.	First performance of Monteverdi's *Orfeo.*
1588	1599	1607

1563–4: Juan de Herrera, El Escorial.
1568–75: G. Della Porta, Church of Gesù, Rome.
1584: Palladio, Teatro Olimpico, Vicenza.
1600: Caravaggio, The Conversion of St Paul, Rome. Church of S. Maria del Populo.
1605: Building starts on the Place Royale (the present-day Place des Vosges) in Paris.
1607: Claudio Monteverdi, first performance of Orfeo.
1617: Building begins on the Plaza Mayor in Madrid by J. Gómez de Mora.
1619: Inigo Jones begins work on the banqueting hall, Whitehall.
1627: Simon Vouet returns to Paris.
1633: Bernini completes the baldachin over the tomb of St Peter in Rome.
1638: Philippe de Champaigne, Le Voeu de Louis XIII.
1642: Rembrandt, The Night Watch. Nicolas Poussin in Paris.
1656: Jean de La Vallée builds the Church of St Catherine of Stockholm, with its cupola on a Greek cross.
1657–63: Bernini: colonnade over the piazza before St Peter's.

1665: Bernini travels to Paris.
1666: Great Fire of London. Foundation of the French Academy of Rome.
1674: Boileau writes his Art poétique.
1675: Christopher Wren, St Paul's (work continues till 1710).

1677: Roger de Piles, Conversations sur la connaissance de la peinture.
1702: Building starts on the Abbey of Melk (Austria).
1703: Founding of St Petersburg.
1705: Sir John Vanbrugh undertakes the

4. The Holy Spirit descending from the cupola, by Francesco Borromini, in the Church of S. Carlo alle Quattro Fontane, in Rome (1641).

2. *The beginnings of the Baroque: the contrast between heaven and earth, as depicted in El Greco's* Burial of Count Orgaz, *1586.*

Bernini dies.   **Watteau, *L'Enseigne de Gersaint*.**   **Christopher Wren dies.**

1680   **1720**   **1723**

building of Blenheim Palace for the Duke of Marlborough.

1707: Foundation of the Society of Antiquaries in London.

1717: Antoine Watteau, *L'Embarquement pour Cythère.*

1717–31: Juvarra's basilica on Superga, near Turin.

1725: John Wood the Elder begins work in Bath.

1730: J. E. Fischer von Erlach, imperial stables in Vienna.

1735: Jean-Philippe Rameau, the opera-ballet *Les Indes galantes.*

1745: G. W. von Knobelsdorff builds Sans-Souci palace in Potsdam.

1749–60: Palace of Amalienborg, Copenhagen.

1750: Giambattista Tiepolo begins his cycle of frescoes decorating the rooms of the Residenz in Würzburg.

1755: Earthquake in Lisbon.

1768–75: Jacques-Ange Gabriel, Place Louis XV in Paris (the present-day Place de la Concorde).

5. *The ecstasy of God's love: St Theresa, as seen by Bernini (1652).*

6. *Dam Square in Amsterdam, by J. Van der Ulft, in 1659.*

7. *The sacristy of the convent-palace of El Escorial, as seen by Claudio Coello in 1690.*

Louis XIV and Absolute Monarchy

THE FRONDE was many things. It marked a moment of crisis in the authority of an under-age king and was a sign of revolt against an unprecedented fiscal onslaught by central government, as well as a period of self-interested agitation on the part of the privileged classes. It saved Spain from disaster and jeopardized the diplomatic and military achievements of Richelieu and Mazarin.

As a true pupil of Cardinal Richelieu, Louis XIV devoted the bulk of his time to foreign policy. Without having any single fixed idea throughout his personal reign of fifty-four years, he nonetheless pursued an anachronistic battle against Spanish hegemony. It was not a dowry that he married (indeed, the 300,000 gold crowns were never to be paid) but a set of political aspirations: upon the death of Philip IV, he claimed the devolution of Brabant, the freehold of the Hainault and the equal partition of the Franche-Comté. To press home his claims he needed to humiliate the United Provinces, and attract England into the French sphere of influence, as well as to support a good part of Europe financially. However, Louis had not reckoned with the surprising longevity of Charles II of Spain. He had, in the end, no alternative but to accept the terms of his last will and testament (16 November 1700).

For the execution of his policy he had at his disposal a large, well drilled army established by Le Tellier and Louvois and protected by Vauban's fortifications. But its cost was so high that, to improve the yield of indirect taxation, Colbert introduced the system of the five great tax Farms (in 1669). Faced with all the various threats of the last years of the reign, it proved necessary to sell offices, to tax the privileged classes by the introduction of *capitation*, a graduated poll-tax, and to follow Vauban's advice in collecting a tithe (1710). A highly centralized administrative structure held the country in its grip: the office-holders had to give way to *commissaires*, and the 'sovereign' courts became merely 'higher' courts (1665). Restored after the Fronde, the *intendants* administered the provinces, which were progressively unified by the Civil Ordinance of 1667, the Criminal Ordinance of 1699 and the setting up of the post of *lieutenant général de police* in the cities.

Fiscal pressure led inevitably to the development of a mercantile and protectionist economy. Communications were improved, with Riquet, completing, for example, the Canal du Midi. The rise in

2. Versailles viewed from the gardens in 1672.

manufacturing output, the foundation of the French East India Company, and the 1664 and 1667 changes in the tariff system, brought about the closing of the borders of Holland to French products in 1670 and, subsequently, war with Holland. The competitive Dutch economy was much weakened as a result, and the only beneficiaries were the English. Alarmed by any action which might possibly have some subversive implication or intent, Louis XIV restricted the papal prerogative, dissolved the Company of the Holy Sacrament and revoked the Edict of Nantes. As a result he impoverished the kingdom by forcing the Protestants (Huguenots) to flee, though he did welcome the Irish, who had been declared outlaws by the penal laws of 1702–1705. More a close descendant of Philip II of Spain than Henry IV of France, Louis imposed the rigid etiquette of a cult of monarchy on a domesticated nobility.

1. Louis XIV, five years after the start of his personal reign, surrounded by Colbert and various members of the Academy of Sciences, as seen by Henri Testelin, 1666.

Death of Richelieu.

Death of Mazarin.   Death of Pascal.

| 1642 | 1661 | 1662 |

14 May 1643: On the death of Louis XIII, Louis XIV comes to the throne.
19 May: Victory of the Prince de Condé at Rocroi.
January 1644: Imposition of the *toisé*, which ordered the destruction of the dwelling-houses built just outside Paris (where building was prohibited for military reasons), or a fine of 50 sous per *toise* (a unit of measure).
1647: Vaugelas, *Remarques sur la langue française*.
15 June 1648: Declaration of the Chambre de St Louis imposing a charter on Anne of Austria, the Queen Regent.
1–2 July 1652: Battle of the faubourg Saint-Antoine during the Fronde.
1660: Company of the Holy Sacrament dissolved.
9 June: Marriage of Louis XIV to Marie-Thérèse of Austria, daughter of the King of Spain, in Saint-Jean-de-Luz.
9 March 1661: Death of Mazarin.
1665: Colbert appointed controller general of finance.
17 September: Death of Philip IV of Spain, the father of Marie-Thérèse.
1667: Racine writes *Andromaque*.

3. An argument in favour of converting to Catholicism after the Revocation of the Edict of Nantes. A Protestant cartoon from 1688.

2 May 1668: The Treaty of Aix-la-Chapelle marks the end of the War of Devolution.
1670: The Criminal Ordinance.
10 May 1678: 1st Treaty of Nijmegen marks the end of the war with Holland.
1681: Annexation of Strasbourg.
1682: Declaration of the Four Articles reaffirming the legitimacy of Gallican customs.
30 July 1683: Death of Queen Marie-Thérèse.
15 August 1684: Truce of Ratisbon between Louis XIV and the Holy Roman Emperor.
18 October 1685: Edict of Fontainebleau revokes the Edict of Nantes.
1688: Setting up of the militia.
1694: First edition of the *Dictionnaire de l'Académie française*.
1695: Introduction of *capitation*.
27 September and 30 October 1697: The treaties of Rijswijk mark the end of the War of the League of Augsburg.
1 November 1700: Death of Charles II of Spain.
16 November: Philip V accedes to the Spanish throne.
1707: Vauban, *Projet d'une dîme royale*.
12 June 1709: Appeal from Louis XIV read out in all the churches in France.

1643–1715

Extent and Defences of the country

	1643 Borders
	Territory acquired by Louis XIV
	1715 Borders
■	Vauban's fortified defences

Political and economic organization: the development of the centralised administration

●	Seats of the *intendants*
	Approximate boundaries of the *intendances*
	Main stage coach routes
---	Canal

Popular discontent

	Major peasant uprisings

Map labels:
Dunkirk, Fort d'Ambleteuse, SPANISH NETHERLANDS, Rhine, HOLY ROMAN EMPIRE, Calais, *Lustucrus*, Lille, Valenciennes, ARTOIS, Namur, Dieppe, Arras, Cambrai, Givet, Amiens, Rocroi, Sedan, Luxemburg, Cherbourg, Rouen, Soissons, Montmédy, Longwy, Bitche, Caen, Verdun, Metz, Toul, Fort Louis, St Malo, *Nu-pieds*, PARIS, Châlons sur Marne, Strasbourg, Brest, VERSAILLES, DUCHY OF LORRAINE, Camaret, Alençon, Seine, Brisach, Rennes, Orléans, FRANCHE-COMTÉ, Neubrisach, *Torreben*, Concarneau, Belfort, Fort Houat, Fort Houedic, Tours, *Sabotiers*, Loire, Besançon, Belle-Ile, NANTES, Loire, Dijon, SWITZERLAND, Bourges, Salins-les-Bains, Poitiers, Moulins, Saône, Ile de Ré, La Rochelle, *Tard-avisés Croquants*, Tournus, DUCHY OF SAVOY, Ile d'Aix, Oléron, Rochefort, Limoges, Clermont-Ferrand, Lyon, *Tard-avisés Croquants*, Angoulême, Grenoble, Exilles, Turin, Rhône, Briançon, Pinerolo, *Croquants*, Mont-Dauphin, Fort Paté, Blaye, Fort Médoc, Bordeaux, *Roures*, Embrun, Barcelonnette, Garonne, *Tard-avisés Croquants*, Sisteron, Colmars, Montauban, *Camisards*, AVIGNON (Papacy), Nice, *Croquants*, Auch, Montpellier, Aix-en-Provence, Antibes, Bayonne, Toulouse, Ile Sainte-Marguerite, *Audijos*, Pau, *Croquants*, Canal du Midi, Marseille, St-Jean Pied de Part, Toulon, ROUSSILLON, Perpignan, Collioure, Mont-Louis, Port-Vendres, 100 km

---

Birth of Voltaire.	Death of Racine.	Death of Louis XIV.
1694	1699	1715

24 July 1712: Battle of Denain.
11 April 1713: Treaty of Utrecht between France on the one hand and England, Portugal, Savoy and the United Provinces on the other, marking the end of the War of Spanish Succession.
6 March 1714: Treaty of Rastatt signed with Emperor Charles VI, thus ratifying the Treaty of Utrecht.
1 September 1715: Death of Louis XIV.

4. The beginnings of realism: a group of French peasants, by Louis Le Nain.

5. Louis XIV as the Sun King.

6. Louis XIV, at the end of his reign, 21 October 1714, welcomes the Elector of Saxony. Painting by Louis de Silvestre.

An Imperial Republic: The United Provinces

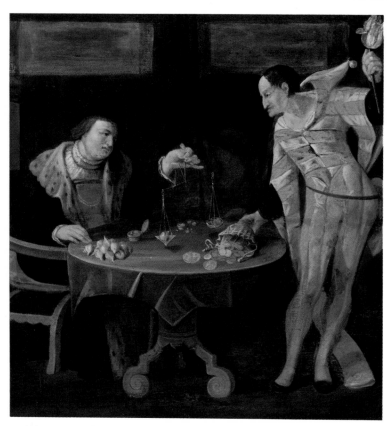

1. Valuing tulip bulbs in gold – picture of the Dutch School, 17th century.

To reach the spices of the Indian Ocean – Lisbon having been closed to the Dutch since 1580 – a first expedition financed by the Far Lands Company and commanded by Cornelius Van Houtman (who had lived in Portugal in his youth) rounded the Cape of Good Hope, made treaties with local rulers and came back with a valuable cargo. In 1602 a number of trading companies were amalgamated to form the East India Company, which was directed by Dutch merchants. In 1605 the company got a foothold in the Moluccas (Spice Islands) and established a garrison at Amboina; in 1616 it obtained the monopoly of trade with Japan, an essential factor in trade with the Far East; in 1619 it occupied Jakarta and established the capital of its colonial empire at Batavia, on the island of Java; in 1624 it founded a settlement on Formosa. The company rid itself of English competition (the massacres of Amboina in 1624), drove the Portuguese from Malacca (1641), Ceylon and the Moluccas and took over the pepper and cinnamon trade. On the spice route, the Dutch stopped periodically at Mauritius and established a station at the Cape of Good Hope (1652), a port of call for its vessels which gradually became a permanent colony. The quest for new routes led Willem Janszoon (1606) and Piet von Nuyts (1628) to Australia, and Tasman to New Zealand and Fiji (1624–44). In 1607 Hudson had tried in vain to find a north-west passage.

The West India Company (1621) set its aims on America. It founded, as stations for the fur trade, both New Amsterdam on the island of Manhattan and, 200 kilometres up-river, Fort Orange (Albany). Disquieted by this, the English invaded New Netherland in 1664 and renamed the colony New York. The company was forced also to relinquish Bahia but nevertheless, between 1621 and 1634 captured 540 Spanish vessels carrying goods worth more than 150 million *livres*. Lured by the sugar of Brazil, the company took Recife from the Portuguese and gradually extended its influence over 2,100 kilometres of coastline. Between 1636 and 1645 it imported 23,000 black slaves. But Portugal's regaining of its independence (1642), the slump in sugar prices in Amsterdam (1644), the uprising – almost nationalist in character – of the *moradores* (Portuguese settlers) in 1644 and the exhausting of sources of black slaves in Angola put an end to the domination of the *Flamengos* (the Dutch). They withdrew to Curacao, a busy centre of smuggling and illegal trade with the Spanish colonies.

In this Protestant society, the profits of trade had to be reinvested; art was the only permitted luxury. But it was a sober luxury, for this art depicted bare churches, quiet interiors and boards of directors and governors. Rembrandt side-stepped such restrictions by making himself the subject of his paintings. ...

THE NARROW, FLAT LANDS of the United Provinces, bordered by the sea, were claimed first by Spain (1621–48), then by France (1672–8). Each was attracted by the area's prosperity, for if ever there was an agricultural revolution, it sprang from Dutch husbandry.

The Dutch were experienced herring-fishermen in the North Sea and well equipped to inherit the legacy of the Hanseatic League in the Baltic: 'Commanding the trade of the Kingdom of Sweden since they command the trade of copper' (Huet, 1694). With a new type of ship (a bulk carrier – the *fluyt*) and a fleet of ten thousand vessels, they carried Baltic corn as far as the eastern Mediterranean. Van Heemskerck and Barents set out to find a north-eastern passage but became ice-bound in the Arctic Ocean and had to return with only geographical information.

Birth of Rembrandt in Leyden.

Birth of Spinoza in Amsterdam and Vermeer in Delft

1606

1632

1595: Expedition (4 vessels, 250 men), financed by Far Lands Company, commanded by Cornelius Van Houtmann.
1602: Founding of one of first great joint-stock companies – Dutch East India Company (*Vereenigde Oost-Indische Companie*).
9 April 1609: Twelve-year truce, signed at Antwerp. In same year, founding of Bank of Amsterdam (*Amsterdamsche Wisselbank*). Publication by Huig Van Groot (better known as Grotius, 1583–1645) of *Mare liberum*.
1621: Founding by Usselincx of West India Company (*West Indische Companie*). First long-term Dutch settlement in Guiana.
10 May 1624: Bahia captured by expedition (26 ships, 450 cannons, 3,300 men), financed by West India Company, commanded by Jakobs Willekens.
1626: Founding of Nieuw-Amsterdam (New York).
7–8 September 1628: Seizure by Piet Heyn of 80 tons of silver (15 million florins) from Plate fleet of New Spain.
1630: Recife taken by Dutch.
1639: Admiral Van Tromp's great victory, off

2. The port of Macassar on the Indonesian coast, after its capture by the Dutch in 1660.

Dover, over Spanish fleet.
1644: Revolt of *moradores* in Brazil.
30 January 1648: At The Hague, independence of United Provinces recognized by Spain. Agreement by Spain to surrender its right to the 'Pais de la Généralité' and to close Antwerp. (Treaty ratified at Münster on 15 May 1648.)
5 August 1651: Navigation Act promulgated by Cromwell.
28 January 1654: Loss of Recife to the Portuguese. Treaty of Westminster with England.
1661: Dutch driven from Formosa by Chinese (Koxinga).
4 September 1662: Treaty with England.
1665: Dutch colonial positions attacked by English.
1667: Peace of Breda: English possession of New York recognized by Dutch.
January 1668: Triple Alliance at The Hague (Sweden, England, Holland) against Louis XIV. In same year, Japanese embargo on export of silver, depriving East India Company of metal money, used to pay in Indies for exports to Europe.

1595–1689

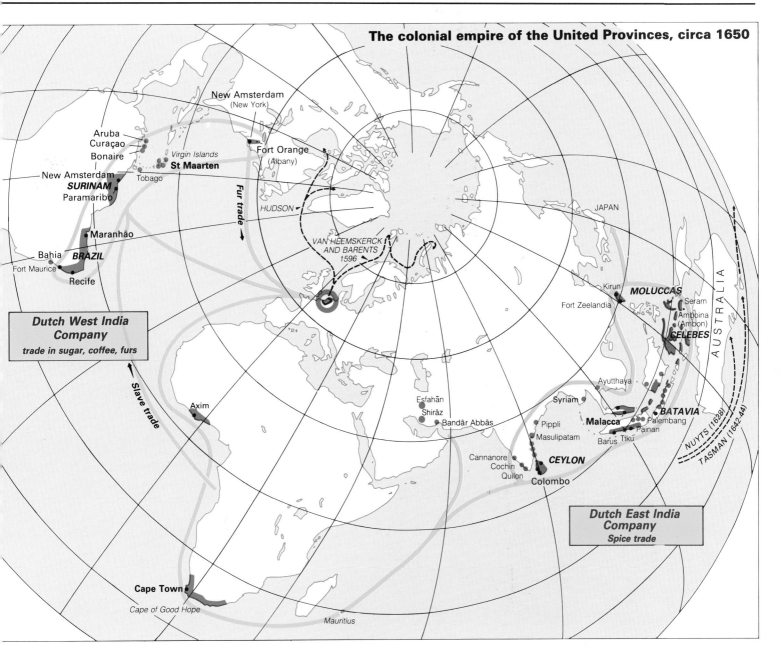

The colonial empire of the United Provinces, circa 1650

New Amsterdam
(New York)

Aruba
Curaçao
Bonaire

Virgin Islands
St Maarten
Tobago

New Amsterdam
SURINAM
Paramaribo

Fort Orange
(Albany)

Fur trade

HUDSON

*VAN HEEMSKERCK
AND BARENTS
1596*

JAPAN

Kirun

MOLUCCAS

Seram

Fort Zeelandia

Amboina
(Ambon)

CELEBES

Maranhão

Bahia *BRAZIL*
Fort Maurice

Recife

**Dutch West India
Company**
trade in sugar, coffee, furs

Slave trade

Axim

Esfahān
Shīrāz

Bandār Abbās

Ayutthaya

Syriam

Pippli
Masulipatam

Malacca

Cannanore
Cochin
Quilon

CEYLON

Colombo

BATAVIA

Palembang
Painan

Barus Tiku

AUSTRALIA

NUYTS (1628)
TASMAN (1642-44)

**Dutch East India
Company**
Spice trade

Cape Town
Cape of Good Hope

Mauritius

Death of Frans Hals in Haarlem.   **Loss of New Amsterdam (New York).**   **Louis XIV in Holland.**

1666	1667		1672

1669: Death of Rembrandt.
1670: Publication by Spinoza (1632–77) of
Tractatus Theologico-politicus.
12 June 1672: Crossing of Rhine by Louis
XIV.
1677: Posthumous publication of Spinoza's
Ethics.
10 May 1678: Peace of Nijmegen.
1689: Accession of William III to English
throne.

3. The governors of the Handbow Archers'
Guild depicted by Van der Helst, 1613–70.

4. Japanese engraving of a Dutch ship,
circa 1700.

The Greatness of Russia

AT THE DAWN OF the modern age, the territory of medieval Muscovy expanded considerably, both as a result of military conquest – the product of a strengthening of the state – and also, more importantly, as a result of a vast spontaneous migration of the population. From the fifteenth century the princes were led increasingly to reduce the peasantry to serfdom in order to satisfy the needs of a new class of 'lesser serving landowners' (*dvoriane*), favoured at the expense of the old aristocracy (the *boyars*). This produced a migratory movement, first of all towards the steppes of the Don region – where communities of Russian Cossacks formed parallel to those of the Ukrainian Cossacks on the Polish marches, then towards Siberia. The discontent of the masses also found expression in rural risings in which the serfs were joined by Cossacks, defending their rights against advancing state structures and foreign immigrants. These revolts were often conducted in the name of a legitimate prince, who had disappeared in mysterious circumstances and been usurped by an adventurer. In effect, the image of an authoritarian sovereign, who was the protector of the weak and whose legitimacy derived from hereditary right, was ever present in the popular consciousness. But this utopia could not survive the evidence of the repression practised against both rural and urban uprisings. Even among the more well-to-do sections of society, the possibilities of participation in government that were offered in the seventeenth century by the 'Assemblies of the Land' (*Zemskie Sobory*) – to whom was entrusted among other tasks the resolution of dynastic crises – had come to nothing, because society was not organized into orders and a 'third estate' could not be easily identified. The power of the church was reduced once and for all by

Peter the Great. His reign saw the culmination of a process whereby all social groups were subordinated to the needs of the state: the nobles were merged into a single class, whose role was to serve the state, in either a military or a civilian capacity; the peasants were called upon to provide the economy with servile labour on the lands of the nobles or the crown or in the first factories, and to provide the army with recruits. Thanks to the decisive role the nobility played during palace revolutions, its obligations were diminished and its rights reinforced. The nobility, a privileged class, which in fact supplied the state with all its officers, became the solid pillar on which the monarchy rested. The army, a caricatural copy of the Prussian model, contributed to the further petrification of social relations. The European dress which the élite chose to wear simply completed their isolation from the rest of the nation. The cultural unity of Russian society had already been compromised in the seventeenth century by the Old-Believers schism, which put an end to the idea of a Christianity identified with the Russian ethnic group and by the Polish, White

2. The Kolichev Estate in the province of Tver, by E. Fedorov, 18th century.

Russian and Ukrainian influences on the Muscovite aristocracy. It was shattered when Peter the Great abruptly introduced a policy of Westernizing the beliefs, manners, way of life and even language of the ruling class. The Russian, with its foreign loan-words, which they had spoken was now supplanted by French. Even literary Russian, a combination of the vernacular language and Slavonic, which in Catherine II's reign had boasted Russia's first great modern writers and poets, had distanced itself from the language of the people, who were left only with traditional oral culture and a religion reduced to rituals.

1. The soldiers of Peter the Great, by Kardovski.

Ivan IV.		Fyodor I.	Boris Godunov.	Fyodor II, then the first False Dimitri.	Mikhail Romanov.	Alexis.
1533		1584	1598	1605	1613	1645

1547: Imperial coronation of Ivan IV ('the Terrible'); official adoption of the title of tsar (from the Latin Caesar).
1549–60: Government of the so-called 'Chosen Council' (Izbrannaya Rada). Administrative, judicial and military reforms.
1553: Arrival in Russia of the English explorer, Richard Chancellor.
1558–72: War of Livonia. General exhaustion of the country.
1564: First book (Acts and Epistles) printed in Moscow.
1565–72: Creation of the *oprichnina*, an instrument of the terror régime, placed under the direct control of the Tsar.
1571: Raid of the Crimean Tartars; burning of Moscow.
1582: Cossack troops under Ermak penetrate into Siberia.
1589: Creation of the Moscow patriarchate.
1603–19: Outbreak of social struggles, fanned by famine, dynastic crises and foreign intervention.
1617–18: Armistice treaties with Sweden and Poland.
1630–2: Creation of army mercenary corps.

3. Muscovite cavalrymen. German engraving, 16th century.

1648: Rising of Ukrainian cossacks against Poland. Social disturbances in Moscow and several other cities.
1649: Promulgation of a new legal code (the *ulozhenie*), laying down judicial procedures and legalizing serfdom.
1654: Proclamation of union of Ukraine with Moscow.
1654–67: Liturgical reforms; Old Believers schism.
1662: Rioting in Moscow against price rises brought about by the introduction of copper coinage.
1682: Abolition of placement in state offices based on internal hierarchy in noble families (*mestnichestvo*).
1687: Creation of the Slavo-Graeco-Latin Academy.
1697–8: Peter the Great's first journey to Europe.
1699–1705: Beginnings of military conscription.
1700: Introduction of the Julian calendar.
1718: Introduction of a poll-tax.
1718–21: Creation of 'colleges', which pre-figured ministries, to replace *prikazy*

(executive bureaux of Muscovite administration).
1721: Creation of the Holy Synod to replace the patriarchate.
1722: Promulgation of the 'Table of Ranks' fixing civil, military and ecclesiastical hierarchies.
1725: Academy of Sciences founded.
1736–9: War against Turkey (Treaty of Belgrade).
1753: Abolition of internal customs duties.
1754: Creation of Commercial Bank in St Petersburg.

4. The first False Dimitri, Tsar in 1605.

The Rise of Russia from Ivan the Terrible to Catherine II

*Map labels:*

BALTIC SEA, Revel 1710, Narva 1710, Vyborg, Riga, St Petersburg, Pskov, Kovno, Viino, Brest, Minsk, Novgorod, Archangel 1584, Kholmogory, Soloveki, Smolensk, Tver, Vologda, Kamenets-Podolsky, Kiev, Chernigov, Moscow, Trinity St Serge, Poltava 1709, Toula, Ryazan, Nijni-Novgorod, Odessa, Voronezh 1586, Kharkov, Kazan 1552, Penza 1660, Perm, Azov 1696, Saratov 1590, Samara 1586, Ufa, Ekaterinburg 1721, Tsaritsyn 1589, Yatskii, Tyumen 1586, Tobolsk 1584, Astrakhan 1556, Orenburg 1735, Cherkessk, Sebastopol 1735, BLACK SEA, CASPIAN SEA, Aral Sea, Amu-Daria, Syr-Daria, Lake Balkhash

Kalmuks, Small and medium Cossack Hordes, Bashkirs, Udmurts, Komis, Samoyeds, Selkups, Mangazeia 1601, Turukhansk 1607, Narym 1598, Tomsk 1604, Kuznetsk 1678, Krasnoyarsk 1628, Bratsk 1630, Yeniseisk 1619, Irkutsk 1652, Lake Baikal, Nerchinsk 1658, Buryats, Evens (or Lamuts), Yakuts, Evens, Yukhagirs, Koryak peoples, Sredne-Kolymsk 1643, Verkhoyansk 1638, Olekminsk 1635, Yakutsk, Okhotsk 1649, Anadyr 1649, Tougursk 1652, Amur, Lena, Yenisei, Ob, Irtysh

1000 km

FRONTIERS

Frontier of the Muscovite State in 1618
Frontier fixed by the Treaty of Nerchinsk
Territory under joint Russian and Chinese administration
Central Asian frontier in 1790
Russian protectorate at the end of the XVIIIth century

Pugachev's Rising (1773-75)
Razin's Rising (1667-71)
Evens Non-Slav peoples
Towns, with date.
□ of military conquest
○ of foundation or fortification
◔ Monasteries

TERRITORIES ANNEXED

Truce of Andrusovo (War of the Ukraine 1654-67)
End of Zaporozhe autonomy - 1686
Peace of Nystadt (Great Northern War 1700-71)
Treaty of Kuchuk-Kainardzhi and Jassy (wars with Turkey 1768-74 and 1787-91)
Annexation of the Crimean Khanate, 1783
Partitions of Poland 1772-1793-1795

Fyodor III.	Ivan V and Peter I.	Peter I alone.	Catherine I.	Anne.	Ivan VI.	Elizabeth.	Catherine II.	Paul I.
1676	1682	1696	1725	1730	1740	1741	1762	1796

1755: University of Moscow founded.

1757: Publication of M. V. Lomonosov's *Russian Grammar.*

1757–62: Participation in the Seven Years' War.

1762: Nobles relieved of the obligation of state service.

1764: Suppression of the *hetman* function; integration of Ukraine into Russia. Secularization of monastic lands.

1775: Reform of local administration.

1783: Extension of serfdom to the Ukraine.

1790: Publication of A. N. Radishchev's *A Journey from St Petersburg to Moscow*, the first literary pamphlet against serfdom; the author is arrested.

5. The Trinity. *Icon by Andrei Roublev, 15th century.*

RURIK DYNASTY
⋮
YAROSLAV VSEVOLDOVICH † 1246

Boyars of Kostromo

ALEXANDER NEVSKY † 1263 — ANDREY † 1264

Muscovite boyars

VASILY III † 1533 Ⓐ
∞ Yelena Glinskaya [1533-38] Ⓐ

IVAN IV † 1584

BORIS GODUNOV 1605 † [1584-98] Ⓑ
FYODOR I Ⓑ † 1598
Tsarevich Dmitry † 1591 — Usurpers (1605-10)
VASILY IV Shuysky † 1612
Fyodor Romanov † 1633 Joint sovereign [1619-33] Ⓒ

FYODOR II † 1605

MICHAEL ROMANOV † 1645 Ⓒ

ALEXIS † 1676

Sophia [1682-89] Ⓓ FYODOR III † 1682 Ⓓ
IVAN V † 1696
PETER I † 1725 Ⓓ, ∞ CATHERINE I † 1727

ANNA † 1740

ELIZABETH † 1761

Anna [1740-41] Ⓔ
PETER II † 1730
PETER III ∞ CATHERINE II † 1762 Usurpers (Pugachev 1773-75)

IVAN VI † 1764 Ⓔ

PAUL I † 1801

[1533-38]: Regency conducted with or in the name of sovereign indicated by the letter in Ⓐ

Emperors (Czars) of the nineteenth century (→1917)

Swedish Expansion and the Rise of Prussia

THE TREATIES OF WESTPHALIA made Sweden a major force in Europe. To go with her Baltic possessions (Ingria, Estonia, Livonia), well secured since 1629, she now received Pomerania, Wismar and the bishoprics of Bremen and Verden, all of which, together with her role in the Empire, exposed her to other nations' jealousies. For his part, the Elector of Brandenburg acquired the bishoprics of Halberstadt (with Magdeburg to follow), Cammin and Minden, the latter a staging-post on the way to the Rhenish territories inherited in 1614. With less than 1.5 million inhabitants (even counting Finland), Sweden was a poor country and its expansion produced internal tensions. The 'alienation' (or acquisition by the nobility) of crown lands (formerly farmed as common land) was endangering the survival of a free peasantry, and the upper aristocracy, who were strong enough to

thwart the intentions of the monarchy, met with hostile reaction from the three lower orders of the Parliament (Riksdag), the clerg bourgeoisie and peasants. King Karl X Gustav, who came to th throne after Queen Kristina's abdication, pushed through a policy 'reduktion' (reclamation) of a quarter of the 'alienated' lands. He als embarked upon a renewed policy of aggressive expansion. His mili ary campaigns in Poland and Denmark both ended in failure. Th maritime powers – the United Provinces and England – could no accept the effective domination of the Baltic by Sweden. The death Karl X left to a regency the arduous task of maintaining a façade greatness with insufficient means. The development of export indu tries (iron, tar) by foreign entrepreneurs augmented resources som what and Sweden's external possessions brought in some revenu but their potential was not integrated into an imperial econom Faced with the vengeful intentions of the Danish monarch, now longer hamstrung by his aristocracy, the Swedish polity had need funds. Alliance with France in 1672 provided them. In 1679 Lou XIV forced the restoration to Sweden of the German provinces sh had lost in battle. This put a check on the aspirations of Brandenbur which Frederick William had built up patiently, establishing h authority at home against the old estates, setting up a permanen administration and army, and winning sovereignty in Prussia b skilfully playing off Poland and Sweden (until 1657 Prussia had bee a Polish fief). In 1685 the Great Elector welcomed Huguenot refugee who provoked new disturbances in Berlin.

Karl XI, who came of age in 1672, fought a fine defence of Skan his reign was distinguished by the completion of the process of 'reduk tion' of former crown lands, which he began in 1680. This was prelude to the installation of an autocratic, thrifty government whic steered clear of alliances. Both the army and the bureaucracy wer efficient instruments in Karl XII's hands and, riding on a stron wave of national feeling, he had some initial success in battle again his united neighbours. He became bogged down in Poland, howeve and even more irremediably so in Russia, obstinately refusing an compromise settlement. An exhausted Sweden viewed the collapse these pretensions to grandeur with some relief. In the new norther balance of power, English maritime dominance was placed in th service of Hanover, the elector of which sat on the English throne; th new element in the situation was the considerable presence of Russi installed on the Baltic. Between these two, Prussia made modes progress. Possessing a taste for dynastic pomp, the Great Elector successor had taken the royal title in Prussia, but his political action had been unremarkable. Going to war only in 1714, his son Frederic William I gained part of Pomerania including Stettin. Until 1740 h was to use his stern sergeant-king's manner to train up his army without, however, taking it to war. The real strength of the Hohenzol lern state was as yet difficult to discern.

1. The Great Elector Frederick William and his mother, or 'Solomon and the Queen of Sheba', Mathias Czwieczek, 1648.

Descartes dies in Stockholm.

1650

1648: Treaties of Westphalia. Gains by Sweden and Brandenburg.
1653: The agreement of the Brandenburg Estates consolidates the power of the Elector and the subservient status of the peasants.
1654: Queen Kristina abdicates. Karl X Gustav becomes king of Sweden (1654–60).
1655: Swedish invasion of Poland ('the deluge'). The Swedish Riksdag votes to reclaim a quarter of alienated crown lands.
1656–7: Danzig protected by a Dutch fleet. Sovereign independence conferred upon the Duchy of Prussia.
1657–8: Unsuccessful Danish attack: by the Peace of Roskilde, Frederik III has to cede six provinces to Sweden.
1658–9: Karl X Gustav reopens hostilities, but his siege of Copenhagen ends in failure.
1660: The Treaty of Oliva with Poland produces no gains for Sweden. The Peace of Copenhagen gives back Trondheim and the island of Bornholm to Denmark. The Danish monarchy becomes hereditary.
1661: The Treaty of Kardis between Sweden and Russia.

Prussia becomes a sovereign state.

1657

1661–3: The Diet of Prussia reduced to a subordinate role.
1662–8: Construction of the Frederick William Canal (Elbe-Oder).
1665: The new constitution of Frederick III codifies absolutism in Denmark.
1666: Foundation of Lund University in Swedish Skanie.
1674–8: Allied to Louis XIV, Sweden's only successful resistance against the attacks of her united enemies is in Skanie; Prussian victory at Fehrbellin (1675).
1679: Louis XIV forces the restitution of all Swedish possessions in the Treaty of Saint-Germain-en-Laye.
1679–1702: Publication of *Atland* by Olaus Rudbeck, 'proving' that Sweden was Atlantis.
1680: The archbishopric of Magdeburg passes to the Elector of Brandenburg. Karl XI wins assent for his policy of *reduktion* of all alienated crown lands.
1682: Swedish monarchy becomes virtually absolute.
1685: The Edict of Potsdam grants asylum to Huguenot refugees from France in the states of the Great Elector.

4. Olaus Rudbeck, as depicted by M. Mijtens in 1696.

Absolutism in Denma

1665

1688: Death of the Great Elector, Frederick William, first architect of the might of the Prussian state.
1694: Foundation of the University of Halle spread of Pietism (August Francke).
1697: At the age of 15, Karl XII inherits uncontested power in an isolated Sweden.
1700: Foundation of the Society of Science at Berlin; Frederick IV of Denmark has to withdraw in defeat from the coalition agains Sweden. Karl XII defeats the Russians at Narva.
1701: The Elector Frederick III has himself crowned king in Prussia (and becomes Frederick I).
1704: Karl XII has Stanislaw Leszczynski elected king of Poland.
1709: Defeated at Poltava in the Ukraine, Kar XII flees into Turkey.
1710–14: All Swedish external possessions are conquered by the allies; desire for peace within Sweden.
1718: Death of Karl XII.
1719–20: New Swedish constitution reduce the monarch's power almost to nothing. The Treaties of Stockholm cede the provinces o

1648–1721

. Leibniz. Late 17th-century engraving.

3. Skokloster Palace in Sweden.

NORWAY

Trondheim

JAMTLAND

KERALIA

KINGDOM OF SWEDEN

Vyborg

Christiania
(Oslo)

Abo

Uppsala

Stockholm

Narva

INGRIA

iron, copper

linen, hemp, copper

Reval

ESTONIA

Novgorod

BOHUSLAN

Göteborg

OSEL

Dorpat
(Tartu)

LIVONIA

RUSSIA

Towards England and
the United Provinces

HALLAND

GOTLAND

Riga

DENMARK

Sund

Dvina

BLEKINGS

Halsingbörg

Baltic Sea

cereals

Lund

Copenhagen

SKANE

cereals

BREMEN AND
VERDEN

Lübeck

BORNHOLM

WESTERN
POMERANIA

Königsberg

POLAND

Bremen

WISMAR

Danzig

Hamburg

Stettin

PRUSSIA

HANOVER

Elbe

BRANDENBURG

Vistula

200 km

Swedish expansion, 1560-1660

- The Sweden of Gustavus I Vasa (1523-1560)
- Acquisitions between 1561 and 1660

  Treaty of Altmark (1629) ⟹ Baltic possessions
  Treaty of Brönsebro (1645) ⟹ Jamtland
  Treaty of Westphalia (1648) ⟹ Pomerania, Wismar, Bishoprics of Bremen and Verden
  Treaty of Roskilde (1658) ⟹ Southern provinces

- Temporary acquisitions
  Trondheim and Bornholmk (1558-60)
- ◆ Great Swedish universities

Decline of Swedish power, 1679-1721

- to the benefit of Russia
- to the benefit of Brandenburg
- to the benefit of Hanover

The Baltic Economy

- ●● Major ports
- → Principal sea-trade routes

Huguenots welcomed by Prussia.

1685

Death of Olaus Rudbeck.

1702

Bremen and Verden to the Elector of Hanover and a part of Swedish Pomerania to Prussia; Denmark makes no territorial gains.
1721: The Peace of Nystad cedes the Baltic provinces and a part of Karelia to the Tsar.

5. Charles XII. Engraving after a painting by Craft, 1701.

6. The war between the Russians and the Swedes, from the Zubov Chronicle.

Colonial Expansion of England and France

THE EIGHTEENTH CENTURY marked a particularly important stage in the history of European expansion in the world. This movement should be considered in terms of its three main features: the development of great voyages of exploration and discovery, the rise of intercontinental trade, and the growth of colonial imperialism.

The great voyages of exploration were made possible by advances in shipbuilding and in navigation techniques. Increasing numbers of expeditions set sail in the second half of the century. The ambitions which inspired these enterprises were born of the spirit of the age: faith in enlightenment and in the advance of knowledge, a passion for science and nature, the desire to make a complete inventory of human activity in the world. The main objective of the expeditions was to explore the uncharted areas of the Pacific Ocean, which some geographers had suggested might hide another continent. By the end of the century, barring a few details, the discovered lands and their coastlines had been mapped definitively. On the other hand, the interiors of both the Asian and African continents – particularly the latter – had been explored very little.

The development of maritime trade was one of the most important factors in the profound economic changes which the countries of Western Europe experienced during this period. Ever-increasing quantities of tropical products – cotton, sugar, coffee, indigo – were sought by Europe and the volume of trade between the continents was growing constantly. The most profitable part of this trade was 'triangular': in exchange for various goods, local rulers on the west coast of Africa handed over slaves; these slaves were sold, on the other side of the ocean, to planters in the West Indies and in both North and South America; the profit from these transactions enabled tropical goods to be purchased and exported at great gain to the markets of Europe. Thus the Atlantic became the centre of international trade, while the ports of Western Europe – Bordeaux, Nantes, Liverpool, London – enjoyed a period of exceptional prosperity.

Bitter commercial rivalry – particularly between France and England – largely explains the lengthy conflicts which ensued over the possession or control of certain colonial territories. When the Treaties of Utrecht were signed, the major colonial powers were still Spain, Portugal and the United Provinces. France and Great Britain began expanding their domains through overseas conquest somewhat later. Each did so during a period of economic expansion, and each was a contender for naval supremacy. So it was, that in the second half of the century, a fierce contest was fought on three fronts: the Caribbean, North America and the East Indies.

The conflict began in 1755 and ended in 1763 with a decisive English victory which was confirmed by the Treaty of Paris. In the West Indies, which were particularly valuable because of their rich plantations, French possessions remained intact. In contrast, however, France lost its vast territories in North America, stretching from the St Lawrence to the Gulf of Mexico. In addition, France renounced its policy of territorial expansion in the East Indies, where it retained only five coastal trading stations. It was the turn of the English to expand their territories in the East Indies, thus marking the beginnings of the British Empire, which would be consolidated in the course of the next century.

1. Loading cargo bound for the colonies in the port of Rochefort in 1762. Painting by Joseph Vernet.

Treaties of Utrecht between England and Holland.

French defeat the Allies at Fontenoy.

1713

1745

2. General Louis-Joseph de Saint-Véran, Marquis of Montcalm, dies outside Quebec in 1759. Engraving by Moret, after a drawing by Desfontaines.

1715: Death of Louis XIV. Beginning of policy of *rapprochement* between France and Great Britain, lasting until 1740.
1740–8: War of Austrian Succession. France in naval conflict with Great Britain.
1742–54: Dupleix, governor of French East India Company's trading stations. Start of policy of territorial expansion.
26 December 1754: Godeheu Treaty (from name of Dupleix's successor in the Indies). Agreement by English and French East India Companies to abandon policies of expansion and conquest.
1755: Beginnings of Anglo-French hostilities in North America. Seizure by English (under Admiral Boscawen) of more than 300 French ships.
1759: Siege and surrender of Quebec.
8 September 1760: Capture of Montreal by English.
1761: Capture by English of French station at Pondicherry.
10 February 1763: Treaty of Paris. Surrender of French territories in North America, with exception of islands of St Pierre and Miquelon and fishing rights off Newfoundland.

1765: Robert Clive appointed governor of English East India Company's trading stations. Extension of company's dominion to Bengal and Ganges Valley.
1766–9: Bougainville's voyage around world.

3. Joseph-François Dupleix (1696–1763), French colonial administrator, and Governor General of the French settlements in India.

1768–71: Captain Cook's first voyage. Discovery of New Zealand and east coast of Australia.
1774: Extension of Dutch territorial power to Java.
1774–83: Revolt of England's 13 American colonies and American War of Independence.
1779: Death of Cook in Hawaii.
1783: Treaty of Versailles. Granting of independence to British colonies in America.
1785–8: La Perouse's voyage of discovery. Expedition wrecked in the New Hebrides.
1788: First English settlement in Australia (Botany Bay).

18th century

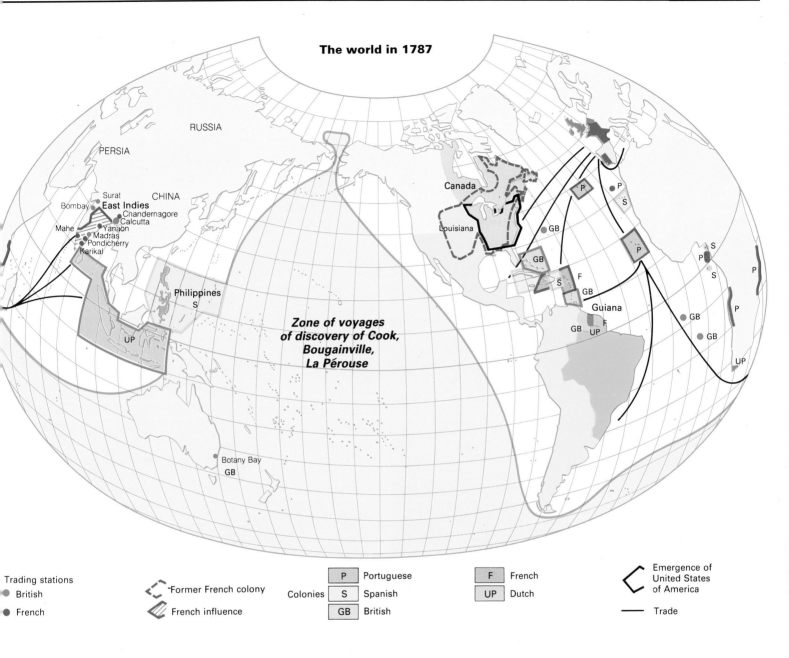

The world in 1787

RUSSIA

PERSIA

CHINA

Surat

Bombay · East Indies

Mahe · Chandernagore

Calcutta

Yanaon

Madras

Pondicherry

Karikal

Philippines
S

Canada

Louisiana

GB

P

P

S

GB

S

F

GB

Guiana

GB

F

GB UP

S

P S

P

GB

P

GB

UP

UP

*Zone of voyages
of discovery of Cook,
Bougainville,
La Pérouse*

Botany Bay
GB

Trading stations
● British
● French

 Former French colony

French influence

Colonies

P	Portuguese
S	Spanish
GB	British

| F | French |
| UP | Dutch |

Emergence of
United States
of America

— Trade

Peace of Paris between France and England.

1763

Cook circumnavigates the earth.

1768–71

La Pérouse's voyage.

1785–8

4. *Plan of Madras, trading post of the British East India Company, on the Coromandel coast,
captured by La Bourdonnais in 1746 and lost again in 1759.*

5. *The English navigator, James Cook, during his second voyage to Tahiti in 1774, looks on at a
human sacrifice.*

The Enlightened Despots

THE EXPRESSION 'enlightened despotism', widely employed in the nineteenth century, has its origin in the *Literary Correspondence* of Melchior Grimm. It is used to designate both a technique of government enabling backward states to become modernized and a propaganda theme. Among the many countries which attempted this form of government (Pombal's Portugal, Spain, Naples, Parma, Poland and Denmark), there are only three which played a significant 'great power' role: Frederick II's Prussia, the Hapsburg Empire of Maria Theresa and Joseph II and Catherine the Great's Russia. The policies of these sovereigns had certain features in common; in particular, they all regarded Louis XIV as an exemplary figure, and the practices of Frederick II (historically the first 'enlightened' ruler) exerted enormous influence over the others. Their principal concern was for the glorification of the state, of which they themselves were the incarnation. To this end, they began by augmenting their own powers. For Frederick II, who was given, now and then, to theorising, the source of political authority resided in a social contract which gave the sovereign very extensive rights indeed; he therefore suppressed the Diet of Prussia and set out to reduce the powers of the intermediary state bodies. In this he was imitated by Maria Theresa, who drastically reduced the privileges of her dominion states, by Joseph II, who centralized power within his empire, and by the Tsarina, who in her *Nakaz* produced an apology for the despotism of law. Following the example of Frederick II, who had built up his civil service and standardized laws and customs, Catherine II and Joseph II proceeded to initiate thoroughgoing reforms. The latter created a genuine 'civil service' and imposed the use of the German language on his various kingdoms; the education provided by the grammar schools (*Gymnasien*) and the universities was reformed to adapt it to the needs of state service. The army was the principal instrument of these rulers' power: in 1780, with some 200,000 men, Frederick II's army was the most powerful in Europe. Russia and Austria took similar steps to build up their military might. The maintenance of so many troops required new sources of fiscal revenue: these rulers increased their resources by means of customs duties, indirect taxes and monopolies (only Joseph II was so bold as to propose equality of liability to taxation, on the basis of a cadastral survey). Alongside these efforts, they also pursued a goal of enriching their countries; they encouraged agricultural colonization, the building of roads and canals and the creation of industries, all within a strictly regulated framework. Such Colbertist measures enabled these states to meet their own needs and even to export to finance their conquests. Austria, which had lost Silesia, did, however, participate in the dismembering of Poland, completed in 1795. These administrative, military and fiscal reforms did not drastically change society, which remained fixed in its archaic ways: the Prussian and Russian nobilities saw their privileges increase in this period. Joseph II alone dared stand up to the privileged classes, as can be seen in his attempt to abolish serfdom and corvées and his reorganization of the secular clergy along the lines of a civil service. Everywhere, however, the bourgeoisie remained weak and urbanization was still in its initial stages. It is, therefore, more accurate to speak of state despotism than enlightenment in this context. Certain themes borrowed from Enlightenment philosophy (reason, tolerance, happiness) served mainly as an excellent fund of propaganda themes. Voltaire and Diderot hailed Frederick II and Catherine II as 'philosophers'. Frederick II, indeed, kept what was positively a 'philosophical menagerie' at Sans-Souci and at the Berlin Academy. The Austrian monarchs showed some reserve in this matter, though it was in fact Joseph II who attempted the most far-reaching and radical reforms, precipitating his states into a revolt that was quelled only when all his reforming measures were revoked after his death.

1. The Marquis of Pombal, by J. Guimaraes.

Frederick II King of Prussia. Maria Theresa Empress.

Voltaire in Berlin.

Catherine II Tsarina.

1740	1750	1762

1736: Correspondence between Voltaire and Frederick II begins.
1739: Frederick II: *Anti-Machiavel*.
1740: Accession of Frederick II (May) and Maria-Theresa (October).
1740–48: Christian Wolff, *Jus naturae*.
1741: First war in Silesia.
1742: Treaty of Breslau. A large part of Silesia becomes Prussian.
1743: Frederick II draws up statutes of the East Berlin Academy, whose director is Maupertuis.
1744: Frederick II introduces the cotton industry.
1745: Construction of the Sans-Souci residence at Potsdam.
1747: Johann Sebastian Bach at Potsdam.
1749: Frederick II's directory and commission for schools.
1752: Maria Theresa creates a system of technical education.
1753: Voltaire and Frederick II quarrel. Maria Theresa institutes a judicial commission.
1756–63: Seven Years' War.
1762: Nationalization of the Bank of Vienna; accession of Catherine II, who corresponds

with d'Alembert; Maria Theresa, Mining College of Hungary.
1764: C. Beccaria-Bonesana, *On Crimes and Punishments*.
1765: Death of Emperor Francis; Joseph II Emperor and co-regent. Catherine II buys Diderot's library. Helvetius at Potsdam; creation of the Bank of Berlin.
1767: Nakaz ('Instruction') by Catherine II; she translates Marmontel's *Bélisaire*; Mercier de la Rivière at St Petersburg.
1769: Catherine II creates the Assignat Banks of Moscow and St Petersburg.
1770: Maria Theresa: Royal Academy of Commerce and Penal Code.
1771: Voltaire, *Épitre à l'impératrice de Russie*; Maria Theresa's patents on the corvée in Silesia.
1772: First partition of Poland.
1773: Pugachov's revolt in Russia; Diderot at St Petersburg; Frederick II decrees education compulsory.
1775: Catherine II issues decrees on administrative reform, freedom of trade and industry.
1778: Equestrian statue of Peter the Great

2. Frederick II at Sans-Souci.

3. The Empress Maria Theresa.

The Age of Enlightened Despotism

FINLAND · *KARELIA*

SWEDEN

St Petersburg

ESTONIA
1721

LIVONIA
1721 · Pskov

DENMARK

EAST
FREISLAND
1744

UNITED
PROVINCES

DUCHY OF CLEVES

UCHY OF GELDERLAND
1713

Antwerp

russels

ETHERLANDS

Aix-la-Chapelle

AUSTRIAN

LOWER
PALATINATE

FRANCE

NEUCHATEL
1707

SWITZERLAND

PIEDMONT
1738

PARMA
1735-1748

SARDINIA
1714-1720

Lübeck

Hamburg

Bremen

Lingen

HANOVER

RAVENSBERG

Dortmund

COUNTY
OF MARK

Cologne

Mainz

Worms

Rothenburg   Nürnberg

UPPER PALATINATE

Heilbronn

Esslingen

Rottweil   Ulm

Menmingen

Kempten

1714

MILAN

Milan

MANTUA
1708

Florence

TUSCANY
1737

Stettin

BRANDENBURG

Magdeburg   Berlin   Potsdam

SAXONY

Leipzig

Dresden

Prague

BOHEMIA

Nördlingen

Augsburg

BAVARIA

Salzburg

TYROL

Trent

REPUBLIC
OF VENICE

Trieste

CARINTHIA

CARNIOLA

POMERANIA

DANZIG

WEST
PRUSSIA
1772

SCHWIEBUS
1742

Breslau

SILESIA
1742

MORAVIA

INNVIERTEL
1779

Vienna

SIYRIA

Buda · Pest

Königsberg

Vistula

POLAND

Warsaw

Cracow

KINGDOM OF
GALICIA AND LODOMERIA
1772

Danube

Tisza

HUNCARY-TRANSYLVANIA

BANATE
1718

SERBIA-WALLACHIA
1718-1739

Danube

Dwina

1772

Smolensk

Pripet

Dniepr

BUKOVINA
1775

CRIMEA
1774

OTTOMAN EMPIRE

KINGDOM OF NAPLES
1714-1735

300 km

▨	**Russia** (Romanov)	▨	**Austria** (Hapsburg)
▨	**Prussia** (Hohenzollern)	▨	Territories acquired temporarily

---- Polish frontier before 1772

SAXONY Electorate

—— Border of the Holy Roman Empire

1744 Date of annexation

· Imperial Free Cities

Towns and cities:

● With more than 100,000 inhabitants

● With more than 50,000 inhabitants

● With more than 25,000 inhabitants

• With less than 25,000 inhabitants

Partitions of Poland

Riga

Courland

Danzig

LITHUANIA

Torun (Thorn)

Vistula

Poland

Cracow

GALICIA   PODOLIA

Kiev

Prussia   **Russia**

Austria

1772

Prussia   **Russia**

Poland

Austria

1793

Prussia   **Russia**

Austria

1795   300 km

Joseph II's Edict of Toleration.

1781

Third partition of Poland.

1795

by Falconet) at St Petersburg.

1778–80: Lessing, *Gespräche für Freimaurer.*

1780: Death of Maria Theresa, who is succeeded by Joseph II.

1781: Frederick II, *Essay on Forms of Government*; Kant, *Critique of Pure Reason*; Joseph II, cadastral survey, Edict of Toleration, reform of the regular clergy and abolition of serfdom.

1782: Joseph II, reform of the secular clergy; Berlin Academy's competition on the universality of the French language.

1786: Joseph II abolishes the guilds. Mirabeau in Prussia. Death of Frederick II (17 August).

1787: Triumphal visit of Catherine II to the Crimea; Josephinian Law Code.

1788: Risings in Hungary and Belgium.

1789: Joseph II, abolition of the corvée; the Austrian Netherlands proclaim their independence.

1790: Death of Joseph II (20 February).

1793: Second partition of Poland.

1795: Third partition of Poland.

1796: Death of Catherine II (17 November).

4. Schönbrunn Palace in Vienna, by Bellotto.

5. Catherine II of Russia.

Europe of the Enlightenment and the Encyclopaedists

ENLIGHTENMENT EUROPE was characterized by French domination and by the awakening of 'Germany' after 1770. Dutch, English and Italian influence declined: the universities of Leyden, Utrecht and Oxford had lost their vitality, and the Dutch republican model was no longer regarded as particularly inspiring by theorists, who saw it as suitable only for small states. English-style parliamentarism was admired by philosophers but not by sovereigns jealous of their power. Italy, the home of the arts, remained the country most visited by lovers of painting, opera and antiquities (the discovery of Pompeii and Herculaneum). According to Gibbon, 40,000 English people toured Italy in 1785, but there was a considerable decline in the overall number of visitors. After 1750, Italian artists were much less in demand and were replaced more often than not by French ones. In the field of the arts, the classical and neo-classical French influence won out over the baroque. The other states built palaces inspired by Versailles and constructed royal squares. In political matters, Louis XIV served as a model, while, culturally, the *philosophes*, who became the zealots of reason, freedom and tolerance, were a dominant force. Enlightenment culture was an élite culture (nobility and upper bourgeoisie) which was transmitted by way of national and provincial academies, masonic lodges (English and Scottish in origin) and salons (particularly those of Mmes Geoffrin, Deffand and Necker and of Mlle Lespinasse, all in Paris). Paris, the 'model for foreign nations' (Caraccioli) was the capital of taste and fashion, wit and good manners. The diaspora of French Protestants in their Dutch, Swiss and German havens ensured the spread of the language and culture. Holland and Switzerland became the great centres for the printing of banned books and Frankfurt a great market for French works. The principal European courts copied the French model: they wrote and spoke in French (which, since the Treaties of Utrecht, was the language of diplomacy) and they engaged the services of French tutors, scholars, actors, artists and architects. They copied Parisian fashions and they created academies. All this represented a court culture, imposed by the rulers. A reaction did, however, set in very early, especially in 'Germany' with Weimar and Dresden, faithful to their local Germanic culture, giving the lead. In Germany's dynamic universities (Leipzig, Halle, Göttingen, Königsberg) a generation was formed which further developed the specific traits of the German *Aufklärung*. This was rationalist in tendency in the work of Kant, for example, but was also characterized by a nostalgia for origins (Herder) and a certain world-weariness. The new generation was that of the *Sturm und Drang* epitomized by Goethe's *Young Werther*. This triumph of sensibility became a European phenomenon which at times developed into a taste for the morbid: the readers of Rousseau's *La Nouvelle Héloise* also appreciated Young's *The Complaint, or Night*

1. From left to right: Condorcet, La Harpe, Voltaire, d'Alembert, Diderot and le père Adam, as seen by J. Huber.

Thoughts, macabre meditations that were translated into all languages. The influence of 'German' culture was strong in the field of music, where Italian supremacy was now fiercely contested. Following on the heels of Handel and Bach, Gluck was a great success in Paris; Mozart, Haydn and, subsequently, Beethoven were also soon to make their reputations. In the later years of the century, the cosmopolitanism of the Enlightenment, illustrated by the diffusion of French culture, was everywhere receding. The first manifestations of nationalism appeared, with the virtues of national languages and heritages being extolled. This was a prelude to a new type of confrontation between states, one unknown in the century of the Enlightenment in which conflicts – localized and few in number (Wars of the Austrian Succession, 1741–8; Seven Years' War, 1756–63) – had remained an affair of princes rather than peoples.

Birth of Voltaire.   **Birth of Rousseau.**

1694	1712

1721: Montesquieu (1689–1755), *Lettres persanes.*
1723: J. S. Bach, *The St John Passion.*
1726: Voltaire (1694–1778), journey to England.
1730: Réaumur's thermometer.
1731: Academy of Surgery. Abbé Prévost, *Manon Lescaut.*
1733: Boerhaave, *Elements of Chemistry*; Pope, *Essay on Man.*
1735: Linnaeus, *Systema Naturae*; Rameau, *Les Indes galantes.*
1742: Young, *The Complaint, or Night Thoughts.*
1744: Piranesi, *Prisons.*
1748: Montesquieu, *L'Esprit des lois*; Hume, *An Enquiry Concerning Human Understanding.*
1749–51: Marigny, Cochin and Soufflet journey to Italy.
1749–67: Buffon, *Histoire naturelle.*
1750: Rousseau (1712–78), *Discours sur les sciences et les arts.*
1751–72: The *Encyclopédie* (banned in France in 1759).
1751: Voltaire, *Le Siècle de Louis XIV.*

1753–90: Grimm, Diderot, Raynal, *Correspondance littéraire.*
1754: Rousseau, *Discours sur les origines et les fondements de l'inégalité.*
1756: Voltaire, *Essai sur les moeurs.*
1757: Academy of Sciences and Fine Arts, Berlin.
1758: Russian Academy of Fine Arts.
1759–81: Diderot (1713–84), Accounts of the Paris Salons.

3. The so-called Temple of Neptune at Paestum, by Piranesi.

18th century

Europe of the Enlightenment

Uppsala
Stockholm
St Petersburg

Glasgow
Edinburgh

Cambridge
London
Greenwich
Amsterdam
Leyden
Copenhagen
Danzig

Arras
Amiens
Soissons
Rouen
Paris
Metz
Caen
Versailles
Göttingen
Halle
Berlin
Leipzig
Warsaw

Lunéville
Auxerre
Orléans
Strasbourg
Vienna
La Rochelle
Dijon
Besançon
Villefranche
Bordeaux
Geneva
Clermont-Ferrand
Montauban
Lyon
Pau
Nîmes
Turin
Venice
Toulouse
Avignon
Arles
Bologna
Béziers
Aix-en-Provence
Montpellier
Marseille
Florence
Lisbon
Madrid
Pisa
Corsica
Rome
Naples
Sardinia
Sicily

500 km

Principal stages in Mozart's musical career

Berlin
London
Brussels
Leipzig
Frankfurt
Prague
Paris
1777-1779
Vienna
Lyon
Geneva
★ Salzburg
Verona
Milan
Venice
Parma
Bologna
Florence
Rome
Naples

→ 1763-1766
→ 1769-1773
→ 1782-1783
→ 1788

Religious observance in XVIIIth Century Europe

500 km

rtistic movements

✱ Palaces designed on the Versailles model

Scientific and literary movements

🏛 Dynamic universities
● Great European academic centres
○ Academies in France at the end of the XVIIIth century
▣ Publication of scientific or philosophical journals
🔭 Creation of observatories

☐ Catholics
☐ Orthodox
▨ Protestants
▪ Moslems
▥ Protestant minorities

des lois.   The *Encyclopédie*.   **Mozart becomes a freemason.**   **Death of Condorcet.**

1748   **1751**   **1784**   **1794**

60: MacPherson, 'Ossian'.
61: Rousseau, *La Nouvelle Héloise*; euze, *L'Accordée du village*.
62: Rousseau, *The Social Contract* and *ile*; Gluck, *Orfeo*; Gabriel, the Petit anon.
63–79: Potsdam, the columns and buildings of Sans-Souci.
64: Winckelmann, *History of the Art of tiquity*; Voltaire, *Philosophical Dictionary*.
64–90: Soufflot, Sainte-Geneviève *antheon*).
65: Cavendish studies hydrogen.
66: Lessing, *Laokoon*; Bougainville's yage.
68: Cook's first voyage. Foundation of the yal Academy (London).
68: Gabriel, Place Louis XV (Concorde).
74: Herschel's Great Telescope; Goethe, *e Sorrows of Young Werther*.
75–9: Ledoux builds the salt-works of aux at Arc-et-Senans.
76: Adam Smith, *The Wealth of Nations*.
77: *Journal de Paris*, daily newspaper; W. Scheele separates hydrogen from rogen.

4. Ledoux's stage set for the theatre at Besançon.

1778: Mozart (1756-91) and Mesmer in Paris.
1781: Herschel discovers Uranus; publication of Rousseau's *Confessions*; Schiller's *Robbers*; Laclos, *Les Liaisons Dangereuses*.
1783: Lavoisier's analysis of water. First balloon flight.
1784: Beaumarchais, *The Marriage of Figaro*.
1785: David, *The Oath of the Horatii*; La Pérouse's voyage.
1787: Mozart, *Don Giovanni*; Bernardin de St Pierre, *Paul et Virginie*.
1788: Monge, *Traité de statistique*.
1789: Kalproth discovers uranium; Abbé Barthélemy, *le Voyage du jeune Anacharsis en Grèce*; William Blake, *Songs of Innocence*.
1791: Polish constitution; Mozart, *The Magic Flute*; Haydn, *Orpheus and Euridyce*.
1793: Suppression of the Paris Academies.

World Population

1500: Population of the world, before its systematic exploration by the Europeans, approximately 470 million. Main centres of population – India (including present-day Pakistan, Bangladesh, Nepal, Bhutan, Sri Lanka), approximately 95 million; China (including present-day Manchuria, Mongolia, western Turkestan, Tibet and Taiwan), 84 million; Europe, 78 million; central Sudan (including present-day Niger and Nigeria), 25 million; Peru and Mexico, each 12 million; Japan, 10 million.

1517: Death of almost one-third of Mexico's population, after spread of smallpox from Haiti. Same fate a little later for other American countries. Smallpox followed by other diseases: measles, typhus, diphtheria in 1531, 1545, 1564, 1576–7 and (the worst epidemic) in 1582. Beginning, nevertheless, of Spanish emigration to New World.

1. Slave ship at Goree, Senegal, late 18th century.

1518: Slaves from Black Africa taken to America by the Spanish to overcome shortage of manpower; from 1520, slave trade established on coast of Guinea.

1522–34: Significant drop in population of Western Europe, caused by famines, wars and epidemics.

1530: Beginning of rise of trade with America and India and of prosperity of Atlantic ports. Decline of Mediterranean trade and of economic role of Ottoman Empire. Population of the East at lowest level.

1542: Arrival of first shipload of African slaves in Brazil.

1556: 800,000 Chinese killed in Shaanxi earthquake.

1563: Plague epidemic throughout Europe; continuing increase in population.

1580–98: Population of France reduced by four million through epidemics and religious conflicts.

1582–3: Famines and serious epidemics in Saharan Sudan.

1588: Growth of Chinese population not hindered by great famine and epidemics affecting almost whole of China.

2. Slave merchants at Goree, Senegal, late 18th century.

1500

1 point: 1 million individuals

1600

16th–18th centuries

THE THREE CENTURIES from 1500 to 1800 form the first phase of an age of transition, the second phase of which we are still living through today: it is the age of the discovery of the world by Europe and of the cultural, technological and biological repercussions of that discovery.

In the sixteenth century the Muslim and Chinese worlds seemed to follow along with the European movements in scientific learning. But from the second half of the seventeenth century the closing of minds – even more than the closing of frontiers – meant that for three centuries (two in the case of Japan) the initiative in both technical progress and cultural development was held by Europe, and Europe alone derived benefit from it. This made for an even greater shock when, from political, commercial, religious or ideological motives, Europe and its influence eventually penetrated into all societies on earth. From the demographic point of view, the exchanges of microbes were particularly deadly to the American peoples: the arrival of smallpox in Mexico in 1517, for example, wiped out more than 30% of the population.

The map for 1500 shows the approximate distribution of the world's population at that date, on the eve of the spate of discoveries and journeys of exploration which would bring all those previously separate worlds into contact with one another. Each had lived until then inside its own system of religion, culture, cosmology and philosophy, which formed a coherent mental whole; its almost complete ignorance of all other societies had preserved this self-sufficiency. The principal centres of population at this time were India, followed by China, Europe, Western Sudan (Niger-Nigeria) and, in the New World, Western Mexico and Peru.

The map for 1600 shows the upheavals which, a century later, followed that initial shock: the terrible reduction – to almost one-fifth – of the American population and the stagnation and, in some cases, decline of the populations of Africa, Asia and the South Sea Islands. Only Europe saw a significant increase in its population.

On the map for 1800, two centuries later, a new demographic order can be seen. The population of Europe was still growing, as was that of China, which had isolated itself from the rest of the world and continued to live at its own rhythm. But the population of India was increasing only slightly, while that of America was stagnating, with the exception of the Atlantic coast of North America, where large numbers of immigrants were beginning to settle. The population of Africa, drained by the slave trade, was decreasing, as was that of the South Sea Islands, decimated by epidemics.

3. The plague in Marseille, 1720, depicted by Michel Serre.

1618–48: German population reduced through Thirty Years' War and epidemics by almost one-third from 15 million to 10 million.
1620: Beginnings of slave trade in English colonies.
1628–31: Terrible plague epidemics in Germany, France, northern Italy. Serious uprisings in China.
1636: Beginning of slave trade in French colonies.
1641–4: Famine, epidemics, uprisings, Manchurian invasions; fall in Chinese population estimated at 13 million.
1648–51: One million people killed by plague in Spain; population level not restored until 18th century.
1650–85: Population of Great Britain reduced by almost one million by civil war and plague.
1651–3: Nearly one million people killed in France by Fronde uprisings and plague.
1654–7: One-third of Polish population lost in wars against Russia and Sweden and in epidemics.
1689: Beginning of policy of repopulation of the Balkans with German settlers.
1690–4: Serious crisis of food shortages and epidemics in almost all Europe. Fall in European population at start of 17th century, from approximately 106 million in 1600 to 103 million in 1650, followed by slight increase to 114 million in 1700. Contrasting rise in Japanese population from 10 million in 1600 to 25 million in 1700.
1699: Sultanate of Oman established on east coast of Africa: new impetus to trade – existing since eighth century – of black slaves to Muslim countries.
1709–10: Severe winter and food shortages in Europe. Repeopling of northern Poland, east Prussia and Lithuania, following loss of half of population through famine, plague and smallpox.
1730: From this date, rapid rise in European population, from 114 million in 1700 to 180 million in 1800. (But in France, beginnings of contraception and fall in birth rate.) Even greater increase in Chinese population, from about 150 million to 330 million in course of century. Population of Japan level at 25 million.
1740–80: Slave trading by European merchants at its height – tripled since 17th century. Trade in Muslim countries doubled. In course of 18th century, population of Black Africa reduced by 10 million through slave trade.
1769–70: Great famine in Bengal, where the population is reduced from 29 million to 19 million.
1787: Beginning of movement in England for abolition of slavery.
1794: Abolition of slavery in French colonies decreed by Convention Nationale. Beginning of decline in European slave trade.

The Beginnings of the Industrial Revolution

THE INDUSTRIAL REVOLUTION – a British phenomenon above all – was at once the product of a specific historical experience limited to a particular geographical area and the result of the very broadest patterns of world historical development. Hence the ambiguous consequences of 'imitating' it and the sometimes tragic setbacks experienced by many of those who have sought to do so. Put simply, it consisted of a wave of particularly significant, sudden innovations, the unexpected, accidental character of which it would be foolish to deny, but which, nonetheless, followed on one from the other in a logical sequence. A series of convergent lines of technical development came together, and, in so doing, formed a new 'system'. Two such 'lines' were of particular importance: developments in textiles (notably the mechanization of the production process and the rise of chemical processes of bleaching and dyeing) and developments in coal fuel technology. Coal now had a double role, both as the principal fuel for treating and refining materials, and as a source of mechanical energy, which it had become thanks to the new 'atmospheric machines'. Each of the significant inventions of the time was in reality only one link in a continuous chain of interactions which continued a developmental process spanning many centuries. The Industrial Revolution was not a 'leap' in technological development; it was the outcome of a long learning process.

Before 1750 Britain was an advanced pre-industrial country: its agriculture was generally more efficient than Continental farming and its industry, which was expanding within a framework of domestic production, was becoming increasingly diversified. From the seventeenth century onwards Great Britain in fact enjoyed a market whose criteria were distinctly higher than those of Continental markets, and which, moreover, was capable of accepting new partially standardized products. Between 1500 and 1750 the growth in industrial production was of the order of 0.2% per head annually and the overall increase in production 0.45%. New technical avenues were evolved because as different types of production developed they came up against the right bottlenecks: a very early shortage of fuel in the case of the coal sector, a localized but marked shortage of labour in the case of textile mechanization. This pressure became more and more constraining after 1760 and especially after 1780: the increase in industrial production rose from 0.7% a year between 1700 and 1760 to 1.5% between 1760 and 1780, and 2.1% between 1780 and 1800. The role of exports, which was by no means negligible in the eighteenth century, now became crucial. The history of the cotton industry is exemplary in this regard: initially started as part of a substitution process – to displace imported Indian articles – after 1780 it was carried along by the very rapid rise in exports that increasing mechanization made possible.

In order to grasp the opportunities offered, on the one hand by the combination of the science and technology of the period and, on the other, by the pressure of demand, it was necessary for a stratum of industrial entrepreneurs to be formed, possessing a minimum of capital and capable of putting the available labour force to work. Even if the rates of capital accumulation did not achieve the wonderful leap forward that has been suggested, they nonetheless rose progressively throughout the period. On the micro-economic level, a minimal initial input was required, together with the will to reinvest the profits systematically. Here once again historical continuity came into play: the initiative was for the most part taken by traders or merchant producers, the most enterprising of whom transformed themselves into industrialists.

1. Open-cast coal mine in Great Britain, c. 1790. Steam pump invented by Thomas Newcomen.

A. Darby smelts iron with coke.

J. Kay invents the flying shuttle.

1709

1733

1698: Thomas Savery (c. 1650–1715) designs a machine aimed at draining water from mines ('the miner's friend').
1700: The rate of capital formation is 4% of gross national product (GNP) and exports represent 8.5% of national revenue.
1709: Abraham Darby (1677–1717) first smelts iron with coke at Coalbrookdale in Shropshire.
1712: Thomas Newcomen (1663–1729), a Dartmouth locksmith, builds the first piston-driven 'atmospheric machine'.
1733: John Kay (1704–64) invents the flying shuttle.
1740–50: B. Huntsman (1704–66) perfects the production of steel in a crucible furnace.
1746: John Roebuck (1718–94) perfects the iron chamber process for manufacturing sulphuric acid.
1748: The Darby process of cast-iron production using coke is improved by selecting ores that contain less phosphor.
1761: Adoption of cast-iron rails in the factories of Coalbrookdale.
1762: Matthew Boulton (1728–1809) builds his factory at Soho.

2. First entirely automatic loom built by Jacques de Vaucanson in 1745.

1767: J. Hargreaves, a Stanhill weaver, perfects the 'Spinning Jenny' for the spinning of cotton.
1769: R. Arkwright perfects his 'Waterframe' spinning machine. J. Wedgwood opens his 'Etruria' pottery works. First patents for J. Watt's steam engine.
1770: The share of exports in national revenue falls back to 7.6% after having reached 11.6% in 1759.
1771: Completion of Richard Arkwright's first factory at Cromford (Derbyshire).
1776: Adam Smith, the father of economic liberalism, publishes An Enquiry into the Nature and Causes of the Wealth of Nations.
1777: Arkwright builds a second factory at Cromford.
1779: Samuel Crompton invents the spinning mule. First cast-iron bridge over the Severn (J. Wilkinson).
1780: The rate of investment as a proportion of GNP reaches 7%.
1780–1800: Average annual growth rate of total production estimated at 1.2%. Growth of industrial production is 2.11%. Production per head is rising by 0.35%.

1782–5: Rotative beam steam engine invented by J. Watt. Henry Cort takes out his grooved rail patent.
1783: Exports as a proportion of national revenue at 7.8%.

3. Joseph Priestley (1733–1804), British chemist and philosopher, who discovered oxygen in 1774.

18th century

Great Britain's supremacy at the end of the XVIIIth century

RUSSIA

HOLLAND   SWEDEN

Ireland   RUSSIA

DENMARK   DANZIG

Channel Islands   GERMANY

Canada   FRANCE

Georgia   FLANDERS

New York   PORTUGAL

SPANISH   Newfoundland   ITALY   CHINA

Honduras   New England   SPAIN   TURKISH   EMPIRE

Pennsylvania   Minorca   LEVANT

Jamaica   Carolina   Virginia and Maryland

Gibraltar   Bengal

COLONIES   French West Indies   Bombay

East Indies

Senegal-Gambia

PORTUGUESE

COLONIES   **Value of British trade**

Accra   £ 2,000,000 sterling
£ 1,000,000
£ 500,000
£ 100,000

AFRICA

SPANISH
COLONIES   ● Imports from Great Britain
○ Exports to Great Britain
▣ Great Britain and colonies

St Helena

Arkwright's spinning machine.   N. J. Cugnot invents the steam road-carriage.   **First steam engine on rails by M. Boulton and J. Watt.**

1769   1770–1   **1785**

1784: Henry Cort takes out patent for the puddling process.
1785: Matthew Boulton and James Watt's first steam engine installed in a Nottingham cotton factory.
1787: Cartwright's semi-automatic weaving machine. Adoption of bleaching process using chlorine, invented by C. L. Berthollet in 1785. Foundations laid for Arkwright's New Lanark factory in Scotland.
1792: First successful attempt at gas lighting by William Murdoch.
1797: Henry Maudsley invents carriage lathe.
1801: Exports represent 17.8% of national income. The rate of investment reaches 7.9%.

4. The workshop at Soho near Birmingham, where Boulton and Watt's steam engines were built, c. 1790.

5. Galleries in the Bradley coal mine, Staffordshire, c. 1800.

Revolutions throughout the World

FROM AROUND 1760 ONWARDS, the revolutionary upheavals which had characterized the middle of the seventeenth century resurfaced on a wider scale and with even more striking effects. Out of the whole period in which the capitalist world market was being formed and rising to its zenith (from the end of the fifteenth century to the beginning of the twentieth), the years 1760–1800 or, more precisely, 1787–94, were the richest in socio-political innovation. The American Constitution of 1787 is still in force and the French Revolution is still a vital factor today. The reigns of Andrianampoinimerina in Madagascar (1787–1810) and the Tay Son brothers in Vietnam (1786–92) constitute major landmarks in the history of those countries; the movement of Tupac Amaru in Peru has been described as 'the greatest social revolution in Latin American history' (before Mexico in the second decade of this century) and Pugachov's was indisputably the greatest peasant revolt in Russia before 1917.

If the place occupied in this crucial period by Pascal Paoli's Corsica, the Tay Son brothers' Vietnam, Stanislaus II (Poniatowski)'s Poland and Tupac Amaru's Peru forces us to reject the expressions 'Atlantic Revolution' or 'Western Revolution', it is nonetheless true that Western Europe and North America were at the centre of the global historical process. And there is no doubt that the French Revolution was at the heart of the Western part of that process.

One should not, though, make too rigid a distinction between genuine revolutions and the many and varied vigorous attempts at reform which followed the Seven Years' War. The 'enlightened despots' of these decades and their ministers were great innovators.

Even though Louis XIV, George III of England and Joseph II of Austria were victims of the upheavals of the age, and the 1780s in particular were hardly favourable to the enlightened despots (some curious 'aristocratic reactions' emerged in the period), and though the first large-scale 'republics' known to history were born at that time, princely or royal 'revolutions' and popular revolutions had as much to unite them as to divide them.

If we ask what the common achievement of these revolutions was, the answer must be a rationalization of societies and cultures, a containment of religious influence and a general re-shaping of reality by the new spirit. They also achieved some democratization, the reduction or abolition of privileges, a reduction of differences in status, the passage from caste to class societies, and, therefore, the embourgeoisement of both the old and new élites. Together with this went a liberation of mercantile and productive energies, with, after the 1780s in particular, periods of anti-trade reaction such as are seen in the French Revolution and counter-revolution with their very marked peasant overtones and in Norway, the Ukraine, Rumania, China, Japan, North and South America etc. Finally, in many cases there was a clear restoration or reinforcement of the spirit of patriotism, to the detriment of colonial or cosmopolitan tendencies: there were moves towards integrating the Jews in Western countries, the first concerted abolitionist activities on the part of the North American Blacks, there were Indian and Creole risings throughout the Americas, and anti-Manchu plots and uprisings in China. Other important patriotic movements which surfaced during this period include the first signs of the assertion of Vietnamese identity, the beginnings of armed resistance by the great African peoples against Boer expansion, Greek insurrections against the Turks, the modest beginnings of the Italian *Risorgimento*, and the development of early German nationalism, not to mention the emergence of 'patriots' in France and elsewhere. ...

1. Emelyan Ivanovich Pugachov, 'Tsar of the Mujiks and Cossacks', anonymous Russian painting.

1755–69: Pascal Paoli is general of the Corsican nation; he is a kind of 'enlightened despot'.
1756–63: Seven Years' War: major turning-point in European and world history.
1759–60 onwards: Numerous peasant uprisings in Russia, Norway etc.
1760s: Democratic stirrings in Geneva, which in 1768 limits the privileges of the oligarchy in favour of the bourgeoisie.
1760–1820: George III King of Great Britain and Ireland. Upsurges of nationalist and democratic feeling in the country, which at times seems on the verge of revolution.
1761–82: Hyder Ali King of Mysore: reforms; war against the British. His son Tippoo (1782–99) continues his policy.
1764: Beginning of the reign of Stanislaus II (Poniatowski) in Poland. End of the nobiliary state. Period of reforms and enlightenment.
1768: Peasant rising in the Polish Ukraine; massacres of nobles and Jews.
1769: Publication begins of Nikolai Ivanovich Novikov's revue, *The Drone*, in Russia. It deals with peasant problem, problem of relations with Western culture.

c. 1769: Beginnings of *Sturm und Drang* literary movement in Germany, with democratic and nationalist tendencies.
1770: Anti-Turkish risings in Greece.
1770–1: Maupéou's reforms in France: attempt at 'Royal Revolution'.

2. The eldest of the three Tay Son brothers, the unifier of Vietnam. Stamp issued by the Democratic Republic of Vietnam.

1771: Beginning of the Tay Son insurrection – a national, popular movement – in Vietnam.
1773–4: Pugachov's revolt in Russia.
1774: Beginnings of anti-Manchu revolts in China – social movements with nationalist tendencies.
1775–83: American War of Independence.
1776: Revolt of Mapuche Indians in Chile.
1779–80: First 'Kaffir War' (Boer expansion comes up against native resistance).
1780s: Peasant risings in Norway, Massachusetts, Rumania, Ukraine, Japan etc., generally directed against merchants and speculators.
1780: Beginning of the social disturbances in Holland, which rapidly grow into the republican revolution. Grave failure of the King of Poland and his reform attempts.
1780–2: Tupac Amaru's rising in Peru.
1781: The Californian Indians massacre the Spaniards. Anti-Spanish movements in Colombia and Venezuela.
1782: Oligarchic reaction in Geneva.
1786–92: Reign of the Tay Son brothers in Vietnam, who carry out an impressive programme of modernization and unification.

3. Andrianampoinimerina, King of Madagascar. Anonymous painting.

1750–1800

BEFORE 1789

1780 *Republican revolution*
1760-80 *Uprisings*
1768 *Insurrection in the Ukraine*
1773 *Pugachov's revolt*
1770 *Anti-Turkish uprising*

1781
Massacre of Spaniards

1775-83
War of Independence

1781
Anti-Spanish movements

1780
Tupac Amaru's rising

1776
Revolt of Mapuche Indians

1780 *Uprising*
1787 *Reforms*

1774
Anti-Manchu revolts

1771
Tay Son insurrection

1761
King of Mysore's reforms.
War against the English

1787
Adrianampoinimerina's
modernization programme

1779 *Kaffir War*

1789 AND AFTER

1789 *French Revolution*

1791
Toussaint
Louverture's revolt

1804-25
Independence of
Latin America

1792
Assassination of
King of Sweden

1793-1802
Repression of the
Anti-Manchu movements

1795
Partition of Poland

1709
Selim III's reforms

1799
Fall of the Kingdom
of Mysore

Populated areas
Reforms
Revolts Revolutions
Revolts put down

4. *Gustavus III, King of Sweden, 'contemplating revolution beneath the gaze of Minerva and Justice'. Engraving by John F. Martin, 1784.*

1787: US Constitution and beginnings of French Revolution. First great democratic reforms in Denmark. Beginnings of the Kansei era reforms in Japan; these had an anti-trade, 'back-to-the-land' aspect.
1787–1810: Andrianampoinimerina becomes King of Madagascar. Great programme of modernization and unification carried out.
1788–92: Four Years' Diet meets in Poland: great debates, reforms.
1788–9: Anti-Portuguese plot in Brazil.
1789: Beginning of Turkish sultan Selim III's reforms directed against the traditionalists. Royal anti-aristocratic *coup d'état* in Sweden, but King Gustavus III is assassinated in 1792.
1793: Vendéan insurrection in France.
1793–1802: Savage repression of anti-Manchu movements in China.
1795: Third partition of Poland.
1799: Fall of the state of Mysore.

5. *Vendéan leader, Henri de la Rochejaquelin, pictured by Baron Guérin, 1817.*

The Age of Railways and Steamships

1. The first French railway, from Lyon to Saint-Etienne, in 1832.

IN 1840 THERE WERE 8,854 kilometres of railway track throughout the world; in 1860 there were 106,000 kilometres; of these, 50% were in North America and 47% in Europe (excluding Russia). In 1900 the figure was 750,000 kilometres, and in 1920, 1,086,000 kilometres; of these, 24% were in Europe (excluding the USSR) and 43% in America.

The lines which were built in the 1840s, 1850s and 1860s for the most part served areas where there was already considerable economic activity and therefore represented a good investment. Gradually, however, there developed a whole ideology of the railway, according to which railways could populate deserts and bring wealth to undeveloped regions. Building them became a concern of the state and largely exceeded simple criteria of economic rationality. The building of railways was, and remained, till just before the First World War, far and away the single most important reason for the export of capital and the main method of developing new territories. The American transcontinental railways constructed between 1864 and 1890 played a key role in populating and developing huge tracts of land, as did the Trans-Siberian Railway after 1891.

Fairly rapidly, however, it became clear that the building of railways could not of itself bring about the hoped-for prosperity. In this respect the history of railways is to some extent a story of lost illusions. Nevertheless, the returns on investment, even long afterwards, were always considerable. The expansion of the network and the rise in traffic gave the impetus to technical progress and made railways one of the main sources of innovation in the nineteenth century. The decisive turning-point came in the 1870s, which saw the simultaneous adoption of steel rails, electric signals, compressed-air brakes, hydraulic handling apparatus and other inventions. The development of

railways thus prompted many of the technical discoveries which were to be fundamental to the civilization of the twentieth century.

The age of sailing ships, which was dominated by American technological expertise, reached its height in the middle of the nineteenth century. It was the era of the clippers which plied from the east coast of America and California, carried on the tea trade with China and shipped convicts to Australia. In the world context the rise of the railway was inseparable from that of the steamship. In 1838 four British steamers crossed the Atlantic. But steam shipping came into its own in a real sense only after 1870, as a result of the completion of the Suez Canal in 1869 and the technical progress which reduced the amount of coal consumed in the steam engine. Sailing ships held their own over very long distances until the 1890s but by 1913 they represented only 8% of world shipping capacity (40% of which was British, whilst the Germans and Americans each controlled 11%).

The economic and geographic consequences of these two innovations complemented one another. Both had the effect of increasing the size of markets as well as the amount of economic activity. The expansion of newly emergent countries like the USA, the Argentine, Siberia and Australia, as well as many others, was closely linked to this. Everywhere new opportunities for trade became available, as was the case, for instance, with wine from the Languedoc or coal from Britain, both of which were exported worldwide. The trade in foodstuffs (which till the 1850s had been an exclusively European concern) now operated within a global market.

But over the same period railways and steamships made competition more acute because of the falls in tariffs. A process of depopulation and deindustrialization had been set irreversibly into motion that was ultimately to cause the Great Depression.

R. Fulton builds the first submarine.

1800

1814: George Stephenson builds his first locomotive.
1825: First line of railway track using steam traction opened in Great Britain.
1827: Marc Séguin invents his multitube boiler.
1829: Stephenson's *Rocket*, using the principle of the fire-tube boiler wins Rainhill Concourse.
1830: First locomotive built and first line opened in the USA. Stephenson develops in same year a locomotive using cylinders arranged horizontally.
1832: First railway line using steam opened in France.
1836: First patents granted for properly efficient steam-driven propellers.
1837: First railway line opened in Russia. In France, line opened between Paris and St Germain.
1838: Isambard Kingdom Brunel's *Great Western* crosses the Atlantic.
1839: First application in France of the guaranteed interest system for the financing of the Paris–Orléans line. R. and W. Hawthorn invent their steam superheater.

1842: French and Prussian laws defining the modes of concession of railway lines.
1846: First three-cylinder locomotive built by Robert Stephenson and William Howe. Concession of the 'ligne du Nord' between Paris and Lille to a consortium headed by Rothschild's Bank. Concession of the Paris–Strasbourg line.
1848: Brunel's *Great Britain*, first iron-built propeller-driven steamship.
1849: Crampton perfects his express locomotive.
1850: First railway line using steam opened in Mexico.

George Stephenson builds his first locomotive.

1815

Building of the Suez Canal.

1859–69

3. St Pancras Station in 1876.

2. A share certificate in a British shipping firm around 1880.

Railways in Europe, 1840

1850

1880

1000 km

The Transcaspian Railway.

1880–8

1850–60: Perfecting of the compound engine, which reduces the consumption of coal by half.

1853: First railway line using steam opened in India.

1854: First railway lines using steam opened in Brazil, Egypt and Australia.

1856: 'La Grande Société des Chemins de fer Russes' formed.

1859: Signing of the Franqueville conventions in France between the state and the railway companies. The railways become a national institution.

1860–70: First use in Britain, France and the USA of Bessemer steel for the manufacture of rails.

1862: The Steamship, *The Banshee*, is the first steel-built ship to cross the Atlantic. First steam railway line opened in Algeria.

1864–9: First American transatlantic service.

1867: First compound engine locomotive by John Lay.

1871: First multiple expansion engines for ships.

1872: First railway line using steam opened in

The Transsiberian Railway.

1891–1906 and 1907–17

Japan. Westinghouse invents his automatic compressed-air brake.

1876: A. Mallet invents his twin-cylinder compound engine.

1883: First railway line using steam opened in China. Signing of conventions between the state and the French railways which were to be seen as models throughout the world.

1891: The Tsar's rescript deciding upon the start of work on the Transsiberian railway.

1894: With the invention of radio, ships were no longer cut off from the outside world. Four-cylinder shipboard compound engine.

1897: First application of the steam turbine.

1909: First fitting of the steam turbine to a cargo ship.

The Birth of a Nation: USA

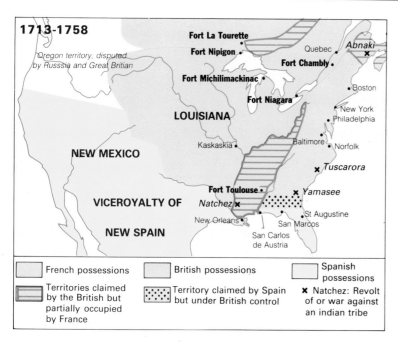

1713-1758

Oregon territory, disputed by Russsia and Great Britian

Fort La Tourette
Fort Nipigon
Fort Chambly
Quebec · Abnaki ×
Fort Michilimackinac
· Boston
Fort Niagara
LOUISIANA
· New York
· Philadelphia
Kaskaskia ·
Baltimore · · Norfolk
NEW MEXICO
× Tuscarora
Fort Toulouse ·
VICEROYALTY OF
Natchez ×
× Yamasee
NEW SPAIN
New Orleans · · St Augustine
San Marcos
San Carlos
de Austria

French possessions

British possessions

Spanish possessions

Territories claimed by the British but partially occupied by France

Territory claimed by Spain but under British control

× Natchez: Revolt of or war against an indian tribe

1763

CANADA

Oregon territory disputed by Russia and Great Britain

NOVA SCOTIA

LOUISIANA

NEW MEXICO

The thirteen colonies

Territory reserved for the Indians

VICEROYALTY OF

NEW SPAIN

500 km

British possessions

Spanish possessions

Boundary line laid down in royal proclamation

1. The American uprising: the statue of George III knocked off its pedestal, 9 July 1776.

PROSPECTS SEEMED VERY BRIGHT for the British Empire in the second half of the eighteenth century. The thirteen North American colonies had considerably expanded their agriculture, forestry and commerce, as well as their fishing and shipbuilding activities. The Seven Years' War (also known as the French and Indian Wars), which stripped France of its American possessions, rid the settlers of a dangerous rival. Nothing seemed to stand in the way of their territorial and economic expansion. And England, after this 'last war for the Empire', also saw the balance of power in Europe swinging in its favour.

But the war left England heavily in debt, and this new extension of the Empire required administrative and political reorganization. The hesitant, erratic and clumsy political actions of the crown came into conflict with colonial interests. The royal proclamation reserving the land west of the Appalachians for the Indians and the Acts of Parliament extending the English monopoly on maritime trade to new commodities and tightening English control over the colonial settlers were met in the colonies with petitions, pamphlets and a boycott of English goods. Tensions increased until, in April 1775, the first military hostilities broke out. The war, in which the settlers received aid from Louis XVI, was to last eight years. In July 1776 the Second

France is driven out of America.

1763

The 'Boston Tea Party'.

16 December 1773

Declaration of Independence

1776

1754–63: Seven Years' War or French and Indian Wars.
1763: Peace of Paris. France loses its possessions on the American continent. War by Pontiac, chief of the Ottawa Indians of the Great Lakes region, against the British. Royal proclamation forbidding the colonists to settle west of the Appalachians.
1764–5: Mercantilist laws on sugar, money and stamp duties. Protests in the colonies, including boycott of British products. Intercolonial Stamp Act Congress.
1766–7: The above-mentioned Acts are revoked, but the Townshend Act introduces duties on other commodities.
1773–5: Boston Tea Party; the Boston 'Sons of Liberty' throw East India Company tea into the sea. Parliament responds with coercive legislation.
1775: First clashes at Lexington and Concord between British troops and Massachusetts militia. The Second Continental Congress appoints Washington commander-in-chief of the colonial armies.
4 July 1776: Signature of the Declaration of Independence.

3. The 'Boston Tea Party', 16 December 1773.

1775–83: War of Independence. The first phase, which produces no definite outcome, ends in 1778 with the coming of the alliance with France (La Fayette and Rochambeau).
1777–81: The Articles of Confederation, the first constitution of the USA, are drawn up, then ratified.
1783: Peace of Versailles. Recognition of the United States.
1786: Revolt of the farmers, led by Shays in Massachusetts.
1787: North-West Ordinance, which regulates the admission of new states into the Union and the administration of the West. The Convention of Philadelphia draws up the Constitution.
1789: The Constitution is ratified and put into practice. George Washington President. Bill of Rights passed (the first ten amendments).
1791–2: Alexander Hamilton's fiscal proposals become law.
1791–4: Armed conflicts against the North-West Indian Confederation. Series of American defeats. Battle of Fallen Timbers: the Indians are defeated.

The War of Independence, 1775-83

Quebec
Montreal
Ticonderoga 1776
Saratoga 1777
Lexington 1775
Bunker Hill 1775
New York
Valley Forge 1777-78
Trenton 1776
Brandywine Creek 1777
Philadelphia
Victory of the Ohio River 1778
Yorktown 1781
King's Mountain 1780
Moores Creek Bridge 1776
Camden 1780
Charleston

→ Movements of British forces
○ Zones occupied by British forces
✕ British victories
→ Movements of American forces
✕ American victories

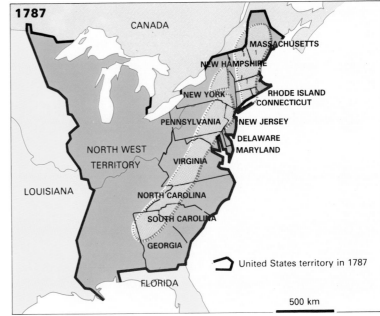

1787
CANADA
MASSACHUSETTS
NEW HAMPSHIRE
NEW YORK
RHODE ISLAND
CONNECTICUT
PENNSYLVANIA
NEW JERSEY
DELAWARE
MARYLAND
NORTH WEST TERRITORY
VIRGINIA
LOUISIANA
NORTH CAROLINA
SOUTH CAROLINA
GEORGIA
FLORIDA

⬠ United States territory in 1787

500 km

Continental Congress signed the Declaration of Independence of the United States.

But the unity of the new states, initially held together by war against the metropolis, was fragile. Apart from the internecine struggles between Loyalists and Patriots, the former colonies were divided over territorial questions, trade and the relative autonomy that was to be accorded to the individual states of the Union by the central government. The leaders also had to deal with revolts on the part of farmers and artisans against crippling taxes and oligarchic power.

The Articles of Confederation which set out the terms of the Union were thought insufficient by the more conservative of the new leaders. Meeting at Philadelphia in 1787, the delegates of the thirteen states drew up a constitution which established a powerful central government, whilst at the same time ensuring, by the federal system, the relative sovereignty of each member. Individual liberties were guaranteed by the first ten amendments, but Black slavery was maintained and the Indians were excluded from the American nation.

In 1789 George Washington became the first President of the United States; the legislative Congress was made up of two chambers and, with the Supreme Court as third power, a clear separation of powers was maintained, with the various institutions exercising a check on each other. During George Washington's two terms and that of John Adams, the 'federalist' conservatives interpreted the Constitution in such a way as to strengthen the position of the central government. Alexander Hamilton laid the bases for economic nationalism with the quasi-public Bank of the United States, a development plan for manufacturing industry, protectionist customs tariffs and the federal government's acceptance of responsibility for war debts. In foreign policy, the federalists conducted a covert war against revolutionary France. At home, they curbed individual freedom. These policies bred discontent among certain sections of the population and, upon being elected third President of the USA in 1801, Thomas Jefferson, the leader of the Democrats (or Radicals), announced a 'Second Revolution'.

2. The English plenipotentiary as seen by an American caricaturist, 1778.

Peace of Versailles.

Constitution. Washington President.

John Adams President.

Thomas Jefferson President.

1783

1789

1797

1801

1794: *Whiskey Rebellion* (Pennsylvania farmers' revolt).
1794–5: The Jay Treaty with England, Pinkney Treaty with Spain and Greenville Treaty with the Indians ease the course of expansion westwards.
1797: The federalist John Adams elected President.
1798: Covert war against France. Congress passes laws on aliens and sedition. Opposition leaders Thomas Jefferson and James Madison have resolutions adopted in Virginia and Kentucky declaring any law which infringes individual liberties null and void.
1800: Thomas Jefferson is elected President on the thirty-sixth ballot of the Congress. He will revoke the centralizing measures passed by the federalists.

4. White America and a young Black keep vigil at George Washington's tomb, c. 1800.

5. William Penn, the father of the constitution of Pennsylvania, a model for American institutions

The French Revolution

1. The storming of the Bastille, as seen by one of those involved, le sieur Cholat.

THE CRISIS which was to sweep away the *Ancien Régime* was born of a combination of three factors: first, a bad harvest, which produced, as usual, food shortages, unemployment, poverty and unrest; second, the financial deficit suffered by a state that had exhausted both its resources and the range of fiscal measures it could apply; and lastly, the resistance of the *'notables'* (representatives of the privileged orders: great nobles, bishops and *parlementaires*) and the *'parlements'* (sovereign courts of justice which were becoming a forum for political debate) to any reform of the royal finances that was not sanctioned by a meeting of the Estates General, where representation by social 'order' assured them of an automatic majority. When this body did meet, the Third Estate, which popular anger, the appeal to natural rights and the claim for equality before the law had momentarily united, became ever more ferocious in its denunciation of the seigneurs, privileges and despotism. The immediate causes of the revolution here met its deeper origins: the inevitable crisis of absolute power and its manifestations, the divorce between the theory and the actual development of a society of 'orders', the cultural transformations that had been taking place for the past century or more, Enlightenment teachings etc.

In summer 1789 an insurrection in Paris, an agrarian revolt and, most importantly, a political revolution all occurred simultaneously.

The political revolution broke with the 'organic' logic of the old social order: sovereignty changed hands, passing from the divine right of the monarch to the nation, the corporate entity was supplanted by the individual and the subject became a citizen. Liberty and equality were established, in theory at least, and privileges abolished. *The Declaration of the Rights of Man and of the Citizen* laid down the principles of a new legal system, that was subsequently enshrined in the constitution of 1791. Meanwhile, the deputies claimed church possessions for the nation and enacted the civil constitution of the clergy.

Successive factions came and went, their various external and internal conflicts all revolving around the same notions of national sovereignty, the popular will and the hydra of counter-revolution. From the monarchists to Robespierre, by way of Feuillants, Girondins, Dantonists and Hébertists, each succeeding group would be either deposed or executed, as Louis XVI was to be in 1793.

This uncontrollable dynamic, periodically re-stimulated by pressure from the street, culminated in the installation of a dictatorship and the Terror, a system of government which created new opponents as fast as it could eliminate old ones (in Paris, Lyon, Nantes, the Vendée etc.) and which finally devoured itself on 9 Thermidor.

These struggles unfolded against a backcloth of foreign war, entered upon, in a wave of enthusiasm, by the Legislative Assembly; the part played in this decision by ideological ambitions was as great as that played by classical reasons of state. Victory at Valmy safeguarded France against invasion; the Battle of Fleurus opened Europe for invasion and led to the subsequent great expeditions of Bonaparte (Italy and Egypt). But between these two dates a long series of reverses (Neerwinden, Valenciennes, Mainz, Toulon) imposed an unprecedented war effort on the young republic. In this regard, Thermidor brought a double respite. However, the advent of the Directory did not restore the republic's institutional stability, nor pacify its citizens. General weariness, an endemic civil war, a crisis of authority and the discredit into which the representative regime had fallen would ultimately sweep it away on 18 Brumaire.

2. Snuff-box of a Parisian sans-culotte, with the inscription, 'Peace to the simple folk, châteaux, death to tyrants', from the Convention period.

Tennis Court Oath.	Fall of the Bastille.	Louis XVI guillotined.
20 June 1789	14 July 1789	21 January 1793

22 February 1787: Assembly of Notables meets.
8 August 1788: The Estates General are called for 1 May 1789.
5 May 1789: Opening session of Estates General at Versailles.
17 June: The Third Estate declares itself a National Assembly.
20 June: Third Estate takes Tennis Court Oath.
14 July: Storming of the Bastille.
July–August: 'Great Fear' and peasant uprisings.
4 August: 'Feudal régime' abolished.
26 August: Declaration of the Rights of Man and the Citizen.
6 October: The King is brought back to Paris. The Assembly declares itself inseparable from the King.
2 November: The clergy's possessions are put at the disposal of the nation.
12 July 1790: Civil constitution of the clergy.
20 June 1791: Flight of the King and royal family; they are stopped at Varennes.
14 September: Louis XVI gives his sanction to the Constitution.

3. The politicization of women during the Revolution: here, in a picture by Lesueur, a patriotic club discusses the decrees of the Convention.

1 October: First session of the Legislative Assembly.
20 April 1792: France declares war on Francis II in his capacity as king of Hungary and Bohemia.
10 August: The people of Paris invade the Tuileries.
2–5 September: Massacres in Paris prisons.
20 September: Battle of Valmy.
21 September: First session of the Convention. Monarchy abolished.
21 January 1793: Louis XVI is guillotined.
1 February: The Convention declares war on Holland and England.
10 March: Revolutionary tribunal created.
11 March: Beginning of the Vendéan War.
18 March: Defeat of Neerwinden; French troops retreat from Belgium.
6 April: Committee of Public Safety formed.
31 May: Day of rioting against the Girondins.
28 July: Surrender to the British forces at Valenciennes.
27 August: Toulon is occupied by the British.
5 September. The Convention puts Terror on the order of the day.
5 October: Republican calendar adopted.

4. End of the Capetian monarchy: execution of the former King Louis XVI on the Place de la Révolution (now Place de la Concorde). Popular print, 1793.

1787–1799

The French Revolution

------ 1789 Frontiers

⊙ Revolutionary centres in 1789

▨ Regions touched by the Great Fear
(July-Aug 1789)

★ Main epicentres of panic
among the peasants

Counter-revolutionary risings

● Principal centres of counter-revolutionary activity

▨ Areas of Royalist insurrections

▨ Areas of Federalist insurrections

➤ Allied offensive, 1792-7

——— Less than fifty per cent
illiteracy rate in the North

Distribution of Jacobin Clubs 1789-1791

● Founded before
August 1790
● Founded between
August 1790 and
July 1791

Based on M.L. Kennedy
The Jacobin Clubs in the French Revolution, Princeton, USA, 1982.

Map labels: BRITISH AND DUTCH; HANOVERIANS AUSTRIANS; Rhine; Lille; Philippeville; Marienburg; PRUSSIANS; Landau; BRITISH; Le Havre; Rouen; Estrées-St Denis; Metz; Strasbourg; Caen; PARIS; Nancy; Versailles; Seine; Romilly; Colmar; Dol; CHOUANNERIE; Rennes; St Florentin; Savenay; Loire; Sancerre; Dijon; Besançon; Quiberon; Nantes; Bourges; Louhans; Émigrés; Cholet; Risings in the Vendée; AUSTRIANS; BRITISH; Ruffec; Lyon; Grenoble; Vizille; Bordeaux; Valence; SARDINIANS; Garonne; Cahors; Rhône; COMTAT VENAISSIN; Avignon; Nîmes; Montpellier; Marseille; SPANIARDS; Toulon; BRITISH; SPANIARDS; 100 km

---

Beginning of the Great Terror. | **Victory at Fleurus.** | **Bonaparte's Coup d'état.**

10 June 1794 | **26 June 1794** | **18 Brumaire Year VIII**

19 December: Recapture of Toulon by French forces.
8 June 1794 (2 Prairial Year II): Festival of the Supreme Being.
10 June (22 Prairial): Beginning of the Great Terror.
26 June (8 Messidor): French victory at Fleurus.
27 July (9 Thermidor): Warrant issued for Robespierre's arrest. He is guillotined the following day with Saint-Just, Couthon and 19 other Robespierrists.
21 January 1795 (3 Ventose, Year III): Freedom of worship granted.
31 May (12 Prairial): Revolutionary tribunal suspended.
23 September (1 Vendemiaire, Year IV): New Constitution proclaimed.
26 October (4 Brumaire): The Convention disbands.
31 October (9 Brumaire): Executive Directory elected.
2 March 1796 (12 Ventose): Bonaparte named commander-in-chief of army in Italy.
4 September 1797 (18 Fructidor, Year V): Coup d'état of the Directory against the

councils.
17 October (26 Vendemiaire): Peace of Campo Formio between France and Austria.
11 May 1798 (22 Floreal, Year VI): Coup d'état of the Directory against the left.
19 May (30 Floreal): Bonaparte sets out for Egypt.
25 July 1799 (7 Thermidor, Year VII): Victory at Aboukir.
9–10 November (18–19 Brumaire): Resignations of Ducos, Barras and Sieyes. Bonaparte, who had returned from Egypt on 9 October, is appointed commander of the French army in Paris. On 10 November Bonaparte, Sieyes and Ducos are appointed consuls.

5. The battle of Jemappes: victory of the French general Dumouriez over the Austrians, 6 November 1792. Popular print.

Bonaparte and the Lure of Empire

NAPOLEON BONAPARTE's 18th Brumaire *coup* discomfited only the Parisian 'political class'. Though he was installing a form of political regime in France that had no parallel in contemporary Europe – the enlightened despotism of a general bathed in military glory – he met with the general consent of the majority of the population, which was at once weary of the succeeding manifestations of the republic and yet unwilling to countenance a restoration of the monarchy.

In terms of the perceptions of their own age, the Consulate and the Empire could be thought of as phases of consolidation. The successive constitutions had gradually come to vest all power in a single man. It was self-evident that the period of France's apprenticeship in democracy (or at least in the operation of a representative regime) had been too chaotic. The pursuit of those goals would now be put off to other generations. Admittedly, the proclamation of the first emperor since Charlemagne might seem disconcerting, but was this not merely a means of continuing the consolidation process? The *Code civil*, the guarantee of the inviolability of the *biens nationaux*, the Concordat, the Legion of Honour, the reintroduction of titles of nobility (hereditary if primogeniture was accepted) satisfied the country's deepest needs, which were the confirmation of private ownership of property, the restoration of the values of authority, religion and the family, together with hierarchy and marks of distinction. These were all things for which the bourgeoisie clamoured. The France of 'orders' and privileges gave way to a France of notables, landowners and heads of families.

1. Bonaparte at the Council of Five Hundred, 19 Brumaire, Year VIII.

Being, at least in his early years, a man of 'consensus', Bonaparte found little opposition when he undertook the formidable task of reconstructing the administrative institutions. This reconstruction – completed around 1808 – was a prelude to the effective unification of France as a modern nation-state which, without doubt, was one of the most surprising consequences of the revolution.

Unfortunately, Napoleon Bonaparte had always had two contending sides to his personality: ultimately, his desire to rival Alexander vitiated the actions of the statesman within him. Internal stability was not accompanied by military and diplomatic stability, except during the truce constituted by the Peace of Amiens (1802).

2. Crossing of the Beresina, late November 1812. Gouache by General Fournier-Sarloves.

Europe saw Napoleon as the dangerous knight of the revolution, and he undoubtedly continued to subscribe to its essential political and social principles. He, for his part, saw the continent as the ideal terrain for building a political edifice in which France's frontiers would be extended with vassal states organized in a pyramid around her, allowing the personal ambitions of his own family to be satisfied and the continent to be unified as a trading area that was at once hostile to English commerce and accommodating to France's interests. The overweening nature of his ambitions, as they stand revealed in his attempts to conquer the Iberian Peninsula and the vastness of Russia, led Napoleon, from 1808–09 onwards, first through a series of partial failures and then to total catastrophe. In the process, he threw away not only his own personal success but also many of the achievements of the revolution.

As for Europe, it came out of the adventure profoundly transformed. It was henceforth hostile to France, which was now perceived to be as much a domineering, exploitative state as a land committed to propagating the ideals of the Enlightenment.

Beethoven: *Pathétique Sonata.*	Chateaubriand, *La Génie du christianisme.*	Fichte: *Addresses to the German Nation.*	Turner, *London seen from Greenwich.*
1799	**1802**	**1807–8**	**1809**

9 November 1799 (18 Brumaire, Year VIII): Transfer of the Assemblies to Saint-Cloud; de facto dissolution of the Directory; Bonaparte made commander of the Paris troops.
10 November (19 Brumaire): Bonaparte forces the Assemblies to cede power to three provisional consuls.
12 December: Bonaparte imposes the text of the Year VIII Constitution and becomes First Consul.
7 February 1800: Results of plebiscite on the Constitution: 3 million vote 'Yes', 1,500 'No'.
13 February: Creation of the Bank of France.
17 February: Creation of prefects and sub-prefects.
3 March: Closure of the lists of émigrés.
14 June: Bonaparte crushes Melas at Marengo.
3 September: The French surrender at Malta.
1 October: San Ildefonso Treaty with Spain: restitution of Louisiana to France.
24 December: Rue Saint-Nicaise assassination plot.
9 February 1801: Peace of Lunéville with Austria: France gains the Left Bank of the Rhine.

15 July: Signature of the Concordat.
25 March 1802: Peace of Amiens with England.
8 April: *Articles Organiques.*
26 April: Amnesty granted to all émigrés returning to France before 1 Vendemiaire, Year XI; creation of lycées.
20 May: Slavery and slave trade restored in the colonies.
2 August: Napoleon Bonaparte appointed First Consul for life.
23 January 1803: Bonaparte suppresses the Moral and Political Sciences class at the Institute.
20 March: Bonaparte declares the Peace of Amiens breached by the English.
21 March: Duc d'Enghien executed. *Code civil* promulgated.
18 May: Bonaparte proclaimed Emperor of the French under the title, Napoleon I (Constitution of the Year XII.)
19 May: Creation of 18 Imperial Marshalls.
2 December: Napoleon I's coronation.
17 March 1805: Napoleon made King of Italy.
21 October: France and Spain defeated at Trafalgar.

2 December: French victory at Austerlitz.
4 April 1806: Publication of the *Catéchisme impérial.*
10 May: University of France, an 'institution of public education', founded.
12 July: Confederation of the Rhine created.
6 August: End of Holy Roman Empire; Francis II resigns the Imperial Dignity and becomes Francis I, Emperor of Austria.
27 October: Napoleon in Berlin.
8 February 1807: Battle ('Butchery') of Eylau.
25 June: Meeting between Napoleon and Tsar Alexander I at Tilsit.
12 October: French enter Spain (with the aim of attacking Portugal).
2 May 1808: The population of Madrid attacks the French soldiers.
22 July: French surrender at Baylen.
13 May 1809: Napoleon enters Vienna.
1810: France annexes Rome (17 February), Holland (9 July), the Hanseatic towns and the Canton of the Valais (10 December).
2 April: Napoleon marries the Archduchess Marie-Louise.
8 February 1811: The French army sets out

discreetly for Russia.
20 March: Birth of the 'King of Rome'.
19 June 1812: Pius VII interned at Fontainebleau.
14 September: Napoleon enters Moscow.
27–29 November: Battle of Beresina.
11 January 1813: 250,000 Frenchmen technically eligible for military service between 1810 and 1815, called up.
21 June: Wellington wins Battle of Vittoria; French forces withdraw from Spain.
16–19 October: Napoleon loses Battle of Leipzig.
31 March 1814: Allies triumphantly enter Paris.
6 April: Napoleon's first abdication.
3 May: Louis XVIII enters Paris.
30 May: First Treaty of Paris: France loses most of the territory gained since 1792.
20 March 1815: Napoleon returns to Paris.
18 June: Napoleon defeated at Waterloo.
22 June: Napoleon's second abdication.

1799–1815

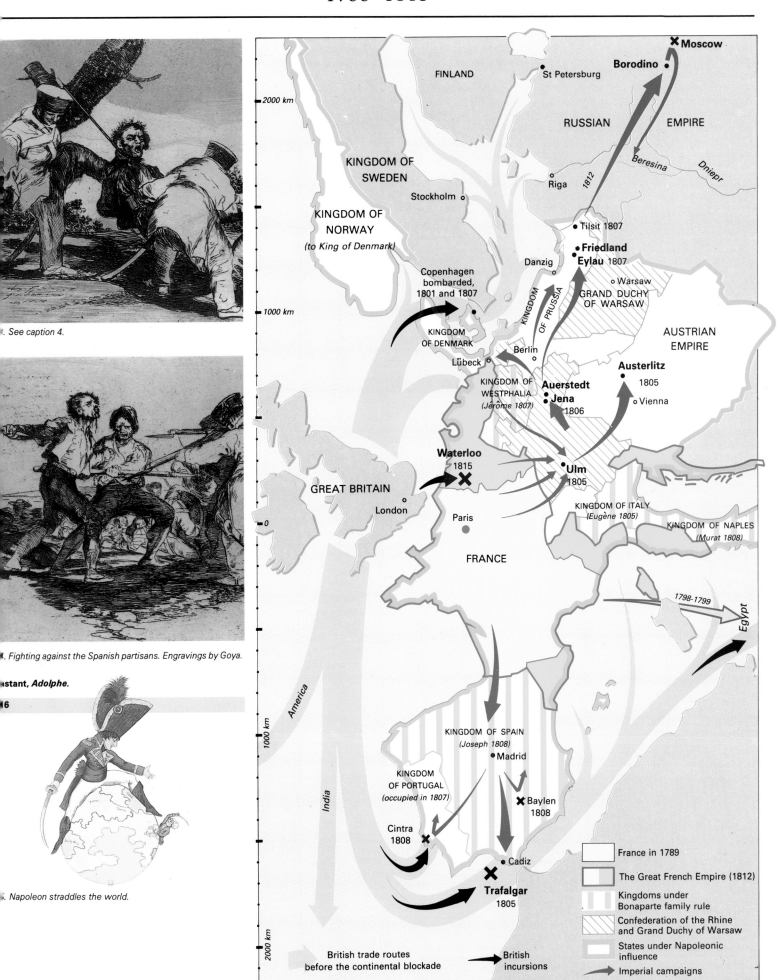

3. See caption 4.

4. Fighting against the Spanish partisans. Engravings by Goya.

stant, **Adolphe.**

6

5. Napoleon straddles the world.

FINLAND

St Petersburg

RUSSIAN EMPIRE

X **Moscow**

Borodino

Beresina

Dniepr

1812

KINGDOM OF SWEDEN

Riga

Stockholm

KINGDOM OF NORWAY
(to King of Denmark)

Copenhagen bombarded, 1801 and 1807

Tilsit 1807

Danzig

Friedland
Eylau 1807

Warsaw

GRAND DUCHY OF WARSAW

AUSTRIAN EMPIRE

KINGDOM OF DENMARK

Berlin

KINGDOM OF PRUSSIA

Lübeck

KINGDOM OF WESTPHALIA
(Jérôme 1807)

Auerstedt
Jena
1806

Austerlitz
1805

Vienna

Waterloo
1815 **X**

GREAT BRITAIN

London

X **Ulm**
1805

KINGDOM OF ITALY
(Eugène 1805)

KINGDOM OF NAPLES
(Murat 1808)

Paris

FRANCE

America

1798–1799

Egypt

India

KINGDOM OF SPAIN
(Joseph 1808)

Madrid

KINGDOM OF PORTUGAL
(occupied in 1807)

X Baylen
1808

Cintra
1808 **X**

Cadiz

X

Trafalgar
1805

2000 km

1000 km

0

1000 km

2000 km

British trade routes before the continental blockade

→ British incursions

France in 1789

The Great French Empire (1812)

Kingdoms under Bonaparte family rule

Confederation of the Rhine and Grand Duchy of Warsaw

States under Napoleonic influence

Imperial campaigns

Nationalism and Revolution

1. The 'Trois Glorieuses', July 1830. Fighting near the Porte Saint-Denis, as depicted by Delondre.

Europe at the time of the Congress of Vienna, 1815

—— Frontier of the German Confederation   Parma   Modena

POLITICAL ENERGIES during this period were, at first, directed towards the exaltation of nationalist sentiment. Romanticism at its height, with its demands for a return to the simple life, its attachment to folklore and its sympathy for oppressed peoples, paved the way for a considerable intellectual and artistic flowering in the period following the Congress of Vienna. It also laid the ground for an affirmation of cultural identity in Italy and Germany – though each was frustrated in its hopes of achieving unity – and among the peoples of Central Europe, who were subsumed against their will within the Turkish, Russian or Austrian Empires or into the Kingdom of Prussia.

The first insurrections bore the marks of this impulsion, though the wave of uprisings of 1820, which was a product of both nationalist and liberal demands, was quickly crushed. The case of Germany was quite specific and contrasts with the demands for independence and for a constitution that inspired the Spanish liberals, the Italian *carbonari* and later the Russian Decembrists. The problem of German unity had two stages to it. There was an initial need to produce an internal coherence within each of the thirty-nine states, whose frontiers con-

tained within them a number of ancient principalities; then to bring into being a greater German state that would have a more genuine existence than the German Confederation. The cause of unification was championed by groups from the universities, gathered together in an association, the *Burschenschaft*. This was suppressed in 1820 after having had some success in the granting of constitutions. It was Prussia, the principal countervailing power to Austria, which took the initiative in bringing about customs union (*Zollverein*), a sign that those states felt they shared common economic interests.

The support the Western powers gave to the Greek independence movement (after some initial reticence) was, however, as much a response to a public opinion that had been awakened to Romantic accounts of the plight of the Christian populations of the Ottoman Empire as it was the result of diplomatic considerations. The success of the movement showed that nationalist rebellions could only hope to succeed where they could ensure, if not the support, then at least the neutrality of the great powers.

It was the July Revolution in France, which was as much national

Rising in Serbia led by M. Obrenovic.

Chios massacres.

1815

3. Anonymous French picture honouring Greek independence fighters, 1821.

1815–17: Serbia gains independence.
1820: In Naples, Piedmont and Spain, officers lead army rebellions and force their sovereigns to grant constitutions. These risings are crushed by the French and the Austrians.
1821–32: First Eastern crisis: Greek independence (7 May 1832).
December 1825: Tsar Nicholas I puts down the insurgents in Moscow who were demanding a constitution.
11 January 1828: Signature of a treaty of customs union (*Zollverbund*) between Prussia and Hesse-Darmstadt. This is in time extended to the majority of the German states and transformed into the *Zollverein* (from 1 January 1834).
1830: Agitation in Germany: the sovereigns of Hanover, Saxony and Brunswick agree to promulgate constitutions. The Diet of the German Confederation presided over by Austria passes six articles limiting the powers of the Constitutional Assemblies and renewing its restrictions on the universities, the press and on the right of assembly.
In Switzerland, the liberal opposition wins

April 1822

4. 'Patriots of all lands, beware!' The execution of two Italian nationalists, 16 June 1831. Lithograph by Daumier.

electoral successes in various cantons and modifies their constitutions. The seven Catholic cantons will form a separatist *Sonderbund* in 1845.
27–9 July 1830: July Revolution in France. After the signature of four reactionary ordinances, three days of rioting and barricades (the 'Trois Glorieuses') leave Charles X no alternative but to abdicate.
7 August: The Chamber of Deputies recognizes the King's abdication and calls on Louis-Philippe, king of the French, to reign with a revised charter. Revolutionary fever spreads throughout Europe.
25 August: An insurrection of the bourgeoisie and the popular classes in Brussels calls on the Dutch king to respect basic law and the separation of powers. A provisional government proclaims independence in October. France threatens to defend Belgium in case of intervention. In December the London Conference recognizes the independence of Belgium and, on 20 January 1831, its perpetual neutrality. After some minor military excursions the Dutch king accepts the *fait*

1815–1832

The revolts of 1816-22

FRANCE
AUSTRIA
Turin
SERBIA
Naples
GREECE
Cadiz

The revolts of 1827-32

RUSSIAN EMPIRE
HANOVER
BELGIUM
Brussels
SAXONY
Paris
AUSTRIA
Parma
Modena
MARCHES
GREECE

))) Revolt   Granting of a constitution   → Repression   C Independence

2. The echo of the 'Trois Glorieuses' in Warsaw. Parisian engraving.

ist as liberal in inspiration and which reflected the frustrations produced by both the Treaty of Paris and the Restoration, that gave the signal for a wave of revolutions in Europe. The accession of a bourgeois king, carried to power by street rioting, gave birth to great hopes, as can be seen from the fact that it was immediately followed by the Belgian revolution. One of the members of the Belgian provisional government arrived in Paris to request material aid from Louis-Philippe. Though that aid was refused, the revolutionaries did receive effective diplomatic protection which, when coupled with a military expedition, would prove sufficient to ensure Belgian independence.

There were stirrings of revolt in a great number of countries, including the southern German states, northern and papal Italy and Poland. In spite of sympathy in some quarters for these movements, France refused to intervene and they were rapidly snuffed out.

The July monarchy did not therefore fulfil the hopes it had aroused, either in France or abroad. 1830 remained a passionate but abortive manifestation of the aspirations of the European peoples.

Battle of Navarino Bay. **Revolution in Paris (the 'Trois Glorieuses').** **Independent Belgian constitution proclaimed.** **Greece wins independence.**

20 October 1827 **27–29 July 1830** **11 February 1831** **7 May 1832**

5. Women appear on the barricades, Paris, July 1830. Painting by Manguin.

accompli.
29 November: Revolt in Warsaw. An insurrectionary government is formed and on 25 January 1831 the Diet of Warsaw announces that Tsar Nicholas has been deposed. Warsaw falls to Russian troops on 8 September and the revolution is crushed.
1831–2: Italian revolutionary movements at Modena, Bologna, Parma, Piacenza and in the Marches. The Austrians occupy the Duchy and the north of the Papal States. A French expeditionary force, designed to prevent them from advancing too far in the peninsula, lands at the port of Ancona and remains there till 1838. Sporadic insurrections occur until 1848.

6. 'Order reigns at Warsaw': a lithograph by Grandville after the crushing of the insurrection.

From the Holy Alliance to the Eastern Question

1815-27: The first nationalist movement

1827-29: Independent Greece

It was at the Congress of Vienna that the political reorganization of Europe was negotiated between the states allied against Napoleon. Two principles regarded as crucial to the maintenance of order governed those negotiations: dynastic legitimacy and the balance of power. To this purely geographical arrangement, there was added the Holy Alliance, which lacked any real force, and the Quadruple Alliance, which affirmed the solidarity of Prussia, Austria, Russia and England against the revolutionary forces. Provision was made for congresses, which were to provide forums for dialogue and platforms for intervention. It was at such congresses that military expeditions were decided upon, such as the Austrian expedition to Italy and the French one in Spain. Though modern in its preoccupation with collective organization, this diplomatic machinery – largely inspired by the Austrian chancellor Metternich – nonetheless revealed a total inability to understand national and liberal aspirations. The basic underlying idea was one that belonged to the *Ancien Régime*.

The first Eastern crisis (Greece, 1821–32) revealed its weaknesses: the crisis involved an implicit challenge to the dynastic principle, but Western pressures on Sultan Mahmud II were connected rather with the problem of Russian access to the Mediterranean through the Black Sea Straits, which posed a threat to British maritime supremacy. The European revolutions of 1830 modified the Vienna balance: France passed into the camp of liberal nations and supported

1. The 'Kings' Cake' or the division of Europe at the Congress of Vienna, as seen by an unknown French caricaturist.

Congress of Vienna.	Death of Byron at Missolonghi.	Navarino.
September 1814–June 1815	**19 April 1824**	**20 October 1827**

23 September 1814–9 June 1815: Congress of Vienna.
26 September 1815: Holy Alliance.
20 November 1815: The Second Peace of Paris settles France's new frontiers and the Quadruple Alliance is signed. France is integrated into it at the Congress of Aix-la-Chapelle (30 September–21 November 1818).
1820–1: The Austrian Empire is mandated to intervene militarily in Turin and Naples by the Congresses of Troppau (2 October–17 December 1820) and Laibach (26 January–12 May 1821). In 1822, France will be entrusted with the mission of restoring order in Spain.
March 1821: The Archbishop of Patras and a member of the Hetaera (a patriotic society) summon the Greeks to insurrection.
1822: Turkish sultan Mahmud calls on the help of the Egyptian Pasha Mehemet Ali (Mohammed Ali) in the fight against the Greek insurrection. He wins victories at Navarino, Missolonghi and Athens (1825–7).
6 July 1827: A treaty between Britain, France and Russia proposes a settlement whereby the Sultan is to remain suzerain of an

3. *Mehemet Ali, Viceroy of Egypt from 1804 to 1849, in the period of his victory over the Mamlukes. Anonymous artist, 1811.*

4. *Prince von Metternich-Winneburg (1773–1859), by Sir Thomas Lawrence, 1818.*

autonomous Greece. After Mahmud II's rejection of this proposal, the British destroy the Turco-Egyptian fleet at Navarino (20 October).
14 September 1829: By the Treaty of Adrianople, the Turks accept Greek independence under Turkish suzerainty and cede various territories to Russia.
1830–1: European revolutions.
7 May 1832: The London Convention makes Greece a *de jure* independent kingdom.
December: War between Egypt and Turkey. The Egyptian army routs the Turks in Syria and at Konieh. Mahmud II calls on the great powers for aid.
1833: At the Conference of Teplitz and Münchengrätz, Russia and Prussia form a conservative alliance. Beginning of the crisis of the Spanish succession.
February: The Russian fleet occupies the Bosphorus. France and Britain put pressure on Turkey and Egypt to come to an early settlement.
May: The Sultan cedes the whole of Syria to Egypt by the Treaty of Kütahya.
July: Treaty of Unkiar-Skelessi (Turkey)

1814–1846

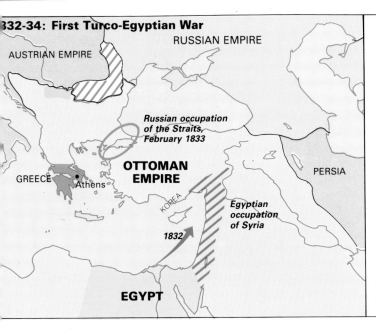

1832-34: First Turco-Egyptian War

RUSSIAN EMPIRE

AUSTRIAN EMPIRE

GREECE ·Athens

OTTOMAN EMPIRE

PERSIA

Russian occupation of the Straits, February 1833

Egyptian occupation of Syria

1832

EGYPT

1839-41: Second Turco-Egyptian War

RUSSIAN EMPIRE

AUSTRIAN EMPIRE

OTTOMAN EMPIRE

GREECE ·Athens

PERSIA

Closure of the Straits (Treaty of London, 1841)

Nezib 1839

British offensives, 1840

·Beirut

Alexandria

EGYPT

e cause of Belgian independence against the Dutch king. The buffer little states that was intended to isolate Central Europe from ssible French contagion crumbled away. In spite of the formation n the pretext of difficulties in the Iberian Peninsula) of a liberal nt to oppose the conservative alliance, Europe in the period after 30 was dominated by two great antagonisms, the one between ussia and England and the other between Russia and France.

The second Eastern crisis (Egypt 1832–41) saw the liberal states at gerheads, with France supporting the Egyptian Pasha, Mehemet i, who had gone to war against his sovereign. The Treaty of nkiar-Skelessi, which established a virtual Russian protectorate er the Ottoman Empire, saved the latter and gave Russia access to e Mediterranean. The defeat of Mahmud II gave England an portunity to propose the establishment of a collective European otectorate over Turkey at the Conference of Vienna, which effec- ely snatched away Russia's newly-won advantage. In the final ase of the Egyptian crisis, the Anglo-French antagonism grew, and ench blunders allowed the British Prime Minister, Palmerston, to tain the neutralization of the Straits, whilst leaving Mehemet Ali reditary Pasha of Egypt.

The key feature of the 1840s was European expansionism. The tente between France and England was re-established, in spite of me colonial differences. The marriage of Queen Isabella II of Spain

to her cousin the Duke of Cadiz in 1846 reawakened a hostility which ruled out the possibility of any middle ground being found; the conservative powers were able to impose their law on the Catholic cantons of Switzerland and on insurgent Polish Prussia.

However, behind the interplay of commercial and territorial rival- ries, the rise of nationalist aspirations was laying the ground for the 1848 'Springtime of the Peoples'.

2. Louis-Philippe, king of the French, welcoming Queen Victoria at Le Tréport in September 1843, as portrayed by François-Auguste Biard.

eek Independence.

The Ottoman Empire defeated at Nezib.

Convention of the Straits.

May 1832

June 1839

13 July 1841

tween the Ottoman Empire and Russia kes provision for mutual assistance and closure of the Straits to any foreign fleet eight years, making the Black Sea a vast ssian roadstead.

April 1834: Signature of a liberal adruple Alliance between France, Britain, ain and Portugal to prevent the return of solutism in Spain (Don Carlos and Dom guel).

ne 1839: Sultan Mahmud II attacks Egypt. dies after the defeat at Nezib. The powers et at Vienna to seek a common solution.

July 1840: After secret attempts at diation by the French, Britain, Prussia, ssia and Austria sign the Treaty of London, ich gives Mehemet Ali hereditary ssession of Egypt and southern Syria for . When he refuses the arrangement, merston bombards Beirut and in cember, after deploying the British fleet Alexandria, wins Egypt's unconditional rrender.

July 1841: Egyptian crisis ended on terms d down by Treaty of London. Convention of Straits is signed, closing them to

warships of all nations.

1846: Austria annexes the Cracow Republic after the uprising in Polish Prussia.

5. Capture of Trocadero, near Cadiz, by the French expeditionary force (31 August 1823). Engraving by Ledoyen.

6. Caricature of Talleyrand, Paris, 15 April 1815.

South America at the time of the Caudillos

1. *San Martín at the battle of Chacabuco (2 February 1817), by Géricault.*

THE OCCUPATION of Spain and Portugal by Napoleon's armies an threats of a French or English conquest of South America prompte certain South American élites to take over the actual running of thei countries and very soon to seek political independence. This move ment towards emancipation was general but not unanimous: it too various and sometimes contradictory forms. Spanish America wa the scene of fifteen years of civil war that divided every stratum c colonial society; the partisans of independence fought for motives a diverse as religious integration (in Quito) and liberal principles (i Buenos Aires and Venezuela). Others sought to free themselves a much from Southern American powers on whom they were depen dent as from the colonial powers; this was the case for Ecuado Bolivia, Paraguay and Uruguay.

The independence of Spanish America resulted first of all in th fragmentation of the sub-continent into small units, sparsely popu lated and weakened by war. Much of the countryside was ruined, th population dispersed and decimated, administration reduced to bare minimum. The new states went through thirty years of instabil ity aggravated by the *caudillos*, local chieftains whose irregular armie fought for domination. Civil wars continued up to the 1860s, wit federalists confronting partisans of a centralized state.

Brazil was free of these wars and disturbances. In January 1808 th Portuguese royal family and government officials took refuge in Ric the administration of the new state was handed over to the Infant Pedro, who was declared Emperor in 1822, and the transition wa thus accomplished smoothly. When Brazil became a republic in 188 this also happened without disruption.

Towards the middle of the century the budding states were able t emerge from their difficulties by exporting their natural resources Peruvian guano, Ecuadorian cocoa, Brazilian and Venezuelan coffee Argentine and Uruguayan cattle, Bolivian and Chilean ores, wer exported to the United States and Europe, particularly Britain, which controlled a great part of the South American market and invested i the sub-continent.

Argentina, which won its 'frontier' by waging campaigns on th Indians of the interior, and, to a lesser degree, Chile and Brazil wer peopled by immigrants from Europe; the gap widened between thes states and the others, some of which, such as Peru, Bolivia and Paraguay, suffered from the expansionist designs of their powerfu neighbours.

At the end of the century South American governments, converted to liberal economics and influenced by positivist philosophy, attemp ted to modernize the societies they controlled. They met with resis tance from a traditionalist population, provoking revolts among th Indians and messianic movements in the Sertão.

Death of Aleijadinho in Brazil.

1814

1807–8: British attempts to conquer the Rio de la Plata meet with resistance from local inhabitants.
1808: Spain occupied by Napoleonic armies. Legitimacy of colonial government in question, communications difficult.
1809–12: First South American insurrections at Chuquisaca, La Paz, Quito, Santa Fé, Caracas, Buenos Aires.
1811: The independent town of Buenos Aires sends expeditionary force to the provinces of the interior to win them over to its cause.
1814–40: Dictatorship of de Francia in Paraguay. Communication with other countries outlawed.
1818: Chilean independence.
1819: Venezuela and Colombia become independent (definitively in 1830).
1821: Precarious independence of Peru; San Martin appoints himself protector.
1822: Guayaquil conference, following which General San Martin retires from South American scene in favour of Bolívar.
1824: Battle of Ayacucho ends war of independence in Peru.
1825: Province of Banda Oriental becomes

Death of Bolivar and Sucre.

1830

independent and takes name of Uruguay (definitive independence in 1828). Bolivia declares its independence against wishes of Peru and Argentina.
1825–c. 1855: Instability becomes general: caudillos engage in civil wars and risk themselves in frontier expeditions.
1828–38: Government of Marshal Santa Cruz in Bolivia.
1830: Partition of Gran Colombia in three states: Ecuador, Colombia and Venezuela. Assassination of Sucre. Death of Bolívar.
1831–89: Reign of Pedro II in Brazil. He abdicates in 1889 and republic is proclaimed.
c. 1850: Abolition of slavery in most states except Cuba (1886) and Brazil (1888). New states adopt their own legal systems and abandon Spanish law in force until then.
1850–60: Presidency of Marshal Castilla in Peru. The country amasses a shortlived fortune by exporting guano.
1864–70: Triple Alliance war. Paraguay is attacked by Brazil, Uruguay and Argentina in coalition and loses nine-tenths of its male population.
1879–83: Pacific war between Chile and an

End of war that destroyed the Triple Alliance.

1870

2. *An imperial philosopher: Don Pedro II, in 1855.*

alliance of Peru and Bolivia; Bolivia loses its coastline and Peru its saltpetre mines. Chile controls Pacific.
c. 1880: End of Indian wars in Argentina and Chile.
c. 1880–1900: Conservative but modernizing régimes in most South American states. Programmes of road, rail and telegraph development. Exportation of natural resources.
1895–1903: Liberal coups d'état, civil wars between liberals and conservatives in Chile in 1891, Ecuador 1895, Uruguay 1897, Bolivia 1899, Colombia 1899–1902; Thousand-Day War in Venezuela 1899–1903.
1897–8: Messianic uprising of the *Canudos* in the hinterland of Bahia, Brazil.

1800–1900

Wars of Independence

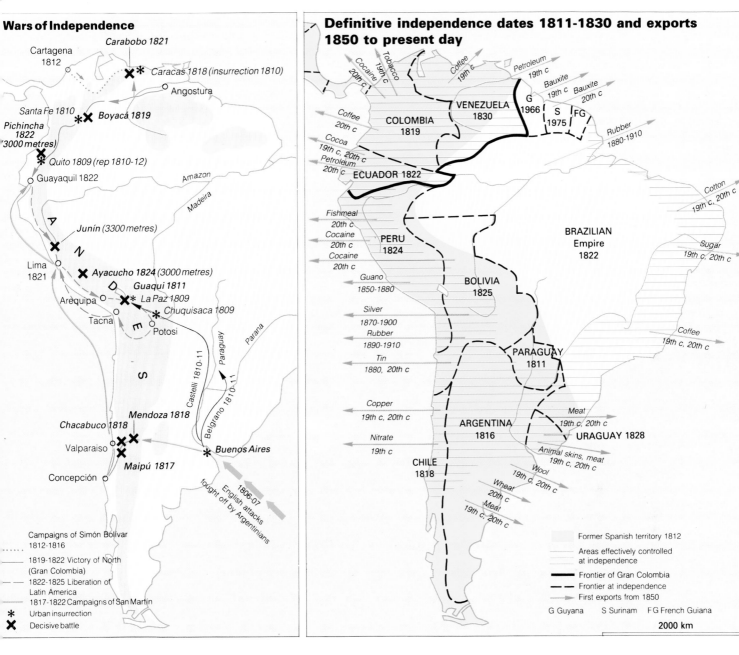

Cartagena 1812
Carabobo 1821
✕✳ Caracas 1818 (insurrection 1810)
○ Angostura

Santa Fe 1810
✳✕ *Boyacá 1819*
Pichincha 1822 3000 metres)
✳ Quito 1809 (rep 1810-12)
○ Guayaquil 1822

Amazon
Madeira

A
N
Junín (3300 metres)
✕
Lima 1821 ○
D
✕ *Ayacucho 1824 (3000 metres)*
Guaqui 1811
Arequipa ○ ✕✳ *La Paz 1809*
E
Tacna ○ ✳ *Chuquisaca 1809*
S ○ Potosi
Paraguay
Parana
Castelli 1810-11
Belgrano 1810-11

Mendoza 1818
Chacabuco 1818
✕✕
Valparaiso ✕✕
Maipú 1817
Concepción ○
✳ *Buenos Aires*
1806-07 English attacks fought off by Argentinians

········ Campaigns of Simón Bolívar 1812-1816
——— 1819-1822 Victory of North (Gran Colombia)
– – – 1822-1825 Liberation of Latin America
—·—· 1817-1822 Campaigns of San Martín
✳ Urban insurrection
✕ Decisive battle

Definitive independence dates 1811-1830 and exports 1850 to present day

Cocaine 20th c
Cocaine 19th c
Tobacco
Coffee 19th c
Petroleum 19th c
Bauxite 19th c
Bauxite 20th c

VENEZUELA 1830
G 1966
S 1975
FG

COLOMBIA 1819
Coffee 20th c
Cocoa 19th c, 20th c
Petroleum 20th c

ECUADOR 1822
Rubber 1880-1910

Fishmeal 20th c
Cocaine 20th c
Cocaine 20th c

PERU 1824
Guano 1850-1880
Silver 1870-1900
Rubber 1890-1910
Tin 1880, 20th c

BOLIVIA 1825

BRAZILIAN Empire 1822

Cotton 19th c, 20th c
Sugar 19th c, 20th c

PARAGUAY 1811
Coffee 19th c, 20th c

Copper 19th c, 20th c
Nitrate 19th c

ARGENTINA 1816
Meat 19th c, 20th c
URAGUAY 1828
Animal skins, meat 19th c, 20th c
Wool 19th c, 20th c

CHILE 1818
Wheat 20th c
Meat 19th c, 20th c

░ Former Spanish territory 1812
≡ Areas effectively controlled at independence
▬▬ Frontier of Gran Colombia
– – – Frontier at independence
→ First exports from 1850
G Guyana   S Surinam   F G French Guiana

2000 km

José Hernandez: *Martin Fierro*
1872

Republican constitution in Brazil.
1891

3. Simón Bolívar frees the Colombian slaves, as portrayed by Luis Cancino Fernandez.

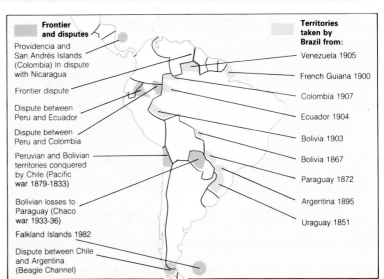

Frontier and disputes

Providencia and San Andrés Islands (Colombia) In dispute with Nicaragua

Frontier dispute

Dispute between Peru and Ecuador

Dispute between Peru and Colombia

Peruvian and Bolivian territories conquered by Chile (Pacific war 1879-1883)

Bolivian losses to Paraguay (Chaco war 1933-36)

Falkland Islands 1982

Dispute between Chile and Argentina (Beagle Channel)

Territories taken by Brazil from:

Venezuela 1905
French Guiana 1900
Colombia 1907
Ecuador 1904
Bolivia 1903
Bolivia 1867
Paraguay 1872
Argentina 1895
Uraguay 1851

Central America

ECONOMIC EXPANSION based on exports made Latin America in the late nineteenth century a reserve for world capitalism. It generated an embryonic middle class whose vast fortunes were spent in Europe while leaving the greater part of the population in extreme poverty, a situation that led to the eventual downfall of the regimes that had created the new order.

This was to happen in 1910 with the Mexican revolution. The long presidency of Porfirio Díaz (1876–1911), supported by ministers with modernizing, anti-clerical attitudes who were fascinated by the North American example, ended in a civil war bringing into play the reaction of a still largely traditional population and the centrifugal tendencies of a vast and poorly administered country. The confrontation between government forces and opposition armies was followed first by clashes between rival factions, then by the religious war of the *Cristeros* (partisans of Christ the King). The Cárdenas government (1934–40) gave some impetus to agrarian reform and the situation became more stable; the only party (the PRI – Institutional Revolutionary Party) now held power unopposed and a state with unprecedented powers was established.

Central America and the West Indies were then under United States protection. Cuba and Nicaragua were ruled by fierce dictatorships for several decades.

The First World War broke the traditional patterns of trade and immigration; it also brought into question European political and cultural models. In addition, with the opening of the Panama Canal in 1914 and the withdrawal of European powers, the United States acquired a much greater hold on the sub-continent, over and above their historical domination of the Caribbean and Central America by such well-known tactics as the 'big stick' and 'dollar diplomacy'.

The crisis of 1929 dealt Latin America a severe blow: the flow of capital stopped, the price of raw materials collapsed. In the larger countries, however, it was useful in stimulating the creation of industries to replace goods until then imported. But social problems were soon overtaken by political ones.

From 1930 onwards instability became the rule; the military, supported by some politicians, plotted to take over government.

Industrial and office workers and sections of the middle classes withdrew their support from the liberal parties in favour of more immediate solutions confidently offered by popular leaders in direct contact with the masses. This marked the rise of populist movements backed by the trade unions, whose policies were progressive and nationalist but whose practices were often quite moderate. Although some real improvements were made, particularly in conditions of life in the cities, and although the regimes did wish to modernize their countries, no real reforms were made in the countryside, powerful vested interests remained unchallenged and the military stayed close to the seat of power.

In Cuba and then in Nicaragua the 'rebels' went much further in overthrowing the old ruling classes and challenging American domination; however, they paid the price of dependence on the USSR, and the revolutionary societies themselves became militarized. The United States in turn provided massive aid to the enemies of Nicaragua's Sandinista government, the Contras.

Meanwhile, from the 1960s the Caribbean states and Central America were going through a rapid process of decolonization: Jamaica and Trinidad and Tobago became independent in 1962, Barbados in 1966, the Bahamas in 1973, Grenada in 1974, Dominica in 1978, Saint Lucia in 1979, Saint Vincent and the Grenadines in 1979, Antigua, Barbuda and Belize in 1981 and St Kitts and Nevis in 1983.

1. March of Castro's forces on Havana, early January 1959.

War between USA and Mexico. Emperor Maximilian shot at Queretaro. Pancho Villa, Mexican revolutionary. D. A. Siqueiros: *The Devil in the Church.* Juan Rulfo: *Pedro Pará*

| 1846–8 | 19 June 1867 | 1878–1923 | 1947 | 1955 |

1810–11: First popular insurrections in Mexico in favour of independence, led by priests Miguel Hidalgo and José Maria Morelos.
1824: Birth of Mexican Republic after an attempt at establishing a Creole empire. In 1833 General Santa Anna sets up a long series of dictatorships punctuated by civil wars (up to 1855).
1839: Central America splinters into many states. In spite of all attempts to form a federation during the century (particularly by Rufino Barrios, President of Guatemala), 'Balkanization' is inevitable.
1861: Mexican liberals defeat conservatives. Their leader, Juárez, suspends repayment of foreign debt, thus provoking French intervention.
1862: French occupation in support of Emperor Maximilian; he is defeated and shot by troops led by Juárez in 1867.
1867–76: Period of reform in Mexico, first modernizing and secularizing measures.
1868–78: Cuba fights for independence and eventually fails.

2. The 1810 War of Independence in Mexico, as seen by Diego Rivera, 1929.

3. The Cristero rebels, opponents of aggressive anti-church measures, Tlalpujahua, 1926.

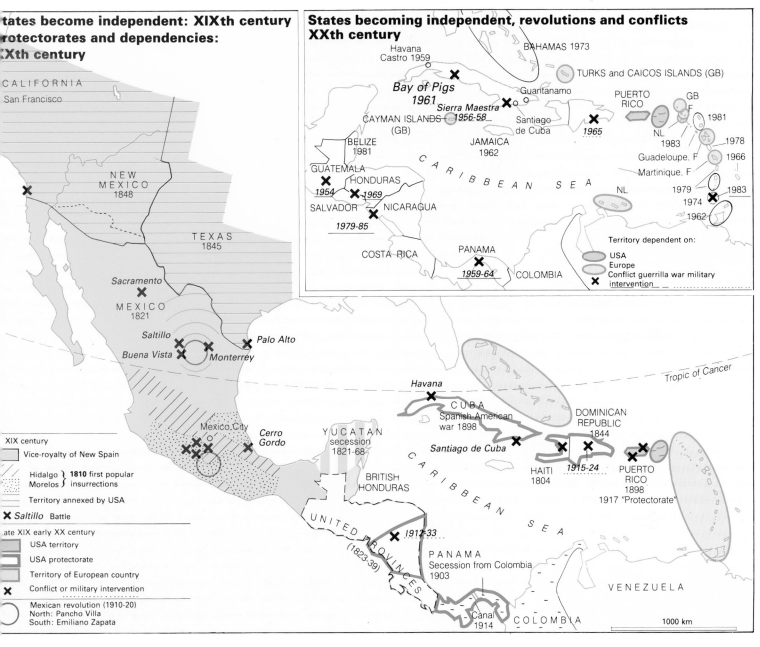

tates become independent: XIXth century rotectorates and dependencies: XXth century

States becoming independent, revolutions and conflicts XXth century

CALIFORNIA
San Francisco

NEW MEXICO 1848

TEXAS 1845

Sacramento

MEXICO 1821

Saltillo
Buena Vista — Monterrey — Palo Alto

Mexico City — Cerro Gordo

YUCATAN secession 1821-68

BRITISH HONDURAS

UNITED PROVINCES (1823-39)

1912-33

PANAMA Secession from Colombia 1903

Canal 1914

COLOMBIA

VENEZUELA

Havana
CUBA Spanish-American war 1898
Santiago de Cuba

HAITI 1804

DOMINICAN REPUBLIC 1844

1915-24

PUERTO RICO 1898 1917 "Protectorate"

CARIBBEAN SEA

Tropic of Cancer

1000 km

Legend
XIX century
- Vice-royalty of New Spain
- Hidalgo } **1810** first popular Morelos } insurrections
- Territory annexed by USA
- ✗ Saltillo Battle

Late XIX early XX century
- USA territory
- USA protectorate
- Territory of European country
- ✗ Conflict or military intervention
- ○ Mexican revolution (1910-20) North: Pancho Villa South: Emiliano Zapata

States becoming independent box
Havana Castro 1959
Bay of Pigs 1961
Sierra Maestra 1956-58
Santiago de Cuba
Guantanamo
BAHAMAS 1973
TURKS and CAICOS ISLANDS (GB)
PUERTO RICO
GB F
1981
NL 1983
1978
1965
Guadeloupe, F 1966
Martinique, F
1979
1974
1983
1962
NL
CAYMAN ISLANDS (GB)
BELIZE 1981
JAMAICA 1962
GUATEMALA
HONDURAS
1954 1969
SALVADOR NICARAGUA
1979-85
COSTA RICA
PANAMA 1959-64
COLOMBIA
CARIBBEAN SEA

Territory dependent on:
- USA
- Europe
- ✗ Conflict guerrilla war military intervention

jo Carpentier: *El Siglo de las Luces.*   Jose Lezama Lima: *Paradiso.*   Gabriel Garcia Márquez: *One Hundred Years of Solitude.*   Miguel Angel Asturias: *Viernes de Dolores.*

62   1966 1967   1972

3–85: Rufino Barrios dictator in atemala.
6–1911: Porfirio Díaz governs Mexico, ining presidency in six successive ctions.
8: Spanish-American War: Cuba gains ependence but ends up an American tectorate in all but name.
3: Panama secedes from Colombia, ported by North American intervention.
0–20: Mexican Revolution.
2–33: United States occupies Nicaragua, i (1915–33) and Dominican Republic 16–24). Founding of APRA (Alianza ular Revolucionaria Americana) in Mexico y by Peruvian Raúl Haya de la Torre, to roup revolutionary tendencies in Indian erica.
5–33: Dictatorship of General Machado Cuba.
7–9: War of the Cristeros in Mexico, a ular reaction against anti-religious policies he revolution.
4–40: Lázaro Cárdenas president of xico; reformist policies.

1936–79: Dictatorship of Samoza family in Nicaragua; this is overthrown by a massive insurrection led by Sandinista party which takes power.
1939–59: Dictatorship of Batista in Cuba; overthrown by guerrilla fighters led by Fidel Castro.
20 August 1940: Assassination of Trotsky in Mexico.

4. Emiliano Zapata.

1950–4: Arbenz Guzman president of Guatemala.
1957–71: Francois Duvalier dictator in Haiti.
21 April 1961: Attempted landing by anti-Castro forces in Bay of Pigs.
1962: International crisis provoked by installation of Soviet missile bases in Cuba. Beginning of Nicaraguan guerrilla war.
1963–9: Crisis in Dominican Republic; military intervention by USA.
1969: War between El Salvador and Honduras.
1978: Dormant civil wars erupt in Central America (Guatemala, El Salvador, Nicaragua).
1982: Unprecedented economic crisis in Mexico.
7 February 1986: Fall of Haitian dictator Jean-Claude Duvalier.
1989. 19 March: In El Salvador, A. Cristiani defeats J. Napoleon Duarte in the presidential elections.
7 May: As a result of fixed elections in Panama, General M. Noriega remains in power.
20 December: The United States invades Panama to oust Noriega and set up a new government.

5. Daniel Ortega on the first day of his presidency, Managua, 1985.

The Springtime of the Peoples

A TANGLED WEB of anti-feudal, democratic, social and nationalist aspirations existed in Europe in 1848. Widespread revolution was the outcome. The economic crisis in Britain in 1847 and the Chartist movement, the hunger riots caused by the food shortages of previous years, the Polish uprising of 1846 signaling the democratization of the nationalist movement, and the civil war in Switzerland, were all precursory signs of the revolutionary explosion. Italy, as yet still an abstract entity, was ablaze from north to south and Hungary was trying to shake off the Austrian yoke. The monarchy in France had been abolished at the end of February, and the outlines of a modern democratic social system were taking shape with the Luxembourg Commission and the setting up of National Workshops. Starting in southern Germany, the democratic revolutionary movement brought about both a pre-parliamentary body (which was to lead to the Frankfurt elected assembly and to a government devoid of power) and the Vienna and Berlin uprisings. Finally, Prague rose up as the effects of the Czech national movement were felt, and formed a pan-Slavic democratic congress in which the only Russian was Bakunin.

Having returned to Cologne, Marx and Engels took part in the revolution and published the *Neue Rheinische Zeitung*. The counter-revolution celebrated its first victories in Paris during the bloody 'June days' that were triggered off by the announcement that the National Workshops were to be closed, whilst in the elections for the Assembly the rural areas had already enabled the moderate elements to win a triumphant victory. There were victories, too, in Prague, where the uprising was crushed and the pan-Slavic congress dissolved, and in Custozza, where the army of Charles Albert was defeated by the Austrians. In contrast, Vienna continued to resist the inconsistencies of government policy and sided with the Hungary of Kossuth, whose armies in turn supported the Viennese rebellion until it was crushed. In Germany the Frankfurt Parliament's acceptance of the armistice with Denmark marked the final abandonment of the German national cause in Schleswig and Holstein and unleashed the second wave of revolution in Frankfurt and in the south-west. The republican idea gained ground in Italy, where, both in Rome and Florence, the Republic was proclaimed, though not in Manin's Venice (a bastion of resistance to the Austrians). Although international intervention by the revolutionaries – by the French in Germany and Belgium and by the Germans on behalf of the Poles in Posen – had been hesitant and contradictory in nature, reactionary intervention was in a much more offensive style. Under cover of containing the Austrian advance, the French got the better of the Republic of Rome, while Russian troops, called to the rescue by the Emperor of Austria,

Liberal movements before February 1848

RUSSIAN EMPIRE

PRUSSIA

Cracow

Paris

AUSTRIA

Ferrara

|)))) Victorious struggle of the liberals | o))) Unrest, civil war | ⌒ Granting of a constitution | → Repressio |

1. The barricades in the Avenue Brigida in Naples, 15 May 1848. Anonymous painting.

Uprising in Paris.	Uprising in Vienna.	Berlin.	Pan-Slavic Democratic Congress of Prague.	Workers' riots in Paris, 'the June Days'
22–25 February 1848	**13–15 March 1848**	**18–22 March 1848**	**2–28 June 1848**	**23–6 June 1848**

12 January: Palermo uprising.
10 February: Constitution granted to Naples and to Florence (17th).
22–5 February: Uprising in Paris, proclamation of the Republic, creation of the Luxembourg commission and national workshops.
March (beginning): Liberal governments in several German states; peasant uprising in the south-west.
5 March: Promulgation of the constitution (Statuto) of Charles Albert, King of Sardinia; German liberals and democrats meeting in Heidelberg decide to assemble a pre-parliamentary body.
5–6 March: Troubles in Glasgow.
13–15 March: Uprising in Vienna, flight of Metternich.
14 March: Rome constitution.
17–22 March: Uprising in Venice; Daniele Manin proclaims the Republic.
18–22 March: In Berlin, Frederick William IV grants a constitution. Uprising in Milan against the Austrian occupation.

3. Allegory of the Republic. Anonymous French painting.

22 March: Charles Albert declares war on Austria.
26 March–7 May: Riots in Madrid.
31 March–3 April: Meeting of the pre-parliamentary body (Vorparlament) in Frankfurt.
12–20 April: Uprising in Baden.
23–4 April: Extreme left defeated in French elections.
April–May: Polish uprising in Posnan.
15 May: Demonstrations in Paris and Vienna.
15–16 May: Popular uprising crushed in Naples.
18 May: First session of the Parliament of Frankfurt.
22 May: Start of the Prussian National Assembly.
2–28 June: Pan-Slavic Congress of Prague.
11–17 June: Prague uprising crushed.
15 June: Workers' riot in Berlin.
23–6 June: Workers' riot in Paris put down by Cavaignac.
22 July: Opening of Austrian Parliament in Vienna.
22–5 July: Austria (Radetzky) defeats Charles Albert at Custozza.

July–August: Irish rebellion fails.
23 August: Uprising in Vienna.
23 August–3 September: Congress of Workers' Associations in Berlin.
7 September: Abolition of feudal régime in Austria.
10 September: Jellačic's Croatian troops attack Hungary.
16 September: Parliament of Frankfurt ratifies the Malmo armistice of 26 August, setting off the 18 September uprising in Frankfurt.
21–4 September: Failure of the republican endeavour in Baden.
6–31 October: Revolution in Vienna.
15–16 November: Republican uprising in Rome.
22 November–7 March 1849: Austrian Parliament sits at Kremsler.
2 December: Franz Josef Emperor of Austria.
5 December: Dissolution of the Prussian National Assembly.
10 December: Louis Napoleon Bonaparte elected President of the French Republic.
February 1849: Republic proclaimed in

1848

iberal movements after February 1848

Berlin
Frankfurt
Paris
Prague
Vienna
Venice
Bucharest

Order restored 1848-1852

RUSSIAN EMPIRE
PRUSSIA
AUSTRIA
FRANCE
Budapest
Novara · Custozza
Ferrara
Rome
Bucharest

)))) Victorious struggle of the liberals	⌒ Granting of a constitution	→ Repression	▨ War of Independence

crushed the Hungarians. The final offensives in Germany – in Saxony with Bakunin, in Baden, in the Palatinate and in the Rhineland with Engels – were launched to support the constitution voted through by the Parliament of Frankfurt, but this was rejected, together with the imperial crown and its 'plebeian' associations, by Frederick William IV. At the same time French intervention in Rome set off the final convulsive movements of the people's revolt in Paris and Lyon.

Despite their general failure, the 1848 revolutions, as well as achieving the abolition of seigneurial privileges, did allow clarification of the division between democrats in general and democratic-socialists, and as the revolutions unfolded the independent organization of the working class began to emerge. But the revolutions also revealed the complexity of radical movements within particular countries; for example, in Hungary, the revolutionaries' refusal to respond to supporters of Slav national liberation – particularly the Croats – made the nationalists allies of the monarchy.

2. Riot scene in Berlin, June 1848. Engraving by P. C. Geissier, Nuremberg.

evolution in Vienna.

Republic proclaimed in Tuscany and Rome.

Proclamation of Hungarian independence.

–31 October 1848

8–9 February 1849

14 April 1849

Tuscany (8th) and in Rome (9th).
15–30 March: Ancient powers re-established in Parma, Modena, Florence.
23 March: Charles Albert abdicates, defeated at Novara by the Austrians.
28 March: The Parliament of Frankfurt adopts the constitution of the Reich and offers the imperial crown to Frederick William, who refuses it (28 April).
14 April: Kossuth proclaims Hungarian independence at Debrecen.
3 May–23 July: Uprisings in Saxony, Baden, Palatinate, Rhineland.
11 May: Restoration of absolute monarchy in the Kingdom of the Two Sicilies.
23 May–13 August: Victorious Tsarist intervention against Hungary.
30 May–18 June: The Parliament leaves Frankfurt and sits in Würtemberg.
15 June: Workers' uprising in Lyon.
1 July: Surrender of Rome.
22 August: Surrender of the Republic of Venice.

. The Viennese watch over the German democrat, Robert Blum, after his execution in October 1848. Lithograph by H. Shanes, 1851.

5. Lajos Kossuth (1802–94), leader of the Hungarian nationalist revolution. Anonymous painting.

Europe: From Romanticism to Positivism

IT MAKES GOOD SENSE to speak of a separate historical entity called the nineteenth century, even if this entity does not fit exactly into the chronological frame of a century. Between the Napoleonic era and the First World War we can identify a relatively homogeneous period easily distinguishable both from the period 1640–1800 and from the twentieth century that followed. It is often said that the nineteenth century was a religious century, a century in reaction against the rationalism of the 'Century of Louis XIV', the Enlightenment and the French Revolution. This observation holds true only if one does not attribute the generally high levels of artistic and scientific creativity found during this period to the burgeoning pioneering and avant-garde movements of the time, which were above all rationalist in inspiration: and further if one separates this high level of creativity from the rise of mass production, which can after all be considered to have spread the spirit of the Enlightenment, albeit in a vulgarized form, rather than to have denied it.

Nonetheless, the nineteenth century did challenge excessive faith in reason in the name of morality and the mystical, and what's more, it also put abstraction in the dock in the name of singularity and sensuality. It was 'realistic' after its own fashion, even if subject to some degree of hallucination. It was the century of the concrete, of the novel in literature, of induction and experimentation in science and of the close study of history and geography. There was a general passion for detail and fine distinctions; the age adored local colour, cultivated a feeling for nature and freely indulged in pantheism and pansexualism. Not least, the nineteenth century exalted the individual over the group and tended to contest the disciplines, rules and norms which the classical spirit (and even the revolutionary spirit) considered indispensable.

These characteristics are essentially those of Romanticism. Some further secondary features can be added to this picture. It is clear, for example, that Romanticism developed links at a very early stage with political liberalism and also with nationalism. In Germany, for example, Romanticism cannot be understood unless one takes into account the desire to be free of French influence. In Spain, 'Romantic' meant the opposite of 'servile'.

Yet, if the nineteenth century was the century of Romanticism, it was also the century of Positivism. That is to say, the philosophical and scientific tendency of the age was towards description and induction, as is illustrated by the strong predeliction for the natural sciences and their methods. Ultimately, the nineteenth century can only be seen as homogeneous in relation to what preceded it and what followed it. It can be broken down into three great sub-periods. The second of these (1855–85) saw a reaction against Romanticism properly so-called (1800–55, the first sub-period), appearing less moralistic and religious, and if anything even more obsessed by natural and material realities but also less indifferent to the demands of commun-

ity, less free in its attitude to conventions. As for the third period (from around 1885: Symbolism, Modernism, Idealism ...), it saw a protest against scientism, a rediscovery of the sacred and a partial rehabilitation of the symbol and the concept. It also saw some staunch battle fought in defence of the individual.

A deeper study would have to go beyond this tripartite chronological schema to produce a more thorough inventory of these longer sub-periods and, in particular, to examine shorter sub-divisions 1828–44 (Romantic freedoms but also rationalist achievements ..., 1869–79 (religious offensives and resistance, flowering of utopian thinking and poetry ...), 1900–10 (movements towards secularizatio and social preoccupations ...). We would also have to show the ver broadly European and worldwide character of these turning-points i collective sensibility.

1. Victor Hugo, standard-bearer of Romanticism. Caricature by Montbard in Gulliver, c. 187C

1797–1804: First German Romantic Movement. A.W. and F. von Schlegel (founders of the review Athenäum (1798).
1798: Beginnings of English Romanticism: W. Wordsworth, Lyrical Ballads; S. T. Coleridge, Recantation.
After 1799: Strong religious revival.
1802: Chateaubriand's Génie du christianisme.
1804: Birth of Russian prophetic monasticism. Rise of German Romanticism.
1805: Chateaubriand's René.
1805–7: Hegel's thought undergoing development. Primacy of history; hostility to the Enlightenment. The Phenomenology of Mind published in 1807.
1812–22: Alessandro Manzoni's Inni Sacri.
1816: The 'Romantic Battle' begins in Italy.
1816–17: Leopold von Ranke, the greatest scholarly historian of the century, has elaborated his method.
1819: Géricault's Raft of the Medusa.
1828: Anti-clerical measures in France.
1830: Success of Berlioz's Symphonie fantastique. The 'battle' over Hernani (Hugo's play) in France. Goethe opposes

3. Georg Wilhelm Friedrich Hegel, German philosopher (1770–1831). Copy of a portrait by E. Born, 1831.

Romanticism. First volume of what will become Balzac's Comédie humaine is a satire of romantic dreams, Scènes de la vie privée (1830–2).
1830–42: Publication of the six volumes of Auguste Comte's Course of Positive Philosophy.
1839–1841: F. Chopin's 25 Preludes.
1842: Publication of the first part of N. Gogol's Dead Souls.
1844–5: Upsurge of Romantic movements in France, Germany and Italy. Realist tendencies developing, especially in painting.
1846–9: The 'Forty-Eighters', Romantic revolutions, Christian socialism.
1853: Verdi's La Traviata.
1855: In Piedmont, Cavour launches an attack on monastic property, Gustave Courbet's Exhibition seen as a Realist 'insurrection' (especially The Burial at Ornans, The Studio). Offensive of biological evolutionism with Herbert Spencer (Principles of Psychology) and A. R. Wallace. L. Büchner's Kraft und Stoff (Energy and Matter). Materialism has some success. N. G. Chernyshevsky's Anti-Romantic

Manifesto. He becomes leader of Nihilist thinkers (A Vital Question or What is to be done?, 1863).
1855–7: Taine's Les philosophes français du XIXe siècle.
1856: First publication of Flaubert's Madame Bovary.
1857: Attacks in Germany on Hegel and metaphysics.
1859: Charles Darwin's The Origin of Species by Natural Selection.
1862: Otto von Bismarck Chancellor. Realpolitik.
1862–3: E. Renan is appointed to the Collège de France and publishes The Life of Jesus.
1863: Failure of insurrection in Poland: end of Polish Romanticism.
1865–9: Tolstoy's War and Peace.
1866: Dostoyevsky's Crime and Punishment.
1869: Meeting between Monet and Renoir. Towards Impressionism.
1869–70: Zola and his friends develop Naturalism.
8 December 1869–18 July 1870: First Vatican Council. Traditionalism affirmed.
1872: Dostoyevsky's The Possessed.

2. Les Énérves de Jumièges, *as imagined by Evariste Vital Luminais (1822–96).*

1874: E. Boutroux's philosophical thesis, *De la contingence des lois de la nature.*
1876: Inauguration of the theatre at Bayreuth. Wagner's *Ring* cycle performed.
1878: Election of Pope Leo XIII, who will attempt to make the church more in touch with the modern world.
1880: The *lois laiques* in France.
1882: Death of Charles Darwin (national funeral). Triumphal reception of H. Spencer in USA.
1885: M. Barrès's *Culte du Moi* (Cult of the Self). Death of Victor Hugo (22 May).
1886: Conversion to Catholicism of Paul Claudel, Charles de Foucauld and Theresa of Lisieux. Tolstoy's *Death of Ivan Illich*. E. M. de Vogüé's *Le Roman russe*. Idealist Manifesto. Crisis of Naturalism. 'Symbolist Revolution'. Discovery of Rimbaud. Wagner fashionable in France.
1886–7: Policy of appeasement towards Catholics in France. Polish Neo-Romanticism.
1887–8: 'Modernism' in Hispanic literature.
1889: Henri Bergson's thesis, *Les Données immédiates de la conscience.*
c. 1890: Hegemony of Marburg School and

Neo-Kantianism in Germany (H. Cohen, P. G. Natorp, E. Cassirer).
1900–10: Neo-Classical and anti-individualist trend in literature, rationalist tendencies in philosophy and theology, and laicising ones in politics.
c. 1910: New wave of religious converts.
1911: Triumph of Bergson at the Bologna Congress.

4. Science and Charity, *by Pablo Picasso, 1897.*

European Migration

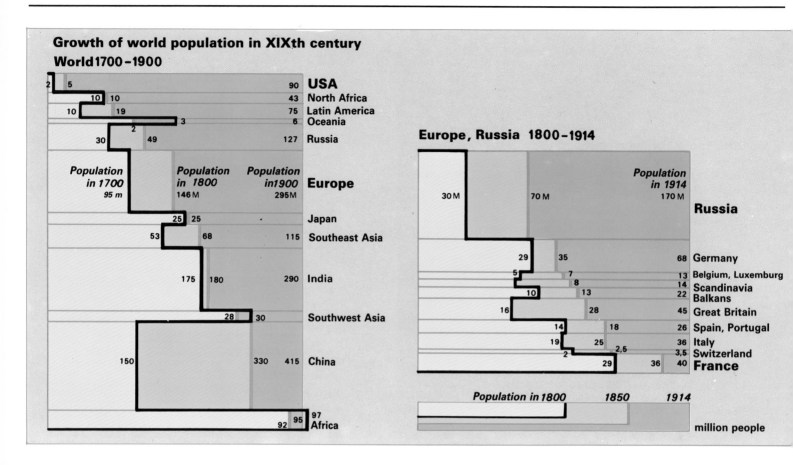

Growth of world population in XIXth century
World 1700–1900

2	5	90	**USA**
	10 10	43	North Africa
10	19	75	Latin America
	3	6	Oceania
30	2 49	127	Russia

Population in 1700 — 95 m   Population in 1800 — 146 M   Population in 1900 — 295 M   **Europe**

	25 25	·	Japan
53	68	115	Southeast Asia
175	180	290	India
	28 30		Southwest Asia
150	330 415		China
92	97 95		Africa

Europe, Russia 1800–1914

Population in 1914 — 30 M   70 M   170 M   **Russia**

29	35	68	Germany
5	7	13	Belgium, Luxemburg
	8	14	Scandinavia
10	13	22	Balkans
16	28	45	Great Britain
14	18	26	Spain, Portugal
19	25 2,5	36	Italy
2		3,5	Switzerland
29	36	40	**France**

Population in 1800   1850   1914

million people

WORLD POPULATION GROWTH, estimated at 18% during the seventeenth century and 40% during the eighteenth, speeded up in the nineteenth century: total population went from 680 million in 1700 to 954 million in 1800, 1,241 in 1850 and 1,634 in 1900, a relative rise of 71% in 100 years.

The main causes of this increase are still in doubt; some attribute it to climatic variations (the Little Ice Age may have limited the spread of microbial infections), others to the mix of populations which may have strengthened immune defences. For nineteenth-century Europeans the effects of anti-smallpox vaccination were of major importance, as were improvements in hygiene, particularly the antiseptic techniques popularized by Pasteur from the late 1880s onwards.

Progress in the fight against mortality enabled the European continent to increase its share of world population considerably. In the seventeenth century demographic growth was only 13% compared with 19% for the rest of the world, but in the eighteenth century it reached 56% (rest of the world 37%) and in the nineteenth 106% (rest of the world 63%). In 1770, with approximately 115 million people, Europe made up only one-sixth of the world total; in 1800 it represented 20% (192 million out of 954) and in 1900, 24% (395 million out of 1,634).

During this same century Europe expatriated to other continents about 70 million emigrants (50 million of these permanently), mostly to North America but many to Siberia, Latin America and Australia. These people then reproduced in their new homelands, bringing the total population of European origin to 210 million at the beginning of the nineteenth century and 560 million around 1900 (166% increase), when it represented over a third of the population of the globe!

All the European countries did not share equally in this expansion nor in the creation of new centres of population. In France the early adoption of birth control practices meant that the population was only just reproducing at replacement level; but for an increase in average lifespan it would not have grown, as it did, from 29 million to 40 million. Consequently France contributed little to the great movement of European emigration.

Most other European countries, on the contrary, witnessed both a demographic explosion and a mass exodus of their population.

The British, and especially the Irish, were among the first to leave. Between 1800 and 1850 the population of the British Isles doubled and that of Ireland reached a record level in absolute terms (8 million around 1845).

Even before the Great Famine the Irish had begun to emigrate in large numbers: half a million crossed the Atlantic from 1820 to 1844 and nearly one and a third million in the decade that followed, at which point they represented half the influx to the USA. As for the English and the Scots, 13 million of them emigrated between 1815 and 1914 in four successive waves (around 1850, 1870, 1885 and 1910). 65% settled in the USA, 15% in Canada, 11% in Australia and 5% in South Africa.

About 6 million Germans emigrated, mostly to the USA, with three peaks (around 1850, 1870 and 1885). Two million Scandinavians left, crossing the Atlantic either with the last wave of Germans or with the fourth wave of British.

Italy expatriated 16 million citizens: 4 million to the US, 4 million to Latin America and the rest to Europe. The beginnings of the twentieth century witnessed a veritable tidal wave, with 873,000 departures in the one year 1913.

At the same time there was an exodus from Central and Eastern Europe: 4 million Austro-Hungarians, 2.5 million Russians and the same number of Poles. Over 15 years about 6 million people emigrated to the USA. Many Russians also left for Asia: in 1914, 4 million of them had settled in the Caucasus and 9,600,000 in Siberia.

Between 1800 and 1914 Europeans had progressively peopled the world.

European emigration

million people

. On the Canadian Pacific Railway: immigrants round 1880.

2. From Genoa to New York: Italian emigrants in 1901.

Immigrants to USA

Population of USA

Immigration

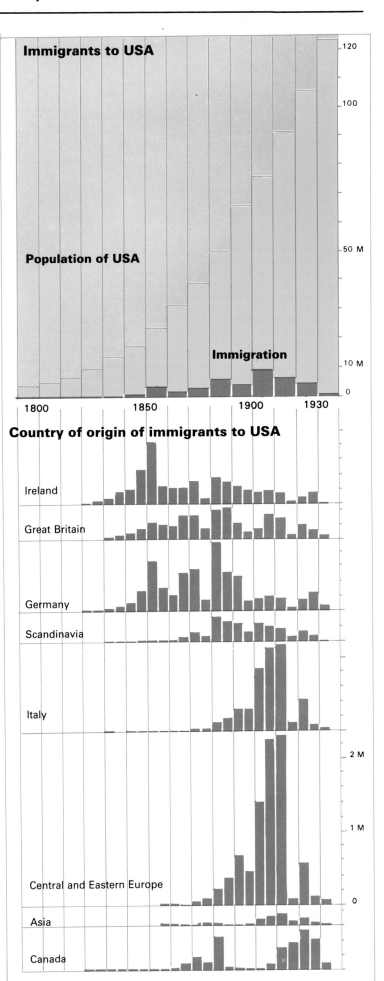

Country of origin of immigrants to USA

Ireland

Great Britain

Germany

Scandinavia

Italy

Central and Eastern Europe

Asia

Canada

Population of the United States of America, 1790–1930

(million people)

790 3.9	1820 9.6	1850 23.2	1880 50.2	1910 92.0
800 5.3	1830 12.9	1860 31.4	1890 66.9	1920 105.7
810 7.2	1840 17.1	1870 38.6	1900 76.0	1930 122.8

Capital, Industry and Banking

1. The new industrial space: a panorama of the Universal Exhibition in Paris in 1867.

THE GROWTH of industrial civilization in the nineteenth century was marked by a gradual shift from a system of production dominated by 'iron and coal' technology towards a model dominated by the technology of electricity, the internal combustion engine and the chemistry of synthetic materials. The turning point in this process came in the 1890s when technological development in all fields began to accelerate exponentially. The spread of industrialization through the century was confined mainly to a number of European countries together with North America, and can be broken down into three stages. The first began in Great Britain at the end of the eighteenth century, and reached France, Belgium, Switzerland and the United States by the first half of the nineteenth century. All these countries, with the sole exception of the United States, experienced a marked slowing down in growth after the 1860s. While Great Britain was responsible for producing one-third of world industrial output in

1873, its share had fallen to 14% by 1913, while that of the United States went from 23% to 36%. The years from 1840 to 1873, those of the first world boom in railway construction, saw a real industrial revolution spread throughout Europe, particularly to Germany. In Germany's case, this was only the first stage in a much greater economic transformation which, after a severe period of stagnation (from 1873 to 1886), took Germany's share of world economic output from 13% to 16% (the second highest in the world). The last wave of industrialization came at the end of the nineteenth century. By this time Russia, the Scandinavian countries, Italy, various parts of Eastern Europe and Japan were also enjoying a strong surge in economic activity, in a series of great leaps forward. In 1913 Europe was responsible for 44% of world industrial production, as opposed to 62% in 1870. But if one adds North America to this, the figure goes up to 82% in 1913, as compared with 86% in 1870.

The growth and spread of new technology were accompanied by deep-seated changes in how the system of production was organized. Until the 1870s the capitalist system, in its actual workings, simply carried on, without any major disturbance, the commercial capitalism of modern Europe. To this extent its social dynamic was founded essentially on the family, and its modes of internal organization rested on the authority of one man, the all-knowing entrepreneur. Gradually, however, mainly in Germany and in the United States, a new model began to emerge, which reflected the system of continuous production and the organization of business around mass distribution. The shift could be defined as the substitution of the 'visible hand' of the integrated company by the invisible hand of the market. It went hand in hand with the growing concentration of firms, which tended to bring together in one unit the activities of production, marketing and research. These huge corporations, with their multi-functional structure, became organized according to the hierarchical model borrowed from the railways. Some of these companies did retain a family structure, while others evolved irresistibly towards a managerial model, and decision-making passed into the hands of salaried executives. The networks of marketing agreements which became ever closer after the 1880s did no more than set these mergers in motion. Nevertheless, the dynamism of the system was due just as much to the continual emergence of new businesses (which introduced new products like the bicycle, the motor-car, cinemas and aeroplanes), as it was to the successful re-organization and rationalization of these large corporations. It was the existence of these two types of activity side by side which guaranteed the smooth progress of the system.

Société Générale de Belgique.	First steam hammer developed in Great Britain.	Bessemer perfects the manufacture of steel.	Zénobe Gramme invents the dynamo.
1822	**1839**	**1856**	**1869**

1822: Société Générale de Belgique founded.
1825–34: Development in Great Britain of the wet puddling process. Richard Roberts invents his automatic loom, and the Neilson process for hot-air blasting in smelting furnaces is developed.
1827: B. Fourneyron develops the hydraulic turbine by applying Carnot's principles.
1839: In Great Britain, Nasmyth builds the first steam hammer. The Daguerrotype is perfected.
1851: The Great Exhibition at the Crystal Palace demonstrates simultaneously British pre-eminence and American expertise in certain techniques like the standardization of parts, which was a fundamental aspect of the American system of manufacturing. First Singer sewing machine built.
1856: Perkin obtains the patent for manufacturing aniline dye, known as 'aniline purple' or 'mauve'. Bessemer process for the manufacture of steel developed.
1859: Laws concerning the setting up of public companies passed in Great Britain.
1867: Siemens develops his open-hearth furnace based on the regenerative principle.

French legislation is enacted concerning the freedom to create public companies.
1869: Zénobe Gramme improves the dynamo. The birth of electromechanics. Synthetic alizarin dye is developed.
1873: Hippolyte Fontaine discovers that the dynamo could be operated in reverse as an electric motor at the Exhibition of Vienna.
1876: Patent granted for the telephone of Alexander Graham Bell.

4. The cup-and-ball telephone invented by Alexander Graham Bell in 1876.

1878: Patent granted for an efficient typewriter (Christopher Sholes had sold his patent to Remington and Sons in 1873).
1880: Edison develops the light bulb.
1881: Patent for the first transformer granted to Lucien Gaulard and John D. Gibbs. First international electricity exhibition held in Paris.
1882: First working public power station put in operation in New York. The Standard Oil Trust is set up by John D. Rockefeller and associates.
1883: Emil Rathenau founds the DEG, which was to become the AEG combine (Allgemeine Elektrizitäts Gesellschaft).
1884: Bayer Research Laboratory founded. Patent for the turbine granted to Charles Algernon Parsons. The CIBA AG founded in Basle. The Comte de Chardonnet granted a patent for artificial silk.
1888: Nikola Tesla granted a patent for his induction motor.
1889: Eiffel Tower built for the Universal Exhibition. The Michelin Company set up as a limited partnership.
1891: First patent granted to the Michelin

5. The Michelin Man is born, 1898.

...he plans for the Eiffel Tower. A satirical engraving in about 1886.

3. Steel being poured from a Bessemer converter, Germany, c. 1880.

...on produces the first electric light bulb.

Michelin brothers are granted their first patent.

Pierre and Marie Curie discover radium.

...880

1891

1898

...factory in the Ruhr, pictured by A. Dressel, ...900.

brothers, which was to be the first of many. The Diesel engine developed. Thomson-Houston and Edison General Electric merge to form General Electric.
1897: Peugeot Automobile Company founded.
1898: Louis Renault begins making motor-cars. Frederick Winslow Taylor develops high-speed steel and Bayer makes aspirin.
1901: J. P. Morgan forms the United States Steel Corporation. General Electric sets up its research laboratory.
1904: The three major German chemical firms (BASF, Bayer and AGFA) form a cartel, the *Dreibund*, later to become I. G. Farben.
1911: The Supreme Court demands the breaking up of Standard Oil under the Anti-Trust Act.
1913: BASF develops an economical process for the synthesis of ammonia.

7. The Chicago Stockyards, c. 1910.

Workers and Socialism in Europe

ONE OF THE MAJOR CONSEQUENCES of European industrialization was the growth of the working class, the development of its forms of organization and its links with those other social strata that were to some degree unwilling to accept integration into bourgeois society. Three principal periods can be distinguished. The first of these, marked by powerful popular movements and harshly repressed mass strikes, runs from the creation of the International Working Men's Association in 1864 to the founding of the Socialist International, which coincided with the explosion of socialism in Western Europe (1889–93). The second period, which came to an end around 1903–5, was characterized by the rise of trade unions and by the entry on to the scene in the newly constituted nation-states of political parties. The dominant feature of the last period, which runs from 1905 to the Great War, was the general expansion of the labour and socialist movement and the appearance of new problems with which it was forced to contend.

The First International, 'a big heart in a little body', as a celebrated expression had it, founded in London in 1864, initially drew its vitality from the British, French, Belgian and Swiss workers' organizations, though subsequently those of Germany, Italy and Spain also became of major importance. It aimed to be a worldwide workers' party, or, at least, a European one. As a breeding-ground of solidarity among workers struggling to improve their conditions, it both radical-

ized many – if only temporarily – and stimulated them to organize themselves. On the paramount need to organize Marx and Bakunin were in agreement, even if the 'anti-authoritarian' faction came into conflict (especially after 1869) with those followers of Marx who led the International's General Council. After the Paris Commune – which was both the end of an era and a new dawn – it was the very development of the working class which led, in a mere twenty years, to the splintering of the movement into national groups. It gradually became clear that the different forms of action and militancy could not develop according to a single model, even if the German Social Democratic Party had the ambition – legitimated by its seniority, its long resistance to Bismarck's Anti-Socialist Laws, its political power (A. Bebel, W. Liebknecht) and its theoretical capacities (K. Kautsky) – of playing the role of the guiding party. The movement polarized around the two opposing elements, unions and parties. The relative importance of these two bodies varied according to the economic situation, the extent of industrial development and the state of civil liberties. In these conditions, it was only possible for the Second

2. 'Proletarians of all lands unite!' Swiss trade union banner from the end of the 19th century.

International, which was born in the years 1889–91, to be a loose federation of organizations.

It did, however, contribute to establishing the tenets of the socialist creed, particularly at the London Congress of 1896. To call oneself a socialist, it was necessary to work for the collective ownership of the means of production and recognize the need for political and parliamentary action. In this way the anarchists were swept aside and with them, in many countries, a number of syndicalists, at a time when renewed expansion was producing a general upturn in the

1. Strike of graders at the Courrières mine in 1911, as seen by one of the participants.

First International.

28 September 1864

1864: International Workers' Association founded.
1869: Large-scale strikes in France at La Ricamarie and St Aubin.
18 March–27 May 1871: Paris Commune.
1875: At the Gotha Congress, the two German socialist parties, founded in 1863 and 1869, form the SPD, the German Social Democratic Party.
1879: The Federation of the Party of the Socialist Workers of France is born at the Congress of Marseille.
1883–9: Bismarck's social insurance laws.
1884: In Great Britain, Social Democratic Federation, Fabian Society and Socialist League founded. In Belgium, Belgian Workers' Party.
1887: Norwegian Workers' Party.
1888: Spanish Socialist Workers' Party. Austrian Social Democratic Party.
1889: Second International founded. Social Democratic Party of Sweden. Dockers' strike in London. New unionism.
1890: First May Day parades.
1891: SPD's Erfurt Programme. Fourmies massacre.

Paris Commune.

March–May 1871

4. The Lyon silk workers live and work in their workshops. Engraving by Moller, 1860.

Second International

1889

1892: Italian Socialist Party. Polish Socialist Party.
1893: Mass strikes in Belgium. Independent Labour Party formed in Britain. Social Democratic Workers' Party founded in Netherlands.
1895: CGT formed in France. Death of Engels.
1896: In London, the Second International expels the anarchists and a section of the syndicalists.
1897: The Bund, the General Jewish Union of Workers of Lithuania, Poland and Russia, is founded.
1898: Milan uprising. Social Democratic Workers' Party of Russia founded. Law on industrial accidents passed in France.
1900: The International Socialist Bureau meets in Brussels.
1901: In Switzerland, the Social Democratic Party is formed; it is an offshoot of the 'Grütli' (the pact founding the Swiss Confederation in 1291). In Russia, the Socialist Revolutionary Party formed.
1903: Split between the two wings of the Bulgarian Social Democratic Party and

The trade unions in 1911

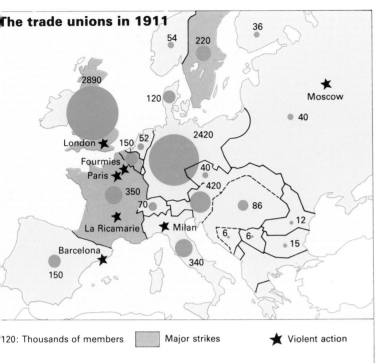

36
54
220
2890
120
Moscow ★
300
40
London ★ 150 52
Fourmies 2420
Paris ★ 40
350 420
70 86
La Ricamarie ★ Milan
6 6 12
Barcelona 340 15
150

120: Thousands of members | Major strikes | ★ Violent action

The Socialist Parties in 1911

120: Thousands of members
✚ National Congresses

36
71
64 ✚ St Petersburg
1400 50
C.
A.
L. • B. •14 1000
220 Erfurt Warsaw • Kiev
•P. Gotha ✚
65 Ba. ✚ S. 130 Nikolayev Kherson
Z. ✚ V Odessa
36 146 30
Marseille ✚ 1 2 5
12 25

Congresses of the IInd International:
P. Paris 1889   L. London 1896   S. Stuttgart 1907
B. Brussels 1891   P. Paris 1900   C. Copenhagen 1910
Z. Zurich 1893   A. Amsterdam 1904   Ba. Basle 1912   V. Vienna 1914

...rtunes of trade unions and political parties. These latter began to ...ppear in the Balkans and they even emerged in tsarist Russia – ...hough with enormous difficulties. From this point on, one has to ...ifferentiate between those countries where the trade unions (and in ...ome cases co-operatives) and the political parties lived in symbiosis ...Great Britain, Belgium, Sweden), where they grew in parallel – ...hough not without difficulties (Germany, Austria, Balkan states) – ...nd those where trade unionism or syndicalism was the vehicle of 'a ...ifferent type of socialism' (France, Italy, Spain). Strikes were ...ncreasingly becoming the union movement's main weapon and the ...uestion of the functions of the general strike was placed on the ...genda.

At the beginning of the twentieth century the labour movement ...roved impotent in the face of the rise of the various nationalisms and ...mperialism. In spite of Jaurès's efforts in France, at the eleventh hour ...e gave in to the declaration of war without a fight.

3. The beginnings of the 'trois-huit'. Advertisement for the Workers' Soap Factory, Paris, 1894.

...econd International expels the anarchists.   First Russian Revolution.   The Stuttgart Congress votes against war.

1905   1907

5. 'Forward, the dawn is breaking!' Labour Party poster, 1910, by Gerald Spencer Pryse.

between the Bolsheviks and the Mensheviks in the Russian SD Party.
1905: First Russian Revolution. Socialist unity achieved in France with the creation of the SFIO, the French section of the Workers' International.
1906: The Labour Representation Committee takes the name Labour Party.
1907: At the Stuttgart Congress, the Second International passes its famous motion against war.
1909: General strike in Sweden. 'Tragic week' in Barcelona.
1910: Upsurge of labour unrest in Great Britain. French railwaymen's strike.
1911: National Confederation of Labour (anarchist) founded in Spain.
1912–14: Social legislation in Great Britain after the election of Lib-Labs and the Labour Party.
31 July 1914: Assassination of Jaurès.

6. Jean Jaurès at the Pré Saint-Gervais in May 1913.

The United States and the Western Frontier

1. Evening meal on the trail going west.

THE TERRITORY coveted by the United States, a domain inhabited by a great number of native communities (there were approximately 10 million American Indians in the fifteenth century), was conquered within a century. In that period the new American nation expanded outwards from the initial narrow Atlantic belt to reach the Pacific coast. This expansion was achieved by negotiation and by purchases from the great powers (Louisiana, Florida, Oregon), by colonization and annexation (Texas), by military conquest (California and New Mexico). In 1867, with the purchase of Alaska from Russia, the

United States eliminated her rivals from North American territory. In 1812–14 a war against England led to the acquisition of the Great Lakes region, and fixed the frontier with Canada. In 1823 President Monroe announced the doctrine of European non-interference in the Western Hemisphere, keeping 'America for the Americans'. There remained only the 'savages', who, it was hoped, would disappear with the onward march of civilization.

The winning of the West was, as Benjamin Franklin had predicted, a spur to demographic growth. From 4 million in 1790 the American population rose to 31 million in 1860 and to 75 million inhabitants by the end of the century. The government encouraged migration westward by liberal land laws: in 1862 the Homestead Act allotted 160 acres to every pioneer family free of charge. As the new territories became inhabited, they passed from the status of colonies under the jurisdiction of Congress to that of equal states within the Union. The 'frontier', which mythology has portrayed as a 'wild' area, a domain of individual dynamism and agrarian democracy, was a powerful factor in capitalist development. To join the eastern states to the West, lines of communication were developed, including river routes, canals and, later, transcontinental railroads. These were the source of intense financial speculation, which gave rise to economic crises throughout the entire country. The westward march of farmers from the North-East, planters from the South, immigrants newly arrived from Europe, adventurers and missionaries, produced some rapid successes which led to growth, though there were also some catastrophic collapses. Towards the end of the century, farmers encountered the 'scissors phenomenon' which favoured industrial over agricultural prices; they organized in populist movements, but their movement failed in the face of opposition from the two political parties which held the reins of industry and finance. The frontier was pushed back at a cost to the native populations who, though they put up tenacious resistance, had in 1830 to take the 'Trail of Tears' across the Mississippi. In the second half of the century, in the great central plains, the railway builders and fur traders massacred 15 million bison, the Indians' chief source of subsistence. Defeated by the army, decimated by epidemics and reduced to poverty, the Indians yielded their territories and were left with nothing but small reservations. They lost their independence and were placed under the administrative supervision of the Bureau of Indian Affairs; with the disappearance of collective property and their conversion to Christianity, they forgot their own cultures. In 1890, after the Ghost Dance attempt at cultural revival, the massacre of 300 Sioux at Wounded Knee marked the triumph of the United States' colonization of the West.

Washington becomes federal capital.	Spain sells Florida.	Beginning of the great removal of the Indians.	Annexation of Texas.	Unification of the railr
1801	1819	1830	1845	18

1803: Thomas Jefferson buys Louisiana from Napoleon.
1803–5: Lewis and Clarke's expedition to the Pacific.
1811: Tecumseh organizes an Indian confederation.
1812–14: US war against England.
1814–18: Expeditions against the Creek and Seminole Indians.
1819: Adams-Onis Treaty: Spain cedes Florida.
1823: Monroe Doctrine: Europe is excluded from America.
1825: Completion of the Erie Canal.
1830–8: The 'Removal Bill': Creeks, Cherokees, Chickasaws, Choctows and Seminoles pushed back towards 'Indian territory'.
1836: Texan settlers proclaim an independent republic.
1841: By the Law of Pre-emption, squatters are given first rights in the purchase of public lands.
1842: The Oregon Trail is opened up: end of the 'definitive frontier' between Whites and Indians.

4. The California gold rush.

1845: Annexing of Texas to the Union in the name of the doctrine of 'Manifest Destiny'.
1846–8: War against Mexico. By the Treaty of Guadalupe-Hidalgo, the US acquires the southwestern regions.
1847: Mormons settle in Utah.
1848: California Gold Rush.
1858: Wells Fargo Company founded.
1858–64: Gold rushes and miners' strikes in Colorado, Nevada, Arizona, Idaho and Montana.
1860: Invention of the Winchester rifle.
1861–5: Cheyenne and Arapaho wars of resistance in the plains. The Cheyenne are massacred at Sand Creek.
1862: Homestead Act; 160 acres allotted free to every pioneer householder. Pacific Railway Act: subventions in the form of land to the transcontinental railroad building companies.
1865: Beginning of the great migrations of cattle from Texas towards the north and the east.
1865–8: Great Sioux Wars against Crazy Horse and his warriors.
1867: Organization of Indian reservations in

Oklahoma and Dakota. Purchase of Alaska. Agrarian movements.
1867–85: Extermination of bisons in the Great Plains.
1869: Completion of the first transcontinental railroad.
1871–86: Military conflicts with the Apaches.
1876: Dakota gold rush. Battle of Little Big Horn against the Sioux: Custer and his regiment are killed.
1877: War against the Indians of the North-West.
1887: End of the open-range cattle industry boom. Dawes Severality Act: the tribal lands are split up and allotted to families; tribal governments are dissolved.
1889: First colonization of Oklahoma.
1890: Ghost Dance; and its repression. Massacres of Wounded Knee. The Superintendent of the Census Bureau announces that the frontier is no longer of statistical relevance.

1800–1890

Pushing back the Frontier

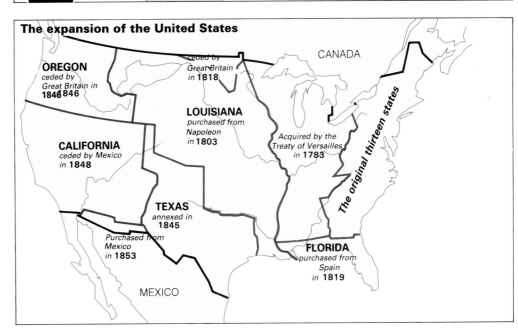

Little Big Horn 1876 ✗

Wounded Knee 1890 ✗

CANADA

MEXICO

500 km

✗ Principal battles with the Indians

The progress of the line marking a population of 1 inhabitant per square kilometre (the 'frontier')

1800 1850 1890

The progress of the line marking the expropriation of Indian lands

1810 1850 1870

The expansion of the United States

OREGON ceded by Great Britain in **1846**

ceded by Great Britain in **1818**

CANADA

LOUISIANA purchased from Napoleon in **1803**

Acquired by the Treaty of Versailles in **1783**

The original thirteen states

CALIFORNIA ceded by Mexico in **1848**

TEXAS annexed in **1845**

Purchased from Mexico in **1853**

FLORIDA purchased from Spain in **1819**

MEXICO

The creation of States between 1783 and 1890

CANADA

WASHINGTON 1889

OREGON 1859

IDAHO 1890

MONTANA 1889

NORTH DAKOTA 1889

MINNESOTA 1858

VERMONT 1791

MAINE 1820

NEW HAMPSHIRE

MASSACHUSETTS

WISCONSIN 1848

MICHIGAN 1837

WYOMING 1890

SOUTH DAKOTA 1889

NEW YORK

RHODE ISLAND

CONNECTICUT

NEW JERSEY

NEVADA 1864

NEBRASKA 1867

IOWA 1846

INDIANA 1816

OHIO 1803

PENNSYLVANIA

DELAWARE

MARYLAND

CALIFORNIA 1850

COLORADO 1876

KANSAS 1861

ILLINOIS 1818

MISSOURI 1821

W.V. 1863

VIRGINIA

KENTUCKY 1792

NORTH CAROLINA

TENNESSEE 1796

ARKANSAS 1836

ALABAMA 1819

SOUTH CAROLINA

GEORGIA

TEXAS 1845

MISSISSIPPI 1817

LOUISIANA 1812

FLORIDA 1845

MEXICO

W.V.: WEST VIRGINIA

Date at which territories formed into States

1783
1803
1845
1860
1890

Territories not formed into States

2. Wild West heroine Calamity Jane.
3. The Apache chief Geronimo, c. 1895.

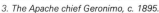
Disappearance of the 'frontier'.

1890

NORTHERN PACIFIC RAILROAD

THE PIONEER ROUTE TO FARGO MOORHEAD

5. When the pioneers took the railroad.

The United States: The North–South Conflict

1. Ruins of Charleston after the Northern victory.

SLAVERY, which in its ethos ran counter to the ideology of independence, disappeared from the northern states in the early years of the nineteenth century. It was, however, implicitly recognized by the US Constitution, where provision for an end to the slave trade was only made in 1808. The North–South conflict over the slavery issue intensified as economic growth produced greater disparities between the two regions. By 1860, the North had become the home of industry, great ports and banks. The South, where 350,000 families (one-third of the white population) owned some 3 million slaves, the planta-

tion economy, where single crops of tobacco, cotton, rice and sugar were grown, determined a way of life and a set of values quite opposed to those of the industrial capitalism of the North and the family agriculture of the West. Slavery was still at the centre of debate in the first half of the century because it involved a wide range of economic, political and ideological rivalries.

Apart from the campaign of the Abolitionists (Quakers, reformers, industrialists) in the North for the suppression of slavery, the conflict centred on three issues. The first of these was the question of who was to have ascendancy over the Congress and the Presidency; this was important because it would enable the dominant party to obtain legislation favourable to their particular type of economic base. The second was the problem of customs tariffs, which the North wished to keep high to protect its industry, but which threatened the exporting South with economic retaliation on the part of its overseas clients. The third was the issue of control over the West, which became the object of conflict between the Southern planters, who wished to extend their system of life to that area and acquire new land, and the North, which saw the West as the natural outlet for its industry and as a provider of meat and cereals to its urban population.

The problem of the slave or free status of the new states of the West was settled by a series of unsatisfactory compromises in 1787, 1820 and 1850. 1854 saw the founding of the Republican Party, which stood for the abolition of all slavery, the granting of land free of charge to settlers in the West and protectionism. The South campaigned for the maintenance of slavery, an issue championed by the Democratic Party. When the Republican candidate, Abraham Lincoln, was elected President, South Carolina seceded, was followed by ten other states and created a new Confederacy.

A minor military clash in April 1861 led to the outbreak of war. The South, though lacking industry, had the better officers, yet was unable to follow up its early successes. It had to capitulate in April 1865 after a savage conflict. This was, in fact, the first modern war; there were more than a million victims, civilian and military; modern means of transport and warfare were employed; and the Southern countryside was devastated. The war set two conceptions of federal government at odds, that of a contractual union between sovereign states on the one hand and that of an indestructible organic nation on the other. The North, with its nascent industrial capitalism, was to bring about the victory of the latter.

It took ten years to reconstruct the Union. Under the Thirteenth Amendment, Blacks were released from slavery and under the Fourteenth they acquired the right to vote. For a long time the South remained in an inferior economic and political position. Cotton only recovered its previous strong position in 1880. Meanwhile, as the Southern states recovered their freedom of action, they began to apply segregation against the Blacks.

Arrival of black slaves.		Outlawing of slave trade.	Birth of Buffalo Bill
1619		1808	1846

1619: First twenty Africans sold in Virginia.
1660–80: Institutionalization of slavery in English colonies.
1787: Slavery is prohibited in the North-West, but the Constitution protects it elsewhere.
1808: Congress outlaws slave trade.
1820: Missouri Compromise; the 36°30′ parallel separates the slave states from the free states.
1828: 'Abominations' tariff; denounced by the South and West.
1829–37: Jackson President. Rise of liberal capitalism.
1848: Free Soil Party: 'free soil, free speech, free labour and free men'.
1850: Clay Compromise: admission of California as a non-slave state. The question of slavery in the new states to be decided by their populations.
1852: The Abolitionist Harriet Beecher-Stowe publishes *Uncle Tom's Cabin.*
1854: The Free-Soilers are absorbed into the Republican Party. Ostende Manifesto under pressure from the Southern states recommending that Spain purchase Cuba;

Kansas-Nebraska Act, which invalidates the Missouri Compromise.
1856: Bloody Kansas. Civil war between pro- and anti-slavers.
1857: Dred Scott affair. The Supreme Court declares Congress incompetent to decide on the right to slavery.
1859: John Brown's raid on the arsenal at Harper's Ferry.
1860: Abraham Lincoln elected President. South Carolina secedes in December.
1861: February–March: Ten states join South Carolina to form the Confederacy with its capital at Richmond. April: Capture of Fort Sumter by the Confederates. Lincoln declares war on the rebels. Potomac front; Southern victories.
1862: March: Missouri front; Lee's Confederates are pushed back towards the South. On the peninsula they fail to break the Northern blockade. September: Proclamation of emancipation of the Blacks by Lincoln. 13 December: Lee is victorious at Fredericksburg.
1863. January–July: Victorious march north by Lee. July: Lee is halted by Federal troops

at Gettysburg. Grant's campaign in the West. 4 July: Northerners victorious at Vicksburg.
1864–5: Northerners, led by Sherman, march towards the South.
9 April 1865: Lee abandons Richmond. The Southern capital is captured by the North. Victory of the Union.
1865: Thirteenth Amendment: Abolition of slavery in the USA. 14 April: Lincoln is assassinated. Johnson becomes President.
1867: Formation of the Ku Klux Klan. Beginning of reconstruction.
1868: Fourteenth Amendment: Congress lays down the rules of citizenship.
1877: End of reconstruction. The Southern states are re-integrated.

3. Abraham Lincoln.

2. Uncle Tom's Cabin. *An illustration from Harriet Beecher-Stowe's famous work.*

The white man, John Brown, leads a rising against slavery.   **Ku Klux Klan.**

1859   1867

4. The Mistress's Visit, *as seen by Winslow Homer.*

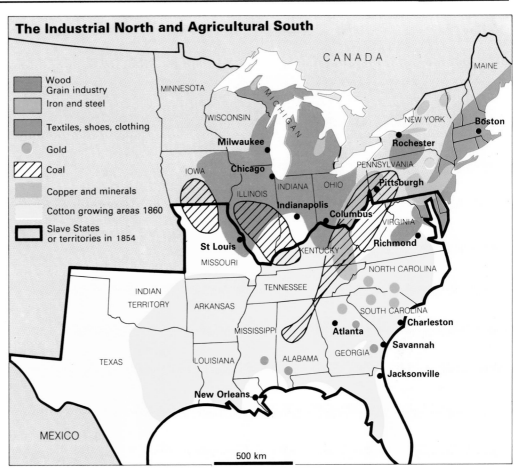

The Industrial North and Agricultural South

Wood Grain industry
Iron and steel
Textiles, shoes, clothing
Gold
Coal
Copper and minerals
Cotton growing areas 1860
Slave States or territories in 1854

CANADA
MAINE
MINNESOTA
WISCONSIN
MICHIGAN
NEW YORK
Boston
Milwaukee
Rochester
IOWA
Chicago
PENNSYLVANIA
Pittsburgh
INDIANA
OHIO
Indianapolis
Columbus
ILLINOIS
VIRGINIA
St Louis
KENTUCKY
Richmond
MISSOURI
NORTH CAROLINA
INDIAN TERRITORY
TENNESSEE
ARKANSAS
SOUTH CAROLINA
Charleston
MISSISSIPPI
Atlanta
GEORGIA
Savannah
TEXAS
LOUISIANA
ALABAMA
Jacksonville
New Orleans
MEXICO
500 km

The Civil War

CANADA

Gettysburg
Washington
Richmond
Norfolk
Lexington
Appomatox
Cairo
Goldsboro
INDIAN TERRITORY
Memphis
Chattanooga
Columbia
Corinth
Fort Sumter
Atlanta
Savannah
Vicksburg
Jackson
Jacksonville
New Orleans
MEXICO

| Conquest of Southern-held territory | | | Northern offensives | Confederate States | States of the Union |
| 1862 | 1863 | 1864 | Southern raids | | |

Italian and German Unification

1815 | **1859** | **March 1860** | **May–October 1860**

- - - - German Confederation ═══ Alliances ▬▬▬ *Zollverein* (customs union) dating from 1 January 1834

FROM THE BEGINNING of the nineteenth century, nationalist and liberal opinion in Italy had grouped together under the banner of the newspaper *Il Risorgimento*, the organ of the industrial and commercial middle classes of the north, who saw in the achievement of unity and in the setting up of a constitutional monarchy the means of satisfying both their patriotic feelings and their own economic interests. Cavour, the Prime Minister of Piedmont, was to be the principal architect of unity. Fully aware of the need to have recourse to the assistance of a foreign power, Cavour turned to Napoleon III, whose sympathies for the Italian patriots were well known. An alliance was concluded between Piedmont and France, and in April 1859 the two countries went to war together against Austria. In June, the Franco-Piedmontese army won the victories of Magenta and Solferino. But Napoleon III, motivated by the slaughter at Solferino and worried at the reaction of French Catholics to the mobilization of Prussia, signed the armistice of Villafranca and then the Treaty of Zurich with the Austrians, according to the terms of which Piedmont was given Lombardy but Venetia was left in the hands of the Austrians. Despite this setback to unity, Cavour took advantage of the cautious complicity of France to found, in less than two years, the Kingdom of Italy, which was proclaimed in March 1861 after the merging of the three duchies of central Italy (Tuscany, Parma and Modena), Papal

1. The end of the temporal power of the Pope: the Italian Bersagliere at the gates of Rome (20 September 1870).

First performance of Verdi's *Nabucco* at La Scala, Milan.   Abdication of Charles Albert in favour of his son Victor Emmanuel II.

9 March 1842 | **23 March 1849**

2. The making of Italian national banners in Piedmont, in April 1859.

14 January 1858: The Italian patriot Orsini makes an attempt on the life of Napoleon III. Orsini's action, which was motivated by a wish to punish the Emperor for abandoning his former comrades-in-arms (in 1831 Louis Napoleon had taken part in an uprising against the Papal States), persuades the Emperor to give military support to the Kingdom of Piedmont.
20–21 July: Cavour and Napoleon III meet in Plombières.
26 January 1859: Franco-Piedmontese Alliance signed in Turin.
April: Austria declares war on Piedmont. France intervenes almost immediately.
4 June: Battle of Magenta.
24 June: Battle of Solferino.
12 July: Unbeknown to Cavour, who resigns the following day, Napoleon III and the Emperor of Austria, Franz-Josef I, sign the Armistice of Villafranca.
11 November: Treaty of Zurich. Austria cedes Lombardy to France, who cedes it in turn to Piedmont.
March 1860: Annexation of the three duchies of central Italy (Tuscany, Parma and Modena)

and of Emilia-Romagna.
24 March: Under the Treaty of Turin, France is awarded Nice and Savoy in exchange for its good will.
May–October: Expedition of the Thousand. The small army of volunteers recruited by

3. Count Cavour, the architect of Italian unity, in a painting by Francisco Hayez.

Garibaldi conquers the Kingdom of the Two Sicilies.
4 November: Annexation of Umbria.
5 November: Annexation of the Marches.
14 March 1861: The Kingdom of Italy is proclaimed, and Victor Emmanuel takes the title of King of Italy.
6 June: Death of Cavour.
29 August 1862: Garibaldi is defeated and taken prisoner at Aspromonte in Calabria by the Piedmontese, who are forced to intervene under pressure from the French.
22 September: Bismarck appointed chancellor of Prussia.
14 August 1865: The Convention of Gastein ends the Danish War. Prussia is given the administration of Schleswig, while that of Holstein is handed over to Austria.
October: Meeting in Biarritz between Napoleon III and Bismarck. France guarantees Prussia its neutrality in the event of a conflict with Austria.
April 1866: Alliance between Prussia and Italy.
21 June: Beginning of the Seven Weeks' War between Austria and Prussia.

1858–1871

November 1860–March 1861

KINGDOM OF PRUSSIA
FRANCE
AUSTRIA
Florence • THE MARCHES
UMBRIA
Rome •

March 1861: Victor Emmanuel crowned King of Italy

1865-1866

SCHLESWIG-HOLSTEIN
KINGDOM OF PRUSSIA
Bismarck
× Sadowa
Prague •
• Vienna
FRANCE
AUSTRIA
× Custozza
Florence •
VENETIA
× Lissa
Rome •
Aspromonte ×

1867-1870

Zollverein
NORTH GERMAN CONFEDERATION
Sedan ×
LORRAINE
ALSACE
P BADEN BAVARIA W
AUSTRO-HUNGARIAN EMPIRE
French Expeditionary Force
Garibaldi
× Mentana 1867
Rome •

P. = Palatinate
W. = Württemberg

1871

NETHERLANDS
Berlin ■
RUSSIA
BELGIUM
GERMAN REICH
SWITZERLAND
FRANCE
AUSTRO-HUNGARIAN EMPIRE
KINGDOM OF ITALY
Rome ■

Emilia-Romagna and the Kingdom of the Two Sicilies which had been conquered by Garibaldi and his army of volunteers (the 'Thousand'). France, as a result of her acquiescence, was rewarded in exchange with Nice and Savoy. Under the pretext of arresting Garibaldi, the Piedmontese troops then occupied the Papal States (excepting Rome and the surrounding areas). Venetia was annexed in 1866 as a result of the alliance with Prussia.

The resolution of the Roman question, however, proved more troublesome and was more protracted. On this occasion the French Catholics mobilized and forced the Emperor to intervene, directly as well as indirectly, against the Garibaldians who, in 1862 and 1867, attempted to take the city. It was not until the recall of the French Expeditionary Force in September 1870 that Rome at last became the capital of the Kingdom of Italy, which it did on 1 August 1871.

In Germany, the failure of the bourgeois liberal revolution of 1848 left the initiative for unity to Prussia, which was in the hands of conservative forces. The architect of German unification was Otto von Bismarck, who was made chancellor in 1862. But the unity of Germany under the aegis of Prussia was impossible so long as Austria continued to exert its influence over the German-speaking lands. Bismarck, who had decided to embark on a trial of strength with the Austrian government, grasped the opportunity given him by the issue of Schleswig-Holstein in 1864. The two duchies of Schleswig and

Holstein, which were inhabited by a mixture of Germans and Danes, and were under the control of the King of Denmark, declared themselves, on the death of Frederick VII in 1863, in favour of a German prince who had the support of the Prussian chancellor. As a result, Bismarck decided to intervene in a joint action with the Austrians. The two allies, at the end of a rapid campaign, obtained the transfer of the two duchies, which henceforth came under joint Austro-Prussian administration. After having assured himself of French neutrality and concluded an alliance with Italy, Bismarck only had to invoke the pretext of the 'poor administration' of Holstein by the Austrians to invade the territory and declare war on the Hapsburgs. The Austrians won a land battle over Italy at Custozza (24 June 1866) and a sea battle at Lissa (20 July). But in Bohemia, the Prussians won a resounding victory at Sadowa. The peace treaty signed in Prague gave the duchies to Prussia and forced upon Austria the dissolution of the German Confederation.

The following year, after annexing the minor states in the centre of Germany, Bismarck set up the North German Confederation, under the presidency of the King of Prussia. The war with France, by uniting the German princes against a common enemy, put the final seal on unity and overcame the lingering reservations of the southern German states. The German Reich was proclaimed in Versailles on 18 January 1871.

tor Emmanuel II crowned King of Italy. Death of Cavour. Prussian victory over the Austrians at Sadowa.   Proclamation of the German *Reich* in the Hall of Mirrors at Versailles.

14 March 1861	6 June 1861	3 July 1866	18 January 1871

3 July: The Prussian army routs the Austrians at Sadowa.
23 August: Under the Treaty of Prague, Austria cedes Schleswig-Holstein to Prussia.
19 October: Under the Treaty of Venice, Austria cedes Venetia to France, who transfers it to Italy.
1 July 1867: Establishment of the North German Confederation.
3 November: The French Expeditionary Force sent to defend Rome disperses Garibaldi's troops at Mentana.
19 July 1870: Napoleon III falls into the trap laid by Bismarck (in the Ems telegram of 13 July) and declares war on Prussia.
2 September: France capitulates after the defeat at Sedan.
20 September: The Italian Army enters Rome.
18 January 1871: Proclamation of the German *Reich*.
1 August: Rome becomes the capital of Italy.

4. 'Be united!' An allegory of Germany according to a patriotic image in 1870.

5. Kaiser Wilhelm II proclaims the German Reich in the Gallery of Mirrors at Versailles. From a German engraving dated 1871.

6. Giuseppe Garibaldi (1807–82), dressed in his red shirt, which became the uniform of the Garibaldian volunteers.

Victoria, Queen and Empress

1. The Great Exhibition of 1851 at the Crystal Palace, by L. Haghe.

THE SIX MILLION PEOPLE who in 1851 visited the Crystal Palace, the central attraction of the Great Exhibition, were more or less conscious participants in the burial of the green England of former times, and were joining together in the self-consecration of a triumphant island full of mystical self-confidence in its mission as the workshop of the world. At the heart of this industrial hall of fame was the railway engine: for twenty years 'railway-mania' had mobilized people's savings and transformed the countryside, and the advance of the rail-

ways symbolized the technological supremacy of a whole nation. London was the unrivalled financial centre of the world as well as being the capital of the first country to have a majority urban population: in 1851, 50.1% of Britons lived in the city, compared with 16.9% in 1801, and outside of London ten other cities had more than 100,000 inhabitants. This proliferating growth appeared to be limitless; and in 1870 more than a third of world production of manufactured goods came from British factories. In the period leading up to the coronation of Queen Victoria, heated political controversies had heralded the changing balance of forces within what was the first industrial society. The 1832 Reform Act had enfranchised only one in five of the population, and the landowning oligarchy were still in control of Parliament. However, the dynamic of reform had begun, and was to promote slow but steady progress towards democracy. Revolutionary stirrings were to be found, most notably present in the guise of Chartism, which worried the ruling class on three occasions, but the movement turned out in the end to be 'much ado about nothing' and paid the price of its own incoherent demands. It is difficult to see how a programme for the restructuring of the electoral system could successfully be mixed up with a call for the abolition of workhouses (set up under the 1834 Poor Law Act), or be consistent with the backward-looking agrarian ideals of O'Connor, one of the movement's leaders. More effective in their aims were the crusades in favour of free trade, the support for which came from the employers in Manchester. The campaigners grouped themselves together under the name of the Anti-Corn Law League. Its victory was precipitated by the Great Irish Famine of 1846.

It is unsurprising that the values of those who defined themselves as 'the industrious middle classes' characterized Victorianism at its height: the attachment to religion, the family, thrift, the spirit of endeavour, 'respectability', all the virtues embodied by the Queen, herself an emblem of security and unity. But this edifice of certainty slowly developed cracks in the face of the emergence of numerous accounts of an 'other nation' of workers whose living and working conditions were not only difficult to reconcile with Christian values but threatened to cause social unrest. Only in the very last decade of the century was a powerful trade union movement to emerge, when socialists begun to organize and unite, albeit more often inspired by the Bible than by Marx. Twenty-five years earlier a wave of reforms had started up once again, under the dual impetus of Disraeli and Gladstone, preserving social stability by absorbing pressures from 'below'. However, an opportunity to make progress on the eternal Irish question had been lost with the failure of the 1886 Home Rule Bill.

The attack of imperialist fervour which filled most minds at the end of the Queen's reign, was, perhaps, a means of exorcizing anxiety at having to compete with the emergent powers, America and Germany.

Birth of Chartism.

Great Famine in Ireland.
Corn Laws repealed.

Gladstone Prime Minis

1838

1846

1

1837: Victoria accedes to the throne, at a time when the prestige of the monarchy is low.
1838: The first Anti-Corn Law League founded. Dickens publishes *Oliver Twist*, describing the depths of low life in London.
1839: Parliament rejects the 1838 People's Charter calling for universal suffrage.
1842: England acquires Hong Kong by the Treaty of Nanking.
1846: Great Famine in Ireland. Over a five-year period there were 800,000 deaths from hunger, and about the same number emigrated. The protectionist Corn Laws are repealed by Parliament.
1847: Ten-hour day introduced for women textile workers.
1848: Definitive failure of Chartism.
1849: Navigation Acts repealed.
1851: First Universal Exhibition in London.
1855: Palmerston Prime Minister. The master of Victorian diplomacy from 1830 to 1865 (with a few brief intervals), he remained the symbol, either hated or revered, of British superiority.
1856: Development of the Bessemer process, which leads to a boom in steel

2. Reformers attack the tree of Rotten Boroughs in 1832.

production.
1857: Indian Mutiny put down with great brutality.
1859: Darwin's *Origin of the Species* causes great scandal. Samuel Smiles publishes *Self-Help*, which was to symbolize Victorian individualism.
1865: William Booth founds the Salvation Army.
1867: 1867 Reform Bill gives the vote to 2,250,000 electors, a third of whom are workers.
1868: Gladstone forms his first Liberal government. Disraeli made leader of the Conservative Party. The Trades Union Congress is formed, and Sir Charles Dilke publishes *Greater Britain*, the gospel of nascent imperialism.
1869: Disestablishment of the Anglican Church in Ireland.
1870–6: Numerous reforms are enacted (legal recognition of trade unions, compulsory primary schooling, secret voting etc.).
1872: Disraeli delivers his imperialist speech at the Crystal Palace.
1873: Onset of economic depression (fall of

1837–1901

The British Empire at the death of Queen Victoria in 1901

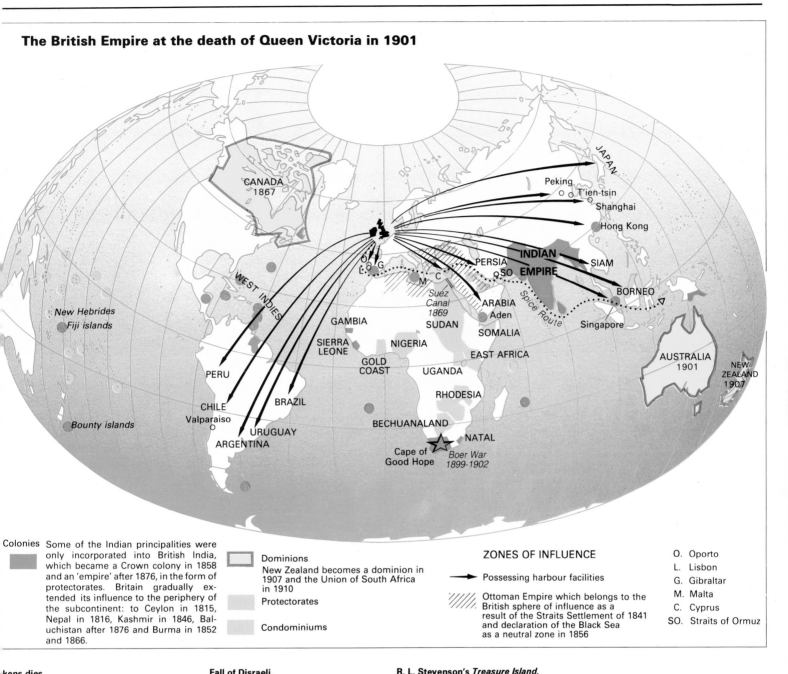

Colonies Some of the Indian principalities were only incorporated into British India, which became a Crown colony in 1858 and an 'empire' after 1876, in the form of protectorates. Britain gradually extended its influence to the periphery of the subcontinent: to Ceylon in 1815, Nepal in 1816, Kashmir in 1846, Baluchistan after 1876 and Burma in 1852 and 1866.

Dominions
New Zealand becomes a dominion in 1907 and the Union of South Africa in 1910

Protectorates

Condominiums

ZONES OF INFLUENCE

→ Possessing harbour facilities

////// Ottoman Empire which belongs to the British sphere of influence as a result of the Straits Settlement of 1841 and declaration of the Black Sea as a neutral zone in 1856

O. Oporto
L. Lisbon
G. Gibraltar
M. Malta
C. Cyprus
SO. Straits of Ormuz

---

kens dies.

Fall of Disraeli.

R. L. Stevenson's *Treasure Island*.

70

1880

1883

world economic indexes and relative slowing down of British economic growth).
1876: Queen Victoria proclaimed Empress of India.
1878: Near Eastern crisis and British invasion of Afghanistan.
1879–82: Irish Land War.
1882: Occupation of Egypt.
1885: Two out of three Englishmen given the vote.
1885–7: Workers' riots as a result of unemployment.
1886: The General Election goes against Gladstone and his Home Rule Bill.
1889: General strike in London docks.
1893: Independent Labour Party founded as a forerunner to the Labour Party (which was itself formed in 1906).
1896: The best-seller *Made in Germany* points out the advances made by Germany in various leading technical domains. Birth of *The Daily Mail*, which was to be a focal point of popular imperialism.
1897: Queen Victoria's Diamond Jubilee.
1899: Beginning of the Boer War.
1901: Death of Queen Victoria.

3. The Queen Engine and the Fairy Electricity. . . . From Queen Victoria's Jubilee album in 1897.

Find Gardeners 'Two' and 'Five' and 'Gardener Seven'.

6

Nº 16.

"OFF WITH THEIR HEADS!" said the QUEEN.

4. ' "Off with their heads!" said the Queen', in Lewis Carroll's Alice in Wonderland.

From the President-Prince to President Poincaré

1. *Execution of the Communards: the* Mur des Fédérés, *28 May 1871, by Alfred-Henri Darjou.*

FRANCE'S POPULATION varied as her territorial boundaries shifted – Nice and Savoy were added in 1860, Alsace-Lorraine taken away eleven years later – but on the whole it grew gradually, from 36 million to 39.7 million, mainly due to the early immigration of Italians and Belgians. The mortality rate was relatively high and the birth and fertility rates exceptionally low for the period, leading to a static, aging population.

Economic growth was irregular and unequal. After the crisis of the mid-nineteenth century, the railways stimulated an average growth in revenue of 2% per annum up to 1865 and French industry appeared to be catching up with Britain's; French capital and engineers contributed to the development of many other countries. But a severe depression followed (1873–1896), and a more rapid decline than elsewhere meant that for three decades the growth rate was a meagre 1% per annum. France lagged behind in spite of renewed economic vitality at the beginning of the twentieth century, when the growth rate rose to 3%. However, the *Belle Epoque* witnessed some remarkable achievements in new sectors, such as automobile manufacture, and capital was exported freely. France's new economy was dualistic: ancient forms of production and exchange subsisted side by side with modern ones.

The rural sector was still of major importance, peasants representing about 40% of the active population. The great number of small-holdings slowed down progress and favoured the survival of traditional polyculture: however, some regions were specialized (e.g. Languedoc for wine); in others, such as Beauce, large farms practised modern agricultural methods. Peasants were now less concerned with the state of their crops than with their market value.

Towns varied greatly. Side by side with slow-moving, traditional towns, manufacturing centres sprang up, such as Le Creusot and Roubaix. Paris stood out by its rapid growth and its size (2.9 million inhabitants in 1911). The capital was enlarged and modernized during the Second Empire; bourgeois neighbourhoods in the west abutted poor and working-class suburbs in the north and east. Marked social inequality characterized the whole of French society. Two-thirds of the population left practically nothing at their death.

Napoleon III Emperor.

The Paris Commune.

2 December 1852		18 March–27 May 1871

2 December 1851: Coup d'état of President-Prince Louis Napoleon Bonaparte.
1852: Setting up of Crédit Mobilier and Crédit Foncier (December 10) and large private railway companies.
1853: Haussmann prefect of the Seine département.
1854–6: Crimean War.
25 February–30 March 1856: Congress of Paris convened at end of Crimean War.
1859: War between Italy and Austria.
23 January 1860: Trade agreement with Britain. Nice and Savoy vote to become part of France.
1862–7: Mexican expedition.
1864: Law on 'combination'.
1865: Bank cheques legally recognized.
1867: Law liberalizing the setting up of limited companies.
1868: Laws restoring freedom of the press and rights of assembly.
1869: Suez Canal opened.
2 January 1870: Emile Ollivier government.
8 May: Referendum approves the liberal Empire.
19 July: War declared on Prussia.

2–4 September: Fall of Sedan. Government of national defence set up.
1871: Armistice 28 January. Thiers heads government.
18 March–27 May: Paris Commune.
10 May: Treaty of Frankfurt.
24 May 1873: Thiers resigns and is replaced by Mac-Mahon.
1875: Wallon amendment (vote on 30 January) and constitutional laws founding Third Republic.
1877: Legislative assembly dissolved, Republican victory in legislative elections.
1878: Freycinet plan aiding economic expansion (railways, canals etc.).
1879: Jules Grévy replaces Mac-Mahon as President.
1880: Amnesty of Communards. Official celebration of 14 July as a national holiday.
1881: Tunisia becomes protectorate. Law introducing free primary education. Laws on public meetings and the press.
1882: Gambetta Prime Minister. Union Générale crashes (economic crisis). Law introducing compulsory lay primary education.

4. La Tache noire: *the cultural heritage being transmitted at a lay school, as seen by Albert Bettanier in 1887.*

2. Factories at Le Creusot in 1866. Watercolour by Ignace-François Bonhomme.

Many working people made a precarious living; over half their revenue was still spent on food, although their diet was now more varied. At the opposite pole, the numerous tiers of the bourgeoisie reached their apogee in the aristocracy of the millionaires, mainly bankers, industrialists and absentee landlords.

The most spectacular changes were in the political field. The Second Empire marked France's first step towards universal suffrage. Then, with hopes of a restoration dashed and those of a revolution fading fast, the French at last enjoyed a stable regime uniting two political principles inherited from 1789 and until now incompatible: democracy and freedom. The Third Republic made France into a great colonial power; she held her rank in Europe thanks to the Triple Entente with Russia and Great Britain. Considerable improvements were made at home, particularly in education. Though there were violent conflicts between radical governments and the Catholics, the Republic did succeed in lessening the age-old differences between the regions and consolidated national unity.

3. The Separation of Church and State. Postcard, 1907.

Emile Zola: *J'accuse.*	**Entente Cordiale.**	**Law on the separation of Church and State.**	**Jean Jaurès assassinated.**
13 April 1898	**8 April 1904**	**9 December 1905**	**31 July 1914**

1883: Second Jules Ferry government. Annam becomes protectorate.
1884: Trade union and divorce laws.
1885: Pasteur administers first anti-rabies vaccination.
1886–9: Boulanger crisis.
1887: Grévy resigns.
1888: First Russian loan.
1889: Eiffel Tower built.
1891: Fourmies incident.
1892: Méline tariff. Panama scandal.
1893: Franco-Russian military convention.
1894: Anti-anarchist laws.
23 September 1895: CGT (Confédération Générale des Travailleurs) formed.
1898: Dreyfus Affair. Crisis between France and Britain at Fashoda.
1899: Waldeck-Rousseau government.
1901: Radical Party founded. Law on associations.
1902: Combes government.
1904: Entente Cordiale with Britain. Law forbidding religious orders to teach. Break with Vatican.
23–25 April 1905: SFIO (Section Française de l'International Ouvrière) founded.

1906: Algeciras conference. 24 hours weekly rest introduced by law. CGT conference at Amiens. Clemenceau Prime Minister.
1907: Languedoc vine-growers' revolt.
1912: Morocco becomes a protectorate.
1913: Poincaré President. Military service increased to three years.
1914: Vote to introduce income tax.
31 July: Jaurès assassinated.
3 August: Germany declares war on France.

5. Pas-à-Quatre: pro-Dreyfus caricature on the Affair.

Bismarck and William II

1. Friedrich Krupp's foundry at Essen. Otto Bollhagen, 1873.

service by a powerful military caste. Bismarck, the Prussian prime minister and chancellor of the Reich, first assured himself of the support of the Liberals and then, in the *Kulturkampf* (campaign for secularization), set about attacking the particularist Catholics of the *Zentrum*. This led to the expulsion of the Jesuits and controls being imposed upon the clergy, which also alarmed Protestants. It was, therefore, a failure. Two attempts on the Kaiser's life then gave Bismarck a pretext for dissolving the Reichstag and promulgating the so-called Anti-Socialist Laws, which were renewed every two years until his fall from power. The great rise in population that the Reich had seen, alongside the disordered growth in investment in the feverish climate of the *Gründerjahre* (foundation years), was temporarily halted by the repercussions of the Viennese Stock Market crash. Expansion continued nonetheless. Heavy industry became more highly concentrated and rapid urbanization was accompanied by a further dramatic population increase, which cannot simply be attributed to decreasing levels of emigration. Agriculture was modernized, in spite of the archaic social relations which still pertained in the east. Germany became the second-strongest world power, practising a unique form of state capitalism. A variety of interest groups stepped into the breach left by the failings of the German parliamentary system: associations of employers and farmers, and colonial and nationalist pressure groups. Falling into line with the aristocracy, the richest industrialists joined in the chorus of hostility to socialists, progressives and trade unionists: hence the repeated attempts to integrate the workers into society by detaching them from the Social Democratic Party (SPD), such as Bismarck's insurance laws and the social legislation passed at the beginning of William II's reign and revamped in the early years of the twentieth century. The Reich was largely dependent for its revenue upon the goodwill of its individual states. It was also faced, on its borders, with a number of national problems, which were aggravated by its policy of Germanization.

In foreign policy, the attempt under Bismarck to consolidate Germany's position in Europe by a series of apparently contradictory treaties was followed, under William II, by the search for 'a place in the sun'. In fact, the colonies were to have more of a strategic than an economic significance, and imperial rivalries posed more of a threat to Germany's ability to carry through a co-ordinated process of modernization and democratization than they did to its overseas empire. The influence of the SPD, the leading force in the Socialist International, increased in this period, and in 1912 it became the largest group in the Reichstag. One of its main objectives, which it backed up by demonstrations and strikes, was to win universal suffrage in the parliaments of those *Länder* where the three-class system was still in force (Prussia, Saxony etc.). This demand figured among its war aims when the SPD accepted Germany's entering the war under a government of national unity on 4 August 1914.

THE CREATION of the German Reich, which symbolically took place in the Hall of Mirrors at Versailles, succeeded in producing German unity around Prussia by joining the southern states to the North German Confederation. In spite of the existence of universal suffrage in the elections to the Reichstag, the Reich remained until its demise an authoritarian state, since the government was not responsible before parliament. The parliament itself was, in any case, dissolved on each of the numerous occasions when it displayed opposition to the government. The predominance of Prussia over the other twenty-four states (which included three city-states) forming the federation meant the imposition of a particular civilization and type of government characterized by Junker conservatism and domination of the civil

Creation of the Reich.	Triple Alliance.	Bismarck dismissed.
18 January 1871	**1882**	**19 March 1890**

18 January 1871: William I, King of Prussia, is proclaimed German Kaiser.
1871: Zentrum (German Catholic Centre Party) founded.
1871–86: *Kulturkampf* – power struggle against Catholicism.
May 1873: Vienna Stock Market crashes.
May 1875: The two German socialist parties unite to form the SPD (Social Democratic Party of Germany) and adopt the Gotha Programme.
1876: German Conservative Party founded.
11 May and 2 June: Assassination attempts on William I.
June–July 1878: Berlin Congress.
October 1878–1890: Anti-socialist laws.
October 1879: Alliance with Austria-Hungary.
June 1881: The Three Emperors' League (William I, Alexander II and Franz Josef).
1882: Triple Alliance (Germany, Austria-Hungary, Italy).
1883: Death of Karl Marx in London (14 March). Law on health insurance.
1884: Law on industrial accident insurance.

2. The founders of the Reich: William I, Crown Prince Frederick William, Prince Frederick-Charles, Bismarck and Moltke. German postcard.

3. Jules Favre and Adolphe Thiers opposite Bismarck, May 1871. Anonymous lithograph.

1871–1914

Political frontiers and national communities in 1848

Norwegians

Finns

Scots

Swedes

Danes

Estonians

Latvians

Lithuanians

Russians

RUSSIAN

English

White Russians

Irish

Welsh

Dutch

MECKLENBURG

PRUSSIA

EMPIRE

HANOVER

Germans

PRUSSIA

Flemings

SAXONY

Poles

Ukranians

Walloons

THURINGIA

Czechs

Slovaks

Bretons

BADEN

BAVARIA

AUSTRO-

French

Hungarians

Hung. Ger

Rumanians

KINGDOM OF PIEDMONT

HUNGARIAN EMPIRE

Slovenes

Basques

SARDINIA

PARMA

MODENA

Croats

Serbs

Bulgarians

TUSCANY

OTTOMAN EMPIRE

Catalans

PAPAL STATES

Italians

Albanians

Spaniards

KINGDOM OF THE TWO SICILIES

Turks

Greeks

Jews

500 km

Mass movement for universal suffrage in Prussia.

Moroccan crisis.

G. Hauptmann wins Nobel Prize for Literature.

First World War.

1905

1911

1912

August 1914

1884–5: Beginnings of German colonial empire.
March 1888: Death of William I. Frederick III reigns for 99 days.
1888–1918: Reign of William II.
1889: Law on old age pensions.
1890–91: Legislation on working conditions.
1890–4: Caprivi Chancellor.
1891: SPD adopts the Erfurt Programme.
1892: Gerhardt Hauptmann's *Die Weber.*
1893: General Commission of German Trade Unions founded.
1894–1900: Hohenlohe-Schillingfürst Chancellor.
1895: Death of Engels in London.
1897–9: Extension of German colonial possessions.
1898: Admiral Tirpitz becomes head of Reich Navy Office.
1899–1907: Social legislation extended.
1900–9: Bülow Chancellor.
1903: A German firm begins the construction of the Berlin-Baghdad railway, which is intended to link Constantinople with the Persian Gulf.

1904: Textile workers' strike at Crimmitschau.
1905: Strike by Ruhr miners, iron and steel and building workers demanding universal suffrage.
March: Moroccan crisis provoked by William II's visit to Tangier and followed by the Algeciras Conference (16 January–7 April 1906).
1906–7: Reichstag refuses to vote military budget for German colonial policy and is dissolved. The 'Hottentot elections' ensue.
1908: Expropriation Law, permitting the confiscation of Polish property.
October: William II's controversial *Daily Telegraph* interview, after which his influence on foreign affairs is curtailed.
1909–17: Bethmann-Hollweg Chancellor.
1910: Progressive Popular Party founded.
February–May: SPD demonstrations for universal suffrage.
May 1911: New constitution for Alsace-Lorraine.
July: Threat of war as a result of German gunboat being sent to Agadir.

4. The town of Mannheim, c. 1910. German postcard.

4 November: Agreements with France on colonial questions.
1913: Saverne affair: conflict between the military and the Alsatian population. Reichstag votes a wealth tax.
4 August 1914: Reichstag votes war credits.

Austria-Hungary and Russia

1854-1856 : The Crimean War:
Creation of Rumania

Occupation of Moldavia and Wallachia (1853) then its abandonment (April 1854). Creation of RUMANIA

MOLDAVIA

WALLACHIA

SERBIA

MONTENEGRO

Siege of Sebastopol (September 1854)

Dardanelles 1853

Gallipoli, April 1854

OTTOMAN EMPIRE

Anglo-French interventions in 1853 and 1854

GREECE

1875-1877 : Bosnian and Bulgarian uprisings
(catalyst of the Congress of Berlin)

RUSSIAN EMPIRE

AUSTRIA-HUNGARY

Bosnian Uprising SERBIA Plevna *Bulgarian Uprising*

MONTENEGRO

Constantinople

OTTOMAN EMPIRE

GREECE

AFTER THE REVOLUTIONS of 1848, the Russian and the Austro-Hungarian Empires emerged as champions of law and order. For both, military defeat proved to be a turning-point, in Russia's case in the Crimean War, in Austria's at Sadowa, ten years later, excluding her from the German Reich. In an age of nation-states, these two multi-national states seemed outmoded even in their style of colonial expansion, Russia finally conquering Caucasia and Central Asia, and Austria-Hungary penetrating deeper into the Balkans. These conquests were accompanied by a policy which encouraged the spread of German, Magyar or Russian national influence, although the controlling nations did not play the same economic role: the Germans were responsible for the development of an essentially finance-based capitalism, whilst in Russia it was the state which encouraged development, with the support of a few large, middle-class, Russian or non-native families. With the accession of Alexander II, the reformist era began; serfdom was abolished and peasants were allowed to buy up land gradually; locally elected councils (*zemstva*) were created; there was legal reform and municipal administrations were established. The assassination of Alexander II can be traced back to the populist movement, *Narodnaya Volya* (the Will of the People), which both originated from and yet constituted an advance over the university youth's campaign of 'going to the people'; but the Polish uprising

1. Naval battle of Petrograd between the Russians and the Germans. Russian illustration 1914.

Fall of Sebastopol.	Peasants freed from serfdom.	Polish uprising.	Assassination of Alexander II.	Beginning of the Russian Revolution.
8 September 1855	**19 February 1861**	**1863**	**1 [13] March 1881**	**9 [22] January 190**

8 September 1855: Fall of Sebastopol during Crimean War.
1855–81: Reign of Tsar Alexander II.
1859: Surrender of Chamil: completion of the conquest of the Caucasus by Russia.

3. The diversity of the Hungarian people. German engraving by H. Veber 1854.

19 February [3 March] **1861:** Promulgation of the 'Edict of emancipation of Russian peasants from serfdom'.
1863: Polish uprising, suppressed the following year.
1864–5: Conquest of Central Asia by Russia.
13 January 1864: Administrative reform in Russia; creation of *zemstva* (local assemblies).
2 December: Reform of the judiciary in Russia.
3 July 1866: Austria is defeated by Prussia at Sadowa.
18 February 1867: 'Compromise' between Austria and Hungary: creation of the double monarchy.
1868: Croatia becomes the Kingdom of Croatia-Slavonia following a 'compromise' with Hungary.
1870: Municipal administrations established in Russia; creation of urban dumas.
1873: Alliance between the three Emperors (William I, Alexander II, Franz-Josef).
May: Vienna Stock Exchange crash.
1874: 'March to the People' in Russia.

4. The Viennese doctor, Sigmund Freud, founder of psycho-analysis with his wife Martha, circa 1890.

19 April 1877–31 January 1878: Russo-Turkish War.
5 February 1878: Vera Zasulič shoots at Trepov, chief of police in St Petersburg.
13 June–13 July: Congress of Berlin.
1879: Occupation of Bosnia-Herzogovina by Austria-Hungary.
1 [13] March 1881: Assassination of Alexander II.
1881–2: Wave of pogroms against the Jews in Russia.
1887: *Numerus clausus* for the Jews: increase of Russian influence in Poland and the Baltic countries.
1888: Founding of the Austrian Social Democratic Party led by V. Adler and O. Bauer.
1891–3: Franco-Russian Alliance.
1 November 1894: Death of Alexander III: accession of Nicholas II.
1897: Creation of the fifth curia (general) for the *Reichsrat* elections. Edicts of K. Badeni (President of the Austrian Council of Ministers) on the equality of languages in Bohemia.
March 1898: Founding of the Russian Social

878-1885 : The Balkans at the time of the Congress of Berlin
(creation of Bulgaria)

RUSSIAN EMPIRE

AUSTRIA-HUNGARY

Protectorate

RUMANIA

BOSNIA
HERZOGOVINA

SERBIA

LESSER BULGARIA
EASTERN ROUMELIA

} *united in 1885*

MONTENEGRO

OTTOMAN EMPIRE

GREECE

CYPRUS
*British
Protectorate 1878*

Greater Bulgaria under
the treaty of San Stefano

1912-1913 : 1st and 2nd Balkan Wars
(Dismemberment of Macedonia)

RUSSIAN EMPIRE

AUSTRIA-HUNGARY

Annexation

RUMANIA

SERBIA

BULGARIA

MONTENEGRO

MACEDONIA

ALBANIA

OTTOMAN EMPIRE

GREECE

Annexation

CRETE

CYPRUS

⇨ 1st Balkan war
⬛➡ 2nd Balkan war

of 1863 had already cooled the movement's reforming zeal, particularly in national affairs.

Within the Hapsburg Empire – founded on clericalism, bureaucracy and the army – recognition of the 'historic Magyar nation' led to the era of 'compromise' (*Ausgleich*). Defence, foreign affairs and their financing were all that Austria and Hungary administered jointly. The Slavs were the overall losers in this arrangement. While the nationalities of Hungary were reduced to silence, the middle classes of the renascent 'nations without a history' were struggling in Austria for a share of power in the state, particularly through obstruction in parliament, which slowed down social progress. Social democracy took its place in the *Reichsrat* (the Austrian parliament) when a fifth curia was created, and in 1907, in the wake of the Russian Revolution of 1905, it won the universal suffrage denied its Hungarian counterpart. A federation of six national parties – German, Czech, Italian, Southern Slav, Polish and Ruthenian (Ukrainian) – set up a model national programme. It was challenged by a strong populist movement which was violently anti-semitic and formed under the wing of the Christian-Social party.

Within the Russian Empire, the socialist parties of the various nationalities also became spokesmen for national demands; the split which occurred between Bolsheviks and Mensheviks in 1903 actually

concealed a rift between nations. Preceded by terrorist attacks and anti-Jewish pogroms, the revolution broke out on 'Red Sunday', the catalysing agent being the Russo-Japanese war. The concessions of the Tsar's October Manifesto had been gradually whittled away by the dissolution of the first two Dumas, the first after the St Petersburg Soviet had been crushed, the second after the Moscow uprising.

The First World War was catalysed by rivalry in the Balkans between two powers which were already suffering internal instability because of national dissensions. Even within the Austro-Hungarian army there were deep tensions and last minute concessions could not stop the rot. In Russia, the 'Sacred Union' of nations could only briefly hold the revolutionary movement in check.

2. Archduke Charles-Louis of Hapsburg, Emperor Franz-Josef, Franz Ferdinand, Hungarian chromolithograph.

Universal suffrage in Austria.

1907

Russian Revolution.

February [March] 1917

Democratic Workers' Party in Russia.
1901: Founding of the Russian Revolutionary Socialist Party.
1902: Confiscation of Armenian Church property in Russia.
1903: Pogroms in Gomel and Kishinev.
8 February 1904: Port Arthur attack (start of Russo-Japanese War).
9 [22] January 1905: Red Sunday; the police open fire on a large popular peace demonstration in front of the Winter Palace in St Petersburg.
14–25 June [27 June–8 July]: Mutiny on the battleship *Potemkin* at Odessa.
5 September: Treaty of Portsmouth between Russia and Japan.
30 October: October manifesto of Nicholas II, which promises a meeting of the State Duma.
December: Uprising in Moscow.
10 May–21 July 1906: First Duma.
1907: Universal suffrage in the Reichsrat.
5 March–6 June: Second Duma in Russia.
1908: Annexation of Bosnia-Herzegovina by Austria.
1912: Striking miners shot in Lena.

December: Start of the Fourth Duma.
28 June 1914: Assassination of Franz-Ferdinand at Sarajevo.
1 August 1915: The Duma calls for a government accountable to parliament.
21 October 1916: The Social Democrat, Friedrich Adler (son of Victor), assassinates Count Sturgh, Prime Minister of Austria.
21 November: Death of Franz-Josef; accession of Charles I.
February [March] 1917: Russian Revolution.
18 October 1918: Charles I announces the creation of a Federal State of Austria.
12 November: Proclamation of the Republic of German Austria.

5. Sailors of the battleship Potemkin, *June 1905. Anonymous Russian painting.*

6. Judith, 1909, by the Viennese Gustav Klimt (1862–1918) co-founder of the Secession (see p. 274).

The New Division of the World

ON THE EVE of the 1914 war, it seemed that the division of the world among a number of great powers was almost complete. In Africa there were only two independent republics: Ethiopia and the small Republic of Liberia. In Asia the remaining great empires – Turkey, Persia, China – were increasingly being threatened by rival foreign ambitions. In Central and South America, the United States was establishing its economic protection. This general movement of imperialism – which involved not only the old colonial powers such as France and Great Britain, but Germany, Italy, Russia, Japan and the United States as well – took various forms, from territorial conquest and colonial domination to the imposition of such less direct methods of control as the enforcement of political allegiance or the setting up of a state of economic dependency. There were various reasons for this, many of which were closely interrelated, though they were of varying importance depending on the countries involved.

The first causes were economic. After the establishment of free trade in Europe from 1860, there followed a general return to protectionism at the end of the century, except in Great Britain. National markets were shrinking and there developed a determination to appropriate overseas territory possessing natural potential for expansion which would provide markets for industrial production and financial investment. Jules Ferry said that 'Colonial policy is the daughter of industrial policy.' In some instances (Italy, for example) strong demographic pressure was exerted in addition to pressure from all-important business interests.

These economic factors, on the other hand, came to be part of a power struggle inseparable from a nationalism that was asserting itself in increasingly violent terms. The great powers needed to acquire naval bases essential to the protection of the commercial sea routes and to the supply of their fleets of coal-carrying ships. It was also something of a race on a global scale to prevent other states from staking their claims over lands that were considered available. 'No time must be lost,' said King Leopold II of Belgium, 'otherwise we shall see nations more enterprising than ours taking up the best positions, and such positions are few in number already.'

Finally, there were the ideological and moral forces in play. Faith in the values of progress and civilization among Western nations led them to argue that colonization would bring the light of reason, democratic principles and the benefits of science and medicine to those tribes of the interior that were thought of as primitive. Also, there was a desire in religious circles to spread the Christian faith in areas which had not yet been converted. The spread of missionaries had been part of colonial expansion ever since the beginning of the century. For those countries involved, expansionist policies would lead to outbreaks of violent controversy. Pressures from certain groups (businessmen, missionaries, the military, nationalist or progressive idealists, travellers and geographers) often met with lively resistance from many and various quarters (humanitarian arguments or suggestions that caution should be exercised where commitment was considered dangerous and of no value compared with the costs involved). Notions of worldwide policy and global strategy nonetheless did finally become accepted thinking in international relationships. Paul Valéry summed up the situation when he wrote: 'The age of the finite world has begun.'

By overturning people's traditional ways of thinking and the old economic and social structures, colonialism soon aroused hostile reactions in the conquered countries, however. Indian nationalism and the reawakening of the Arab world were direct consequences of this.

1. The Sudan war: the British Army marching against the Khartoum uprising in 1898.

Anglo-French Free Trade Treaty.

1860

1859–79: Conquest of the Caucasus and Russian expansion to the south of the Aral Sea in Central Asia.
1873–4: French attempt to conquer Tonkin. Hanoi is taken, then evacuated.
1874–8: Exploration of the Congo area by Savorgnan de Brazza and Stanley.
1879–82: Competition between Brazza and Stanley (acting in the name of the King of the Belgians, Leopold II) for the control of the Congo basin. Question of the Egyptian debt. This brings about increasing political intervention by France and Great Britain in Egyptian internal affairs.
1881: French intervention in Tunisia. 12 May: signing of the Bardo treaty by which the *bey* recognizes French protectorate. Touaregs massacre the French reconnaissance mission in the Hoggar.
1882: Military intervention and establishment of British control in Egypt. Crisis in Anglo-French relations.
1883–95: Conquest of Tonkin and recognition of French protectorate by Annam.
1883–95: French rule over the Niger, Guinea, Ivory Coast and Dahomey areas established.

Leopold II, King of the Belgians.

1865–1909

2. The march of African slaves according to the accounts of Dr Livingstone, c. 1860.

Colonial Conference in Berlin.

1884

1884–5: Colonial Conference in Berlin. Establishment of a procedure to settle frontier conflicts in Africa and the recognition of the independent state of the Congo under the sovereignty of Leopold II.
1885: Franco-Chinese war. China renounces suzerainty over Annam. Anglo-Russian tension over Afghanistan.
1886: Burma becomes a province of the Indian Empire.
1890–1: Italy conquers Eritrea and Somalia.
1894–5: Sino-Japanese war. Victory for Japan, established by the Treaty of Shimonoseki.
1894–6: Conquest and annexation of Madagascar by France.
1895–6: Attempted Italian take-over of Abyssinia. Disaster at Adowa (1 March). Under the Treaty of Addis Ababa, the Italians recognize Ethiopian sovereignty.
1898: Anglo-French crisis over the control of the Upper Valley of the Nile. Marchand mission reaches Fashoda then leaves, 7 November.
1899: Establishment of Anglo-Egyptian joint rule over the Sudan. Fouteau-Lamy mission

1860–1914

The division of the world circa 1900

Colonies
- British
- French
- German
- Others
- Russian expansion

Colonies
- P: Portuguese
- S: Spanish
- D: Dutch
- B: Belgium
- Da: Danish
- U.S.: United States
- I: Italian

Treaty of Tiantsin between China and France.

Fashoda.

1898

Algeciras Conference.

1906

crosses the Sahara. Definitive establishment of French rule over the Sahara.
1899–1902: Boer War originating from opposition between the Boer Republics in Orange Free State and Transvaal, and the British colonies in Southern Africa. The defeated Boers accept the suzerainty of the King of England at Vereeniging 31 May 1902.
1900: Boxers attack the foreign legations in Peking, China. An international expedition led by the German general, A. von Waldersee relieves the legations, 14 August.
1904–5: Russo-Japanese war. Japan is victorious on land and sea and ensures its own freedom of action in Manchuria and Korea.
1905: First Moroccan crisis. Germany opposes French ambitions in Morocco. The Algeciras conference (16 January–7 April 1906) makes the Moroccan question an international issue.
1910: Annexation of Korea by Japan.
1911–12: Italian-Turkish war and Italian occupation of Libya. Second Moroccan crisis. Germany accepts the principle of French protectorate against certain territorial

concessions in the Congo.
30 March 1912: Fez Convention. Establishment of French protectorate over Morocco.

3. One picture of colonialism: a white teacher in Senegal c. 1860.

The Break-Up of the Chinese Empire: Contacts with the West

AT THE END of the reign of Ch'ien-lung two major factors were already in evidence which were to undermine the basis of imperial society at the very moment when, on its borders, the threat from Western imperialism was becoming plain. The first, and most important problem, was the extent to which China's mandarin system and its centralized administration were ill-adapted to pre-industrial society. Secondly, difficulties arose as a result of what has been termed the 'handicap of a prematurely high level of social equilibrium': the agricultural and industrial progress of the eighteenth century brought in its train a demographic explosion which hampered any attempt to industrialize the country, firstly by making mechanization unnecessary, and secondly by causing the pauperization of the whole of society when production stagnated. In this way a chronic economic cycle was set into being, of which China remained the prisoner for more than a hundred years. In the rural areas, for example, poverty gave rise to the endemic problem of peasant revolts, which in their turn made poverty more acute.

In addition to these internal causes were external factors. The

1. 'Shoot the Christian Pig!'. A popular propaganda engraving from around 1810.

opium trade, forced on China by the British, created such a heavy balance of payments deficit that the result was almost catastrophic. This was at the root of the two major events in the history of China in the twentieth century, which were to have a decisive effect on its destiny. The Opium Wars not only left the way open for the foreign penetration of China, they also marked the end of a movement of trade (which till then had always been favourable to the West) and

provoked a haemorrhage of capital, which in turn created a financial crisis of the most severe sort.

The collapse of the economy was sparked off by the Taiping Rebellion. This gigantic movement of revolt, under the leadership of Hung Hsiu-ch'uan (who was also a convert to Christianity), had its roots in ancient tradition. It caused irreparable damage in the Yangtze basin which was the most prosperous area in China. It went hand in hand with other peasant uprisings (of the Nien, for example) with which it at times converged, while it was given further momentum by secessionist moves on the part of the Hui (who were Muslims) in Yunnan and Kansu, then in Sinkiang. In truth, the whole Empire was in turmoil for more than fifty years. These rebellions, which demonstrated the inability of central government to react to the crisis, marked the rise to power of a new generation of provincial administrators who were both reformers and traditionalists, such as Tseng Kuo-fan or Tso Tsung-t'ang. They met, however, with hostility on the part of the imperial court and total lack of sympathy on the part of Empress Tzu-hsi. The inability of Chinese society to effect its own modernization was mirrored in the liquidation of its reforming leaders (the most important of whom, Kan Yu-wei and Liang Ch'i-Ch'ao, were only in government for a hundred days) and in the destruction of the Chinese fleet at the hands of Japan. The Western countries took advantage of China's weakness and divided the country up into zones of influence. The awareness that it had proved impossible to reform traditional society from within led to the emergence of a radical movement which saw the only hope as being total Westernization. The Boxer uprising was only to be the last, archaic convulsion of an empire whose days were numbered. Even though the Republic, proclaimed by Sun Yat-sen, was taken over by General Yüan Shih-k'ai, it did enough to destroy the dynasty for ever.

2. Empress Tzu-hsi in her sedan chair.

The Mirror of the Hundred Flower Women by Li Ru-chen, the phonetician.

Taiping Rebellion.

1800: A decree is passed, banning the importation of opium and the planting of poppy fields.
1810: Christian preaching is banned.
1812: The population of China reaches 361 million inhabitants.
1820–5: A growing balance of payments deficit is caused by the development of the opium market by the East India Company.
1839: Energetic measures taken by Lin Tse-hsü to ban the importing of opium cause British retaliation and mark the beginning of the First Opium War.
1842: Display of strength by the British leads to the Treaty of Nanking, setting up trading links between China and the West and providing for the transfer of Hong Kong to Britain.
1843: China recognises the territorial independence of Hong Kong. Shanghai and Ning-po are declared open ports.
1850: The Taiping Rebellion begins. Hung Hsiu-chüan proclaims himself Heavenly King in the Celestial Kingdom of Great Peace.
1853–4: After spreading to Hunan and the Yangtze basin, the Taiping establish their

capital in Nanking. The Nien uprisings begin. The Taiping movement spreads to the North and threatens Peking.
1855: Muslim uprisings in Yunnan.
1857–60: Second Opium War, leading to the sack of the Summer Palace by French and British troops and to the ratification of the Peking Treaty.
1861–2: Muslim uprisings in Shensi and Sinkiang.
1863: The sea-board customs network passes under British control.
1864: Nanking is captured and Hung Hsiu-chüan commits suicide.
1865: The Nien counter-attack.
1866: The Taiping are defeated.
1867: Li Hung-chang defeats the Nien as they threaten Peking.
1876–8: The Secessionist revolt of Sinkiang is put down.
1879: Under the Treaty of Livadia the major part of the area around Ili passes under Russian control.
1883–5: War breaks out between China and France as a result of the French intervention in Indochina and ends under a treaty signed

after the siege of Ning-po.
1888: An armaments factory is set up in Wuhan.
1894–5: War between China and Japan, leading to the Treaty of Shimonoseki (under which Taiwan and the Pescadores Islands are given to Japan). China must pay extensive reparations.
1897: Chiao-chou Bay in Shantung is annexed by Germany.
1898: Wei-hai-wei is annexed by the British, and Dalian by the Russians. The liberal policies followed by K'ang Yu-wei come to an end and reformist circles are repressed.
1900: The Boxer uprising breaks out as a result of Western harassment. It leads to the capitulation of the Imperial Court and the paying of reparations.
1905: Sun Yat-sen founds the United League (T'ung-meng hui) in Japan.
1907: The imperial system of recruitment by written examinations is abolished.

3. The passengers of a British steamship arriving in Canton: mid-nineteenth-century Chinese painting.

1800–1916

Central China

Territory conquered
by the Ch'ing

Temporary Conquests

1910 Borders

Foreign occupation of China

Ports open to foreign powers
in 1842

from 1842 to 1911

Territory ceded by China

Railways built by foreign companies

Internal revolts

Taiping Rebellion and other peasant risings (1850-1880)

Boxer Uprising against foreign powers (1900)

First centre of republican uprising (October 1911)

400 km

The Great Commonwealth by K'ang Yu-wei.   **Reform of teaching.**   **The magazine *New Youth* is launched.**

1896   1912   1915

1908: Death of Empress Tzu-hsi.
1910: Northeast China is divided up between the Russians and the Japanese.
1911: Insurrection in Wu-han leads to the secession of South China.
1912: Sun Yat-sen proclaims the Republic in Nanking, and the Emperor Pu-yi abdicates. Sun Yat-sen hands the presidency of the Republic over to General Yüan Shih-k'ai. The education system is reformed.
1916: Death of Yüan Shih-k'ai.

4. *Yüan Shih-k'ai before his death in 1916.*   5. *The revolution is also a matter of hair-style.*

British Colonial Settlement

1. Queen Victoria visits the Australia exhibit, in May 1886.

SINCE 1791 CANADA HAD BEEN under the control of a governor appointed by London and an executive council made up of leading citizens and British civil servants. But there were growing demands for a representative system, and Canadians of French descent continued to protest at their exclusion from power. By 1837 the need for change had become clear to all. Lord Durham was commissioned to undertake an inquiry into the roots of the disturbances. His report recommending the granting of responsible self-government was only partly put into effect, though in reality Governor Elgin allowed the assembly elected in 1848 to form the government itself, and this type of self-government quickly created a precedent for other countries. Moreover, the annexationist overtures being expressed by the United States led to the growth of the idea of a federal structure: as a result, in 1867, the Dominion of Canada was created from the joining together of four provinces, including Quebec, with institutions on the British model. The integration of the west and the completion of the Canadian Pacific Railway gave the country a continental dimension.

In the case of Australia, the country had at first been little more than the penal colony of New South Wales. After 1840, the crown made official the settling of vast areas in the country by squatters whose main interest was in wool production, and later in gold mining as the gold rush got under way. The granting of self-government took place smoothly and a second dominion came into being at the start of the twentieth century. Similarly, in New Zealand, where agricultural development took the form of the confiscation of Maori land, the path to self-government was quickly followed and dominion status finally granted in 1907. Durham and those who came after him had understood that as far as the 'White' colonies were concerned the interests of trade and profit were best served by the abandonment of unwieldy and expensive colonial rule.

The strategic importance and mineral wealth of Southern Africa, its ethnic diversity, and the growing number of politicians invoking the supremacy of the Empire, resulted in different conflicts and took the whole region down a different evolutionary path. In the Cape, the attempted process of anglicization and the emancipation of the slaves had, in the years after 1833, sparked off the Great Trek, that is the migration towards the north-east of the country of 10,000 Boers (these were colonial settlers of Dutch descent). After limiting the extent of these movements by the declaration of Natal as British territory, Britain recognized the independence of the Boer states of the Orange Free State and the Transvaal. But the problem became more complicated after the discovery of diamonds along the borders of the Orange Free State in 1867. The British extended the sovereignty of the Cape Colony before granting it self-government. Unrest on the part of the black workers, the mining interests involved and the appeal of the Transvaal for German capital dragged Britain into an abortive project for a South African Federation, and then in 1877 into a disastrous

The first convicts arrive in Botany Bay, near Sydney.

Ottawa has its first Parliament.

Diamonds discovered in the Orange Free Sta

1788

1848

1867

3. The Last of England by Ford Madox Brown.

1788: The first shipment of convicts arrives in Sydney.
1791: Constitutional Act of Canada.
1815: Britain has its title to the Cape Colony confirmed.
1825–1836: Five new colonial states are founded in Australia.
1829–1836: William Lyon Mackenzie launches his campaign for Canadian self-government.
1834–9: The Great Trek by the Boers.
1837: Rebellion put down in Montreal.
1839: The Durham Report is published, opening the way to responsible self-government in Canada.
1840: Annexation of New Zealand.
1841: Union Act passed, by which the different provinces of Canada are unified.
1843: The British occupy Natal. The Orange Free State is founded.
1848: Beginnings of parliamentary government in Canada.
1851: Gold discovered in Australia.
1852: The Transvaal founded. The British recognize its independence (and that of the Orange Free State in 1854).

1854–9: Five Australian colonies gain responsible self-government.
1867: The Dominion of Canada is established. Diamonds are discovered in the Orange Free State.
1868: Basutoland becomes a British protectorate.
1870–3: Three new provinces, including British Columbia, join the Dominion of Canada.
1871: The diamond mining district of Kimberley is transferred to the Cape Colony.
1872: The Cape Colony gains responsible self-government.
1876: The British plan for a South African federation fails.
1877–9: Disraeli adopts an aggressive policy: the Transvaal is attacked, then the Zulu War breaks out.
1880: The Transvaal rises up against the British, and Boer, or 'Afrikaner', nationalism emerges.
1881: The British are defeated by Transvaal forces at Majuba Hill.
1882: The first cargoes of refrigerated meat leave New Zealand for Britain.

1885: Gold is discovered in the Transvaal. Kruger greets the Germans from South West Africa as allies.
1886: Completion of the Canadian Pacific Railway.
1889: The British South African Company,

4. President Kruger as seen by Caran d'Ache.

attempt to annex the Transvaal. The country, vastly enriched by the mining of gold after 1885, rallied around President Kruger to reject any abandonment of sovereignty. The fate of the Uitlanders, who were (often British) workers in the Transvaal mines and enjoyed no political rights, added to the dispute. When in 1899 war broke out, international opinion regarded the Boers as the innocent victims of British imperialism. Two and a half years, 400,000 soldiers and the invention of concentration camps were needed to break their resistance. The annexation of the Boer states was tempered by the assurance that self-government would be granted before long. At last, the Union of South Africa was established. It had the status of a dominion, but one in which the Boers demanded that all civil rights be reserved for the Whites. Racial segregation had found a homeland.

2. The British Lion and the Boer Bull.

uger becomes dent of the Transvaal.	Gold rush in the Transvaal.	Australia becomes the second dominion.
1883	**1885**	**1901**

founded by Cecil Rhodes in 1887, is given the territories soon to be named Rhodesia to administer.
1895: Failure of the Jameson Raid against the Transvaal.
1897: The ultra-imperialist Sir Alfred Milner is appointed High Commissioner in the Cape Colony by the Colonial Secretary Joseph Chamberlain.
9 October 1899: The Orange Free State and the Transvaal declare war.
1900: In the British General Election the supporters of Empire win a convincing victory.
1901: The Commonwealth of Australia is founded. This was the second dominion, after Canada.
31 May 1902: The Peace of Vereeniging leads to the annexation of the Boer States.
1906–7: The Transvaal and the Orange Free State are given self-government.
1907: The Dominion of New Zealand is established.
31 May 1910: The Union of South Africa is established, on the basis of racial segregation.

5. Terminus of the Canadian Pacific Railway in Vancouver.

Map 1 (Canada) legend:

- 1837 Canada / Other British Colonies
- 1867 Dominion of Canada
- 1870-1905 Provinces formed or joined to the Dominion
- 1895-1912 Establishment of federal territories
- 1912 Territories joined to the Canadian provinces
- Canadian Pacific Railway

1000 km

Map 2 (Australia) legend:

- Territory inhabited in 1860
- 'Profitable zones' at the end of the XIXth century, in descending order of importance
- ▼ Gold
- ◢ Ore
- ▬ Seaport activities
- Sheep Farming
- Less than 250 mm of annual rainfall
- Journeys of exploration

1000 km

NEW ZEALAND

Auckland
Wellington
Christchurch

1700 First Dutch settlements	**1840** British settlements and the Great Trek	**1850** Policy of encirclement and isolation of the Boers	**1899-1902** Boer War ✗ Battles
Cape Town	NATAL	Majuba Hill / Zulu War	

Map 3 (South Africa) legend:

- Great Trek
- Boer States: Natal 1839 / Orange Free State 1843 / Transvaal 1852
- British Settlements
- Territories annexed or controlled from 1843 to 1899
- Borders of the Republic of South Africa in 1985 and government-controlled towns in 1910
- ▽ Gold and diamonds
- J. Johannesburg
- P. Pretoria
- V. Vereeniging

500 km

The United States and Global Expansion

FOLLOWING THE CIVIL WAR, over a period of some twenty years, the United States, which at the time was still mainly an agrarian country, entered the industrial era. The need for war materials, the temporary absence of the Southerners from the political scene and the conquest of the far West stimulated the exploitation and transformation of resources. The rise of the food, textile and iron and steel industries and the growth in coal, mineral and oil production was such that by the end of the century the United States was able to compete with the European powers. Its success was due to the concentration of its industry, both the concentration of its resources – geographic, economic and human – and the financial concentration that came with the formation of trusts and holding companies, which liberal legislation would not succeed in checking. A monopoly capitalism, from which several major figures (Rockefeller, Carnegie, Morgan) had an impact upon political life, became superimposed upon the brute capitalism of the 'robber barons'. Between 1900 and 1920 the movement of reformers fighting against the abuses of capitalism was outflanked by the political strategy of Theodore Roosevelt, who represented a progressive position, and Woodrow Wilson, a Democrat. The First World War, which the US entered in 1917, increased foreign demand for its goods and made the USA the leading world power.

The American industrial revolution would not have been possible without the contribution from immigrant labour. Thanks to that immigration, the American population rose from 31 million in 1860 to 92 million in 1910. At the beginning of the twentieth century, more than a million people a year (in peak years) were entering the USA. Brought there by economic demand, the immigrants – most of whom came from Central and Southern Europe, though there were some from Asia – were badly received by the more established population, who resented them for accepting lower wages and for having different cultures. From 1882 onwards, nativist and trade union movements succeeded in having the Congress pass discriminatory immigrant legislation. The 'melting-pot' was now to admit only those who were by their colour and culture close to the 'White Anglo-Saxon Protestants'. Part of the effect, however, of the newcomers' influence was that the traditionally elitist and reformist American trade unions became radicalized, a process which culminated in the great days of the Haymarket Affair in 1886 and the Pullman strike in 1894 and in the revolutionary movement of the IWW (Industrial Workers of the World) at the beginning of the twentieth century.

Whilst protecting itself from outside influences, in foreign affairs the USA conducted a policy of expansion by investing capital as far afield as Oceania, by implanting colonial settlers in Puerto Rico, the island of Guam and the Philippines, by exerting political, military and financial influence in Cuba, and by its military expedition against Spain in 1898. In the wake of this venture, Hawaii was annexed. Theodore Roosevelt justified this policy in terms of a doctrine of the 'big stick'. Under his leadership, the US participated in the actions of the European powers in China, a decision which was made in the name of the 'open door' theory.

The age of imperialism did not end with the election of the Democrat, Woodrow Wilson, for he intervened in Latin America, combating the Mexican peasant revolution to establish bourgeois democracy. In 1917 the United States entered the First World War on the side of the democracies, but the politics of Wilson's 'Fourteen Points' was to be disavowed by public opinion and Congress, which in 1919 refused to ratify signature of the Treaty of Versailles.

1. Immigrants arriving at Ellis Island c. 1900.

Blacks granted civil rights.	Economic crisis and monetary disorder.		Protectionism.
1866	**1873**		**1890**

1866: Creation of the Freedmen's Bureau; assistance to the emancipated Blacks. The Civil Rights Act guarantees them civil rights.
1868: Burlingame Treaty: admission of Chinese workers.
1869: C. Vanderbilt organizes the New York Central Railroad Company. Creation of the Knights of Labour, an industrially based union.
1873: Crisis caused by railroad speculation.
1875: Greenback Party, supporting an inflationary policy.
1876: Centenary Exhibition in Philadelphia. Alexander Graham Bell invents the telephone.
1877: Major strike by workers in the Baltimore and Ohio Railroad Company.
1879: Formation of the Standard Oil Trust.
1880: Chicago becomes the capital of meat packing.
1882: Formation of the Standard Oil Company. Act prohibiting Chinese immigration (renewed in 1892 and again, definitively, in 1902 when it is extended to all Orientals).
1886: Haymarket Riot; explosion of a bomb during a public meeting in Chicago. Four anarchists hanged without evidence. Creation of the American Federation of Labour (A.F. of L.), a federation of craft unions.
1887: The Interstate Commerce Act regulates national transport.
1890: McKinley protectionist tariff. Anti-Trust Act of Senator Sherman.
1892: Homestead strike in the Carnegie works.
1894: Strike in the Pullman factories in Chicago.
1898: War against Spain in Cuba and the Philippines; annexation of Hawaii.
1900: McKinley assassinated. Theodore Roosevelt President.
1901: Currency Act: gold made the sole monetary standard.
1903: Revolution in Panama: United States accorded contract for management of a trans-isthmian canal.
1905: The appearance of revolutionary syndicalism in the shape of the Industrial Workers of the World (IWW).
1908: Appearance of *The Octopus* by Frank

3. In the streets of New York: barrel organ c. 1910.

Norris, *The Jungle* by Upton Sinclair and *The Iron Heel* by Jack London, all critiques of capitalism.
1912–20: Woodrow Wilson President.
1912–25: Occupation of Nicaragua.
1913: Federal Reserve Act: government control over money supply.
1914: US intervention in Mexico.
1915: Intervention by the marines and occupation of Haiti.
1917: Literacy Test Act: immigrants have to be able to read. 6 April, US declares war on Germany.
1919: Volstead Act on the prohibition of alcohol.
November 1919: The Senate rejects the Treaty of Versailles.
1920: 20th Amendment. Women granted the right to vote. Election of the Republican, W. G. Harding.
1921 and 1924: Quota Acts fixing the number of immigrants at 3% of nationals of the same country in the USA in 1910, then at 2% of the 1890 figure.

1865–1920

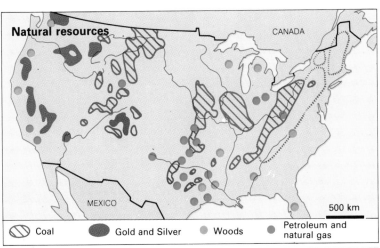

Natural resources

Coal	Gold and Silver	Woods	Petroleum and natural gas

500 km

Areas of high population density

Seattle
Salt Lake City
San Francisco
Detroit
Chicago
Boston
New York
Philadelphia
Pittsburgh
Cincinnati
Kansas City
St Louis
Birmingham
Atlanta
Dallas
New Orleans
MEXICO
CANADA

Population density (inhabitants per square kilometre): Between 17 and 35 | More than 35

Industry

Milwaukee, Flint, Rochester, Buffalo, Boston
San Francisco, Omaha, Chicago, Detroit, Cleveland, Philadelphia
Columbus, Pittsburgh, Baltimore
Indianapolis, Cincinnati
Los Angeles, Kansas City, St Louis
Atlanta
New Orleans
MEXICO, CANADA

Industrial cities	Textiles	Iron and steel Automobiles	Abattoirs and meat packaging

2. First view of America.

Wilson is elected President.   USA enters First World War.
1912   1917

U.S. expansion in the Pacific and the West Indies

Alaska 1867
Hong Kong
Philippines 1898
Marcus I
Midway 1867
Hawaii 1898
Guam 1898
Wake I
Johnston Atoll
Palmyra Atoll
UNITED STATES
Cuba
Haiti
Puerto Rico 1898
Nicaragua
Panama 1903
NETHERLANDS
Tutuila 1899
FRANCE
UNITED KINGDOM

Social Movements

Coeur d'Alene 1892-1899
Pullman Factories (railways) 1894
Haymarkets Riots 1886 7 policemen killed, 4 anarchists hanged
1877-1878 1902
Pittsburgh
Homestead (steelworks) 1892
Paterson (textiles) 1877-1879
Martinsburg
10 Irish miners hanged, 1876 "Molly Maguires"
New Orleans 1894-1895
1894
MEXICO
CANADA

Strikes: Miners | Railway workers (1877) | Others | Disturbances involving fatalities

The World Market before 1914

1. The New York Stock Exchange in 1899.

THE EXPANSION in international trade prior to 1914 was unprecedented, and developed at a much greater rate than in the succeeding decades of the twentieth century. The volume growth of world trade was 4.6% per annum from 1820 to 1913. Growth slackened somewhat in the years from 1873 to 1896, but picked up very strongly over the last twenty years preceding the War. This was only possible because of the rise in the number of steamships after 1870. The opening of the Suez Canal in 1869 resulted in major changes in commercial shipping routes. Sailing ships were banished from the routes to the Far East. Steam gave a considerable boost to the various Atlantic routes and increased the number of opportunities for new lines in the Pacific.

On the eve of the First World War, international trade was characterized by a dual hegemony: first, that of Europe itself, though it was in slight decline (from 67% in 1876–80 to 62% in 1913), and secondly that of the whole of the 'developed' world (the northwestern countries of Europe, North America and Australia: 63.5% in 1913). Two basic trading patterns, working in tandem, lay behind this twofold superiority. First, there was a 'classic' trading pattern based on the exchange of primary goods (raw materials and foodstuffs) in return for industrial products, which is what made the developed countries into the 'workshops of the world'. Second, there was a more recent trading pattern based on the trade in industrial products between the industrialized countries themselves. These two patterns complemented each other within the multilateral trading network that existed at the outbreak of the War. The industrial success of countries such as Germany, Sweden or the United States, with their efficient exploitation of technical innovations, fostered the development of exports from countries which were producers of primary products and gave them the means to purchase more traditional industrial goods (textiles in particular) which came from Great Britain, Belgium or France. In this way the system maintained its equilibrium in spite of its rapid growth: Great Britain had a trading deficit with continental Europe, the United States and Canada, and a surplus with India, Australia and the colonies in Africa. The equilibrium was restored by the deficit which, in turn, continental Europe and North America had with this third group of countries. Essentially, then, the equilibrium rested on the British trade surplus with the developing world, which reflects the somewhat 'archaic' nature of the structure of the country's exports, as it was also a major importer of German or American industrial goods. It must be said, too, that the British were the only country to maintain free trade in spite of the rising tide of protectionism which, after the great age of the free market in the 1850s and 1860s, spread across the world in the years following 1879, though the extent of European protectionism was much less wide-ranging than that in Russia or America.

International investment increased by a factor of approximately 7.5 times between 1870 and 1914. This was complementary to the growth in trade, as it enabled the development of the infrastructure necessary for the production and transportation of primary products. Great Britain owned 43% of these assets before the outbreak of war, while France had 20%, Germany 13% and the United States already 7%. These investments were traditionally directed towards infrastructure and public works, and towards the modernization of those emerging countries which had for the most part European populations (Russia in the case of France, and the dominions in the case of Britain). The colonies and countries with non-European populations were relatively neglected, but it was also the case, since the 1870s, that industrial investment was made directly by companies, which thus became 'multinational' companies, within the context of the transfer of technology amongst industrialized countries, at the head of which was the United States.

3. The loading of cotton bound for New Orleans on the Mississippi river, as seen by an American newspaper at the end of the nineteenth century.

4. The export of German products. An advertisement for Liebig's meat extract in Britain towards the end of the nineteenth century.

19th and 20th centuries

2. Opening of the Suez Canal, 17 November 1869.

5. The Frigorifique, the first cargo-ship able to store food-stuffs by refrigeration. It crossed the Atlantic in 1876.

6. The establishment of Swiss companies in Britain: an advertisement for Nestlé's condensed milk.

Towards the First World War

AFTER ITS VICTORY over France in 1871, Germany dominated European diplomacy to such a degree that, when a congress was arranged in 1878 to settle problems in the Balkans it was quite naturally held at Berlin.

Bismarck wished above all to maintain the European balance of power. France, isolated and weakened, was no longer a danger, even if she did experience periodic crises of revanchist nationalism. The major danger to stability lay in the fragility of the two great multinational empires, the Ottoman and the Austro-Hungarian. The Turks still controlled part of the Balkans, which the Austro-Hungarian Empire and Russia harboured designs upon, whilst in Austria-Hungary, the Slavic minorities – discreetly supported by Russia – were demanding independence. By arranging numerous meetings and agreements, Bismarck managed to prevent any direct confrontation between the Austrians and the Russians.

After 1890, William II broke with this prudent policy and openly opted for an alliance with Austria. Russia, which needed French capital to develop its industry, resigned itself to signing a military convention with Paris. Since the 1860s European expansion in Africa and Asia had greatly intensified, though Germany had played no part in it: it was William II's intention to acquire the military and economic means to enable Germany finally to pursue a genuinely global politics. In the Far East, and particularly in China, where they encountered competition from the USA and Japan, the Europeans managed to divide the country up quite comfortably into zones of influence. On the other hand, in the Near East and Africa they came into open confrontation. The reinforcement of the German war fleet and the territorial expansion sought by William II directly threatened Great Britain in Africa – where German possessions were sandwiched between territories under British control – and in the Persian Gulf. Although Germany was its principal trading partner in Europe, Britain accepted a *rapprochement* with France.

Europe found itself split into two coalitions, but the Triple Entente (Great Britain, France, Russia) was weakened by the internal difficulties experienced by Russia and was unable to co-ordinate its plans for military reorganization. William II, aware of the temporary superiority of the Triple Alliance (Germany, Austria-Hungary, Italy), applied increasing pressure. In Morocco, where he wanted to stem the tide of French penetration, he ran into concerted opposition from the other powers, who did not wish to see the African status quo threatened. By contrast, his unconditional support allowed Austria-Hungary to extend its territory and influence in the Balkans.

At the beginning of 1914, the Balkan peninsula constituted the only politically sensitive area in Europe. Russia had only one ally left there, Serbia, to whom she gave wholehearted support. The Austro-Hungarian Empire, encouraged by Bulgaria, was on the lookout for a pretext to remove this final obstacle. Ten years of tension had caused all the powers to reinforce their armed forces considerably, to tolerate fanatical support for war among the public, and to bind themselves by a complex system of accords which, if once triggered, might unleash a chain reaction that would prove irreversible. War was not in sight, but neither of the two coalitions was in a position to halt the mobilization process if it should once be set in motion.

1. Colonial rivalry between France and Germany. A German cruiser blockades Agadir in the summer of 1911.

Wagner's *Ring* cycle performed at Bayreuth.

Nietzsche's *Genealogy of Morals*.

Kipling, *The Jungle Book*.

1876	1887	1894

10 May 1871: Treaty of Frankfurt. France loses Alsace and part of Lorraine.
1872: Alliance between the three Emperors – German, Austrian and Russian – against revolutionary threats of any kind.
1876–8: Agitation in the part of the Balkans still under Ottoman rule. Russia goes to war against the Turks and, after her victory, seeks to consolidate her influence in the Balkans. Austria-Hungary and Great Britain displeased. In July 1878, the Congress of Berlin seeks to balance out influence within the Balkan peninsula. Bulgaria becomes independent. Austria-Hungary obtains control over Bosnia-Herzegovina.
7 October 1879: Dual alliance between Austria and Germany.
1882: Triple Alliance: Austria, Italy and Germany strike military pact.
1885: Germany forces recognition of her colonial rights in Africa.
1887: French nationalism revived under General Boulanger: tension between France and Germany.
1889: First French loan granted to Russia.
1890: William II dismisses Bismarck.

December 1893: The ratification of a Franco-Russian military agreement establishes a de facto alliance between the two powers.
1894–5: Sino-Japanese War. Japan acquires Formosa and protectorate over Korea.
1898: Germany, Great Britain, France and Russia come to an accord on the siting of naval bases in China. In the Sudan, French and British troops come face to face at Fashoda. The French troops, led by Marchand, withdraw. Hague Conference to restrain the arms race. The International Court will be founded two years later.
1899–1902: The Transvaal, the richest independent state in South Africa, refuses to submit to British influence. Great Britain subjugates it by force.
1900: Nationalist rising in China (Boxers), crushed by an international expeditionary force. The Ottoman Empire concedes to Germany the right to build a railway from Berlin to the Persian Gulf.
1904–5: Russo-Japanese War for control of Manchuria: the Japanese are victorious.
8 April 1904: Entente Cordiale: colonial

agreement between Britain and France marks beginnings of a *rapprochement*.
9 Jan 1905: Revolution in Russia.
1908: Austria-Hungary annexes Bosnia-Herzegovina.

4. Setbacks to Britain's imperial rule: the revolt of the Boers in the Transvaal and of the Boxers in China.

1912: Balkan states fight victorious war against the Ottoman Empire.
10 August 1913: Treaty of Bucharest confirms Turkish withdrawal from the Balkans. Serbia fails to acquire access to the coast.
1914. 28 June: Assassination of an Austrian Archduke at Sarajevo in Bosnia. Austria-Hungary holds Serbia responsible. William II promises his support to the Austro-Hungarians in case of war.
28 July: Austria-Hungary declares war on Serbia.
1st August: Germany declares war on Russia.
3rd August: Germany declares war on France and enters Belgium.
4th August: Great Britain declares war on Germany.

Fashoda: the English wolf and the French Little Red Riding
Hood, as seen by a German cartoonist.

3. Beginnings of the Entente Cordiale. Edward VII visits Paris,
May 1903.

erzl, *The Jewish State.* Romain Roland's *Jean-Christophe.*

95   1904–12

5. Franco-Russian rapprochement. The French fleet putting in
at Kronstadt, July 1891.

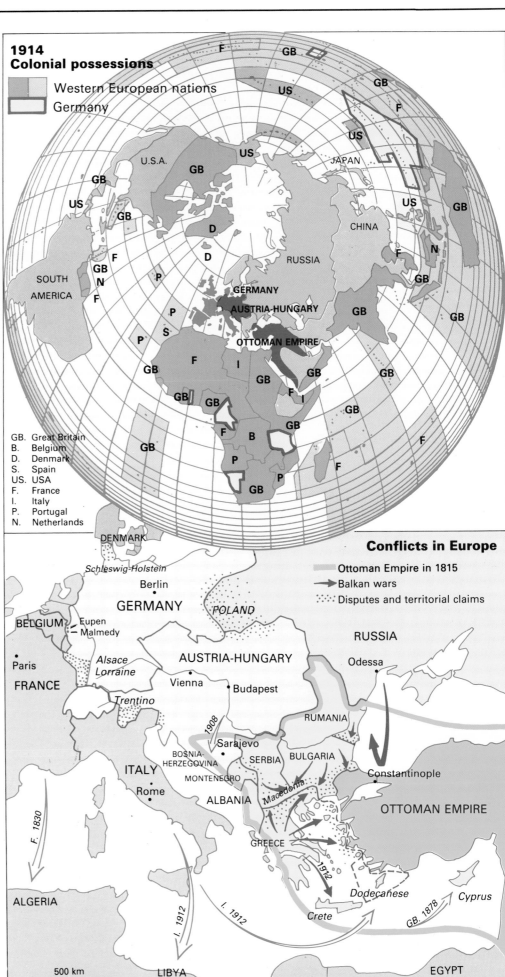

1914
Colonial possessions

Western European nations
Germany

GB. Great Britain
B. Belgium
D. Denmark
S. Spain
US. USA
F. France
I. Italy
P. Portugal
N. Netherlands

U.S.A.

SOUTH
AMERICA

JAPAN

CHINA

RUSSIA

GERMANY
AUSTRIA-HUNGARY
OTTOMAN EMPIRE

Conflicts in Europe

Ottoman Empire in 1815
Balkan wars
Disputes and territorial claims

DENMARK
Schleswig-Holstein
Berlin
GERMANY
POLAND
RUSSIA
BELGIUM
Eupen
Malmedy
Odessa
Paris
Alsace
Lorraine
AUSTRIA-HUNGARY
FRANCE
Vienna
Budapest
Trentino
RUMANIA
1908
Sarajevo
BOSNIA-
HERZEGOVINA
SERBIA
BULGARIA
Constantinople
ITALY
MONTENEGRO
Rome
Macedonia
OTTOMAN EMPIRE
ALBANIA
GREECE
1912
Dodecanese
Cyprus
F. 1830
I. 1912
I. 1912
Crete
GB. 1878
ALGERIA
500 km
LIBYA
EGYPT

The Great War in the West

1. The Chemin des Dames disaster, after the failure of the French offensive in April 1917, depicted by François Flameng.

2. 'Down with war!': anti-militarist poster before Italian intervention in 1915.

BETWEEN 1914 AND 1918 the high commands of both sides switched repeatedly between the strong point strategy – which consisted of attacking the enemy in an effort to break his resistance – and the weak point strategy, which aimed to disorganize him and reduce the number of his allies.

In 1914 the Germans attacked at the strong point in the west: this was the Schlieffen plan, which sought to encircle and destroy the British and French armies by an attack from the west. They failed in this, however, Joffre halting them on the Marne. Simultaneously, the Russians attacked at Gumbinnen, but the Germans repulsed them and Hindenburg was victorious at Tannenberg. Each side's powerful hammer blows, struck at the principal enemy's strongest point, proved costly and ineffective. No decisive victory was possible; in fact, they merely produced a general paralysis of fronts (the trenches). In 1915 both the Allied offensives in Champagne and Artois and the German and Austrian attacks in Poland came to nothing.

Given these conditions, it is not surprising that the protagonists thought up another strategy which aimed at the weak point in the enemy coalition. However, did the Allies really have to mount a massed attack on the Turks in the Dardanelles, while the enemy was camped at the gates of Noyon? And, in the opposing camp, was it

really necessary for the Germans and Austrians to pursue the Serbs with such ferocity or seek to punish the Italians who had changed sides, at a point when the Cossacks were able at a stroke to reach the Hungarian frontier? In 1916 it was back once again to the strong point strategy, but neither at Verdun nor on the Somme nor in the east, nor for that matter on the Isonzo or at Asiago did anything decisive occur. It was the same in 1917 when even the Chemin des Dames or Passchendaele hardly changed the respective armies' positions and even the Russian Revolution left things unchanged in the east.

The war then took on a global dimension as the British mounted offensives in Egypt, Iraq and elsewhere in the Arab world, and as first Japan, then China entered the war and, even more importantly, as submarine warfare brought America into the conflict.

In Europe, the strong point strategy produced another failure for the Germans on the Marne. It was at its weakest points that the Central Powers' alliance was to fall apart, in spite of the Russian armistice. These were the Bulgarian and Turkish fronts. At the same time the Italians gained revenge for Caporetto at Vittoria Veneto and the massive arrival of the Americans showed the Germans that they could no longer hope to turn the situation in their favour. The first armistices were signed at the end of October and in November 1918.

Sinking of the *Lusitania*.	Year of Verdun		V. Blasco Ibanez: *The Four Horsemen of the Apocalypse*
7 May 1915	**1916**		**1916**

3. British militarist poster, 1914.

1914. 4 August: The Germans advance on Paris by way of Belgium.
*19 August: Russian offensive aimed at relieving the French front.
26–30 August: German counter-offensive; Russian defeat at Tannenberg.
6–12 September: The Germans, halted on the Marne, withdraw to the Aisne.
10 October–10 November: The Germans and the Anglo-French seek to outflank each other on the west ('The race for the sea'). The front settles down on a line running through Ypres, Soissons, Reims and Verdun.
5 November: The Allies declare war on Turkey.
1915. February: German offensive; Russians defeated at Masurian Lakes.
24 April: Allies land in the Dardanelles.
24 May: Italy enters the war against Austria.
August: Austro-German offensive; Russians lose whole of Poland.
October: Austro-Bulgarian offensive against Serbia; fall of Belgrade (9 October).

*Dates relating to Russia given according to the Gregorian Calendar adopted in January 1918.

1916. 9 January: Allies evacuate the Dardanelles.
21 February: Verdun offensive. German gains.
June–August: Russian offensive against Austria, repulsed with very heavy losses. Russian Army begins to break up.
24 June: Franco-British offensive on the Somme. Attempt to make a breakthrough thwarted.
27 August: Rumania declares war on Austria and Italy enters the war against Germany. Austrian offensive: fall of Bucharest.
October–December: French regain the positions captured by the Germans around Verdun. End of the Battle of Verdun.
1917. 1 February: Germany announces unrestricted naval warfare.
12 March: February Revolution in Russia. End of Tsarism. Provisional government promises to fight with Allied cause.
6 April: USA declares war on Germany.
16 April–17 May: French offensive between Soissons and Laon. German front holds fast.
May–June: Mutinies in the French Army.
July: Russian offensive. Total failure.

7 November: October Revolution in Russia.
1918. 3 March: Russia signs separate peace treaties with the Central Powers.
May: Germans break through Allied lines and reach the Marne.
18 July–3 August: Second Battle of the Marne; Germans are fought back.
14 October: Independence of Czechoslovakia: proclamation of union of Serbs, Croats and Slovenes; 24 October: secession of Hungary.
27 October: Italian victory at Vittorio Veneto.
3 November: Austro-Italian Armistice.
11 November: Armistice signed at Rethondes between the Allies and Germany.

1914–18

'All Quiet on the Western Front'

NETHERLANDS

Zeebrugge

Antwerp

Ghent

Niewpoort

LANDERS
9.14
5-12.17

Dixmude (Diksmuide)

Dunkirk

Yser Ypres

Passchendaele

Lys

Calais

April 1918

Lille

ARTOIS
5,9.15

VIMY
5-7.15
4,7,9.17

Lens

Vimy

Arras

Cambrai

Doullens

SOMME
7-11.16

Péronne

Albert

St Quentin

German retreat to the Siegfried line

Somme

Amiens

March 1918

Noyon

CHEMIN DES DAMES
4.17

CHAMPAGNE
9-10.15

ARGONNE
5-10.15

VERDUN
2-12.16

Montdidier

Oise

Aisne

Hill 304

September 1914

Beauvais

Soissons

Tahure

Verdun

Les Éparges

Reims

May 1918

Marne

Château-Thierry

St Mihiel Nancy

Meaux

Coulommiers

Vitry-le-François

Paris

Bombon
(Allied High Command H.Q.)

Seine

Seine

BELGIUM

Brussels

Liège Eupen

Meuse

Spa
(German High Command H.Q.)

Malmedy

Mons Charleroi

Sambre

11 November 1918

Luxemburg

GERMANY

Moselle

Rhine

Saar

Morhange

Strasbourg

Lunéville

Meurthe

Charmes

LINGE
7-8-15

St Dié

Épinal

VOSGES

HARTMANNS-WILLERKOPF
1-3-15

8.14

Mulhouse

Belfort

SWITZERLAND

Legend:
- Sept. 1914 Furthest German advance
- Settled front, late 1914
- Massacres
- German advance in 1918

100 km

Siegfried Line (called the Hindenburg Line by the French)

Pirandello: *Ciascuno a suo modo.* 1917

Death of Wilfred Owen.
4 November 1918

Death of Guillaume Apollinaire.
9 November 1918

4. French soldiers in the trenches, Verdun front, 1917.

5. Death of Baron Manfred von Richtofen, the German fighter ace, shot down near Corbie, 21 April 1918. Painted by an Allied soldier.

The Great War in the East and Across the World

1. In the British rear: nationalist insurrection in Ireland. The Dublin General Post Office after the Easter Rising of 1916.

DURING THE GREAT WAR both sides employed strategies designed to disrupt or to stifle the other's efforts. Of these methods, the most widely employed was that of seeking to break up the opposing coalition. The main thrust of the Central Powers' policy consisted in an attempt to provoke non-Russian nationalities to revolt against the Tsarist empire. To this end, they published a Bulletin of the Nationalities of Russia, formed a Finnish legion and proclaimed the independence of Poland (in 1916). No one was deceived by these actions, but they nonetheless represented a blow against the Entente. Against Great Britain, the Germans lent support to the Irish nationalists, precipitating the 'Easter Rising' of 1916. In Belgium, Germany sought to weaken the Allied coalition by reawakening the ideal of Flemish nationhood: they even went so far as to form a National Council of Flanders. Lastly, the Austrians and the Germans attempted to provoke holy wars within their enemies' empires and, in Libya at least, they succeeded in fomenting a revolt against the Italians. They also lent aid to the Boer, St Moritz, who had hopes of regaining independence for his country. For their part, the Allies also acted in an indirect fashion against Hapsburg domination in Central Europe, promising independence, if they were victorious, to the oppressed nationalities (Croats, Slovenes, Czechs and Slovaks etc.). The only practical result of this policy was one massive desertion, that of the 29th Regiment of Prague, but it nevertheless weakened the morale and the cohesion of the Central Powers. The same policy produced more tangible effects in the Ottoman Empire, where the hopes raised in Armenia by the advance of the Russians led to the collective deportations and massacres of 1915, in which over a million people were killed. By contrast, the rising of the Arabs, aided by Colonel T. E. Lawrence, had positive effects for the insurgents, who entered Damascus alongside the British and reconstituted a nation that had been lost for several centuries.

To this general strategy of undermining the enemy's unity, we may add a second strategy, the attempt to suffocate him. From 1914 onwards the Allies sought to ruin the Central Powers' seaborne trade, thus destroying the foundations of their economy and provoking a crisis by creating shortages. The historical example set by Napoleon helped to revive the idea of blockade. When there seemed some danger that this strategy might have fatal consequences, the Austrians and the Germans responded with submarine warfare, which became rife after 1917. Instead of causing the Allies to throw in their hand and terrorizing the neutrals, this counter-attack merely stimulated the Allied naval effort and provoked US entry into the war.

These economic measures certainly had effects, but they are difficult to evaluate. No break-up of alliances occurred, and the war was won by military rather than economic means. Germany was able to offset the effects of the blockade for a long period, mainly because Great Britain, which believed its chances of victory would be improved by increasing its wealth, carried on 'business as usual' with the Germans through the neutral countries and also because Germany mobilized and rationalized its economy more quickly than the other belligerents. Through its attempts to imitate the German practice in this latter respect, the Russian economy deteriorated, and the resulting shortages were a major cause of the February 1917 revolution. The negative effects produced by submarine warfare had one essential consequence: the part played by US supplies and the arrival of a large contingent of American fighting men contributed to the Central Powers' demoralization and hastened their capitulation.

Russians crushed at Tannenberg.	The Germans take Warsaw.	Freud, *Introductory Lectures on Psychoanalysis*; H. Barbusse, *Le Feu*.
26 August 1914	**5 August 1915**	**1916**

1914. 25 August: Allies establish blockade of Germany.
December: At Mecca, Arabs proclaim a holy war against the Sultan.
8 December: German naval defeat off the Falkland Islands.
1915. January: German zeppelins overfly London.
18 March: The Allies guarantee the Russians control of the Black Sea Straits.
22 April: First use of poison gas by the Germans.
22 May: Germany extends its submarine campaign to include merchant ships.
July–August: Massacres in Armenia.
6 August: Allies define their war aims at Chantilly: Alsace-Lorraine to be returned to France, German colonies to be divided up among the Allies with Britain as the principal beneficiary.
1916. April: Nationalist insurrection in Ireland – the 'Easter Rising' – repressed by the British.
June: The smaller nationalities meet at Lausanne.
6 June: Allies blockade the coasts of Greece.

30 August: Venizélos instals a government in Salonica.
26 December: The German government declares its willingness to participate in a peace conference.
1917. 10 January: Allies announce their war aims: restoration of Alsace-Lorraine to France, Belgian and Serbian sovereignty to be restored; principle of nationalities to be applied to all minorities.
29 January: Indirect response from Germany, which accepts modifications to its frontiers in favour of France and the establishment of an independent Poland under German influence.
1 February: Germany declares unrestricted submarine warfare.
16 April: Return to Russia of Lenin, whom the Germans have allowed through in the hope that he will hasten the onset of negotiations between Russia and the Central Powers.
18 May: Opening of a socialist conference at Stockholm which debates ways of bringing the war to an end.
Spring–Summer: British offensive in the

Near East. Occupation of Baghdad.
June: Under Allied pressure, King Constantine of Greece, who is sympathetic to the Central Powers, is forced to abdicate. The new government declares war on Germany.
22 December: Beginning of peace negotiations between Russia and the Central Powers.
1918: American President Wilson defines the conditions for a durable peace, the Fourteen Points, which have to do mainly with the principle of nationalities.
3 March: Brest-Litovsk treaty between Russia and Central Powers: Russia accepts great territorial losses.
11 November: Armistice signed at Rethondes on the basis of Wilson's Fourteen Points.

4. A scene from the British conquest of Palestine: Field-Marshal Edmund Allenby enters Jerusalem.

1914–18

The Armenian massacres of 1915, as depicted in the French Petit Journal.

Colonel Thomas Edward Lawrence – 'Lawrence of Arabia' – at the head of troops allied to Great Britain in 1917.

Ernst Jünger, The Storm of Steel.

20

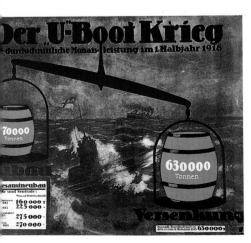

5. Submarine warfare, as seen by German propaganda in the early months of 1918.

The War in the East

Paris • Brussels

FRANCE
11.18
Luxembourg

GERMANY
1.8.14 11.11.18

• Berlin

Tannenberg
26–30.8.14   Riga
Gumbinnen   Petrograd

Vittorio Veneto
10.18
Caporetto
10.17 • Vienna

ITALY
5.15

AUSTRIA-HUNGARY
28.7.14 4.11.18

Brest-Litovsk
1.15
9.15
10.17

RUSSIA
1.8.14 2.17

7.16
1914

• Moscow

Belgrade
Czernowitz

SERBIA

UKRAINE

RUMANIA
8.16

ALBANIA
Evacuation
of Serbian
army to
Corfu,
1915

Sofia
Bucharest

Salonica
BULGARIA
10.15 9.18

GREECE

Gallipoli
Athens   • Constantinople
1915 *Dardanelles*

Limits of German occupation 12.17.

Ankara

OTTOMAN EMPIRE
10.14 10.18

Trebizond

Deportation of Armenians
1915 1916 *ARMENIA* 1918

Aleppo

• Baku

Cairo Damascus
• Suez 10.18 Mosul
Jerusalem
10.17

*Arabian
Desert*

EGYPT

Baghdad

Kut al-Amara
9.15 PERSIA

1000 km

1.8.14 Date of entering war
11.11.18 Armistice date

Brusilov Offensive   Allied offensive

Summer 1916   before 1918   In 1918

Basra
4.15

Revolution and Civil War in Russia

1. From left to right: Stalin, Lenin and Kalinin in February 1918.

2. Russian poster caricaturing the enemies of the revolution, 1917.

MILITARY DEFEATS, shortages and the hatred of autocracy constituted an explosive mixture, which, within five days in Petrograd, sealed the triumph of the revolution and the abdication of Nicholas II. A Soviet of Workers and Soldiers' Deputies was constituted which shared power with a provisional government made up of former Duma representatives. A. Kerensky was the living embodiment of the alliance between the 'bourgeois' and 'proletarian' revolutions. The new regime, which was incapable of winning the war and yet unable to put an end to it, and unable also to carry through the reforms which would have transformed the social order, found itself up against opposition from, on the one hand, the factory and soldiers' committees headed by Bolsheviks or anarchists and, on the other, that of the military high command and the big industrial bourgeoisie, who were intransigent in their resistance to the reforms desired by the socialists in the Provisional Government and the Soviets. The Mensheviks and Socialist-Revolutionaries were, as it turned out in any case, soon to lose their majority in these assemblies.

This situation explains why, after General Kornilov's failed *putsch*, the Soviets and workers' and soldiers' committees – led by the Bolsheviks under Lenin's guidance – were easily able to overthrow the Provisional Government in the October rising.

Subsequently, Lenin and Trotsky concluded the Treaty of Brest-Litovsk, which detached the Baltic states, Poland and part of the Ukraine from the old empire. At the same time the Bolsheviks, by dissolving the Constituent Assembly where they were in a minority, incited opposition from the other socialists and democrats, whilst the White generals raised the standard of rebellion in the south and, not long afterwards, in Siberia. The Allied powers gave assistance to the (White) volunteer army and landed British and Canadian troops at Archangel, Japanese and later American troops at Vladivostock and French troops at Odessa who, though they were still nominally at war, joined up with German forces in the Ukraine even before 11 November 1918. This foreign intervention discredited the White forces and contributed to the defeat of Denikin, Kolchak and Wrangel.

The revolution, which was for Russia a political and social phenomenon, seemed a good opportunity for the other nations of the old empire to recapture their freedom, an impression reinforced by the Bolsheviks' declaration of the peoples' right to self-determination. However, once the revolution was accomplished, it was pointed out that 'the right to divorce did not mean the necessity of divorce'. Lenin and Stalin accordingly broke up the nationalist movements in Georgia, the Ukraine, the Tartar regions and in Armenia (after they had saved the Armenians from being massacred by the Turks). At the end of the war and the civil war, only the Baltic states, Poland and Finland had succeeded in preserving their independence.

V. Mayakovsky, *Man.*	In Finland, Lenin writes *The State and Revolution.*	Dissolution of the Constituent Assembly by the Bolsheviks.
1916	August 1917	6 January 1918

*1917. 8 March: Strikes begin in Petrograd: the situation gets out of the government's control.
9 March: Constitution of a Provisional Government with the support of the elected assembly (Duma). The soviet and government were to find themselves in competition.
12 March: Constitution of a Soviet (Council) of Worker and Soldier Representatives.
16 April: Return of Lenin, who takes over as leader of the most hard-line faction (Bolsheviks) of the Russian Workers' Social Democratic Party.
17 April: Lenin publishes his *April Theses*: calling for an immediate peace treaty, establishment of a republic of Soviets.
16 June: All Russia Congress of Soviets.
July: Provisional Government launches an offensive against the Germans; it is a total failure and a complete break-up of the army ensues.

September: Attempted counter-revolutionary *putsch*. The Provisional Government has to call on the Soviets to overcome it.
6–7 November: Bolshevik insurrection. Dissolution of the Provisional Government.

3. Kerensky, as a minister in the Provisional Government in March 1917.

4. Assault on the Winter Palace in Petrograd (today Leningrad) by the Bolsheviks, November 1917.

*Dates are from the Gregorian Calendar.

Russian frontiers in 1914
--- --- Limits of German occupation
Frontiers of U.S.S.R. in 1922
☐ Regions remaining under Soviet control
▒ Secessionist territories

Offensives
1918 and Summer 1919 ⟹
Autumn 1919 ⟹
1920 ⟹
1921-22 ⟹

Foreign interventions: ⟹
F: France G.B.: Great Britain G: Greece
J: Japan U.S.: United States

1000 km

A. Kollontai, *Communism and the Family.*   L. Trotsky, *Terrorism and Communism.*

| 1919 | 1920 |

8 November: Constitution of a Council of People's Commissars presided over by Lenin, who will exercise executive power. Confiscation of the large domains; end of war announced.

1918. 6 January: An elected Constituent Assembly meets. The Bolsheviks, who are in the minority, disperse it.

15 January: Creation of the Red Army based on the principle of voluntary service and the election of officers. These principles will not survive the pressures of the Civil War.

3 March: Treaty of Brest-Litovsk with the Central Powers: Russia cedes the Baltic provinces, its part of Poland and its protectorate over Finland.

March–April: The Allies land an anti-Bolshevik expeditionary corps at Murmansk.

1919. 2 March: Foundation of the Communist International (Comintern).

May–September: Counter-revolutionary offensive (supported by the Allies) against Petrograd and Moscow and on the Volga. In August, the victory of the Bolsheviks on the Volga marks the collapse of the

5. The cruiser, Aurora, *the sentinel of the revolution, on the Neva, October 1917.*

counter-revolution.

1920. July: 2nd Comintern Congress. 21 points adopted which lay down strict conditions of membership for Communist parties.

September: Baku Congress for the liberation of the Eastern Peoples. Definition of a strategy to mobilize the East against the West.

November: The last Allied troops withdraw.

1921. February: Demonstrations by workers at Petrograd. Revolt of Bolshevik sailors at Kronstadt. The two movements are repressed.

17 March: The Congress of the Bolshevik party adopts a New Economic Policy (N.E.P.) tolerating private property and trade on a capitalist basis.

18 March: Treaty defining frontiers with Poland: commercial accord with Great Britain.

The Aftermath of the First World War

SIGNED AFTER MONTHS of laborious negotiation, the treaties that are given the name 'Treaty of Versailles' were almost immediately contested and were to end up being repudiated within two decades. Four of the principles which were invoked at Versailles explain this failure.

The first of these was the principle of nationalities. For centuries, within the Austrian, Russian and Ottoman Empires there had been oppressed minority groups labouring under the rule of a dominant community, which accorded them only minimal guarantees. In the nineteenth century these groups sought to emancipate themselves. During the war, the Western Allies took up their cause again, hoping thereby to weaken the Central Powers. However, within the Empires the minorities were intermingled; in fact it proved impossible to draw up political frontiers that were also linguistic ones. In only one case was the problem resolved by a massive population transfer: 400,000 Turks moved from Macedonia into Turkey and 1,300,000 Greeks were shipped from Asia Minor to Greece. This did not, however, diminish the hostility the two nations felt towards each other. Elsewhere, the minorities remained in their original homes. A large German population that had settled in the outer reaches of Bohemia became Czech; another group of Germans found themselves included in Poland, and in this case the problem was complicated by the granting of the port of Danzig, which had a mainly German population, to Poland. Paradoxically, the Treaty of Versailles would provide Hitler with one of his most effective propaganda themes.

To this thorny question of nationalities was added the problem of non-European territories. German colonies and the non-Turkish ter-

ritories of the Ottoman Empire were divided up (in the form of colonies or mandates) between the victors. From this time onwards, the Middle East became a source of permanent difficulty for Britain and France.

The third problematic clause in the Versailles Treaty was the one dealing with Germany. Being judged responsible for the war, she was disarmed and condemned to pay reparations. A series of convoluted plans for paying reparations over half a century were devised and then abandoned. Germany, whose territory the Allies had not even reached at the signing of the Armistice in 1918 (the fighting took place on French soil), was still regarded, a decade after the Treaty, as the guilty party. The rejection of the Versailles *diktat* was to be the Nazi's first priority.

The final source of tension was the fact that no one was able to ensure that the new territorial divisions and the payment of reparations were respected. The United States immediately refused to ratify

2. The surviving orphans arriving in Greece in 1922, after the Turkish massacres of Greeks and Armenians.

the Treaty. The League of Nations – a sort of world parliament – was not provided with any means of external action. As early as 1920, the Turks rebelled against their treaty (the Treaty of Sèvres), forcing its revision in the Treaty of Lausanne.

Between 1935 and the outbreak of war, Hitler's initiatives would be aimed at simply abolishing the Treaty (reintroduction of military service, remilitarization of the left bank of the Rhine, *Anschluss*, annexation of the German border region of Bohemia, claim upon the Polish corridor). It was the spirit of Versailles the Nazis sought to erase.

1. 'To arms! To arms!': poster by R. Berény, for the Budapest Commune in 1919.

Eisenstein, *Battleship Potemkin.*
Charlie Chaplin, *The Kid.*
Hitler, *Mein Kampf.*

E. M. Remarque, *All Quiet on the Western Front.*
E. Hemingway, *A Farewell to Arms.*

1920   **1925**   **1929**

5. Rosa Luxemburg, the revolutionary whose life took her from a Jewish community in Poland to the Berlin uprising of 1919.

1919. 18 January: Peace negotiations open in Paris.
16 June: Allied ultimatum demands Germany signs treaty.
28 June: Signature of the Treaty of Versailles. Germany loses Alsace-Lorraine to France and cedes Western Prussia to Poland: she accepts the existence of a 'corridor' across her territory that will give Poland access to the port of Danzig. She loses her colonies. Her army is limited to 100,000 men; the left bank of the Rhine is demilitarized. Germany acknowledges its responsibility for starting the war and undertakes to pay reparations.
10 September: Treaty of St. Germain-en-Laye. Austria, limited to its German-speaking territories, will not be allowed to unite with Germany.
27 November: Treaty of Neuilly. Bulgaria cedes Thrace to Greece and loses all access to the sea.
1920. 4 June: Trianon Treaty. Hungary is reduced to Magyar territory.
10 August: Treaty of Sèvres. Turkey loses its non-Turkish territories: the Straits and the

Mediterranean coast of Asia Minor are occupied by the European powers. The Turkish national assembly refuses to ratify the treaty. A section of the army led by Mustafa Kemal decides to resist and the Greeks, given the task of implementing the treaty are defeated by the Turkish Army.
25 August 1921: After the rejection of the Versailles Treaty by the American Senate, the U.S. signs a separate pact with Germany. They neither recognize the League of Nations nor German reparations.
1923. 11 January: Because Germany fails to make its reparations payments, France and Belgium occupy the Rhineland. This action is fiercely criticized in Europe and the USA.
24 July: Treaty of Lausanne: Turkish sovereignty over whole of Asia Minor and the western region around Istanbul recognised.
1924: After American mediation, the Dawes Plan sets a total figure for German reparations payments and states how they are to be broken down.
16 October 1925: Locarno Pact: Germany guarantees French and Belgian frontiers, but refuses to give any commitment on its

Eastern frontiers.
1929: Germany requests a re-scheduling of its debt, a revision of the Treaty which provides for payments until 1988.
1932: Lausanne Conference: reparations finally abandoned.
14 October 1933: Disarmament Conference. Germany, unable to obtain parity with other powers, leaves the conference and withdraws from the League of Nations.
16 March 1935: Re-introduction of compulsory military service in Germany – first open violation of the Treaty of Versailles.

1919–35

3. Josef Pilsudski (1867–1935), Commander in Chief of the Polish Army and provisional Polish head of state in 1918.

4. Mustafa Kemal (later Attaturk). After serving as a general in the First World War, he was elected president of Turkey in 1923.

ert Musil,
Man without Qualities.

L-F. Céline,
Journey to the End of the Night.

1930–1943   1932

The Peace Treaties

☐ New States

FRANCE
1. Alsace-Lorraine
2. Military occupation of the Rhineland
3. Saarland: League of Nations, then plebiscite after 15 years

BELGIUM
Eupen and Malmedy after plebiscite

DENMARK
Schleswig after plebiscite

LEAGUE OF NATIONS

NORWAY   SWEDEN   FINLAND

Danzig Memel

Helsinki

Tallin
ESTONIA
Petrograd

Riga
LATVIA

FRANCE

GERMANY
VERSAILLES
28 June 1919

LITHUANIA

Kaunas

Corridor

POLAND

Vilna

Warsaw •

RUSSIA
BREST-LITOVSK
3 March 1918
Russia renounces all sovereignty over these countries

• Brest-Litovsk

BUCHAREST
7 May 1920
gives Bessarabia to Rumania

CZECHOSLOVAKIA

Upper Silesia after plebiscite

RIGA
18 March 1921
Eastern frontier of Poland

AUSTRIA
SAINT-GERMAIN
10 September 1919

Galicia

Alto Adige

HUNGARY
TRIANON
4 June 1920

Trieste

Croatia

ITALY

Zadar

Bosnia

Transylvania

Bessarabia

Lagosta

YUGOSLAVIA

Montenegro

Serbia

RUMANIA

ALBANIA

BULGARIA
NEUILLY
27 November 1919

GREECE   Thrace

TURKEY
SÈVRES
10 August 1920
Abandons all rights to Egypt
1920 frontiers: ••••

Smyrna

(Italy)

LAUSANNE
24 July 1923
1923 frontiers: ▬

Kars

Armenia

T'sing-tao- acquired without mandate   **JAPAN**

Mariana Islands

Marshall Islands

Caroline Islands

Bismark Archipelago

Nauru

Samoa

GREAT BRITAIN

AUSTRALIA

NEW ZEALAND

SYRIA
French Mandate

Damascus

PALESTINE
Jerusalem •

Amman •

IRAQ

IRAN

Baghdad •

TRANSJORDAN

British

Mandate

ARABIA

League of Nations Mandates
over former German colonies

GREAT BRITAIN

Togo

Cameroons

Rwanda-Burundi

BELGUIM

FRANCE

Tanganyika

South West Africa

UNION OF SOUTH AFRICA

Japan Opens its Frontiers and Embarks on a Policy of Conquest

1868

1. Emperor Meiji arriving at the palace, print, late 19th century.

IN 1858, UNDER PRESSURE from the Western countries, the shogunate, despite its reservations, signed a number of unfavourable trade treaties with the foreign powers. Ports were opened up to trade, but traditional groups like the samurai, especially in the fiefs in the south-west, responded with a wave of xenophobia. Inflation made working conditions for ordinary people more difficult, and sparked off a number of revolts and violent protests. Those who argued for the end of the old regime of the Tokugawa prevailed and in 1867 the Shogun restored power to the Emperor.

Over a fairly short period of time the new Meiji state achieved major structural reforms, which aimed to put into operation the slogan 'Enrich the country, strengthen the army', and thus, it was thought, create the conditions necessary for the preservation of national independence. To guarantee the success of the slogan, it was argued, the country had to assimilate 'Western technology' without at the same time abandoning the 'Japanese spirit'. Within a generation, Japan was able to emerge successfully from its industrial revolution. The traditional social stratum of the samurai, who were already trained in the upkeep and management of feudal estates, occupied key positions in the civil service and in industry, with the aid of foreign

experts. Japan's leaders, starting with Emperor Meiji himself, encouraged the adoption of Western methods and manners while some intellectuals translated and discussed books and ideas coming from the West.

By the very early years of the twentieth century Japan had become a major modern power. Over the period since 1890 the country had become a constitutional monarchy with a parliament. Legal reforms made it possible to model the legal system on that of the Europeans and to renegotiate the unfavourable treaties. Educational reforms were successful and all young Japanese enjoyed a school education. And, in the domain of scientific research, Japan enjoyed its first successes in this period. Japanese industrial growth, which up till then had been concentrated in textiles, from now on accelerated in the heavy industry sector. Like Western countries, Japan went through its moments of nationalist fervour and socialist trades union agitation. Symbolic of the country's success on the international stage were the Anglo-Japanese Alliance of 1902, the victory in the Russo-Japanese War of 1905, and the arrival of Japan as a colonial power with its annexation of Korea in 1910. From then on, Japan was able to have its voice heard internationally, as was for instance the case when

MODERN TIMES		CONTEMPORARY PERIOD		
1850	1860	1870	1880	1890
	PERIOD OF 'THE END OF THE SHOGUNATE'			MEIJI ERA
	1853	1868		

1854: Japanese–American Friendship Treaty signed. Japan ends its policy of isolation from the outside world.
1858: Trade treaties are signed with the major Western powers.
1860: Japanese Embassy opens in Washington.
1866: Military alliance formed between the fiefs of the south-west against the shogunate. There are more and more popular rebellions.
1867: Restoration of imperial power.
1868: First year of the new Meiji imperial régime. The last followers of the shogun capitulate.
1869: Tokyo, the former city of Edo, becomes the imperial capital.
1871: The fiefs are abolished and prefectures established. Emancipation of the *Eta Hinin*, or subordinate castes, is made official.
1872: Introduction of universal education. A conscript army is formed. The first railway line, from Tokyo to Yokohama, is inaugurated.

Fukuzawa Yukichi publishes *Gakumon no susume*, supporting the idea of introducing Western science and ways of thinking.
1873: Land Tax reform.
1876: It is made illegal for former samurai to wear the sabre.
1877: A group of samurai, disappointed by the policies of the new régime, rebel in the south of the country. The new Imperial Army wins a victory over them.
1881: First paper money issued. The Liberal Party is formed, and the movement in favour of civil freedoms grows larger.
1882: Nakae Chomin translates Rousseau's *Social Contract* into Japanese.
1884: Popular rebellion in Chichibu to claim 'the freedom and rights of the people'.
1885: Tsubouchi Shoyo publishes *The Essence of the Novel*, which marks the beginnings of modern Japanese literature.
1889: Imperial constitution is promulgated. A rail link is established between Tokyo and Osaka.

3. A Chinese ship is destroyed by the Japanese.

1890: Parliament opens. The first major workers' strike takes place in Osaka.
1895: Japan defeats China.
1897: A team of Japanese scientists discover the dysentry bacillus.
1901: The Social-Democratic Party is formed.
1902: Anglo-Japanese Alliance is signed.
1905: Japanese victory over Russia. Treaty signed between Russia and Japan in Portsmouth, New Hampshire. Natsume Soseki publishes *I am a Cat*.
1907: Reform of primary schooling. All children now enjoy full-time education.
1910: Annexation of Korea. The first Japanese aeroplane is built.
1914: Japan declares war on Germany.
1915: Akutagawa publishes *Rashomon*.
1919: Japan takes part in the Conference of Versailles on the side of the victorious powers.
1921–2: Washington conference takes place. Japan is forced to reduce the power of its fleet.

1854–1941

1910
After the wars with China and Russia

Late 1931
The invasion of Manchuria

500 km

1938
The invasion of China

2. Old Japan: a group of young Japanese dressed as samurai warriors in 1910.

it sat with the victorious powers at the Conference of Versailles in 1919.

Between 1910 and 1920 public life was made more democratic. From 1913 onwards, parliamentary parties became the basis for government, while the trades union movement also grew stronger. Individualist values were the order of the day, and in the cities mass culture began to make an appearance. But this trend was blocked from the beginning of the 1930s by a resurgence of authoritarian and ultra-nationalistic views, which held sway amongst the military in particular. The economic slump, which affected the country after 1927, led some politicians to look to expansionism as a means of resolving the crisis. Losing control over their own rank-and-file activists, political parties were led into various military adventures on the continent of Asia, while, in the name of imperial values, repressive measures were taken against all those who disagreed with this change of direction, which was in fact supported by the majority of the population. Embroiled since 1937 in an unsuccessful war against China, in 1941 the military leaders launched the country into war against the United States by the attack on Pearl Harbor.

1900	1910	1920	1930	1940
		TAISHO ERA	SHOWA ERA	

1926

4. Modern Japan: students at work in an armaments factory during World War Two.

1922: Formation of the Japanese Communist Party.
1923: Earthquake in Kanto.
1925: Formation of a united trades-union movement. Repressive laws on the maintenance of public order are passed. Universal male suffrage is introduced.
1926: Hirohito becomes Emperor. He will be given the name Showa after his death.
1931: Japan invades Manchuria.
1932: 15 May, an attempted ultra-nationalist coup fails.
1933: Japan leaves the League of Nations.
1936: A further attempted right-wing coup fails on 26 February. Anti-Comintern Pact is signed with Germany.
1937: War with China breaks out.
1940: All political parties are banned.
1941: Japan declares war on the United States and Britain.

STEEL 5 800 000 t
RAILWAYS 23 000 km
45 200 000 t
COAL
600 000 t
30 km
1 000 t

1870 80 90 1900 10 20 30 40

China: From Nationalism to Communism

1926-1927
The Expansion of the Kuomintang

U.S.S.R.

OUTER MONGOLIA
(autonomous region in 1911)

Peking □

KOREA

TIBET
(autonomous region in 1912)

Huang Ho

Nanking

1927:
Shanghai uprising put down

Wu-han

Yangtze

Ch'ang-sha

Chi Shiang

Canton

FORMOSA

JAPAN

Areas under the control of military chiefs

Areas under the control of the Kuomintang

July 1926 — End of 1926 — April 1927

1927-1935.
The Civil War

U.S.S.R.

Peking 1929.
CHIANG KAI-SHEK

MANCHOUKUO
1932

Ch'iang-T'ang.
Under Soviet influence 1928

JEHOL
1933

1931

SHENSI

The Long March.
October 1934
October 1935

Yenan

Shanghai

1932

Ching-kan-shan
MAO TSE-TUNG

HUNAN *KIANGSI*

Canton Commune crushed. 1928

JAPAN

Underground Communist Bases

THE REPUBLIC, which was transformed almost immediately into a dictatorship by overthrowing the dynastic order of the Manchus and the imperial system of government, deprived China of the last elements of cohesion. The sense of imperial unity having been torn away, society began to fall apart, revealing all the underlying contradictions which were at its centre. China's centrifugal tendencies re-emerged with the proliferation of warlords, held in check, however, by the dominant personal rule of Chiang Kai-shek. The penetration of foreign influences into Chinese society, in the dual shape of economic exploitation and political domination, produced their own antidote in the guise of the modernist and revolutionary ideas developing in the minds of the intellectuals and workers in the major ports. Urbane and sympathetic to Western ideas, the May Fourth Movement attacked all the outdated ideas of Confucianism and the Chinese tradition, while at the same time it reflected a genuine moment of national awareness. The same period as that which saw the gap widening between those enclaves of (relative) prosperity like Shanghai, Hong Kong, Canton, Tientsin etc., which were under foreign control, and the much poorer rural areas which were still very backward, also witnessed the confrontation between the China of the south, which was republican and progressive, and the China of the north, which was in the hands of a military clique. The confrontation between these

1. March 1944. Modern warfare and the Great Wall of China.

May Fourth Movement of Modernist students and intellectuals.   Chinese Communist Party founded.   Death of the writer Lu Hsün   Nanking massacres perpetrated by the Japane

4 May 1919	1921	1936	1937

1916: Period of the warlords begins.
4 May 1919: Students demonstrate against the decision taken at the Versailles peace conference to leave the territories in China taken from the Germans in the hands of the Japanese.
1921: Chinese Communist Party founded. Sun Yat-sen proclaims the nationalist government in Canton.
1924: The Whampoa Military Academy established.
1925: Establishment of the General Labour Union for the whole of China. Death of Sun Yat-sen. Wave of strikes and boycotts of foreign goods.
1926: Chiang Kai-shek organises the Northern expedition. The Nationalist government moves its headquarters to Wu-han.
1926–7: Peasant revolts in Hunan. Mao Tse-tung argues they should be left to run their course.
1927: Shanghai uprising crushed. The Nationalist government established in Nanking. The Communists set up their base at Ching-kan-shan.

1928: Canton Commune is put down amidst much bloodshed, after the Huifeng uprising.
1929: Second Northern Expedition. Peking captured. Kiangsi Soviet declared.
1930: Failure of the policy advocated by Li Li-san, whom the Soviet Union repudiates.
1930–4: Nationalist campaigns to surround the bases of the Kiangsi Soviet.
1931: Japanese invasion of Manchuria.
1932: Shanghai attacked. Manchukuo set up by the Japanese with P'u-yi enthroned as emperor.
1933–5: Penetration of the Japanese in North China.
1934: Beginning of the Long March to break out of the Nationalist encirclement.
1935: Tsun-i conference adopts Mao Tse-tung as leader and acknowledges his leading role. Mao reaches Shensi with 8,000 survivors.
1936: Sian Incident. Chiang Kai-shek is captured and released only in return for a promise that he would join with the Communists in a common front against the Japanese.
1937: After a general offensive, the Japanese

overrun all the major cities in North China. Shanghai, and then Nanking are occupied and 500,000 people are massacred by the Japanese.
1938: The Nationalists retreat to Chungking. The Japanese occupy Hankow and Canton. The Communists establish bases behind the Japanese lines (in Honan, Shantung and Chekiang).
1940: Wang Ching-wei establishes a collaborationist government with Japanese support in Nanking.
1944: Series of Japanese campaigns giving them control over Honan and South China.

3. The Bridge over the Tatu River during the Long March.

4. The schoolteacher and the Mandarin: Chou En-lai and Mao Tse-tung in 1937.

1935-1945
The Common Front against the Japanese

U.S.S.R.

MANCHUKUO

Peking

Yenan

KOREA

SHANTUNG

JAPAN

TIBET

HONAN Nanking
Hankow 1937
1938 •Shanghai 1937
CHEKIANG

Chungking
1938

•Canton

→ Japanese
→ Communists
→ Nationalists

500 km

1946-1949:
The Communist Victory

U.S.S.R.

PEOPLE'S REPUBLIC
OF MONGOLIA

Shenyang •Ch'ang-ch'un

CH'IANG-T'ANG
1949-50

Peking

DEMOCRATIC PEOPLE'S
REPUBLIC OF 1948

Tianjin

REPUBLIC OF KOREA
1948

Jinan Tsingtao

TSINGHAI
1950

JAPAN

TIBET
1950-51

Nanking

Wu-han

1949

Chungking

• Towns held by the
■ Nationalist forces in 1946
Communist-held areas

YUNNAN

FORMOSA
(TAIWAN),
refuge of
Chiang Kai-shek

in Autumn 1945
in July 1948
in December 1949
Territory controlled by the
Communists after 1949

Canton
October 1949

HAI-NAN
1950

wo forces changed, with the northern expedition of Chiang Kai-shek,
nto a civil war between the two allies of the democratic front, the
Kuomintang and the Chinese Communist Party, and finally culmi-
ated in the destruction of the workers' movement in a series of
bloody massacres inspired by Chiang Kai-shek in Shanghai, Canton
and Hunan. From Peking, from which he came in triumph after
mposing his will on the generals, the Generalissimo returned to the
outh with nothing more to offer than bureaucratic corruption. It was
he destiny of the Communist Party which would prove to be closest
o that of China itself during the years to come, for it reflected most
clearly the contrasts and paradoxes at work in the country. Forged in
he urban environment, the revolutionary movement (helped a lot in
his by the mistakes and dogmatism of their advisers in the Commun-
st International) came to realize the impossibility of bringing about a
workers' revolution, and forged itself into a peasant movement. P'eng
Pai, in Canton, and Mao Tse-tung, in Hunan, were discovering the
evolutionary potential of the rural areas at the very time when the
movement of rebellion was being crushed in the cities. Later, Mao
Tse-tung, in Kiangsi, by relying on traditional agrarian structures,
found a rich fund of troops and activists as well as an operational base.
The peasant revolution seemed threatened in its turn, though, when,
driven back from their base, the communists were pushed back into

the disinherited fringes of North Shensi (later to be known as the
Yenan region). The Japanese invasion of China gave them a second
chance by allowing them to apply the principles of guerilla warfare on
a larger scale through opening a second united front against the
Japanese. The day after the Japanese capitulation, the communists
had at their disposal an infinitely greater number of soldiers and
activists than they had ever had, even at the high
point of the revolutionary period. Sapped by corruption, conservat- ism, and disorder, the nationalist regime, in spite of its initial military
superiority, collapsed, leaving China
in the hands of the com-
munists.

2. 'The Golden Age of Yenan': Mao Tse-tung talking with the peasants. Propaganda painting,
1939.

Mao Tse-tung's lectures at the Yenan conference 'On Problems of Literature and Art'

1942

1945: Japan capitulates. Manchuria is
occupied by the Soviet Union. The Chinese
Nationalists, with American support, take up
the positions abandoned by the fleeing
Japanese.
1946: The Soviets withdraw from Manchuria,
after dismantling and shipping back to Russia
much of the industrial machinery. The
Marshall Mission delays the confrontation
between Nationalists and Communists.
1947: The Nationalist forces go on the
offensive after the failure of the conciliation
mission, but the Communists win victories in
Manchuria and North China.
1948: Lin Piao crushes the government
forces in the whole of Manchuria.
1949: The victory at Huai opens the way to
the Yangtze to the Communist armies. South
China is conquered. The People's Republic of
China is proclaimed in Peking. Chiang
Kai-shek flees to Taiwan.

5. Scene of destruction after a Japanese
bombing raid in Hankow, 1938.

6. The rout of the Nationalist armies, a scene from the 1949 War.

The Great Depression

RECENT RESEARCH has made it clear how (if one excepts the USSR, which was undergoing its own specific crisis) the universal influence of the 1929 slump was at once the result of deep-seated strains and stresses in world capitalism, and the result of difficulties specific to certain countries. The crisis began in the United States, but it was also a continuation of the great European crises of the second half of the nineteenth century. Though fundamentally it was brought about by the low level of consumer spending, it was at the same time closely linked both to structural phenomena characteristic of the various countries and to the crisis in currency, credit and international trade which had been slowly developing since the Great War.

Indeed, even from before 1929, there had been many worrying symptoms. In France, for example, the warning signs had been flashing since 1928, in spite of the country's prosperity, as a result of the contradiction between a level of production which had entered into the 'capitalist' age and a level of consumption which was still held down by traditionally low wages. Inflation, which had been particularly spectacular in Germany, had ruined people living off savings or capital almost everywhere. The under-industrialized colonies suffered from the growing gap between agricultural and industrial prices. The financing of the war by inflation and the fall in the gold reserves kept the currencies, who had apparently been stabilized at the end of 1920, in a state of great fragility. The power of the bank which specialized in the short-term investment of floating capital, ha increased. It was eventually a fairly ordinary spate of speculation o Wall Street which, on 24 October 1929, sparked off the great crash Stocks and shares continued to plummet until 1932.

In its acute form, the crisis quickly spread throughout the world Bankruptcies followed one after the other in all those countries tha the credit system had tied to the United States, i.e. Austria (in Ma 1931), Germany (where the banks were forced to go 'on holiday' i the summer of 1931), Great Britain and then France. Trade col lapsed, falling by 25% in three years.

The banking and business crisis precipitated the industrial crisi and made the plight of agriculture, already in a precarious position even worse: the fall in agricultural prices was in excess of 50% in th United States, and that in world industrial output close to 40%. A enormous number of workers were thrown on to the dole: some 4 million in 1932. The Great Depression affected farmers not only i those countries where the capitalist economy was most highl developed (the United States and Canada), but also in those whic were dependent on colonial powers. The lack of social security sys tems in many countries, and the weakness of independent trade union organizations for farm workers in the colonies or in the fascis countries (such as Italy) made the scale of human tragedy greate still.

As a result, social and political unrest was widespread. There wer marches by the unemployed in the United States, in Great Britai and in France. There were uprisings in the colonies (like Vietnam) and a general radicalization of the suffering masses who could se with their own eyes the absurdity of a system in which, to 'maintai prices', corn was being burned and oranges destroyed while childre were starving.

Confidence in the virtues of free enterprise was deeply shaken. I the world of business there was an urgent call to get the econom moving again at almost any price. In these conditions new politica forces came to power almost everywhere. State intervention wa advocated by businessmen and farmers, as well as workers, to a unprecedented degree. Almost everywhere the talk was of state plan ning of the economy.

Sometimes spurred on by violence spilling on to the streets (i Germany in 1931–2, in Vienna and Paris in 1934), different 'solu tions' were devised according to how deep the crisis was and how th various forces in society lined up. What form these solutions took depended on the amount of support given to the various ideologies o the time, such as the New Deal in the United States, Nazism i Germany, or the Popular Front in France and Spain.

Total withdrawal into isolationism proved impossible. Nonethe less, the return to protectionism was general, notably in Great Bri-

1. The New York unemployed in the dole queues, November 1933.

'Black Thursday' on Wall Street.	Great Britain abandons free trade.	Hitler comes to power.	Beginning of the New Deal
24 October 1929	February 1932	30 January 1933	4 March 1933

1929. October: Failure of the Hatry Bank in England.
24 October: 'Black Thursday' on Wall Street.
1930. June: Severe customs restrictions imposed in the United States.
1931: In Japan, the military forces the government to intervene in Manchuria.
May: The Kreditanstalt fails in Vienna.
July–August: The banks 'go on holiday' in Berlin.
20 September: Great Britain leaves the gold standard.
December: Germany embarks upon a policy of rapid deflation. On 13 December, Japan goes off the gold standard.
1932. February: Great Britain abandons free trade.
August: The Ottawa Imperial Conference sets preferential trade tariffs between Britain and the dominions.
November: F. D. Roosevelt elected President of the United States.
1933. 30 January: Hitler becomes chancellor of Germany.
12 May: The Agricultural Adjustment Act gives new powers to the American President.

3. A Gaul defends the French franc against the pound and the dollar. Cartoon by A. R. Moritz, January 1924.

4. The good ship Europe turns in distress to the dollar. German cartoon of 1926.

5. Zeus the capitalist: work or thunderbolts Cartoon by Theodor Heine, December 192

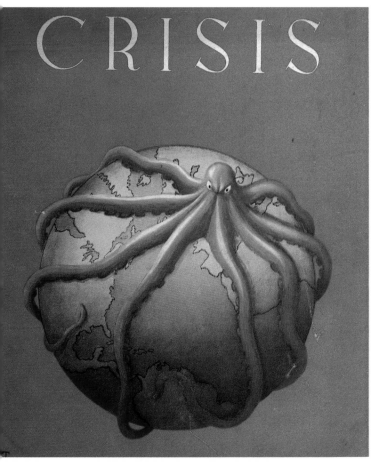

. *The World Crisis as viewed by the German cartoonist Theodor Heine in 1941.*

ain, the home of free trade. The free convertibility of currencies was bandoned. All countries devalued their currency, France being the ast to do so. Gradually, policies of deflation and austerity having hown their ineffectiveness, the wealthy nations turned towards ublic works (in the United States), towards increases in wages (in rance) or closer links with the colonies (as in Great Britain), while in he 'proletarian countries' (Germany, Italy, Japan) governments hose the path of rearmament and preparation for war. Given such an conomic climate, in some countries war had come to be considered s the 'natural' way out of the crisis.

Matignon Accords.

7–8 June 1936

6 **June:** The National Industrial Recovery ct sets the United States on a policy of ublic works.

934. January: The dollar is devalued.
February: Right-wing extremists riot in aris.

935: France undertakes a policy of rapid eflation.

936 February: J. M. Keynes, *The General heory of Employment, Interest and Money.*
June: In France, the Popular Front overnment comes to power with Léon lum as prime minister.
–8 June: A broad strike movement in rance leads to the Matignon Accords etween the Confédération générale de la roduction française (C.G.P.F.) and the onfédéderation générale du travail (C.G.T.).
st October: The French franc is devalued.

. *'When will the crisis end?' Drawing by utriac, October 1931.*

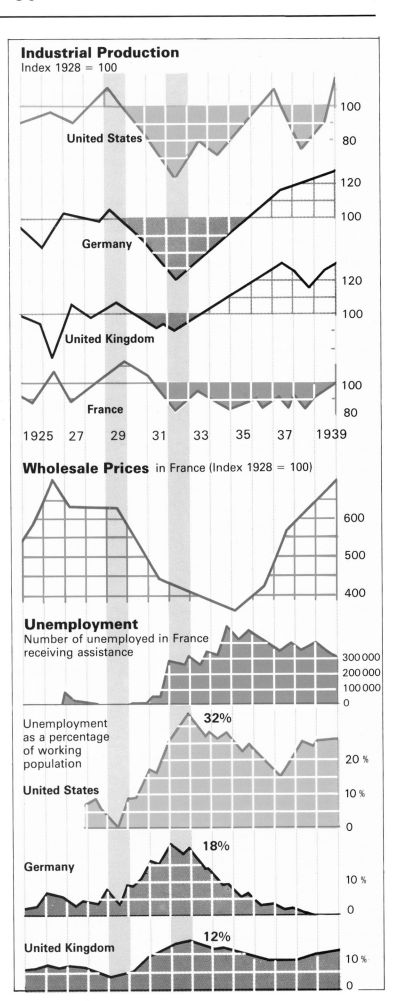

Industrial Production
Index 1928 = 100

United States

Germany

United Kingdom

France

1925   27   29   31   33   35   37   1939

Wholesale Prices in France (Index 1928 = 100)

Unemployment
Number of unemployed in France receiving assistance

Unemployment as a percentage of working population

United States   32%

Germany   18%

United Kingdom   12%

Fascism and the Popular Fronts in Europe

THE DAY AFTER the March on Rome in October 1922, Benito Mussolini was named head of government by King Victor Emmanuel III. After the Matteotti affair of 1924, which unsuccessfully attempted to strike a lethal blow against fascism, an initial period of uncertainty and 'legal dictatorship' was succeeded by the inauguration of a regime of personal power based on a single party, whose aim was the integration and regimentation of the Italian masses. Gradually, as the mechanism of dictatorship was set in place, Italy completed its transformation into a totalitarian state, the political centre extending its control over all sectors of economic, social and cultural life. This tendency increased after 1936 when the Ethiopian War – by means of which the regime sought to link up with the tradition of national grandeur inherited from the Roman past – forced the Duce to launch Italy on the road to autarchy and drove him to strengthen his ties with Nazi Germany.

2. The Italian fascists celebrate the anniversary of the March on Rome in 1939.

1. Striking workers dance at the Argenteuil car factories in Lorraine, 1936.

The wave of counter-revolution which submerged Europe after the First World War reached as far as Hungary, Lithuania, Poland, Spain and Portugal, all of which, in the twenties, were ruled by dictatorial regimes that had come to power in military coups. By contrast with Italian fascism, these deeply conservative regimes aimed only to consolidate or restore the power of the traditional social forces. In the course of the following decade there were indeed open conflicts between certain authoritarian regimes and the fascist movements representing the interests of the peasantry and the petty bourgeoisie. For example, King Carol II, faced in Rumania with the fascist upsurge embodied in Codreanu's Iron Guard (1931), dissolved all political parties by force (1938). In Bulgaria, Khimon Georgiev suppressed political parties and, in May 1934, set up a

March on Rome.	Primo de Rivera.		Seventh Comintern Congress.	Victory of *Frente Popular* in Spa
27–28 October 1922	**13 September 1923**		**August 1935**	**16 February 1936**

1922. 27–28 October: March on Rome.
29 October: Mussolini becomes head of government.
13 September 1923: Miguel Primo de Rivera y Orbaneja comes to power in Spain following a military 'pronunciamento'.
10 June 1924: Socialist deputy Giacomo Matteotti murdered by fascists. In response, a section of the deputies refused to sit in the chamber ('withdrawal to the Aventine'), whilst many fascists left the party.
3 January 1925: Mussolini's speech to the Chamber claiming responsibility for events and proclaiming a dictatorship.
1926. 3 April: Rocco law on trade unions, which gave birth to the corporate state in Italy.
May: A coup d'état brought Gomes da Costa to power in Portugal. In 1928, Antonio de Oliveira Salazar emerged as the regime's 'strong man'. Became President in 1932 and introduced the nationalist, Christian *Estado Novo* constitution in March 1933.
12–14 May: Marshal Pilsudski's coup d'état in Poland; he marches on Warsaw at the head of soldiers faithful to his cause.

November: Laws for the defence of the state – so-called *fascistissime* laws. These set in place the apparatus of dictatorship.
21 April 1927: The Charter of Labour laid down the basic principles of the fascist regime's social organization.
11 February 1929: Lateran Treaty. Mussolini resolved the Roman question, which had remained in suspense since 1870. The Pope's sovereignty over the Vatican was recognized and a concordat established the position of the Catholic Church within the Italian state.
28 January 1930: Resignation of Miguel Primo de Rivera.
March 1933: Authoritarian, traditionalist regime comes to power in Austria. Chancellor Dollfuss outlaws all political parties in 1934.
1934: General Georgiev establishes a monarcho-military dictatorship in Bulgaria.
16 May: Karlis Ulmanis, head of the Peasant Union, carries out a coup d'état in Latvia.
27 July: Signature of a unity pact between the SFIO and PCF in France.
October 1935–May 1936: Italy conquers Ethiopia.

1936. 16 February: Victory of the Popular Front in Spain.
3 May: Victory of the French Popular Front.

3. A Republican dies during the Spanish Civil War.

4. Armband of the Croix-de-Feu, a French Rightist political organization created in 1927 under the leadership of Colonel de la Rocque. It was to be outlawed in 1936.

ictatorship similar to that which Metaxas – ith the assent of the sovereign – introduced 1 Greece (August 1936). In Austria, the uthoritarian and traditionalist regime of Chancellor Dollfuss and of his successor, chuschnigg, rid itself in 1936 of the Heim-ehr, a fascist grouping that had been ounded after the war.

Drawing the lessons from Hitler's rise to ower, which had been aided by divisions ithin the Left in Germany, the Comintern dopted the strategy of Popular Fronts, in hich it was no longer social democracy that as the main enemy but fascism. The com-unists had then to move closer not only to he socialists, but also to the bourgeois democ-atic parties. Several pacts on united action ere signed in 1934, particularly in France, pain and the Saarland and within the Italian migré communities. In France, the Popular ront, which came to power in May 1936, mmediately embarked upon important struc-ural reforms and measures of social legisla-ion. But economic difficulties and the unre-itting hostility of the Right quickly put paid o Blum's government, which was forced out f power in June 1937. In Spain, after the Republicans' crushing electoral victory over he Monarchists, a republic was proclaimed. The elections of 16 February 1936 confirmed he victory of the *Frente Popular*, a combined novement of anarchists, communists and rad-cals, supporting the demands of the workers nd peasants. But the assassination of the Monarchist leader, Calvo Sotelo, on 13 July ave the signal for a military rising under General Franco. A bloody civil war which asted for three years until the capture of Mad-id by Franco, was to set the Republicans gainst the Nationalists, who had their power base in the army, the clergy and the Phalange. This latter was a fascist-style movement ounded in 1933 by José Antonio Primo de Rivera and backed with men and material by Germany, Italy and Portugal.

Political regimes in Europe in 1938

400 km

Liberal democracies

Countries governed at some point by Popular Fronts

Communist regimes

Fascist regimes

Authoritarian regimes

First Blum government.

4 June 1936–21 June 1937

Franco's forces capture Madrid.

28 March 1939

The Left coalition won 369 seats against 236 won by the Right.
17–18 July: Beginning of the Spanish Civil War.
4 August: Metaxas's coup d'état in Greece.
1 November: Rome–Berlin Axis.
1938. February: King Carol II strikes to eliminate Codreanu's Iron Guard in Rumania.
July: Publication of the Manifesto for the Defence of the Race in Italy.
October: Education Charter.
1939. 28 March: General Francisco Franco takes Madrid and, on 18 October sets up his government there. The Civil War left more than one million dead.
7 April: Italy invades Albania.

5. Adolf Hitler and Count Ciano sign the Pact of Steel on 22 May 1939, which transforms the political entente into a military alliance.

6. Léon Blum, miner's lamp in hand, acclaims the workers, 1937.

The USSR in the Age of Stalin

1. Iosif Vissarionovich Stalin. Propaganda poster.

THE 'RUDDERLESS YEAR', 1928, marks the irreversible passage from the Leninist to the Stalinist period. The forces of opposition to the one-party system were broken and the other institutions tamed. From this point on, the various oppositions within the Communist Party itself were destroyed (Bukharinite Right, Trotskyite Left), in confrontations which produced more surprise and indignation abroad than had previous efforts to bring factions into line. The same was true of the executions that accompanied these 'purges', which were more extensive than any previously carried out.

The Stalinist era was, moreover, characterized by great transformations which shaped the country for half a century.

The adoption of five-year plans to organize economic production was a spectacular innovation and one which seemed particularly rational when the crisis of 1929 broke in the West. The Soviet example was soon imitated, and several other countries adopted the idea of economic plans, whether of five years or some other period.

Industrialization gave priority to the production of heavy plant, which received three-quarters of investment. The symbols of this period of major public works, which were a subject of intense propaganda, were the great Zaporozhe and Dniepr dams, the huge Urals and Kuzbass industrial complexes, and the newly-built giant communications routes, such as the Turksib railway.

The collectivization of the countryside began with dekulakization, i.e. the persecution and extermination of the better-off (or merely refractory) peasants. This collectivization aimed at grouping peasants into the *sovkhozy*, which were organized as industrial enterprises, or into the *kolkhozy*, where the peasants retained a little individual plot of land but devoted the greater part of their time to the collective's land.

The reinforcement of the machinery of the state showed itself in the growing importance of the organs of control and repression, and in particular the NKVD (and the OGPU at its centre). This organization provided the inmates for the labour camps (known as Gulags), such as Kolyma, Karaganda, etc. The numbers of prisoners in these camps reached a figure of between five and eight million, depending on whose estimates one believes.

At the same time, the 1936 Constitution established the map of the Federation of the Republics of the Union, which rose from seven in number to eleven (fourteen after the war with the annexation of the three Baltic republics and Moldavia), whilst the number of autonomous republics rose to twenty, sixteen of which were in Russia.

This whole period can be summed up in three words: mobilization, reaction, repression. Society as a whole was mobilized in the most relentless manner and at a considerable cost in human sacrifice, symbolized in the emergence of such figures as the *Udarniki* (shock workers), the Stakhanovites and the *Mnogostanochniki* (elite workers), not to mention the *zeks* (Gulag deportees).

In the same period a traditionalist reaction occurred in favour of the family, academicism, the Soviet motherland and its new army. This phenomenon was connected with the slow 'plebeianization' of the army, following the accession to the state apparatus of popular elements who had entered the Soviets in 1917.

Lastly, the intensification of political terror on the eve of the war found expression in the 'show trials' which eliminated a number of Lenin's companions (Zinoviev, Kamenev, Radek, Bukharin) and generals like Tukhachevsky.

1933	1934	1935	1936	1943
Birth of I. A. Yevtushenko.	Maxim Gorky organizes the Writers' Union.	Boris Souvarine publishes a biography of Stalin.	André Gide publishes his *Return from the USSR*.	Birth of Lech Wałę

April 1922: Stalin becomes General Secretary of the Communist Party.
21 January 1924: Death of Lenin.
24 April 1926: Treaty with Germany.
November 1927: Trotsky expelled from the Communist Party: two years later, he will be exiled from the Soviet Union.
October 1928: Beginning of first Five-Year Plan. Suppression of private trade; collectivization of the countryside; iron and steel production doubled.
February 1930: Beginning of the campaign against the kulaks (so-called rich peasants); massive destruction of harvest, entire villages deported (10 million dead?).
1933: Second Five-Year Plan; call for emulation amongst workers.
1934: A. Zhdanov fixes the norms of Socialist Realism at the First Writers' Congress.
18 September: USSR enters League of Nations; in this way it marks its *rapprochement* with the democratic nations against Nazi Germany.
1 December: Kirov, a member of the Politburo, is assassinated; his death serves as a pretext for the incarceration of a large number of political prisoners.
2 May 1935: Franco-Soviet treaty of mutual assistance.
1936: 'Trial' of 'Left' opposition leaders (including G. Zinoviev and L. Kamenev).
1937: 'Trial' of Marshal Tukhachevsky and 31 other higher officers; the whole of the Soviet high command, which is suspected of opposition to Stalin, is disrupted.
1938: 'Trials' of 'Right' opposition, including Bukharin and Rykov.
23 August 1939: Non-aggression pact between Germany and the Soviet Union. Its secret clauses provide for a partition of Poland between the two countries.
1941. 22 June: Germans invade the USSR, encircle Leningrad and advance on Moscow.
5 December: Soviet counter-offensive. Moscow relieved.
1942: Germans attack towards the Black Sea and the Caucasian oil fields; in September, Stalingrad is encircled; in November, the Soviets relieve the town and launch a counter-offensive. From this point on, the Germans are constantly in retreat.
1944. 1 August: Warsaw rising.

9 October: Moscow conference. Britain and the Soviets divide up Europe into zones of influence.
2 May 1945: Berlin falls into Soviet hands.
1946: Stalin is Secretary of the Central Committee of the Communist Party, Prime Minister and Minister of War. Beginning of the fourth Five-Year Plan directed towards repairing the damage caused by the war.
June 1948: The Soviets blockade Berlin, forcing the Americans to organize an air bridge; the blockade lasts until May 1949. Split between Soviet Union and Yugoslavia in June.
June 1950: Outbreak of the Korean War.
1951: Launch of fifth Five-Year Plan directed towards the provision of electricity by huge hydro-electric dams.
5 March 1953: Death of Stalin. End of June, arrest of Beria.

3. Lavrenty Pavlovich Beria, the second most eminent Georgian, chief of the secret police.

The barque of love has shattered on the reefs of the daily ...nd.' Vladimir Vladimirovich Mayakovsky, photographed at ...offices of Izvestia in 1927.

L. Rajk is condemned to death.

24 September 1949

Lev Davidovich Bronstein, known as Trotsky, arrives in ...exico, 1936.

ALASKA

PACIFIC OCEAN

Petropavlovsk

JAPAN

Anadyr

Sakkhalin Island

Pevek

Sovietskaya Gavan

Kolyma

Okhotsk   Komsomolsk   Vladivostock

CHINA

Yakutsk   *Lena*

Sea frozen over all year round

Chita Shilka

Oz Baykal

Yenissey   Irkutsk

Norilsk

TUVA

Sea frozen in winter

KUZBASS

Novaya Zemlya   *Ob*   *Ob*   Novosibirsk

CHINA

Vorkuta

Turksib

Murmansk   Omsk   Karaganda

Archangel   **URALS**   Sverdlovsk   Alma Ata

Leningrad   Tashkent

Kuybyshev

Moscow

AFGHANISTAN

Minsk   Stalingrad

Kharkov   *Volga*

Kiev   **DONBASS**   Baku

Tbilisi   Yerevan

Odessa   IRAN

TURKEY

0 km

2000

4000

6000

8000 km

	Tundra	● Iron deposits	Main railway lines built between 1917 and 1953
	Forest	● Coal deposits	
	Mountains	▲ Oil ❱ Dams	★ Labour camps in 1953

The United States: Prosperity, Crisis and Reform

IN THE DECADE after the First World War, the US enjoyed unprecedented prosperity, sustained by the Republican governments of Harding, Coolidge and Hoover. These were the boom years, during which the new industries (automobiles, aeronautics, electrical goods) began mass production, employing new, rationalized methods (Taylorism, production-line working).

This prosperity, however, concealed a number of weaknesses: incomes increased less (by 17%) than output (35%) and company profits (62%). Out of 27 million households, 6 million – most of them Black or immigrant households – lived in poverty. Agriculture experienced a permanent crisis of overproduction. The old sectors of industry stagnated. Profits were diverted towards frantic speculation on the Stock Exchange. In October 1929, the exaggerated rise in share prices relative to their real value caused the Wall Street Crash, which ushered in the Great Depression from which the USA would only recover thanks to the New Deal and war.

The Stock Exchange crisis quickly spread to the whole of the economy. Between 1929 and 1932, national revenue collapsed from 87 billion dollars to 39 billion. The unemployment figures rose from 1.5 million to 12 million. Ruined farmers lost their lands. This new poverty found its expression in the soup kitchens, shanty towns, the sight of homeless people wandering the streets, and general despair. In 1932, given the failure of Hoover's policies, the electorate put its faith in the Democrat, Franklin D. Roosevelt's promise of a New Deal.

The aim of the New Deal was to bring about a revival of free enterprise by means of pragmatic federal government intervention in all sectors of the economy: the control of the banking and monetary systems; aid to farmers and a reduction in agricultural production (AAA); the development of codes of fair competition in industry, together with collective agreements on reduced working hours and a minimum wage (NIRA); the commencement of huge public works schemes such as the Tennessee Valley Authority project. These initial measures were resisted by the business community and the Supreme Court ruled them illegal; but after 1936 Roosevelt called upon the support of broader sections of public opinion to push through bolder policies that were Keynesian in inspiration. He applied the principle of deficit funding to create new wealth and increase consumption levels. Thanks to a reshuffle of the Supreme Court, the principal measures of the first 'Hundred Days' were taken up again and reinforced.

1. In the days of Prohibition. *Anonymous painting, New York.*

2. *Work progressing on the world's biggest dam, Boulder City, Nevada, 1934.*

The 'Red Scare'.   **The Model T Ford.**   **The Wall Street Crash.**

1921	1924	October 1929

1920: First commercial radio station.
1921: The 'Red Scare'. N. Sacco and B. Vanzetti are sentenced to death for murder, in spite of the lack of evidence. They will be executed in 1927.
1924: The Model T Ford priced at less than 300 dollars.
1927: First 'talking' cinema.
1929: 48 airlines in operation, serving 355 American airports. October: panic on the Stock Exchange. Hoover signs the Agricultural Marketing Act.
1929–1932: 85,000 companies bankrupted.
1932: 12 million unemployed. March of the 'Bonus Army' of ex-servicemen and civil servants on Washington. Reconstruction Finance Company founded. Norris-La Guardia Act restricts the use of injunctions in labour disputes.
1933–1945: Franklin D. Roosevelt President.
1933 March–June: The 'Hundred Days'. Emergency Banking Act: the banks are closed and reorganized by the President. National Industry Recovery Act (NIRA): accords between industry, the federal government and the unions. Agricultural

4. *The anarchists Sacco and Vanzetti in court, 1921.*

5. *Franklin D. Roosevelt.*

These measures brought recovery in 1937, but it was short-lived. As soon as the federal government balanced its budget again, depression set in once more. From 1938 onwards the arms industry took up the slack from the industries that were in difficulty. The New Deal was a set of policies designed to attack the problem of depression; it was not a revolution. Though it succeeded in saving the American economy from bankruptcy, it was not able to find a market for the enormous productive potential of the USA. But for the Americans – and for the outside world – it represented a model for restoring harmony to a crisis-ridden economy and society. By imposing two countervailing forces to capitalism (trade unionism and the federal government), it reconciled a section of the intellectuals and workers to the American system. But confidence was still fragile, and it would take Pearl Harbor to persuade the American people to ally with the democracies in their war against Hitler.

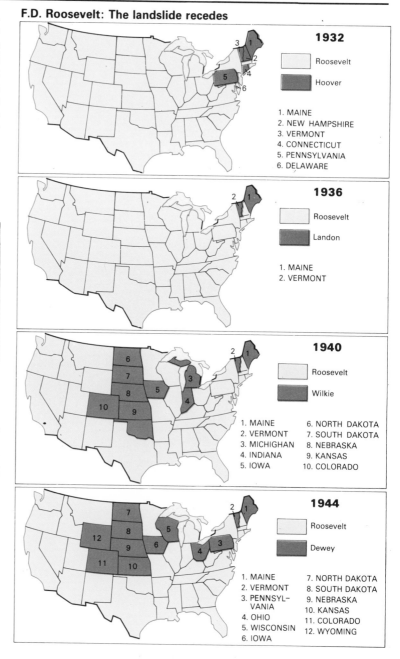

F.D. Roosevelt: The landslide recedes

1932
Roosevelt
Hoover

1. MAINE
2. NEW HAMPSHIRE
3. VERMONT
4. CONNECTICUT
5. PENNSYLVANIA
6. DELAWARE

1936
Roosevelt
Landon

1. MAINE
2. VERMONT

1940
Roosevelt
Wilkie

1. MAINE   6. NORTH DAKOTA
2. VERMONT   7. SOUTH DAKOTA
3. MICHIGHAN 8. NEBRASKA
4. INDIANA   9. KANSAS
5. IOWA   10. COLORADO

1944
Roosevelt
Dewey

1. MAINE   7. NORTH DAKOTA
2. VERMONT   8. SOUTH DAKOTA
3. PENNSYL-   9. NEBRASKA
   VANIA   10. KANSAS
4. OHIO   11. COLORADO
5. WISCONSIN   12. WYOMING
6. IOWA

3. As the 'grapes of wrath' ripen . . . Refugees from Oklahoma reach California, August 1936.

osevelt elected President.   **New Deal**

              1932   1933

                                          Pearl Harbor.

                                          7 December 1941

Adjustment Act (AAA): price control and assistance towards reducing agricultural production. Tennessee Valley Authority (TVA) giving development a regional dimension.
1934: Devaluation of the dollar. Abrogation of the Platt Amendment which had allowed the U.S. to intervene in Cuba.
1935: Creation of the Committee for Industrial Organization (CIO) and the Works Progress Administration, which, by 1939, will have employed 8.5 million people. The Supreme Court declare the AAA and the NIRA unconstitutional. The Wagner-Connery Act extends trade union rights and lays down the principle of collective conventions under the aegis of the federal government. First social security legislation.
1935–7: 'Neutrality' laws, prohibiting the sale of arms to a warring nation.
1936: Re-election of Roosevelt with a large majority. Second New Deal. Federal budget deficit of 3,500 million dollars.
1937–41: Roosevelt appoints 7 new judges to the Supreme Court.
1937 spring: Brief economic upswing. Sit-in strikes in the car industry. In a speech at

Chicago, Roosevelt warns his fellow countrymen of the danger of a war in Europe.
1938: Unemployment reaches 19% of the employable population. Budget deficits accumulated over a five year period total 1 billion dollars.
1939: Modification of 'neutrality' laws.
1941 spring: The USA establishes a naval base in Greenland. 7 December: Japanese attack on the American base at Pearl Harbor. The USA goes to war against Japan.

6. Eleanor Roosevelt (right) and a New Deal supporter in front of a poster for the National Industrial Recovery Act in August 1933.

7. The gangsters Bonnie and Clyde.

Hitler's Conquests: The Prelude to War

1. The 'Cathedral of Light', Nuremberg, 1st May 1939.

2. Hitler in Berlin, 1939.

IT TOOK THE FÜHRER less than a year to have his party declared the only legal one and bring into line all sectors of public life by intimidation and violence (the 'experimental' camp at Dachau was opened in March 1933 and was to be followed by five others before 1939). Once assured of compliance on the 'home front', Hitler then had the means to strike the final blows against the Versailles *diktat*, which he did with the reintroduction of compulsory military service and the remilitarization of the Rhineland. These shows of strength allowed him to assess Franco-British inertia and to achieve a *rapprochement* with the states of Southeastern and Central Europe, which the crisis had pushed into dictatorship. The (aerial) support that the Reich gave to Franco's forces in the Spanish Civil War laid the ground for a *rapprochement* with fascist Italy (the 'Axis'), which was formalized in the Pact of Steel.

Enjoying military superiority over the Western democracies, Hitler was able to move progressively towards the solution of the 'problem of Greater Germany'. The first stage in that solution consisted in annexing the lands inhabited by Germans. In the spring of 1938 the entry of the Wehrmacht into Austria provoked only verbal protestations in London and Paris. In Czechoslovakia, the last military and parliamentary bastion in Central Europe, Hitler supported the claims of the German-speaking Sudeten minority.

France and the USSR were prepared to honour their obligations on Czech independence (May 1938); however, out of a desire for 'appeasement', the British government refused to give any assurances. Once Prague had resolved to yield over the autonomy of the

Sudetenland, Hitler doubled the stakes and called at the Nuremberg Congress for their annexation to the Reich. After the British prime minister, Neville Chamberlain, had made two trips to Germany, negotiation carried the day. Britain, France, Italy and Germany endorsed the Munich Agreement, which compromised the security of the democracies and dismantled Czechoslovakia (delivered up shortly afterwards to the appetites of the Poles and the Hungarians). On 15 March 1939, Bohemia-Moravia disappeared from the map. This new show of strength rounded off the second stage of Hitler's programme, the conquest of *Lebensraum* in the east. Now master of the Memel territory, occupied a week after Prague, Hitler's actions raised the question of what was to become of Danzig and the Polish Corridor. On this occasion, Paris and London could not retreat for fear of losing face among the smaller nations threatened by the Axis powers. The British government associated itself with the French guarantees to Poland, and negotiations commenced which even included the Soviets. These progressed slowly on account of reciprocal mistrust and as a result of the Polish refusal to allow the Red Army on to its soil. During this period, talks began in Moscow which were to lead to the Nazi-Soviet non-aggression pact, the secret clauses of which made provision for the division of Poland.

Hitler, therefore, had a free hand. After vainly attempting to sway the attitude of the British, with whom he offered to divide up the world, he ordered his forces to enter Poland on 1 September 1939. A final intervention by Italy could not prevent the outbreak of hostilities on 3 September.

Hitler to power.	Reichstag fire.	Dachau camp opened.		Night of the Long Knives.
30 January 1933	27 February 1933	March 1933		30 June 1934

1933. 30 January: Hitler becomes chancellor.
19 October: Germany leaves the League of Nations Disarmament Conference.
1934. 26 January: German-Polish non-aggression treaty.
1935. 13 January: The Saarland returned to the Reich by plebiscite.
16 March: Reintroduction of compulsory military service.
14 April: Stresa Front (Britain, Italy, France) condemning the unilateral revision of treaties.
2 May: Franco-Soviet Pact.
18 Nov: League of Nations votes sanctions against Italy which had gone to war against Abyssinia on the 3rd October.
1936. 7 March: Military occupation of the Rhineland.
18 July: Beginning of the Spanish Civil War (–28 March 1939).
1 November: Proclamation of the Berlin-Rome Axis.
25 November: Anti-Comintern Pact between Germany and Japan.
1937. 26 April and 31 May: Guernica and

3. 'Strength through Joy', Nazi poster of 1936.

Almeira.
5 November: The 'Hossbach Protocol' which lays down Hitler's future intentions.
1938. 12–13 March: Anschluss.
24 April: The Sudeten programme, 'the eight points of Karlovy Vary'.
3 August: Lord Runciman's mission to Prague.
12–13 September: Hitler's anti-Czech speech at Nuremberg and the Sudeto-Czech split.
15 and 22–4 September: Neville Chamberlain and Hitler meet at Berchtesgaden and Bad Godesberg.
29–30 September: Four-way international conference and Munich Agreement.
2 October and 2 November: Teschen ceded to Poland and Southern Slovakia ceded to Hungary with German backing.
1939. 14–15 March: Disappearance of Czechoslovakia. Slovakia proclaims its independence. Bohemia-Moravia becomes a Reich protectorate.
23 March: Lithuania cedes the Memel territory to the Reich.
23 March: British guarantees to Poland and

Internment camps

1. Ravensbrudck
2. Buchenwald
3. Dachau
4. Mauthausen
5. Ponza Is.
6. Miranda da Ebro
7. Gurs

NORWAY
Stockholm
SWEDEN
DENMARK
Copenhagen
ESTONIA *1934*
LATVIA *1934*
Riga
LITHUANIA *1926*
Memel
Kaunas
Danzig
Moscow
USSR
Nazi-Soviet Pact 8.39

IRELAND
Dublin
GREAT BRITAIN
London
HOLLAND
Amsterdam
BELGIUM
Brussels
LUXEMBOURG
Paris
FRANCE
GERMANY
Hitler 1933
Berlin
Warsaw
POLAND
Pilsudski 1926

RHINELAND *3.36*
3.35
SAARLAND
Rome-Berlin Axis
11.36
3.38
SUDETEN GERMANS
BOHEMIA
Prague
CZECHOSLOVAKIA
MORAVIA
SLOVAKIA *11.36*
RUTHENIA *3.39*
Odessa

SWITZERLAND
Munich
AUSTRIA
Dollfuss 1933
Vienna
Budapest
HUNGARY
Horthy 1929
RUMANIA
Carol II 1938
Bucharest

Genoa
Belgrade
YUGOSLAVIA
Alexander I, 1929
BULGARIA
Boris III 1934
Sofia

Oviedo
Guernica *4.37*
Bilbao
Burgos 6
SPAIN
Franco 1936
Madrid *3.39*
Toledo
Teruel
Valencia
Cordoba
Granada *7.36*
Cadiz
PORTUGAL
Salazar 1928
7
Barcelona
1.39

ITALY
Mussolini 1922
Rome
4.39
ALBANIA
Tirana
GREECE
Metaxas 1936
Athens
Angora *(Ankara)*
TURKEY
Mustafa Kemal 1920
(Italy)

5

Supply line to the Nationalists
Supply lines to Republicans

500 km

End of Parliamentary rule

Date of events | 1936 | 1937 | 1938 | 1939

◇ Rome-Berlin Axis
➔ Civil War in Spain

Conquest of Ethiopia by Italy (10.35)

Nuremberg Laws.

15 September 1935

Remilitarization of the Rhineland.

7 March 1936

Freud goes into exile in London.

4 March 1938

Rumania.
31 March: Pledge of Permanent Mutual Guarantee between the United Kingdom and Poland.
7 April: The Italians occupy Albania.
28 April: Hitler repudiates his agreements with Britain and Poland.
22 May: Signing of the Pact of Steel, the military alliance between Germany and Italy.
11 August: Arrival of the Franco-British military mission in Moscow.
23 August: Nazi-Soviet Non-aggression Pact signed in Moscow.
1 September: Invasion of Poland. Danzig annexed by the Reich.
3 September: United Kingdom and France declare war on Germany.

4. Hitler portrayed by Charlie Chaplin in The Great Dictator, *1940.*

5. The Nazis in Prague, 15 March 1939.

6. An orthodox Jew is arrested in Berlin, 1935.

The War in Europe and Africa

AFTER INITIAL SUCCESSES in Poland (September 1939), the lightning war (*Blitzkrieg*) began again the following spring, enabling the Germans to seize the Danish straits and the Norwegian coast, and subsequently the north-west of Europe (the Netherlands, Belgium and France were overrun in six weeks). After unprecedentedly heavy bombing raids on England, the focus of the war shifted for a year or two into the eastern Mediterranean and the Balkans, where Hitler wanted both to ensure that his Italian ally did not lose face and to prevent Great Britain re-establishing a foothold on the Continent. On 22 June 1941 the attack on the USSR (Operation Barbarossa) began,

1. Searching for the dead after a massacre in the Crimea, 1942.

but after five months of the offensive the *blitz* began to show signs of petering out, the Germans having to confront, simultaneously, the problems of the Russian winter, the vastness of the territory and the weight of numbers ranged against them. Nevertheless, neither the Soviet counter-attack nor the Russian winter prevented the German's from advancing, between May and November 1942, as far as the Caucasus and the Volga.

Treated with varying degrees of harshness, either according to the imperatives of the conflict (as was the case with Vichy France and the puppet regimes of Norway and Croatia) or as a result of the exercise of the Nazi's racial doctrines (Poland, the USSR and Eastern Europe), the occupied countries were subjected to an implacably oppressive regime (eleven new concentration camps were built within the Greater Reich) and to intensive economic exploitation: this exploitation was most severe in the 'Ostlands' (the Ostland system organized agricultural production particularly in the east). The 'New Order' thus generated internal resistance movements which were to play an important role in the eventual liberation of Europe.

A turnabout in fortunes first became apparent at the end of 1942 and the beginning of 1943 with Montgomery's victory at El Alamein, the British and American landings in North Africa and Paulus's surrender at Stalingrad. Total war, to which the USA and the USSR (east of the Urals) had become converted, gave the Allies a superiority which they put to good effect, taking the initiative on all fronts. Whilst the Soviets forced their enemies into an 'elastic retreat' over the greater part of Russian territory, the Allied landings in Sicily (July 1943) brought about the fall of Mussolini, the capture of southern Italy and the surrender of the Badoglio government. In combination with the Red Army's operations, the landings in Normandy and Provence (6 June and 15 August 1944) made possible the liberation of a vast part of 'Fortress Europe' and forced Germany's satellites to sign armistices (autumn 1944).

The recourse to V1 and V2 rockets – first against England, then against Antwerp – and the counter-offensives in the Ardennes and around Budapest, did not halt the Allied advance. This began again, both in the east with a drive towards the Oder (January 1945), and in the west with the British, French and American forces crossing the Rhine (March). The desperate resistance of the leaders of the Reich could not prevent either the invasion of the country nor a general exodus of the population.

Powerless either to prevent the Allied armies from meeting up or to stop the Russians entering Berlin, Hitler took his own life in his bunker on 30 April. He left to his chosen successor, Admiral Doenitz, the task of negotiating with the Allies. The unconditional surrender of the German armies was ratified in Berlin on 8 May, having been signed at Reims on the 7th. It left a 'Year Zero' Germany in the hands of the Allied commanders-in-chief (USSR, USA, Britain, France).

Fall of Warsaw.	German offensive in the west.	Operation Barbarossa.	German capitulation at Stalingrad.
26 September 1939	**10 May 1940**	**22 June 1941**	**2 February 1943**

1939. 26 September: End of the Polish campaign. The country is partitioned between Germany and the USSR.
1940. 30 November–12 March: USSR attacks Finland.
10 May: General German offensive: the Netherlands and Luxembourg are invaded.
14 May: French defences pierced near Sedan.
28 May–4 June: Battle of Dunkirk.
7–8 June: French lines breached.
10 June: Italy enters the war.
22 and 24 June: France signs armistice with Germany and Italy.
10 July–31 October: Battle of Britain.
28 October: Italians invade Greece.
1941. 19 January–18 May: British victories in East Africa.
31 March–29 April: Rommel's offensive in Libya.
6 April–31 May: German campaigns in Balkans and Crete.
2–31 May: Failure of anti-British coup in Iraq.
22 June: Germany and her allies invade the USSR.
2 October–5 December: Siege of Moscow.

4. Stukas over the Acropolis, May 1941.

6 December–March 1942: Soviet counter-offensive on the Moscow front.
1942. 21 January–2 September: Rommel's second offensive in Libya.
8 May–2 July: German offensive in the Crimea.
12 May: Fall of Sebastopol.
5–10 July: Rommel advances to El Alamein.
23 October–4 November: British victory at El Alamein. Afrika Korps routed.
8 November: Allied landings in North Africa.
19 November–2 February 1943: Battle of Stalingrad. German surrender.
1943. 13 May: Axis troops forced out of Tunisia.
10 July–7 August: Sicily campaign.
25 July: Fall of Mussolini (executed 28 April 1945).
3 September: Italian armistice. Allies in Calabria.
Late 1943–Early 1944: USSR's 1939 frontiers restored.
1944. 11 May: Allies assault the Gustav line in Italy.
6 June: Normandy landings.
15 August: Landings in Provence.

2. *The Red Poster, 1944. The Nazi occupiers denounce terrorists among the immigrant labour force before shooting them.*

3. The dead at Auschwitz.

ration of Paris.   Liberation of Auschwitz.

ugust 1944   25 January 1945

July–October: Soviets penetrate into German satellite states, which sign peace treaties (October–January 1945).
16 December–27 January 1945: German counter-offensive in the Ardennes.
26 December–13 February 1945: Soviets besiege Budapest.
1945. 13 January: Beginning of Soviet offensives in Germany.
7 March: Allies cross the Rhine.
26 April: Soviet and American forces meet.
30 April: Hitler commits suicide in his bunker.
2 May: Soviets enter Berlin. The Americans take Munich.
7–8 May: German surrender.

The War: A Global Perspective

THE PLANISPHERE reveals the great disparity in size between the Axis partners and the Allied nations. The latter formed a bloc covering huge land masses, with the result that in some areas the Allies were able to develop their industrial potential safe from the enemy's strategic bombing campaigns (Canada, USA, the USSR east of the Urals). Their arms production (Great Britain included) was twice as great as the figure for the Greater Reich and Japan combined in 1941 and rose to three times that figure in 1943.

The Americans, who possessed the most powerful arms factories in the world, not only equipped themselves for a war on two fronts, they also became the 'arsenal of the democracies', and the Lease-Lend Bill (11 March 1941) was extended to include all their allies. The question of long-distance transport, therefore, became crucial. Two conditions had to be met for the United States to come to Britain's assistance. First, they needed ports backed up by air bases in the Middle East and Southern Africa in order to convey the material. Up until November 1942, when West Africa and Madagascar entered the war, the impossibility of using Dakar and Diego Suarez proved to be a stumbling-block. The British (and in September 1940 at Dakar the 'Gaullists') were ultimately forced to intervene, with varying levels of success. They succeeded only in occupying Diego Suarez, which fell on 6 May 1942.

The second condition was success in anti-submarine warfare, which was necessitated by the German *Rudeltaktik* (hunting in packs) in the Atlantic (and also in the Mediterranean and the Arctic Ocean). The situation was very difficult for the Allies until the beginning of 1943, when it began to improve as a result of technological developments and a naval building programme that outstripped losses. As a consequence, the Allies were able to carry out amphibious operations in Europe in 1944 and provide supplies for the forces on the Continent in the autumn.

By contrast, in the Pacific it was American submarines which held the initiative, attacking a Japanese merchant fleet that was ill-prepared for this type of warfare and whose losses soon exceeded the number of new ships launched. By the early months of 1945, Japan had lost all but 10% of the ships it possessed before the war (and these were its smallest vessels) and was threatened with economic asphyxiation.

The Second World War was fought out over long distances. Transport problems, therefore, assumed enormous importance and, as a further consequence, both submarine warfare and strategic bombing became particularly intense theatres of conflict.

1. Identity checks in the Warsaw ghetto.

2. 'This war is a world war', De Gaulle, 18 June 1940.

3. Americans landing at Omaha Beach on D-Day.

1939–45

French military establishments in the Pacific

Pearl Harbor
Hawaii
Midway
Dutch Harbor
Auckland
NEW ZEALAND
New Caledonia
Brisbane

San Diego
Vancouver
AUSTRALIA
Darwin

USA
CANADA
Tokyo
JAPAN

Washington
Halifax
Greenland
Spitsbergen
USSR
Beijing (Peking)
Chonging (Chungking)
CHINA

Cuba
Guantanamo
Bermuda
French West Indies
Mumansk
Narvik
Archangel
Moscow
Calcutta

Georgetown
Azores
London
GREAT BRITAIN
Berlin
Rome
Yalta
AFGHANISTAN
INDIA
Bombay
Cocos Islands

Paramaribo
French Guyana
Gibraltar
Casablanca
North Africa
Malta
TURKEY
Tehran
Damascus

Natal
Marzuq
Cairo
SAUDI ARABIA
Trincomalee
Chagos Archipelago

Dakar
French West Africa
Aden
Djibouti
Seychelles

Freetown
Fort Lamy
Lagos
Addis Ababa 9.41
Diego Suarez
Mauritius

Accra
Douala
French Equatorial Africa
Reunion

Accension Island
Brazzaville
Madagascar

St Helena
Angola
MOZAMBIQUE

UNION OF SOUTH AFRICA
Cape Province

Scale at centre of map = 3000 km

Legend

▨ Allies at the end of 1940	⬤ Major Allied bases
▧ Free French Forces (General de Gaulle)	→ Supply lines
Territories loyal to the Vichy Government	→ Allied assaults or landings
States passing over to the Allied cause during the conflict	∴ Principal zones of submarine warfare
Territories occupied by Axis powers	
→ Major Japanese raids	
Neutral	

Monthly allied tonnage

from P.K. Lundberg

sunk
built

1 300 000
800 000
200 000
0

NOVEMBER

1942   1943

Jan Apr Jul Oct Jan Apr Jul Oct Dec

The War in the Pacific

THE SURPRISE ATTACK on Pearl Harbor demonstrates the astonishing eagerness of the Japanese military establishment to take on the United States, who were hostile to Japanese penetration into China. It also reveals their determination to seize the resources of both Indochina and the Dutch East Indies, whose colonial rulers in Europe had fallen to the German Reich in 1940. The military occupation of Indochina, which posed a threat to Singapore and the South Seas (summer 1941), brought retaliatory measures from Roosevelt and the Commonwealth, spurring the bellicist party (Tojo) into action.

In a lightning war of only a few months' duration, the Japanese gained control of the American bases in the eastern Pacific and the main sources of raw materials in the south, and even threatened India and Australia. They may perhaps have expected to achieve a compromise peace with the Americans. The USA, however, riposted by bombarding Tokyo for the first time in the spring of 1942 and by fighting the air and sea battles of the Coral Sea and Midway. With its best units removed from the action, the Japanese navy was unable to prevent an Allied landing at Guadalcanal (Solomon Islands) in August of the same year.

1. The Australians and Japanese do battle in the jungle of New Guinea (July 1943), painted by Ivor Hele.

From then on the Japanese, with their communication lines over-extended and their forces too dispersed (in spite of temporary help received from the peoples they had 'liberated'), were unable to prevent the Allies carrying out a 'pincer' operation (1942–5). With General MacArthur at their head in the south, the Allies went from island to island, 'leapfrogging' those where the enemy contingents were too strong (these would later be forced to surrender when they had become encircled), and, eventually, reached the Philippines.

With his 'task forces' (groups of aircraft-carriers, protection vessels and landing craft), Admiral Nimitz led the attack in the central Pacific, advancing from the Gilbert Islands as far as the Ryu Kyu. Like the British in Burma, the Americans came up against stubborn Japanese resistance (kamikaze suicide squads). At the beginning of 1945, as the Chinese were also launching an offensive, the US forces captured Iwo Jima and Okinawa, islands lying near to the Japanese archipelago. From these bases, their Flying Fortresses were able to bomb the nerve centres of Japan's war effort, as well as the supply ships arriving from Southeast Asia.

In spite of these threats, the Japanese leaders were not prepared to capitulate (they still held Indochina, the Dutch East Indies and the Chinese coasts): the American high command did not expect to be able to launch the final assault until 1946 and even then expected to suffer heavy losses (a million men).

The situation was resolved by President Truman's decision to drop the atomic bomb on Hiroshima and Nagasaki (6 and 9 August) and by the entry into the war of the USSR – it had been neutral since the treaty of 13 April 1941 – which marched into Manchuria and Korea. Emperor Hirohito decided to intervene personally and force his ministers and military leaders to agree to their country's surrender.

The act of capitulation, signed on 2 September aboard the battleship *Missouri* in the Bay of Tokyo, set the seal on bellicist Japan's defeat, but left a number of problems unresolved: Japanese occupation had dealt a fatal blow to European domination in Southeast Asia; in China, victory over the Japanese was to be followed by a confrontation between Chiang Kai-shek's nationalists and the communists led by Mao Tse-tung.

2. Hiroshima six months after the bomb.

Pearl Harbor.	Fall of Singapore.	First American victory.
7 December 1941	15 February 1942	7 June 1942

1941. Spring–end of autumn: US-Japanese negotiations.
13 April: Soviet-Japanese non-aggression pact.
26 July: Japanese assets in USA 'frozen'.
29 July: Japan obtains forces from Vichy France for the war in Southern Indochina.
1 August: Embargo on petrol exports.
16–17 October: The Tojo cabinet succeeds that of Prince Konoye in Tokyo.
7 December: Attack on Pearl Harbor;
8 December: Japan declares war on USA, Britain and the Commonwealth.
10–11 December: Japanese landings in the islands of Guam and Luzon.
20 December: Destruction of the *Prince of Wales* and the *Repulse*.
1942. 18 January–17 March: Occupation of Burma.
15 February: Capitulation of Singapore.
8 March: Occupation of Java; 7 April: Occupation of Sumatra.
18 April: First American bombing of Tokyo.
4–8 May: Battle of the Coral Sea (air and sea forces).
8 May: Surrender of Corregidor (Philippines).

3. Destruction of the American fleet by the Japanese, 7 December 1941.

3–7 June: American victory at Midway.
12 June: Japanese occupy Kiska (Aleutian Islands).
7 August: US landing at Guadalcanal (Solomon Islands).
1943. 8 February: Japanese evacuation of Guadalcanal.
15 August: Americans recapture Kiska.
20 November: American landings at Tarawa.
1944. 31 January: American landings in the Marshall Islands.
20–23 May: American landings in New Guinea.
14 June: Allied landings at Saipan.
21 July: Americans land at Guam.
20 September: Americans land at Leyte (Philippines).
22–25 October: Americans win air and sea battle at Leyte.
1945. 23 January: Reopening of the Burma Road to China.
16 February–1 March: Siege and capture of Corregidor.
19 February–16 March: Capture of Iwo Jima.
1 April–21 June: Battle of Okinawa.

1941–45

B. Biak
H. Hollandia
J. Jaluit
K. Kavieng
L. Lae
N. Nanning
R. Rabaul
T. Truk
W. Wotje
We. Wewak

2000 km

Furthest advance of Japanese forces — Japanese raids — Territories under Japanese control at capitulation, 2 September, 1945. — American landings and Allied attacks — Naval battles ✕ — Burma Road

Fall of General Tojo.

16 July 1944

Atomic bomb.

6 and 9 August 1945

14 April: Americans take Bataan (Philippines).
2 May: Australians land in Borneo. British re-capture Rangoon.
18 May: Chinese re-take Fuchow.
27 May: Recapture of Nan-ning.
14 July: First naval bombardment of Japanese coasts.
2 August: Liberation of Burma completed.

6 and 9 August: Atomic bombs dropped on Hiroshima and Nagasaki.
8 August: USSR enters war against Japan.
9 August: Beginning of Soviet campaign in Manchuria.
15 August: Japanese delegation surrenders to the American general MacArthur at Manila.
2 September: Signature of Japanese capitulation aboard the *Missouri*.

5. The Japanese plenipotentiaries surrender on the battleship Missouri, 2 September 1945.

From Cezanne to Beckett

THE FIRST DECADES of the century saw a remarkable blossoming of artistic schools and movements. In Paris, after Seurat had given an intellectualist turn to Impressionism, the *fauves*, who were influenced by Van Gogh and Gauguin, rediscovered the expressive and emotive power of colour. The Cubists of the *Bateau-Lavoir* (Picasso, Braque, Juan Gris) took up Cézanne's legacy and transformed it, particularly through the use of collage. In Germany, the Expressionists (Kokoschka) enrolled poetry and painting in the cause of an anguish-laden rebellion, whilst Kandinsky and Klee (*Der blaue Reiter*) sought in pure colour the manifestation of an 'inner necessity'. Mondrian and Malevich were to extend this line of development into the most rarefied abstraction, whilst the Surrealists, more concerned with the imagination than with questions of technique, went in search of the 'convulsive beauty' of the dream-state which they hoped to find in 'transfigured' objects from everyday life (Ernst, Dali, Miró). After 1945 the United States was the most lively centre of avant-garde activity, particularly with movements like Pollock's 'Action Painting', even if certain tendencies there such as Pop Art maintained a somewhat ambiguous relationship with industrial society. It must be added that a list of schools and tendencies does not do complete justice to the contributions of the century's truly creative personalities, such as Matisse, Kandinsky, Klee and, above all, Picasso, who masterfully transmuted the various conflicting movements into 'periods' of his own life.

After the arabesques of Art Nouveau, architecture discovered the potential of reinforced concrete (Perret) and the beauty of stark forms. But the elegant and daring innovations of Van de Velde, Le Corbusier, Mies van der Rohe and Frank Lloyd Wright would subsequently give way to the monumental public architecture of Stalin's Russia, fascist Italy and Nazi Germany (Speer). After the Second World War, in spite of certain projects conceived on a grand scale (e.g. Niemeyer's Brasilia), the 'international style' came to dominate and, although design exerted a widespread influence, the Bauhaus ideal of a synthesis of all the plastic arts remained a utopian dream.

In the period in which Debussy, Ravel and Stravinsky were composing for the *Ballets russes*, Schoenberg and Webern launched music on the adventurous course of the atonal 'series'. In the same spirit, with his *Wozzeck*, A. Berg created twentieth-century opera. In France, the Group of Six (whose leading members were Poulenc, Honegger and Milhaud) were innovators who, nonetheless, respected traditional forms. After 1945, Messiaen seemed the master of contemporary music, though certain composers, while remaining faithful to the atonal (e.g. Boulez), were to experiment with radically new techniques, including concrete music (Schaeffer) and electro-acoustic or aleatory music (Berio, Stockhausen, Maderna, Xenakis). Finally, we should not forget the role played by jazz since its birth in New Orleans around 1910.

The hermetic but ambitious art of poetry sparkled with a rare brilliance in this period, both in France (Apollinaire, Valéry, Claudel, Breton, Éluard and Char) and in the rest of Europe (Rilke, Eliot, Yeats, Mayakovsky). Moreover, Expressionism and Surrealism sought to bring together poetry, painting and cinema in a common quest. In the work of Proust, Joyce and the Austrian, Musil, the traditional forms of narration were broken down. The novel remained, nonetheless, the privileged instrument of psychological analysis (Gide, Thomas Mann, Mauriac) and of social and political criticism (Aragon, Orwell, Céline), whilst also opening itself up to philosophical reflection in the work of Sartre and Camus and to phenomenological abstraction in the Nouveau Roman. It is through the novel, nowadays, that the Columbian writer (Garcia Marquez) or the Russian (Solzhenitsyn) makes his voice heard.

1. Les Demoiselles d'Avignon *by Picasso, 1907.*

Death of Rimbaud	Debussy's *Pelléas et Mélisande.*	Proust, *Swann's Way.*	Death of Modigliani.	Kafka, *The Trial.*	Bunuel, *Un chien anda*
1891	1902	1913	1920	1925	1928

2. La Montagne Sainte-Victoire *by Cezanne, c. 1905.*

1890: Death of Van Gogh.
1891: Gauguin in Polynesia.
1895: The Lumière brothers invent the cinematograph.
1896: Puccini, *La Bohème* (verismo).
1897: Klimt and the Vienna Secession.
1900: Exposition universelle (Paris).
1902: Debussy *Pelléas et Mélisande.* Rilke meets Rodin.
1905: *Die Brücke* (Dresden). Les fauves (Paris).
1906: Death of Cézanne.
1907: Picasso, *Les Demoiselles d'Avignon.*
1908: Richard Strauss, *Elektra.*
1909: *La Nouvelle Revue francaise.* The *Ballets russes* in Paris.
1910: *Der Blaue Reiter* (Munich), Marinetti, Futurism (Turin), Acmeism (Moscow).
1912: Schoenberg, *Pierrot Lunaire.*
1913: Stravinsky, *The Rite of Spring.* Proust, *Swann's Way.* Apollinaire, *Alcools.*
1917: Satie, Picasso, Diaghilev, *Parade.* Mondrian founds 'De Stijl'. Valéry, *La jeune Parque.*
1918: Cocteau and the Group of Six. Dada Manifesto.

1919: Gropius founds the Bauhaus.
1922: Joyce, *Ulysses.* Mural paintings in Mexico.
1924: Breton, *Surrealist Manifesto.*
1925: Berg, *Wozzek.* Kafka, *The Trial.*
1926: Éluard, *Capitale de la douleur.* Aragon, *The Paris Peasant.* Gide, *The Counterfeiters.*
1928: Brecht-Weill, *The Threepenny Opera.* Bunuel-Dali, *Un chien andalou.*
1929: Talking cinema. Faulkner, *The Sound and the Fury.* Claudel, *Le Soulier de satin.*
1930: Breton, *Second Surrealist Manifesto.* Musil, *The Man without Qualities.*
1932: Céline, *Journey to the End of the Night.*
1933: Malraux, *The Human Condition.*
1934: Socialist realism in the USSR. Aragon, *Les Cloches de Bâle.* Char, *Le marteau sans maître.*
1937: Picasso, *Guernica.* Exhibition of 'degenerate' art organized by the Nazis (Munich).
1938: Eisenstein-Prokofiev, *Alexander Nevsky.*
1944: Sartre, *In Camera.* Existentialism.
1945: Carné-Prévert, *Les Enfants du paradis.*
1946: Rossellini, *Païsa* (Italian neo-realism).

ART NOUVEAU (MODERN STLYE, JUGENDSTIL)

Paris, Guimard. *Nancy*, Gallé. *Barcelona*, Gaudi. *Brussels*, Horta, Van de Velde *Munich, Vienna*, Kilmt, *London*. Morris, Arts and Crafts. *Edinburgh*

EXPRESSIONISM

Oslo, Munch. *Brussels*, Ensor. *Arles*, Van Gogh. *Dresden*, Die Brücke. *Munich*, Der blaue Reiter. *Berlin*, Der Sturm, Neue Sachlichkeit around 1920. *Paris*, The Fauves Derain, Matisse, Vlaminck.

DADA

Zurich, Tzara 1916. *Berlin*, 1917. *Cologne*, Max Ernst, 1918. *Hanover*, Schwitters, Merz, 1919. *Paris*, 1920

BAUHAUS

Darmstadt, Behrens. *Weimar, Dressau*. *Berlin*, Le Corbusier.

SURREALISM

Paris, Brussels, Prague.

FUTURISM

Turin, Moscow.

CUBISM and ORPHISM

Paris.

SUPREMATISM

St Petersburg, Malevich.

'DE STIJL'

Amsterdam, Mondrian.

CONSTRUCTIVISM

Moscow, Pevsner.

Camus, *The Outsider*.　　Beckett, *Molloy*.　　Death of Nicolas de Staël. Georges Perec, *Les Choses*.　　Marguerite Duras, *L'Amant*.　　Death of René Char.　　Death of Salvador Dali.

1942	1951	1955	1965	1985	1988	1989

1947: Camus, *The Plague*. Pollock, Action Painting.
1950: Discovery of Japanese cinema (Kurosawa).
1953: Beckett, *Waiting for Godot*.
1954: Fellini, *La Strada*.
1955: Boulez, *Le Marteau sans maître*.
1956: Bergman, *The Seventh Seal*.
1957: The Nouveau Roman.
1959: Godard, Truffaut, the *nouvelle vague*.
1960: Pop Art (Andy Warhol). *Tel Quel*.
1967: Garcia Marquez, *One Hundred Years of Solitude*. Hyperrealism.
1968: *Living Theatre* at Avignon. Solzhenitsyn, *Cancer Ward*.
1969: Beckett, Nobel Prize for Literature.
1973: Death of Picasso.
1985: Claude Simon, Nobel Prize for Literature.

. *Watery Paths* by Jackson Pollock, 1947.

4. *The National Gallery of Art, Washington, by the architect Pei, built in 1978.*

From Riemann to Sartre

THE CLASSICAL PICTURE of a world regulated like clockwork has given way to a new vision of a constantly shifting universe. The phenomenology of the radiation, emission and absorption of light by matter has revealed a paradoxical entity, now wave, now particle, discontinuous and indeterminable: yet it is nonetheless subject to only four fundamental forces (gravitational, electromagnetic, weak and strong interactions), structured by a universal constant (Planck) and invariant for the observer in relative motion (Einstein).

This entity is Niels Bohr's atom. It contains a nucleus (protons and neutrons) which is positively charged, around which orbit negatively-charged electrons that balance its mass. These jump from one orbit to another, radiate, spin on their own axis and are magnetically charged, all according to Planck's constant. An atomic number can now be given to each of the elements in Mendeleyev's table of atomic weights: the periodic system indicates the orbits and the groups the electronic structure.

The experimental creation of energy-matter exchange by radiation gave rise to new industrial and medical techniques. Now the mainstay of the television set, the cathode tube was invented by Hittorf in 1869. At the phosphorescent end of a tube containing a vacuum, at the other end of which was an incandescent cathode, he observed the projected shadow of a cross placed in the middle; he thus discovered the cathode ray. In 1895 Röntgen studied the phenomenon of fluorescence on the outside of a cathode tube and discovered X-rays; thus was radiology born. In 1897 J. J. Thomson calculated the mass of these cathodic particles and discovered the electron; this was the beginning of electronics.

These results were only reached through new mathematical schemata: the notion of variety, the geometric object generalized to any number of dimensions, notions of metrics in Euclidian spaces with nil curvature and non-Euclidian spaces with positive or negative curvatures (Riemann); matrix theory (Cayley), theory of invariance

1. The chemist and biologist Louis Pasteur towards the end of his life (c. 1890).

2. The physicist Albert Einstein in the USA in 1934.

Riemann's hypotheses on the basic principles of geometry.

H. Bergson's Matière et Memoire.

Einstein discovers special relativity

| 1854 | 1896 | 1905 |

1864: Maxwell's equations governing the electromagnetic field, the transverse wave of which is light.
1865: Mendel's laws describe the discontinuous transmission of genetic inheritance.
1869: Periodic table of elements (Mendeleyev). The properties of chemical elements are periodic functions of their atomic weights. Elements are classified in order of increasing atomic weight, forming a table, with vertical columns representing the broad chemical groups (alkali metals, alkaline-earth metals etc) and the horizontal lines the periods. The gaps in the table have since been filled by the discovery of elements as predicted (scandium, gallium etc) and the artificial creation of elements beyond uranium, such as neptunium and plutonium.
1888: Institut Pasteur founded by international public subscription after the invention of rabies vaccination.
1896: Becquerel discovers radioactivity by neutralizing the phenomenon of phosphorescence and observing the spontaneous radiation of uranium salts.

4. The French mathematician Henri Poincaré (1854–1910), founder of algebraic topology.

1900: Planck's constant: energy is constituted of discrete units, quanta of energy, determined by a universal constant. $h = 6.55 \times 10^{-27}$ erg-second.

5. The French philosopher Henri Bergson c. 1911.

1905: Einstein's theory of special relativity. Measurements made with instruments in uniform relative motion are invariant under a given group of transformations of frames of reference (space–time co-ordinates) that vary in speed compared to the ultimate speed, that of light. Frames of reference will hardly be affected by motion on a human scale, where speed is low compared to that of light (300,000 km per second in a vacuum). But they are affected by motion at the atomic level, where speeds approximate to that of light; we can only conclude that rulers will shrink and clocks slow down.
1916: Einstein's theory of general relativity. Extends the principle of relativity to the accelerated motion of a frame of reference; this leads to the definition of gravitation by the curvature of space.
1924–7: Quantum mechanics: mathematical laws governing the movement of elementary particles in which wave and particle phenomena are linked through Planck's constant. The same equations, obtained with different mathematical schemata, led to different interpretations. For some people

3. Scales of atomic weights of the Russian chemist Dmitry Ivanovich Mendeleyev: the blank spaces correspond to elements unknown at the time and discovered subsequently. From Le Bulletin Scientifique, *Paris, 1879.*

	GROUPE I	GROUPE II	GROUPE III	GROUPE IV	GROUPE V	GROUPE VI	GROUPE VII	GROUPE VIII
	—	—	—	—	—	—	—	—
				RH^4	RH^3	RH^2	RH	
SÉRIES	R^2O	RO	R^2O^3	RO^2	R^2O^5	RO^3	R^2O^7	RO
—	—	—	—	—	—	—	—	—
1	H = 1	»	»	»	»	»	»	
2	Li = 7	Be = 9.4	B = 11	C = 12	N = 14	O = 16	Fe = 19	
3	Na = 23	Mg = 24	Al = 27.3	Si = 28	P = 31	S = 32	Cl = 35.5	
4	K = 39	Ca = 40	— = 44	Ti = 48	V = 51	Cr = 52	Mn = 55.....	Fe = 56; Co = 59; Ni = 59; Cu = 63;
5	(Cu = 63)	Zn = 65	— = 68	— = 72	As = 75	Se = 78	Br = 80	
6	Rb = 85	Sr = 87	?Yt = 88	Zr = 90	Nb = 94	Mo = 96	— = 100.....	Ru = 104; Rh = 104; Pd = 106; Ag = 108.
7	(Ag = 108)	Cd = 112	In = 113	Sn = 118	Sb = 122	Fe = 125	I = 127	
8	Cs = 133	Ba = 137	?Di = 138	?Ce = 140	»	»	»	
9	»	»	»	»	»	»	»	
10	»	»	?Er = 178	?La = 180	Ta = 182	W = 184	»	..... Os = 195; Ir = 197; Pt = 198; Au = 199.
11	(Au = 199)	Hg = 200	Tl = 204	Pb = 207	Bi = 208	»	»	
12	»	»	»	Th = 231	»	Ur = 240	»	» » » »

under a given group of transformations (Klein), set theory (Cantor); the theory of dynamic systems (Poincaré).

Then there are the philosophical questions: firstly, determinism. A phenomenon is determined if, knowing its initial state and its rate of change, we can deduce its successive states, its trajectory. But the observation of elementary particles implies a margin of error of the same magnitude as the measurement to be effected (a photon is needed to spot an electron), so that the localization of the phenomenon and the determination of its velocity become incompatible, and the trajectory can only be arrived at statistically. The knowledge of a phenomenon cannot be both accurate and complete (Copenhagen School).

A second, more metaphysical question is that of meaning: the world is no longer the work of a rational God; yet subject to the laws of chance, with neither cause nor goal, it seems absurd. To the analytical philosopher (Russell, Wittgenstein, the Vienna Circle) such a question, like any metaphysical question, cannot be posed because it is meaningless. To the phenomenological philosopher (Bergson, Husserl, Heidegger, Sartre), man is the bearer of meaning because he chooses to be, because he is free.

Bohr's atom.

1913

Quantum mechanics.

1924–27

Manhattan project produces atomic bomb.

January 1943

(Broglie, Schrödinger), waves and particles are real, albeit mysterious, space–time entities. For others (Heisenberg, Dirac), they are only the probable outcome of particular measurements and have no physical reality.
1934: Frédéric and Irène Joliot-Curie discover artificial radioactivity.
1939: *Eléments de mathématique* (Bourbaki) A group of French mathematicians writing under the collective pseudonym of Bourbaki undertake the axiomatic reconstruction of the whole body of mathematics from a few key structures.

The British philosopher and logician Bertrand Russell, (1872–1970), author of the Principia Mathematica, *towards the end of his life.*

7. Ludwig Wittgenstein (1889–1951), Viennese philosopher who became a naturalized British citizen. A student of Russell, famous for his research on the foundations of mathematics.

8. The French philosopher and writer, Jean-Paul Sartre (1905–1980).

From Alliance to Cold War

IT IS GENERALLY BELIEVED that Roosevelt, Stalin and Churchill met at Yalta in February to divide up the world between them. Roosevelt, who was the initiator of the Conference, had, in reality, quite different objectives. In the first instance, he needed to ensure that the USSR would in fact enter the war against Japan once the Reich had capitulated. Stalin was happy to conclude a secret agreement with him to that effect, which involved in exchange the restitution to the USSR of the territory ceded by Tsar Nicholas II after the Russo-Japanese War of 1904–5.

Another objective was to build a 'United Nations Organization' whose goal was the indefinite preservation of the alliance between the victors over the Reich. Roosevelt had no doubt that America, which alone was capable of being an honest broker between 'British imperialism' and 'Soviet communism', would be its real leader. And in fact he had no difficulty in obtaining from Stalin and Churchill the formation – alongside a General Assembly open to all members on an equal footing – of a Security Council possessing broad powers for the maintenance of peace within which the five great powers (USA, Great Britain, USSR, France and China) would each have a permanent seat and a right of veto. The incessant interventions of this Council, particularly on the initiative of the USSR, paralysed the United Nations, which has proved powerless to prevent the outbreak of some 130 local conflicts since its inception.

The UN has been no more successful in preventing the formation, in the East and in the West, of two great antagonistic power blocs, which have no doubt only been restrained from coming into direct conflict on the battlefield by the fear of nuclear apocalypse. These blocs were, in fact, already in the course of being formed before Yalta, Stalin being clearly determined to conserve within his ambit all the territories occupied by the Red Army. Churchill himself had been to Moscow in the previous October and had reached an agreement on how the Balkans were to be divided up into zones of influence. This gave a free hand to the British in Greece, left Rumania and Bulgaria to the Soviets and divided Hungary and Yugoslavia equally between the two powers.

The agreement did not cover Poland, where two rival bodies – one in London, the other set up in liberated Poland by Soviet troops – disputed the government of the country. One of the major subjects of discussion at Yalta concerned the fusion of these two groups, which would not occur until the following June. The Americans then had to yield over the essential question for fear of endangering the prospects of Soviet participation in the war against Japan. There remained Czechoslovakia, which was not discussed at Yalta, Austria, on which the three great powers had reached an agreement (at Teheran in 1943) to restore its independence, and Germany.

1. The three men of Yalta from left to right: Churchill, Roosevelt, Stalin.

At Teheran, there had been a plan for Germany to be dismembered into several regional states. This project was taken up again at Yalta. But, subsequently, Stalin had an unexpected change of mind. At Potsdam in July he met Truman, successor to Roosevelt (who had died in April), and Attlee, who had defeated Churchill at the polls; they decided to maintain a united but permanently demilitarized Germany, whose industrial power would be limited. Maintaining this unity would, however, have presupposed the continuing unity of the victor nations. From the moment the Cold War began to develop, the demarcation line from Czechoslovakia to the Far East between the occupying Soviet forces on the one hand and the British, French and American forces on the other ineluctably became a frontier between two Germanies, two Europes and, ultimately, two different worlds. To use Churchill's expression, it became an 'Iron Curtain'.

Atlantic Charter.

Teheran Conference.

14 August 1941

28 November–2 December 1943

1941. 22 June: Germany invades USSR.
14 August: Roosevelt and Churchill sign Atlantic Charter, recognizing the principles of self-determination for all peoples and excluding any territorial settlements that do not have the agreement of the parties concerned.
7 December: Attack on Pearl Harbor by the Japanese. United States at war.
1 January 1942: 26 countries at war against the Axis adopt a 'United Nations declaration', which echoes the terms of the Atlantic Charter and adds a clause on freedom of worship.
1943. 22 May: Dissolution of the Comintern (the Communist International founded at Moscow in March 1919).
28 November–2 December: Stalin-Roosevelt-Churchill Conference at Teheran. USSR adds its name to 'United Nations Declaration'. Agreement on the re-establishment of Austria's independence and on the principle of the division of Germany. Discussions on Poland come to no clear conclusion.
1944. 1–22 July: Bretton Woods

2. De Gaulle in Moscow, December 1944. Molotov is to his left.

Conference, which establishes the Gold Exchange Standard.
23 July: Constitution of a pro-Soviet Polish provisional government in opposition to the government in exile in London.
9 October: Agreement between Churchill and Stalin in Moscow on zones of influence in the Balkans.
14 November: Agreement between USSR, USA and Britain on zones of occupation in Germany.
3 December–12 January: First civil war in Greece. Bound by the agreement with Churchill, the USSR allows the British to crush the Communists.
10 December: De Gaulle signs a Mutual Aid pact with Stalin.
1945. 4–11 February: Stalin-Roosevelt-Churchill conference at Yalta. Agreement on the creation of the United Nations. Adoption of a 'declaration on post-war Europe' promising democratic institutions to all countries liberated from Nazi occupation. Confirmation of the return to the USSR of the eastern part of Poland that had been annexed since 1939 (as a result of the secret clauses in

The Europe of Yalta and Potsdam, 1945

The Churchill-Stalin share-out, November 1944 or 'the art of disposing of the fate of others'

HUNGARY		
50%	50%	

RUMANIA		
10%	90%	

YUGOSLAVIA		
50%	50%	

BULGARIA		
25%	75%	

GREECE		
90%	10%	

Russia
Others
Great Britain in accord with the USA

Legend:
- Fronts on 4 February 1945
- Current borders
- ---- 1937 borders
- Neutral countries on 4 February 1945

Territories annexed
- by the Soviet Union
- by Poland
- by Bulgaria
- by Yugoslavia

- Countries under military occupation
- Borders of the occupied zones
- Quadripartite occupation
- Territories evacuated by the Western nations

Population displacement after the war
(principal population movements, figures for millions of persons displaced):
- Germans
- Poles
- Balts and Finns
- Russians
- Italians

Yalta Conference.
4–11 February 1945

Potsdam Conference.
17 July–2 August 1945

Churchill's Fulton speech.
5 March 1946

the Nazi–Soviet Pact of the previous August), it being understood that Warsaw would receive substantial compensation at German expense. Long discussions on the merging of the two Polish governments and on the sum of reparations to be paid by Germany. Agreement on the conditions on which Russia was to join in the war against Japan.
12 April: Death of Roosevelt. Truman becomes President of USA.
25 June: Signature of the United Nations Charter.
6 July: The USA and Great Britain recognize the Polish government of national unity, of which S. Mikolajczyk, the president of the government in exile, becomes vice-president.
17 July–2 August: Conference at Potsdam between Stalin, Truman and Churchill (who is replaced during the conference, after his electoral defeat, by Attlee). Germany is to be permanently de-militarized and its industrial

capacity reduced, but its unity will be maintained, power being provisionally exercised by the four Allied military commanders. Poland is to be allowed to continue to administer the part of Germany occupied by its troops. The definitive settlement of the frontier question is postponed till the negotiation of the peace treaty.
6 August: Hiroshima.
8 August: Soviet intervention against Japan.
15 August: Japan surrenders.
17 August: Soviet-Polish agreement on the Oder-Neisse frontier.
1946. 5 March: Churchill's anti-Soviet speech at Fulton. Beginning of the Cold War.

3. Signature of the United Nations Charter at San Francisco.
– Andrei Gromyko and the Soviet delegation, 26 June 1945.
– Secretary of State Stettinius and President Truman, 28 June 1945.

4. General MacArthur and Emperor Hirohito, 15 October 1945.

Establishment of the Soviet Bloc

IN MAY 1945 the Red Army was present in Romania, Bulgaria, Hungary, Poland, Czechoslovakia, Yugoslavia, Germany, and Austria. In most of these countries the communists (who had played a crucial role in the resistance movement against the Nazis) were very influential. In Yugoslavia and Albania the communists were sufficiently strong to govern without the support of the Soviet army. In the other countries the communists came to power as members of coalition governments and introduced significant reforms. Land that had belonged to large land owners or that had formerly belonged to Germany was distributed to the peasants, major industries were nationalized, and planned economies based on the Soviet model were set up.

The diversity of the political situations and the need for reconstruction had led certain countries like Poland, Czechoslovakia, and Hungary to turn toward the West. After 1947, the USSR responded to the Truman Doctrine and the Marshall Plan, which it considered to be threats to its influence, by consolidating its hold over Eastern Europe. This led to the founding of the Cominform (Communist Information Bureau). At its creation, Zhdanov (Moscow's representative) stated that the world had split into two antagonistic blocs: the imperialist bloc, headed by the United States, and the anti-imperialist bloc, controlled by the USSR. The Yugoslavs, who were strong activists (they had already proclaimed their loyalty to the Soviet model, the dictatorship of the proletariat, and had introduced the first five-year plan) blamed their moderation on parties in the other popular democracies. Thus Cominform instigated a radicalization of communist parties and brought other party members of coalition governments into line. In particular, socialists were forced to merge with the communists into a single party that was controlled by the latter in several countries.

It was against this background, intensified by power struggles in Germany, that the "Prague Putsch" and Yugoslavia's break with the Soviet Union occurred. Tito's activism offended Moscow (for example, he negotiated with Bulgaria hoping to create a common state). Moscow had no intention of sharing control of the bloc; at a meeting in Bucharest in June 1948, the Cominform condemned Tito and the direction his party had taken. One month later, during the Yugoslav party's congress, all pro-Soviet elements were eliminated.

The USSR speeded up its attempt to gain control over the other parties. According to the Stalinist line, they were to serve as "transmission channels" for the CPSU. Trials reminiscent of those in Moscow in the 1930s were organized. Their main victims were communist members who had lived in the West for a long time, for example, past volunteers in International Brigades in Spain and veterans of anti-fascist resistance movements in Europe, or those individuals who had defended the economic and political interests of

their own countries too vigorously. Several hundred people we subjected to torture, long imprisonment, or execution. In Polan Gomulka was dismissed from his function as General Secretar thrown out of the party, and placed under house arrest. The tria that had the greatest repercussions were those of Rajk in Budapes Kostov in Sofia, and Slánsky in Prague. All three were sentenced death for being "Trotskyites," "Titoists," "spys for the imperialists, and "Zionists." (One of the main features of the Slánsky trial, whe eleven of the fourteen accused were Jews, was anti-Semitism.)

1. Stalin at the age of 70; ceremony at the Bolshoi, 1949. With him are Mao Tse-tung and N.S. Khruschev.

Creation of Comecon

January 1949

1944–45: Central and Eastern Europe are liberated from Nazi occupation by the Red Army supported by the national resistance movements.
1945. 4–11 February: Yalta Conference.
2 May: Berlin is taken by the Red Army.
17 July–2 August: Conference of the Allied Powers at Potsdam.
11 November: In Yugoslavia the People's Front, controlled by the communists, wins the elections to the National Assembly. Tito controls the government.
December: In Albania, the Democratic Front, led by the Albanian Workers' Party (communist) wins the elections to parliament.
1946. February: Mutual Aid Treaty between the USSR and Mongolia, which had been controlled by the communists since the revolution of 1921 (at that time the Red Army invaded at the request of the "provisional government").
August: Zhdanov, who was responsible for the ideological division of the central committee of the CPSU, launches an

offensive against the intelligentsia in the name of pure ideology.
22 November: In Bulgaria communist G. Dimitrov heads the government following parliamentary elections.
1947. 19 January: In Poland the Workers' Party (communist) wins the parliamentary elections.
12 March: Truman Doctrine.
5 June: Introduction of the Marshall Plan.
22–27 September: Founding of Cominform (Communist Information Bureau).
November–December: In London, failure of the "Last Chance" Conference between the foreign ministers of France, Britain, America, and the Soviet Union.
1948: Campaign against "cosmopolitans" (scientists, writers, and artists) in the USSR. This continues up to Stalin's death.
25 February: the "Prague Putsch": Communists seize absolute power in Czechoslovakia.
February–March: In Romania, the communists absorb the socialists and form a Workers' Party, which wins the

2. K. Gottwald, who executed the "Prague Putsch."

parliamentary elections with the alliance of the People's Democratic Front.
June: The Hungarian Workers' Party (communist) absorbs the socialists and the governs the country alone. Yugoslavia is expelled from Comintern at the Conference of Bucharest.
July: The USSR blockades Western zones in Berlin. This continues for approximately one year.
1949. 25 January: Creation of the Council for Mutual Economic Assistance (Comecor in Moscow.
4 April: Signing of North Atlantic Treaty Organization (NATO) in Washington.
8 May: Creation of the Federal Republic of Germany (FRG).
September: The USSR denounces its friendship treaty with Yugoslavia. Trial of L. Rajk, Minister of Foreign Affairs, in Hungar
7 October: Creation of the German Democratic Republic (GDR).
7 November: Moscow demonstrates its power: Rossokovski, a marshal in the Red Army, is appointed Marshal of the Polish

1944–53

Administrative Divisions and Nationalities of the Soviet Union

Popular Democracies

A - ALBANIA
B - BULGARIA
CZ - CZECHOSLOVAKIA
GDR
H - HUNGARY
P - POLAND
R - ROMANIA
Y - YUGOSLAVIA

Federal Republics

— Frontier ● Capital

I - R.S.F.S.R. (Russian Soviet Federal Socialist Republic) (Moscow)
II - UKRAINE (Kiev)
III - BELORUSSIA (Minsk)
IV - UZBEKISTAN (Tashkent)
V - KAZAKSTAN (Alma Ata)
VI - GEORGIA (Tbilisi)
VII - AZERBAIDZHAN (Baku)
VIII - LITHUANIA (Vilnius)
IX - MOLDAVIA (Kishinev)
X - LATVIA (Riga)
XI - KIRGIZSTAN (Frunze)
XII - TADZHIKISTAN (Dushanbe)
XIII - ARMENIA (Yerevan)
XIV - TURKMENISTAN (Ashkhabad)
XV - ESTONIA (Tallinn)

Autonomous Republics

---- Boundary ● Capital

In R.S.F.S.R.
1 - Kabardino (Nalchik)
2 - N. Osetinsk (Ordzhonikidze)
3 - Checheno Ingush (Groznyy)
4 - Dagestan (Makhachkala)
5 - Kalmytskaya (Elista)
6 - Mordov (Saransk)
7 - Chuvash (Cheboksary)
8 - Tatar (Kazan)
9 - Mariy (Yoshkar Ola)
10 - Bashkir (Ufa)
11 - Udmurt (Izhevsk)
12 - Karelia (Petrozavodsk)
13 - Komi (Syktyvkar)
14 - Tuvin (Kyz)
15 - Buryat (Ulan-Ude)
16 - Yakutskaya (Yakutsk)

In Georgia
17 - Abkhaz (Sukhumi)
18 - Adzhar (Batumi)

In Azerbaidzhan
19 - Nakichevan (Nakichevan)

In Uzbekistan
20 - Karakalpaks (Nukus)

Autonomous Regions

------- Boundary ● Main Town

In R.S.F.S.R.
21 - Adygeysk (Maykop)
22 - Cherkessk (Cherkessk)
23 - Upper Altaysk (Gorno-Altaysk)
24 - Khakassk (Abakan)
25 - Yevreysk (Jewish) (Birobidzhan)

In Georgia
26 - South Osetinsk (Tskhinvali)

In Azerbaidzhan
27 - Upper Karabakh (Stepanakert)

In Tadzhikistan
28 - Upper Badakhshan (Khorog)

Nationalities

Europeans
Slavs
- Russians
- Ukranians
- Belorussians (White Russians)

Baltic Peoples
- Letts
- Lithuanians

Latins
- Moldavians

- Caucasians
- Armenians
- Iranians
- Finno-Ugrians
- Turco-Tartars
- Ural-Altaic
- Paleo-Asiatics

First Atomic Bomb in the USSR
5 September 1949

Birth of the People's Republic of China
1 October 1949

Death of Stalin
5 March 1953

Army and Polish Minister of National Defense.
December: Trial of T. Kostov, General Secretary of the Bulgarian Communist Party.
1952. November: Trial of R. Slánsky, General Secretary of the Czechoslovak Communist Party.
1953. January: L. Beria, Minister of the Interior and member of the Politburo of the USSR Communist Party, is arrested and executed after being blamed for the reign of terror in the USSR and in Eastern Europe since 1938.

Laslo Rajk, on the right, Brankov on the left, confessing their "crimes." Budapest, 1949.

4. Marshal Tito votes beneath his portrait, 1952.

Decolonization: Beginnings

To PARAPHRASE Lenin's famous words, it might be said that, 'a colonial power gives its colony the rope with which to hang it'. By imposing a new economic and social system, colonialism causes the break-up of traditional societies, but at the same time it produces agents of decolonization: networks of village leaders (the Indian maliks, the Algerian rural leaders), trade unionists in the towns (Tunisia), a civil and military petit bourgeoisie (Egypt and Black Africa). It introduces its colonies into the world economy, bends them to its needs, leaves them open to exploitation and arbitrary power. But it also exposes them to the wind of change, to new influences and models. Its schools, universities and factories create a group of men in its own image, cultural hybrids prone to feelings of frustration and malaise but also skilled in manipulating the ideas and weapons of the rulers. Eventually they will return to their own cultural heritage to forge a national identity: the Indian nation for which Gandhi fought was a Hindu *maharani*, Jinnah's Pakistan a Muslim 'Land of the Pure'; for Arab peoples seeking independence (with the exception of Syria and Iraq) Islam was the guiding principle (this was also the case for the followers of the Riff leader Abd el-Krim). But these élites are also – perhaps essentially – Western intellectuals; their model is the nation-state, their ideologies those of the West. This is the greatest paradox of colonialism. Western values inevitably lead to a condemnation of the colonial phenomenon.

We need only think of the influence of Marxism, of the republican values inculcated by colonial French schoolteachers or the British liberalism absorbed at Oxford or Cambridge by Indian and African élites. The efficiency of the West, its sophisticated political and military organizations were imported by the colonies and eventually turned against the colonial powers themselves. Political parties sprang up everywhere to take on the political and ideological leadership of the masses, armies on the Western model assumed the lead in liberation struggles and lawyers employed all the sophistry of French or British law to argue their cause. Last, but not least, the language of the colonial powers and their cultural system proved an admirable way of unifying vast and disparate areas such as India, Africa and Southeast Asia.

As the West suffered repeated crises – the First World War, the Russian Revolution, the Depression, the Second World War – and became less and less sure of its moral position, colonized people found effective allies in anti-colonialist militants of all tendencies: progressive intellectuals, liberal politicians and churchmen. Even before the first wave of decolonization, colonialism had already lost the moral battle at home. It was considered economically out-of-date, politically unreformable and morally indefensible. The era of Kipling gave way to the idealism of Woodrow Wilson and the determined anti-colonialism of the Atlantic Charter. After the Bandung Conference there was no turning back: the Third World had made its appearance on the historical scene, and an era begun five centuries before with the dawn of European expansion had now come to an end.

1. Gandhi at the spinning wheel.

President Woodrow Wilson's Fourteen Points.	Speech by Nguyen Ai Quoc (Ho Chi Minh) at Congress of Tours.	Lyautey resident-general in Morocco.
8 January 1918	**December 1920**	**1912–25**

1855: Indian Congress Party founded.
8 January 1918: Woodrow Wilson's 14 Points for Peace.
1919: Massacre at Amritsar (13 April) in India; Afghan independence war (Armistice 8 August). Emir Khalid's action in Algeria.
1920: Speech by Nguyen Ai Quoc (Ho Chi Minh) at Congress of Tours (25–30 December) in favour of liberation of colonial peoples. Founding of Liberal Constitutional Party in Tunisia (Destour). Congress of Eastern Peoples in Baku.
21 February 1921: Independence of Iran.
1921–6: Riff War in Morocco waged by Abd el-Krim against the Spanish and French.
1922: British create Emirate of Transjordan (July–September).
1927: Founding of Vietnamese National Committee (*Viet Nam Quoc Dan Dang*, VNQDD). Anticolonialist Congress of Brussels. Sukarno founds Indonesian National Party.
1930. 10 February: Yen Bai uprising in Vietnam at instigation of VNQDD.
30 June: (Relative) independence of Iraq.

2. Algerian sharp-shooters during the First World War.

1931: Association of Algerian Reformist Ulamas.
1934: Split between *Destour* and *Neo-Destour* in Tunisia. Founding of Moroccan Action Committee.
1935: Granting of limited autonomy in India: Government of India Act.
1936: Independence of Egypt (26 August). Founding of Algerian Muslim Congress. Treaties ending French mandate over Syria and Lebanon; French parliament refuse to ratify these. Arab anti-British and anti-Jewish revolt in Palestine.
1937: Founding of Algerian People's Party (Messali Hadj), offshoot of the *Mouvement de l'Etoile Africaine* (founded in 1926 by Ali Abd el-Kader).
1939: Indonesian People's Congress founded.
1941: Front for the Independence of Vietnam (Viet Minh) founded in May. Atlantic Charter plans emancipation of peoples under foreign domination (14 August). Abortive Nationalist and pro-German coup in Iraq by Rashid Ali.
1943: Ferhat Abbas: Manifesto of the Algerian People (10 February) demands end

3. Moroccan nationalist leader Abd el-Krim.

1885 . . .

USSR

KAZAKHSTAN

TURKMENISTAN

UZBEKISTAN

MONGOLIA

Hawaii

IRAN

KIRGHIZISTAN

TAOJIKISTAN SINKIANG

NORTH KOREA

AFGANISTAN

SOUTH KOREA

JAPAN

OMAN 70

PAKISTAN 47

Amritsar ✳

TIBET

CHINA

Wake Island

INDIA 47

NEPAL BHUTAN

BANGLADESH 47-71

Haiphong

Dien Bien Phu

Macao (Port)

Hong Kong (GB)

MARIANA ISLANDS

MARSHALL ISLANDS

KIRIBATI 79

Easter Island (Chile)

Diu

Portuguese territories until 1961

Daman

Goa Y

BURMA 48

C

LAOS 54 ✳ ✳

Guam

Federal State of Micronesia (Carolines)

Gilbert Islands

Portuguese territories until 1961

M

THAILAND

VIETNAM 54-76

PHILIPPINES 46

French Polynesia

French trading stations until 51-56

P

KAMPUCHEA 54

Belau

PAPUA

NAURU 68

(Ellice Island) 78 TUVALU

SAMOA 62

Pitcairn Island (GB)

K

MALDIVES 65

SRI LANKA 48

MALASIA 63

B

57

INDONESIA 49

NEW GUINEA 75

SOLOMON ISLAND 78

WF

TONGA 70

Chagos Islands (GB)

SINGAPORE 58

Bandung

Surabaya ✳

Timor

VANUATU (New Hebrides) 80

FIJI 70

Cocos Islands

New Caledonia

AUSTRALIA 1901

Amsterdam and St Paul Island

NEW ZEALAND 1907

Kerguelen Island

2000 km

Independence dates before 1960 1960 onwards	Ex-colonial states	Possession	⬡ Independence war	B Brunei 83

WF Wallis Island and Futuna Island

F GB US

✳ Major confrontation

Litigation

Trust Territory of the Pacific Islands (EU)

French trading stations in India:
C = Chandernagore K = Karikal M = Mahe
P = Pondicherry Y = Yanan

lgerian People's Manifesto.

General de Gaulle's Brazzaville speech.

Creation of Arab League.

10 February 1943

30 January 1944

22 March 1945

to French colonial rule. Dismissal of Muhammad al-Munsif, Bey of Tunis (May).
1944: General de Gaulle's Brazzaville speech (30 January) praises colonial achievements, makes a brief allusion to necessity of 'emancipation'. Moroccan *Istiqlal* party issues independence manifesto.
1945: Arab League founded (22 March) by Saudi Arabia, Egypt, Iraq, Lebanon, Syria, Transjordan and Yemen. Publication of Leopold Sedar Senghor's *'Defense de l'Afrique noire'* in French revue, *Esprit*, July 1945.

4. 24 March 1946: meeting between Ho Chi Minh and Sainteny.

5. Mural illustrating the Indonesian revolution of 1945.

Decolonization: The Main Stages

DECOLONIZATION is not a unitary phenomenon; it takes almost as many forms as there are countries seeking liberation. Forms of colonial domination varied from one power to another: the French, for example, practised active assimilation, while the British attitude was culturally élitist and tended to ignore the local cultures. 'Colonies' varied also, from old, sophisticated civilizations such as India and Southeast Asia to the tribal societies of Black Africa. Some were territories that sizeable European minorities regarded as their homeland such as Algeria, South Africa, and Palestine, not to mention South America where 'decolonization' began in the nineteenth century; some were colonies of pure exploitation; finally, there were lands directly under colonial administration, there were protectorates (Morocco, Tunisia) and there were territories under mandate (Syria, Lebanon, Palestine) enjoying a certain autonomy.

Four phases do stand out, however, taking into consideration the areas concerned, the degree of violence involved and the international context, these three variables being, of course, related.

Up to the end of the forties a few territories gained independence without actual liberation wars; these were countries under British or Dutch rule where élites had been ready to take over for some time (Egypt, India, Pakistan).

Next in line, in the fifties – with the Cold War contributing to a hardening of positions – were North Africa and Indochina. In Southeast Asia and Algeria the colonial power was only prepared to surrender after wars of extreme violence, which explains, at least partly, the militant character of the emergent states that took over.

The third phase, in the sixties, marks the emancipation of Black Africa: this usually took place without incident and with the consent of the outgoing colonial power.

Finally, the last of the Western empires were dismantled, comparatively painlessly, in the wake of the Portuguese 'carnation' revolution.

The effects of decolonization have been complex and ambiguous. It is easy to contrast the dignity of those still bound to the ex-colonial powers with ties of dependence (though Franz Fanon termed these neocolonials 'the wretched of the earth'), with the tinpot dictatorships that have sprung up in Africa and elsewhere, suffering tribal conflicts, famine and the suppression of human rights. Inadequately prepared and clumsily effected, decolonization forced societies into the ill-fitting mould of the nation-state. It tied them to a world market which drained their subsistence economies and exhausted them in the race to close the ever-widening technological, industrial and agricultural gap between themselves and the more developed countries. The various forms of fundamentalism appearing everywhere (Qaddafi, Khomeini, the Muslim Brotherhood, Ethiopian and Khmer Marxism) must be seen as the result of mismanaged transition to independence.

Decolonization may not have been a smooth process, but it is pointless to argue that it could have been easier. Freedom is not given, said Ferhat Abbas, it has to be fought for. Conditions of struggle are not conducive to the development of a well-regulated state. Even where independence was granted voluntarily, as in India or Africa, the colonial phenomenon left too deep a mark on the society and its way of thinking, the gap between ideal and reality was too great for the dream of 'successful' decolonization to come about. Rather than blame the past we ought now to turn our attention to the struggle for development, which undoubtedly will be a hard task.

(For a more detailed account of the decolonization of Southeast Asia see pp. 306/307.)

1. Dream of an Algerian child, 1958.

Brazzaville Conference.	Independence of State of Israel.	Coup d'état of "free officers" in Egypt.
30 January–8 February 1944	14 May 1948	23 July 1952

1944: Brazzaville Conference (30 January–8 February).
1945: Riots and massacres of Setif and Kabilie in Algeria (8 May). MacArthur receives Japanese surrender (15 August). Sukarno and Haata proclaim independence of Indonesia (17 August). Ho Chi Minh proclaims independence of Vietnam (2 September).
1946: Autonomy of Cambodia (Kampuchea) within the framework of the French Union (7 January). King Abdullah ('Abd Allah) proclaims independence of Transjordan (25 May). Independence of Philippines (4 July). Autonomy of Laos within French Union (27 August). Bamako conference and founding of RDA (Rassemblement Démocratique Africain, 18–21 October).
1947: Nationalist riots in Madagascar (30 March) and bloody repression. Independence of Indian Union and Pakistan (15 August). Populations are exchanged, communal conflicts. United Nations accepts plan for partition of Palestine (29 November).
1948: Independence of Burma (4 January). Gandhi assassinated by Hindu fanatic (30 January). Independence of Ceylon (Sri Lanka

in 1971) (4 February). Creation of State of Israel (14 May), Arab invasion and start of first Arab-Israeli war (up to 20 July). Transjordan annexes West Bank of Jordan intended as nucleus of future Palestinian state; Israel and Egypt occupy the rest (16 December).
1949: Hashemite Kingdom of Jordan (January).
1951: Libyan independence (24 December).
1952: Coup d'état by 'Free Officers' in Egypt (23 July). King Farouk abdicates, beginning of Nasser government. Mau Mau terrorists in Kenya, British state of emergency (20 October).
1953: Muhammad Ben Yusuf, Sultan of Morocco, deposed (20 April).
1954: Fall of Dien Bien Phu (7 May). Geneva Accords put an end to French phase of Indochina war (20–21 July). Speech by Pierre Mendès France in Carthage recognizes Tunisian autonomy (31 July). Beginning of armed insurrection in Algeria. FLN (National Liberation Front) issues programme; declaration demanding independence (1 November).
1955: Afro-Asian conference of Bandung

2. French-held prisoners after Dien Bien Phu.

BANGLADESH 47-71

BELIZE 81
CUBA 1898
GB
JAMAICA 62
BAHAMAS 73
St-Pierre-et-Miquelon
HAITI 1804:
DOMINICAN
REPUBLIC 1821
US-GB
NL
VENEZUELA
WEST INDIES 62-81
Azores (Port.)
GUYANA 66
SURINAM 75
Maderia (Port.)
BRAZIL
French Guiana
Canaries (Spain)
CAPE VERDE
REPUBLIC 75

INDIA 47
PAKISTAN
47

MOROCCO 56
TUNISIA
56
ALGERIA 62
LIBYA 51
EGYPT
36
CYPRUS 60
SYRIA
45
LEBANON 45
MALTA 64
ISRAEL 48
IRAQ
30
JORDAN 46
B
Q
K
UAE
OMAN
70
REPUBLIC OF
SOUTH YEMEN
67
YEMEN
62
MALDIVES
65

MAURITANIA
GAMBIA 65
SENEGAL
GUINEA
BISSAU
74
GUINEA 58
SIERRA LEONE 61
LIBERIA 1848
MALI
NIGER
BURKINA FASO
IVORY COAST
GHANA
57
Togo
Benin
NIGERIA
NAMBIA
CAMEROON
SUDAN
56
DJIBOUTI 77
ETHIOPIA
SOMALIA
SEYCHELLES
76

CENTRAL
AFRICAN REPUBLIC
UGANDA 62
KENYA
63
MAURITIUS
68

SAO TOME 75
G
GABON
CONGO
ZAIRE
RUANDA 62
BURUNDI 62
TANZANIA
64
COMOROS
75
M
Réunion

ANGOLA
75
MALAWI
64
ZAMBIA
64
ZIMBABWE
80
MOZAMBIQUE
75
MADAGASCAR

BOTSWANA
66
SWAZILAND 68
LESOTHO 77
Namibia

SOUTH AFRICA
61

2000 km

West Indies

B-US
GB
US
NL
GB
St Martin (F-NL)
St Barthelemy (F)
ANTIGUA 81
Guadeloupe
DOMINICA 78
Aves
(Ven.)
Martinique
ST LUCIA 79
ST VINCENT 79
BARBADOS
66
GRENADA 74
TRINIDAD
AND TOBAGO
62
VENEZUELA

Independence dates		Ex-Colonial state	Possessions		Independence war	M = MAYCOTTE	UAE = UNITED ARAB EMIRATES
before 1960	in 1960	after 1960		France	GB US NL	* Major conflict	B = BAHRAIN 71	G = EQUATORIAL GUINEA 68
						⋯ Litigation	Q = QATAR 71	K = KUWAIT 61

| eferendum on Algerian independence. | Independence of Bangladesh. | Independence of Angola and Mozambique. | Independence of Zimbabwe. |
| July 1962 | 16 December 1971 | June and November 1975 | 18 April 1980 |

7–24 April) attended by 29 countries. Talks
La Celle–Saint-Cloud in France recognize
Moroccan sovereign (6 November); Sultan
turns to Rabat as Muhammad V, King of
Morocco (16 November).
956: Sudanese independence (1 January).
eds-noirs riot in Algiers (6 February). French
ime minister Guy Mollet resigns.
dependence of Morocco (2 March) and
unisia (20 March). Suez crisis.
ationalization of canal by Nasser (26 July)
d Anglo-French-Israeli campaign from
ctober to December.
957: Battle of Algiers (January to October).
dependence of Ghana (5 March).
958: Conference of Independent African
ates at Accra, Ghana (15–22 April). De
aulle visits Madagascar, French Equatorial
frica and French West Africa (20–28
ugust). Second Brazzaville speech
roclaims right of colonized peoples to
dependence.
960: Independence of Belgian and French
ack African territories, Nigeria (Britain) and
auritania (France).
61: Independence of Sierra Leone (27

April), Tanganyika (9 December). Coup by
Generals in Algiers (22–25 April).
Anti-Algerian pogrom in Paris (17 October).
1962: Evian Accords (18 March). At the cost
of thousands of victims, mainly Algerian, and
the uprooting of one million *Pieds-noirs*,
Algeria gains independence (1 July
referendum). Independence of Ruanda and
Burundi (1 July).
1963: Creation of Malaysia (Malaya and
Singapore) on 16 December and
independence of Kenya (12 December).
1964: Creation of Tanzania (Zanzibar and
Tanganyika, 26 April). Independence of Malta
(21 September), Malawi (ex-Nyasaland) on 6
July and Zambia (ex-Northern Rhodesia) on
24 October.
1967: Independence of People's Republic of
South Yemen (29 November).
1968: Independence of Mauritius (12 March).
1975: 'Carnation' revolution in Portugal leads
to independence of Angola (25 June) and
Mozambique (11 November). Independence
of Papua New Guinea (September).
1976: Spain leaves Western Sahara:
beginning of Saharan question.

1977: Independence of Republic of Djibouti
(27 June).
1980: Independence of Zimbabwe
(ex-Southern Rhodesia) on 18 April.

3. General Idi Amin, President of Uganda, 1972.

Fronts of the Cold War

THE PRINCIPAL VICTORS of the Second World War, the United States and the Soviet Union, now dominated the world. A rift between them quickly occurred, and the ex-allies began jealously to guard their zones of influence at the cost of a relentless arms race. Eventually, the balance of terror meant that the world's 'policemen' were forced into good behaviour; Cold War became 'peaceful coexistence', and the certainty that a nuclear holocaust would destroy them both resulted in a tactical neutralization of the ambitions of both sides. In the meantime, from 1946 to 1962, their rivalry shaped the history of international relations, in spite of efforts to rouse the conscience of the rest of the world against their hegemony (the United Nations was formed in 1945, followed by the Universal Declaration of Human Rights in 1948), and in spite also of the promising emergence of a 'non-aligned' movement in the Third World (the term dates from 1952), challenging the rationale of the power blocs, in particular since the Bandung Conference of 1955.

1. Nuclear obsession in the US: gas mask practice.

In reality the two super-powers were opposed in every way. From the Atlantic to the Pacific, the maritime empire of the 'free world' contrasted with the continental dominion of the 'socialist camp'. In the West, capitalism and freedom reigned. The East retorted with the 'classless society' and the endeavour to create a 'new man'. Moscow-style totalitarianism was loudly denounced in the West; the Atlantic camp took pride in its rapid recovery after the war and its economic vitality, often due to state intervention encouraging growth and a

high standard of living. In answer to Western economic dynamism the Eastern bloc upheld the intrinsic superiority of 'peaceful' socialism over warlike imperialism. It invoked its concern to raise the consciousness of the masses and its tactical alliance with 'progressive elements fighting 'Americanization' within Western societies. Conflict, both economic and territorial, between two world views assumed ideological and cultural dimensions, fuelling rival propaganda and mobilizing all forms of communication and mass culture which were at that time developing to the furthest corners of the globe.

In the Cold War years (1946–62), confrontation several times came to a head. East-West relations became strained over Germany and the Marshall Plan for the reconstruction of Europe, and reached breaking point over the future of Berlin. In Korea and Indochina the confrontation became an armed one. 1956 was a pivotal year: crises within the People's Democracies and in the Near East revealed the capacity of the super-powers to 'contain' the antagonism. From 1956 to 1962, up to the short-lived but grim crisis brought about by the Soviet attempt to install missile bases in Cuba, directly threatening the United States, the loci of potential clashes became more decentralized. Decolonization, the emancipation of the People's Republic of China, and African and South American interests played a role in this process. The nuclear balance and the fact that the power blocs were no longer seen as monolithic paved the way for 'peaceful coexistence', which was a mark of the 1960s.

2. Arrival of American planes during the Berlin blockade, 1948.

Marshall Plan.	Communist coup in Prague.	North Atlantic Treaty Organization.
5 June 1947	25 February 1948	4 April 1949

1946. 20 January: De Gaulle resigns from government.
5 March: At Fulton Churchill talks of an 'iron curtain' dividing Europe
1947. 11 March: Truman doctrine of containment of Communism.
5 June: Launching of Marshall plan.
22–7 September: Creation of Cominform (dissolved 17 April 1956).
1948. 25 February: Communist coup in Prague.
20 June: Berlin blockade (to 12 May 1949).
28 June: Exclusion of Yugoslavia from Cominform.
1949. 25 January: Economic union of Eastern countries in Comecon.
4 April: Signature of North Atlantic Treaty.
5 May: Creation of German Federal Republic (West Germany).
14 July: First Soviet Atomic bomb.
1 October: Proclamation of People's Republic of China.
October: End of civil war in Greece.
25 June 1950–27 July 1953: Korean War.
1951. 1 September: Defence treaty for

4. Massacres in Korea. *Painting by Picasso, 1951.*

Pacific between Australia, New Zealand and USA (ANZUS).
8 September: Peace declared between USA and Japan.
1952. 1 November: First American H bomb.
1953. 12 August: First Soviet H bomb.
3 September: Nikita Khrushchev becomes First Secretary of the Communist Party of the Soviet Union (until 15 October 1964).
1954. 7 May: Fall of Dien Bien Phu.
20–1 July: Geneva agreements on Indochina.
8 September: Creation of the Southeast Asia Treaty Organization.
1955. 24 February: Baghdad pact.
17–24 April: Bandung Conference.
14 May: Warsaw Pact.
1956. 23 October–13 November: Budapest rising and Soviet intervention in Hungary.
29 October–6 November: Second war between Egypt and Israel.
5 November–22 December: Suez expedition.
1957. 25 March: Treaty of Rome.
1958. 4 November: Khrushchev demands demilitarization of Berlin.

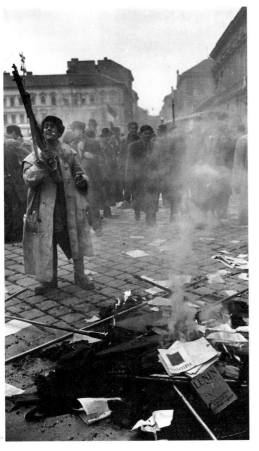

3. Budapest in revolt: burning of Soviet books, 9 November 1956.

The Cuban Missile Crisis 1962
An international crisis can be analysed step by step through tracing the decisions each protagonist makes in response to the other. The Cuban crisis is a good example.
Actual decisions are taken from many possible decisions, which are ranked according to their gravity, or the danger of war they represent. The succession of such bands of possibility provides a backdrop against which actual decisions mark the ups and downs of the conflict, its main stages and its most critical moments. On the chart, the role of various agencies is also shown, e.g. external agencies such as the UN.
From A. Joxe, La crise cubaine de 1962: Eléments de décision au cours de la crise chaude.

Budapest uprising.

23 October 1956

The Cuban crisis of 1962

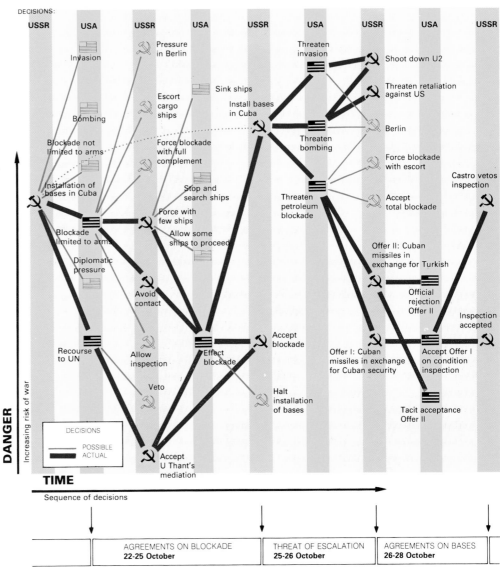

DECISIONS:

| USSR | USA | USSR | USA | USSR | USA | USSR | USA | USSR |

Invasion
Pressure in Berlin
Threaten invasion
Shoot down U2
Sink ships
Threaten retaliation against US
Bombing
Escort cargo ships
Install bases in Cuba
Berlin
Blockade not limited to arms
Force blockade with full complement
Threaten bombing
Force blockade with escort
Installation of bases in Cuba
Stop and search ships
Castro vetos inspection
Blockade limited to arms
Threaten petroleum blockade
Accept total blockade
Force with few ships
Diplomatic pressure
Allow some ships to proceed
Offer II: Cuban missiles in exchange for Turkish
Avoid contact
Accept blockade
Official rejection Offer II
Inspection accepted
Recourse to UN
Allow inspection
Effect blockade
Offer I: Cuban missiles in exchange for Cuban security
Accept Offer I on condition inspection
Veto
Halt installation of bases
Tacit acceptance Offer II
Accept U Thant's mediation

DANGER
Increasing risk of war

DECISIONS
—— POSSIBLE
━━ ACTUAL

TIME

Sequence of decisions

| AGREEMENTS ON BLOCKADE 22-25 October | THREAT OF ESCALATION 25-26 October | AGREEMENTS ON BASES 26-28 October | |

Berlin wall.

12 August 1961

5. Khrushchev and Eisenhower at the White House, September 1959.

1959. 15–18 September: Khrushchev visits United States.
1960. 13 February: First French Atomic bomb.
1 May: American U2 spy plane shot down over USSR.
June: Founding of Lumumba University in Moscow.
1961. 12 August–20 November: Building of Berlin wall.
1962. 18 October–2 November: Cuban Missile Crisis.

6. The French at Port-Said during the Suez crisis, 5 November 1956.

Problem-Ridden Europe

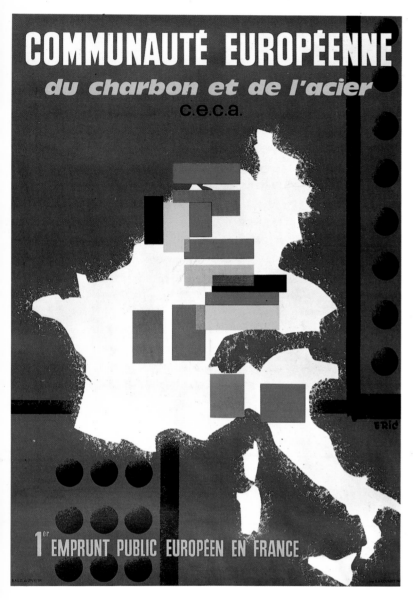

1. Poster for the European Coal and Steel Community (ECSC), 1964.

UNTIL THE BERLIN WALL FELL, Europe underwent inevitable decline. Its old supremacy over the world was lost as a result of two world wars, decolonization, the Cold War, and two major economic crises one in the 1930s and one following the monetary and oil upheavals of 1971-73. In the East, which was cut off by the Iron Curtain in 1948, and despite the dissent within the bloc, so tragically evident in Hungary, Czechoslovakia, and Poland, communism, in the grip of the USSR, drained the fertility of Central Europe from which the continent had frequently obtained much of its energy and dynamism in the past. In the West, protected by the nuclear umbrella of NATO since 1949, state nationalism has put an end to any hopes for a federation and has made the creation of a United States of Europe impossible.

However, as early as 1943 Jean Monnet, one of the founding fathers of Europe, observed that, "The countries of Europe are too cramped to ensure prosperity for their people." From the ECSC to the ECU, from the EEC to ambitious space research, starting with funds available under the Marshall Plan and later creating a (primarily agricultural) Common Market, and ultimately allowing citizens to participate in parliamentary elections since 1979, Europe has succeeded in rising from the ashes, experienced the "Thirty Glorious Years," and has helped establish the welfare state that has begun to iron out differences in society. But France's rejection of the EDC in 1954 put a stop to its political ambitions. From General de Gaulle to Mrs. Thatcher the logic of sovereignty has run counter to any real delegation of power to supra-national entities, thus favoring the old controversy between France and the Federal Republic of Germany, and stimulating divisive national interests.

Therefore the European community was based on strengthening the economy. Not without success: the Europe of the Twelve made up one-third of world exports and its 320 million inhabitants enjoyed the revenues from this evolution and the countries attained high GNPs. However, it was unable to save depressed sectors such as the iron and steel industry and textiles. It was slow to implement a true social policy or widespread scientific and cultural cooperation. It included the countries of the South that had weaker economies.

With a decreasing birthrate, indicating a lethargic attitude toward the future; a crisis that continues while the world shakes; apathetic pacifism in the face of the Soviet threat; stagnating inventiveness and research; and with unemployment and immigration causing serious problems everywhere: the future of Europe does not look very auspicious at the end of the 1980s.

However, the upheavals that have occurred since the beginning of 1989 have certainly changed the outlook: though the continent of Europe will comprise less than 6% of the world population in the year 2000 (compared to 12% in 1959), it may have the opportunity to become the largest production and consumption market in the world.

Treaty of Paris leads to the founding of the ECSC.	Treaty of Rome leads to the founding of the EEC.	Franco-German Treaty.	General de Gaulle dies.
18 April 1951	**22 March 1957**	**22 January 1963**	**9 November 1970**

16 April 1948: OECE set up, later becoming, in December 1960, the OECD, Organization for Economic Cooperation and Development.
9 May 1950: Schuman plan for the European Coal and Steel Community (ECSC) put forward.
18 April 1951: ECSC established by the Treaty of Paris. First European steel produced in May 1953.
30 August 1954: Failure of the EDC (European Defence Community).
1–3 June 1955: Agreement signed in Messina, Sicily, for the formation of a Common Market. On 13 October Jean Monnet launches the Action Committee for the United States of Europe.
25 March 1957: Treaties of Rome and founding of the EEC and the European Atomic Energy Community (Euratom). Europe of the Six.
1 June 1958: General de Gaulle takes power in France. Appointed the first president of the French Fifth Republic, 8 January 1959.
January 1960: Great Britain launches EFTA (European Free Trade Association).

1963. 14 January: de Gaulle vetoes British entry into the Common Market.
22 January: Franco-German Treaty.
19 December 1965: de Gaulle is re-elected president.
19 April 1967: Konrad Adenauer dies.
1968: World-wide protest movement against Western society. 1 February sees the international student meeting in Berlin, and 22 March marks the beginning of the Paris 'événements'. By 22 May, Six million strikers. 25-27 May: Grenelle Accords. 30 May: Parliament dissolved. 23-30 June: Gaullists re-elected. Fall: "Tempestuous May" in Italy.
1969. 28 April: General de Gaulle resigns.
15 June: Georges Pompidou elected President of France.
21 October: Willy Brandt elected chancellor of West Germany.
30 January 1972: 'Bloody Sunday' in Londonderry (Northern Ireland).
1 January 1973: Europe of the Nine (Denmark, Ireland and the United Kingdom).
1974. 2 April: Death of Georges Pompidou.
25 April: Military coup in Portugal restores democracy.

3. Three of the Junta of Colonels who took power in Greece on 21 April 1967.

16 May: Helmut Schmidt becomes West Germany chancellor.
19 May: Election of V. Giscard d'Estaing.
24 July: Democracy restored in Greece following 7 years of dictatorship.
1975. 1 August: Final Act of Helsinki Conference.
20 November: Juan Carlos I accedes to the throne of spain.
1976. 2 and 25 April: Constitution drawn up and parliamentary elections in Portugal.
23 November: Death of A. Malraux.
18 October 1977: Death of two leaders of the Red Army Faction: A. Baader and G. Ensslin.
9 May 1978: Aldo Moro discovered assassinated by the Red Brigades.
1979. 3 March: Creation of the ECU.
16 March: Death of Jean Monnet.
3 May: Mrs. Thatcher elected Prime Minister.
7–10 June: First elections to the European Parliament with universal franchise.
1981. 1 January: Europe of the Ten (Greece).
10 May: Election of F. Mitterrand.

1948-89

This is because the countries of the East, rid of communism, are aiming to rejoin the world of liberty and capital. The end of the Cold War made the problem of security less acute. And, above all, the fall of the Berlin Wall in November 1989 allowed the reunification of Germany, which could prove to be the driving force behind the renewal of European power.

European Organizations in 1986

O.E.E.C (Organization for European Economic Cooperation) set up in 1948

O.E.C.D. (Organization for European (Cooperation and Development) set up in 1960

COMECON in 1949 — in 1986
• State having associate status within COMECON
• State having associate status within the O.E.C.D.

Albania leaves Comecon in 1961

N.A.T.O. (North Atlantic Treaty Organization) set up in 1949

WARSAW PACT, set up in 1955

— 'Iron curtain'

France leaves the military command structure of NATO in 1966

E.C.S.C. (European Coal and Steel Community) set up in 1951

C.E.R.N. (European Council for Nuclear Research) set up in 1854

EURATOM (European Atomic Energy Community), set up in 1957

E.E.C. (European Economic Community) sometimes known as the Common Market

1957   1981
1972   1986

E.F.T.A. (European Free Trade Association)
• in 1960
• in 1986

2. Three of the founding fathers of Europe: A. De Gasperi, Konrad Adenaeur and Robert Schuman, pictured here in Strasbourg, 11 January 1951.

Margaret Thatcher elected prime minister.	Beginning of the Europe of the Twelve.
3 May 1979	**1 January 1986**

1 October 1982: H. Kohl becomes Chancellor.
2 December 1985: The Twelve agree on a law on the unification of Europe.
1986. 1 January: Europe of the Twelve (Spain and Portugal).
September: Wave of terrorist attacks in

Paris (11 dead, 150 injured).
1988. 8 May: Re-election of F. Mitterrand.
9 November: Jean Monnet's ashes transferred to the Pantheon.
1989. 15–18 June: Widespread abstentions (41%) in European parliamentary elections.
9 November: The Berlin Wall falls.

4. Anti-nuclear demonstration in Germany, 23 October 1983.

Soldiers and Populists in South America

RELATIONS WITH THE United States intensified during the Second World War: willingly or not, all the countries in South America participated in the economic mobilization (or military mobilization in the case of Brazil, which sent a contingent). The continent was able to industrialize superficially and American interests were predominant everywhere.

At the end of the war there were revolutionary attempts to find solutions to social and economic problems. This was the case in President Arbenz's Guatemala in 1944, in Bolivia in 1952, and in Cuba in 1959. The first two ventures failed following profound structural changes (nationalization, agricultural reforms); the latter culminated in the adoption of Soviet-style communism. The rural and urban guerilla movements, which attempted to extend the revolution throughout the entire continent, were crushed at the end of the 1960s and the beginning of the 1970s. The 'legal Marxist' experiment of Allende's Chile also failed. A victim of economic crisis and 'social contradictions', weakened by the clandestine intervention of the CIA and undermined by its own errors and internal divisions, it was brutally brought to an end by a military coup. Authoritarian regimes under military control then became established in the cause of anti-communism (Brazil in 1964, Argentina in 1966, Chile in 1973...). Elsewhere other so-called 'progressive' military forces (in Peru in 1968, in Ecuador in 1972), often originating from the nationalist middle classes, but for all that still 'military', set about extending the role of the state. Between 1965 and 1985 economic and social structures changed; some countries began living less off their mining and farming exports (apart from oil) and began to become industrialized (Brazil, Argentina). Towns grew phenomenally with the influx of rural migrants; unemployment and crime grew, and shanty towns sprang up.

Traditional governing groups such as the land-owning oligarchy gave way to newcomers who were in some cases connected with national industry, multinational companies and in others with overseas trade, because South America depends on equipment, technologies, and capital from more developed countries. By the beginning of the 1980s this dependence had led to enormous debts, which in some instances brought countries to the brink of bankruptcy. At the end of the 1970s, military factions of the Left and of the Right had been discredited because they had so profoundly failed to solve the problems of countries in the grip of a crisis which was without precedent. Gradually democracy returned everywhere—especially in Chile—and, by 1992, Cuba and Haiti were almost the only exceptions. To some extent the guerrillas laid down their arms, and the influence of the United States was stronger than ever before, especially in Panama where they intervened militarily at the end of 1989 to establish the party that had won the elections. However,

though democracy has been re-established, this does not mean that the problems connected with economies that are in ruins and societie that have been torn apart have been resolved. Since the end of th 1980s, Latin America has abandoned the model of developmen favored during the last 40 years, and is returning, rather abruptly, t a liberalism that will re-integrate it into the international market.

1. Argentine democracy passes judgement on its military leaders, 12 September 1985.

E. Pettoruti paints *Quintet*.

1927

1930: Following the economic crisis a series of military uprisings (Argentina, Brazil, Peru...)
1932–35: Chaco war between Bolivia and Paraguay.
1937: In Brazil, Getulio Vargas proclaims 'Estado Novo', a corporatist dictatorship, similar to European fascist regimes. He was overthrown in 1945 by a military coup d'état.
1939: Latin American neutrality in the Second World War.
1942–5: Progressive commitment of the South American continent to the United States. Strong reservations on the part of Argentina (coup d'état in 1943). Brazil sends an expeditionary force to Italy.
1944: *Fictions* by J. L. Borges.
1945: Peron's triumph in Argentina. Populist 'Justicialism' until 1955. Military government in Peru (until 1964).
30 March-2 May 1948: 'Bogotazo' in Columbia: riots in the capital: civil war spreads to the countryside ('La violencia' 1949-57).

J. Amado: *The Violent Land*.

1942

2. Juan Peron giving his speech of 1 May 1946.

Gabriela Mistral: Nobel Prize for Literature.

1945

1951–2: Vargas elected president in Brazil on a programme of reforms (he commits suicide in 1954). Start of the Bolivian revolution: the National Revolutionary Movement in power until 1964.
5 May 1954: General Stroessner takes over power in Paraguay.
1961–9: Alliance for Progress created on President Kennedy's initiative.
1964–7: Military coup d'état in Brazil: anti-communist and technocratic dictatorship. Military coup d'état in Argentina.
9 October 1967: Ché Guevara, Castro's lieutenant, dies in Bolivia. Supression of guerilla forces organized by him.
22 August 1968: Paul VI at Medellin (Colombia): South American 'Vatican II'.
1968–1975: 'Progressive' militarism (nationalizations, land reform, educational reforms...) in Peru under General Velasco. Urban guerrillas in Argentina (the 'montoneros') and in Uruguay (the 'tupamaros'). Repression and military dictatorship in both countries.

Ernesto Sabato: *Alejandr*

1967

1970–3: Experiment of Salvador Allende's Popular Unity government in Chile, overthrown by General Pinochet's coup d'état (11 September 1973).
September 1973: Death of the Chilean poet N. R Reyes, known as Pablo Neruda.
1973–8: Succession of very repressive military governments. National security 'anti-subversive' doctrine.
1978–85: Return to pluralist democracy in most of the South American countries. Serious economic crisis bringing with it an escalation in and reapportionment of foreign debt, especially in Mexico, Brazil, Argentina.
28 January–1 February 1981: Border conflict between Peru and Ecuador.
1982: Falklands war between Argentina and United Kingdom. Occupation of the Islands by Argentina, 2 April. Surrender of Argentine forces 13 June.
1983: Assassination of Maurice Bishop, Prime Minister of Grenada, 19 October. Military intervention by America.
18 October 1984: Settlement of the Beagle

1930–92

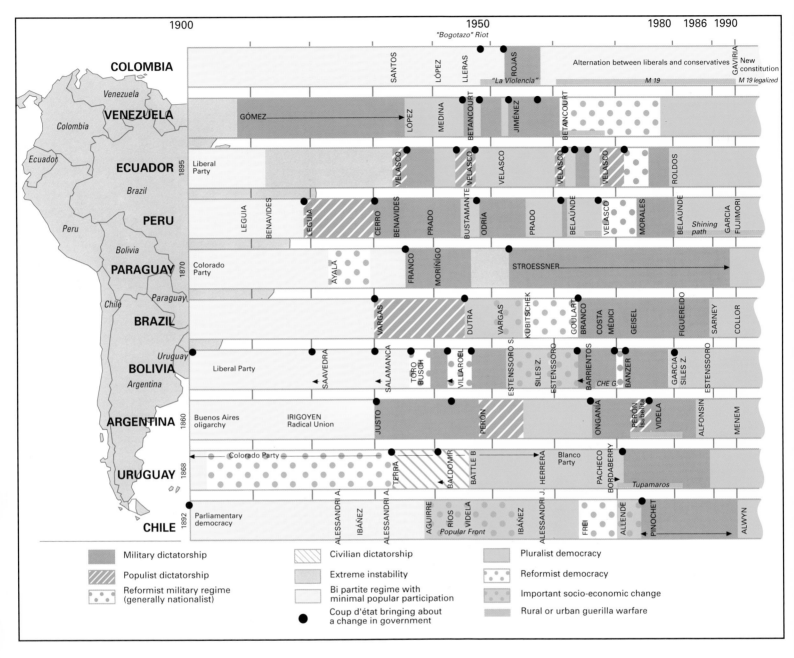

Timeline chart (1900–1990) showing political regimes of South American countries:

COLOMBIA — "Bogotazo" Riot — SANTOS, LÓPEZ, LLERAS, ROJAS, "La Violencia", Alternation between liberals and conservatives, M 19, GAVIRIA, New constitution, M 19 legalized

VENEZUELA — GÓMEZ, LÓPEZ, MEDINA, BETANCOURT, JIMÉNEZ, BETANCOURT

ECUADOR (1895) — Liberal Party, VELASCO, VELASCO, VELASCO, VELASCO, VELASCO, ROLDOS

PERU — LEGUIA, BENAVIDES, LEGUIA, CERRO, BENAVIDES, PRADO, BUSTAMANTE, ODRIA, PRADO, BELAÚNDE, VELASCO, MORALES, BELAÚNDE, Shining path, GARCIA, FUJIMORI

PARAGUAY (1870) — Colorado Party, AYALA, FRANCO, MORINIGO, STROESSNER

BRAZIL — VARGAS, DUTRA, VARGAS, KUBITSCHEK, GOULART, BRANCO, COSTA, MÉDICI, GEISEL, FIGUEREIDO, SARNEY, COLLOR

BOLIVIA — Liberal Party, SAAVEDRA, SALAMANCA, TORO BUSCH, VILLAROEL, ESTENSSORO S., SILES Z., ESTENSSORO, BARRIENTOS, CHE G., BANZER, GARCIA SILES Z., ESTENSSORO

ARGENTINA (1860) — Buenos Aires oligarchy, IRIGOYEN Radical Union, JUSTO, PERÓN, ONGANÍA, PERÓN Isabelita, VIDELA, ALFONSIN, MENEM

URUGUAY (1868) — Colorado Party, TERRA, BALDOMIR, BATTLE B, Blanco Party, HERRERA, PACHECO, BORDABERRY, Tupamaros

CHILE (1892) — Parliamentary democracy, ALESSANDRI A., IBÁÑEZ, ALESSANDRI A., AGUIRRE, RÍOS, VIDELA, Popular Front, IBÁÑEZ, ALESSANDRI J., FREI, ALLENDE, PINOCHET, ALWYN

Legend:
- Military dictatorship
- Populist dictatorship
- Reformist military regime (generally nationalist)
- Civilian dictatorship
- Extreme instability
- Bi partite regime with minimal popular participation
- Pluralist democracy
- Reformist democracy
- Important socio-economic change
- Rural or urban guerilla warfare
- ● Coup d'état bringing about a change in government

Beginning of Transamazonian Highway.

1970

M. Vargas Llosa : *The War of the End of the World.*

1981

Earthquake in Ecuador.

5 March 1987

3. Strike in the tin mines, Bolivia.

canal conflict between Chile and Argentina: signing in the Vatican of a treaty ending the territorial differences which had existed between the two States since 1891.
1985: Election of T. Neves in Brazil—return to democracy.
3 November: First free elections in Argentina two years after the return to democracy.
5 October 1988: Despite the defeat of his referendum, General Pinochet of Chile announces his intention to finish his mandate in 1990.
1989. 1 May: First free elections in Paraguay following the overthrow of General Stroessner on February 2.
14 May: C. Menem succeeds R. Alfonsin in Argentina.
14 December: P. Alwyn elected in Chile; return of democracy.
15 December: F. Collor elected in Brazil.
20 December: United States' intervention in Panama. General Noriega arrested (3 January 1990) and democratic process restored.

1990. 25 February: Mrs V. Chamorro elected in Nicaragua: pluralist democracy restored.
27 May: C. Gaviria elected in Colombia.
10 June: A. Fujimori elected in Peru.
27 June: President G. Bush announces an "Initiative for the Americas," an economic development program based on free trade.
30 September 1991: Father J. B. Aristide, democratically elected president in 1990, is overthrown in a military coup d'état in Haiti.
1 January 1992: End of guerrilla war in El Salvador.

The Destructuring and Restructuring of China

Density of population (1982)

SINKIANG
KANSU
NINGSIA
INNER MONGOLIA
HEILUNGKIANG
KIRIN
PEKING
TIENTSIN
HOPEH
SHANSI
SHANTUNG
TSINGHAI
TIBET
SHENSI
HENAN
KIANGSU
SZECHWAN
HUBEI
ANHUI
SHANGHAI
HUNAN
CHEKIANG
KWEICHOW
KIANGSI
YUNNAN
FUJIAN
KWANGSI
TAIWAN
KWANGTUNG

30   inhabitants/km²
100
230
350
700
1913   (Shanghai)

Birth rates (1982)

National average
1970 : 35,7 ‰
1975 : 27,6 ‰
1982 : **20,9** ‰

SINKIANG
KANSU
NINGSIA
INNER MONGOLIA
HEILUNGKIANG
KIRIN
TIENTSIN
B
SHANSI
HOPEH
SHANTUNG
TIBET
TSINGHAI
SHENSI
HENAN
KIANGSU
SZECHWAN
HUBEI
ANHUI
SHANGHAI
CHEKIANG
HUNAN
KWEICHOW
KIANGSI
YUNNAN
FUJIAN
KWANGSI
TAIWAN
KWANGTUNG

16 ‰
18 ‰
19 ‰
20,9 ‰
26 ‰
31 ‰

CHINESE POLITICS, after the arrival of the communists, were to fluctuate from one extreme to another and undergo a series of crises which in practice did no more than reflect the fundamental contradiction of the revolution, based as it was on a proletarian ideology but one reworked and subverted by the peasantry. The early years were spent in improving the economy and ensuring the obedience of the people (3 million executions took place to serve as an example). The currency was stabilized, moderate agrarian reform ensured satisfactory harvests, and a programme for industrial reconstruction was carried out, while at the same time campaigns for the mass mobilization of the population consolidated the power of the state and the party over the whole of society. The restoration of national unity allowed China to resume its ancient desire to attain supremacy in the Far East: intervention in Korea where it defeated the Americans; Vietnam, which it invaded after aiding the Viet-Minh and Hanoi first against the French and later against the Americans; Tibet, where it repressed the desire for real autonomy and risked an armed conflict with India. This local imperialism came into conflict with Soviet expansionism (Ussuri incident and support for Cambodia [Kampuchea], etc.).

The second phase in the Chinese revolution was marked by the extension of the socialist system of production, corresponding to the first five-year plan of Soviet inspiration. This led to the nationaliza-

tion of industry and to the development of the farm co-operatives. With the achievement of the goals set out in the plan, which, in spite of some outstanding successes in some areas, Chinese leaders later had to admit were fundamentally unsuited to the reality of China, the time had come for what turned out to be the great agrarian disaster of the Great Leap Forward.

The plan was to bring about industrialization no longer at the expense of the rural areas but in the countryside itself, hand in hand with the peasants. The basic tool for this miracle was to be the people's commune: a huge economic, administrative, and policing entity, that would facilitate the mobilization of workers for ambitious projects. The end result was catastrophic. After Mao's overthrow, the ruling group began to adopt a more realistic approach. But just as the country was recovering from the difficulties which the Great Leap Forward had caused (which ranged from famine to disorganized production and apathy on the part of the population), Mao was readying himself for the counter-attack. He embarked upon a series of mobilizing campaigns, each more popular than the one before, which eventually turned into the Cultural Revolution. While the Cultural Revolution did lead to the overthrow of Mao's main adversaries, it rapidly proved uncontrollable, and threw the country into total chaos. A semblance of order was restored only at the cost of fearsome

The Great Leap Forward.   *The General History of Chinese Thought*, under the editorship of the historian Hou Wai-lu.   **The Cultural Revolution begins.**

1958   1960   1966

June 1950: Agrarian Reforms leading to the elimination of land-owners and the redistribution of land. Chinese intervention in Korea.
1953: First Five-Year Plan announced. The Korean War ends. The population of China is 583 million.
1954: New Constitution adopted.
1955: Co-operative farms developed.
1956: Total nationalization of industry and collectivization of 90% of the peasant population.
1957: The Campaign of a Hundred Flowers ends.
1958: The Great Leap Forward begins.
1959: The Lushan Plenum acknowledges the failure of the Great Leap Forward. Mao Tse-tung is replaced as head of state by Liu Shao-ch'i. The rising in Tibet is severely put down.
1959–61: Famine in the whole of China.
1963: Conflict between China and India.
1964: China explodes its first atom bomb.
1966: The Cultural Revolution begins. China is thrown into chaos. Liu Shao-ch'i is eliminated.

4. *During the 'rectification campaign' in 1958, the putting up of wall-posters.*

5. *Building of a dam near the Ming tombs, photographed by Henri Cartier-Bresson in 1958.*

Birth control and birth rate

In *1953*, the population of China was 583 inhabitants; in *1982* it had risen to *1,008 million inhabitants*. The aim for the year *2000 is not to exceed 1,200 million inhabitants.*

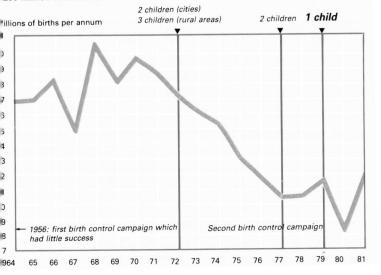

Millions of births per annum

2 children (cities) / 3 children (rural areas) — 2 children — **1 child**

— 1956: first birth control campaign which had little success

Second birth control campaign

1964 65 66 67 68 69 70 71 72 73 74 75 76 77 78 79 80 81

1. Chou En-lai (1896–1976).

2. Teng Hsiao-p'ing (born in 1904).

3. Tien An Men Square during the night of 3–4 June 1989.

repression on the part of the army. The factional struggles which had been rife in the party since the disasters of 1966 were to come to an end only with the total liquidation of the group who emerged from the Cultural Revolution, after the death of Mao Tse-tung. The victory of the realists and pragmatists, who represented the class of managers, technicians, and workers, made it possible to implement more flexible and better adapted policies. Starting in 1979, under the leadership of Teng Hsiao-p'ing, China underwent fast economic development and became self-sufficient in food production. But the lack of true liberalization in the government gave rise to opposition movements culminating in the "Beijing Spring" of 1989, which ended in a bloodbath. Large numbers of intellectuals and students found refuge in the West and established democratic resistance movements. After a period of relative isolation due to negative public opinion in the West, China, which was attempting to liberalize its economy at the same time as it was implementing political repression, re-entered the international exchange system.

Campaign against Confucius and Lin Piao.

1974

Chiang Ch'ing is given a suspended death sentence.

25 January 1981

"Beijing Spring"

May–June 1989

1967: Production falls back. China explodes its first H-Bomb.
1969: IXth Congress of the Chinese Communist Party marks a wish to return to normal. Lin Piao designated as Mao's successor. Frontier incidents between China and the Soviet Union over the disputed border territories on the Ussuri river.
1971: Lin Piao dies in mysterious circumstances after attempting to overthrow Mao and take power.
1973: Teng Hsiao-p'ing rehabilitated. The campaign against Confucius and Lin Piao launched, masking the conflict between (on the one hand) the 'Gang of Four', the architects of the Cultural Revolution, and (on the other) the pragmatists (Chou En-lai, Teng Hsiao-p'ing).
1975: New Constitution promulgated. Chou En-lai, with the support of the moderates, consolidates his position.
1976: Death of Chou En-lai. Teng Hsiao-p'ing is disgraced. Hua Kuo-feng, the head of the secret police (the quivalent of the soviet KGB), is appointed Prime Minister and Vice-President, showing that some

6. Mao and his fourth wife, the actress Chiang Ch'ing.

compromise had been reached with the 'Gang of Four'. Violent riots break out in Peking in T'ien-an men Square on 5 and 6 April on the occasion of the funeral of Chou En-lai, as a sign of the wish to put an end to the dictatorship of Mao's wife, Chian Ch'ing. The death of Mao (9 September) brings about the fall of the 'Gang of Four' and the recall to power of Teng Hsiao-p'ing.
1977: XIth Congress of the CCP officially puts an end to the Cultural Revolution and sets out a programme of modernization.
1978: New Constitution. Teng Hsiao-p'ing consolidates his position. Peace treaty with Japan.
1979: New Democracy Movement (the Peking Spring) denounces the abuses of the régime and is severely repressed (Wei Ching-sheng is put on trial and sentenced to 15 years in prison); there are arbitrary arrests of dissidents such as Liu Ch'ing. Invasion of Tonkin. Relations between China and America are normalized. Special economic zones are set up in the Canton region and firms established with joint Chinese and foreign capital.

1986: Despite the stated policy of "only one child," demographic growth is larger than predicted as the population exceeds one billion one hundred million.
December 1986–January 1987: Following student demonstrations in Shanghai and Peking, resignation of Hu Yao Bang, Secretary General of the CCP, replaced by Chao Tzu-yang.
1989. 5–7 March: Repression of the anti-Chinese uprising in Tibet.
May–June: "Beijing Spring." Massacre at Tien An Men Square (3–4 June). Removal of Chao Tzu-yang.
January–February 1992: Prime Minister Li Peng, who was primarily responsible for the repression, visits the United States and Europe.

Crises in the Communist System

AFTER STALIN'S DEATH, the strength of the Soviet Bloc increased. The rearmament of Germany became the main object of confrontation with the West. West Germany became a member of NATO. The USSR created the Warsaw Pact. Moreover, the latter's relations with its satellites expanded. On the economic level, for instance, mixed societies, accused of robbing the latter of their wealth, were broken up. On the political level, Khruschev recognized Yugoslavia's right to follow its own path toward socialism and reconciled with Tito.

The Twentieth Congress of the Communist Party of the Soviet Union upset the communist movement. More certain of itself, and conscious of the stalemate caused by the Cold War, the USSR promised not to export revolution, to promote peaceful coexistence with imperialism, and to look toward a peaceful transition to socialism in some countries. But, above all, Khruschev's secret report caused an upheaval; it listed show trials, torture, mass arrests, deportation of entire populations, and elimination of the Polish Communist Party in 1938. Khruschev strongly and vehemently denounced Stalin's "personality cult." Destalinization was initiated. The Congress' decisions became the focal point of the schism because the Chinese leaders objected to "Soviet revisionism."

In Eastern Europe, preceding the Twentieth Congress, the army had already put down the workers' uprising in East Berlin and in Czechoslovakia. The most serious crises broke out in Poland and Hungary after the Congress. These countries were in the midst of transition: collectivization injured the peasants and limited the flow of supplies to the towns, while industrialization confined thousands of rural immigrants in temporary housing. The Soviets put pressure on Warsaw while their troops crushed the Hungarian revolt. In the GDR, the tension around West Berlin continued and thousands of East Germans fled there. Starting in 1961, the Wall put an end to free exchange between the two parts of the city. Fearing that it would be relegated to the status of an agricultural country, Romania rejected the acceleration of economic integration and international division of labor within the bloc. Strengthened by the support of China, it received satisfaction before distancing itself from Moscow in its foreign policy.

Brezhnev inherited a divided socialist camp. There were breaks in relations with China and Albania, cool relations with Belgrade and Bucharest, and Mao's influence was strong in North Korea, Vietnam, and Cuba. On the other hand, the USSR extended its influence in Black Africa and in the Arab world but was subjected to increased anti-Soviet sentiments within its own camp. In Czechoslovakia, the "Prague Spring" was crushed by Warsaw Pact forces. In Poland the announcement of a price increase resulted in uprisings in 1970, 1976, and 1980. The free trade union Solidarity, led by Lech Walesa was founded during the 1980 uprising. By the time General Jaruzelski declared martial law in December 1981, it had over 10 million members.

The USSR ended this decade by invading Afghanistan, thus plunging into a war that would ultimately cause thousands of casualties.

1. Soviet troops in the streets of Prague, August 1968.

Launch of Sputnik.

4 October 1957

1953. June: Workers' demonstrations in Czechoslovakia. Workers' uprising put down by Soviet troops in East Berlin (17 June).
7 September: Khruschev elected First Secretary of the Communist Party of the Soviet Union.
May 1955: Signing of the Warsaw Pact, military alliance of European communist countries under Soviet control on 14 May. Khruschev's trip to Belgrade; reconciliation with Yugoslavia.
1956. 14–15 February: Twentieth Congress of the CPSU. Khruschev's secret report.
18 April: Official announcement of the dissolution of Cominform, which had not met since 1950.
June–July: Workers' uprisings in Poznan, Poland.
20 October: Gomulka becomes the head of the Workers' Party in Poland. Marshal Rokossovski returns to Moscow.
23 October–4 November: Revolt brutally put down in Budapest, Hungary.
1957. 14–19 November: In Moscow, the international conference of communist and

2. Bronze statue of Stalin dismantled in Budapest, late October 1956.

workers' parties proclaims the USSR's leading role in the socialist camp and defines the relations between the parties along the principles of equality, independence, sovereignty, and nonintervention.
1959. January: Victory of the revolution in Cuba.
1960. 11–25 November: In Moscow the second international conference of communist and workers; parties discuss the Sino-Soviet conflict and agree on a compromise. Only Albania totally supports China.
1961. 13 August: Berlin Wall erected.
17–31 October: Twenty-second Congress of the CPSU. Stalin's body is removed from the mausoleum. The city of Stalingrad becomes Volgograd. Break with Albania.
14 July: Ideological break between China and the USSR.
1964. 27 April: The Romanian Communist Party staunchly confirms its right to choose its own path.
14 October: Khruschev dismissed; Brezhnev takes over leadership of the CPSU.
1968. 3 January: A. Dubcek replaces Novotn

1953–80

Soviet influence in the world at the end of the 1970's

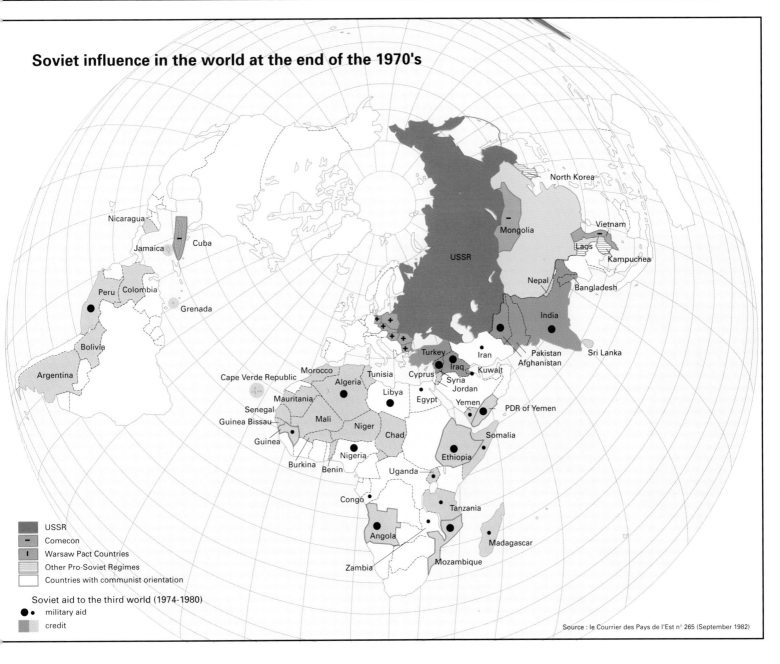

Map labels:
Nicaragua, Cuba, Jamaica, Peru, Colombia, Grenada, Bolivia, Argentina, North Korea, Mongolia, Vietnam, USSR, Laos, Kampuchea, Nepal, Bangladesh, India, Sri Lanka, Turkey, Iran, Pakistan, Afghanistan, Iraq, Kuwait, Cyprus, Syria, Jordan, Morocco, Tunisia, Cape Verde Republic, Algeria, Libya, Egypt, Yemen, PDR of Yemen, Mauritania, Senegal, Guinea Bissau, Mali, Niger, Chad, Somalia, Guinea, Nigeria, Ethiopia, Burkina, Benin, Uganda, Congo, Tanzania, Madagascar, Angola, Mozambique, Zambia

Legend:
- USSR
- Comecon
- Warsaw Pact Countries
- Other Pro-Soviet Regimes
- Countries with communist orientation

Soviet aid to the third world (1974-1980)
- ● ● military aid
- ▨ credit

Source : le Courrier des Pays de l'Est n° 265 (September 1982)

Establishment of secret publications (samizdat).

1960-1970

A. Solzhenitsyn : *The Gulag Archipelago.*

1973

3. L. Brezhnev presenting a decoration to his predecessor, N.S. Khruschev.

as the head of the Czechoslovak Communist Party. Beginning of reforms.
20 August: The "Prague Spring" is crushed. Warsaw Pact armies occupy Czechoslovakia.
1970: The first group of Soviet Jews is permitted to leave for Israel. The emigration reaches its peak in 1979.
December: W. Gomulka is replaced by E. Gierek at the head of the Polish Workers' Party.
1973. February: A. Solzhenitsyn is expelled from the USSR.
1975. 1 August: Signing of the Helsinki Accords during the Conference on Security and Cooperation in Europe (CSCE).
October: A. Sakharov receives the Nobel Peace Price.
1976. May: The Group for the Recognition of the Helsinki Accords is founded in the USSR.
1977. 7 January: The dissidents organize around Charter 77 in Czechoslovakia.
2-3 March: Official creation of Eurocommunism during the summit between the general secretaries of the Italian, French, and Spanish communist parties.

27 April 1978: Communist coup d'état in Afghanistan.
27 December 1979: The Red Army invades Afghanistan.
July-August 1980: Founding of the trade union Solidarity in Poland.

4. Marx has a choice: the army or Solidarity.

The End of the Soviet Empire

BY THE END OF THE 1970S economic growth had slowed down considerably. The USSR could no longer ensure a constant increase in the standard of living (however low), or full employment, on which the social system was based, especially since its needs had increased significantly. The population had become urbanized and educated. The infrastructure was threatened by generalized malfunctioning. The invasion of Afghanistan proved to be a great drain on resources as well as dangerous political short-sightedness.

The arrival of Mikhail Gorbachev marked the turning point. Aware that the society would not make any great effort to help the economy without an atmosphere of true freedom to make the reform plan credible, he gave priority to political liberalization. Freedom of the press was demanded by publishers and journalists, and granted. A historical review of the painful and adulterated past was encouraged and the victims were rehabilitated. Gradually political prisoners were

released from the camps and mental institutions. Parliamentary elections, which for the first time offered several candidates in each district, gave the Soviets the feeling that they were playing an active role in politics. Hundreds of political clubs and parties formed. The election of Boris Yeltsin as president of Russia (in the first presidential election with universal suffrage in the history of Russia) demonstrated a fundamental change in the collective mentality. The society began to feel that it could grant power, a role that had been ascribed to God under the czars, and then to "scientific ideology" under the Soviet regime.

But the process advanced so rapidly that the progressives of yesterday became the conservatives of today, and conflicts tore apart those who had supported perestroika in 1985–1986. Gorbachev held on to his communist convictions and believed that the system could be reformed. As a result, he was permanently at variance with the most democratic elements of society. A disastrous past, fear of a free market, as well as the lack of a true governmental organization explain why perestroika failed economically.

The plan for a Treaty of the Union ended in convincing the "rightists" that Gorbachev was incapable of keeping the democratic movement and centrifugal forces in check; they decided to get rid of him, believing that his unpopularity would ensure the success of the coup. The 1991 coup was badly organized and ignored the previous developments in Russia; it failed due to the determination of a handful of democrats and the brutality of a group of security forces and of the army. At this point it was the democrats who no longer needed Gorbachev.

It is difficult to resolve the national-religious conflicts that subject various peoples to violence. The issue of self-determination in Upper Karabach, which is primarily Armenian, in the conflict with the inviolability of the borders of Azerbaidzhan. And the issue of universal suffrage (in the Asiatic and Moslem republics where the party apparatus and the fundamentalists maintain or seize power) is in conflict with the issue of human rights. Agriculture needs to be revitalized, the industrial sector needs to be revived. There is a large foreign debt; inflation is rising faster than income, and unemployment is growing rapidly. The military forces believe they have been abandoned and could easily be tempted to become involved in political intrigues. Russia and its CIS neighbors (made up of the ex-USSR republics excluding Lithuania, Estonia, Latvia, and Georgia) are becoming a part of the Third World.

1. Gorbachev's return to Moscow.

Perestroika or Restructuring.	Glasnost or Openness.	Ouster of M. Gorbachev.	Price liberalization in Russia.
1985	**1987**	**25 December 1991**	**2 January 1992**

1982. 10 November: Death of L. Brezhnev, replaced by Y. Andropov (former head of the KGB) on the 12th.	Politburo. **20 February:** The Upper Karabach Soviet (population 75% Armenian) demands that the region be separated from Azarbaidzhan and reunited with Armenia. As a result, there are anti-Armenian pogroms in Sungait.	state by the Supreme Soviet. **7 December:** Earthquake in Armenia. **1989. March:** Central Committee of the CPSU investigates B. Yeltsin, who calls for a multiparty system. Demonstrations supporting him in Moscow.	support the preservation of the Union. **9 April:** Georgia declares independence. **12 June:** B. Yeltsin elected President of Russia by universal suffrage (60% of the votes). **19–21 August:** Failed conservative putsch in Moscow.
1984. 9 February: Death of Y. Andropov, replaced by K. Chernenko. **1985. 11 March:** Following death of K. Chernenko, M. Gorbachev is elected Secretary General of the CPSU Central Committee.	**13 March:** The spokesperson for the conservative opposition, N. Andreeva, publishes a manifesto. **23 March:** USSR Supreme Soviet resolution rejecting reunification of Upper Karabach with Armenia.	**26 March:** Elections for Congress of People's Deputies according to a new law authorizing a number of candidates. **July:** Miners strike in Kuzbass, Donbas, and Vorkuta.	**29 August:** Supreme Soviet suspends activities of CPSU. **20 August–31 September:** 10 republics declare independence. **21 December:** Founding meeting of the Commonwealth of Independent States (CIS) at Alma-Ata.
1986. 25 February–6 March: Twenty-Seventh Congress of the CPSU initiates perestroika. **26 April:** Explosion at Chernobyl nuclear plant. **11–12 October:** Reagan-Gorbachev meeting at Rejkjavik. **16 December:** Dissident A. Sakharov returns to Moscow following six years of exile in Gorki.	**14 April:** Agreement on the withdrawal of troops from Afghanistan. **29 April:** M. Gorbachev receives the patriarch of the Orthodox Church and signs a new policy on religion. **June:** Rehabilitation of the victims of the 1936-1937 trials.	**1990. 25 February:** Demonstration in Moscow against the CPSU and in support of accelerating the reforms. **11 March:** Lithuania declares independence. **25 March:** Soviet Army invades Vilnius, Lithuania.	
1987. January: Policy of openness (glasnost) adopted. **June:** Self-management permitted in enterprise. Cooperative and private sectors encouraged in agriculture and services. **1988. 18 February:** B. Yeltsin dismissed from his position as deputy member of the	**28 June–2 July:** Nineteenth Party Congress approves the reform of the political system and the organization of semi-democratic elections to a new Congress of People's Deputies. **1 October:** M. Gorbachev elected head of .	**15 July:** In Moscow, demonstration demanding the dissolution of the Ryjkov government and the dissolution of the CPSU. **15 September:** Nobel Peace Prize awarded to M. Gorbachev. **1991. January:** Soviet troops besiege parliament in Vilnius, Lithuania. **17 March:** The "yes votes" in the referendum	

2. A trembling dynasty: L. Brezhnev.

3. Y. Andropov

4. K. Chernenko

The CIS at the beginning of 1992

Countries of the CIS — Pollution of waters

1 Russia
2 Kazakstan
3 Kirgizstan
4 Tadzhikistan
5 Uzbekistan
6 Turkmenistan
7 Azerbaidzhan
8 Armenia
9 Moldavia
10 Ukraine
11 Belorussia

B - Lake Baikal
D - Dnepr
K - Kara Sea
L - Lake Ladoga and Neva
V - Volga

Deterioration of surrounding soils

A - Aral Sea
Volga delta

Conflicts between ethnic groups

Radioactivity

T - Chernobyl
S - Semipalatinsk
Tc - Chovkotka

The United States from Truman to Bush

DURING THE GOVERNMENTS of Harry Truman and Dwight Eisenhower, the United States was at the height of its power. Economically, militarily, and even culturally the country was at its peak. However, there were some negative aspects: the American economy suffered several economic recessions during the 1950s, there was still significant social inequality (22% of the population lived below the poverty level in 1959), McCarthyism had left its mark on the political climate, and the "problem of the blacks" was more acute than ever, since American blacks had started to rebel against the segregation to which they were subjected.

After John F. Kennedy, the first catholic President, was elected to the White House, the 1960s started along a road toward revival. Kennedy launched his "New Frontier" program, which was intended to combat poverty and inequality in the United States and throughout the world, abolish segregation, and which, literally, aimed at the moon with its Mercury, Gemini, and Apollo space exploration programs. To be sure, aid to Latin America was not without political motivation: in Cuba the CIA attempted unsuccessfully to land at the Bay of Pigs and, one year later, Kennedy resolved the missile crisis by forcing the Soviets to back down. Simultaneously, in order to block the communist advance, the President sent the first American military contingents to South Vietnam, and involved his country in a long and expensive conflict. Assassinated in 1963, Kennedy passed into legend. But his successor, Lyndon B. Johnson, was left with the task of translating Kennedy's projects into reality.

Against a problem-ridden background, marked by riots in the black ghettos and by the Vietnamese war, he completed the social agenda with his "Great Society" program, which financed the fight against poverty, the construction of low income housing and the establishment of social security systems.

Johnson's successor, Republican Richard Nixon, assisted by his Secretary of State Henry Kissinger, launched various successful foreign policy initiatives: he renewed relations with China, signed the SALT agreements with the USSR and negotiated America's withdrawal from Vietnam. But the Watergate affair forced him to resign and created a crisis of confidence, which his successors Gerald

2. Racist demonstration by the Ku Klux Klan in the sixties.

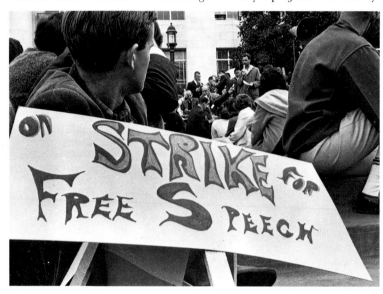

1. Student sit-in at Berkeley in 1964 for freedom of speech.

Death of Roosevelt.	Outbreak of Korean War.	Eisenhower President.	Kennedy becomes first Catholic President.
12 April 1945	**1950**	**1953**	**1961**

1945–53: Harry S Truman, President.
June 1947: Taft-Hartley Act restricting the right to strike.
1950–53: Korean War and McCarthyism.
19 June 1953: Execution of the Rosenbergs.
1953–61: Dwight D. Eisenhower, President.
1953–4, 1957–8, 1960–61: Economic recessions.
May 1954: Supreme Court rules social segregation in schools unconstitutional.
9 February 1955: Merger between AFL and CIO, the two major trade union federations.
1958: NASA created.
1960: CORE, Congress for Racial Equality.
1961: John F. Kennedy, President. Failure of the Bay of Pigs (Cuba) landing.
1961–1969: Economic expansion.
1962: Organization of the Peace Corps and of the Alliance for Progress in Latin America. Cuban missile crisis.
22 November 1963: John F. Kennedy assassinated in Dallas.
1964: Lyndon B. Johnson has 'Law against poverty' and law on Black civil rights passed.
1964–7: Riots in the Black ghettoes of Harlem, Los Angeles, Newark, Detroit.

4. John Fitzgerald Kennedy in the White House during the Cuban Missile Crisis.

1965: Immigration law: quotas abolished; immigration of scientists and intellectuals promoted. Assassination of Malcolm X, ex-leader of the black Muslims.
4 April 1968: Assassination of Martin Luther King.
1969–74: Richard Nixon, President.
1969. 21 July: Americans land on the moon.
15–17 August: Woodstock festival.
9 May 1970: 100,000 students demonstrate in Washington against the war in Vietnam.
1970–2: Environmental protection law.
15 August 1971: Dollar inconvertible.
1971–2: Bombing of Vietnam resumed.
1971–3: Devaluations of the dollar.
21–28 February 1972: Nixon visits China.
1972–9: SALT I and II agreements.
1973: Roe v. Wade decision by Supreme Court legalizing abortion.
27 January: Paris Accords on ceasefire in Vietnam.
1973–4: Watergate Affair; Nixon resigns after Senate investigation.
1974–7: Gerald Ford is President.
1974: Rise in price of imported oil.

5. Poster depicting Martin Luther King, winner of the Nobel Peace Prize in 1964.

The Black population in 1965 and Black revolt, 1964-67

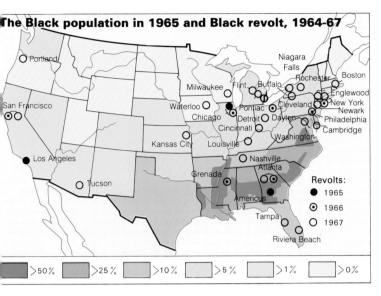

Portland
Niagara Falls
Milwaukee Flint Buffalo Rochester Boston
Waterloo Pontiac Cleveland Englewood New York
San Francisco Chicago Detroit Dayton Newark
Kansas City Cincinnati Philadelphia Cambridge
Louisville Washington
Los Angeles
Tucson Nashville
Grenada Atlanta
Americus
Tampa
Riviera Beach

Revolts:
● 1965
◉ 1966
○ 1967

>50% >25% >10% >5% >1% >0%

The proportion of black mayors in the USA in 1985

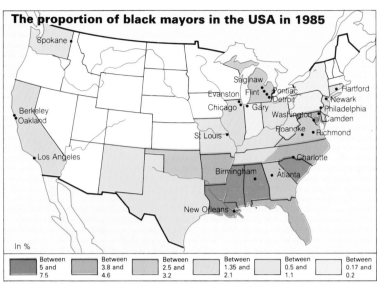

Spokane
Saginaw
Evanston Flint Pontiac Hartford
Berkeley Chicago Detroit Newark
Oakland Gary Washington Philadelphia
St Louis Roanoke Camden
Los Angeles Richmond
Birmingham Charlotte
Atlanta
New Orleans

In %

| Between 5 and 7.5 | Between 3.8 and 4.6 | Between 2.5 and 3.2 | Between 1.35 and 2.1 | Between 0.5 and 1.1 | Between 0.17 and 0.2 |

Ford and Jimmy Carter were unable to surmount. Carter, a little-known Democrat before his election, played an active role in the Israeli–Egyptian negotiations and acted resolutely when the Soviets invaded Afghanistan. But the hostage affair at the American Embassy in Teheran cost him a second term. The man who defeated him, Ronald Reagan, embodied the conservative tradition of the "silent majority." He governed the country for eight years and attempted to re-establish trust and confidence. Although, generally speaking, the economic results were successful, the social cost was high as were the deficits in the balance-of-payments and Federal budget. Reagan's successor, George Bush, has had to deal with this situation since 1989. His steadfastness in foreign affairs, especially during the Gulf War, has been accompanied by a relative indifference toward critical domestic problems, such as homelessness, drugs, racial tensions and the renovation of the basic infrastructure (bridges, roads, etc.) which is in urgent need of repair. These issues will have to be dealt with—and the costs financed—during the 1990s.

3. Edwin Aldrin, the second man to set foot on the moon, during the Apollo 11 mission in 1969.

Nixon resigns.	Re-election of Reagan.	Stock Exchange Crash.
9 August 1974	6 November 1984	19 October 1987

1975: Onset of recession.
July 1976: Bicentenary celebrations.
1977–81: Jimmy Carter's Presidency.
7 September 1978: Camp David Accords between Egypt and Israel.
1979: Carter attempts to control American companies' oil prices.
1979–81: Iran hostages affair.
1980: Beginning of agricultural difficulties. Carter interrupts the shipping of wheat to the USSR to protest against invasion of Afghansitan.
1981–5: Ronald Reagan's first term.
1981: Wheat shipments to USSR recommence.
1982: Unemployment reaches 10% of the total employable population and 20% among Blacks.
3 October 1983: 230 American soldiers are killed in a terrorist attack in Beirut.
1985–1989: Ronald Reagan's second term.
1986. 28 January: Explosion of the Challenger space shuttle.
December: The beginning of two investigative commissions on the "Iran-contra" affair.

22 January 1987: Andy Warhol dies.
1988. May: Unemployment reaches 1974 levels.
8 November: George Bush elected.
1989: D. Dinkins elected as first black Mayor of New York.
August 1990–March 1991: Crisis in the Persian Gulf followed by Gulf War. Activation of American public opinion.

6. First feminist demonstrations in New York.

7. Ronald and Nancy Reagan descending from the presidential plane.

Détente and Nuclear Strategy

THE POST-WAR ERA witnessed the birth of two new empires: the American empire, based on the free market economy, and extending throughout the world by virtue of its sea-power; and the Soviet empire, dependent on the idea of the centrally planned economy, and existing as a continental entity, primarily a Eurasian one. Within a short space of time the two military alliances, NATO and the Warsaw Pact, both maintaining an integrated command structure in peacetime, began to treat Europe as an arena of confrontation, but also of possible equilibrium. The two leading countries in the alliances, the USA and the USSR, adopted the policy of using nuclear weapons in case of attack, which produced reciprocal nuclear stalemate. Each country remains free, nonetheless, within its own sphere of influence, to carry out repression by military force or impose military dictatorship in any area where political or social movements threaten the Eastern or Western empire. As a result military strength has become one of the foundations of co-existence, and the arms race has become a permanent feature. The arms race itself has followed three phases, each based on a different type of military technology and each more expensive than the one before. Each of these phases has in turn been accompanied by wars and –fruitless – negotiations on disarmament. After the destruction of Hiroshima, the nuclear bomb was considered as a weapon of war, more powerful than any other. During the Cold War, the bombers of the Strategic Air Command (SAC) threatened 300 Soviet cities with destruction, thus claiming to deter any attack from the other side (the strategy depended on the threat of massive retaliation). The nuclear monopoly initially enjoyed by the United States, and later, after the Soviet Union had its own bomb, its nuclear superiority over the Soviet Union, did not lead to the use of nuclear arms in Korea; rather, it was thought that the role of the atomic bomb was to compensate for the regional superiority of the USSR within Europe. Prospects for disarmament seemed remote.

After 1955 the American mainland became vulnerable to attack from Soviet bombers and especially from Soviet missiles. The era of peaceful coexistence had begun. With Sputnik, the Soviets at first had a technical lead in the field of intercontinental ballistic missiles (ICBMs), but the Americans were able to produce more modern medium range missiles, such as their submarine-launched ballistic missiles (SLBMs) which were invulnerable to attack and which were targeted on the Soviet Union from the seas surrounding Europe and Asia. The Americans effectively prevented the Soviet Union from threatening the USA from Cuba and at the time gave up the idea of targeting the USSR from within Europe. Both countries abandoned the development of anti-missile missiles. The balance of power rested on the enormous destructive power of thousands of missiles, accumulated in great numbers to maintain sufficient forces for reprisal even if the enemy were to attack by surprise (the strategy known as deterrence by MAD or 'mutually assured destruction'). Britain, France and

1946-57: Bombers and Military Divisions

✈ Soviet Advances	Number of Warheads in 1955
✪ Western Repression	USA 1,050
Neutral	USSR 340

KOREA

GUATAMALA

Indo-China

Algeria   Suez

Kenya

Bombers
Divisions

China took the course of maintaining a national nuclear capability, independent of the two superpowers. The American doctrine of 'flexible response' did nothing to stop the United States from losing the Vietnam war. The two superpowers first presented grand 'plans for general and total disarmament'. Then after 1962 they moved towards more limited agreements which were to be called Arms Control Agreements. The SALT I and SALT II (Strategic Arms Limitation Talks) agreements were signed simply as a way of moderating the arms race.

From 1974 weapons, whether nuclear or not, became 'intelligent', meaning that they began to incorporate computerized automatic guidance systems. The technology of multiple warheads became more important, as the number of missiles had been fixed in the SALT II agreement. In addition, cruise missiles are now being deployed on land and at sea, and American B-52s and B-1s equipped with them. Weapons have become more accurate, more reliable and

War in Indo-China.	Korean War.	Suez Crisis. Crushing of the Hungarian uprising by Soviet tanks.		Cuban Missile Crisis.
1946–54	**1950–3**	**1956**		**1962**

1 December 1959: Antarctic Treaty prohibiting nuclear explosions or disposal of radioactive waste in Antarctica.
20 September 1961: Soviet Union–United States Statement of Agreed Principles concerning disarmament negotiated by Zorin and McCloy.
1963. 16–25 July: Agreement on the establishment of the 'hot line' between the United States and the Soviet Union.
5 August: Partial Nuclear Test – Ban Treaty signed (by Great Britain, the Soviet Union and the United States) banning nuclear tests in the atmosphere, in outer space and under water.
1967. 27 January: Outer Space Treaty demilitarizes space.
14 February: Tlatelolco Treaty prohibits nuclear weapons in Latin America.
1 July 1968: Treaty on the Non-Proliferation of Nuclear Weapons signed.
1971. 11 February: Sea-bed Denuclearization Treaty.
30 September: Agreement on measures to reduce the risk of outbreak of nuclear war between USA and USSR (Nuclear

Accidents Agreement).
1972. 10 April: Biological Warfare Convention prohibits the development or possession of biological weapons.
16 May: SALT I Treaty signed, on the use of anti-ballistic missiles (ABMs).
November: Opening of the SALT II negotiations.
22 June 1973: US–USSR Agreement on the Prevention of Nuclear War.
1974. 3 July: US-USSR Treaty on the limitation of underground nuclear weapons tests.
24 November: Joint declaration by the United States and the Soviet Union on strategic arms (Vladivostock Agreement).
1 August 1975: Final Act of the Helsinki Conference on Security and Co-operation in Europe.
16 July 1976: Agreement between France and the Soviet Union on the prevention of the accidental or unauthorized use of nuclear weapons.

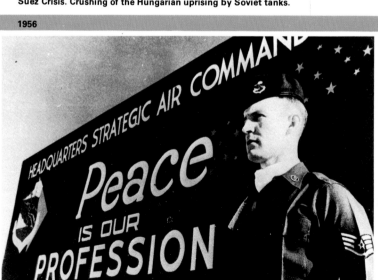

2. Headquarters of the Strategic Air Command.

1959–89

6-74 ICBMs

Armed National Liberation Movements
Communist Revolutions
Western Repression
Progressive Military Regimes
Neutrals

Warheads in 1967
USA 25,800
USSR 6,350

Oct. 1962
CUBA
PERU
BOLIVIA
HILE

VIETNAM
INDONESIA

Palestine
Algeria
GUINEA-BISSAU
ETHIOPIA
ZAIRE
TANZANIA
ANGOLA
RHODESIA (ZIMBABWE)
MOZAMBIQUE

Intercontinental Ballistic missiles
Intermediate Range Ballistic missiles
Polaris submarine-launched missiles

Firing Range

1975-85 Multiple Warheads

Warheads in 1982
USA 30,400
USSR 17,500

Pearl Harbour
Okinawa
Da-Nang
NICARAGUA
CUBA
VIETNAM
Azores
AFGHANISTAN
CAPE VERDE ISLANDS
LEBANON
ADEN
Diego Garcia
ETHIOPIA
CONGO
ANGOLA
MOZAMBIQUE
Walvis Bay
SOUTH AFRICA

Major bases
Western
Soviet

ore numerous (there are now about 10,000 on each side). Deterr-ace is no longer guaranteed by MAD, and, according to present-day ATO strategists, can be maintained only by the alliance's belief in s own 'capacity to win a limited nuclear war'. 40,000 targets have een assigned in the USSR.

These developments continue to be the source of great alarm to ublic opinion (especially after 1980), in particular in the United tates (with the Nuclear Freeze Movement), in Great Britain (with e Campaign for Nuclear Disarmament and other peace groups) and the German Federal Republic (with the Peace Movement and the reen Party). Major demonstrations have been held to call a halt to e arms race. Despite this, early 1987 saw the Reagan administration eaching the SALT II agreement (signed under President Carter ut never ratified by Congress) and thus far the Strategic Arms eduction Talks (START) have made little progress. With the eployment of Cruise and Pershing in Europe, and the research

undertaken for the Strategic Defence Initiative (SDI), or 'Star Wars', the arms race has been set off on a new spiral. The dealings between Reagan and Gorbachev in 1985, reinforced by subsequent Soviet initiatives, perhaps represent new hope of détente in East-West relations. But the growth in the sales of arms to the Third World and the wars in the Southern Hemisphere, increase the dangers of non-nuclear conflict.

1. French nuclear explosion on Muroroa Atoll, 1983.

etnam War.   **Invasion of Czechoslovakia by the Warsaw Pact nations.**   **War in Afghanistan.**

3–75   1968   1979–

18 June 1979: SALT II Treaty between the Soviet Union and the United States on the limitation of strategic arms.
11 November 1980–9 September 1983: Madrid Conference.
13 May 1982: President Reagan makes proposals for START (discussions on the reduction of strategic arms).
1983. 23 November: Deployment of Pershing II missiles begins in the Federal Republic of Germany.
8 December: Suspension *sine die* of START talks.
17 January 1984: Stockholm Conference.
19–20 November 1985: Talks held in Geneva between Gorbachev and Reagan.
11–12 October 1986: U.S.-Soviet summit at Reykjavik.
7 December 1988: M. Gorbachev announces a unilateral reduction of 500,000 Soviet armed forces and the withdrawal of 10,000 tanks from Eastern Europe by 1991.

Missiles on parade in Red Square, 7 November 1984.

4. Meeting between Reagan–Gorbachev, 19–20 November 1985.

The Indian and Pacific Oceans

1. The skyscrapers of Hong Kong facing the China Sea.

THOUGH THEY ARE ADJACENT to each other and closely connected, the Indian Ocean (75 million square kilometers) and the Pacific Ocean (176 million square kilometers) have developed very differently during the twentieth century. One-fourth of the world population is concentrated around the Indian Ocean. It juxtaposes the rich oil empires with the poorest countries (from Ethiopia to Bangladesh)—today almost half of the least-developed countries in the world. Social and demographic disequilibrium, overall under-industrialization (with the exception of South Africa, some Indian states, and Australia), food shortages, famines (Horn of Africa, Bangladesh), recurring hydrological, ecological, and chemical disasters, and uncontrolled migrations toward the Gulf, dictatorships, and fundamentalist endeavors make the shores of the Indian Ocean

the least stable area in the world. This instability increases the ocean geopolitical importance; 60% of the world oil reserves are distribute around it and 50% of oil supplies of Europe and 90% of Japan a transported through it. In the hinterland of the Pacific, the Indi Ocean is an extremely strategic region. It is controlled—witho competition due to Russia's loss of power—by the ships of the 6th–7 American fleets from a dense network of bases (Bahrein, Diego Ga cia, Seychelles, and soon Singapore). Due to the superabundance military presence in the Indian Ocean, attempts to make it into peace zone are unlikely to succeed even if the nations in this are gradually acquire a feeling of mutual belonging.

Has the Pacific become the "Mediterranean of the Future" durin the twentieth century as predicted by the Russian philosoph Alexander Herzen? The reality is more complex because the peopl crowded around the largest ocean are extremely heterogeneous. Th economic growth of the last 35 years has in fact been localized in th North Pacific—from Singapore to Los Angeles via Taiwan, Hor Kong, the eastern provinces of China, and, above all, Tokyo ar Seoul.

During the last 100 years, the geopolitical importance of the regic has repeatedly been confirmed. In 1900 American Senator Beveridg commented: "Whoever controls the Pacific controls the world." Th was confirmed by the outbreak of World War II. In 1945 the Pacif was the only region in the world to be hit by a nuclear bomb; became an American ocean, protected by the strongest fleet ar largest military base in history. As for the process of modernization, started with the Meiji Era in Japan, the mining and oil operations California, and industrialization in Manchuria. Since the 1950s it h. accelerated due to uninhibited increases in exchange between th densest populations and the strongest industrial nations in the worl

During the last half century, the impressive movements of wor. growth favored the northern half of the Pacific. Initially they we stimulated by the overflow of the political and social structures in th countries in the region: the decolonization of Southeast Asia ar Korea; constitutional reform in Japan; agrarian reform in Japa South Korea, and Taiwan; the "green revolution" in Southeast Asi anti-communist massacres of 1965 in Indonesia; and the failure of tl communist revolution in Vietnam, despite its military victory. Toda the North Pacific is beginning to be the focus of the world market, has been proved by the recent reversal of the prevailing America foreign trade flows. For the first time in 1980 trade between tl United States and the Pacific Rim ($117.6 billion) exceeded trac between America and Western Europe ($115.6 billion). This chang started with the shift of the center of gravity of American capit: toward the countries on the West Coast during World War II. It wa

Japan opens its frontiers and attempts conquest of the world.	Opening of the Suez Canal.	P'anmunjam Armistice.	Creation of Malaysia.
1868	**1869**	**27 July 1953**	**16 September 1963**

1868: Beginning of Meiji Era and start of industrialization in Japan.
1894: Japan annexes Korea.
1904–1905: Manchurian War between Russia and Japan.
1931: Japan occupies Manchuria and establishes heavy industry there.
1941–1945: War in the Pacific; Japanese attempt to establish the "Sphere of Co-prosperity of Greater Eastern Asia"; industrial boom in California.
1946. 21 October: Agrarian reform in Japan initiated by American authorities.
3 November: New Japanese constitution.
1949. 21 June: Agrarian reform in South Korea.
9 December: Chinese nationalist government is set up.
1950–1953: Korean War and consolidation of the partitioning of the country into two states.
1950: Peace treaties signed by the Allies (with the exception of the Soviets) and

Japan; San Francisco Peace Treaty signed between Japan and the United States on 8 September.
1953: Agrarian reform in Taiwan.
1954. September: Creation of the Southeast Asia Treaty Organization (SEATO).
1956. 26 July: Nasser nationalizes the Suez Canal.
1959: Lee Kuan Yew forms government in Singapore; policy of industrialization adopted.
1961: General Park Chung Hee comes to power in South Korea; beginning of accelerated industrialization of the country.
1963. 16 September: Creation of Malaysia.
1963–1975: Vietnamese War stimulates the economic expansion of neighboring countries.
1965. 11 February: First Japanese satellite.
9 August: Singapore leaves Malaysia and becomes an independent state.
November: F. Marcos elected president of the Philippines.

1966. 12 March: In Indonesia, General Suharto establishes military rule.
1967 June–5 June 1975: Suez Canal closed following the Six-Day War.
1967. August: Creation of the Association of Southeast Asian Nations (ASEAN).
1968: Beginning of industrial expansion in Indonesia (textiles, plastics, etc.)
1970. 25 November: Yukio Mishima, the Japanese author, commits suicide.
1971. 31 October: The British Far East Command ceases to operate.
18 December: Re-evaluation of the yen.
1972. 23 September: The Marcos government declares martial law in the Philippines.
30 September: Normalization of relations between Tokyo and Peking [Beijing].
1972–1980: Second stage of industrial development (heavy industry, chemicals, automobiles) in the four Newly Industrialized Asian Countries (NICs).
1984. 26 September: Anglo-Chinese

2. Futuristic architecture in Singapore.

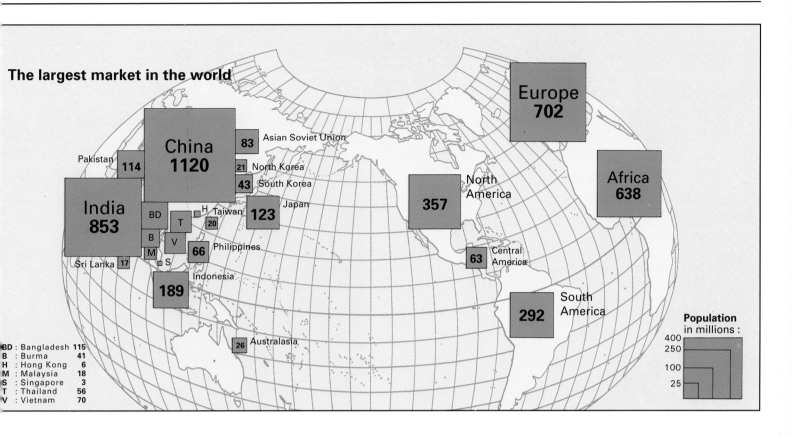

The largest market in the world

Europe
702

China
1120

Asian Soviet Union 83

Pakistan 114

North Korea 21

South Korea 43

Japan 123

India
853

BD

H Taiwan
T 20

Africa
638

North America
357

B
V

M
S

Philippines
66

Sri Lanka 17

Indonesia
189

Central America
63

South America
292

Australasia
26

Population in millions:
400
250
100
25

BD : Bangladesh 115
B : Burma 41
H : Hong Kong 6
M : Malaysia 18
S : Singapore 3
T : Thailand 56
V : Vietnam 70

---

llowed by the miraculous economic growth of Japan starting in the
960s, by the impressive industrial development of the four newly
ndustrialized Asian countries (NICs): South Korea, Taiwan, Hong
ong, Singapore—and by slower and more random industrialization
f Thailand, Malaysia, Indonesia, and the Philippines.

It was during the 1973-1982 decade that the growth of these
workshop" countries and of Japan broke all historical records, with
n average annual rate of 8% (North America, 2.7%; EEC, 1.9%). The
ndustrialization of the NICs was implemented along identical lines:
lanning by military and civilian technocracies that were powerful
omestically but were vulnerable to the advance of communism in

Asia, authoritarian control of proletarian labor and systematic exploitation of their low prices, massive inflow of foreign capital, the downward trend of some industries (consumer goods) and upward trend of other industries (raw materials and high-tech; semiconductors, data processing, telecommunications). Thus a new economic, technological, cultural, and political axis formed around the United States and Japan. The growth of technology and world industry shifted toward the "teletronic commonwealth" of the North Pacific in less than a half a century. The third Industrial Revolution was the first that did not start in the Atlantic states of Europe. The Greenwich Meridian has ceased to be the axis of the world.

---

dependence of Singapore.

9 August 1965

cord on the return of Hong Kong to the
eople's Republic of China in 1997.
86: End of F. Marcos' dictatorship in the
hilippines. C. Aquino becomes president
26 February.

Corazon Aquino's victory salute.

Sino-Japanese Peace and Friendship treaty

12 August 1978

1987: In Japan the balance of payments releases a surplus of $87 billion (twice that of the FRG).
10-26 June: In South Korea demonstrations and "peace marches" against President Chun and his designated successor Roh Tae Woo.
1988. 26 June: Matignon agreements between the RCPR and FLNKS on the future of New Caledonia.
1990. September: Start of normalization of Sino-Vietnamese relations.
24 October-1 November: The Burmese military junta crushes the democratic opposition that won the elections on 27 May.
1991: Soviet withdrawal fro mthe Indo-Chinese peninsula.
1992. 27-28 January: ASEAN Summit in Bangkok. Vietnam and Laos plan to join the association, which decides to create a free-trade zone in Southeast Asia over 15 years.

Anglo-Chinese Accord on Hong Kong

26 September 1984

Death of Hiro-Hito

7 January 1989

4. Diego Garcia American military base in the Indian Ocean.

Africa: The Problems of Independence

AFTER EXPERIENCING almost total subjection, most of the world's colonies acquired their independence within a few years: a new era began around 1960. In contrast, it is those areas where decolonization was not achieved that stand out: Portugal did not yield until 1974, White Rhodesia did not give way to Zimbabwe until 1980. The last wave is still continuing: White South Africa gave up Namibia in 1990 and is beginning to make changes itself.

But the simple listing of when independence was achieved and on what legal terms can be misleading. Relations of dependence, which are built into the world market, the political choices for investments, power interests and geopolitics, the distribution of technological expertise and ideologies, and linguistic necessities still remain. Neo-colonialism is not a policy like any other: it is the global situation of the age, though it takes different forms in different places, with varying implications and social costs. Moreover, two generations of colonization have dismantled and re-formed territories, societies and cultures. The new states have been unable to return to their pre-colonial traditions, and yet have found it equally hard to adopt the modern nation-state model of government, as this did not evolve from their own historical processes.

The moderate/revolutionary distinction, which is entirely a matter of ideology is inadequate for understanding an emerging political reality where the functions and absence of the state and the relation between a dispersed society and a concentrated political societ prevail. Ethnic particularisms are not stubborn vestiges of the pas they enable present-day social groups to affirm their identity i relation to current issues.

1. UN soldiers in the Congo 1961.

2. Guerrillas from Bissau, Guinea 1974.

Independence of Ghana.

Leopold Sedar Senghor.

1957

1960–1981

1947: Founding of the review *African Presence* under the aegis of Alioune Diop.
1956: First Congress of Representatives of Black Culture in Paris.
15–22. April 1958: Nkrumah calls the conference of Independent African States in Accra (Ghana), then the conference of African people.
1958–72: Rebellion in Southern Sudan. In 1972 the Nimeiri government recognizes its cultural and administrative autonomy.
3 March 1960: Rubgangwa the first black cardinal (Tanganyika).
1960–5: Clashes in Leopoldville, Congo; Katangan secession (11 July 1960–January 1963); assassination of Lumumba (17 January 1961); rebellion in the provinces; Western intervention; coupd'etat by Mobutu (24 November 1965).
1963–1964: Chou Enlai tours Africa.
22–23 May 1963: Creation of the OAU in Addis Abada.
1965: White independence in Southern Rhodesia. Uprising in Northern Chad; beginning of a series of still-existing troubles.

24 February 1966: Nkrumah ousted from power in Ghana.
1967: Nyerere expresses the socialist economic principles of Tanzania in a speech at Arusha.
1967–70: Secession of the Ibos (30 May 1967) in Nigeria; Biafra gives in (12 January 1970) after a terrible war.
1969: Siyad Barre comes to power in Somalia (21 October); socialist regime friendly to Russia (co-operation agreement, 1977); but geographic and political factors force him to seek American support (21 August 1980). Pan-African Festival, Algiers.
1969–73: Droughts and famines; political repercussions.
1969–85: Ganfar el-Nimeiri in the Sudan; political changes; he is outsted after demonstrations; provisional military Council.
18 May 1972: P. Tsiranana eliminated in Madagascar.
1973: UN and OAU recognize SWAPO (South West Africa People's Organization) as the sole representative of the Namibian people.
12 September 1974: Ethiopian revolution

4. The OAU conference at Lome in 1981. From left to right: E. Eyadéma, D. Dacko, A. Ahid F. Houphouet-Boigny

1950–92

Black Africa is a political arena for the great powers. France and reat Britain remain active and influential there, both by providing d and by initiating projects. They are present in the economic, ultural, military and political spheres, both in bilateral relations and rough large regroupings of states. The two super-powers have also eveloped their modes of intervention, the United States becoming assively involved, the USSR having a more discreet—and, initially . least, less successful—presence. The East-West confrontation in its ore pronounced form reached Africa around 1975, when the Por-uguese withdrawal and radicalization of the Ethiopian revolution ave the USSR and Cuba the opportunity to acquire a firm foothold . Ethiopia and Angola. But this communist support is beginning to isappear. Interests originating in Mediterranean Africa and the ear East also still exert considerable influence.

The decolonization process has gone against the Pan-African ideal. Vherever the union of states has not been achieved, regional, flexible r technological regroupings have been more successful. Since 1963 e Organization of African Unity (OAU) has offered all the African ates a structure for concerted action which provides a solid response a deeply felt aspiration, even though it also reveals the divisions etween its members and fails to settle all their differences.

The most serious internal and international tensions have involved neighbouring countries and external powers, namely: sharp conflicts in Congo-Kinshasa (1960–5); defeat of the Ibo secession in Nigeria; recurrent troubles in Chad; two uprisings in southern Sudan; rebellion in Eritrea (1961–1991); the strains on the Somali frontiers, too narrow for its large people; the destiny of the former Spanish Sahara; resistance movements in Angola and Mozambique; uprisings among apartheid's subjects; and the various forms of pressure exercised by South Africa on all her neighbours, most notably Angola, Zambia and Malawi. But the white stronghold had to give way and is now beginning to overhaul its structures; where this will lead is still uncertain. The 1990s were characterized by internal conflicts in Africa. Wars followed, some of which led to the brink of the total collapse of the state (Liberia, Somalia...). The almost dictatorial systems of many of the state-nations that resulted from independence were faced with serious issues in relation to food and politics: some truly liberalized, many resisted or conceded to some form of pacifying and superficial multiparty system and political debate. These aspirations and the beginnings of democracy, in any case, ran up against the limits of the very restricted room for manouevering that the African countries have on the economic level in the world order.

First Black ghetto uprising in Soweto, 16 June 1976.

li Amin ruler of Uganda.	Independence of Mozambique.	Race riots in Soweto.	independence of Zimbabwe.	Independence of Namibia
971–80	**25 June 1975**	**June 1976**	**18 April 1980**	**21 March 1990**

itiated by the army; deposition of Emperor aile Selassie; land reform.
975: Malagasy socialist revolutionary harter. Inauguration of Tanzam (Tanzania-ambia) Railway built by the Chinese, pening south west Zambia economically nd providing an outlet for Zambian copper.
975–6: Spanish withdrawal from the ahara: shared between Morocco, the olisario Front and Mauritania: complex ilitary and political development: Republic f the Western Sahara recognized and isputed.
976: Uprising in Soweto, a Black African uburb of Johannesburg (South Africa). eturn to multi-party system in Sengal einforced in 1983) which had been ejected in 1966.
1 February 1977: Mengistu takes over in thiopia: the USSR supports his regime.
977–8: Ogaden war between Somalia and thiopia.
980: First intensive raids by South Africa nto Angola.
984: Death of Sékou Touré in Guinea and nd of his rule. Signing of a cease fire

between South Africa and Angola; Nkomoti agreement: Mozambique and South Africa agree not to support action against each other.
27 March 1987: Recapturing of Faya-Largeau, last stronghold held by Libyans in

Northern Chad. Cease-fire between Colonel Qaddafi and Hissène Habré on 11 September.
April 1988: Erytrean Af-Abed victory over the Ethiopian army, which begins to implode.

1990. 11 February: Nelson Mandela, leader of the African National Congress liberated in South Africa.
7 August: Pretoria Agreement between the South African government and the ANC: the ANC halts the armed conflict.
1991. 27 January: General Zaid Barre driven from power in Somalia.
February–June: Main legislative pillars of apartheid torn down.
21 May: In Ethiopia Mengistu's government falls as a result of several rebel fronts.
31 May: Cease-fire agreement between the president of Angola, J.E. Dos Santos, and J. Savimbi, leader of the UNITA rebels.
17 March 1992: The white community in South Africa approves the reformist policies of president F. de Klerk in a referendum.

5. An artist's evocation of the massacres under the regime of A. S. Shagari, Nigeria 1981.

The Third World and Third World Independence Movements

In 1952, ALFRED SAUVY, drawing an analogy with the Third Estate in 1789, called those states and peoples who belonged neither to the West nor to the East the "Third World." Today, the term is occasionally used in the plural to emphasize the heterogenous nature of the different countries involved. Sometimes it is rejected altogether because the Third World will never be a unity, or a force, or an autonomous political entity. The idea of the Third World has always merely been a utopia. The argument about an appropriate expression to be used in connection with a changing reality that is difficult to define, causes a genuine problem for close to 4 billion people to shape their own history.

1. Aswan Dam in Egypt.

The Third World movement, as set out at its moment of inception at Bandung (1955), was anticolonialist and neutralist. Its aim was to bring together dominated peoples and states in the common defence of their territorial integrity and their political interests, to influence the relations between states and the work of international agencies in order that greater priority be given to developmental issues. In the 1960s the Cuban revolution, the independence of Algeria, the guerrillas in South America, the war in Vietnam, and the Palestinian movement gave rise to radical and "tricontinental" trends.

Several key ideas defined this theory of twentieth-century revolution. It was argued that the peasant masses, the "wretched of the earth," constituted a huge force; "power comes out of the barrel of a gun," and there must be more Vietnams, and more centers of insurrection must be created (Che Guevara's *focos*). "The global countryside" had to surround the "global city" (Mao Tse-Tung): the internationalism of the three continents became the main focus of the

2. The dry season near Makanah, in Senegal.

Bandung Conference.	Formation of the Organization of African Unity.	War in Biafra.	Anti-imperalist coup d'etat in Ethiopia.	L.S. Senghor: *Elégies majeure*
17–24 April 1955	25 May 1963	July 1967–January 1970	12 September 1974	19

April 1951: Mosaddeq nationalizes Iranian oil.
17–24 April 1955: Bandung Conference brings together 29 Third World countries for the first time and adopts a charter (equality of races and nations, special United Nations Development Fund). The symbolic personalities of Nehru, Tito, Sukarno, and Nasser are brought to the attention of the world.
1960: Sino-Soviet split. China rejects the notion of peaceful coexistence and claims leadership of the 'storm zone' between the two superpowers.
1961. 17 January: Patrice Lumumba, the figurehead of the independence and unity of the Congo, is assassinated. He becomes the first martyr of the Third World.
1–6 September: Conference of the nonaligned in Belgrade. The 25 initial countries increased to 95 at the meeting in Havana in 1979. At the United Nations U Thant becomes its first non-Western Secretary General (3 November).
22–28 October 1962: Cuban Missile Crisis. The Soviet Union backs down in the face of

American protests and the image of 'Castroism' suffers its first blow.
3–15 January 1966: Conference of Solidarity between the peoples of Africa, Asia and Latin America held in Havana. It puts forward the idea of a revolutionary Third World movement spreading beyond the boundaries of individual countries.
May 1968: Protest movement is born of the struggle against American involvement in Vietnam and solidarity with the Third World.
25 October 1971: The People's Republic of China is admitted to the United Nations. Taiwan is expelled.
1975: Victory of the Khmer Rouge in Cambodia (17 April). The Vietcong arrive in Saigon on 30 April after 11 years of American involvement.
1975–6: Start of Vietnamese involvement in bordering countries: Laos, then Cambodia. Tension grows with China.
1979: Shah of Iran is overthrown (16 January). Ayatollah Khomeini returns to Tehran on 1 February. The Islamic Revolution announces upheavals in the

muslim states (Khartoum revolution in 1985) and demonstrates the ability of fundamentalism to mobilize the population.
1980: Start of the Iran-Iraq war. UNESCO adopts a report calling for a 'new world order' in information. This is opposed by the Western states.
1982: Falklands War between Argentina and Great Britain. In August the PLO is forced out of Lebanon.
1983: 146 national liberation organizations are counted in the Third World. Nigeria decides to deport one and a half million immigrants (17 January).
1984. June: The issue of immigration is used extensively in the campaign debates leading to the European elections in France.
31 October: Indira Ghandi assassinated by Sikhs. Clashes between communites in India.
1985: Vatican condemns the liberation theology. In Latin America democracy spreads to the detriment of military governments: Following Argentina (December 1983), presidential elections held in Brazil (January) and in El Salvador.

25 February 1986: F. Marcos' dictatorship in the Philippines ends.
9 December 1987: Start of the Intifada (War of Rocks) in the Israeli occupied territories.
14 April 1988: Agreement on the withdrawal of Soviet troops from Afghanistan.
May-June 1989: Beijing "Spring".
11 February 1990: Nelson Mandela set free in South Africa.
1991. 17 January–27 February: Gulf War.
27 June: In South Africa, president F. de Klerk signs the abolition of the last laws supporting apartheid.
11 January 1992: In Algeria a coup d'etat deprives the ISF (Islamic Salvation Front) of probable victory in the parliamentary elections.

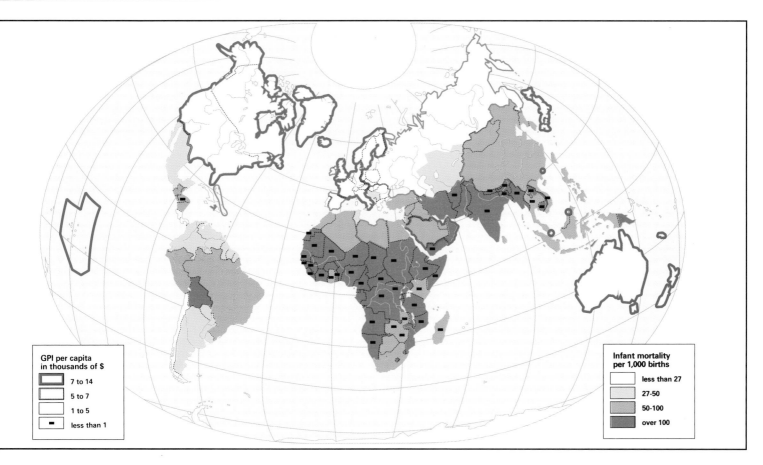

GPI per capita
in thousands of $

7 to 14
5 to 7
1 to 5
less than 1

Infant mortality
per 1,000 births

less than 27
27-50
50-100
over 100

ti-imperalist struggle. The Third World was inventing new storical paths, new models of development, creating a ''new Man,'' exemplified by the Chinese Cultural Revolution.

This body of doctrine did not survive beyond the 1970s. The Third orld countries do not constitute a unified geopolitical bloc due to e extreme diversity of their social structures, their cultures, and story—each of which has its own specific differences. In addition, e situations of the various countries have become increasingly verse because of economic strategies and different experiences and sults. On the one hand, there are oil-producing countries and, on e other, countries that suffer from oil crises, on the one hand untries suffering from famines and, on the other, new industrial untries.... Finally, wars between the forces of the same ideologies

demonstrate the ancient ethnic tensions and the *Realpolitik* that inspires the States. In the absence of a global plan and clear leadership, neither tricontinentalism nor neutrality are sufficiently unifying forces. Contrary to the prophecies, Marxist revolutions often established tropical gulags, or they failed. The weakness of democratic traditions, the oppression of minorities, the political importance of the military, and bureaucracies: the totalitarian state is the largest current problem, and human rights remain the key issue.

Finally, did the Gulf War announce a new type of South-North conflict? Though the idea of a Third World was born, in fact, due to the conflict between the free and the communist world, and though the communist bloc has collapsed, the North-South problems continue to be greater than ever.

Restoration of democracy in Brazil.

1985

4. The encirclement of the capitalist world as viewed by Chinese propaganda.

4 April 1955: Bandung Conference, the leaders latform.

The Indian Union since Independence

AT THE VERY MOMENT of independence, the Indian subcontinent began to break up. The first step in this process was the partition of India and Pakistan. In spite of Gandhi and Nehru, who were both passionately committed to national unity, the Muslim League, under the leaderhsip of Ali Jinnah, achieved its aim of setting up a separate Pakistan, 'the country of the pure', in those territories, in the Indus basin and in Bengal, where the majority of the population were Muslims. The partition sparked off several massacres of minority groups, and led to considerable waves of emigration: 7 million Muslims left the Indian Union to take refuge in Pakistan, and 5 million Hindus and Sikhs left Pakistan for the Indian Union. But while Pakistan became an almost exclusively Muslim country, the Indian Union retained a large Muslim minority (one tenth of the population). In addition, the princely states (of which there were 562) occupied 45% of the territory of the Indian Union. The task of absorbing these different states into one and creating a solid and homogeneous federation was undertaken by Patel and brough to completion by 1956. The basic principle was that the different federal states should coincide with language areas. The federal language itself is English, though periodic attempts have been made to include Hindi as well, but this has always been rejected by the southern states. India is proud of its reputation as the largest democracy in the world. Each state has its own assembly, directly elected by universal suffrage, as well as its own government. The people also vote for the lower house of the central parliament (Lok Sabha), and the state assemblies choose a state chamber (Rajya Sabha). The central government is accountable to these twin chambers. In cases of emergency it can dissolve a state assembly and impose the President's rule, and the procedure has often been used. India remains a member of the Commonwealth. Its constitution, carrying on the work of Gandhi, makes it illegal to discriminate on grouds of religion, race or caste. The avowed goal of the government and the administration has been to abolish 'untouchability' and, by a system of quotas and facilities for university admission, to promote the integration of the disadvantaged castes. Marriage laws and laws concerning inheritance provide, at least in theory, for equality between the sexes. To these provisions must be added measures, which, in the spirit of Nehru, aimed both to reduce social inequality and to expand production: for instance the huge complex of agrarian reforms (abolition of the *zamindar* system, in which the landowner was also responsible for collecting taxes; the setting of a maximum limit for the ownership of lands and the various attempts made to eliminate the problem of absentee landlords).

These were the ideals that inspired the founders. What effect did they have in practice? Admittedly, the goals were not fully realized, and features of underdevelopment certainly continue to exist: the excessive growth of the population (361 million in 1951, 797 million in 1988), the predominantly rural nature of the country (70%), vulnerability to natural disasters (droughts, floods), the extreme poverty of a large section of the population, the often corrupt and inefficient administration, the undermining of the democratic system by system of patronage and the disproportionate influence wielded by special interest groups. In some rural areas, the untouchables are over exploited and are also the victims of physical violence. Slave labour has not yet entirely disappeared everywhere and the village money lender remains a powerful figure. And yet, India has become one of the great nations of the world. It has been able to maintain its territorial integrity and its unity, despite all the forces working against it, the democratic system (except for the interlude of the State of Emergency) has worked properly, and the numerous and often violent clashes between different ethnic groups and religious communities have not challenged the secular character of the institutions of the state. Due, above all, to the development of irrigation and technical innovation of the 'Green Revolution', the production of food has increased more quickly than the population (120% as compared to 90%), and India seems free of famine and enjoys self sufficiency in food production. The road network has been extended five-fold. Production of electricity tripled between 1970 and 1990 and went from 68 to 200 million FET. The modernization of rural areas and the development of industry have created a powerful and varied bourgeoisie. India exports not only industrial products, but also qualified workers, engineers, and "brains." A fresh Indian exodus has joined that, already centuries old, of its shopkeepers and tradesmen. Finally, up to the present, India has been able to follow course of diplomacy which has allowed it to assert itself as a dominant force in the region, to be a leader for the countries of the South, and to survive the oil crises and the upheavals caused by the disintegration of the Soviet bloc unharmed.

1. A meeting in support of Bangladesh.

First Five-Year Plan: irrigation construction, beginning of agrarian reform.

The Bandung Conference: India emerges as leader of the Third World.

Second Five-Year Plan: heavy industry.

1951–6

1955

1956–61

15 August 1947: British India is granted independence and partitioned: the Indian Union and Pakistan are formed.
30 January 1948: A Hindu fanatic assassinates Gandhi.
26 January 1950: Constitution of the Indian Union promulgated.
1952: First general elections. The victory of the Congress Party is overwhelming. Nehru remains prime minister.
1954: Sino-Indian Agreement. Nehru and Chou En-lai proclaim the 'Five Principles of Peaceful Coexistence'. France's territories in India are transferred to the Indian Union. Pakistan joins the Southeast Asia Treaty Organization (SEATO).
1957: The Congress Party is once more victorious in the elections, except in Kerala, where the Communists are swept to power.
1958: General Ayub Khan takes power in Pakistan.
1959: The central government dissolves the State Assembly in Kerala and imposes the President's rule.

2. Offerings after the death of Nehru in 1964.

1961: The Indian Army forces the Portuguese to leave Goa.
1962: War breaks out along the Himalayan frontier between China and India. China shows its superior strength.
1964: Death of Nehru, 27 May. He is succeeded by Lai Bahadur Shastri.
1966: Shastri dies in Tashkent during the conference called to settle the conflict between India and Pakistan over Kashmir. Indira Gandhi, Nehru's daughter, becomes prime minister.
1967: Elections. The Congress Party wins in national parliament, but in the majority of state assemblies various opposition parties are elected. Split in Communist Party: the rightist "Marxist" faction heads the governments of Kerala and Bengal. The Maoist Party of "Naxalities" engages in guerrilla warfare in Bengal.
1968: The policy of five-year plans is abandoned. Greater support is given to private capital. The 'Green Revolution' enables the country to become self-sufficient in wheat.

1969: The banks are nationalized. Indira Gandhi has the right wing of the Congress Party expelled. In Pakistan, Yahya Khan takes power.
1971: Indira Gandhi wins the elections after campaigning with the slogan 'Eliminate Poverty'. Friendship treaty signed with the Soviet Union. East Pakistan rebels, India intervenes, defeats the Pakistani army and sees the setting up of an independent Bangladesh. In Sri Lanka, the rising of revolutionary youth violently quelled.
1972: Relations with Pakistan are restored. Zulfikar Ali Bhutto sets about reorganizing Pakistan after the war over Bangladesh. His aim will be to sever the country's links with the Americans.
1974: In May India explodes its first nuclear device.
1975: Indira Gandhi declares a State of Emergency. Elections are put off for a year, civil rights are suspended, and her opponents are put in prison.
1977: Elections. The Janata party, created by a follower of Ghandi, Jayaprakash Narayan, takes power. Morarji Desai, a strict Hindu,

One India or several ?

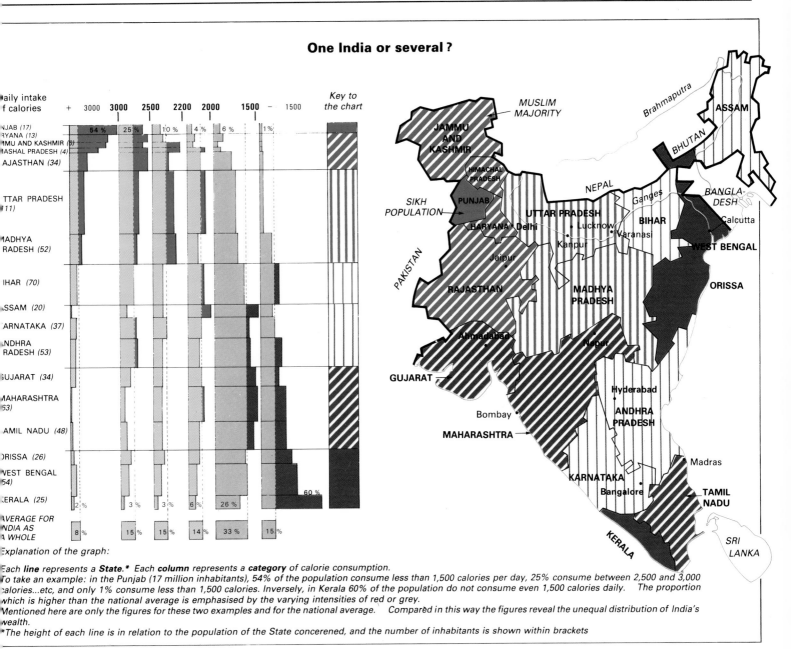

Daily intake of calories

Key to the chart

	+ 3000	**3000**	**2500**	**2200**	**2000**	**1500**	– 1500
PUNJAB (17)	54 %	25 %	10 %	4 %	6 %	1 %	
HARYANA (13)							
JAMMU AND KASHMIR (6)							
HIMACHAL PRADESH (4)							
RAJASTHAN (34)							
UTTAR PRADESH (111)							
MADHYA PRADESH (52)							
BIHAR (70)							
ASSAM (20)							
KARNATAKA (37)							
ANDHRA PRADESH (53)							
GUJARAT (34)							
MAHARASHTRA (63)							
TAMIL NADU (48)							
ORISSA (26)							
WEST BENGAL (54)							
KERALA (25)	2 %	3 %	3 %	6 %	26 %	60 %	
AVERAGE FOR INDIA AS A WHOLE	8 %	15 %	15 %	14 %	33 %	15 %	

Explanation of the graph:

*Each **line** represents a **State**.* Each **column** represents a **category** of calorie consumption. To take an example: in the Punjab (17 million inhabitants), 54% of the population consume less than 1,500 calories per day, 25% consume between 2,500 and 3,000 calories...etc, and only 1% consume less than 1,500 calories. Inversely, in Kerala 60% of the population do not consume even 1,500 calories daily. The proportion which is higher than the national average is emphasised by the varying intensities of red or grey. Mentioned here are only the figures for these two examples and for the national average. Compared in this way the figures reveal the unequal distribution of India's wealth.*

*The height of each line is in relation to the population of the State concerened, and the number of inhabitants is shown within brackets

---

Third Five-Year Plan for the development of anciliary industries for agriculture.	**The 'Green Revolution' begins.** **The policy of Five-Year Plans is abandoned.**	**India begins exporting technical goods.**	**Increased separatist agitation.**
1961–6	**1968**	**1980**	**Since November 1984**

...becomes president (March). In Pakistan, General Zia ul-Haq deposes Ali Bhutto who is sentenced to death and hanged in 1979. The new regime intends to create a "truly Islamic" state.
1980: After a series of political crises, the central parliament is dissolved, and the elections see the triumphant, though unexpected, return to power of Indira Gandhi.
1984: Sikh nationalists in the Punjab embark on a policy of insurrection and terrorism. The Golden Temple in Amritsar, held by militants is stormed and taken by Indian Army. Consequence: on 31 October, Indira Ghandi is assassinated by one of her Sikh body-guards. She is succeeded by her son Rajiv Ghandi. At the end of December, new elections give him a clear victory.
3 December 1984: In Bhopal, toxic gases escaping from a chemical plant cause the deaths of thousands of local inhabitants.
October 1987: Intervention of Indian troops in Sri Lanka to separate the Tamils and the Sinhalese.

December 1988: In Pakistan Benazir Bhutto, Ali Bhutto's daughter, succeeds to power.
1989: Unrest among the muslims of India as a result of the publication of Salman Rushdie's *Satanic Verses*.
18 September: The government of Sri Lanka succeeds in attaining the withdrawal of Indian troops that had invaded the Island in 1987 to act as barrier between the Tamils and Singhalese.
November: Rajiv Ghandi defeated in the elections. A Janata government, headed by V.P. Singh, is established with the help of the communists.
30 October 1990: Huge demonstration at Ayodhya, holy place of Hinduism, to secure the destruction of a mosque. Fundamentalist Hinduism becomes a political force.
1991. 13 March: Dissolution of parliament.
21 May: Rajiv Ghandi is assassinated at an election rally: the crime is ascribed to Tamil separatists.
12–15 June: Parliamentary elections; relative victory of Congress Party.

3. Gandhi in 1947.

4. A Sikh demonstration, 1984.

War in Southeast Asia

TOWARDS THE END OF THE 1950s, with the rivalry between the superpowers having crossed the nuclear threshold, and with the beginnings of détente in Europe, the axis of international conflict shifted to Southeast Asia. The geopolitical notion of 'Southeast Asia' only appeared around 1942, but this 'corner of Asia' had in reality been an unsettled part of the world for many years. In the nineteenth century the region was at once the most profitable area for the colonial expansion of classic imperialism (Great Britain, France, the Netherlands) and the theatre for their confrontation with China. From 1925–30 strong communist parties were at work while the peasantry in Java, the Philippines, and Vietnam lapsed into under-development and poverty. The overthrow of the European colonial empires by the Japanese between 1940 and 1945, the First Indochina War and the painful process of decolonization in Indonesia and Burma numerous important issues were concentrated in this region: the future of the French Union, the nature of the social hegemony in the new states, opportunities for neutralism, the credibility of the models of national construction and development that the United States wished to see imposed in the Third World, power relations between the United States, the USSR, and China. The Indochina War became a 'world war fought on local territory'.

At the centre of the conflict was Vietnam. After the collapse of the plans for unification of the country provided for in the Geneva Accords of 1954, which Washington refused to support, the war resumed in the south of the country. From 1955 the government led by Ngo Dinh Diem, with US backing, tackled the task of annihilating the communist opposition. In 1958 the National Liberation Front (NLF) was set up, and its guerilla army made rapid progress. Diem, unable to deal with it and tempted by neutrality, was overthrown in 1963 as a result of pressure from Washington, which sought through massive intervention to create a military state in South Vietnam similar to that in South Korea. The massive communist offensive at Tet in 1968 put an end to American policies, which had already been paralyzed by the antiwar movement in the United States and throughout the world. As a result, negotiations began in Paris.

It was feared that the whole region would become embroiled in the Indochinese conflict. This is indeed what happened to Laos after 1959, and to Cambodia in 1970. At the same time as large sections of the previously powerful Indonesian Communist Party were being massacred by the government, communist guerillas were gaining ground in Thailand, and the Maoist 'New People's Army' was formed in the Philippines. The need to stop this process led the Nixon-Kissinger administration to negotiate directly with Beijing in 1971—which thus saw its own Indonesian ambitions recognized—and to "Vietnamize" the conflict by exacerbating the tensions that existed between the Indochinese and Chinese communists. The war in Vietnam thus culminated in a conflict where the fronts were reversed, in the establishment of the bloodthirsty pro-Chinese Pol Pot regime in Phnom Penh (between 1 and 2 million dead), in the expansion of Soviet influence throughout the rest of the peninsula of Indochina, and, finally, in a war that, despite the intervention of Beijing (Peking) ended with the transformation of Kampuchea (Cambodia

1. *Vietnam in 1967: Vietcong prisoners during the battle for the Mekong Delta.*

Ho Chi Minh proclaims the independence of Vietnam.	Dien Bien Phu.	Communist Tet Offensive.	Paris Conference.	North-Vietnamese troops enter Saigon.
2 September 1945	**7 May 1954**	**January—March 1968**	**May 1968—March 1973**	**30 April 1975**

1926: Workers' uprising organized by the Communist Party (PKI, Parti Kominis Indonesia) in Java.
1930–1: Indochinese Communist party formed, village 'Soviets' set up in Nghe Tinh (North Annam). Peasant revolt in Burma.
1940–5: Overthrow of the colonial powers by the Japanese, and various countries declare their independence. In Indochina, the August 1945 Revolution leads to the proclamation of the Democratic Republic of Vietnam under the leadership of Ho Chi Minh (25 September). Anti-Japanese independence fronts are formed by the Communist Parties in Malaysia, the Philippines and Burma.
19 December 1946: Indochina War (Battle of Hanoi).
1946–9: Dutch fail to reconquer Indonesia, which becomes independent under President Sukarno.
1948–60: Emergency declared in Malaysia—the British put down the communist guerrillas. In the Philippines the Hukbalahap movement is put down. In Burma communist insurrection and uprising

by minorities.
7 December 1949: Chinese People's Army reaches the borders of Indochina.
1954. 7 May: Defeat of the French at Dien Bien Phu.
20–1 July: Geneva Accords on Indochina.
March 1958: The NLF is formed in South Vietnam and the war resumes.
July 1959: War resumes in Laos.
1 November 1963: Ngo Dinh Diem is toppled and assassinated. He is followed by a succession of military governments (Nguyen Van Thieu in 1965) in South Vietnam.
1965. 31 July: Tonkin Gulf Incident leads to American escalation of the conflict in Vietnam.
1 October: Indonesian communists massacred in "Operation Gestapo".
1968. 31 January–beginning of March: In Vietnam, communist Tet Offensive launched against 33 towns (including Hue) and the Battle of Khe Sanh (21 January) takes place in the Central Highlands.
1968–70: Phoenix plan in Vietnam: the destruction of the communist network in the South.

2. *Indonesian communist survivors in Salembra prison in 1965.*

18 March 1970: In Cambodia, Prince Sihanouk is overthrown in a coup. Lon Nol takes power.
21–8 February 1972: President Nixon visits China.
27 January and 2 March 1973: Paris Accords: Cease-fire in South Vietnam, gradual reunification of country, American withdrawal.
1975. 9 March: North Vietnamese military offensive in Ban Me Thuot; military collapse of the Saigon regime.
17 April: The Khmer Rouge enter Phnom Penh. The deportation of town populations to the country begins.
30 April: The North Vietnamese Army takes Saigon.
1976: Socialist Republic of Vietnam: incidents start between the Khmer Rouge and the Vietnamese (diplomatic relations are broken off on 31 December 1977).
1978. June: Beginning of the exodus of the Vietnamese 'boat people'.
1979. 1 January: Vietnamese army launches an offensive against Kampuchea.

to a ''sister republic'' of Viet[n]am in 1979.

China henceforth had to con[te]nt itself with 'bleeding Viet[n]am dry' by arming the Khmer [r]ouge guerillas. With the excep[ti]on of the Philippines, the com[m]unist guerilla movement in [s]outheast Asia began to lose [gr]ound, and the 'corner of Asia' [fo]und itself firmly cordoned off. [T]he disintegration of the USSR [in] 1990–1991 left Vietnam—[w]hose shores were strategically [im]portant for ports on the Indian [Oc]ean—drained, isolated, and [un]protected. Hanoi was forced [to] withdraw from Kampuchea in [19]89 and, two years later, to [ac]cept the Paris Agreement on [th]e settlement of the Kampu[ch]ean conflict, to seek help from [th]e West, and to normalize rela[ti]ons with Beijing, and, finally, [to] request entry into ASEAN [(A]ssociation of Southeast Asian [N]ations) in 1992. In Southeast [As]ia, revolutions connected with [de]colonization turned into con[fl]icts between states, communism [ha]d certainly won the wars in [In]dochina but it had destroyed [pe]ace in the process.

[V]ietnamese troops enter Phnom Penh.

7 January 1979

[1]7 February–beginning March: Chinese [m]ilitary offensive in North Vietnam.

[1]8 February: Kampuchea concludes treaty [w]ith Hanoi.

[1]3 March: Treaty signed between [K]ampuchea and Laos.

[2]–4 December 1987: First meeting [b]etween Prince Sihanouk and the [K]ampuchean Prime Minister Hun Sen.

[2]6 September 1989: Last Vietnamese [tr]oops leave Kampuchea.

[5]–7 September 1990: Secret visit to China [b]y Secretary General of the Vietnamese [C]ommunist Party in preparation for Sino-[V]ietnamese rapprochement.

[2]3 October 1991: International Agreement [s]igned in Paris on the settlement of the [K]ampuchean conflict.

Far East before 1942

Colonial possessions

1942-1945

Japanese invasion

1945-1980

Wars
Independent States

The Korean War 1950-1953

P'yongyang
NORTH KOREA
38°
Seoul
SOUTH KOREA
Sept. 50
Pusan
June 1950

Yalu
Nov. 50
Wonsan
Inch'on

CHINA
Jan. 51

P'anmunjom
Armistice
1953
April 1951

500 km

First Indochina War (French period: 1945-1954)

Lao Cai
Cao Bang
Dien Bien Phu
Lang Son
Hanoi
Haiphong
Luang Prabang
TONKIN
LAOS
Vientiane
ANNAM
Mekong
Hue 17°
Bangkok
Angkor
CAMBODIA
Dalat
Phnom Penh
Saigon
COCHINCHINA

Regions controlled by the Viet Minh in 1954
✕ Battles

American Period 1956-76

Hanoi
Xam Nua
Vinh
Ho Chi Minh Trail
Khe San
Da Nang
An Khe
Ban Me Thuot
Cam Ran
Saigon

● American Bases
Areas Bombed

War between communists

Refugee camps 1979-1982

Xiang Khoang
Hanoi
Hong Kong
Nong Khai
Paracel Islands
PHILIPPINES
Manila
Si Khiu
Ubon
Sa Kaeo
VIETNAM
Bataan
Bangkok
KAMPUCHEA
Khmers rouges
Leam Sing
Ho Chi Minh City
Palawan
Songkhla
MALAYSIA
Kuala Lumpur
Pulau Redang
Pulau Tenggol
Anambas
Kuching
SARAWAK
Singapore
Pulau Bintan
BORNEO
SUMATRA
INDONESIA
Jakarta

500 km

Refugee camps (according to G. Condominas)

Vietnamese   Boat People   Khmers   Hmong   Lao

The Muslim World

A TENDENCY to try to remedy social ills by recourse to ethical and religious norms is a recurring feature of Muslim societies in time of crisis. The rise of Islamic fundamentalism, which is often referred to rather hastily as the 'political awakening of Islam', follows in this tradition. The steady forward march of secularization has not reduced the importance of religion, which continues, as before, to provide the terms by which the political authorities are judged.

The 'Islamic revolution' in Iran and the religious political movements which have put Islam at the centre of the world stage are, in the main, the consequence of a threefold failure: that of the reformist body of opinion within Islam, that of the nation-state, and that of the major economic models of our time, free-market capitalism and state socialism.

Since the eighteenth century the Muslim countries have seen a number of broad popular uprisings take place which were inspired and led by puritanical reformers such as Muhammad ibn 'Abd al-Wahhab (1703-97) in the Arabian Peninsula, Muhammad Ahmad ibd 'Ali al-Sanusi (1787-1857) in Libya, and Mahdi Muhammad Ahmad ibn Abd Allah in the Sudan. In each case the purpose of the uprising was to restore the true faith and to lay the foundations for a political order which would carry out divine law. The modern states of Saudi Arabia, Libya and the Sudan have their roots in these movements.

At the end of the nineteenth century a major attempt was made b the Persian Jamal al-Din al-Afghani (1838-97) and the Egyptia Muhammad 'Abduh (1849-1905) to reform Islam and to awaken th Muslim peoples. Their aim was to respond to the challenge c Western colonial power and to restore to Islam the 'splendours of it early greatness'. They had the effect of preparing the way for futur nationalist movements throughout the Islamic world, from India t Morocco.

Confronted with the tasks of modernization and economi development, the newly independent Muslim states—since Ataturk abolition of the Caliphate in 1924—had been unable to emancipat themselves from religious ideology or to find an original course t follow. From 1928 onward, the association of the Muslim Brother hood appealed to the spontaneous beliefs of the masses and ushered i the age of fundamentalist protest against the secular modern stat and compromises made between the ruling groups and the imperialis powers. On the eve of the Nasserite revolution (1952), it was the mos powerful movement in Egypt and had followers in most of the Ara countries.

The rise of Arab nationalism, anti-imperialist and largely populis in emphasis, eclipsed for two decades all other politico-religiou movements in the Middle East. But defeat in the Arab-Israeli war i June 1967, together with the death of Nasser (1970), left the wa open for the return of religious activism, usually supported by Saud Arabia and even by Pakistan. Nevertheless, the eruption of th "Islamic Revolution" in Iran which allowed the Shi'ite religiou hierarchy to seize power and to install a regime in keeping with th ideals of the followers of Islam, ushered in a new era in the history o the Muslim world.

During the 1980s, the countries of Magreb and Sudan were th primary victims of the politico-religious conflicts. The Islamic Tendency Movement (later to became the *Al-Nahda*, the "Renais sance," after the arrival of President Ben Ali) in Tunisia and th Islamic Salvation Front in Algeria followed a strategy of seizing power and jeopardized the "democratic beginnings" of President Ben Ali and Chadli.

They are now running into harsh repression, while their ghos continues to haunt the political scene. In the Sudan, General E Bechir's military coup (30 June 1989) made it possible for Hassar Turabi's National Islamic Front to take control of the country and t become the focus of a new Islamic "international," which ha become hostile to Saudi Arabia and close to Iran since the Americar intervention in the Gulf. However, the goals of the Arab Islamic movements (Sunni) and those of the Iranian Shi'ite state are by fa not the same.

1. Trial of the Muslim Brotherhood in Cairo 1954.

Ottoman caliphate abolished.	Attempt on Nasser's life by the Muslim Brotherhood.	Coup d'état of Colonel Qadhafi in Libya.	Formation of the 'Amal'.
1924	**1954**	**September 1969**	**1975**

March 1924: Mustafa Kemal Pasa, President of the Turkish Republic, abolishes the Ottoman caliphate. Abd al-Aziz III Ibn Sa'ud (Ibn Sa'ud) drives Sharif Hussayn from Mecca.
1926: Failure of the caliphate congress in Cairo and in Mecca.
1928: Association of Muslim Brotherhood (AMB) is formed in Egypt.
1932: Ibn Sa'ud becomes King of Saudi Arabia (died 1953).
1941: Association of Muslims is formed in what is to become Pakistan.
1948: Egyptian Prime Minister an-Nuqrashi is assassinated.
1949: The Supreme Guide of the Muslim Brotherhood is murdered as an act of reprisal.
1952: In Jordan, the Islamic Liberation Party (ILP) is first formed.
1954: Attempt on Nasser's life. The Muslim Brotherhood is dissolved, and five of its leaders executed.
December 1958: Shi'ite religious leaders react strongly against the introduction of 'foreign ideas' into Iraq.

2. Nasser on the walls of the Aswan Dam which was opened in 1964.

1963: Pro-Islamic activist groups formed in Syria. In Iran, there are demonstrations against the Shah.
1964. April: In Algiers, Sheikh Bashir el-Ibrahimi attacks socialism.
4 November: The Shah forces Ayatollah Khomeini into exile.
1965: In Tehran, Ali Shariati is the new influential force within Islam.
1966: In Egypt, Sayyid Qutub, the leading theoretician of the Muslim Brotherhood is executed.
1968: The shi'ite group al-Da'wa is formed in Iraq. Wave of arrests of Islamic activists in Turkey.
22 October 1973: Imam Sadr founds the "Movement of the Deprived" in Lebanon. In Syria, Hafez el-Assad (Hafiz al-Assad) abandons the secular state.
1975: "Amal" formed as a military wing of the Movement of the Deprived. Shi'ite riots in Iraq. Civil war in Lebanon.
1977: In Cairo, pro-Islamic terrorists kidnap and murder Sheikh Dahabi, spokesman for official Islam.

3. A suicide squad demonstrates in Iran. January 1984.

1. Western Europe
2. Eastern Europe less (3)
3. Albania, Bulgaria, Yugoslavia
4. USSR less the Caucasus and (6)
5. Caucasus
6. Kazakhstan, Kirgiziya, Tadzhikistan, Turkmenistan, Uzbekistan
7. Lebanon
8. Israel

2000 km

	Muslim areas		Sunnites		Secular states		Muslim population
Areas with Muslim minorities		Shi'ites		Islamic states		non-Muslim population
	Kurds

100
50
20
10
2

millions of inhabitants

President Sadat assassinated.

6 October 1981

Death of Khomeini.

3 June 1989

1979: Khomeini in Iran; Islamic Revolution (January–February). The Mosque at Mecca is occupied by fundamentalists. N. Nuass founds the Party of God in Senegal. Several uprisings against the communists in Afghanistan; Soviet invasion (27 December).
1980: Violent clashes in Aleppo. About a thousand Islamic activists are massacred in Palmyra Prison.
6 October 1981: The al-Jihad group assassinates Anwar al-Sadat. Creation of the Islamic Tendency Movement in Tunisia.
1982: In Syria, test of strength between the army and the Islamic activists at Hamah. Allegedly there were 30,000 civilian casualties.
1983: Islamic activists demonstrate in Algiers. Islamic law (*Charia*) in applied in Sudan.
1985: In Khartoum Sheikh Muhammad Taha who opposed the implementation of *Charia* is executed. Nimayri's government is overthrown.
7 November 1987: Removal of Bourgiba by Zine el Abidine Ben Ali.
October 1988: Bloody riots in Algeria. Putting them down ends in hundreds of deaths. Islamic leaders appear in the open.
1989: Democratic reforms in Algeria.
30 June: Pro-Islamic military coup in Sudan.
June 1990: FIS asserts itself as the leading political party in Algeria as a result of municipal elections.
1991. 17 January–28 February: Gulf War. Islamic movements support Iraq and denounce Western intervention.
26 December: FIS wins the first round of parliamentary elections.
1992. 11 January: The army suspends the electoral process in Algeria.
4 March: Dissolution of FIS.

4. The attack on the American Embassy in Beirut, 18 April 1983.

5. Kurdish guerrillas in Iran, May 1985.

Wars in the Middle East

1. *Egyptian president Anwar Sadat in Jerusalem with Israeli prime minister Menachim Begin, November 1977.*

- ⌒⌒ Israeli boundaries 1949
- • • Palestinian refugee camps
- ⋯•⋯ Kibbutzim

- Shi'ites
- Christians
- Alawites
- Druzes

El Quantara
Ismailia — Suez Canal — Port
Suez
Gulf of Suez
Oil
EGYPT
Mitla Pass
El Ar
Oil
Mt Sinai
✝ Convent of St Catherine
Sharm el Sheikh
Strait of Tiran Gulf of Aqaba Elat Petra
Tiran SAUDI ARABIA Aqaba

THE SPECTACULAR RISE of Nasserism which followed the nationalization of the Suez Canal in 1956 seemed to Israel and her Western allies a threat which had to stopped. Three main factors determined the Israeli leaders' choice of a military course of action: Arab intransigence, Syria's ever more uncompromising stance and the birth of an autonomous Palestinian resistance movement. As a result, just a few weeks after the military putsch in Athens, the Six-Day War broke out. This event was to transform the political map of the Middle East profoundly. From this point on, Israel was to control the whole of what had been Palestine (Western Jordan, Gaza), as well as Sinai and the Golan Heights.

Aware of his military inferiority, Nasser was content to wage a war of attrition while he rebuilt his army. Sadat, his successor, continued this policy until October 1973, when his troops crossed the Suez Canal, causing the Israeli army to suffer its first setback. But this was

only a tactical battle with limited objectives and Israel was not slow to reverse the situation. As a result of the Camp David Accords, Egypt recognized the state of Israel, while, in its turn, Israel withdrew from Sinai. Cut off by the Arab world, Egypt turned to the Americans, who had gained most from the war. The Soviets, the Syrians, and the Palestinians had been the main losers. The armed Palestinian resistance organizations now took over the baton from defeated Nasserism, endangering the political balance in the countries where they were offered refuge. They clashed first with King Hussein of Jordan and were defeated. Forced to take refuge in Lebanon, they made that country their principal battlefield in the war with Israel. But at the same time they aroused old religious conflicts among the Lebanese, which were soon to develop into out-right civil war.

There were as many objectives in this war as there were protagonists. For the Phalangists and their allies the Maronites, it was

Six Day War.		**Jordanian–Palestinian confrontation.**	**Start of civil war in Lebanon.**
5–10 June 1967		**September 1970**	**1976**

28 May–2 June 1964: Founding of the PLO (Palestine Liberation Organization).
1967: Syrian-Israeli frontier incidents and Palestinian attacks on Israel. The crisis puts Egypt in the front line.
16–27 May: Egypt obtains the evacuation of the UN peace-keeping force. Blockade of the Strait of Tiran and closing of the Gulf of Aqaba.
5–10 June: Surprise attack by Israel. Six Day War; annexation of Jerusalem.
22 November: Resolution 242 of the UN Security Council. Israeli forces retreat. Each state in the area is to have the right to defined and recognized frontiers.
1968: Jordanian-Israeli incidents. Battle of Karama (21 March). Iraq refuses to share the Shatt-al-Arab waters with Iran.
1969: Stepping-up of the war of attrition in the Suez zone. Lebanese-Palestinian confrontations and the Cairo agreements on Palestinian presence and the action of the fedayeen in Lebanon.
1970. 17 September: Jordanian-Palestinian confrontations. Cairo agreement between Hussein and Arafat (Yassar Arafat) 27

September.
28 September: Death of Gamal Abdul Nasser. Anwar el-Sadat succeeds him.
13 November: Coup d'état in Syria in Hafiz al-Assad.
30 November 1971: Iran annexes 3 islands in the Persian Gulf.
1972. July: Expulsion of Soviet military advisers from Egypt.
5 September: Palestinians kill 11 Israeli athletes at the Olympic Games.
6–25 October 1973: Fourth Israeli-Arab war (war of Yom-Kippur or war of Ramadhan).
1974: The belligerents agree to disengage.
28 October: Arab summit at Rabat: PLO is the only representative of the Palestinians.
22 November: U.N. General Assembly proclaims the "Right to Return" for the Palestinians.
1975: Several encounters between Palestinians and Israeli in Lebanon. Algiers agreement between Iraq and Iran.
13 April: Clashes between Palestinians and Phalangists near Beirut.
5 June: Re-opening of the Suez Canal.
1976: Civil war in Lebanon. At the request of

2. *Egyptian soldiers during the Yom Kippur war, October 1973.*

the Lebanese Christians, Syria invades the country on 31 May.
1977. 21 June: Menachem Begin, Israeli prime minister. Active intervention by Israel in Lebanon. Iran-Iraq agreement and Khomeini is asked to leave Najaf.
19–21 November: Visit of President Sadat to Jerusalem.
2–5 December: Formation of a Solidarity Front between Algeria, Libya, Syria, Southern Yemen and the PLO.
1978. 14–21 March: Israeli intervention in Southern Lebanon. United Nations peacekeeping force established in Lebanon.
1979. February: Islamic revolution in Iran.
26 March: Signing of the Israeli-Egyptian peace treaty in Washington.
1980. July: Jerusalem is proclaimed the capital of Israel.
23 September: Start of the Gulf War between Iraq and Iran.
December 1981: Annexation of Golan Heights by Israelis.
1982: Israel invades Lebanon (6 June); Palestinian troops leave the country. Fez summit and adoption of King Fahd of

1967–92

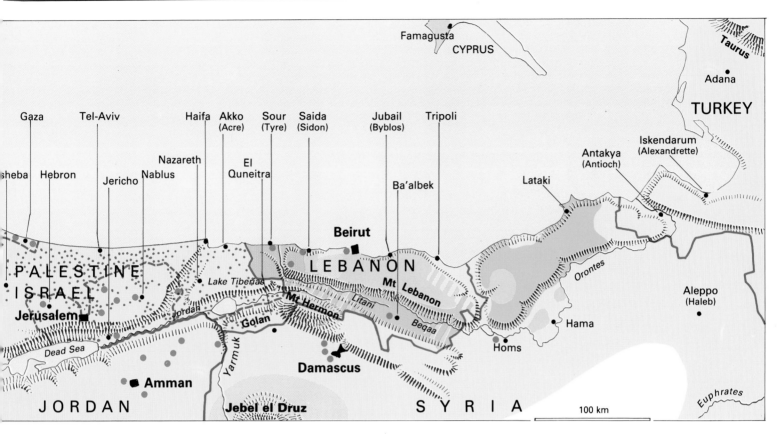

important to preserve the special identity of a Lebanon governed by Christians and turned towards the West, and hence to expel the Palestinians. The latter had initially enjoyed the support of the Moslem factions, the Sunnis, Shi'ites and Druzes. But for the intervention of Syria in 1976, they would have gained the upper hand. The Israeli army's invasion of Lebanon in 1982 eliminated Palestinian resistance in the Lebanese arena and, in objective terms, gave the advantage to the Druzes and Shi'ites. The presence of Iran became more tangible with the appearance of the Hezbollah on the military and political scene. In 1989 the Conference of Taef ended with the elaboration of a compromise that preserved the status quo in Lebanon but gave Syria the right to oversee all political matters in the country.

Taking advantage of the political and military chaos that accompanied the Islamic revolution in Iran, the Baasist government in Bagdad sent its army against that country in 1980 and engaged in

one of the most deadly wars of the century. Intervention by a combination of different world powers (in the form of military aid) prevented the victory of either side. The conflict came to an end in 1988 with neither victory nor defeat. The Bagdad army thus turned its military strength against Kuwait, which it occupied on 2 August 1990. The massive and spectacular reaction by the United States destroyed the infrastructure of Iraq, decimated its offensive ability, and left it to suffer an endemic civil war, where the Kurds in the north and the Shi'ites in the south attempted to overthrow Saddam Hussein's government. The most important consequence of the Iraqi defeat is the elimination of the Arabs from military issues in the region, which is now dominated by Israel, Turkey, and Iran. The Palestinians were the first victims of this change. But the power relations have not yet been consolidated.

Camp David Agreements.	Iran-Iraq War	Opening of Middle East Peace Conference in Madrid
17 September 1978	**1980–1988**	**30 October 1991**

3. The ravages of the Iran-Iraq war seen from the Iranian side, October 1980.

Arabia's peace plan, which unconditionally recognizes Israel.
14 September: Beshir Gemayel, President-elect of Lebanon is assassinated. Massacre of Palestinians by Phalangists at Sabra and Shatila, encircled by Israeli forces (16–17 September). Demonstrations in Israel against the war in Lebanon. Multinational intervention force (France, United States, Italy) enters Beirut.
23 October 1983: Attacks on the multinational force (288 deaths). Shortly thereafter it withdraws from Lebanon.
1984–1985: The PLO resumes links with Egypt and Jordan.
1985–1988: French hostages held in Lebanon.
9 December 1987: Beginning of War of Rocks (Intifada) in the occupied territories.
1988. 8 August: End of the Iran-Iraq War.
15 November: The National Palestinian Council approves United Nations resolution 242 and proclaims an independent state in Palestine.
22 October 1989: Taef Agreement rejected by General Aoun. General Aoun defeated

4. The Chatila refugee camp in Beirut after the massacres perpetrated by the Phalangists, September 1982.

(surrenders on 13 October 1990) and final attempts at Christian hegemony in Lebanon.
August 1990–February 1991: Crisis in Persian Gulf and Gulf war. Defeat of Iraq.
30 October 1991: Opening of Middle East Peace Conference in Madrid.
February 1992: Leader of the Hezbollah, Sheikh Abbas Moussaoui assassinated by Israeli army.

The New Problem of the Balkans

PERESTROIKA AND THE SOVIET policy of nonintervention gave the reformists in the East European communist parties and opposition groups greater freedom of action. But public pressure crossed all imaginable limits among the upper-level staff although it would be easy to believe that Gorbachev was also playing his cards right domestically. Once the bloc no longer existed, his rivals in the Politburo were no longer able to mobilize allied countries against him. The fact remains that by the end of the years 1989–1991, the political scene in Central Europe had changed drastically. The communist parties in power gave way to pluralist democracies (as in Poland, Czechoslovakia, and Hungary) or attempted to save what they could by changing their names and renouncing the past (as in Romania).

"Wir sind das Volk!" (We are the people!), chanted during German demonstrations in 1989, changed to "Wir sind ein Volk!" (We are one people!) after the fall of the wall. Demands for political changes turned into demands for changes in borders—a symbolic shift marking the reversal of old problems through the breakup of the empire that had imposed peace for over 40 years. The rift between the democratic currents desiring European integration and nationalist-populist currents replaced the rift that set communists against their opponents. But the situation is not the same everywhere. In the Balkans the dispute over Moscow's authority as well as the quest for a new legitimacy was often conducted in the name of nationalism (Tito and Ceausescu) while the stronger democratic traditions in Central Europe used political means to express their conflicts with the USSR. Today, in what used to be the Yugoslav federation and in Romania, leaders are stirring up nationalist emotions in order to secure their power. Finally, one should make a distinction between national problems (changes in borders, erection of independent states) and those of ethnic minorities (recognition of their identity).

In Poland the Silesian minority brings back memories of the German threat (five deputies at the Diet in 1991), and traditional anti-Semitism has again begun to make itself felt, although there is only a very small number of Jews left. In Czechoslovakia, Slovak separation is creating a tense situation despite President Havel's good will. The situation of Hungarian minorities in Slovakia (560,000), Subcarpathian Ukraine (200,000), Vojvodina (400-500,000), and Transylvania (2 million) could lead to violent clashes (if they have not already occurred, as in Romania and Yugoslavia). The fate of Moldavia/Bessarabia threatens to cause conflicts between Russia, the Ukraine, and Romania. The situation of other minorities such as the Gagauzes in Moldavia, the Macedonians (about 240,000 in Bulgaria and 150,000 in Greece), and the gypsies (primarily in Romania) are also a source of conflict.

In this Balkan powder keg, the Serbo-Albanian conflict over Kosovo intensified Serbian, Slovene, and Croatian nationalism, and finally caused the disintegration of Yugoslavia. The war that set the Serbs against the Croatians ended temporarily when all parties accepted the deployment of United Nations troops, a decision made in February 1992. In the meantime Slovenia and Croatia have declared their independence. In Bosnia-Hercegovina, following a referendum in which advocates of independence won, armed conflicts set Moslems (Islamic Serbs and Croatians) against the Serbs.

1. *The Romanian flag with the symbol of communism removed, Bucharest, January 1990.*

Dissolution of the Stasi in GDR.

18 December 1989

1989. 6 February–5 April: Negotiations between the power and the opposition in Poland. Plurality of trade unions re-established and reforms announced.
28 March: Violent clashes between Serbian and Albanian forces at Kosovo.
June: Expulsion of Turks (over 300,000) from Bulgaria.
12 September: T. Mazowiecki becomes head of the first noncommunist government in Poland.
18 October: Resignation of E. Honecker, General Secretary of the Central Committee of the East German communist party.
23 October: Declaration of the Republic of Hungary. The new constitution adopts the multiparty system.
9 November: Fall of the Berlin Wall.
10 November: T. Zhivkov, leader of the Bulgarian communist party since 1954, is replaced by P. Mladenov.
17 November: In Prague, student demonstrations mark the beginning of the "Velvet Revolution."
11 December: Abolition of the leading role of the communist party in Bulgaria.

2. *Václav Havel: a philosopher in power.*

16 December: At Timisoara revolt put down by the Romanian police force.
21–26 December: Downfall, hasty trial, and death of N. Ceausescu and his wife. I. Iliescu is elected president of Romania by the National Front Council.
29 December: V. Havel elected president of the Czechoslovak Republic.
1990. January–February: Violent riots in Kosovo.
22 January: In Yugoslavia the League of Communists authorizes pluralism. On 4 February the Slovene communists leave the League.
20 March: Several deaths at Tirgu-Mures (Romania) due to confrontations between Romanians and Hungarians.
March–June: Free elections in Hungary and Czechoslovakia. Victory of anticommunist opposition groups.
April–May: Free elections in Slovenia and Croatia. Anticommunist and autonomist coalitions come to power.
2 July: Monetary union between the FRG and the GDR.

L. Walesa, President of the Polish Republic.

9 December 1990

1 August: Zh. Zhelev elected president of Bulgaria.
3 October: Reunification of Germany.
1991. January–February: Anticommunist demonstrations in Albania.
April: Creation of the European Bank for Reconstruction and Development (EBRD).
15 May: Beginning of violent confrontations between Serbs and Croatians.
25 June: Slovenia and Croatia declare independence.
28 June: Official dissolution of Comecon.
June–July: Thousands of Albanians flee to Italy.
1 July: Following the Briani Island Agreements signed in the presence of EC representatives, a three-month moratorium is imposed regarding the independence of Slovenia and Croatia.
18 July: Yugoslav federal troops (in the service of Serbia) leave Slovenia.
8 August: The two Serbian regions in Croatia, Slovenia and Krajina, declare their autonomy.
November: The federal army bombs Dubrovnik, a historic city on the Adriatic coast.

1989...

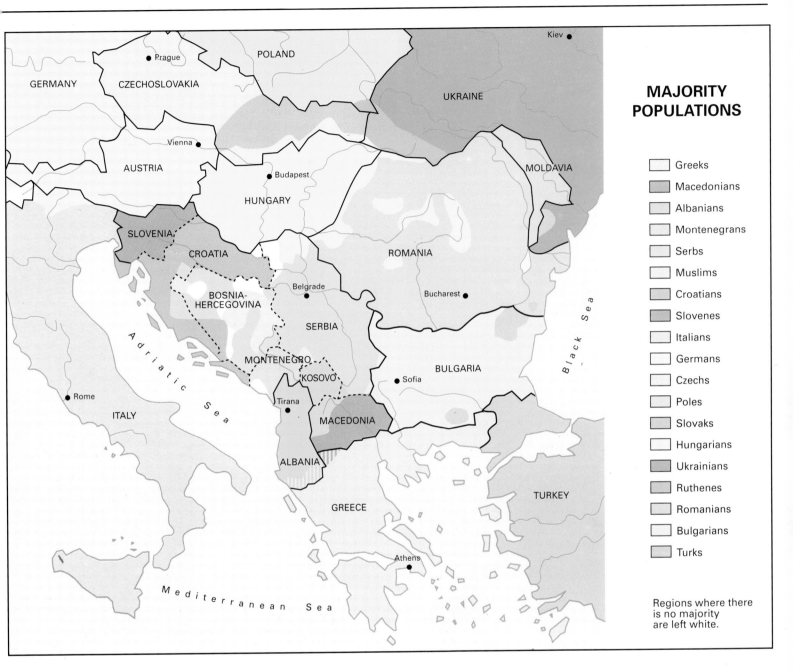

MAJORITY POPULATIONS

- [ ] Greeks
- [ ] Macedonians
- [ ] Albanians
- [ ] Montenegrans
- [ ] Serbs
- [ ] Muslims
- [ ] Croatians
- [ ] Slovenes
- [ ] Italians
- [ ] Germans
- [ ] Czechs
- [ ] Poles
- [ ] Slovaks
- [ ] Hungarians
- [ ] Ukrainians
- [ ] Ruthenes
- [ ] Romanians
- [ ] Bulgarians
- [ ] Turks

Regions where there is no majority are left white.

Dissolution of Comecon.

28 June 1991

Dissolution of the Warsaw Pact.

1 July 1991

21 December: Germany, Italy, and Iceland recognize the independence of Slovenia and Croatia.
1992. 21 February: The United Nations Security Council decides to send 14,000 men to Croatia.
1 March: "Yes" to independence triumphs in Bosnia-Hercegovina.

3. Civil or ethnic war? Yugoslavia, 1991.

4. The Albanians vote with their feet: exodus in Brindisi (Italy), 1991.

The Reunification of Germany

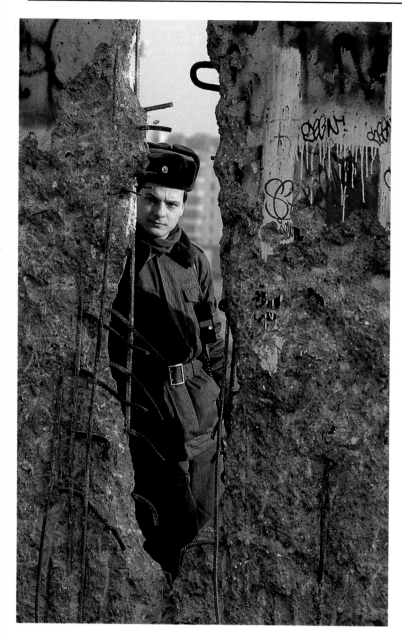

1. *The East German border guards through an opening in the Berlin Wall, December 1989.*

THE EVENTS IN THE USSR helped to destabilize Erich Honecker's government even further, as the GDR had depended on Soviet support to protect its sovereignty and independence since 1949. The controversy worsened and the churches gathered together large numbers of GDR citizens who wished to change their regime. The flow of emigrants kept increasing via Poland, Czechoslovakia, Hungary, and the FRG representation in East Berlin. On the eve of its fortieth anniversary, the GDR was cut off from the East.

Starting in September 1989, the opposition movement became organized. Braving arrests and provocations by the police, it increased the number of demonstrations. The Soviet forces based in the GDR did not intervene. Events succeeded one another so quickly that they took the whole world by surprise. Within two months, the leading government officials had been removed and the roundtable debates that took over the communist party (SED) demonstrated the stalemate in the dialogue between the communists and the democratic movements. They also brought to light the reality of a police state established by the Stasi (the political police of the GDR). One single topic united the political forces present at the roundtable: the desire to keep a separate GDR state based on revitalized socialism that would be more democratic and better adapted to the new economic problems.

But the first free elections on 18 March 1990 disappointed the groups at the roundtable and proved that the parties in the FRG inspired more confidence than those in the GDR. Chancellor Kohl's coalition (CDU-CSU) won 48.1% of the votes, the SPD 21.8%, the PDS 16.3%, and the FDP 5.3%, while "Alliance 90," made up of the GDR democratic movement, fell to 2%. The new government, headed by Lothar de Maizière (CDU-East) followed the Bonn line.

The "2 + 4" negotiations started in May between the FRG and the GDR on the one hand, and the USSR, United States, France, and Great Britain on the other. The Oder-Neisse border with Poland was confirmed.

However, the political breakup of a state that had been reputed to be powerful and irreversible and the alarming realities of the economic consequences of a few decades of planned management were worse than expected. The chasm between the wealth of the FRG and the dilapidation of the GDR could not be eliminated quickly. The negotiations about the monetary reform were just as sensitive as the "2 + 4" negotiations. On 3 October 1990 the ex-GDR Länder adopted the Basic Law of the FRG. On 2 December the Bundestag elections confirmed that Kohl's government had a majority despite a setback.

The reunification forced the Germans to question their national identity. The FRG had nothing to do with the collapse of the GDR and the material and moral disaster of the communist system. Most

Opening of the Berlin Wall.

9 November 1989

1989. 17 May: Municipal elections in the GDR. The government asserts that 98.5% of the votes were for the communist party (SED) and its allies.
mid-September: Creation of political opposition movements: New Forum, Democracy Now, and Democratic Change in the GDR.
6–7 October: M. Gorbachev visits East Berlin for the fortieth anniversary of the GDR.
18 October: E. Honecker, Secretary General of the SED and head of state, resigns. He is succeeded by E. Krenz.
8 November: W. Stoph's government in the GDR resigns. H. Modrow forms a new government on 13 November.
9 November: Opening of the Berlin Wall.
28 November: FRG chancellor, H. Kohl, proposes a 10-point plan for a gradual reunification.
6 December: E. Krenz resigns. A roundtable provides a kind of transition stage.
10 December: Extraordinary congress of the SED (later called the PDS), chooses a new president, G. Gysi.

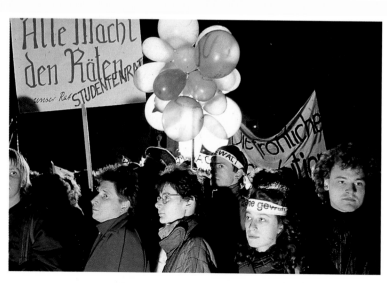

2. *In support of free elections: Leipzig (GDR), November 1989.*

Reunification of Germany.

3 October 1990

20–22 December: F. Mitterand visits the GDR. He emphasizes the need to link reunification of Germany to the reorganization of Europe.
1990. 30 January: H. Modrow visits Moscow. M. Gorbachev accepts the reunification of the two Germanies in theory.
18 March: First free elections to the GDR parliament. The Christian Democratic party (CDU) wins.
12 April: L. de Maizière (CDU) forms a government in the GDR.
6 May: Municipal elections in the GDR. The CDU suffers a setback.
18 May: Signing of an agreement instituting a monetary, economic, and social union between the GDR and the FRG in Berlin on 1 July.
July: At the end of the "2 + 4" negotiations, the USSR removes the last obstacles to German reunification.
12 September: Signing of the treaty permitting German reunification in Moscow.
17–18 September: Franco-German summit in Munich gives France the opportunity to

1989–92

DENMARK
LITHUANIA
Memel
1867-1920
1919-1939

1919-1945
1919-1945
1815-1919

① SCHLESWIG-HOLSTEIN

Bremen Hamburg

② LOWER SAXONY

⑨ MECKLENBURG-WEST POMERANIA

NETHER-LANDS

⑩ BRANDENBURG

Berlin

⑪ SAXONY-ANHALT

1945

POLAND

③ RHINELAND-WESTPHALIA

⑫ SAXONY

⑬ THURINGIA

Bonn

1816-1919

④ HESSEN

1938-1945

CZECHOSLOVAKIA

LUX

⑤ RHINELAND-PALATINATE

⑥ SAAR

1870-1919

⑧ BAVARIA

FRANCE

⑦ BADEN-WURTEMBERG

Munich

AUSTRIA

SWITZERLAND

1938-1945

HUNGARY

LIECHTENSTEIN

ITALY

0 100 200

CITIES
■ 1M
● 500 000
· 100 000

LÄNDER
① SCHLESWIG-HOLSTEIN
② LOWER SAXONY
③ RHINELAND-WESTPHALIA
④ HESSEN
⑤ RHINELAND-PALATINATE
⑥ SAAR
⑦ BADEN-WURTEMBERG
⑧ BAVARIA
⑨ MECKLENBURG-WEST POMERANIA
⑩ BRANDENBURG
⑪ SAXONY-ANHALT
⑫ SAXONY
⑬ THURINGIA

Germans still have serious doubts about the state-nation. The break-up of the GDR turned out to be the betrayal of a utopia and the revelation of an illusory national identity. The identity of the FRG was also upset by the reunification. Some people fear that the new Germany will not be able to overcome the inequality between the West and the East Germans or the xenophobia toward Poland and the immigrants from the East. The resurgence of neo-Nazi violence has revealed a deep moral crisis.

The geopolitical structure of Central Europe has revived "German doubts" between the East and the West. For the moment, the reunification is forcing the FRG to neglect the European Community in order to concentrate on improving the conditions in the new Länder.

Berlin, capital of reunified Germany.

20 June 1991

3. Neo-Nazi rally at Bayreuth, August 1991.

voice some apprehensions about German reunification.
3 October: The ex-GDR Länder officially join the FRG. Germany now has a population of 79.1 million (of which 16.4 million live in the ex-GDR). The average salary in East Germany is about 50% the average salary in West Germany.
14 November: Confirmation of the Moscow treaty in Warsaw. Germany does not question the German-Polish border.
17 November: CSCE conference in Paris. 34 countries participate in the meeting, which confirms the breakup of the Warsaw Pact.
2 December: Elections in the new Bundestag. CDU-CSU keeps its majority. The Social Democrats and the Greens are defeated.
1991. 20 January: Regional elections in Hessen. CDU suffers a setback (40.2% of the votes).
January-February: Germany is not directly involved in the Gulf War and questions its new international responsibilities.

March: First signs of the economic and social problems caused by reunification. The unemployment rate reaches 9.2% while the number of part-time workers exceeds 2 million.
21 April: Regional elections in Rhineland and Palatinate. CDU suffers another setback (38.7% of the votes).
20 June: The Bundestag chooses Berlin as the capital of reunified Germany (by 338 to 320 votes).

4. H. Kohl and M. Gorbachev confirm friendship between the USSR and reunified Germany, 10 November 1990.

European Unification Approaching the Year 2000

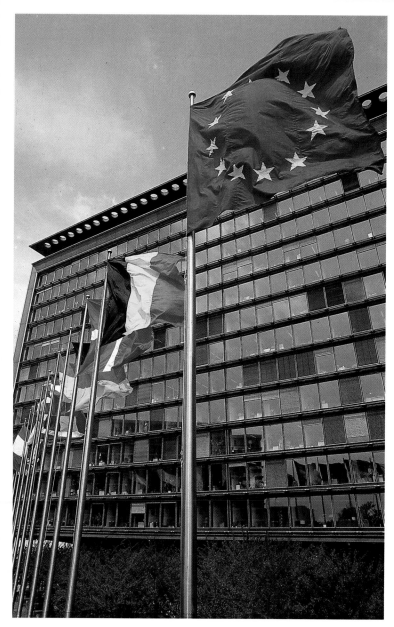

1. *The Foundation of the Europe of the Twelve in Brussels.*

By SIGNING THE Treaty of Maastricht, which will become effective on 1 January 1993, the heads of states and governments (and subsequently the ministers of foreign affairs) of the 12 member countries of the European Economic Community (EC) started a process that should lead to the unification of Europe at the beginning of the twenty-first century. Subject to ratification by the parliaments of all the signatories, the treaty proposes a plan for the gradual implementation of an economic and monetary union (ECU) that will start using the ECU in 1999: one foreign policy, one security (i.e., joint defense) policy, more liberal social policies, an increase in the power of the European parliament, and ultimately European citizenship. Great efforts have been made since 1957 to create a unified Europe on an economic basis; in the future it expects to combine all the attributes that always made the countries strong.

The "post-Maastricht" period involves convincing the 12 nations (especially Great Britain, which is insular and hesitant) of the merits of the decision imposed from above and the advantages of extended citizenship. It involves persuading them to follow labor relations right through to the enterprises as well as the movement of people, the circulation of knowledge and culture, the scientific, economic, and monetary goals that created the EC; and finally to find and regulate the financing of the unification. It is a difficult task because the crises left very tangible economic, social, and ecological scars. Furthermore, the new trade flows and international rates stabilize extra-European products. In addition, if the world order is no longer bipolar, Europe should use the opportunity and make the best of what is being offered. In the present situation that characterizes the end of the century, when the world is being restructured, how important can a European ideal be if it has never been democratically discussed by each of the 12 members?

Above all, the unification has deep roots and exhibits truly Western ambitions. Strengthened by the community, it is merely good sense to begin the unification before exploring the future. But since 1989 the speed of the changing events in the East and South have partly ruined the plan. The southern and eastern Mediterranean regions are vacillating more than ever between a dialogue and a confrontation with Europe under the pressure of the wave of emigration toward the other, wealthier shore, in the midst of the instability and resentment of the Mahgreb and the Middle East. The end of communism in the ex-USSR and its satellites in central and eastern Europe not only increased the number of countries that would like to be integrated "into the West," but reversed the geographic disposition of the European organization by shifting its center of gravity toward the east. This poses a danger because the West's glorious history of the continent has always been based on a dialogue between the West, the Center, the East, and the South. Nevertheless, with the "springtime

The pound sterling is included in the EMS.

8 October 1990

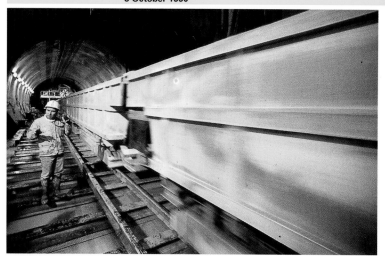

2. *The Channel no longer exists; work on the Chunnel, 1989.*

1990. 28 April: The extraordinary European Council of Dublin reinstigates political Europe.
3 October: German reunification.
8 October: The pound sterling is included in the European Monetary System (EMS).
14 November: Treaty between Germany and Poland confirming the border between the two countries.
19–21 November: The second summit of the Conference on Security and Cooperation in Europe (CSCE) in Paris.
2 December: First parliamentary election in reunified Germany.
1991. 17 January–28 February: Gulf War.
15 April: Creation of the European Bank for Restructuring and Development (EBRD) to provide assistance to Eastern Europe.
25 June: Beginning of confrontations between the Serbs and Croatians in Yugoslavia.
28 June: Dissolution of the Comecon.
1 July: Dissolution of the Warsaw Pact.
26 July: Agreement between the EC and Japan on importing automobiles.

3. *Franco-German brigade created in 1988.*

1990...

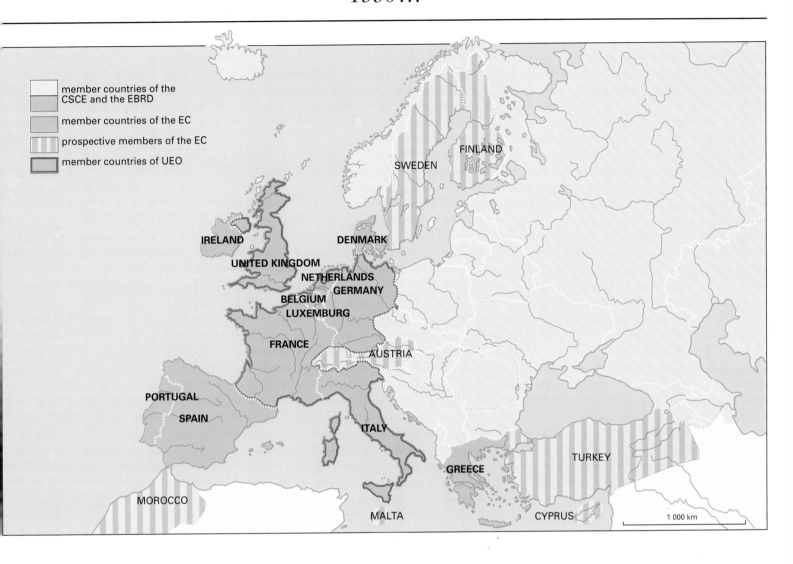

member countries of the
CSCE and the EBRD

member countries of the EC

prospective members of the EC

member countries of UEO

IRELAND DENMARK UNITED KINGDOM NETHERLANDS GERMANY BELGIUM LUXEMBURG FRANCE AUSTRIA PORTUGAL SPAIN ITALY GREECE PORTUGAL SWEDEN FINLAND TURKEY MOROCCO MALTA CYPRUS

1 000 km

of the nations," national ambitions are awakened and mutually destroy each other, populism increases rapidly, the borders are questioned, and political models create conflicts.

As a result, the Europe of the Twelve has found it difficult to form a common front against the new events that could raise the stakes in its unification "deal." There has been disequilibrium in the relations between France and reunified Germany, unequal investment in the Gulf War on the part of the Americans against Iraq, the inability to intervene in a unified manner in the breakup of Yugoslavia, competition in providing aid for the restructuring of the East. In the historic years of 1990-1991, this Europe that has the ambition to become unified has been anything but unified.

Maastricht Summit.

9-10 December 1991

17 October: NATO announces an 80% reduction of stockpiles of tactical nuclear weapons in Europe.
22 October: Agreement between the EC and the European Free Trade Association (EFTA) on the creation of a common economic zone in 1993.
22 November: Hungary, Poland, and Czechoslovakia sign associate members' agreements with the EC.
9-10 December: Maastricht Summit between the heads of states and governments of the Twelve.
1992. 7 February: The ministers of foreign affairs of the Twelve sign the European Unification Treaty in Maastricht.

4. Anti-nuclear demonstration in the FRG, May 1986.

5. Europe at odds; Maastricht, 9 December 1991.

Science and the State

1. Dwarf mouse, the result of genetic manipulation at the Jackson Laboratory in Maine, United States, 1982.

SCIENCE HAS BECOME a concern of the state because it lies at the heart of contemporary military and civil technology. There follow, by way of illustration, three examples of this, extreme cases where state-sponsored programmes are linking together both research laboratories and industrial plants in common ventures.

Our first example is to be found in the development of the atom bomb. Fearing the worst from the uranium project of their German colleagues during the Second World War, a group of European émigré scientists in the United States, supported by their British colleagues who wanted to devote their time to developing radar, persuaded Roosevelt to adopt a project for the development of nuclear weapons. Set up in 1943 under the leadership of General Groves and the physicist J. Robert Oppenheimer, the Manhattan Project had as its object the development and construction in Los Alamos of two nuclear bombs, one to be made from uranium 235 at Oak Ridge, and the other from plutonium at Hanford. 150,000 people were employed at the Experimental Research Centre and in the factories producing fissile material. The project itself cost two billion dollars (the equivalent of the entire output of the motor-car industry at the time) and resulted in 1945 in the explosion of a plutonium bomb in the New Mexico desert. The scientists had suggested to President Truman that the experiment be carried out in public so that it might have a deterrent effect, but this was not done, and so on 6 August 1945 'Little Boy' was dropped on Hiroshima, killing half of the population over an area of 12.5 square kilometres. On 9 August 'Fat Man' was exploded over Nagasaki, with the same devastating effect, but spread over only 3.5 square kilometres, since a mountain spur divided the city into two and protected it in part from the force of the blast.

Our second example is to be found in the field of rocket technology. After the Second World War the United States and the Soviet Union each took over a part of the German research team responsible for developing the V2 rocket, but whereas the Americans were to rely on their B-52s to deliver the atomic bomb, the Soviet Union used rockets which in 1955 Korolev was able to adapt for use in space and for the putting into orbit of man-made satellites. The A1 rocket, developed from the R7 missile, put Sputnik I into orbit, then, on 12 April 1961, Vostok I, with Yury Gagarin on board. A month later, recognizing the Soviet lead in manned flight and pressing for the introduction of piloted missions, President Kennedy launched the Apollo moon programme, announcing that its goal was the landing of a man on the moon before the end of the decade. In carrying out the project, NASA spent 20 billion dollars (half of its entire budget), undertaking ten trials, four of which were manned, and co-ordinated the work of 400,000 people in several hundred different universities. On 21 July 1969 Neil Armstrong became the first man on the moon, with, he said, what was 'one small step for a man, one giant leap for mankind'.

Our final example focuses on the so-called 'Star Wars' programme. While today the dissident scientist Andrei Sakharov, the father of the Soviet H-bomb, continues to experience severe restrictions on his activity despite his recent release from internal exile, Edward Teller, his American counterpart, is the guiding force behind the Strategic Defence Initiative (SDI) announced by President Reagan on 23 March 1983. The aim of SDI is to deploy both on the ground and in space, before the end of the century, laser beam weapons capable of destroying Soviet missiles at each of the three stages of their trajectory. In 1985 1.4 billion dollars had been spent on it, and 5,000 people were at work on it in 260 companies and laboratories.

First atomic reactor built in the USA.

1942

1942: First atomic reactor built in the United States. Such reactors work by setting off a controlled nuclear chain reaction by bombarding fissile material with neutrons. The heat given off is used to drive turbines to generate electricity (1951) or for the propulsion of submarines (1953). Canada (1945), USSR (1946), Great Britain (1947) and France (1948) will follow ...

1945: First atomic bomb exploded in the United States. A non-nuclear explosive charge is used to bombard fragments of fissile material which thus reach a critical mass and spark off a chain reaction in a fraction of a second. The USSR (1949), Great Britain (1952), France (1960), China (1964) and India (1974) will later join the nuclear club ...

1946: First generation of electronic tube computers based on the model of the Electronic Numerical Integrator and Calculator (ENIAC) and having a computing speed of 1/40 second.

1952: First thermonuclear H-bomb exploded in the USA. The A-bomb uses the fission of heavy nuclei, while the H-bomb uses light

First laser invented.

1960

nuclei. The USSR (1953), Great Britain (1957), China (1967) and France (1968) will all explode H-bomb devices in turn. Research is under way to achieve sufficient temperature for fusion by other methods than the explosion of an A-bomb. The aim is to harness for peaceful civil uses the very same thermonuclear energy as that which powers the sun.

1957: First man-made satellite put into orbit by rocket power by the Soviet Union. The United States (1958), France (1965), Japan and China (1970), Great Britain (1971) and India (1980) will follow.

1959: Second generation of transistorized computers based on the IBM 1401 with a computing speed of 10 microseconds.

1960: Invention of the laser. The laser is an apparatus for the amplification of a light wave passing through a layer of excited atoms and stimulating the emission of a light beam of the same frequency, in the same direction, and in phase, in accordance with the equations of quantum mechanics. Contained within two reflective surfaces, the stimulated

3. Portrait of Yury Alekseyevitch Gagarin, first Soviet citizen into space, as pictured on the cover of his official biography published in Moscow in 1981.

4. France opts for atomic power: here one sees the production of plutonium at Marcoule (Gard) where the factory has been in production since 1958.

2. Industrial application of the laser: here the laser is being used to cut steel.

Neil Armstrong becomes the first man on the moon. **Launch of the European space rocket *Ariane*.** **Launch of the American Space Shuttle.** **AIDS: identification of the disease.**

21 July 1969 **1979** **1981** **Summer 1981.**

5. Cape Canaveral: the departure of the American Space Shuttle, 18 June 1983.

light passes through the layer of excited atoms several times, which has the cumulative effect of transforming the amplifier into a generator of coherent light of such a small degree of divergence and such intensity that the laser may be used as a surgical instrument, industrial tool, or even a ray gun ...

1965: Third generation of computers with integrated circuits, an off-shoot of the Apollo project, based on the IBM 360, having a computing speed of 5 nanoseconds. The fourth generation will appear in 1981.

1967: Soviet Soyuz-Saliut-Progress space programme for a manned spacecraft, manned orbiting space station and automatic cargo ship.

1979: Launching of the European space rocket *Ariane*. First satellite put into orbit in 1981. Studies begin on the project for a manned orbiting space station.

1980: World-wide eradication of smallpox. The smallpox virus, which has no animal carriers, is eliminated after an international vaccination campaign organized by the World Health Organization (WHO).

1981: Launching of the American Space Shuttle, which is propelled by rockets into space, orbits like a manned cargo vessel and lands like a glider and thus can be reused.

199?: Fifth generation of computers with artificial intelligence becomes indispensable for the planned American SDI.

6. Explosion of the Space Shuttle, Challenger, *a few seconds after firing, January 27 1986.*

Oil and Raw Materials

UNTIL AFTER the Second World War, mankind drew upon nature's resources with an easy conscience. But at the beginning of the seventies it became clear that supplies of certain strategic raw materials were finite, and concern about this has become a major source of disquiet.

In terms of mineral ore, more than 90% of world production is supplied by only two or three countries. The main areas specializing in particular ores are: the ex-USSR, South Africa and Canada for platinum; Australia and Brazil for titanium ore; South Africa, Zimbabwe and the ex-USSR for chromium ore; Zaire, Zambia, and Cuba for cobalt; North Africa, the ex-USSR and Gabon for manganese ore; the United States, Canada and Chile for molybdenite.

Raw materials providing energy – coal, oil and natural gas – pose different problems.

Coal was the key source of energy for nineteenth-century industrialization, and it will doubtless be of vital importance in the twenty-first century. It is found in many parts of the world and reserves are nearly one hundred times greater than those of oil. In 1984 they represented 11,606,382 million tonnes, to which can be added a further 2,528,944 million tonnes of lignite. 60% of all coal is to be found in the ex-USSR alone, and 90% of world reserves occur in the ex-USSR, and USA and China.

But in the space of a century it is oil that has come to occupy the predominant place. Its 'flexibility' and above all its price, which is constantly falling in absolute terms (and sometimes even in money terms), make it the most highly taxed raw material (at twice the rate of luxury goods) and the one that attracts most controversy. The largest reserves were, in fact, discovered by foreign companies. Production was in the hands of the 'seven sisters' (Exxon, Mobil, Socal, Gulf, Texaco, Shell, BP) before the producing countries awoke to realities – a situation which led to frequent confrontations, and to the creation in 1960 of OPEC (Organization of Petrol Exporting Countries). It was established that oil is still far from recovering the lag accumulated since 1948 compared to other basic products. The tempting prices for crude oil encouraged countries to invest, even at the risk of running heavily into debt (as in the case of Mexico).

But the amount of extra oil produced and the decrease in consumption forced OPEC initially to reduce production and then subsequently to flood the market, which brought about the fall in the price of crude oil. As a result, developing countries are not gaining from their resources in real terms: since they are not sufficiently diversified, they allow no freedom in managing them. The concentration of oil wealth is, however, striking: 85% of the oil discovered to date has been found in twenty-two oil-rich areas which contained initially more than 1.5 billion tonnes of oil. The largest is the Arab–Iranian basin in the Middle East, which forms what amounts to a 'ring' with the other large oil-producing areas. During the last few years the average cost of discoveries by the most active international oil companies has been between five dollars and fifteen dollars per barrel.

Natural gas, which is more widely distributed than oil, was thought to be a cheap replacement fuel until recently. In the long term the largest known deposits which have not yet been developed are in the Middle East and the ex-USSR. By the year 2000 OPEC, holding 72% of world supplies, will have control of the world oil market and joint control with the ex-USSR of the world's gas supplies. A progressive increase in world consumption is likely and alternative energy (coal and nuclear energy) cannot completely replace oil (as we approach the year 2000 some forty to fifty reactors a year are to be closed).

In the final analysis, energy is less a problem of wealth than of power: in spite of sensationalist declarations, quite obviously there is no lack of resources; there are only conflicts between nations for domination.

1. The Soviet Urengoi–Novopskov gas pipe-line under construction.

Creation of the Anglo–Persian Oil Company.	'Red Line' agreement between Americans and British.	Nationalization of Iranian Oil.	First Oil Crisis.
14 April 1909	31 July 1928	February 1951	16 October 1973

29 May 1901: Concession contract granted by the Shah of Persia to W. K. D'Arcy which grants him the 'special and exclusive right', amongst others, 'to prospect for, obtain, work, develop, render suitable for trade, remove and sell oil, natural gas, asphalt, ozocerite throughout the entire Persian Empire for a period of 60 years'. In fact, the Shah excluded five provinces - Azerbaijan, Gilàn, Màzandaran, Astarabad and Khorosan - in order not to upset Russia.

31 August 1907: Great Britain and Russia conclude an agreement relating to Persia, Tibet and Afghanistan.

14 April 1909: Founding of the Anglo–Persian Oil Company which buys the companies founded by D'Arcy. Its capital is fixed at 2 million pounds.

23 October 1912: Agreement between the Turkish Petroleum Company and the Deutsche Bank. The capital of the Turkish Petroleum Company increases from £50,000 to £80,000, divided as follows; Deutsche Bank 25%, National Bank of Turkey 20%, Gulbenkian 15%, Sir Ernest Cassel 15%, Royal Dutch Shell 25%.

3. The Kofflefontein diamond mines, South Africa.

9 May 1915–15 May 1916: Sykes-Picot agreements.

19–26 April 1920: San Remo conference which draws up the Treaty of Sèvres between the Allies and Turkey (10 August 1920).

24 July 1923: Lausanne Treaty. The protocol refers to certain concessions.

5 June 1926: Treaty between Great Britain, Iraq and Turkey.

31 July 1928: British and Americans sign the so-called Red Line Agreement by which the American monopolies obtain 23.75% of the shares of the TPC (Turkish Petroleum Company).

8 June 1929: TPC becomes IPC (Iraq Petroleum Company). The IPC and its subsidiaries are made up of 5 companies: Anglo-Iranian Oil Company (23.75%), Compagnie française de pétroles (CFP) (23.75%), Royal Dutch Shell (23.75%), Near East Development Corporation (American) comprising Standard Oil (11.875%), Socony-Vacuum and Gulf Oil (11.875%), Calouste Sarkis Gulbenkian (5%).

1938: Nationalization of oil in Mexico.

1900–92

2. Rotterdam, Holland, the main oil importing port in the world.

Second Oil Crisis.

1979

Sheik Yamani, Saudi Oil Minister dismissed.

29 October 1986

February 1951: Mossadeq nationalizes Iranian Oil.

3 February 1954: IPC and the Iranian government sign a fifty-fifty agreement.

September 1960: Creation of OPEC which brings together Venezuela, Iran, Iraq, Saudi Arabia and Kuwait.

16 October 1973: Unilateral decision to fix the price of oil taken by OPEC at Teheran.

Between January 1979 and November 1980: The price per barrel rises from 13.3 to 32 dollars.

1985-1986: Oil counter-crisis; drop in oil prices.

2 August 1990: Iraq invades Kuwait. Start of the Persian Gulf crisis.

17 January-27 February 1991: Gulf War. Defeat of Iraq. The price per barrel of oil stabilizes around 20 dollars.

4. A power station in Pennsylvania.

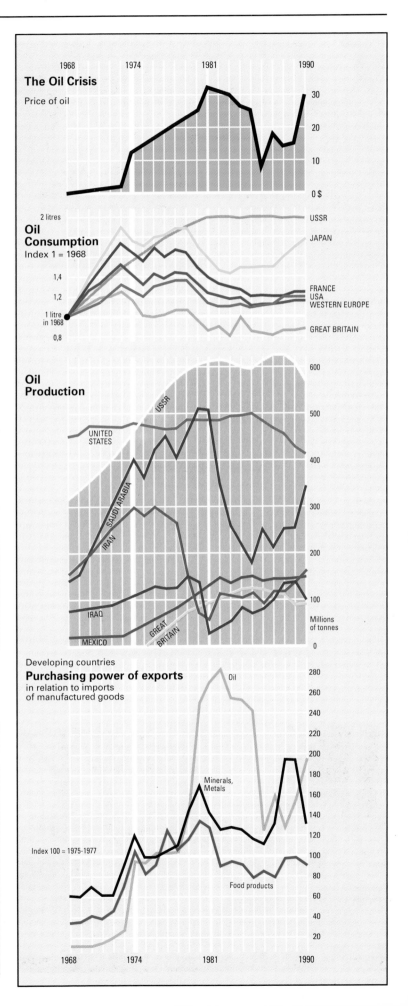

The Oil Crisis

Price of oil

Oil Consumption

Index 1 = 1968

2 litres

1,4

1,2

1 litre in 1968

0,8

USSR

JAPAN

FRANCE
USA
WESTERN EUROPE

GREAT BRITAIN

Oil Production

USSR

UNITED STATES

SAUDI ARABIA

IRAN

IRAQ

GREAT BRITAIN

MEXICO

Millions of tonnes

Developing countries

Purchasing power of exports

in relation to imports of manufactured goods

Oil

Minerals, Metals

Index 100 = 1975-1977

Food products

World Population Development

1. Indian women.

SINCE THE BEGINNING of this century population growth has speeded up. In 1900 there were 1,634 million people in the world; there were 2,530 million in 1950, and today there are 4,845 million. A figure of six billion is forecast for the end of the century, and it is unlikely that it will level off at less than eight or nine billion in the middle of the next century.

In the nineteenth century, Europe and its colonial populations had the highest growth rate in the world. An initial drop in fertility (1880–1940) was followed by a short-lived recovery in 1945–65. Now these areas are in crisis: the birth rate is nearly everywhere too low to ensure replacement, which inevitably means an aging population. Although these countries, along with the USSR and Japan, make up 24% of world totals, they only account for 13.9% of births.

Third World countries, on the other hand, are still at stages two and three of demographic evolution: mortality fell rapidly up to 1970 and only then did fertility begin to drop in some countries. Their population went from around 1,700 million in 1950 to around 3,600 million in 1985, their proportion of world totals from two-thirds to three-quarters.

At present China and the whole of Southeast Asia are heading for a state of equilibrium: their natural population growth only remains a positive figure because of the inertia of demographic phenomena. In Latin America, too, fertility is on the decline. The term 'population explosion' can only really be applied to the Arab world and to Africa, which beats all world records for birth (and death) rates.

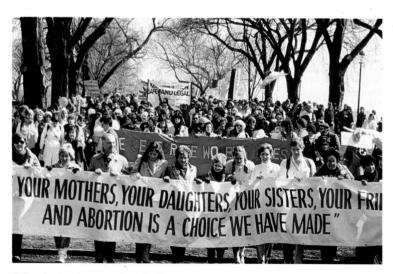

2. Pro-abortion demonstration, Washington, 3 September 1985.

A: Fertility rates in 1985
The figures represent the average number of children a woman would have in her lifetime according to fertility rates recorded in a given year. The replacement of generations is only ensured if this figure is at or above 2.1.

WORLD	**3.7**
Africa	**6.3**
North Africa	6.0
West Africa	6.4
East Africa	6.8
Central Africa	6.1
Southern Africa	5.2
Asia (minus USSR)	**3.7**
Southwest Asia	5.9
South Asia	5.0
Southeast Asia	4.5
East Asia	2.1
Oceania	**2.7**
South and Central America	**4.2**
Central America	4.9
Caribbean	3.3
Tropical South America	4.2
Temperate South America	3.1
Northern America	**1.8**
Europe (minus USSR)	**1.8**
Northern Europe	1.8
Western Europe	1.6
Eastern Europe	2.1
Southern Europe	1.9
USSR	**2.4**

Population et sociétés bulletin July–August 1985.

B: Yearly natural population increase 1950–85 by main region
The natural rate of increase is the difference between the birth rate and the death rate. It is expressed here in percentages.

	1950–55	1965–70	1984–85
WORLD	**1.8**	**2.1**	**1.7**
More developed regions	1.3	0.9	0.6
Less developed regions	2.1	2.6	2.0
Africa	**2.2**	**2.6**	**2.9**
Algeria	2.0	3.0	3.3
Kenya	2.8	3.3	4.1
Asia	**2.0**	**2.5**	**1.8**
Japan	1.4	1.1	0.7
China	2.2	2.8	1.1
India	1.8	2.2	2.1
Oceania	**2.4**	**2.0**	**1.3**
Latin America	**2.6**	**2.7**	**2.3**
Mexico	2.8	3.2	2.6
Brazil	2.9	2.8	2.3
Northern America	**1.8**	**1.1**	**0.7**
Europe	**1.5**	**0.9**	**0.3**
France	0.8	0.8	0.4
West Germany	0.9	0.7	−0.1
USSR	1.7	1.0	1.0

C: World population at the end of the century
Demographic projections are estimates of the future size of populations based on the hypothetical evolution of their fertility and mortality. The United States Bureau of Census published three sets of projections in 1978 based on data recorded in 1975.

Population in year 2000

	upper estimate	medium estimate	lower estimate
World	**6796**	**6350**	**5921**
More developed regions	1377	1323	1274
Less developed regions	5419	5027	4647
Africa	**847**	**814**	**759**
Asia and Oceania	**3951**	**3630**	**3359**
Latin America	**677**	**636**	**580**
USSR and Eastern Europe	**480**	**460**	**442**
Western countries and assimilated immigrant populations	**842**	**809**	**781**

1950–2000

World population in 1985

• = 500,000 people

Fertility*

6	
4	
2,1	

Natural increase

(difference between birth and death rate)

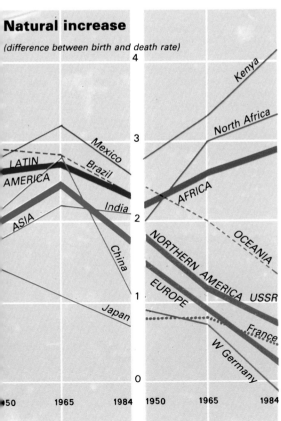

LATIN AMERICA

ASIA

Mexico

Brazil

India

China

Japan

Kenya

North Africa

AFRICA

OCEANIA

NORTHERN AMERICA   USSR

EUROPE

France

W Germany

1950   1965   1984   1950   1965   1984

World population in year 2000

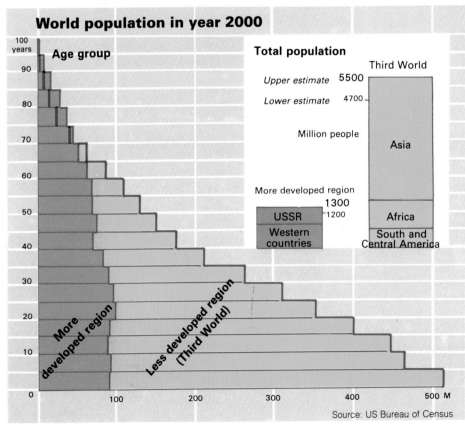

Age group

100 years
90
80
70
60
50
40
30
20
10
0

More developed region

Less developed region (Third World)

0   100   200   300   400   500 M

Total population

Third World

Upper estimate   5500
Lower estimate   4700

Million people

Asia

More developed region
1300
1200

USSR

Western countries

Africa

South and Central America

Source: US Bureau of Census

Average live births per woman based on the fertility rate for a given year (in this case 1985). Below 2.1 replacement is not ensured.

Megalopolis, Suburbs, One-Fourth of the World

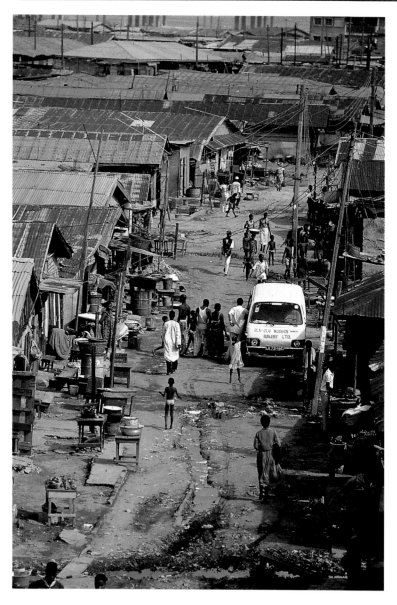

1. Shanty town in Nigeria.

Percentage of the urban population

	1950	1970	1990	2000
World	29.4%	37.0%	43.6%	48.2%
Industrial countries	53.6%	66.4%	74.2%	77.7%
DC*	17.4%	25.3%	34.4%	40.4%
Africa	14.8%	22.9%	35.5%	42.2%
Latin America	41.1%	57.4%	72.1%	76.9%
Eastern Asia	17.8%	26.3%	30.2%	34.2%
Southern Asia	16.1%	21.2%	30.4%	36.8%

* developing countries

AT THE BEGINNING OF the twentieth century, 3% of the world population lived in towns. By the year 2000, more than half will be living in them—or will be trying hard to survive in them. This is already the case for three-fourths of the people in Latin America, a proportion equivalent to that of the Europeans. This transition can take on many forms, but the most striking is the enormous rise of the megalopolis. Within 10 years the 15 largest will have a population concentration larger than that of the ex-USSR or of North America.

Such a change in scale reflects a number of demographic and migratory factors; above all, it reflects a system that contains everything that could be called modern. The West, as the birthplace of this process leading to a world city and having experienced the Industrial Revolution, will remain the center. A new universal geography and a division of labor that will increasingly cross national borders will be organized into a network of material and information flows, and the towns will become the connecting points. Beyond the consequences this will have on the overall economic situation (when the stock exchange in Tokyo sneezes...), a model that will have the same architecture, the same orientation, and the same cultural references will unify the planet in a cosmopolitan syncretism. The thousand-year-old symbols of the European and Asiatic cities or of the native quarters will lose their significance and their individual functions.

But a demarcation line separates those who live in the interconnected world and those who camp at its gates. The metropolises of the North have their ghettos and their suburbs to which those who are superfluous are relegated—the victims of decimation through unemployment. Far from helping the societies of the South to develop, suburbanization ultimately contributes to the elimination of the peasants without integration. The incomes of the 12 to 14 million inhabitants of Cairo are double that of the fellaheen and are based on urban bias, on a political price of essential commodities that intensifies the rural crisis. Shanty towns, slums, "gecekondu" (Turkish: literally, 'constructed overnight')—the outskirts of town will collect those excluded from the countryside as a sector of the urban order. An increasing number of the people will not be able to become integrated into the framework of labor markets, and of urban living and services. Illicit living quarters, the gray sector, an underground economy, one-fourth of the world—these recent concepts strive to take into account a poverty that searches ardently to find its place in the sun. One billion people in the world live below the poverty line.

The middle classes, weakened by inhibited development and limited foundations of modern times, will not succeed in becoming integrated into the dominant sphere in a stable manner. And urbanization makes the masses politically conscious. The towns will unquestionably be the epicenters of the social upheavals. That is where the hunger riots, the pressure from the opposition, and the revolutions will break out. That is where the opportunities for democratization and the danger of totalitarian populism and communal confrontations will demonstrate the problems of our model of a modern system and of the introduction of a new citizenship.

2. Searching for food in the garbage cans of Lima, Peru, 1990.

1900–2000

Population in the year 2000: ⬤ over 20 million inhabitants ● over 10 million inhabitants • over 5 million inhabitants

Los Angeles
Chicago
Mexico
New York
London
Paris
Madrid
Casablanca
Algiers
Caracas
Bogotá
Lima
Belo Horizonte
Rio de Janeiro
Sao Paulo
Santiago
Buenos Aires
Lagos
Kinshasa
Cairo
Baghdad
Istanbul
Teheran
Karachi
Bombay
Bangalore
Delhi
Ahmadabad
Hyderabad
Madras
Lahore
Dacca
Calcutta
Bangkok
Medan
Jakarta
Manila
Hong Kong
Shanghai
Beijing
Tianjin
Shenyang
Seoul
Pusan
Osaka
Kobe
Tokyo
Yokohama
St-Petersburg
Moscow
Milano

Los Olvidados". Peru, 1991, during a cholera epidemic.

4. Skyscrapers and hovels in Sao Paulo, Brazil.

The Second World Crisis

THE LONG PERIOD of post-war prosperity produced an atmosphere [of] heightened optimism. In the West, economists were interested [in] growth, not in crises. In the East, vague generalizations on t[he] 'overall crisis of capitalism' made it possible to avoid any precise vie[w] of the future. Gierek had even laid plans, from 1970 on, to build, wi[th] money borrowed from the West and paid back with goods sold [in] the West, and industrial 'second Poland'. The economic crisis of 19[ ] was a failure in thinking. The possibility of a major recession w[as] misjudged.

Today, one thing seems certain: long-term economic depressions [do] exist, and short-term crises, in the context of such breakdowns in t[he] economic system, take on a seriousness that they do not have durin[g] periods of prolonged expansion.

But pointing up former illusions should not lead one to paint a ro[sy] picture of the 'thirty glorious years' (1945–1974) and a bleak on[e] during the years that followed. The years from 1957 to 1961 and t[he] years from 1964 to 1967 produced noticeable recessions, while 1976[ ] and 1987–89 were clearly better than other moments in the crisis. [In] the same way it would be wrong to underestimate the differenc[es] between the present crisis and earlier crises. In the first place, soci[al] security systems, at least in the more developed countries, are clear[ly] much better.

Secondly, the important role played by the "undergroun[d]

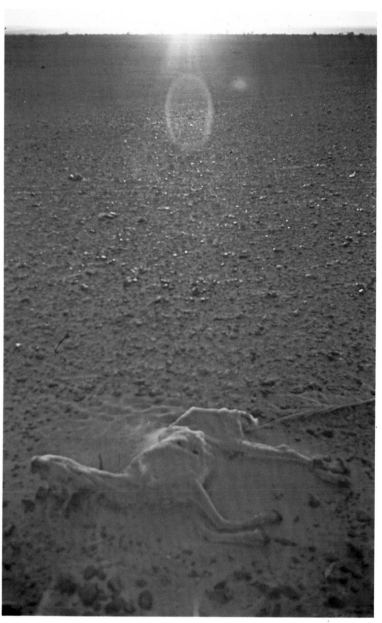

1. Drought in the Sahel: livestock is decimated.

2. A meeting of OPEC.

1945–74: The "Thirty Glorious Years" (J. Fourastié). Long period of economic prosperity.
1945–9: Years of reconstruction.
1950: Korean War breaks out. Huge surge of economic activity takes place in the West. Investments in communist countries increase.
1950–7: Years of rapid growth in communist China.
1967: Devaluation of the pound.
15 August 1971: Devaluation of the dollar, collapse of the international monetary system set up at Bretton Woods in 1944.
1973: The price of oil increases sharply—"first oil crisis"—as a result of the devaluation of hard currencies and the breakup of the international monetary system, and because it was used as a weapon by the Arab world following the 1973 war with Israel. American oil companies made enormous profits and Western banks began recycling petro-dollars (particularly in the form of loans to Third World countries).
1974: Beginning of problem-ridden years. Slowdown of growth throughout the world.

4. A family in Harlem.

Between 1971–1975 and 1976–1980, the annual rate of growth of the GDP of the USSR fell by several points; "Brezhnev stagnation." From 1972 to 1982 the rate of growth in the wealthy capitalist countries (including Japan) is on average 2.5%. In 1983–84 this rises to 3.3%. Stock prices plummet temporarily. Famine rages in Ethiopia and the Sahel.
1974–5: Industrial production in the West falls considerably. First marked rise in unemployment figures.
1976–9: Uncertain years with contradictory trends.
1978–79: Fall of the monarchy in Iran. Islami[c] Revolution.
1978–83: Serious famine in northeast Brazil.
1979–80: Second Oil Crisis brings a fresh increase in oil prices.
The beginning of the 1980s: The dollar, weakened in the 1970s at the same time as American influence itself, reinforces its position. American interest rates rise and capital pours into the country. The consequences of these events are often likened to those of a third 'oil crisis'. The

conomy suggests that statistical results cannot be taken too literally. Finally trade, especially international trade, suffered relatively little.

The forms and intensity of the crisis have varied greatly from country to country. Thus the industrialized West suffered most from the first crisis (1974–75) and the long-term recession. The South, which incurred such international indebtedness that the world, at times, was on the verge of a *krach* of unprecedented dimensions, suffered seriously from the second (approximately 1980–82). The economic and political disintegration of the communist countries (China, which was undergoing full pragmatic readjustment, should not be included) since 1989, constitutes the third, and maybe last, crisis of the recession phase that started in 1974.

There has been, of course, no shortage of attempts to explain or to find the meaning of the current crisis. Some observers are content simply to compare the present recession with various long-term cycles which can be seen to have existed in the past: from 1849 to 1873 there was a positive phase, from 1873 to 1893 a negative one; 1893 to 1913 was positive once more, 1913 to 1945 was negative, 1945 to 1974 was positive....

Other commentators point to demographic factors: according to this view, the baby boom of the 1940s and 1950s was the reason for post-war prosperity, and the fall in the birth-rate is said to have brought about a breakdown in growth. It is worth noting, however, that affluence in the West was quite unaffected by demographic decline in the 1960s and the first half of the 1970s. Many other analysts place the emphasis on changes in technology, since these, it is argued, are what sparked off and sustained expansion after the Second World War, and the upturn in the economy will be correspondingly dependent on the arrival of a fresh wave of technological innovation. But had the latter not already started before the onset of the economic crisis, at the end of the 1960s (nuclear, computer, etc.)? And is it not at its highest point now (biotechnology, robotics...)?

Finally, it is worth considering that the socio-political and cultural changes at the end of the 1960s and 1970s (the questioning of the value of work and industrial disciplines, the decline or collapse of economic planning and of the planned system itself, and the breakdown in the international monetary system under pressure from ethnic and national emotions...) are not an insignificant factor.

According to some analysts, the borderline or hard times will not start to ease until 1992, and true recovery cannot be expected earlier. Nevertheless, one can say that the recovery will be more localized and more limited in area than the boom of 1945–1974, which benefitted the Third World to varying degrees.

3. Ayatollah Khomeini, the head of the Iranian Islamic revolution.

Steelworkers demonstrating for their jobs at Longwy (France) in August 1979.

recession worsens in the West. The economic situation in Poland gets worse.
1982: Mexico defaults on its international debt. Bankruptcy is only barely avoided.
1983: Third World debts increased more than three-fold since 1975. World agricultural production falls (as a result of drought and crisis). Riots and looting in Brazil (Sao Paolo) Polish industrial production falls to its 1973 level.
1983–4: Partial economic recovery, particularly in the USA.
1984: Drought and famine in Black Africa and Ethiopia (where forced displacement of populations increases the number of victims).
1985: America voices its concern about the strength of the recovery. In 1985, the number of unemployed as a percentage of the working population reaches 7 or 8% in the United States and the Federal Republic of Germany, 11 or 12% in France, Great Britain and Italy.
1987–1989: Period of economic improvement in the industrialized countries.
October 1987: Stock exchange crash. Little impact on the economy.

23 July 1989: First application of Brady plan (plan to mitigate the debts of developing countries) in Mexico.
August 1990: Crisis in the Gulf erupts. It accentuates the economic slowdown that has affected the industrialized countries since the end of 1989.
End of 1991: Total foreign debt of all developing countries increases to 1,350 billion dollars.

From East-West Confrontation to North-South Duality

- ● intercommunal confrontations
- ✳ drug trade, mafias
- ⊤ countries that harbor or support terrorism
- ⩊ major wars
- ○ UN troops
- ← boat people

- pro-Turkish countries
- pro-Iranian countries
- Kurdish zone
- borders of the CIS

A	ARMENIA
AL	ALBANIA
AU	AUSTRIA
AZ	AZERBAIDJAN
B	BELGIUM
CZ	CZECHOSLOVAKIA
G	GEORGIA
K	KIRGIZ
L	LUXEMBURG
M	MOLDAVIA
N	NETHERLANDS
SW	SWITZERLAND
T	TADZHIKISTAN
U.A.E.	UNITED ARAB EMIRATES

Under development — Indicator: infant mortality ‰ of births

Wealthy — Poverty

12   26   50   100

0 — 1,000 km

Washington Treaty on the elimination of INF (intermediate missiles) in Europe.

10 December 1987

Opening of the Berlin Wall.

9 November 1989

Breakup of the communist system.
Process of political liberalization

1989–*Poland* 6 February: "roundtable" talks start (Party, Church, opposition); 4 June: Solidarity wins the parliamentary elections; 29 December: abolition of the POUP's leading role. *Hungary* 16 June: solemn funeral for Imre Nagy; 23 October: Declaration of the IV Republic of Hungary. *Czechoslovakia* 21 August: demonstrations in Prague on the anniversary of the 1968 invasion; 17 November: beginning of the large Civic Forum demonstrations; 29 November: abolition of the leading role of the party by the Czechoslovak deputies; 29 December: V. Havel becomes president of the Republic. *Bulgaria* 11 December: demonstrations in Sofia; promises of free elections and abolition of leading role of the party; 29 December: persecution of Turkish minority ends. *Romania* 22 December: the government is overthrown; 25 December: Ceausescu is executed.

1990–*Hungary* 8 April: parliamentary

elections are held, led by the Democratic Forum (right of center). *Lithuania* 24 February: free elections, independents win the majority; 11 March: parliament votes for the restoration of "the sovereignty that was lost in 1940"; V. Landsbergis becomes president; 29 June: under economic and military pressure, parliament suspends the declaration of independence. *Estonia* 20 March: parliament votes for independence. *Latvia* 4 May: parliament votes for independence with a "transition period." *Albania* 8 May: parliament votes on liberalization measures. *Romania* 20 May: I. Illiescu is elected president (85 of the votes) and the National Salvation Front wins the majority in both houses. *Bulgaria* 10-17 June: free parliamentary elections; the socialist party (ex-communist party) wins an absolute majority. *Russia* 29 May: B. Yeltsin elected president of the RSFSR; 12 June: deputies vote 907 to 13 for the "sovereignty of the state" of the RSFSR. *Ukraine* 16 July: parliament declares sovereignty. *USSR* July 1990-December 1991: all the republics

declare sovereignty.

1991–25 February: dissolution of the military structures of the Warsaw Pact. 1 July: dissolution of the administrative structures of the Warsaw Pact. *USSR* 12 June: B. Yeltsin is elected president of the Russian Republic through universal suffrage. 19-21 August: attempted coup d'état against M. Gorbachev. 29 August: the Supreme Soviet dissolves itself. 21 December: all the republics with the exception of Georgia and the Baltic states agree to join the CIS (Commonwealth of Independent States) under the assumption that they will preserve some joint functions (defense, nuclear safety). 30 December: the armed forces of the ex-USSR are disbanded.

Violent intercommunal uprisings

1986–*Kazakhstan*: anti-Russian riots.
1988–*Armenia*. 12-28 December: Azeris vs. Armenians in the Upper Karabach and at Sumgaib, Azerbaidzhan.
1989–*Yugoslavia* 28 March: Serbs vs. Albanians at Kosovo. *Georgia* 8 April: repression by Russian troops; 15 July: Abkhaz.

Bulgaria 1 May-29 December: persecution of Turkish minority. *Uzbekistan* 3 July: Uzbeks vs. Meskhets.
1990–*Azerbaidjan* 20 January: intervention of the army at Baku. *Tadzhikistan* 12-14 February: clashes at Duchanbe; 22 Armenians and Russians killed. *Romania* 2 March: confrontations between Romanian and Hungarian nationalists in Transylvania. *Kirgizia* 4 June: confrontations that set Kirghizis against Uzbekis. *Kazakstan-Usbekistan* June: border clashes. *Moldavia* 26 October: Gagauzes vs. Moldavians.

2. Soldiers in Saudi Arabia.

EAST-WEST: Between 1988 and 1992 the world underwent a severe change. The Soviet Union disappeared both as the center of world communism and as an empire. Within a matter of months, 73 years of October Revolution, 45 years of nuclear bipolarity, and 10 years of the "Second Cold War" came to an end. Gorbachev avoided the type of military interventions that had been advocated by the "Brezhnev doctrine," and the communist regimes, no longer able to rely on that basic support, crumbled almost without violence. They were replaced by pluralist systems moving toward a market economy. The GDR fell with the Berlin Wall and Germany was reunified in 1990, peacefully destroying what remained of the Iron Curtain.

At the same time, disarmament was accelerated and the speed with which the CFE (Conventional Forces in Europe) talks were initiated, followed by START (Strategic Arms Reduction Talks), changed the whole strategic picture. The CSCE (Conference on Security and Cooperation in Europe) created the institutional framework for new European security. The Warsaw Pact has disappeared and NATO's function has vanished, but the organization still exists, and the United States is striving to provide a new guarantee for order in the countries of the North faced with the chaos in the countries of the South by permitting the ex-USSR to be associated with NATO.

The attempt to take part in "harsh capitalism" has aggravated the economic situation in the countries in the East since 1990. The Soviet republics first demanded autonomy and then independence. On 19 August 1991 a coup d'etat against Gorbachev failed for lack of military support, discredited the authoritarianism of the old guard, and made Boris Yeltsin definitely the leader of Russia. The CIS (Commonwealth of Independent States) inherited the obligations of the ex-USSR in regard to security and disarmament, but the status of nuclear arms located in the Ukraine, Bielorussia, and Kazakhstan has still not been completely resolved in 1992. In addition, the United States is emphasizing the idea of a "threat from the South": the "uncontrolled sale" of nuclear materials or Soviet rockets as well as the emigration of scientists could lead to nuclear proliferation in Third World countries.

NORTH-SOUTH: Infant mortality, the general indicator of "underdevelopment," is widespread throughout Soviet Eurasia and extends into the Mediterranean. On both sides of this dividing line between wealth and poverty, there is an increase in intercommunal conflicts and in drug dealers' networks as side-effects of social tensions.

The war in the Caucasus sets Azeris (Turks) against Armenians. In Georgia and some autonomous regions of Russia, uprisings or civil wars have broken out. A new regional diplomacy, based on Turkish and Iranian influence, could stabilize the region or unleash a war in Central Asia. In the Middle East since the time of "peaceful coexistence," the rivalry between East and West has intensified the tensions. The modern issues of oil and armaments have a destabilizing effect when confronted with the archaic issue of the states (monarchies, Islamic republics, dictatorships). The Israeli-Palestinian conflict still continues despite the Camp David Accords with Egypt and the cease-fire with Syria. Israel never abandoned the annexation of East Jerusalem nor the colonization of the West Bank. However, the Gulf War emphasized the need to establish regional security based on different principles. Under pressure from the United States, the Madrid Peace Conference brought the Israelis and Palestinians together at the same table for the first time. On its part, the Maghreb is experiencing social problems and authoritarian political regimes. In Europe itself, the chaos in the Balkans culminated in Yugoslavia.

Entrenched on its continent, the United Sates views the South less as a "neighbor" than as a distant, militarily controllable "environment." But the security of Europe, reunified from Gibraltar to Vladivostok, depends on other methods and puts up with the development in the South rather than exerting force or using surveillance satellites.

1. Opening of the Berlin Wall in November 1989.

START Treaty, planning a 25–30% reduction of strategic nuclear arms.

Treaty on Chemical Disarmament.

CFE Treaty on reduction of conventional forces.

| 1 June 1990 | 21 November 1990 | 30–31 July 1991 |

1991—*Chechen-Ingush:* 8 November. *Moldavia* 13 November. *Georgia* 21 December.

German Reunification
1989—10 September: Hungary opens its border with Austria; 10,000 East Germans escape to the FRG. 28 November: Kohl proposes a 10-point reunification plan. 1 December: The GDR parliament decides to abolish the leading role of the SED party.
1990—14 March: First "2 + 4" Conference in Bonn (GDR, FRG, United States, France, Great Britain, USSR). 18 March: Elections held in the GDR; M. Lothar de Maziere's Christian Democratic Party holds 164 of the 400 seats in the People's House. 18 May: State treaty instituting a monetary, economic, and social union between the GDR and the FRG (on 2 July). July: The USSR accepts the integration of the GDR in NATO. 12 September: Moscow treaty definitively regulates the German question. 3 October: Unification of the GDR and FRG.

Conflicts in the South
Lebanon October 1986–8 July 1988: The "Camp War" ends with the expulsion of the "Carafists" of Beirut by pro-Syrians. October–30 August 1989: Beirut War between General Aoun and the Syrians. 22 October 1989: The Taef agreement (Saudi Arabia) among the Lebanese deputies (political reforms, no date for the withdrawal of Syrian troops) is rejected by General Aoun. 24 November 1989: After the election and the assassination of President Moawad, President Hraoui is elected in Chtaura, a zone controlled by Syria. 31 January 1990: Christian War (Aoun against the Lebanese forces). 13 October 1990: General Aoun surrenders.

Iran-Iraq War
20 July 1987: Resolution 598—the United Nations Security Council demands that hostilities cease; only Iraq accepts. July–December 1987: First Gulf crisis; American and French intervention. 28 February–18 April 1988: The "war of the cities"; 250 ground-to-ground missiles fired at Baghdad, Teheran, and other cities. 8 August 1988: Cease-fire agreement between Iraq and Iran. End of August–beginning of September 1988: Chemical attacks against the Iraqi Kurds by Iraq. 3 June 1989: Death of Khomeini.

Israel-Palestine
9 December 1987: Beginning of the Intifada in the Palestinian territories occupied by Israel. 31 July 1988: Break in legal and administrative relations between Jordan and the West Bank. 15 November 1988: National Palestinian Council declares an independent state in Palestine and accepts United Nations Security Council Resolution 242. 16 December 1988–20 June 1990: Meeting between Americans and Palestinians in Carthage. 2 May 1989: During his visit to Paris, Yasser Arafat declares that the PLO charter has become "null and void." 14 May 1989: Shamir's plan for elections in the occupied territories. 18 September 1989: Egyptian President Mubarak presents his plan to Israeli Minister of Defense, I. Rabin, in Cairo. 10 October 1989: American Secretary of State Baker presents his plan after Israel rejects Mubarak's plan. 5 November 1989: Baker's plan is accepted with reservations by Israel. 8 October 1990: Shooting in Jerusalem close to the Oman Mosque (several dozen Palestinians killed). 3 November 1991: Beginning of peace conference in Madrid. The United States, Israel, and the Arab countries, including a "Jordanian-Palestinian delegation," participate.

War in Afghanistan
14 April 1988: Agreement on the withdrawal of Soviet troops from Afghanistan. 15 February 1989: The last Soviet troops withdraw.

The Gulf War

THE GULF WAR MARKS the beginning of a strategic period that follows the bipolar nuclear order. Since the 1980s the countries of the Middle East were living according to the terrorist logic of "the deterrent of the poor." Both during the Lebanese war and during the Iran-Iraq war, hostages were taken, citizens of towns were subjected to gunfire, and stockpiles of chemicals were made available. Military nuclear research (Pakistan, Iraq) continued because of Israel's nuclear arms and customary reprisal attacks. This chaos turned into a threat not only for the Western world's oil interests but also for the weakened USSR.

The invasion of Kuwait led to a serious conflict: Kuwait and the Arab Emirates had dropped the price of crude oil through sales that exceeded the guides set by OPEC. Crushed by the debt it had to service, Iraq was neither able to cope with the reconstruction (after the Iran-Iraq war) nor to mobilize its soldiers, who faced unemployment due to the recession. Through diplomatic and military pressure, Saddam Hussein attained an increase in prices and a loan of $10 billion from Kuwait and Saudi Arabia. But Kuwait demanded that its borders be changed. Since there was a true partnership between Iraq and the United States against Iran, Iraq believed it could depend on being given the go-ahead or at least the assurance that America would remain neutral. Iraq made a major mistake when it seized Kuwait: the freedom of action of the bipolar era no longer existed. A further mistake was that Iraq believed it could break up the "UNO" coalition by threatening to intensify the Arab-Israeli conflict.

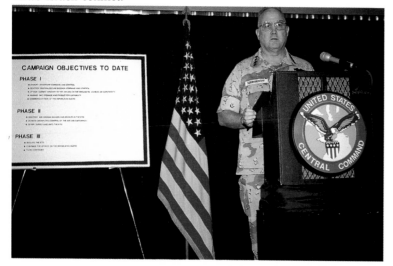

The War. In November 1990, asserting the (highly disputed danger of Iraqi nuclear weapons, the advocates for the war in the United States gained the upper hand over the advocates of a long embargo. On 19 August, President Bush decided to send 250,000 men to Saudi Arabia. He thus obligated himself to launch an offensive before the necessary relief for the professional expeditionary force could lead either to an effective reduction of tension or to a reinstitution of the draft. Operation *Desert Shield* was planned to protect the Saudi government, to safeguard control over the oil reserves, and to sanction the aggressive war that President Bush intended to be a turning point that would introduce a "new world order," which would be "administrative" rather than military (Bush's speech on 11 September 1990). The embargo against Iraq, the projection of force by 450,000 American soldiers, followed by the extended air campaign (*Desert Storm*) and the exhausting ground battle (*Desert Saber*), were the practical application of a tactical exercise the Pentagon had been preparing since Carter's presidency to ward off Soviet or Iranian aggression. It ended in extremely unequal losses (150 American military personnel vs. 150,000 Iraqi military personnel).

Having become the sole world leaders, the Americans, though economically weakened, tried to make the best of their military superiority. They used the Gulf War to define a **new strategic doctrine** based on the following principles:

1. The disappearance of the Soviet enemy made it possible to disarm and reduce the forces to "basic forces" that would permit technological surveillance and an increase in industrial and military power if another major threat were to occur.

2. The localization of responsibilities was to take place under American control. In Southeast Asia the war led to their permanent military presence and thus, in the long run, to placing the regional military role of Israel and Turkey under their supervision.

3. A new kind of strategic pre-eminence: the era of *space power* relegated the Navy to second place following the era of *sea power*. The "stealth" of airplanes (difficulty in tracking the F 115 on radar), "precision guidance" (Tomahawk cruise missiles), operational control, and targeting via observation satellites provide global ascendancy and absolute military superiority.

Faced with this new deal, a mid-sized nuclear power like France is forced to renew the source of its strategic autonomy by equipping itself with its own means of observation.

1. General Schwarzkopf (Commander of the United States Central Command) making a speech in January 1991.

Iraq invades Kuwait.	UN Security Council Resolution 678 authorizes the use of force against Iraq starting on 15 January 1991.	Beginning of the Coalition's offensive.	United Nations Resolution 686 terminates the fighting.
2 August 1990	**29 November 1990**	**17 January 1991**	**2 March 1991**

1990. 2 April: S. Hussein declares that Iraq has binary chemical weapons and will destroy half of Israel if the latter attempts any military action against Iraq.
28 May: At a summit of the Arab League, Iraq condemns the overproduction of oil by Kuwait and the United Arab Emirates, which had made the price drop to $13 per barrel.
2 August: Iraq invades Kuwait. The United Nations Security Council adopts Resolution 660 demanding unconditional withdrawal.
6 August: The United Nations Security council votes for an economic embargo against Iraq and Kuwait (Resolution 661). Saudi Arabia requests American soldiers to be deployed in its territory.
8 August: Iraq annexes Kuwait.
10 August: Iraq orders all embassies in Kuwait to be closed. The Arab countries vote 12 to 8 to send an Arab force to Saudi Arabia.
15 August: Iraq announces its withdrawal from the Iranian territories it occupies.
20 August: Iraq announces that all foreign hostages will be placed at strategic sites.

25 August: The United Nations authorizes the deployment of a force against ships violating the blockade (Resolution 665).
14 September: The Iraqis attack the French embassy in Kuwait.
25 September: The United Nations imposes an air embargo (Resolution 670).
2 October: French troops arrive in Saudi Arabia.
8 November: G. Bush announces that he will double the number of U.S. troops in Saudi Arabia.
19 November: M. Gorbachev says he will refuse to support a resolution authorizing the use of force.
29 November: The United Nations Security Council passes Resolution 678 authorizing the use of force against Iraq unless it implements all preceding resolutions before 15 January 1991.
6 December: S. Hussein announces that all hostages will be set free.
1991. 9 January: In Geneva, talks fail between J. Baker, American Secretary of State, and

T. Aziz, Iraqi Minister of Foreign Affairs.
17 January: An attack by the coalition begins in Iraq and Kuwait. Turkey authorizes raids from its territory.
18 January: Iraq launches its first Scud missile against Israel.
19 January: In order to counter the Iraqi Scuds, the United States sends ground-to-air Patriot missiles to Israel.
26 January: Iraqi planes start to seek refuge in Iran.
29 January: J.-P. Chevènement, French Minister of Defense, resigns.
1 February: France authorizes B 52s to fly over its territory.
13 February: American F 115s bomb an underground shelter in Baghdad causing 300 civilian deaths.
22 February: Iraqis set fire to oil wells in Kuwait. The Soviets announce an 8-point peace plan that is rejected by G. Bush.
24 February: The coalition's ground attack begins.
25 February: S. Hussein orders his troops to

withdraw to the position they held on 1 August 1990. The Soviets propose another peace plan, which is rejected by the United States.
26 February: The Iraqi forces retreat; 63,000 Iraqi prisoners are taken. The coalition troops reach the Euphrates Valley, completing the encirclement of Iraqi forces.
27 February: G. Bush announces that the operation has ended at 5 o'clock Greenwich Mean Time on 28 February.
28 February: Iraq accepts America's cease-fire conditions.
2 March: United Nations Resolution 686 terminates the fighting.
20 March: The Kurds confirm that they have taken Kirkuk. Iraqi armored divisions stream toward the north of the country.
6 April: Humanitarian aid operation to the Kurds by the armed forces of the Coalition begins. It continues until July.

1990–91

Targets and air war

The Coalition

NEW ZEALAND
JAPAN
SOUTH KOREA
AUSTRALIA
HONDURAS
CANADA
USA
UNITED KINGDOM
GERMANY
AFGHANISTAN
E.C. FRANCE
PAKISTAN
ARGENTINA
EGYPT
SAUDI ARABIA
SENEGAL
SYRIA
UNITED ARAB EMIRATES
NIGER
GULF COUNCIL
KUWAIT

MILITARY CONTRIBUTION

□ troops and material
▪ symbolic contingent
∥ air supplies
∥ bases
∥ naval supplies

FINANCIAL AID

to the USA
to countries penalised by the embargo

Incirli
Akrotiri
SYRIA
TURKEY
USSR
LEBANON
Damascus
Mosul
Arbil
Ba'iji
Kirkuk
Jerusalem
Amman
Samarra
Tikrit
ISRAEL
JORDAN
Rutba
Faludja
Karbala
Baghdad
EGYPT
Elat
IRAQ
Al Jaira
IRAN
Ar'ar
Nasiriyya
Tabuk
Basra
Rafa
Abadan
KUWAIT

**SOME DATA
WAR STATISTICS**

oil
pipelines
refineries
air bases
chemical weapons
enriched uranium
SCUD
warning systems
land bases
naval bases
facilities
Kurds
Shi'ites

Yanbu'
Medina
submarines that launch "Tomahawk" missiles
Hafar al Batin
Jiddah
Mecca
Al Jubayl
Dhahran
Damman
BAHRAIN
Ta'if
Riyad
QATAR
Al Khasab
SAUDI ARABIA
UNITED ARAB EMIRATES
Abu Dhabi
OMAN
Sulayyil

0   200   400 km

American deployment

28 August:	50,000	soldiers
2 October:	170,000	
5 November:	230,000	
26 December:	300,000	
19 January:	460,000	
30 January:	500,000	
28 February:	539,000	

Air sorties

18 January:	2,000
23 January:	12,000
30 January:	30,000
25 February:	97,000
28 February:	110,000

Scuds launched by Iraqis

17 January:	4 against Israel and Saudi Arabia
30 January:	53 against Israel and Saudi Arabia
11 February:	61 against Israel and Saudi Arabia
25 February:	78 against Israel and Saudi Arabia

Troop movements

Ⓐ Anglo-saxons
Ⓕ French
Ⓔ Egyptians and Syrians
Ⓢ Saudis, Kuwaitis, and others

As Samawah
Euphrates
Nasiriyya
swamps
Tigris
IRAN
Shatt al-Arab
Basra
Abadan
IRAQ
G
Fao
Rafa
actual border
defences facing west
airborne division
KUWAIT
Kuwait
SAUDI ARABIA
Khafqi

0   50   100 km

○ destroyed bridges
Iraqi forces
G Republican Guard
Allied forces 17.1.91
Allied forces 23.1.91

movements:
according to general H.N. Schwarzkopf

17 - 23   24   25 - 26   27

Local Drug Wars

EVER SINCE ANCIENT TIMES through to the Opium War in China, the history of numerous conflicts is intertwined with that of drugs, the driving force and the goal of wars. Between 1950 and 1975 the center of the first major networks of opium and heroin in the modern era was in Southeast Asia, especially in the mountainous jungles located at the borders of Burma, Laos, and Thailand, which is known as the Golden Triangle. The French, American, and national Chinese foreign secret services used other minorities in these areas, which traditionally were opium consumers, to finance their agencies and to wage a war from the rear against their communist enemies.

At the beginning of the 1980s, the drug wars reached Latin America after the Colombian dealers had monopolized the American cocaine market. The CIA used the services of drug dealers to provide aid to the "contras" in Nicaragua; in exchange, it turned a blind eye to their illegal activities. In the same way, General Noriega's dealings were tolerated for a long time in exchange for services rendered to different United States governments fighting communism in the region. Similarly, the Marxist guerrillas in Colombia and Peru never stopped making a profit from their drug resources. Even Fidel Castro's government, while condemning and executing four high government officials in 1989 for dealing in cocaine, tried unsuccessfully to assert that it was ignorant of their activities.

During the same period, heroin continued to play an important role in the conflicts in Asia and the Middle East. Starting in 1979 the war in Afghanistan encouraged the expansion of poppy cultivation. The secret service of the Pakistani army, Inter Services Intelligence (ISI), which had a monopoly on delivering weapons to the mudjahadeen (supplied by the United States, China, and Saudi Arabia), helped stimulate the processing of Afghani opium into heroin in laboratories located in the tribal regions of Pakistan. The money from these deals augmented the secret funds of the Pakistani army; this primarily served to buy weapons and to provide support for the rebels fighting in the territories of the Kashmir and Punjab Indians. In Lebanon the civil war encouraged the expansion of illegal cultivation and an increase in the number of laboratories for the militias and Syrian troops, especially in the Bekaa Valley.

In Burma, different army groups took part in the heroin trade up to 1989. There were war lords like Khun Sa, ethnic rebels like those of the Kashin, political opposition like that of the communist party (the largest producer), and, finally, sections of the military dictatorship. But in 1989, the communist party broke up and the junta in power (SLORE), having made agreements with most of the regional commanders of the former communist party, assumed control over the trade. Thus it was able to buy weapons in China for more than one billion dollars between 1988 and 1992 to fight in ethnic rebellions. In the Philippines the Marxist rebels of the Mindanese National Liberation Front (MNLF) and in Indonesia those of the Aceth province in northern Sumatra protect the cultivation of cannabis.

Since the breakup of the communist regimes, the regional powers abandoned by the superpowers found the resources needed for their

1. Poppy field under surveillance, Thailand.

Burma enters the drug "spiral."

1951

1951–1954: The Joint Group of Airport Commandos (GMCA) of the French army use the opium trade to finance the Méos (anticommunist partisans belonging to a mountain minority) operations.
1952–1954: The remnants of General Chang-kai Shek's army (Gnomindang), which took refuge in Burma and then in Thailand and Laos, turn to the opium and heroin trade.
1965–1970: The CIA again assumes the practices of French secret services and uses the opium and heroin networks to finance clandestine operations to hit the communists in Laos and Vietnam from the rear.
1967. June: Chan Chi Fu, alias Khun Sa, Sino-Burmese, who started to trade in opium three months earlier, suffers a severe defeat in Ban Kwan (Laos). The troops of his rival, General Onare Rattikare, commander of the Laotian army, take possession of all of his caravans transporting 16 tons of opium.
1971: United States President R. Nixon launches the first "war on drugs."
1975–1992: In Lebanon the civil war and foreign intervention encourage the expansion

2. The Bolivian army destroys a cocaine laboratory, 1991.

R. Nixon launches the first "war on drugs."

1971

of the production of hashish, the appearance of the poppy, and an increase in the number of heroin and cocaine laboratories, especially in the Bekaa Valley.
1979–1992: Prohibition of poppy production and traditional consumption of opium in Pakistan, the Islamic Revolution in Iran, and resistance to the Soviet invasion of Afghanistan cause a rapid increase in heroin production in the region.
1980: Drug dealers finance General Garcia Meza's coup d'etat in Bolivia (7 July). For one year, Minister of the Interior Luis Arce Gomez uses his office to organize cocaine trade.
1984–1986: In order to bypass the supervision of military aid to the "contras" in Nicaragua decreed by the United States Congress (Bolan Amendment), the CIA uses the services of drug dealers. In exchange, it closes its eyes to the infiltration of cocaine and hashish into the United States.
1989. 14–16 July: As a consequence of the Arche Summit in Paris that brought together the seven most industrialized countries, a financial action group to stop money

3. Poppy cultivation in Pakistan.

Production Regions:	Coca (cocaine)	Poppy (opium, morphine, heroin)	*Conflicts
	Cannabis (marijuana, hashish)	Khat	*Conflicts linked to drugs

autonomy in drug money. In Afghanistan, since America announced that it would stop the arms supplies at the end of 1991, the mujahadeen increased drug production in the regions they control. Different militias do the same in the territories of the former Yugoslavia. Several local conflicts in Africa—Senegal, Liberia,

Somalia, Ethiopia—are supported by money from cannabis or khat and their aim is to control the cultivation of these plants. It is to be feared that the Moslem republics in Central Asia (traditional producers of cannabis and the poppy), will find it to be a good means of financing their autonomy and conflicts with their neighbors.

"The Golden Crescent" (Pakistan, Afghanistan, Iran).

1979

Antidrug Summit in Carthagena.

15 February 1990

Pablo Escobar's surrender.

19 June 1991

laundering (GAF) is created.
18 July: General Ochoa and three other high officials are tried and shot in Cuba for trading in drugs.
18 August: In Colombia the Medellin cartel's hitman assassinates Luis Carlos Galan, who is running for election as president of the republic.
20 December: The United States invades Panama in order to arrest General Noriega and put him on trial in the United States.
15 February 1990: Carthagena antidrug summit brings together the presidents of Bolivia, Peru, Colombia, and the United States.
1991. March-May: Appearance of poppy cultivation on a large scale in Colombia.
19 June: The Godfather Pablo Escobar surrenders to the Colombian authorities.
5 July: The activities of the Bank of Credit and Commerce International (BCCI) are suspended. The bank had been convicted of laundering drug money two years earlier.
9 October: Swiss police announce the dismantling of a large network of Yugoslav dealers who sell heroin and supply the

Croatian militia with weapons.
1992. 26-27 February: The Second Continental Antidrug Summit in San Antonio (Texas). The presidents of Ecuador, Venezuela, and Mexico join those of the other Andean states who were present in Carthagena.

4. Presidents Fujimori (Peru), Salinas (Mexico), and Bush (United States) at the San Antonio Summit.

Picture Credits

VI-IX
1. Paris, Bibl. nat./Ph. H. JOSSE
2. London, British Museum/Archives LIDIS-BREPOLS.
3 and 4. Paris, Bibl. nat./Ph. EXPLORER ARCHIVES.

2-3
1, 2 and 3. Ph. CH. LÉNARS-EXPLORER.
4. Liège, Musée Curtius/Ph. CH. MAHAUX-EXPLORER.
5. Ph. CH. LÉNARS-EXPLORER.

4-5
1. Vienna, Naturhistorisches Museum/Ph. E. LESSING-MAGNUM.
2. Ph. G: MARTIN-GUILLOU-EXPLORER.
3. Ph. CH. LÉNARS-EXPLORER.

6-7
1. Ph. A. BORDES-EXPLORER.
2. Ph. H. JOSSE.
3. Ph. M. CAMBAZARD-EXPLORER.
Saint-Germain-en-Laye, Musée des Antiquités nationales/Ph. E. LESSING-MAGNUM.
Périgueux, Musée du Périgord/Ph. J.-M. LABAT-EXPLORER ARCHIVES.
Saint-Germain-en-Laye, Musée des Antiquités nationales/Ph. GIRAUDON.

8-9
1. Paris, Musée de l'Homme/Ph. E. LESSING/MAGNUM.
2. Ankara, Archaeological Museum/Ph. G. DAGLI ORTI.
3. People's Republic of China, Ph. BULLOZ.
4. Stockholm, Historiska Museet/Ph. G. DAGLI ORTI.

10-11
1 and 2. Ph. G. DAGLI ORTI.
3. Ph. FERRERO-J.-M. LABAT-EXPLORER.
4. Paris, Musée de l'Homme/Ph. E. LESSING-MAGNUM.
5. Ph. G. DAGLI ORTI.
6. Athens, National Archaeological Museum/Ph. G. DAGLI ORTI.
7. Ph. J.-M. LABAT-EXPLORER.

12-13
1 and 2. London, British Museum/Archives LIDIS-BREPOLS.
3. Baghdad, Iraq Museum/Ph. E. LESSING-MAGNUM.
4. London, British Museum/Archives LIDIS-BREPOLS.
5. Ph. I. MORATH-MAGNUM.

14-15
1. Ph. G. DAGLI ORTI
2. Ph. P. TÉTREL-EXPLORER.
3, 4 and 5. Cairo, Egyptian Museum/Ph. G. DAGLI ORTI.

16-17
1. Ph. S. FIORE-EXPLORER ARCHIVES.
2. London, British Museum/Ph. BRIDGEMAN-GIRAUDON.
3 and 4. London, British Museum/Archives LIDIS-BREPOLS.
5. London, British Museum/Ph. E. LESSING-MAGNUM.

18-19
1 and 2. Ph. G. DAGLI ORTI.
3. Ankara, Archaeological Museum/Ph. G. DAGLI ORTI.
4. Damascus, National Museum/Ph. G. DAGLI ORTI.
5. Ph. G. DAGLI ORTI.
6. Ankara, Archaeological Museum/Ph. G. DAGLI ORTI.

20-21
1. Ph. G. DAGLI ORTI.
2. Iraklion, Archaeological Museum/Ph. G. DAGLI ORTI.
3. Athens, National Archaeological Museum/Ph. G. DAGLI ORTI.
4 and 5. Athens, National Archaeological Museum/Ph. BRIDGEMAN-GIRAUDON.
6. Athens, National Archaeological Museum/Ph. G. DAGLI ORTI.

22-23
1. Ph. S. FIORE-EXPLORER.
2 and 3. Ph. CH. LÉNARS-EXPLORER.
4. Ph. S. FIORE-EXPLORER.
5. Ph. J.-L. NOU-EXPLORER.
6. Ph. S. FIORE-EXPLORER.
7 and 8. Ph. J.-L. NOU-EXPLORER.

24-25
1. Ph. CH. LÉNARS-EXPLORER.
2. London, British Museum/Archives LIDIS-BREPOLS.
3. Ph. RODGER-MAGNUM.
4. Paris, Musée du Louvre/Archives LIDIS-BREPOLS.
5. Vienna, Kunsthistorisches Museum/Ph. E. LESSING-MAGNUM.
6. Paris, Bibl. nat./Archives LIDIS-BREPOLS.

26-27
1. Ph. E. LESSING-MAGNUM.
2. London, British Museum/Archives LIDIS-BREPOLS.

3. Ph. E. LESSING-MAGNUM.
4 and 5. London, British Museum/Archives LIDIS-BREPOLS.

28-29
1. Ph. PH. BEUZEN-EXPLORER.
2. Ph. E. LESSING-MAGNUM.
3. Ph. S. FIORE-EXPLORER.
4. Luxor, Museum/Ph. G. DAGLI ORTI.
5. Cairo, Egyptian Museum/Ph. G. DAGLI ORTI.
6. Paris, Musée du Louvre/Archives LIDIS-BREPOLS.

30-31
1. People's Republic of China/Ph. H. JOSSE.
2. People's Republic of China/Ph. BULLOZ.
3. People's Republic of China/Ph. CH. LÉNARS-EXPLORER.
4. People's Republic of China/Ph. E. LESSING-MAGNUM.
5. People's Republic of China/Ph. LAUROS-GIRAUDON.

32-33
1. Copenhagen, Nationalmuseet/Ph. E. LESSING-MAGNUM.
2. Ph. E. LESSING-MAGNUM.
3. Graz, Steiermärkisches Landesmuseum/Ph. E. LESSING-MAGNUM.
4. Aix-en-Provence, Musée Granet/Ph. G. DAGLI ORTI.
5. London, British Museum/Ph. E. LESSING-MAGNUM.

34-35
1. Paris, Musée du Louvre/Ph. R.M.N.
2. Ph. CH. LÉNARS-EXPLORER.
3. Tunis, Musée du Bardo/Ph. EDIMEDIA.
4. Carthage, Musée nationale/Ph. CH. LÉNARS-EXPLORER.
5. Paris, Bibl. nat./Ph. EXPLORER ARCHIVES.
6. London, British Museum/Archives LIDIS-BREPOLS.

36-37
1. Paris, Bibl. des Arts décoratifs/Ph. G. DAGLI ORTI.
2 and 3. Ph. G. DAGLI ORTI.
4. Baghdad, Iraq Museum/Ph. G. DAGLI ORTI.
5. Paris, Bibl. nat./Photothèque HACHETTE.
6. Athens, Acropolis Museum/Ph. G. DAGLI ORTI.

38-39
1. Rome, Museo Nazionale Romano/Ph. G. DAGLI ORTI.
2. Vienna, Naturhistorisches Museum/Ph. E. LESSING-MAGNUM.

40-41
1. Ph. CL. BÉRARD.
2. Iraklion, Archaeological Museum/Ph. G. NIMATALLAH-ARTEPHOT.
3. Photothèque HACHETTE.
4. Athens, National Archaeological Museum/Ph. G. NIMATALLAH-ARTEPHOT.
5. Thebes, Archaeological Museum/Ph. E. LESSING-MAGNUM.
6. Athens, National Archaeological Museum/Ph. G. NIMATALLAH-ARTEPHOT.

42-43
1. Ph. G. DAGLI ORTI.
2. Athens, Acropolis Museum/Ph. G. DAGLI ORTI.
3. Istanbul, Archaeological Museums/Ph. E. LESSING-MAGNUM.
4. Châtillon-sur-Seine, Archaeological Museum/Ph. G. DAGLI ORTI.
5. Paris, Bibl. nat./Ph. E. LESSING-MAGNUM.

44-45
1. Ph. G. DAGLI ORTI.
2. Teheran, Archaeological Museum/Ph. H. JOSSE.
3. Teheran, Archaeological Museum/Ph. G. DAGLI ORTI.
4. Ph. G. DAGLI ORTI.
5. Teheran, Archaeological Museum/Ph. G. DAGLI ORTI.

46-47
1. Ph. G. DAGLI ORTI.
2. Paris, Bibl. nat./Ph. EXPLORER ARCHIVES.
3. Boston, Museum of Fine Arts/Ph. EXPLORER ARCHIVES.
4. Athens, National Archaeological Museum/Ph. G. DAGLI ORTI.
5. Ph. R. PERCHERON-ARTEPHOT.
6. Athens, Acropolis Museum/Ph. L.-Y. LOIRAT-EXPLORER ARCHIVES.

48-49
1. Paris, Bibl. nat./Photothèque HACHETTE.
2. Naples, National Archaeological Museum/Ph. G. NIMATALLAH-ARTEPHOT.
3. Paris, Bibl. nat./Ph. EXPLORER AR-

CHIVES.
4. Mexico, National Anthropological Museum/Ph. G. DAGLI ORTI.
5. Rome, Capitoline Museum/Ph. G. DAGLI ORTI.
6. Dijon, Chartreuse de Champmol/Ph. G. DAGLI ORTI.
7. Naples, National Archaeological Museum/Ph. G. DAGLI ORTI.
8. Paris, Musée du Louvre/Ph. H. JOSSE.

50-51
1. Paris, Bibl. nat./Ph. EXPLORER ARCHIVES.
2 and 3. Thessalonika, University Museum/Ph. T.A.P.-EXPLORER ARCHIVES.
4. Ph. P. VIDAL-NAQUET.
5. Delphi, Archaeological Museum/Ph. BRIDGEMAN-GIRAUDON.

52-53
1. Rome, Museo Nazionale di Villa Giulia/Ph. G. DAGLI ORTI.
2. Ph. CH. LÉNARS-EXPLORER.
3. Capua, Museo Provinciale Campano/Ph. G. DAGLI ORTI.
4. Rome, Museo Nazionale di Villa Giulia/Ph. G. DAGLI ORTI.

54-55
1. People's Republic of China/Ph. E. LESSING-MAGNUM.
2. People's Republic of China/Ph. LAUROS-GIRAUDON.
3. Ph. R. BAUMGARTNER-EXPLORER.
4. People's Republic of China/Ph. E. LESSING-MAGNUM.
5. Paris, Musée Cernuschi/Ph. EXPLORER ARCHIVES.
6. PEOPLE'S Republic of China/Ph. CH. LÉNARS-EXPLORER.

56-57
1. Ph. C.B.O.-GIRAUDON.
2. Ph. J.-L. NOU-EXPLORER.
3. Ph. G. DAGLI ORTI.

58-59
1. Ph. F. SCIANNA-MAGNUM.
2. Benevento, Museo del Sannio/Ph. G. DAGLI ORTI.
3. Paris, Musée du Louvre/Ph. H. JOSSE.

60-61
1. Ph. CH. LÉNARS-EXPLORER.
2. Mainz, Römisch-Germanisches Zentralmuseum/Ph. E. LESSING-MAGNUM.
3. Paris, Musée du Louvre/Ph. H. JOSSE.
4. Paris, Musée du Louvre/Ph. EXPLORER ARCHIVES.

62-63
1. Lyon, Musée de la civilisation gallo-romaine/Ph. H. JOSSE.
2. Ph. J. DUPONT-EXPLORER.
3. Trier, Rheinisches Landesmuseum/Ph. LAUROS-GIRAUDON.
4. Nîmes, Maison Carrée/Ph. P TÉTREL-EXPLORER.

64-65
1. Archives LIDIS-BREPOLS.
2. Paris, Bibl. nat./Archives LIDIS-BREPOLS.
3. Rome, Museo Cristiano Lateranense/Ph. ALINARI-GIRAUDON.
4. Urbino, Museo Arcivescovile/Ph. ALINARI-GIRAUDON.
5. London, by courtesy of the Bible Society/Ph. BRIDGEMAN-GIRAUDON.

66-67
1. Rome, Vatican Museum/Ph. E. LESSING-MAGNUM.
2. Ph. H. CARTIER-BRESSON-MAGNUM.
3. Ph. R. BAUMGARTNER-EXPLORER.
4. Sarnath, Museum/Ph. LAUROS-GIRAUDON.
5. Mexico, National Anthropological Museum/Ph. G. DAGLI ORTI.

68-69
1 and 2. Brescia, Museo dell'Età Cristiana/Ph. GIRAUDON.
3. Ph. R. PERCHERON-ARTEPHOT.
4. Troyes, Musée des Beaux-Arts et d'Archéologie/Ph. G. DAGLI ORTI.

70-71
1. Teheran, Archaeological Museum/Ph. G. DAGLI ORTI.
2. Ph. S. FIORE-EXPLORER ARCHIVES.
3. Paris, Musée du Louvre/Ph. H. JOSSE.
4. Paris, Musée Guimet/Ph. LESSING-MAGNUM.
6. Paris, Musée Guimet/Ph. LAUROS-GIRAUDON.

72-73
1. Paris, Bibl. nat./Archives CLAM!
2. Ph. LAUROS-GIRAUDON.
3. Berne, Bernisches Historisches Museum/Ph. F. FAILLET-ARTEPHOT.
4. Paris, Musée de Cluny/Ph. H. JOSSE.
5. Berne, Bernisches Historisches Museum/Ph. F. FAILLET-ARTEPHOT.

74-75
1. Venice, Biblioteca Nazionale Marciana/Ph. G. DAGLI ORTI.
2. Ph. G. DAGLI ORTI.
3. Ph. G. DAGLI ORTI.
4. Paris, Musée de Cluny/Ph. H. JOSSE.
5. Paris, Bibl. nat./Ph. EXPLORER-ARCHIVES.
6. Ph. E. LESSING-MAGNUM.

76-77
1. Ph. CH. LÉNARS-EXPLORER.
2. Ph. PH. BOUSQUET-EXPLORER.
3. Paris, Musée du Louvre/Ph. LAUROS-GIRAUDON.
4. Ph. G. DAGLI ORTI.
5. Tunis, Bibl. nat./Ph. LAUROS-GIRAUDON.

78-79
1. London, Victoria and Albert Museum/Ph. BRIDGEMAN-GIRAUDON.
2. Paris, Bibl. nat./Ph. EXPLORER ARCHIVES.
3. Ph. G. DAGLI ORTI.
4. London, British Museum/Ph. BRIDGEMAN-GIRAUDON.
5. Paris, Bibl. nat./Ph. EXPLORER ARCHIVES.
6. Parisn Bibl. nat./Archives TALLANDIER.

80-81
1. Oslo, Norsk Sjøfartsmuseum/Ph. KNUDSENS-GIRAUDON.
2. Ph. P. TÉTREL-EXPLORER.
3. London, British Museum/E.T. ARCHIVE.
4. Oslo, Norsk Sjøfartsmuseum/Ph. KNUDSENS-GIRAUDON.

82-83
1. Ph. JAFFRE-DUROU-EXPLORER.
2. Paris, Musée Guimet/Ph. GIRAUDON.
3. People's Republic of China/Ph. BULLOZ.
4. Ph. JAFFRE-DUROU-EXPLORER.
5. People's Republic of China/Ph. LAUROS-GIRAUDON.
6. Paris, Musée Guimet/Ph. E. LESSING-MAGNUM.
Commission for the Protection of Japan's Cultural Heritage/Ph. EXPLORER ARCHIVES.

84-85
1. Nara, Todai-ji/Ph. OGAWA-ARTEPHOT.
2. Rome, Museo Nazionale d'Arte Orientale/Ph. G. DAGLI ORTI.
3. Ph. CH. LÉNARS-EXPLORER.
4. Kyoto, Horyu-ji/Ph. OGAWA-ARTEPHOT.
5. Paris, private collection/Ph. G. DAGLI ORTI.

86-87
Illustration BERTIN.
1. Paris, Musée Guimet/Ph. G. DAGLI ORTI.
2. Ph. INVERNIZZI-GIRAUDON.
3. Ph. G. DAGLI ORTI.
4. Ph. CH. LÉNARS-EXPLORER.
5. Ph. G. BOUTIN-EXPLORER.

88-89
1. Aix-la-Chapelle, Trésor de la cathédrale/Ph. E. LESSING-MAGNUM.
2. Paris, Musée de Cluny/Ph. E. LESSING-MAGNUM.
3. Ph. B. BARBEY-MAGNUM.
4. Paris, Bibl. nat./Ph. EXPLORER ARCHIVES.

90-91
1. Paris, Bibl. nat./Photothèque HACHETTE.
2. Ph. CH. LÉNARS-EXPLORER.
3. Istanbul, Topkapi Library/Ph. G. DAGLI ORTI.
4. Paris, Musée Guimet/Ph. G. DAGLI ORTI.
5. Ph. CH. LÉNARS-EXPLORER.
6. London, British Museum/E.T. ARCHIVE.
7. Paris, Bibl. nat./Ph. EXPLORER ARCHIVES.

92-93
1. Paris, Bibl. nat./Ph. H. JOSSE.
2. Conques, Trésor de l'église Sainte-Foy/Ph. GIRAUDON.
3. Paris, Archives nationales/Ph. BULLOZ.
4. Paris, Musée du Louvre/Ph. LAUROS-GIRAUDON.
5. Ph. J.-L. CHARMET.
6. Ph. G. MARTIN-GUILLOU-EXPLORER.

94-95
1. Paris, Bibl. nat./Photothèque HACHETTE.
2. Ph. D. DORVAL-EXPLORER.
3. Paris, Musée de Cluny/Ph. H. JOSSE.

96-97
1. Moscow, State Tretyakov Gallery/Ph. J. MASSON-ED. CERCLE D'ART.

2. Ph. C. CAPA-MAGNUM.
3. Moscow, State Tretyakov Gallery/Ph A.P.M.
4. Ph. A.P.N.

98-99
1. Paris, Musée de Cluny/Ph. H. JOSSE
2. Paris, Bibl. nat./Photothèque HACHETTE.
3. Vienna, Kunsthistorisches Museum Ph. E. LESSING-MAGNUM.
4. Ph. M.-J. LEROY-EXPLORER.

100-101
1. Paris, Bibl. nat./Photothèque HACHETTE.
2. Paris, Musée du Louvre/Ph GIRAUDON.
3. Ph. LAUROS-GIRAUDON.
4. Paris, Bibl. de l'Arsenal/Ph. GIRAUDON.
5. Paris, Musée de Cluny/Ph. H. JOSSE.
6. Paris, Bibl. nat./Photothèque HACHETTE.

102-103
1. Ph. PUJEBET-EXPLORER.
2. London, British Museum/E.T. ARCHIVE.
3. Bayeux, Musée de la Tapisserie de la Reine Mathilde/Ph. G. DAGLI ORTI.
4. Ph. F. MAYER-MAGNUM.
5. Ph. B. GÉRARD-EXPLORER.
6. Paris, Musée de Cluny/Ph. H. JOSSE.

104-105
1. Paris, Musée du Louvre/Ph. H. JOSSE.
2. Dublin, Trinity College Library/Ph. BRIDGEMAN-GIRAUDON.
3. Paris, Bibl. nat./Archives TALLANDIER.
4. Paris, Archives nationales/Ph. J.-L. CHARMET.
5. Montecassino, Abbey Library/Ph. GIRAUDON.
6. Admont, Abbey Library/Ph. E. LESSING-MAGNUM.

106-107
1. Urbino, Galleria Nazionale delle Marche/Ph. LAUROS-GIRAUDON.
2. Ph. CH. MAHAUX-EXPLORER ARCHIVES.
3. Paris, Archives nationales/Ph. BULLOZ.
4. Ph. L.-Y. LOIRAT-EXPLORER.
5. Madrid, Museo del Prado/Ph. G. DAGLI ORTI.
6. Berne, Burgerbibliothek/Burgerbibliothek photo.

108-109
1. Ph. G. DAGLI ORTI.
2. Paris, Bibl. nat./Ph. GIRAUDON.
3. Ph. G. DAGLI ORTI.
4. Ph. E. LESSING-MAGNUM.
5. Ph. G. DAGLI ORTI.
6. Ph. E. LESSING-MAGNUM.

110-111
1. Ph. CH. LÉNARS-EXPLORER.
2. Istanbul, Topkapi Library/Ph. G. DAGLI ORTI.
3. Oxford, Bodleian Library/Ph. EXPLORER ARCHIVES.
4. Toulouse, Musée Paul Dupuy/Ph. LAUROS-GIRAUDON.
5. Paris, Bibl. nat./Ph. J.-L. CHARMET.

112-113
1. Paris, Archives nationales/Ph. BULLOZ.
2. Paris, Musée Guimet/Ph. H. JOSSE.
3. Istanbul, Topkapi Library/Ph. G. DAGLI ORTI.
4. Ph. M. KOENE-EXPLORER.

114-115
1. Tokyo, National Museum/Ph. ZAUHO PRESS-ARTEPHOT.
2. Paris, private collection/Ph. G. DAGLI ORTI.
3. Ph. G. ZAWADZKI-EXPLORER.
4. Lyon, Musée historique des tissus/Ph. GIRAUDON.

116-117
1. Ph. G. DAGLI ORTI.
2. Ph. S. FIORE-EXPLORER.
3. Bombay, Prince of Wales Museum of Western India/Ph. J.-L. NOU-EXPLORER.
4. Ph. J.-L. NOU-EXPLORER.

118-119
1. Ph. G. PERESS-MAGNUM.
2. Castres, Musée Goya/Ph. G. DAGLI ORTI.
3. Oxford, Bodleian Library/E.T. ARCHIVE.
4. Agen, Bibl. municipale/Ph. H. JOSSE.
5. Paris, Archives nationales/Ph. J.-L. CHARMET.

120-121
1. Ph. F. JALAIN-EXPLORER.
2. Ph. H. VEILLER-EXPLORER.
3. Paris, Musée du Louvre/Ph. G. DAGLI ORTI.
4. Gerona, Cathedral Museum/Ph. ORONEZ-ARTEPHOT.
5. Ph. B. BORAUD-EXPLORER.

Picture Credits

122-123
1. Ph. J.-P. LAMOUR-EXPLORER.
2. Ph. M. CAMBAZARD-EXPLORER.
3. Ph. LAROUS-GIRAUDON.
4. Chantilly, Musée Condé/Ph. GIRAUDON.
5. Lyon, Musée du Louvre/Ph. G. DAGLI ORTI.
6. Lyon, Musée historique des tissus/Ph. GIRAUDON.
7. Paris, Archives nationales/Ph. GIRAUDON.

124-125
1. Paris, Bibl. nat./Ph. EXPLORER ARCHIVES.
2. Siena, Palazzo Pubblico/Ph. G. DAGLI ORTI.
3. Paris, Musée du Louvre/Ph. G. DAGLI ORTI.
4. Paris, Bibl. nat./Ph. EXPLORER ARCHIVES.
5. Ph. G. DAGLI ORTI.
6. Paris, Bibl. nat./Ph. EXPLORER ARCHIVES.

126-127
1. Paris, Bibl. nat./Archives TALLANDIER.
2. Avignon, Palais des Papes/Ph. G. DAGLI ORTI.
3. Paris, Bibl. polonaise/Ph. J.-L. CHARMET.
4. Naples, Museo e Gallerie Nazionali di Capodimonte/Ph. GIRAUDON.

128-129
1. Palermo, Galleria Regionale di Sicilia/Ph. LAUROS-GIRAUDON.
2. Paris, Bibl. nat./Archives TALLANDIER.
3. Madrid, Museo del Prado/Ph. G. DAGLI ORTI.
4. Paris, Bibl. de l'Arsenal/Ph. J.-L. CHARMET.
5. Modena, Biblioteca Estense/Ph. GIRAUDON.

130-131
1. Ph. J. VALENTIN-EXPLORER.
2. Paris, Bibl. nat./Ph. EXPLORER ARCHIVES.
3. Ph. BOUTIN-EXPLORER.
4. Ph. CH. LÉNARS-EXPLORER.
5. Ph. CL. WEINMANN-A.A.A. PHOTO.
6. Ph. CH. LÉNARS-EXPLORER.

132-133
1 and 2. Ph. G. DAGLI ORTI.
3. Oaxaca, Regional Museum/Ph. G. DAGLI ORTI.
4. Madrid, Museo de América/Ph. G. DAGLI ORTI.
5. Jalapa, Anthropological Museum/Ph. G. DAGLI ORTI.

134-135
1. Ph. G. DAGLI ORTI.
2. Lima, Museo del Oro del Peru/Ph. G. DAGLI ORTI.
3. Lima, Museo Nacional de Antropologia y Arqueologia/Ph. G. DAGLI ORTI.
4. Ph. G. DAGLI ORTI.

136-137
1. Lisbon/Ph. H. JOSSE.
2. Philadelphia, Museum of Art/Museum photo.
3. Vienna, Kunsthistorisches Museum/Ph. H. JOSSE.

138-139
1. Madrid, Museo de América/Ph. ORONOZ-ARTEPHOT.
2 and 3. Lisbon, Monastero de Jeronimos/Ph. H. JOSSE.
4. Paris, Bibl. nat./E.T. ARCHIVE.
5. Madrid, Bibl. Nacional/Ph. G. DAGLI ORTI.

140-141
1. Amsterdam, Rijksmuseum/Ph. A. HELD-ARTEPHOT.
2. Paris, Bibl. nat./Ph. EXPLORER ARCHIVES.
3. Paris, Bibl. des Arts décoratifs/Ph. EXPLORER ARCHIVES.
4. Paris, Bibl. nat./Ph. GIRAUDON.
5. Versailles, Musée national du château/Ph. GIRAUDON.

142-143
1. Vienna, Österreichische National Bibliothek/Ph. Bibliothek.
2. Paris, Ecole nationale supérieure des Beaux-Arts/Ph. BULLOZ.
3. London, Victoria and Albert Museum/Ph. BRIDGEMAN-GIRAUDON.
4. Florence, Uffizi/Ph. GIRAUDON.
5. Paris, Bibl. nat./Ph. LAUROS-GIRAUDON.
6. Clermont-Ferrand, Musée du Ranquet/Ph. LAUROS-GIRAUDON.

144-145
1 and 2. Paris, Bibl. nat./Ph. EXPLORER ARCHIVES.
3. Private collection/Ph. J.-L. CHARMET.
4. Paris, Bibl. nat./Photothèque

HACHETTE.
5. Paris, Bibl. des Arts décoratifs/Ph. J.-L. CHARMET.

146-147
1. Palermo, Galleria Regionale di Sicilia/Ph. LAUROS-GIRAUDON.
2. Paris, Bibl. des Arts décoratifs/Ph. EXPLORER ARCHIVES.
3. Ph. EXPLORER ARCHIVES.
4. Florence, Santa Maria Novella/Ph. SCALA-FIRENZE.
5. Paris, Bibl. nat./Ph. EXPLORER ARCHIVES.
6. Orléans, Musée des Beaux-Arts/Ph. LAUROS-GIRAUDON.

148-149
1. Florence, private collection/Ph. ZUCCONI-ARTEPHOT.
2. Lima, Museo de Arte/Ph. G. DAGLI ORTI.
3. Siena, Pinacoteca Nazionale/Ph. EXPLORER ARCHIVES.

150-151
1. Paris, Bibl. du Protestantisme/Ph. J.-L. CHARMET.
2. Heidelberg, Kurpfalzisches Museum/Ph. LAUROS-GIRAUDON.
3. Paris, Bibl. du Protestantisme/Ph. LAUROS-GIRAUDON.
4. Winterthur, Kunstmuseum/Ph. BURKHARD-ARTEPHOT.
5. Ph. J.-L. CHARMET.
6. Florence, Uffizi/Ph. BRIDGEMAN-GIRAUDON.
7. Munich, Alte Pinakothek/Ph. ARTOTHEK-GIRAUDON.
8. Lugano, Thyssen-Bornemisza collection/Ph. BRIDGEMAN-GIRAUDON.

152-153
1. Paris, Musée Carnavalet/Ph. LAUROS-GIRAUDON.
2. Ph. J.-L. CHARMET.
3. Paris, Bibl. nat./Ph. J.-L. CHARMET.
4. Paris, Bibl. nat./Ph. I.R.L.
5. Rome, Palazzo Barberini/Ph. A. HELD-ARTEPHOT.

154-155
1. Moulins, Musée d'art et d'archéologie/Ph. LAUROS-GIRAUDON.
2. Madrid, Museo del Prado/Ph. BRIDGEMAN-GIRAUDON.
3. Madrid, Museo de América/Ph. GIRAUDON.
4. Ph. GIRAUDON.

156-157
1. Greenwich, Royal Naval College/Ph. EXPLORER ARCHIVES.
2. Amiens, Musée de Picardie/Ph. LAUROS-GIRAUDON.
3. Versailles, Musée national du château/Ph. GIRAUDON.
4. London, Guildhall Library/Ph. BRIDGEMAN-GIRAUDON.

158-159
1. Naples, Museo Nazionale di San Martino/Ph. G. DAGLI ORTI.
2. Clermont-Ferrand, Musée Bargoin/Ph. LAUROS-GIRAUDON.
3. Paris, Bibl. des Arts décoratifs/Ph. J.-L. CHARMET.
4. Paris, Bibl. nat./Ph. J.-L. CHARMET.

160-161
1. Paris, Musée du Louvre/Ph. H. JOSSE.
2. Paris, I.N.R.P./Ph. J.-L. CHARMET.
3. Paris, Bibl. nat./Ph. J.-L. CHARMET.
4. Munich, Bayerische Staatsgemäldesammlungen/Ph. BLAUËL-Photothèque HACHETTE.
5. Paris, Archives du Quai d'Orsay/Ph. J.-L. CHARMET.

162-163
1. Istanbul, Topkapi Library/Ph. G. DAGLI ORTI.
2. Venice, Museo Correr/Ph. GIRAUDON.
3. Ph. G. DAGLI ORTI.
4. London, Victoria and Albert Museum/Ph. BRIDGEMAN-GIRAUDON.
5. Ph. G. DAGLI ORTI.
6. Istanbul, Topkapi Palace/Ph. G. DAGLI ORTI.

164-165
1. Private collection/E.T. ARCHIVE.
2. Ph. M. PELL-MAGNUM.
3. Lisbon/Ph. H. JOSSE.
4. Paris, Bibl. nat./Archives TALLANDIER.
5. Paris, Bibl. nat./Ph. J. DESMARTEAU-EXPLORER.

166-167
1 and 2. Ph. CH. LÉNARS-EXPLORER.
3. Paris, Musée Guimet/Ph. GIRAUDON.
4. Paris, private collection/Ph. G. DAGLI ORTI.
5. Oporto, Museu Nacional de Soares dos Reis/Ph. GIRAUDON.

168-169
1 and 2. London, Victoria and Albert Museum/Ph. BRIDGEMAN-GIRAUDON.
3 and 4. Ph. J.-L. NOU-EXPLORER.

170-171
1. Ph. J.-L. CHARMET.
2. Paris, Bibl. nat./Ph. J.-L. CHARMET.
3. Ph. G. DAGLI ORTI.
4. London, Museum of Mankind/Ph. BRIDGEMAN-GIRAUDON.

172-173
1. Ph. E. LESSING-MAGNUM.
2. Toledo, San Tomé/Ph. LAUROS-GIRAUDON.
3. Granada, Cathedral/Ph. ORONOZ-ARTEPHOT.
4. Ph. SCALA-FIRENZE.
5. Rome, Santa Maria delle Vittorie/Ph. G. NIMATALLAH-ARTEPHOT.
6. Chantilly, Musée Condé/Ph. LAUROS-GIRAUDON.
7. Madrid, Escorial/Ph. ORONOZ-ARTEPHOT.

174-175
1. Versailles, Musée national du château/Ph. H. JOSSE.
2. Versailles, Musée national du château/Ph. LAUROS-GIRAUDON.
3. Paris, Bibl. nat./Ph. LAUROS-GIRAUDON.
4. San Francisco, The Fine Arts Museums, California Palace of the Legion of Honor/Ph. H. JOSSE.
5. Paris, Hôtel des Monnaies/Ph. LAUROS-GIRAUDON.
6. Versailles, Musée national du château/Ph. H. JOSSE.

176-177
1. Rennes, Musée des Beaux-Arts/Ph. H. JOSSE.
2. Paris, Bibl. nat./Ph. LAUROS-GIRAUDON.
3. Paris, Musée du Louvre/Ph. H. JOSSE.
4. Paris, Bibl. des Arts décoratifs/Ph. J.-L. CHARMET.

178-179
1. Moscow, State Historical Museum/Ph. A.P.N.
2. Moscow, State Historical Museum/Ph. EDIMEDIA.
3. Paris, Bibl. nat./Ph. LAUROS-GIRAUDON.
4. Moscow, State Historical Museum/Ph. A.P.N.
5. Moscow, Rublyov Museum/Ph. A.P.N.

180-181
1. Photothèque HACHETTE.
2. Paris, Bibl. nat./Ph. J.-L. CHARMET.
3. Paris, Institut Tessin/Ph. J.-L. CHARMET-EXPLORER ARCHIVES.
4. Uppsala Universitet/Ph. Universitet.
5. Paris, Institut Tessin/Ph. J.-L. CHARMET-EXPLORER ARCHIVES.
6. Ph. A.P.N.

182-193
1. Paris, Musée de la Marine/Ph. G. DAGLI ORTI.
2. Paris, Bibl. nat./Ph. EXPLORER ARCHIVES.
3. Paris, Bibl. nat./Ph. GIRAUDON.
4. Paris, Archives nationales, section outremer/Ph. J.-L. CHARMET.
5. Ph. GIRAUDON

184-185
1. Oporto, Museu Nacional de Soares dos Reis/Ph. G. DAGLI ORTI.
2. Postdam, Sans-Souci/Ph. LAUROS-GIRAUDON.
3. Paris, Bibl. nat./Archives TALLANDIER.
4. Vienna, Kunsthistorischesmuseum/Ph. MEYER-ARTOTHEK-GIRAUDON.
5. Versailles, Musée national du château/Ph. LAUROS-GIRAUDON.

186-187
1. Geneva, Institut et musée Voltaire/Ph. EXPLORER ARCHIVES.
2. Paris, Bibl. des Art décoratifs/Ph. J.-L. CHARMET.
3 and 4. Private collection/Ph. EXPLORER ARCHIVES.

188-189
1. Ph. G. KREMER-EXPLORER ARCHIVES.
2. Paris, Bibl. des Arts décoratifs/Ph. J.-L. CHARMET.
3. Montpellier, Musée Atger/Ph. G. DAGLI ORTI.

190-191
1. Liverpool, Walker Art Gallery/Ph. Photothèque HACHETTE.
2. Paris, C.N.A.M./Ph. H. JOSSE.
3. London, British Library/Ph. FLEMING-Photothèque HACHETTE.
4. Paris, Bibl. nat./Photothèque HACHETTE.
5. Stafford, Staffordshire County Council/Ph. P. ROGERS-Photothèque

HACHETTE.

192-193
1. Moscow, State Historical Museum/Ph. A.P.N.
2. Private collection.
3. Éd. HOA-QUI.
4. Paris, Institut Tessin/Ph. J.-L. CHARMET-EXPLORER ARCHIVES.
5. Cholet, Musée des Guerres de Vendée/Ph. LAUROS-GIRAUDON.

194-195
1. Paris, Bibl. nat./Ph. H. JOSSE.
2. London, Trade Union Congress/Ph. BRIDGEMAN-GIRAUDON.
3. Ph. MARY EVANS.

196-197
1. Paris, Bibl. nat./Ph. J.-L. CHARMET.
2. Paris, Bibl. nat./Ph. EXPLORER ARCHIVES.
3. THE BETTMANN ARCHIVE.
4. Blérancourt, Musée national de la co-opération franco-américaine/Ph. G. MULLER-PHOTOTHÈQUE HACHETTE.
5. Washington, The National Gallery of Art/Ph. LAUROS-GIRAUDON.

198-199
1. Paris, Musée Carnavalet/Ph. H. JOSSE.
2. Private collection/Archives TALLANDIER.
3. Paris, Musée Carnavalet/Ph. H. JOSSE.
4 and 5. Paris, Musée Carnavalet/Ph. LAUROS-GIRAUDON.

200-201
1. Versailles, Musée national du château/Ph. LAUROS-GIRAUDON.
2. Paris, Musée de l'Armée/Ph. H. JOSSE.
3 and 4. Ph. EXPLORER ARCHIVES.
5. Paris, Bibl. nat./Ph. LAUROS-GIRAUDON.

202-203
1. Paris, Musée Carnavalet/Ph. H. JOSSE.
2. Paris, Bibl. nat./Ph. EXPLORER ARCHIVES.
3. Paris, Bibl. des Arts décoratifs/Ph. J.-L. CHARMET.
4. Paris, Bibl. nat./Ph. EXPLORER ARCHIVES.
5. Paris, Musée Carnavalet/Ph. LAUROS-GIRAUDON.
6. Paris, Bibl. nat./Ph. EXPLORER ARCHIVES.

204-205
1. Paris, Musée Carnavalet/Ph. J.-L. CHARMET.
2. Versailles, Musée national du château/Ph. G. DAGLI ORTI.
3. Paris, Bibl. des Arts décoratifs/Ph. G. DAGLI ORTI.
4. Vienna, Federal Chancellery/Ph. ALPENLAND-Photothèque HACHETTE.
5. Paris, Bibl. nat./Archives CLAM!
6. Paris, Bibl. nat./Ph. EXPLORER ARCHIVES.

206-207
1. Callao, Military Museum/Ph. G. DAGLI ORTI.
2. Rio de Janeiro, Museu Histórico Nacional/Ph. G. DAGLI ORTI.
3. Bogotá, Museum of 20 July/Ph. G. DAGLI ORTI.

208-209
1. Ph. HENRIQUES-MAGNUM.
2. Mexico/Ph. G. DAGLI ORTI.
3. J. Meyer Collection.
4. Mexico, Museo de Historia Natural/Ph. G. DAGLI ORTI.
5. Ph. S. MEISELAS-MAGNUM.

210-211
1. Naples, Museo Nazionale di San Martino/Ph. G. DAGLI ORTI.
2. Frankfurt, Historisches Museum/Ph. H. JOSSE-Photothèque HACHETTE.
3. Paris, Musée Carnavalet/Archives TALLANDIER.
4. Paris, Bibl. nat./Ph. LAUROS-GIRAUDON.
5. Rome, Museo del Risorgimento/Ph. G. DAGLI ORTI.

212-213
1. Paris, Musée Carnavalet/Ph. J.-L. CHARMET.
2. Rouen, Musée des Beaux-Arts/Ph. LAUROS-GIRAUDON.
3. Berlin, Nationalgalerie/Ph. BILDARCHIV PREUSSISCHER KULTURBESITZ.
4. Barcelona, Museo Picasso/© SPADEM, 1986.

214-215
1. Ph. MARY EVANS.
2. Ph. G. DAGLI ORTI.

216-217
1. Paris, Bibl. Hist. de la Ville de Paris/Ph. GIRAUDON.

2. Paris, Musée Carnavalet/Ph. J.-L. CHARMET.
3 and 4. Ph. J.-L. CHARMET.
5. Société Michelin/Archives CLAM!
6 and 7. Ph. J.-L. CHARMET.

218-219
1. Artist's collection: Grand-Mère-Paris © SPADEM, 1986/Ph. J.-L. CHARMET.
2 and 3. Ph. J.-L. CHARMET.
4. Paris, Bibl. nat./Ph. H. JOSSE.
5. Essen, Deutsches Plakatmuseum/Ph. J.-L. CHARMET.
6. Ph. J.-L. CHARMET.

220-221
1, 2 and 3. THE BETTMANN ARCHIVE.
4. Private collection/Ph. GIRAUDON.
5. Chicago, Historical Society/Archives TALLANDIER.

222-223
1. Ph. G. N. Barnard, 1865/THE BETTMANN ARCHIVE.
2. Ph. EDIMEDIA.
3. Ph. EXPLORER ARCHIVES.
4. Washington, National Collection of Fine Arts/Ph. EDIMEDIA.

224-225
1. Brescia, Museo del Risorgimento/Ph. G. DAGLI ORTI.
2. Ph. H. JOSSE.
3. Milan, Pinacoteca di Brera/Ph. GIRAUDON.
4. Paris, Musée Carnavalet/Ph. J.-L. CHARMET.
5. Paris, Musée Carnavalet/Ph. G. DAGLI ORTI.
6. Budapest, Museum of Military History/Ph. J.-L. CHARMET.

226-227
1. London, Victoria and Albert Museum/Ph. E.T. ARCHIVE.
2. Ph. E.T. ARCHIVE.
3. Ph. J.-L. CHARMET.
4. Private collection/Ph. J.-L. CHARMET.

228-229
1. Paris, Musée Carnavalet/Ph. J.-L. CHARMET.
2. Private collection/Ph. J.-L. CHARMET.
3. Éd. IRIS-Archives TALLANDIER.
4. Paris, Bibl. des Arts décoratifs/Ph. J.-L. CHARMET.
5. A. Fildier Collection/Archives TALLANDIER.

230-231
1. Essen, coll. Friedrich Krupp Gemeinschaftsbetriebe/Ph. coll.-Photothèque HACHETTE.
2. A. Fildier Collection/Archives TALLANDIER.
3. Paris, Bibl. nat./Ph. H. JOSSE.
4. Ph. J.-L. CHARMET-EXPLORER ARCHIVES.

232-233
1. Paris, Musée des Deux Guerres mondiales/Ph. G. DAGLI ORTI.
2. Private collection/Ph. J.-L. CHARMET.
3. Paris, Bibl. nat./Ph. J.-L. CHARMET.
4. Sigmund Freud Archive/Archives TALLANDIER.
5. Moscow, State Historiical Museum/Ph. A.P.N.
6. Venice, Galleria Internazionale d'Arte Moderna di Ca' Pesaro/Ph. G. DAGLI ORTI.

234-235
1. *The Illustrated London News*/Ph. G. DAGLI ORTI.
2. Paris, Musée national des Arts africains et oceaniens/Ph. H. JOSSE.
3. Ph. A.D.P.C.-EXPLORER ARCHIVES.

236-237
1. Private collection/Ph. EDIMEDIA.
2. Paris, Bibl. nat./Archives TALLANDIER.
3. Vincennes, Bibl. du Service historique de la Marine/Ph. G. DAGLI ORTI.
4. Paris, Bibl. nat./Archives TALLANDIER.
5. C. Dars Collection/Ph. EDIMEDIA.

238-239
1. *The Illustrated London News*/Ph. J.-L. CHARMET.
2. *Le Petit Journal*/Ph. J.-L. CHARMET.
3. Liverpool, City Museum and Art Gallery/Ph. J.-L. CHARMET.
4. Paris, Bibl. des Arts décoratifs/Ph. J.-L. CHARMET.
5. Collection SIROT-ANGEL.

240-241
1. THE BETTMANN ARCHIVE.
2. Private collection/Ph. F. G. MAYER-Photothèque HACHETTE.
3. THE BETTMANN ARCHIVE.

242-243
1. The Bettmann Archive/Photothèque HACHETTE.
2. Compiègne, Musée du Second Empire/Ph. H. JOSSE.
3. Paris, Bibl. nat./Ph. H. JOSSE.
4. Paris, Bibl. des Arts décoratifs/Ph.

Picture Credits

J.-L. CHARMET.
5. Photothèque HACHETTE.
6. Paris, Bibl. des Arts décoratifs/Ph. J.-L. CHARMET.
244-245
1. Photothèque HACHETTE.
2. Le Petit Journal/Ph. J.-L. CHARMET.
3. Le Petit Parisien/Archives TALLANDIER.
4. L'Illustré National/Ph. J.-L. CHARMET-Archives TALLANDIER.
5. Paris, Bibl. nat./Ph J.-L. CHARMET.
246-247
1. Paris, Musée de l'Armée/Ph. H. JOSSE.
2. Nanterre, B.D.I.C./Photothèque HACHETTE.
3. Ph. E.T. ARCHIVE.
4. Photothèque HACHETTE.
5. Canberra, Australian War Memorial/ Ph. E.T. ARCHIVE.
248-249
1. Ph. J.-L. CHARMET.
2. Le Petit Journal/Ph. J.-L. CHARMET.
3. Archives TALLANDIER.
4. Ph. KEYSTONE.
5. Essen, Deutsches Plakatmuseum/Ph. J.-L. CHARMET.
250-251
1. Nanterre, B.D.I.C./Ph. G. DAGLI ORTI.
2. Paris, Musée des Deux Guerres mondiale/Ph. G. DAGLI ORTI.
3. Nanterre, B.D.I.C./Ph. G. DAGLI ORTI.
4. Ph. KEYSTONE.
5. Paris, Musée des Deux Guerres mondiales/Ph. G. DAGLI ORTI.
252-253
1. Private collection/Ph. J.-L. CHARMET.
2. Ph. KEYSTONE.
3. Paris, Bibl. polonaise/Ph. J.-L. CHARMET.
4. Archives TALLANDIER.
5. Coll. VIOLLET.
254-255
1. Paris, Bibl. nat./Ph. J.-L. CHARMET.
2. Ph. HARLINGUE-VIOLLET.
3. Private collection/Ph. J.-L. CHARMET-EXPLORER ARCHIVES.
4. Ph. LAPI-VIOLLET.
256-257
1. Archives TALLANDIER.
2. Ph. J.-L. CHARMET.
3. Ph. MAGNUM.
4. Ph. J.-L. CHARMET.
5. Ph. R. CAPA-MAGNUM.
6. Washington, National Archives and Records Service/Ph. EDIMEDIA.
258-259

1. Ph. ASSOCIATED PRESS-Photothèque HACHETTE.
2. Ph. J.-L. CHARMET.
3. Le Petit Journal/Ph. J.-L. CHARMET.
4. Kladdezadatsch/Ph. J.-L. CHARMET.
5. Simplicissimus/Ph. J.-L. CHARMET.
6. Lecture pour Tour/Ph. J.-L. CHARMET.
260-261
1. Paris, Bibl. nat./Photothèque HACHETTE.
2. A. Brissaud Collection/Archives TALLANDIER.
3. Ph. R. CAPA-MAGNUM.
4. Private collection/Ph. J.-L. CHARMET.
5. Paris, Bibl. nat./Ph. S.A.F.A.R.A.-Archives TALLANDIER.
5. Ph. R. CAPA-MAGNUM.
262-263
1. Paris, Bibl. nat./Ph. J.-L. CHARMET.
2, 3 and 4. Ph. KEYSTONE.
264-265
1. New York, Museum of the City of New York/Photothèque HACHETTE.
2. Ph. KEYSTONE.
3. Ph. D. Lange, Washington, Library of Congress/GAMMA.
4. Ph. UPI/BETTMANN NEWSPHOTOS.
5. Archives TALLANDIER.
6. Ph. KEYSTONE.
7. Ph. THE BETTMANN ARCHIVE.
266-267
1. Ph. USIS-Archives TALLANDIER.
2. Ph. LIFE-Archives TALLANDIER.
3. Stuttgart, Würtembergische Landesbibliothek/Ph. J.-L. CHARMET-EXPLORER ARCHIVES.
4. Archives INTERPRESS.
5. Silvain Collection/Archives TALLANDIER.
268-269
1. Ph. D. BALTERMANTS-ICP-MAGNUM.
2. Ph. J.-L. CHARMET.
3. Ph. KEYSTONE.
4. Private collection/Ph. J.-L. CHARMET.
270-271
1 and 2. Ph. KEYSTONE.
3. Ph. CAPA-MAGNUM.
272-273
1. Canberra, Australian War Memorial/ Ph. E.T. ARCHIVE.
2. Ph. U.S. AIR FORCE/E.T. ARCHIVE.
3. Ph. USIS-Archives TALLANDIER.
4. Private collection/Ph. J.-L. CHARMET.
5. American Cultural Centre/Archives TALLANDIER.
274-275

1. New York, MOMA/Photothèque HACHETTE. © SPADEM. 1986.
2. Tokyo, Bridgestone Bijutsukan/Ph. LAUSAT-EXPLORER ARCHIVES.
3. Rome, Galleria Nazionale d'Arte Moderna/Ph. G. DAGLI ORTI, D.R.
4. Ph. M. RIBOUD-MAGNUM, D.R.
276-277
1. Archives LAROUSSE-GIRAUDON.
2. Ph. KEYSTONE.
3. Ph. J.-L CHARMET.
4. Paris, Bibl. nat./Ph. EXPLORER ARCHIVES.
5. Paris, Bibl. nat./Archives TALLANDIER.
6. Ph. M. RIBOUD-MAGNUM.
7. Coll. C. SJÖRGEN D.R.
8. Ph. H. CARTIER-BRESSON-MAGNUM.
278-279
1. Ph. UPI-BETTMANN NEWSPHOTOS.
2. Archives TALLANDIER.
3. Ph. UPI-BETTMANN NEWSPHOTOS.
4. Ph. KEYSTONE.
280-281
1. Ph. L'ILLUSTRATION-SYGMA.
2. 3 and 4. Ph. KEYSTONE.
282-283
1. Ph. A.F.P.
2. Autochrome Lumière/Archives TALLANDIER.
3 and 4. Archives TALLANDIER.
5. Ph. F. MAYER-MAGNUM.
284-285
1. Coll. J. Charby/Ph. EDIMEDIA.
2. Ph. E.C.P./ARMÉES-Archives TALLANDIER.
3. Ph. MAGNUM.
286-287
1. Ph. Keystone.
2. Ph. UPI-BETTMANN NEWSPHOTOS.
3. Ph. E. LESSING-MAGNUM.
4. Paris, Musée Picasso/Ph. R.M.N. © SPADEM, 1986.
5. Ph. UPI-BETTMANN NEWSPHOTOS.
6. Ph. D. SEYMOUR-MAGNUM.
288-289
1. Paris, Bibl. nat./Ph. LAUROS-GIRAUDON.
2. Ph. KEYSTONE.
3. Ph. B. BARBEY-MAGNUM.
4. Ph. J. GAUMY-MAGNUM.
290-291
1. Ph. R. WOLLMANN-GAMMA.
2. Ph. KEYSTONE.
3. Ph. S. SALGADO-GAMMA.
292-293
1. Ph. E. HAAS-MAGNUM.
2. Ph. XINHUA-GAMMA.
3. Ph. K. IMAEDA-MAGNUM.
4. Ph. CHRIS MARKER-EDIMEDIA.

5. Ph. CARTIER-BRESSON MAGNUM.
6. Coll. C.J. Bucher/TALLANDIER.
294-295
1. Ph. J. KOUDELKA-MAGNUM.
2. Ph. KEYSTONE.
3. Ph. S. RASKIN-MAGNUM.
4. Ph. COLL. SNARK-EDIMEDIA.
296-297
1. Ph. URSS-GAMMA.
2. Ph. D. SIMON-GAMMA.
3. Ph. D. CHARLON-GAMMA.
4. Ph. NOVOSTI-GAMMA.
298-299
1. Ph. UPI-BETTMANN NEWSPHOTOS.
2. Ph. S. LISS-LIAISON GAMMA.
3. Ph. UPI-BETTMANN NEWSPHOTOS.
4. Ph. E. ERWITT-MAGNUM.
5. Ph. EDIMEDIA.
6. Ph. UPI-BETTMANN NEWSPHOTOS.
7. Ph. C. HIRES-GAMMA.
300-301
1. Ph. E.C.P./ARMÉES-GAMMA.
2. Ph. KEYSTONE.
3. Ph. JASMIN-GAMMA.
4. Ph. GAMMA.
302-303
1. Ph. PH. J.-P. NACIVET-EXPLORER.
2. Ph. F. MAYER-MAGNUM.
3. Ph. S. MEISELAS-MAGNUM.
4. Ph. US NAVY-LIAISON GAMMA.
304-305
1. Ph. M. RIBOUD-MAGNUM.
2. Ph. G. CARON-GAMMA.
3. Ph. KOSI-GAMMA.
4. Ph. D. LAINÉ-GAMMA.
5. Ph. ABBAS-GAMMA.
306-307
1. Ph. G. DAGLI ORTI.
2. Ph. H. VEILLER-EXPLORER.
3. Ph. E. HAAS-MAGNUM.
4. Ph. Washington, Library of Congress/Ph. EDIMEDIA.
308-309
1 and 2. Ph. M. RIBOUD-MAGNUM.
3. Ph. H. CARTIER-BRESSON-MAGNUM.
4. Ph. R. RAI-MAGNUM.
310-311
1. Ph. J. GRIFFITHS-MAGNUM.
2. Ph. F. MAYER-MAGNUM.
312-313
1. Ph. KEYSTONE.
2. Ph. B. BARBEY-MAGNUM.
3. Ph. JEUNE AFRIQUE-GAMMA.
4. Ph. AN NAHAR-GAMMA.
5. Ph. B. BARBEY-MAGNUM.
314-315
1. Ph. A. DE BORCHGRAVE-GAMMA.
2. Ph. J.-P. BONNOTTE-GAMMA.

3. Ph. A. MINGAM-GAMMA.
4. Ph. CH. HIRES-GAMMA.
316-317
1. Ph. L. FREED-MAGNUM.
2. Ph. I. BERRY-MAGNUM.
3. Ph. ZORO-MAGNUM.
4. Ph. F. SCIANNA-MAGNUM.
318-319
1. Ph. S. MC CURRY-MAGNUM.
2. Ph. G. PERESS-MAGNUM.
3. Ph. CH. HIRES-GAMMA.
4. Ph. P. PIEL-GAMMA.
320-321
1. Ph. P. H. VERSELE-PHOTONEWS-GAMMA.
2. Ph. R. KALVAR-MAGNUM.
3. Ph. CH. VIOUJARD-GAMMA.
4. Ph. P. PIEL-GAMMA.
5. Ph. M. DEVILLE-LEBRUN-PHOTONEWS-GAMMA.
322-323
1. Ph. E. HARTMANN-MAGNUM.
2. Ph. A. HOWARTH-DAILY TELEGRAPH-EXPLORER.
3. Ph. J.-L. CHARMET.
4. Ph. H. CARTIER-BRESSON-MAGNUM.
5. Ph. GREEWOOD-LIAISON GAMMA.
6. Ph. EDWARD-LIAISON GAMMA.
324-325
1. Ph. Agence TASS.
2. Ph. A. SAUCEZ.-EXPLORER.
3. Ph. K. KRAFFT-EXPLORER.
4. Ph. F. GOHIER-EXPLORER.
326-327
1. Ph. B. GLINN-MAGNUM.
2. Ph. 1. SENNETT-MAGNUM.
328-329
1. Ph. W. CAMPBELL-SYGMA.
2. P. C. CARRION-SYGMA.
3. Ph. A. BALAGUER-SYGMA.
4. Ph. P. FRIDMAN-SYGMA.
330-331
1. Ph. J.-P. PAIREAULT-MAGNUM.
2. Ph. J. GRIFFITHS-MAGNUM.
3. Ph. ABBAS-MAGNUM.
4. Ph. R. BURRI-MAGNUM.
5. Ph. R. KALVAR-MAGNUM.
332-333
1. Ph. P. PIEL-GAMMA.
2. Ph. S. FERRY-GAMMA.
334-335
1. Ph. G. BASSIGNAC-GAMMA.
336-337
1. Ph. PHANSAK-SIPA PRESS.
2. Ph. S. MEISELAS-MAGNUM.
3. Ph. P.J. GRIFFITHS-MAGNUM.
4. Ph. HALSTEAD-LIAISON GAMMA.

Index